PREHISTORY AND HUMAN ECOLOGY OF THE DEH LURAN PLAIN

PLATE 1

The Deh Luran plain. View south across the tamarisk-filled floodplain of the Mehmeh River toward the Jebel Hamrin.

MEMOIRS OF THE MUSEUM OF ANTHROPOLOGY
UNIVERSITY OF MICHIGAN
NUMBER 1

PREHISTORY AND HUMAN ECOLOGY OF THE DEH LURAN PLAIN

An Early Village Sequence from Khuzistan, Iran

By

FRANK HOLE, KENT V. FLANNERY
JAMES A. NEELY

Paleoethnobotany by Hans Helbaek
Contributions by Cyril S. Smith, Colin Renfrew, I. W. Cornwall

ANN ARBOR
1969

ISBN (print): 978-1-949098-47-1
ISBN (ebook): 978-1-949098-64-8

Browse all of our books at sites.lsa.umich.edu/archaeology-books.

Order our books from the University of Michigan Press at www.press.umich.edu.

For permissions, questions, or manuscript queries, contact Museum publications by email at umma-pubs@umich.edu or visit the Museum website at lsa.umich.edu/ummaa.

FOREWORD

With the appearance of "Prehistory and Human Ecology of the Deh Luran Plain" the Museum of Anthropology at the University of Michigan begins a new publication series. *The Memoirs of the Museum of Anthropology* are designed as a series for major anthropological monographs whose size and format require a larger volume than was available in either the *Occasional Contributions* or the *Anthropological Papers* series, also a part of thc Muscum's publications.

This first Memoir by Frank Hole of Rice University, Kent V. Flannery of the University of Michigan, and James A. Neely of the University of Texas, as the primary authors, is an excellent example of the need for the Memoir series. One of the important considerations in the establishment of the Memoirs is to provide relatively rapid publication following completion of the manuscript and another is to make the Memoirs available at a price substantially below that of many comparable publications.

It is appropriate that the new series begins with a report which provides data from Iran on that important period in Near Eastern prehistory which resulted in the transition from food gathering to the domestication of plants and animals.

This report is the result of the collaborative effort and support of private and governmental institutions, and of a group of individuals who brought their special skills to the project. The Museum of Anthropology serves as the instrument of this complex research operation to make available the information recovered from the excavations and the interpretations provided by the participants.

The Museum of Anthropology and the authors gratefully acknowledge the financial assistance provided by income on the endowment of the Horace H. Rackham School of Graduate Studies of the University of Michigan for a portion of the funds for publication.

June 10, 1968 | Dr. James B. Griffin

PREFACE

The studies reported in this volume were made possible through the willing cooperation of many friends, colleagues, and institutions, in America and abroad. It is with pleasure that we make the following acknowledgements.

The government of Iran, through the offices of the Ministry of Education and the Archeological Service, granted us permission to conduct surveys and excavations, and helped us in many ways. We especially thank the General Directors of the Archeological Service, Mr. Hassan Mashoon and Mr. A. Pourmand; Technical Director, Dr. Ezat O. Nagahban; and Director of Excavations, Mr. Sayid M. Khorramabadi, all of whom gave us valuable assistance and advice. The representatives assigned to us in the field were Messrs. Mohammad Moushirpour, Abdul Hussein Shahidzadeh, and Bahrami. They lived with us under often trying conditions, helped in supervising the excavations, and represented the government's and our interests with local officials.

A number of Americans, resident in Iran, also contributed greatly to the success of our project. Both Mr. Theodore A. Wertime and Dr. John C. Reinhardt, Cultural Attaches with the United States Embassy, gave us considerable help in Tehran, and acted as liason for us with the Iranian Government while we were out of the country.

The Khuzistan Development Service, through its director, Mr. Leo L. Anderson, provided us with facilities for drafting maps in Ahwaz and loaned us a truck (with water trailer) which made possible our first trip to Deh Luran. Mr. Charles Simkins of KDS arranged for analyses of soil and water, and gave us much information and advice about agriculture and related problems in west Iran. Finally, Messrs. Rashidian and Fazli, who were attached to the Andimeshk office of KDS, welcomed us periodically with hospitality and air conditioning when we arrived, hot and tired, from our desert retreat.

Our morale and health were bolstered more than once when we traveled in the vicinity of Kermanshah and were able to stay for a few days with the resident missionaries. Blackie and Harriet Burris and Ed and Belle Jaeger all made us feel very much at home, and we thoroughly enjoyed their company and good cooking.

The Director of the British School of Persian Studies, Mr. David Stronach, gave us the benefit of his wide experience in Iranian archeology and the use of his library and swimming pool. Dr. and Mrs. Joseph Caldwell, Illinois State Museum, visited us briefly in Deh Luran, briefed us on their excavations and surveys, and supplied much-needed succor in Tehran at the end of the season.

The work reported here was, of course, supervised by the authors, but we were ably assisted in the field by our wives—Barbara Hole, Nancy Flannery, and Mary Ann Neely—who actually did most of the processing, labelling and rough-sorting of the artifacts. Their patience in the face of isolation in a land with blistering heat, dust storms, biting insects, precarious water supply, tents that leaked and sometimes blew down, and finally freezing weather, was indeed exemplary.

A special note of appreciation must also go to Mohammad Ali Nargasi, our multilingual cook and spiritual advisor who, in spite of his own prior hearsay knowledge that Deh Luran was "the worst place in Iran," accompanied us and managed to survive all the natural and human hardships which were placed in his way. His son, Mustafa, was surely the most eager cook's helper, lighter of Coleman lanterns, errand runner and pusher of recalcitrant Jeeps in west Iran.

Most of the work in archeology lies in the analysis of materials excavated. The Iranian government very generously allowed us to borrow and bring to the United States all the artifacts and animal bones we needed to study, thereby greatly facilitating our analysis. This kind of cooperation is uncommon in archeology today, and we therefore wish to express our special thanks.

Several specialists, whose reports have been included in Appendices to this volume, analyzed important parts of the Deh Luran collections. We were fortunate in having Dr. Hans Helbaek, Danish National Museum, in the field with us for six weeks while the plant material was being excavated and separated by flotation. Helbaek's initial study of the tens of thousands of carbonized seeds from Deh Luran appears as Appendix I.

Dr. Cyril S. Smith, Massachusetts Institute of Technology, reports on his examination of our copper bead from the preceramic Ali Kosh phase. Dr. Colin Renfrew, University of Sheffield, reports on his analyses of our obsidian samples, undertaken in collaboration with Messrs. J. E. Dixon and J. R. Cann, Department of Mineralogy and Petrology, Cambridge University. We greatly appreciate their efforts.

The following zoologists, all at the Smithsonian Institution, helped with various aspects of the faunal analysis: Dr. George Watson, Division of Birds; Dr. James Peters, Division of Reptiles and Amphibians; Dr. William Taylor, Division of Fishes; Dr. Joseph Morrison, Division of Mollusks; and Dr. Fenner Chace, Division of Crustacea. Prof. Elso S. Barghoorn, Harvard University, kindly examined some of our carbonized plant material.

Radiocarbon dates were processed for us by laboratories at Shell Development Company, Houston; Humble Oil and Refining Company, Houston; the Isotope Laboratory of the Institute of Geophysics and Planetary Physics, University of California at Los Angeles; the Smithsonian Institution; and Isotopes, Inc.

We should also like to acknowledge Prof. Robert J. Braidwood, who gave us our first exposure to Near Eastern archeology when we participated in the Oriental Institute Iranian Prehistoric Project. Among the many other colleagues who deserve mention are Ralph and Rose Solecki, Patty Jo Watson and Peder Mortensen, all of whom kindly allowed us to see relevant unpublished data.

We are indebted to James B. Griffin who arranged for publication of this study as the first of a new series of anthropological memoirs of the Museum of Anthropology, and to the Executive Board of the Horace H. Rackham School of Graduate Studies for substantial support which made possible the inauguration of the series.

The processing of artifacts in the laboratory at Rice University was done with the help of several students: John Durham, Charlene Krause, and Carlos Schubert of Rice University. Miss Susan Mauss, Bennington College, assisted with the sorting of animal bones at the Smithsonian Institution.

All line drawings in this volume are the work of Nancy H. Flannery, with the following exceptions: Figs. 116-121, 123-125, 128, 130, and 132-133, which were prepared by George Robert Lewis, Smithsonian Institution, and Figs. 137-141, which were provided by Hans Helbaek.

Last, and perhaps most important, we acknowledge the sources of our financial support. Various parts of this research were supported by National Science Foundation grants GS-67 and GS-724; by the Oriental Institute, University of Chicago; by Rice University; and by the Smithsonian Institution.

Rice University FAH
University of Michigan KVF
University of Texas JAN

June 15, 1967

CONTENTS

FIGURES

PLATES

I

OBJECTIVES AND RESEARCH DESIGN

INTRODUCTION

This is the report of a series of investigations carried out in the extreme southwestern corner of Iran, and related to the beginnings of successful plant and animal domestication, village life, and irrigation agriculture in that region.

The time span involved is approximately the period from 8000 to 4000 B.C. At the start of that period, man in southwest Iran was a seminomadic herder who subsisted partly on domestic goats, sheep, wheat, and barley, and partly on wild animals and seasonally-available wild plants. At the end of the period, he was a fully sedentary irrigation agriculturalist, who cultivated more than a dozen strains of cereals and legumes, and raised goats, cattle, and sheep. We will deal with the tangible evidence of plants and animals used by these people, and attempt to reconstruct something of their way of life from their artifacts and architecture.

Investigations into the beginnings of food production are nothing new. The long sequence of agricultural developments uncovered by MacNeish (1964*a,b*) in Nuclear America is the New World's most outstanding example, and in southwestern Asia the last fifteen years have seen a number of important excavations along these lines. First, and best known, are the three field seasons at Jarmo in Iraqi Kurdistan (Braidwood, Howe, *et al.,* 1960), which produced skeletal evidence of animal domestication and botanical evidence of plant domestication which are beyond dispute. Our sample of prehistoric floral and faunal remains from southwest Iran simply adds one more chapter to the story which began at Jarmo.

Since 1948, expeditions from the United States, Great Britain, Denmark, France, and Japan have recovered material relating to early village life in the Near East. In the course of their work, many of these groups have also touched on the later problems of irrigation and urban life, or reached back into the paleolithic period for the background to food production. The result is that we now have a series of early village sites spanning nearly 2500 airline miles, from Macedonia to Afghanistan. Most investigators, for purposes of continuity or political expediency, have confined their investigations to one country, sampling sites where their interest led them within those political borders. A conspicuous exception has been the expeditions led by Braidwood, which ranged through three different countries while staying largely within the confines of the oak-pistachio woodland belt, between 800 and 1500 meters in elevation.

Not all sites, however, are within the oak-pistachio belt. Over the wide area mentioned above, there are early villages at desert oases and in fertile mountain valleys, on grassy steppes and on the borders of stagnant marshes. The diversity of environments in which these sites occur suggests to us that the answers to problems as complex as the beginnings of agriculture and the establishment of urban life cannot be sought in a single ecological zone or in a single set of causes. The answers must be sought in the interrelationships of environment, society, subsistence, and economy.

Our suspicions about the way cultures

change and develop suggest that the most fruitful approaches are those which attempt to understand the individual factors determining the course of each local sequence. We would expect that even such factors as "climatic change" and "dessication" would have to be described and understood in terms of their effect on local sequences.

It was formerly believed that there was one environmental zone which was "optimum" for the beginnings of food production–the zone in which the natural ranges of the wild ancestors of the early plant and animal domesticates overlapped (Harlan and Zohary, 1966). Today we doubt that any one zone, no matter how optimum, held all the answers. There seems to have been not only an interaction between man and his environment in southwest Asia, but an equally important interaction between men of one zone and men of neighboring zones. And the routes of interaction between zones became corridors of exchange, along which information about the early domesticates traveled.

Early evidence of such interaction between areas can be seen far back in the beginnings of village life, when obsidian, turquoise and copper from the high plateaus of Anatolia and Iran, sea shells and natural asphalt from the Mesopotamian lowlands, and almonds and pistachios from the Kurdish mountains were widely traded. We were therefore intrigued by the possibility of a long-term project (of which the present report is the first stage), restricted to one small area of Southwest Asia, which would sample each of four or five adjacent environmental zones in an effort to identify and understand the nature of the interrelationships of people living in them.

Western Iran, which displays examples of all the major environmental zones found in Southwest Asia, from sea level to 2000 meters, contains the data we need to test our ideas. In some ways, it is the Near East in miniature. A transect from the Persian Gulf to the high central plateau crosses areas with 100 mm. of annual rainfall, and others with 600 mm. (see Wright, 1961:Fig. 1). Surveys by Jeep and on foot (Hole, 1962) reveal that early village sites cluster in regional "nuclei," areas where favorable soil and surface water are available: at 150 to 300 meters in Khuzistan, 800 to 1500 meters in Luristan and Kurdistan, perhaps higher on the fringes of the high plateau near Hamadan and Kashan. Evidence from traded artifacts (such as pottery) supports the contention that by 6000 B.C., all these regional nuclei, different as their respective traditions may have been, were at least tenuously linked into an economic and social network.

Of all the provinces mentioned above, none has a denser concentration of early villages than Khuzistan, in the southwest corner of Iran, north of the head of the Persian Gulf. Located just across the Iranian border from Mesopotamia proper, Khuzistan is known to contain an extraordinary number of sites from the sixth millennium B.C. (Adams, 1962). Lying at altitudes of 150 to 300 meters and with an annual rainfall of 300 to 350 mm., the plains of northern Khuzistan were eminently suitable for early dry farming, grazing, and irrigation. In view of these facts, Khuzistan seemed like a reasonable place to begin systematic work on the various environmental zones of western Iran.

OBJECTIVES OF THE DEH LURAN PROJECT

We chose the Deh Luran plain for archeological investigation in the hope that work there would shed light on the culture history of Khuzistan and perhaps, in general, on the alluvial lowlands where the first urban civilizations seem to have begun. Deh Luran, although a relatively small and circumscribed area, had a sufficiently large number of sites so that we could be confident of obtaining an adequate sample of the local cultural materials with a minimum of travel. Temporarily, we have left aside the question of whether Deh Luran should be considered part of, or marginal to, the impressive prehistoric developments in central Khuzistan some 100 km. to the southeast. Only more work in each area will tell whether the conclusions we gain from Deh Luran will be generally applicable to adjacent areas.

In attempting to accomplish our long-range goals, we have expanded the traditional emphasis of archeology in Khuzistan to include the remains of plants and animals, although of course artifacts still retain an important place in our overall analysis of the culture sequences. With those artifacts, we have attempted to define a stratigraphic sequence of about 4000 years, but this is no more than a necessary skeleton on which we can hang new data. In the future, we hope to be able to investigate village plans and regional settlement patterns much more extensively than at present. These data should ultimately give us a base on which to make inferences about the social and political changes which attended the development of food production.

Given the fact that Deh Luran is relatively small but well-supplied with sites, we imagine our project there having the following stages, of which as yet only the first two have been investigated in any detail:

1) Survey for sites, and the collection of surface materials (essentially completed).
2) The stratigraphic excavation of sites especially chosen because they contain relatively low segments of the regional sequence. (Two sites are now dug and one is briefly tested.)
3) The piecing together of the various segments of that sequence, including additional excavations where necessary to fill-in gaps or breaks.
4) The excavation of wide exposures of each phase at sites where the architecture is readily accessible, in order to examine housing units and partial village plans. (One house plan of the Mehmeh phase is mapped.)
5) The correlation of observations on changes in artifacts, subsistence, technology, trade, settlement and populations, and inferences about social, political, and religious activities.

Survey of the prehistoric mounds in Deh Luran was done in 1961 and 1963, and our selection of sites was based on the surface collections obtained. One site was tested, and two or three others identified as prime targets for future stratigraphic excavations. In 1963, two stratigraphic trenches were excavated, one (7 meters deep) at Ali Kosh and one (11 meters deep) at Tepe Sabz. Future trenches in Chagha Sefid and Tepe Farukhabad should, on the basis of surface indications, complete the rough outline of the prehistoric village sequence at Deh Luran.[1] Investigation of village plans at Tepe Ashrafabad, Tepe Sefid and other shallow sites can then begin. We are still a long way from the stage of "correlation and interpretation."

EXCAVATION OF STRATIGRAPHIC COLUMNS

Although a hundred years of archeology have gone by in the Near East, and scores of prehistoric site excavations have been undertaken by skilled and thoughtful archeologists, it is difficult to point to valleys or regions where the complete local prehistoric sequence has been worked out and published in detail. This lack of stratigraphically-based regional sequences of artifacts has greatly hampered the work of scholars like Lines (1953), Perkins (1949),

[1]Since this report went to press, Hole and Neely have discovered (at Chagha Sefid) at least one new cultural phase which seems to fall between our Mohammad Jaffar and Sabz phases; and Henry T. Wright's excavations at Tepe Farukhabad have extended our sequence on from the Bayat phase to the Jemdat Nasr period.

McCown (1942) and Dyson (1965), who have attempted to correlate one area with another. These authors have been able to point out instances where two or more areas shared certain pottery design elements, and they have compiled chronological guideposts based on careful comparative studies. In this sense they have constructed regional sequences, but none of them has been able to set forth just what "Halaf," "Ubaid," "Giyan V-A," or "Susiana *b*" means in terms of whole assemblages of artifacts, which can be described as different from preceding or subsequent assemblages. The periods are even less defined in terms of settlement pattern, architecture, agriculture, or domestic animals. Although most excavators possess the techniques for recovering such data, for the most part they do so only if they consider it worth doing.

One area for which the steps in the regional prehistoric sequence have indeed been worked out and published is the plain of Antioch near the Syro-Turkish border (Braidwood and Braidwood, 1960). On the basis of materials from a series of step-trenches at deep, stratified tells, the Braidwoods have defined a sequence of phases—A through J—based mainly on changes in pottery, but also on ground and chipped stone, beads, copper tools, and other artifacts (including even wheat and barley). A similar sequence in Anatolia is currently being published (Mellaart, 1964*a*:114-19; 1965:77-114).

In northern Iran, another sequence has been excavated, though not yet published in full detail: materials from three multi-period stratified tepes (Hajji Firuz, Dalma, and Pisdeli) were used to verify the three oldest prehistoric phases tentatively discerned in basal levels at Hasanlu (Dyson, 1960, Dyson and Young, 1960, Young, 1962).

The careful definition of these sequences, based both on controlled stratigraphic excavations and assemblages of artifacts, emphasizes that good sequences can only be obtained from sites relatively close to one another, dug by archeologists who see the solution of chronological problems as a preliminary framework on which to build the results of more extensive work on particular periods. Dependable sequences can only be obtained and defined on the basis of artifacts which can be dated relative to one another through their stratigraphic position. Digging extensively in the spectacular ruins of one period or confining one's activities to shallow, easily-dug sites precludes establishing the stratigraphic relationships that are so essential to know as one tries to develop the history of an area.

It was our concern with the latter problem that determined how we dug and where we dug in the Deh Luran plain in 1963. We chose to defer exposing large areas of sites until after we had dug them in depth to obtain the stratigraphy. Precisely defining the phases in our sequence in terms of their characteristic artifacts and activities enables us to relate them to other sites throughout southwest Asia; it also forces us to explain why certain complexes of tools appear in some, but not all, phases of the sequence. To the extent that these tool complexes reflect a specific regional way of life, we need to be able to relate them to the kinds of agriculture and animal husbandry they accompanied, and to contrast them with contemporary tool complexes from regions where the way of life was somewhat different.

For the reasons given above, we selected the deepest areas on Ali Kosh and Tepe Sabz, and sent relatively narrow shafts down to virgin soil by means of the techniques described in later chapters. We confess a little amusement at the thought that, while most Near Eastern archeologists have dug for buildings and incidentally recovered a few seeds in the process, we dug for seeds and incidentally recovered a few fragments of buildings in the process.

HOW THE PHASES IN THE CULTURAL SEQUENCE WERE DETERMINED

Our 1963 excavations at two sites uncovered sufficient changes in the Deh Luran sequence to allow us to discern seven "phases" or "periods." Our phases have been given names (like Bus Mordeh, Sabz, and Khazineh) rather than numbers or letters of the alphabet in order to allow us to fit in new phases before them, between them, or after them as they are discovered in the future. It will also allow us to refer to culturally comparable strata in different sites by the same term. Each name was chosen because it was in some way connected with the phase involved, and most are local names for sites, or villages near sites. Although the stratigraphic sequence is clear, the equivalences with sites in other areas are based on artifact ties which are not always clear, and the dates are based on the radiocarbon determinations presently available to us.

Our present impression of the sequence in the Deh Luran plain is that it represents a series of gradual changes in almost every category of artifacts and activities. No drastic, catastrophic breaks occur in the segment we have recovered. The single "gap" in the sequence—between the Mohammad Jaffar phase and the Sabz phase—is partly an artifact of our own digging; the lower levels of Tepe Sabz did not reach far enough back in time to yield materials of the Mohammad Jaffar phase. Surface survey indicates that there may be sites nearby which probably will bridge the gap when they are excavated. Until that gap is filled, we will not know whether it will be necessary to intercalate another phase between Mohammad Jaffar and Sabz.

The evidence now suggests that each phase grew, at least partially, out of the one that preceded it. Of course, we can detect new ideas and new artifacts from other regions at periodic intervals; but our sequence is, in essence, the story of the internal regional development within the Deh Luran plain. How does one divide such a continuum into "phases?" The task was tailored to clarifying the successive ways of life which characterized the peoples of the Deh Luran plain as they changed from primitive herders and plant collectors at 7500 B.C. into sedentary irrigation agriculturalists at 4000 B.C. Obviously, any division of a continuum can only be arbitrary, but we think the over-all picture becomes sharper if we break the continuum into convenient segments which represent different periods within our particular region.

The criteria we used to set up the phases are based on the two kinds of change we see in the Deh Luran sequence: (1) "adaptive" change, involving certain aspects of economic life and social organization, and (2) "non-adaptive" change, or gradual changes in non-economic aspects of the culture, such as decorative styles. These two types of change were not strictly independent of one another, but at times they operated as if they were: during a long period of stable, unchanging economy, change in styles continued, often at a very rapid rate; on the other hand, a really significant change in economy, reflected in the plant and animal remains, sometimes seemed to have no effect on style changes. Apart from these examples, however, there seems to be a consistent correlation between changes in the basic economic adaptation of a group and many aspects of their material culture. At points where such correlations occurred, it was fairly easy for us to draw the line between phases. Elsewhere the decision was harder to make, but our criteria remained those of economic change, or the appearance of an easily-recognized new complex or assemblage of styles and/or artifacts. In some instances, we suspect that the appearance of these new style complexes went hand-in-hand with changes in the social and political organization of the group, but it will be many field seasons before we have concrete evidence on this point.

Of the two types of change mentioned above, it is of course the "adaptive" change which is most important in terms of human culture history, and wherever possible we have made our breaks in the continuum correspond to those changes. For example: from 7900 to 6500 B.C. at the site of Ali Kosh, we see an economy in which systematically-collected winter-ripening legumes constituted the bulk of the plant food supply, while agricultural products and dry-season plants were decidedly secondary, and one attempt at cultivation—involving flax—met with failure. We have referred to this economic period as the "Bus Mordeh phase," using one local name for the site. After 6500 B.C., we see a definite upsurge in the relative amounts of agricultural products, which reduced wild legumes to a smaller percentage of the food supply, and our limited exposure shows us a community with a more "settled" aspect: larger, sturdier dwellings, domed ovens, plastered walls, brick-lined roasting pits, and so forth. We have called this period of economic development the "Ali Kosh phase," using another local name for the site. Finally, after 6000 B.C., we see an increase in domestic animals, as well as an increase in seeds of a plant called *Prosopis* which ripens in the dry summer season and is intimately associated with fallow agricultural land (Adams, 1965:5). Still more substantial stone-founded houses appear during this period, which we have labeled the "Mohammad Jaffar phase," using the name given to the site by Gautier and Lampre in 1903. Our impression is that this was a time of prosperity and of settlement which, judging by the abundant use of dry-season plants, was year-round.

With our special interests in the history of agriculture and the social consequences of effective food production, it is important for us to be able to distinguish economic phases. For us they are more important than phases which might be based mainly on burial styles, house types, or design elements on pottery.

It was much harder to define "economic phases" at Tepe Sabz than at Ali Kosh because already by the time the site was founded, in the "Sabz phase," the Deh Luran plain was the scene of a competent irrigation economy, with free-threshing wheat, naked barley, and a successfully-grown flax joining the previously cultivated races of grain. Through the succeeding Khazineh, Mehmeh, and Bayat phases, this economy remained relatively stable, the major change being an increase in barley over wheat during the Bayat phase, perhaps indicating that the irrigated areas were already becoming salty. Our phases at Tepe Sabz are, therefore, defined on the basis of changes in styles of artifacts to a larger extent than are those at Ali Kosh—though no phase is defined on the basis of its artifacts alone.

Some of our colleagues may wonder how our economic phases can be related to the well-publicized (but not necessarily well-known) "periods" already distinguished in neighboring areas, or to materials found on the surface of sites as survey in Khuzistan and Mesopotamia is continued. Obviously there is little likelihood that archeologists will be able to tell, on the basis of flints and sherds picked up during survey, whether agricultural products constituted 20 per cent, 50 per cent or 80 per cent of the plant food of the sites they have discovered. For this reason, our phases are also defined in terms of artifacts which can be recovered from the surface. Our definition of each phase (Chapter 21) contains a description of certain artifact types whose "life span," or distribution in time, corresponds closely to that of the phases we have distinguished.

These artifact types can be regarded as "index fossils" or "horizon markers" which, although they themselves may tell us little about the economy or community structure of the time, enable us to relate newly-discovered surface collections to the more fully investigated sites. And, as our tests at Tepe Sabz and Musiyan "E" have demonstrated, there is a very good chance that when strata at two different neighboring sites show identical horizon markers, they also show identical plant and animal economies; but we would not expect this to be the case at more widely-separated sites.

PHASES AND CULTURE CHANGE IN THE NEAR EAST

At no point in our investigations of the prehistoric sequence in the Deh Luran plain did we feel it necessary to postulate migrations, invasions, plagues, famines, warfare, or the sacking of towns by barbarian hordes to explain the observed changes. A quick perusal of the literature of the prehistoric Near East would lead one to believe that castrophies are more the rule than the exception in human history. Such catastrophic occurrences have been invoked to explain most culture changes—changes that, we feel, often might better have been explained in less drastic terms. Students of anthropology, who are accustomed to studying the intricate processes of culture change, are surprised to read that stratified sites, where four or five changes in pottery styles can be detected during the course of some hundreds of years, must therefore have been sacked, abandoned and reoccupied four or five times. We are no less surprised to read that multiple burials of ten or twelve persons in a single grave—a not uncommon custom among preliterate, kinship-oriented persons all over the world—constitute "evidence of a massacre." In part, these explanations suggest an uncritical projection onto prehistoric communities of 5000 B.C., of the behavior patterns more properly associated with Assyrian armies or the legions of Xerxes; in part, they seem to stem from the incredible belief (actually held, it appears, by some investigators) that a single "race" of people produced a single pottery type. Thus we see Baron von Oppenheim wondering whether two races of man were present in the lowest levels at Tell Halaf, where both plain and painted pottery were found (von Oppenheim, 1931); we read of Sialk where the "bearers of a red-ware culture (were) under the influence of light-ware design" and "the red-ware culture began to influence the light-ware culture" (McCown, 1942:2). According to such beliefs people cannot change unless they are conquered, migrate, or come in contact with people whose ceramics are a different color. In fact, in popular thought, pots come to have a life of their own.

As a matter of principle, we are slow to invoke catastrophism or racial change to explain what happened in southwest Asia between 10,000 and 4,000 B.C. We feel that each regional development must be seen in its own light and that internal, "adaptive" change was, more often than not, the change that mattered. Each of the prehistoric regional cultures of the Near East developed its own set of behavior patterns aimed at exploiting the grazing and farming potential of the ecological zone in which it lived. The specific adaptation depended on each group's technology, and its contacts with neighboring groups who had different techniques to solve their own ecological problems. It matters little that people occasionally borrowed a painted "red-ware" pot from people in the next valley. It matters a great deal that, on the basis of their own experiences, they learned through the years that their particular valley was best suited to semi-nomadic sheep grazing, or to intensive irrigation of six-row barley. Once the latter discovery had been made, drastic changes in culture took place if and when they made possible a more efficient exploitation of local resources; and we should attempt to see the changes in those terms before we resort to plagues, famines, and invasion.

By way of explanation we give a simple example. The Mohammad Jaffar phase is characterized by the manufacture of literally tens of thousands of flint microblades, many of which were secondarily retouched into drills, scrapers, backed bladelets, and dozens of other interesting tools. The Sabz phase, which follows shortly after the Mohammad Jaffar, has almost no vestige of this flint industry; a few bladelet cores showed up, but the bulk of the blades at the bottom of Tepe Sabz are crude and relatively large. The flint tools and the manner of chipping flint were both fundamentally different from what we found in the Mohammad Jaffar phase at Ali Kosh. The Deh Luran sequence is not unique in this respect, for much the same contrast is seen between the microlithic industry at Jarmo and the flints of Hassuna and Matarrah, which follow.

In the past, such differences might have been (and sometimes were) explained by saying that the Mohammad Jaffar flintmakers had reached "a peak of productive intensity," while those of the Sabz phase "had leveled off from that peak and were simply producing in a rather spiritless way" (compare Braidwood, Howe, *et al.*, 1960:49-50). Today we know that a really basic adaptive change took place in the Deh Luran plain between the Mohammad Jaffar and Sabz phases: competent irrigation began, and an economy divided between primitive farming, wild plant collecting, and hunting was replaced by the growing of an elaborate complex of irrigated plants. Accompanying this change were corresponding changes in material culture, of which the change in flint industry was only one example; well-fired pottery was an innovation of the same period. There was nothing "spiritless" about the people of the Sabz phase. The flint microliths of earlier times were apparently not essential to the new adaptation the people had made toward better exploiting the potential of the Deh Luran plain.

We do not claim that the causes for all observable changes in prehistoric culture can be deduced from the evidence available to archeologists. We claim only that our chances of understanding those changes are better if we attempt to see them in terms of the cultural ecology of the group in question, rather than as the result of catastrophe, degree of "cultural intensity," or racial mixture.

PREVIOUS WORK IN KHUZISTAN AND DEH LURAN

One hundred years of archeology preceded our arrival in Khuzistan. Early in the nineteenth century. H. C. Rawlinson (1839) had traveled through Susiana in search of the traces of ancient civilization there—especially inscriptions whose translation might throw light on the now-buried empire of the Elamites. William Kenneth Loftus (1857) reached Susiana not long afterward, and his early excavations at Susa revealed that the massive mound there was indeed the ruin of "Shushan the Palace," winter capital of the Achaemenian kings.

In the 1890's, Jacques de Morgan began systematically testing the depths of Susa, and the French Archeological Mission was underway. In 1903, during this same phase of archeological activity, Gautier and Lampre visited the Deh Luran plain to make test trenches at Tepe Musiyan, Tepe Khazineh, and a small mound they referred to as "Tepe Mohammad Djaffar." It appears that this latter site was the one we call Ali Kosh—and that, ironically enough, Ali Kosh (unbeknownst even to Gautier and Lampre) was the first "prepottery Neolithic" mound ever tested in the Near East.

Another key period of prehistoric investigations in Khuzistan was 1934 to 1939, during which the French Archeological Mission excavated at Tepes Jaffarabad, Jowi, Bandibal, and Bouhallan. (This was a period of intense archeological activity in the Near East in general; Dorothy Garrod was at work in the Mt. Carmel caves, Ghirshman excavating at Tepe Sialk, and Mallowan surveying the Khabur plain.) Eventually, the task of studying the pottery collections from Jaffarabad and the other prehistoric sites near Susa fell to Louis Le Breton (1947, 1957).

In the 1930's in the Near East, "sampling technique" was unknown, sieves unheard of, and undecorated body sherds considered a crushing bore. Despite the poor stratigraphic control used by the original excavators at Jaffarabad, Jowi, Bandibal, and Bouhallan, Le Breton managed to make sense out of the collections and even discern chronological changes. During roughly the same time period, Donald McCown (1941) in his doctoral dissertation attempted to relate the vessel shapes and painted designs to the Susiana pottery collections to sites in nearby Iraq.

Le Breton (1957) presented a five-period sequence for prehistoric Khuzistan: Susiana *a, b, c, d,* and *e.* Although based on selected ceramics from arbitrary levels of up to three meters, the sequence in general appears to be valid, and has been used as the basis for more recent syntheses (*e.g.*, Dyson, 1965). Our work at Deh Luran in 1961 and 1963 included the definition of four phases which we feel can now be substituted for Susiana *a* through *d*, inasmuch as they are (1) based on natural stratigraphy and (2) include more than ceramics; such as economic plants, domestic animals, stone artifacts, house construction details, and radiocarbon dates.

Robert M. Adams (1962) surveyed Susiana recently and has presented data on population growth and settlement patterns during all the periods mentioned above. Adams, a keen observer of human geography, formulated a number of hypotheses about prehistoric subsistence on the basis of his survey data: for example, that irrigation was practiced during Susiana *b* to *c* times, that goats and sheep were the most common domestic animals, that gazelles were hunted, and so on. In virtually every case, our excavations at Deh Luran have confirmed Adams' hypotheses.

All archeological investigations are preludes to further work, and ours is no exception. It will be many years before the point of diminishing returns is reached at Deh Luran, or anywhere in Khuzistan. Even as these words are being written, British archeologists, working just across the Iraqi border from the Deh Luran plain, are extending knowledge of many of our types and phases, and gaining entirely new data on the complex relationships between Deh Luran and adjacent regions. Our seven-period sequence is just the initial chronological framework on which, we hope, will be built a much broader picture of the development of early agriculture and animal domestication on the Assyrian-Khuzistan steppe.

Table 1

THE SEVEN PHASES OF THE DEH LURAN SEQUENCE, COMPARED WITH THEIR EQUIVALENTS IN THE "SUSIANA SEQUENCE" OF LE BRETON (1957) AND THE SOUTHERN MESOPOTAMIAN SEQUENCE OF OATES (Lines, 1953)

Estimated Absolute Date in Years B.C.	Phases of Deh Luran Sequence	Le Breton's "Susiana" Periods	Equivalent Periods in Southern Mesopotamia
3500....	...	...	...
4000....	Bayat	*d*	Ubaid II (Ubaid 4 of Oates)
4500....	Mehmeh	*c*	Ubaid I (Ubaid 3 of Oates)
5000....	Khazineh	*b*	Hajji Muhammad (Ubaid 2 of Oates)
5500....	Sabz	*a*	Eridu (Ubaid I of Oates)
6000....	Mohammad Jaffar	...	...
6500....	Ali Kosh	...	...
7000....	Bus Mordeh	...	...
7500....	...	...	...

II

THE ENVIRONMENTAL SETTING

One of the key environmental zones in the prehistory of the Near East is a belt of low piedmont and alluvial plain which stretches from the east bank of the Tigris River to the base of the distant Zagros Mountains. Within this zone of rolling, semi-arid steppe, at elevations of 100 to 500 meters above sea level, occur some of the highest densities of prehistoric archeological sites in the world.

Southwest of the piedmont lie the arid plains of southern alluvial Mesopotamia. To the northeast rise the wooded mountains of Kurdistan and Luristan, where the wild ancestors of all the early plant and animal domesticates in the Near East are at home. The piedmont is the zone of transition between Mesopotamia and the mountains, but it is also more than that: it combines many of the best features of both of the latter two regions.

Like the mountains, the piedmont has sufficient rainfall for dry farming. Like Mesopotamia, it has large rivers which can be used for irrigation. It is superb winter grazing land. Its summers are hot and dry, but not as hot and dry as Mesopotamia's. Its winters are cool, but not as cold as Kurdistan's. Once, before the advent of motorized hunting techniques, it supported enormous herds of wild herbivores. Perhaps most importantly, it was an environment where the cultivation techniques necessary in Southern Mesopotamia could be learned at slight risk to the farmer, because of the adequate rainfall. It was in this zone, as pointed out by Adams (1962:112), that the crucial transition from dry-farming to irrigation was probably made.

Four-fifths of the piedmont zone occurs within the political boundaries of modern Iraq, where it is known as the Assyrian Steppe. One-fifth lies in Iran, where it is known as Northern Khuzistan.

For thousands of years the plains of Northern Khuzistan have been, developmentally and politically, one of the nuclear areas of Iran. In ancient times, Khuzistan was the heartland of the Elamite empire, one of the great "first generation" civilizations of the Near East. Here lay the walled city of Susa—"Shushan the Palace"—where Esther was crowned queen, and where Darius and Xerxes made their winter capital. Among the hundreds of other archeological mounds which cover the Northern Khuzistan plain are the ziggurat of Chogha Zambil, now reconstructed by the French; the large prehistoric town of Chogha Mish, currently undergoing excavation by a University of Chicago expedition; and the sprawling ruin of Jundi Shapur, site of one of the world's great pre-Islamic universities.

Khuzistan's prehistory is no less impressive than her history. In 1961, a survey by Robert M. Adams of the University of Chicago revealed no fewer than 130 prehistoric sites in the vicinity of Susa (Adams, 1962:110). Four of these—Jaffarabad, Jowi, Bendibal, and Bouhallan, already excavated by the French in the 1930's—had yielded a five-period sequence which antedated the lowest levels of Susa (see Fig. 1). To these, the present report adds three antecedent periods which carry the Khuzistan sequence back to before 7000 B.C.

Most of the great prehistoric developments in Northern Khuzistan took place in

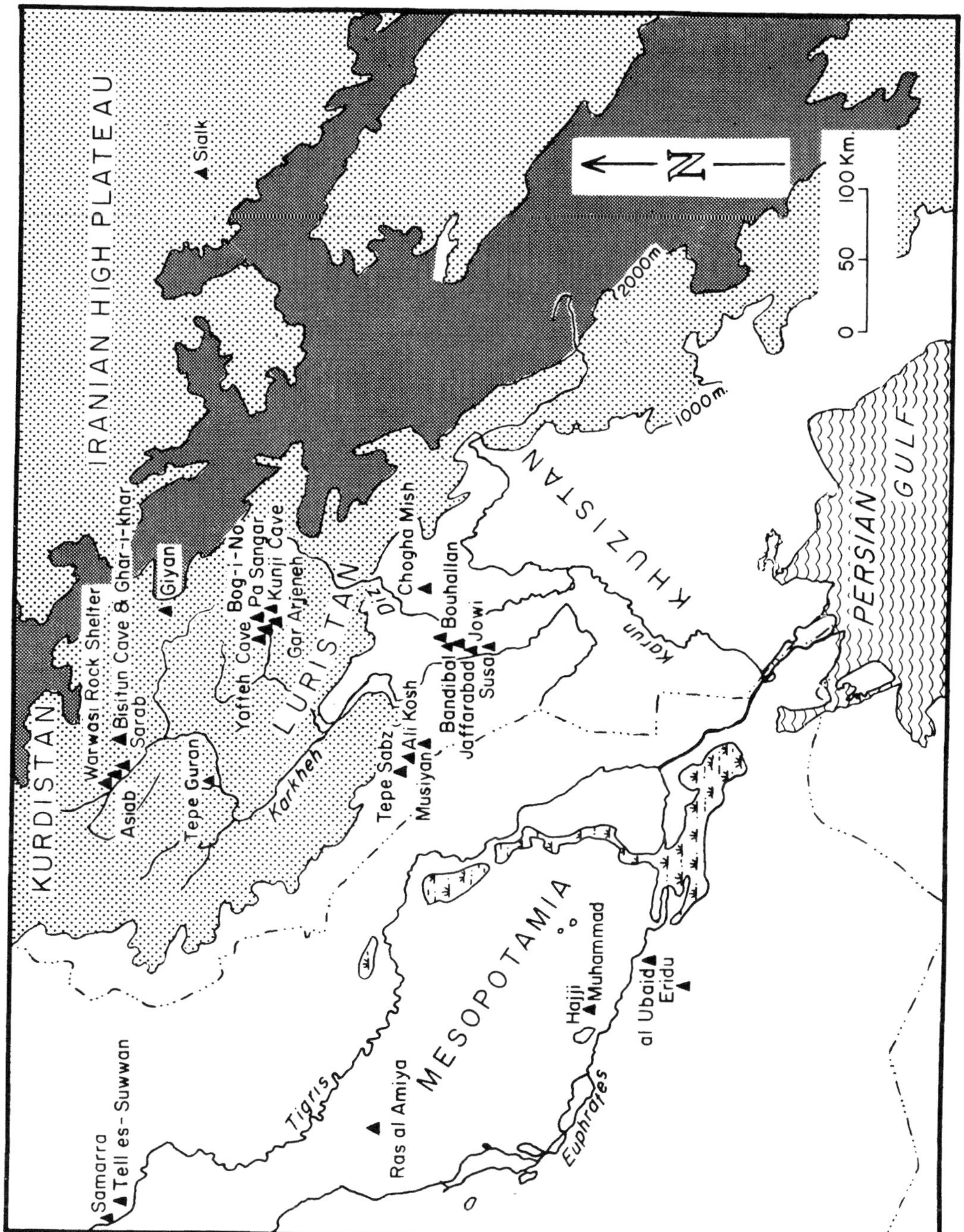

Fig. 1. Map of southwestern Iran and adjacent Mesopotamia, showing some of the archaeological sites mentioned in the text. (Small, isolated mountain ranges of over 2000 meters not shown.)

this "heartland" between the Karkheh, Shaur, Diz, and Karun rivers. This subregion of Khuzistan was called "Susiana" by the French archeologists, after the type site of Susa. Yet developments in "Susiana proper" are echoed in the region of Ram Hormuz, 90 km east of the Karun, and in Deh Luran, 60 km. west of the Karkheh. In terms of settlement patterns, architecture, ceramics, and artifact styles, the whole of Northern Khuzistan is a single coherent culture area.

One purpose of our excavations at Deh Luran was to determine how man had adapted to the Khuzistan steppe, and how dry farming, animal herding, and irrigation had begun there. Because of the general unity of the Northern Khuzistan environment, we feel that the Deh Luran evidence probably is relevant for an understanding of the early sequence in Susiana as well, and parallels between the two subregions will be drawn throughout this report. In this chapter, we will consider first of all the environment of Khuzistan in general, and finally the environment of the Deh Luran plain in particular.

THE GEOLOGY OF KHUZISTAN

In considering the geology of Khuzistan, it is necessary to consider the genesis of the whole Mesopotamian Depression, as summarized most recently by Lees and Falcon (1952). The entire area is an unstable geosyncline, which was produced late in the Pliocene by movements of the earth's crust, forcing the Iranian Plateau closer to the central massif of Arabia. The more mobile strip of land between these plateaus was compressed and pleated like an accordion. The effects of this pleating can still be seen in aerial photographs of the Zagros Mountains, which take the form of parallel ridges running in a generally northwest-southeast direction, at right angles to the lines of pressure from the two plateaus.

The center of this pleated area was depressed, subsided, and began to fill with the erosion products of the parallel mountain ridges. In this still-subsiding geosyncline, thousands of feet of sediment have accumulated. The rivers draining the Zagros Mountains—Tigris, Euphrates, Karun, and Karkheh—annually carry several million tons of silt down to the Depression. The result is that many parallel ridges lie buried in central Mesopotamia, giving the illusion of a relatively level plain. As one travels northeast toward the Zagros, gradually the parallel ridges begin to rise out of the plain: first as low hummocks, then ranges of fifty or a hundred meters, then as true mountains (see Fig. 2).

The first truly substantial range is a series of sandstone hills called the Jebel Hamrin, which forms the border between Iran and Iraq for part of its course (see Fig. 3). Broken in many areas by tributaries of the Tigris, it forms no barrier to travel between the piedmont and Mesopotamia.

The next range to the northeast is considerably higher, and constitutes the first tier of the Zagros Mountains. In Northwestern Khuzistan (near Deh Luran), this series of mountains is known as the Kuh-i-Siah ("Black Mountain"), and rises to elevations of 1450 meters, forming the northeast frontier of the plain. In north-central Khuzistan ("Susiana"), this same range is known as the Shaur Anticline, and it marks the boundary between the piedmont and the Zagros.

These first parallel ridges are composed of Cenozoic sandstones, conglomerates, and gypsiferous marls. Their erosion products, which form the Khuzistan plain, are therefore sands and clays of various types. Many of the springs which originate in these hills are so full of dissolved gypsum salts as to be undrinkable and of little use for irrigation. In this case, intensive use is made of streams which have come from farther away, in the higher limestone

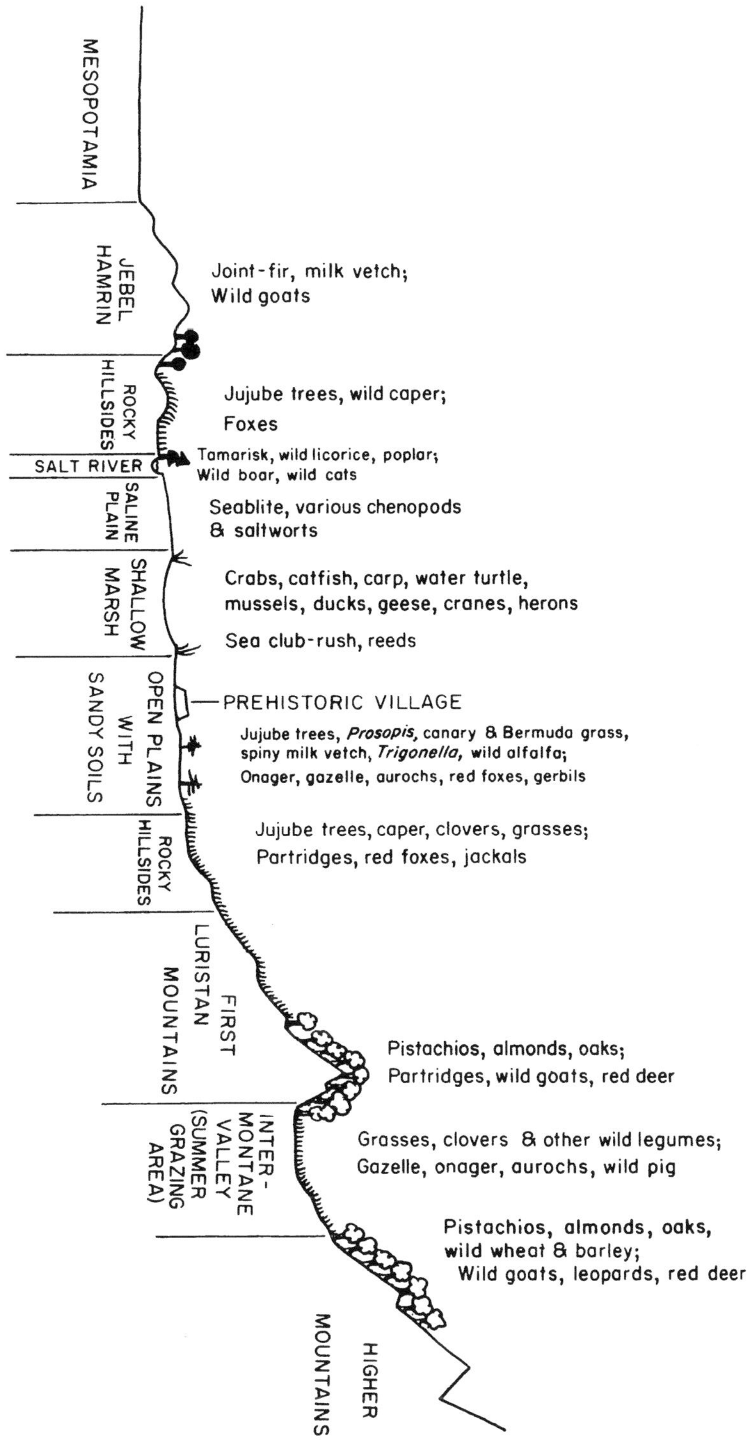

Fig. 2. Idealized cross-section of northern Khuzistan, between the Jebel Hamrin and the first Luristan mountains, showing "microenvironments" with some of their characteristic flora and fauna.

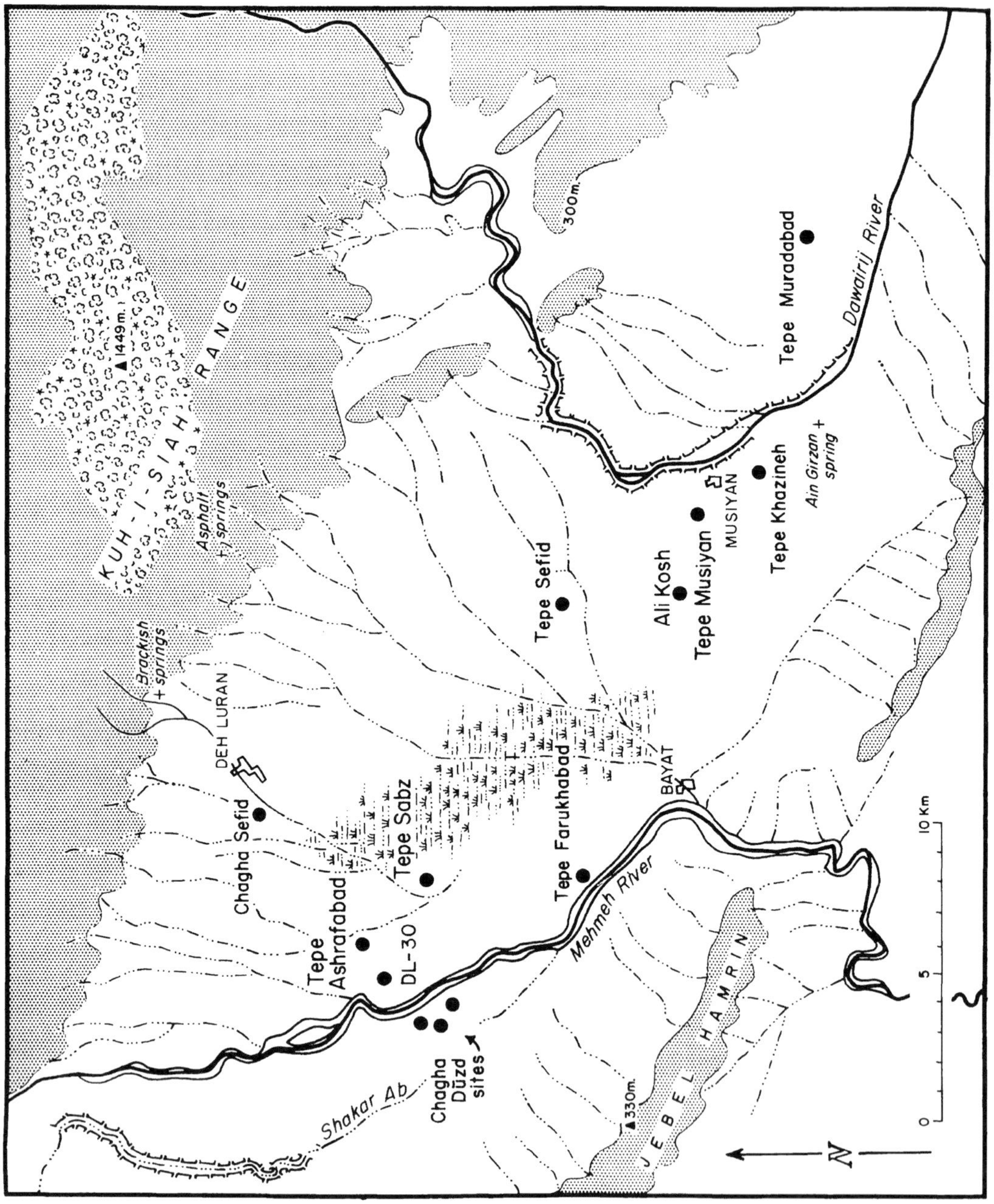

Fig. 3. Map of the Deh Luran plain, showing prehistoric sites located in 1961 and 1963.

mountains of Luristan and Kurdistan.

Wind and water have sculptured the face of Khuzistan with these raw materials. In some areas, long lines of stabilized sand dunes follow the Jebel Hamrin; in others, water stands in low depressions of gypseous clays. In some areas, rivers have cut their way far below the surface of the plain and are useless for irrigation; in others, the rivers flow above the level of the plain, held in check only by natural levees which, when breached, will open the way to extensive irrigation. Adams' survey in north-central Khuzistan (1962) makes clear how important such areas were in the prehistoric period. He also stresses one further point: in the northern part of Khuzistan, the belt of piedmont at the very base of the Zagros Mountains,

> . . .increased surface gradients and widespread underlying gravel deposits provide sufficient natural drainage over most of the area to minimize the problems of salinization and waterlogging that usually attend irrigation agriculture (p. 110).

THE CLIMATE OF KHUZISTAN

To the casual observer, the most striking aspect of the Khuzistan climate is the marked contrast between summer and winter. Throughout the summer months, dry air blows out of Eurasia and crosses Khuzistan on its way to the low-pressure areas in Arabia and India. Descending from a subtropical high-pressure area near latitude 30 degrees North, this air contains no moisture, and hence no rain can be expected. The evaporation rate is extremely high (see Cressey, 1960:99).

In addition, the area is scorched by local winds like the northwesterly *shamal,* which may blow hot and dry for nine days out of every ten, raising temperatures to 120 degrees Fahrenheit (de Morgan, 1900, mentioned 138 degrees on one occasion). Still worse is the *simoon* or "poison wind," which is believed by villagers to have caused fatalities in the past. The *simoon* is a hot wind from the southeast which blows for three or four days with the intensity of a blast furnace, raising great clouds of dust which darken the sky for days.

The summers of Khuzistan appear to have left an indelible stamp on all who have experienced them. William Kenneth Loftus, first excavator of the site of Susa, on entering the area in the 1850's was struck by the fact that:

> It was now only the 19th of May, and yet the grass was scorched to a bright yellow, which. . .gave to the imagination a vivid idea of the intense heat reigning in that region three months later in the season. . . . During nine months in the year the whole country is burned up by the sun's heat, with an intensity which gives some credance to Strabo's report, that lizards and serpents could not crawl across the streets at mid-day without being burnt (Loftus, 1857:307, 346).

Late in the autumn the pattern begins to change. Westerly winds circulate irregularly across the middle latitudes, and where the polar and tropical air masses meet, weak cyclonic storms are produced. Some cyclonics traverse the entire Mediterranean, pass through the gap between the Taurus and Labanon Mountains, and move southeast across the Syrian desert. Reaching the Zagros Mountains—the series of parallel ridges which separate Mesopotamia from the Iranian plateau—they rise, cool and condense. Some of these storms may be quite violent, and although their pattern is erratic and unpredictable, such low pressure areas move into Khuzistan on an average of once every two weeks. Once they have passed, there is clear, cool weather as cold air from the plateau to the north and east breaks over the mountains and descends on Mesopotamia (see Wright, 1961:136; Cressey, 1960:97-102).

The violent rains of the Mediterranean cyclonics are particularly typical of autumn and spring in Khuzistan. At times they are preceded by a wall of red dust which only settles with the arrival of the rains. In mid-winter, more gentle and warmer rains may come to the area by means of anticyclonic storms from Arabia. Thus the winter passes in a succession of violent brief squalls, clear balmy days, cool drizzly nights, and occasional dust storms. When it is all over, an average of 350 mm. of rain have fallen on Northern Khuzistan.

The effect of this precipitation on the parched northern plains is frequently spectacular, as described by Loftus:

> At the beginning of January. . .the young grass, brought into existence by the heavy rains, makes its appearance, and increases with a truly tropical rapidity and luxuriance; nowhere have I ever seen such rich vegetation as that which clothes the verdant plains of Shush, interspersed with numerous plants of a sweet-scented and delicate iris (Loftus 1857:346).

An equally impressive description is that of Rawlinson, who wrote that in March of 1836 "it was difficult to ride along the Shapur (Shaur) for the luxuriant grass that clothed its banks, and all around, the plain was covered with a carpet of the richest verdure" (Rawlinson, 1839:71).

THE VEGETATION OF KHUZISTAN

The Susiana that Loftus and Rawlinson explored was, like today's Northern Khuzistan, a pale shadow of its former self—overgrazed, overcultivated, and salinized for many thousands of years. We glimpse the original vegetation of Khuzistan only vaguely through the writings of botanist Henri Pabot (1960), who attempted to reconstruct it from the surviving vestiges of the ancient steppe flora. Helbaek's studies of the ancient plant remains from our Deh Luran sites (Appendix I) contribute further data which was unknown to Pabot.

Pabot maintains that the original arborescent vegetation of Northern Khuzistan was sparse, with widely spaced jujube trees (*Zizyphus*) on the dry rolling plains. In the humid river bottoms grew forests of tamarisk (*Tamarix*), Euphrates poplar (*Populus euphratica*), and wild licorice (*Glycyrrhiza*). All these aborescent genera remain in the area today.

Because of the relatively low precipitation and the extremely high summer temperatures, few herbaceous perennials survived; but tough, hardy plants like camel thorn (*Alhagi*), *Prosopis* (a woody legume related to American mesquite), and bitter wild melon (*Citrullus*) grew all year. So did tough grasses like *Aristida* (needle grass), *Aeluropus* (cat's claw grass), *Hyparrhenia*, and *Cymbopogon* (oilgrass).

With the winter rains, the herbaceous vegetation of the plain grew richer from the addition of annual grasses, small legumes, and chenopods. Clovers and burnets, wild alfalfa (*Medicago*), spiny milk vetch (*Astragalus*), *Trigonella* (a member of the pea family, and plantain (*Plantago*) reached maturity by the end of March. Canary grass (*Phalaris paradoxa*), Bermuda grass (*Cynodon dactylon*), meadow grass (*Poa*), and feather grass (*Stipa*) provided forage for herds of wild ungulates. Asphodels, iris, and wild narcissus added color to the "rich carpet of verdure" described by the early British explorers of Northern Khuzistan. However, Helbaek's study of the carbonized plants from Tepe Sabz (Appendix I) indicate that some of the grasses and legumes may have been introduced as crop weeds during the sixth millennium B.C.

"MICROENVIRONMENTS" OF NORTHERN KHUZISTAN

The part of Khuzistan with which this report is concerned is the belt of northern plains receiving 200 to 350 mm. of annual precipitation, lying at elevations of 100 to 300 meters above sea level, and classified as semiarid steppe. This has been called the "dry zone" of Khuzistan by Pabot (1960); zoogeographically, it is the Iranian equivalent of Hatt's "Assyrian plains and foothills" biotic province (Hatt, 1959). In this report we will refer to it simply as "Northern Khuzistan."

This belt is far from uniform; it can be divided into a number of biotopes or "microenvironments" (Coe and Flannery, 1964) each of which is characterized by a particular plant community and certain species of animals. These biotopes are, in effect, "resource areas" which were exploited in different ways by the ancient inhabitants of Khuzistan. They include features as different as sand dunes, sandstone and gypsum hills, reed marshes, and saline and non-saline plains (both humid and dry). The data on Khuzistan suggest that, in the words of Adams (1962:109), "gross descriptive categories like 'semiarid steppeland'. . .may be as inadequate for a deeper historical understanding as they are for the contemporary planner."

In this section, we will present a brief description of Northern Khuzistan's major biotopes, emphasizing the potential resources of each from the standpoint of human exploitation. In our descriptions, we will draw heavily on the work of Hatt, Helbaek, and Pabot.

Open Plains with Sandy Soils

This is one of the largest resource areas, and the one with the highest agricultural potential. These sandy soils are the best drained and allow better infiltration of rain; evaporation is lower than in silty soils, and the surface cannot form a compressed crust. Consequently, the sandy plains support the most varied plant complex of any soil area, and they were probably a more extensive habitat before cultivation began. Today, alluviation due to agriculture and deforestation have covered many previously sandy areas with silty alluvium, greatly decreasing permeability and reducing their potential for plant growth.

The dominant tree is the "christ's-thorn" or jujube (*Zizyphus*); perennial grasses include *Aristida* and *Poa.* Annual herbs include spiny milk vetch (*Astragalus*) and *Trigonella,* two small legumes eaten at 7000 B.C.; wild alfalfa or medick (*Medicago*), also eaten; and a variety of clovers, plantains, and annual grasses (*Schismus, Stipa,* etc.) which are useful for grazing. Bermuda grass and canary grass are also common.

These plains are grazed by the Persian gazelle (*Gazella subgutturosa*) and in prehistoric times also had herds of onager or wild ass (*Equus hemionus*). Red foxes (*Vulpes vulpes*) and jackals (*Canis aureus*) are active nocturnally. The Karun desert gerbil (*Meriones crassus*) and the Indian gerbil (*Tatera indica*) burrow into well-drained areas or archeological mounds. Hyenas (*Hyaena hyaena*) make dens in the dry wadis cutting across the plain. Two large lizards, *Uromastix* and *Varanus,* are also residents.

The open plains had a high potential for gazelle and onager hunting, collecting of wild legumes, and cultivation of cereals. During the winter season, good pasturage was available for herds of domestic sheep and goats. This habitat was very heavily exploited in prehistoric times.

Shallow Marshes

Many low areas of the Khuzistan plain are seasonally-flooded to permanent marshes. The more permanent sloughs have a border of reeds (*Phragmites communis*), cat's claw grass (*Aeleoropus*), club-rush (*Scirpus*), spike rush (*Eleocharis*), and common sedge (*Cyperus*). Most of these sloughs are shallow bodies of water with low oxygen content, inhabited by various genera of catfish and cyprinids (members of the carp family) who can tolerate such conditions. Water turtles (*Clemmys caspica*) and fresh-water crabs (*Potamon*) are among the edible aquatic resources. Sloughs untimately connected to the freshwater rivers of the alluvial plain may have various genera of mussels (*Unio, Leguminaea, Pseudodontopsis*). In this habitat, otter (*Lutra lutra*) and wild boar (*Sus scrofa*) abound.

During the winter, these marsh areas are visited by great quantities of water fowl. Ducks, geese, cranes, herons, and storks are among the birds which arrive in September and October and stay until March or April. These waterfowl were widely eaten in prehistoric times, as they are today.

The aquatic resources of the marshes and sloughs figured prominently in the ancient diet in Khuzistan. Fish, crabs, mussels, and water turtles were important to the first permanent settlers of the plain, and reeds and club-rushes are still used today in manufacturing mats and baskets.

Riverine

The sluggish rivers of Khuzistan meander across the plain, winding between sand bars and normally occupying only a small portion of their beds. The remainder of the bed is taken up by low forests of tamarisk (*Tamarix*), licorice (*Glycyrrhiza*), poplar (*Populus*), bramble bushes (*Rubus*) and other woody plants. There are carp, catfish, crabs, turtles, and freshwater mussels in the rivers, and along the banks live abundant small mammal populations—the Indian gerbil (*Tatera*), long-eared hedgehog (*Hemiechinus auritus*), otter, and various wild cats (*Felis chaus* and *F. libyca*). Until 1923, there were lions in the riverine thickets of Khuzistan (Hatt, 1959:51).

In the tamarisk forests there are black partridges (*Francolinus francolinus*), marten (*Martes foina*), and wild boar. Such forests are today the last stronghold of the Mesopotamian fallow deer (Haltenorth, 1961), an animal thought until recently to be extinct. In the Deh Luran plain, at least, there is no prehistoric evidence for fallow deer, and we are uncertain about its role in the diet of ancient Khuzistan.

The riverine habitat seems to have been used mainly for its aquatic resources. In addition, tamarisk was used for firewood; and (although we have no concrete evidence to this effect) it is possible that poplar, when present, was used prehistorically as a building material, just as it is today.

Rocky or Gravelly Hillsides

The rocky hillsides flanking the Northern Khuzistan plain have a distinct vegetation. At the northern margin of the steppe, where the talus rises toward the Luristan Mountains, chenopods and salt-resistant plants decrease and there is a substantial increase in perennial grasses, and arborescent and bushy species. Jujube trees (*Zizyphus*), *Prosopis,* and wild caper (*Capparis*) are among the woody plants with edible fruit. Plantains, clovers, burnets, mints, spurges, and small members of the mustard family are seasonally abundant. Good forage for domestic animals can be found on these slopes, including *Hyparrhenia, Cymbopogon* (oil grass), *Aristida, Aegilops,* and some varieties of wild *Hordeum* (including the ancestor of domestic barley).

These rocky hillsides are roamed by jackals and red foxes, porcupines (*Hystrix indicus*), gerbils and bandicoot-rats (*Nesokia indica*), and partridges (*Ammoperdix* and *Alectoris*). For the most part, the wild plant resources of this habitat outweigh the animals.

Habitats of Little Utility

Within the plains of Northern Khuzistan are localized habitats of low potential for human exploitation. These include areas of highly saline soils; sand dunes; eroded gypsum hills; and bare outcrops of sandstone.

Poorly-drained areas within the open plains biotope can be readily converted to saline conditions, and many areas have been so converted in the past. Such places then become agriculturally unproductive, featuring only a low cover of salt-tolerant chenopods or saltworts (*Salsola, Bassia,*

Halocharis and others). *Aeluropus* and *Atriplex* also take over. The mammalian fauna of these areas is virtually nonexistent.

Sand dunes are seized and fixed by the sedge *Carex*. Once stabilized, they support a cover of needle grass (*Aristida*), bindweed (*Convolvulus*) and thistle (*Echinops*). Such stabilized dune areas are the haunt of the jerboa (*Jaculus jaculus*) who forages nocturnally for seeds and is able to go long periods without water.

The eroded gypsum hills at the north edge of the Khuzistan plain are an unpromising region of salt-tolerant chenopods, joint fir (*Ephedra*) and low perennial herbs. A few species of *Astragalus* colonize both these localities and the sandstone outcrops of the Jebel Hamrin. Partridges, foxes and jackals, and bandicoot rats are the dominant mammals. On the higher sandstone cliffs there are wild goats (*Capra hircus aegagrus*).

The Higher Mountains to the North

One other habitat must be considered. This is the zone of the Shaur anticline or Kuh-i-Siah range, which occurs at elevations of 600 to 800 meters, visible from the plain of Khuzistan but reached only after an all-day climb. This higher mountain area, which lies fully 300 meters above the steppe, receives somewhat more precipitation and has summer temperatures which are not so fatal to the vegetation as are those of the plain. Here stands of pistachio (*Pistacia atlantica*) and almond (*Amygdalus spartioides*) can be found, interspersed with good forage species like goat-face grass (*Aegilops*) sage (*Salvia*), wild members of the barley group (*Hordeum murinum* and *bulbosum*), brome grass (*Bromus*), *Hyparrhenia, Cymbopogon,* and clovers. Preserved pistachios and almonds in the prehistoric sites of the Deh Luran plain indicate that the ancient inhabitants of Khuzistan occasionally ascended to this zone, and it is reasonable to assume that they made use of this good forage by taking their sheep and goats up to the mountains. This habitat has a high potential for wild plant collecting and grazing, but is too steep and rocky for successful agriculture. Wild goats can also be hunted in this area.

GEOGRAPHY OF THE DEH LURAN PLAIN

The plain of Deh Luran is situated in the extreme northwest corner of Khuzistan, between 32 degrees 15 minutes and 32 degrees 30 minutes north latitude and 47 degrees 08 minutes and 47 degrees 24 minutes east longitude. It is bounded on the south by the Jebel Hamrin, the last landmark before the Iran-Iraq border. To the north, it is bounded by the Kuh-i-Siah, first of the high mountain ranges leading up to Luristan. Two shallow rivers, the Mehmeh and the Dawairij, constitute its western and eastern borders respectively (see Fig. 3). The occupied portion of the Deh Luran plain is about 300 square km.

The soils of the Deh Luran plain, like those of northern Khuzistan in general, are composed of sands and clays, which are the erosion products of the sandstones and gypseous marls which flank them. Today these soils range periously close to the limits of cultivation because of salinity, and archeological evidence suggest they have always been in this situation—that the history of the plain has been one of localized worsening of the soil through agricultural activity, combined with the shifting of settlements to areas not previously cultivated and hence still fertile. The areas with the highest densities of prehistoric villages appear to be the localities with the worst salinity problem today.

In 1961 we took a series of soil samples from both fallow land and cultivated land in the vicinity of the site of Ali Kosh, in the southeast portion of the plain. The samples were analyzed for us by Dr. Charles Simkins of the Khuzistan Development Service, who has provided us with the following description:

Sample 06246:
Soil from a random series of points along a one-kilometer line in fallow land near Tepe Ali Kosh, in the Southeast Deh Luran plain
pH 8.0 (mildly alkaline)
Conductivity 4.2 millimohs per cm. (very high salt content)
Oxidation value 0.44 (very low organic matter)
Phosphorus 3.0 parts per million (low available phosphorus)
Potassium 160 parts per million (relatively high potassium content)

Sample 06247:
Soil from a random series of points in a 200 meter square of planted field near Tepe Ali Kosh, in the southeast Deh Luran plain
pH 8.1 (mildly alkaline)
Conductivity 5.6 (very high salt content)
Oxidation value 0.66 (very low in organic content)
Phosphorus 4.0 parts per million (low available phosphorus)
Potassium 290 parts per million (relatively high potassium)

Dr. Simkins' letter, evaluating these soil samples, reads: "Based on this analysis, we can be sure that the yields of most crops would be quite restricted in growth. A conductivity reading from 2 to 4 millimohs indicates that yields of very sensitive crops may be restricted due to salt content. Readings from 4 to 8 indicate yields of most crops restricted."

Soil salinity is not the only agricultural problem in the Deh Luran plain. Both the Dawairij and the Mehmeh Rivers are brackish, so filled with dissolved salts from the gypsum beds north of the Deh Luran plain that they are virtually useless for irrigation. In 1961, Dr. Simkins also analyzed for us a sample of water from the Mehmeh River, and provided us with the following report:

Sample 1241:
Water from the Mehmeh River, near Deh Luran
Conductivity 7700 EC x 10^6
Per cent sodium 51.7
pH 7.31
total hardness 1852.0
Classification: "The above sample of water from the River Mehmeh comes under the classification of C4-S-4 water, possessing very high salinity and very high sodium hazard."

Of this sample, Simkins writes: "This water is not suitable for irrigation under ordinary conditions. It can only be used when the soils are very permeable; drainage must be adequate; irrigation water must be applied in excess to provide leaching, and only salt tolerant crops should be grown."

In spite of these limitations, it appears that the Deh Luran plain was a relatively favorable place for settlement during the period from 7500 B.C. to 3000 B.C. From this time span, we have thus far located at least thirteen mounds marking the eroded remains of prehistoric villages or towns. At their smallest, these mounds may be only a hectare in extent and a meter or two in height; the largest prehistoric site, Tepe Musiyan, is 1.5 km. in circumference and stands 17 meters high. To a very real extent, therefore, it would seem that the present barren and saline character of the Deh Luran plain is the result of misuse by man, who through intensive cultivation, overgrazing, and irrigation with brackish water, destroyed what may have been a reasonably fertile plain at 7500 B.C. We would guess that Deh Luran lay too close to the limits of tolerable salinity, and that once its natural equilibrium was destroyed it never recovered.

The prehistoric sites in the Deh Luran plain fall geographically into two clusters. Eight mounds occur in the northwestern part of the plain, on both sides of the Memeh River. The remaining five mounds lie west and east of the Dawairij River in the southeast part of the plain. These two clusters are separated by a low-lying depression which floods periodically during the winter rains, and has no evidence of prehistoric settlement. There are reasons to believe that in prehistoric times, before it filled in with silt, this depression was a shallow marsh or slough. Prehistoric agricultural activity seems to have centered on the higher and better drained areas to either side of this slough.

The northwestern cluster of sites lies in a region of rolling steppe cut by shallow, intermittent wadis. The northernmost site (Chagha Sefid) appears as a dull white mound on the outskirts of the village of Deh Luran, but all the remaining sites are in areas without permanent habitation. These areas, however, have local names ("Ashrafabad," "Chagha Dūzd," "Haft Tepe," etc.) and are used during the winter rainy season by Lurish nomads. These nomads descend from the mountains in October and set up black-tent encampments near shallow natural depressions where run-off from the rains tends to collect (see Pl. 2*a*). They plow and plant these moist depressions with barley and wheat, obtaining one crop each winter. In addition, they graze their sheep and goats on the higher ground to either side of the depressions (Pl. 2*b*). Because of the extensive network of small stream courses and old silted-in irrigation canals in the Ashrafabad-Haft Tepe area, at least some of which are presumably prehistoric, a considerable amount of runoff is carried south to the vicinity of the prehistoric sites, where it accumulates in the depressions farmed by the nomads. Such was the case in the immediate area of Tepe Sabz, one of the prehistoric villages described in this report.

Today the vegetation of this area is meager. Camel-thorn (*Alhagi*), woody legumes (*Prosopis*), and bitter wild melon (*Citrullus*) are dominant on the high, flat steppe all year; in the winter, Bermuda grass (*Cynodon*) and canary grass (*Phalaris*) sprout in the moist depressions. In the deeper wadis and in the Mehmeh River are stands of tamarisk (*Tamarix*). Many areas of the plain are today without any evidence of vegetation during the heart of the summer dry season.

The village of Deh Luran is the only permanent settlement in the vicinity of these sites. Deh Luran (which means, literally, "village of the Lurs") is a relatively recent enclave of exnomadic Kurds and Lurs who were resettled by the Reza Shah; there was no village there when Gautier and Lampre passed through in 1903. The unsuitability of the spot for a village of 1500 people is indicated by the fact that sweet water must be brought to the town daily by tank truck from a spring near Musiyan; the only springs at Deh Luran are either brackish or sulphurous. The majority of the villagers drink this water for lack of anything better, and irrigate a little barley and sesame. In the winter season, when rain water collects in small depressions and wadi bottoms near Ali Kosh, our Deh Lurani workmen eagerly filled their goatskin water bags from these mud puddles and carried the rainwater home with them.

Northeast of Deh Luran, on the southern talus of the Kuh-i-Siah range, lies another series of springs; but these produce natural asphalt. Once commercially exploited by the British, these tar pits were eventually abandoned because of their small yield in proportion to the expense of transporting the asphalt. The Deh Luranis use the tar for waterproofing and minor roof repairs, and archeological evidence shows that it was used far back into prehistory for hafting tools and mending and waterproofing baskets. It is probable that asphalt from the Deh Luran springs (often incorrectly referred to in archeological reports as "bitumen")[1] was widely traded by the ancient villagers of the area.

The southeastern cluster of five prehistoric sites includes Ali Kosh, one of the sites we excavated, and Tepes Musiyan and

[1] True "bitumen" is free of impurities.

Khazineh, excavated by the French in 1903. This area is somewhat less dissected by intermittent wadis, but the number of silted-in channels which may be ancient irrigation canals is very high. The village of Musiyan (from which many of our workmen came) farms many square kilometers of this region, using both naturally-flooded depressions[2] and drier areas which are irrigated with water pumped up from the Dawairij River. In addition, water from Ain Girzan, a fresh water spring in the foothills leading up to the Jebel Hamrin, is channeled north toward Musiyan for irrigation. Ain Girzan is the only spring of any size in the entire Deh Luran plain which is not saline.

The Musiyan area produces barley, wheat, sorghum, and sesame, though not in excess of its needs. Each year many Musiyanis cross the Jebel Hamrin to find work at Amara or Baghdad in Iraq.

Only one other permanent settlement exists in the Deh Luran plain. This is the village of Bayat, a small hamlet near the police border post where the Mehmeh River leaves the plain and cuts through the Jebel Hamrin. The people of Bayat keep cattle and water buffalo, and trade milk and yoghurt to the village of Deh Luran. In addition, there seems to be some relationship between the people of Bayat and the seasonal nomads who settle the Ashrafabad-Haft Tepe area each winter. The region is one of low agricultural potential, where stabilized sand dunes flank the river and gravelly hills with jujube trees (*Zizyphus*) climb to the crest of the Jebel Hamrin.

We excavated or tested mounds in both the northwest and southeast site clusters in 1963. In addition, we observed many other localities in these cluster-areas where prehistoric sherds are strewn across the surface of the plain with no evidence of an archeological mound. These localities probably mark the site of villages of brief duration, and their number may be double that of the actual mounds. Because we know from our own excavations that the Deh Luran plain has received at least three meters of alluvium since 7000 B.C., it is probable that many small villages, occupied for only a generation or two, lie totally buried below the surface of the plain.

Our survey did not record sites occupied later than 3000 B.C., although many such sites can be found at Deh Luran. The most impressive of these is Tepe Garran, a high tower-shaped mound a kilometer north of Ali Kosh; and Tepe Musiyan, of course, has considerable material in its upper layers which postdates 3000 B.C. These materials were not germane to the problems of early food production, and we have left them for others to investigate.

[2]Our workmen told us that in 1962, a winter of very heavy rains, water stood "as deep as a man's head" in fields surrounding Tepe Musiyan.

III

EXCAVATION TECHNIQUES IN 1963

INTRODUCTION

Some archeologists in southwestern Asia maintain that there is only one method for digging a Near Eastern tell. Others restrict this to mean that there is one proper method for each region, or one proper method for each type of site. We have the feeling that these statements put the cart before the horse by failing to take into account the purpose for which the excavation is being made. In the course of a single excavation at a single site, a Near Eastern specialist may resort to three, four, five, or possibly even more sets of field techniques depending on the problem he is attempting to solve. He has to improvise freely. He knows he cannot dissect a temple or expose a building complex by the same techniques he uses to work out the stratigraphy of a deep surrounding to virgin soil. We, like others, adapted our techniques to the specific problem we were attempting to solve. The best characterization we can give to the excavation methods we used in 1963 is to say that they were adapted to recover minute stratigraphic changes and to correct for the mistakes that we made in 1961.

Our objective in digging these initial stratigraphic trenches was to observe the complexes of artifacts, plants, and animals which succeeded one another in the Deh Luran area. In order to catch the successive changes in these complexes with any precision, it was to our advantage to proceed downward by the smallest steps feasible. At the same time, we needed to adhere as closely to the natural stratigraphy of the mound as possible, so that the complexes we recovered would be truly valid assemblages of objects which had actually coexisted in time. Many archeologists have done this simply by regarding each stratum of house floors and wall stubs (commonly referred to as a "building level") as the "natural unit." To do this at Ali Kosh and Tepe Sabz would have been to close our eyes to the fact that most of the debris was not buildings at all, but middens, ash lenses, clay lenses, or featureless fill washed in from disintegrated walls outside the excavated area. Many of the changes we wished to pinpoint took place during the deposition of such non-architectural strata.

Many archeologists who dig by the "building level" method find it expedient to excavate rapidly with larger tools until they arrive within some prearranged distance (e.g., 10 or 15 cm.) above a house floor; at this point, small tools are used and the floor debris sieved to recover small objects. At Ali Kosh, we were faced with the necessity of observing changes in microlithic flint tools as well as recovering small fish vertebrae and other objects which occurred not merely on house floors but throughout the stratigraphic column. We therefore had to excavate with small tools from top to bottom and sieve all the dirt through two sizes of screens, regardless of whether or not it had come from a floor. Use of the same techniques at Tepe Sabz also yielded necessary small objects like carbonized almonds, fish bones, flint blade fragments, and other artifacts. When the complexes of small items have been worked out in detail for all the prehistoric phases, it will no longer be necessary to use screens with a mesh as fine as 3 by 3 mm., as we did in 1963.

How we went about digging in 1963 was greatly influenced by some of the difficulties we had encountered in 1961. These included: (1) the peculiar nature of the prehistoric room walls in the Deh Luran sites; (2) the nature of the deposits in which carbonized seeds occurred; (3) the need for a large number of readable "sections" or "profiles" going north-south and east-west through the excavation at close intervals in order to keep track of the stratigraphic relationship of houses, middens, ash dumps, and other features; and (4) the need for a system which would allow us to keep one small part of the excavation moving downward ahead of the rest, "previewing" the coming natural strata so we could prepare ourselves ahead of time for dealing with them. "Digging down into the unknown" may be a romantic and exciting concept, but it makes for clumsy and poorly-planned archeology.

The walls of the prehistoric buildings in the Deh Luran plain are not made of packed, chaff-tempered *tauf* or *pisé* as are those of contemporary sites in Kurdistan and Mesopotamia, and we sometimes found it difficult to deal with them as *tauf* walls are commonly dealt with. The usual technique is to pick up to the *tauf* wall with a sensitive, light-tined pick, feeling for the difference in density between the wall stub and the surrounding fill; with a careful tap, the experienced workman can cause the last bit of fill to flake away from the wall stub and leave it standing. Unfortunately there is little or no difference in density between the wall stub and its surrounding fill in the Deh Luran sites. The Ali Kosh walls were made of unbaked, non-chaff-tempered clay or silt slabs, and they were closely surrounded by clay or silt of the same texture, which had formed as a result of the disintegration of the upper part of the wall. It may be for this very reason that virtually no traces of architecture were detected by the French in their excavations at Tepes Jaffarabad, Jowi, Bandibal, and Buhallan, in central Khuzistan (see Le Breton, 1947). Scraping with a sharp trowel, however, reveals a color difference between the silt slabs or "bricks" and the adjoining fill, and this color change is strong enough so that the wall can be easily traced by additional scraping. In several cases (especially in zone B_2 at Ali Kosh), it proved possible to leave such wall stubs standing 50 cm. high by a combination of picking and scraping (see Pl. 9).

A second problem, mentioned above, was the recovery of carbonized seeds. We needed such seeds in bulk so that we could observe, in some detail, changes in subsistence which took place during the sequence. The reader will note that our preliminary report on the 1961 season states confidently that "plant remains were scarce at Ali Kosh" (Hole and Flannery, 1962: 125). Nothing could be farther from the truth. The mound is filled with seeds from top to bottom; all that was "scarce" in 1961 was our ability to find them, and when we had added the "flotation" technique (Struever, 1965)[1] in 1963 we recovered a stratified series of samples totaling over 40,000 seeds. Part of the problem was our expectation that such seeds would be found in burned granaries, hearths, or ovens, when in reality they were almost everywhere but those places. The thinnest smear of ash on a house floor might contain as many as ten species of plants. The mottled earth of a small midden outside a doorway often yielded a thousand seeds. What we needed was a technique that

[1]We began the season by using the technique described by Struever but it proved impractical due to the scarcity of water at Ali Kosh. More frugal (but also more tiring) was the technique introduced by Helbeck (see Appendix I), based on his laboratory methods in Copenhagen.

would allow us to test all such potentially important deposits, determine which were the most rewarding, and carefully work out their stratigraphic relationship to the houses above, below, and beside them. Hand-in-hand with this approach went our knowledge that these "non-architectural" deposits really constituted more of the debris at Ali Kosh and Tepe Sabz than did houses.

The method of excavating which we finally settled on in 1963 was to lay out a grid of one-meter squares over the whole of the area to be excavated, and begin by digging alternate squares so that a section drawing of deposits could be made every two meters throughout the site, running both east-west and north-south. As soon as a square had been excavated to a depth of ten cm. all four of its walls were shaved vertically with a sharp, square-ended shovel, and the stratigraphy examined. When it appeared that the pickman had encountered a wall, attention turned to the adjoining square through which the wall ran. This square would be taken down to the level at which the top of the wall appeared, and the wall traced by scraping. Even when the wall had been fully traced out and it was clear where the corners of the room were, the system of one-meter squares was not abandoned; for some squares lay inside the room, others outside, others in a corner or doorway, and by labeling the artifacts according to square as well as depth we could always tell whether they had come from some particular part of the room or from a midden outside. Moreover, the groundwork was thus laid for future analysis, by which it could be determined whether the repeated associations of certain tools with other tools or with certain grains or animal bones, was due to chance or had functional significance. A beginning toward such analysis was made in the field with the discovery that clusters of flint-nodule choppers repeatedly occurred in squares with clusters of the butchered limb bones of wild ox and onager (see Pl. 10*b*).

When walls were not encountered in the course of digging through one part of the deposits in an exploratory one-meter square, work proceeded by means of ten-centimeter levels. Ten cm. were the least that could conveniently be removed at a time (just as a one-meter square proved to be the smallest space in which a native pickman could squat). The pickman carefully loosened the dirt with a small, light-tined pick; a dirt carrier transported his dirt to the sieving area, where it was passed through two sizes of sieves, operated by a pair of workmen. The pickman, dirt carrier, and two sievers were a team of four men (often from a single family) who habitually worked together, so that there would be no possibility for the dirt from a given square to be transported to the wrong sieves. At the end of a ten-centimeter level, all the objects recovered either by the pickman or his sievers were bagged together, washed, and labeled according to square and depth. The code numbers written on each artifact or animal bone might indicate, for example, that the object had been found at "Ali Kosh; Square 21; at a depth of 260 to 270 cm. below the surface." Reference to the section drawings would immediately show whether such a provenience had been a midden, an ash lens, the corner of a room, or some other feature, as well as relating it (according to its natural stratum) to ten-centimeter levels in adjacent squares.

Adherence to ten-centimeter levels was not so rigid as to ignore the clear natural stratigraphy of the sites. A gray ash bed would be troweled out separately from the buff floor below it. When a house floor was reached, at whatever absolute depth in centimeters, excavation ceased and the pickmen cleaned around the heavy stone tools (choppers, pounders, grinding slabs, etc.) resting on the floor so they could all be mapped *in situ* (see for example Fig.

10). When we reached an old mound surface or courtyard surface (as we did at the break between zones B_1 and B_2 at Ali Kosh), all squares were scraped with sharp trowels just to the level of this natural feature. In other words, our sites were excavated (and analyzed) by natural strata, as is customary today in the Near East; our main departure from custom was that, even when there was no evident break in the "natural" strata, we refused to remove levels of more than ten (or occasionally twenty) cm. at a time, and all artifacts were saved and labeled separately by such units. This was done so that we could observe even changes which took place during the filling of a single collapsed house, and place all seed samples in the exact ash beds from which they had come.

The first one-meter squares excavated, if they encountered no walls, were allowed to proceed downward in order to give us a glimpse of the strata that were to come. Their sections would be drawn, and then the adjoining squares could be dug down more skillfully, anticipating the strata below. This had a number of obvious advantages. First of all, if the exploratory square revealed a meter and a half of nearly sterile washed-in building debris, the adjoining square could be excavated fairly rapidly. If, on the other hand, the exploratory square revealed a series of ash beds, samples of these could be floated to see whether they contained seeds. If a particular bed turned out to be rich, a note was made before the adjoining square was dug, and the whole of the ash deposit collected when the appropriate depth was reached in the latter square. This was vital to the success of our work, because it could not be determined by means of a simple "by eye" inspection in the field whether a given ash deposit was rich in seeds or not; this had to be determined in the field laboratory days later, after the flotation samples had dried. To evaluate each ash lens subjectively and dig through the ones which did not appear useful at first glance would have cost us a good deal of information.

The marking of tens of thousands of microlithic flints, tens of thousands of sherds, and tens of thousands of animal bones with symbols designating the square and depth at which they were found was a tedious task that kept us up until midnight on more than one occasion. We were pleased, however, by the fact that this allowed us to reconstruct the contents of any natural stratum anywhere in the site, even if that stratum was sloping or irregular. To a certain extent, the micro-techniques we used may reflect a subconscious "over-reaction" against the gross techniques which had previously been used in parts of Khuzistan. Within the time range of our interest, the only prehistoric mounds which had been excavated there were the type sites of the "Susiana" sequence: Jaffarabad, Bandibal, Jowi, and Buhallan. Work there seems to have been a quarrying operation in which arbitrary levels of up to three meters were removed, and even the most rudimentary attempts to keep artifacts separate by level were ignored. Painfully slow as our methods have been, we feel they spared us that kind of disaster.

Our system of alternate one-meter squares should not in any sense be considered a counterpart of the "balk" system used in some parts of southwestern Asia. Such balks, although useful for section drawings, are somewhat less flexible than our alternate squares. Our squares stood no longer than it took to draw their sections, and then they, too, could be dug to whatever level we wished. If we needed to leave a block of ten of them, surrounding a particular room which was to be dug later, we could leave them. If we needed to dig a block of ten of them in order to remove some important burials intact, it could be done (see Pl. 4*b*).

The system has unmistakable drawbacks in a village site, one of which is exposure of architecture. We would never have attempted to clear a temple or a building complex by such methods, but this was not our objective in 1963. That season, our problem was complex stratigraphy, and in this respect the one-meter squares were one possible solution to that problem. When the time comes for us to expose houses, temples, and courtyards, we hope to be able to do so by different techniques, but with the assurance that all artifacts found within them can be keyed to our master stratigraphic column.

THE ESTABLISHMENT OF STRATIGRAPHIC "ZONES" FOR PURPOSES OF ANALYSIS

Once the stratigraphy of our operations at Ali Kosh and Tepe Sabz had been worked out, the sections drawn and the artifacts all washed and labeled, we were faced with the necessity of seeing how changes in tools correlated with the natural strata, and determining how many "periods" or phases were represented in our sequence. Our section drawings showed literally dozens of superimposed natural strata, including the floors, ash dumps, clay lenses, middens, and layers of washed-in building debris mentioned above. Some of these strata were filled with artifacts, and we left them to stand alone as stratigraphic zones; others were nearly sterile. It seemed a little fruitless to assign a title like "level 5" to a thin clay layer which contained no artifacts. Our job therefore was to find out which of the less productive strata could safely be lumped together as stratigraphic "zones" for purposes of artifact analysis. We decided to let the artifacts themselves tell us how to do it.

Let us take, as one convenient example of how this was done, the artifact frequently called "bent ceramic nail" (Fig. 91*a*). This tool has a wide geographic distribution, occurring at sites throughout Khuzistan and Mesopotamia. It also has a definable distribution in time: with two exceptions, all the "bent nails" we recovered at Tepe Sabz occurred between 350 and 620 cm. below the surface. Reference to the squares and ten-centimeter levels from which they had come revealed that, in terms of natural strata, virtually all these objects had been deposited between the time of the laying down of an ash-coated floor, which filled the trench at a depth of 620 cm., and the deposition of an orange compost dump which filled the trench at a depth of from 330 to 350 cm. Further analysis revealed that many other artifact types were similarly confined to the area above the ash-coated floor and below the orange compost. A number of Susiana Black-on-buff bowl types, such as fine bell-shaped bowls with external "dancing men" designs, or large bowls with internal "rows of wild goats" panels, also showed much the same distribution. Tentatively, therefore, the area between 330 to 350 cm. and 620 cm. was regarded as a series of natural strata whose artifact content was sufficiently similar to suggest that they probably belonged to the same phase. It should be stressed that we could not have known this while we were digging; it became apparent only after the precise distributions of a number of artifact types had been plotted and compared with each other. This plotting, in turn, could only be done because the location of each artifact was known to within ten cm. vertically and within a meter horizontally.

What the above analysis showed was that, if necessary because of insufficient sample size, we could probably combine artifact counts from some of the natural strata from the area between 350 and 620 cm. without risk of mistakenly totalling together counts of materials of two different cultural phases. Our area between 350 and 620 cm. at Tepe Sabz eventually came to be divided into three "stratigraphic zones." The boundaries between those zones were designed to follow natural strata, as follows: (1) from 350 to 430 cm., a layer of building debris overlain by compact orange compost; (2) from 430 to 500 cm., the ashy room fill and wall stub of a white brick house; (3) from 500 to 620 cm., the ashy floor, wall stubs, and overlying building debris of another house.

These stratigraphic zones at Ali Kosh and Tepe Sabz were given tentative numbers to distinguish them during the period of analysis of artifacts, seeds, and animal bones. Finally, when the cultural phases in the sequence were decided upon, the stratigraphic zones were renumbered so as to reflect those phases. For example, Ali Kosh was divided into six stratigraphic zones designated A_1, A_2, B_1, B_2, C_1, and C_2. They are numbered from top to bottom of the stratigraphic column, with A_1 being the highest (and youngest) zone, C_2 the lowest (and oldest). The letters refer to the phase involved; both A_1 and A_2 belong to the Mohammad Jaffar phase, B_1 and B_2 to the Ali Kosh phase, and so on. The same system was used at Tepe Sabz, although there were ten zones and four phases at the latter site.

SUMMARY

This introduction has been perhaps too lengthy, but we felt that we should explain the techniques by which we excavated and analyzed so that our work can be evaluated—and our raw data perhaps reanalyzed—by future workers in Khuzistan. Let us briefly review the essential points.

The units by which we removed dirt from the ground were 10-centimeter or 20-centimeter levels within one-meter squares, depending on natural stratigraphy. A system of many section drawings and written notes was used to key these small units to the larger natural strata from which they were taken.

The units used for analysis of artifacts were stratigraphic "zones" composed of natural strata. When a stratum contained an adequate sample of artifacts, it stood alone as a stratigraphic zone. When a stratum was sterile or contained too few artifacts, counts of its artifacts were combined with those of adjacent strata to form an analytical unit only if those artifacts within it indicated it did not belong to a different cultural phase.

The units used as cultural phases within the sequence, insofar as data are available, are units of time characterized by stratigraphic zones whose subsistence activities (plants raised or gathered wild, animals herded or hunted) are the same. In a few cases, where long periods of stable and relatively unchanged economy are indicated, we have defined periods mainly on the basis of differences between complexes of artifacts, although no phase is defined on the basis of artifacts alone.

IV

THE EXCAVATIONS AT TEPE ALI KOSH

DESCRIPTION OF THE SITE

Ali Kosh is a roughly circular mound some 135 meters in diameter and 7 meters in depth, with a fairly flat summit rising 4 meters above the surrounding plain. Its lower slopes blend almost imperceptibly into the alluvium, which has completely buried the lower 3 meters of the site since it was founded. Continuous erosion, whose traces can be seen most clearly on the south side, is reducing the height of the mound and leaving behind a carpet of gravel, flints, and tiny sherd fragments, which cover its surface over an area of a little more than one hectare.

There are a few suggestions that Ali Kosh may be a "double" mound. First, the greatest surface concentration of Susiana Black-on-buff sherds occurs on the west and northwest slopes of the site, while the greatest concentration of flint tools characteristic of the preceramic Ali Kosh and Bus Mordeh phases can be found on the east and southeast slopes. Second, a long east-west test trench made in 1963 made it appear that the very center of the mound might contain only sterile mud wall debris which had run into a depression between two adjoining mounds. Future excavations may determine whether or not this is the case.

EXCAVATIONS IN 1903

Gautier and Lampre of the French Archeological Mission in Iran apparently visited Ali Kosh in 1903 and collected flints and sherds. An old, eroded pit (roughly 7 by 7 meters) on the northeast side of the mound may represent a test excavation made at that time. They illustrated flint cores typical of the site, which they referred to as a midden built up of the remains of reed and branch huts (Gautier and Lampre, 1905:81-83).

Gautier and Lampre named the mound "Tepe Mohamad-Djaffar," after a local tribal leader. Today the Musiyan villagers refer to the site as Bus Mordeh ("dead goat"), while inhabitants of Deh Luran call it Ali Kosh ("the place where Ali was killed"). We have used all these titles as names for the various cultural phases represented at the site.

EXCAVATIONS IN 1961

Ali Kosh was visited by Richard Watson and Robert J. Braidwood of the University of Chicago's Iranian Prehistoric Project in 1960. Stimulated by their surface collections, we tested the site briefly in 1961. As previously reported (Hole and Flannery, 1962), our 3 by 5 meter test pit did not reach sterile soil. We had explored to a depth of only 495 cm. below the surface before winter rains led us to terminate work.

Our excavations in 1963 have considerably clarified what we found in 1961. Our "upper mixed zone" (*Ibid.*), we now know, contained artifacts from two phases. We excavated an unmixed component of the earlier of these, the "Mohammad Jaffar phase," at the top of our 1963 pit. The so-called "brick wall" and "pit-house" zones have been combined into components of the "Ali Kosh phase." It seems probable now that what we considered the possible trace of a pit-house wall was the subterranean foundation stub of a badly-destroyed packed mud wall. Lastly, we now have materials from a still earlier "Bus Mordeh phase" which occurred at a depth not even reached by our 1961 test pit.

EXCAVATIONS IN 1963

On our return to Deh Luran in 1963, we resurveyed Ali Kosh and prepared a more accurate map of the site. Next, two narrow exploratory trenches were laid out alongside the 1961 test pit. One trench, a meter wide, ran north-south for 20 meters following the west wall of the 1961 test; the second, also a meter wide, ran east-west for 45 meters following the north wall of the test (see Fig. 4). On September 22, 1963, we began excavation in these trenches and proceeded downward to the first signs of clear stratigraphy, which usually appeared only after 50 cm. of featureless overburden had been removed.

One of the main purposes of these trenches was to locate an area on the mound where materials of the earliest pottery-bearing phase occurred unmixed with later ("Susiana *b-c*") pottery. Our trenches disclosed that (*a*) such mixing as there was, took place mainly in the upper 50 cm. of the site (probably due to rodent activity and erosion of the "Susiana *b-c*" houses which have now disappeared), and (*b*) the place of worst mixture was our 1961 pit and the area immediately to the west of it. It soon appeared that the area of clearest stratigraphy and least disturbance lay to the east of our old test; here there were patches of ash, wall stubs, tools and pottery like those from the upper levels at Jarmo (Braidwood, Howe *et al.,* 1960), without a single sherd of Susiana "buff-ware."

During the first week of October, we laid out a block of 100 one-meter squares in the 10-by-10-meter area immediately to the east of our 1961 pit (Fig. 5). The south wall of the 1963 excavation area was made a continuation of the south wall of the 1961 test, so that the "profiles" or section drawings of the two pits could be linked together. This was done, insofar as the now badly-eroded and rain-washed walls of the 1961 test could still be seen, so that the walls, floors, and tools found in 1961 could be stratigraphically related to those we hoped to find in 1963.

The uppermost 50 cm. of our 1963 excavation (like that of the 1961 test) was, in general, grayish dust with no observable stratigraphic features. The combination of rain water penetration and the leaching of soluble salts into the upper 50 cm. effectively destroyed bone, carbonized plant remains, and even the surfaces of sherds. We therefore stripped off this upper 50 cm. before staking out our 100 one-meter squares.

Next, excavations of the one-meter squares began. Each pickman was equipped with a small, light-tined pick, a sharp screwdriver and trowel, and a paintbrush for cleaning features. At first, only the three or four best Deh Luran workmen from our 1961 season were allowed to pick; then, one by one, Musiyan villagers who had demonstrated the necessary alertness and interest were allowed to try their hands at picking. Competiton was keen, for picking was regarded as a high-prestige

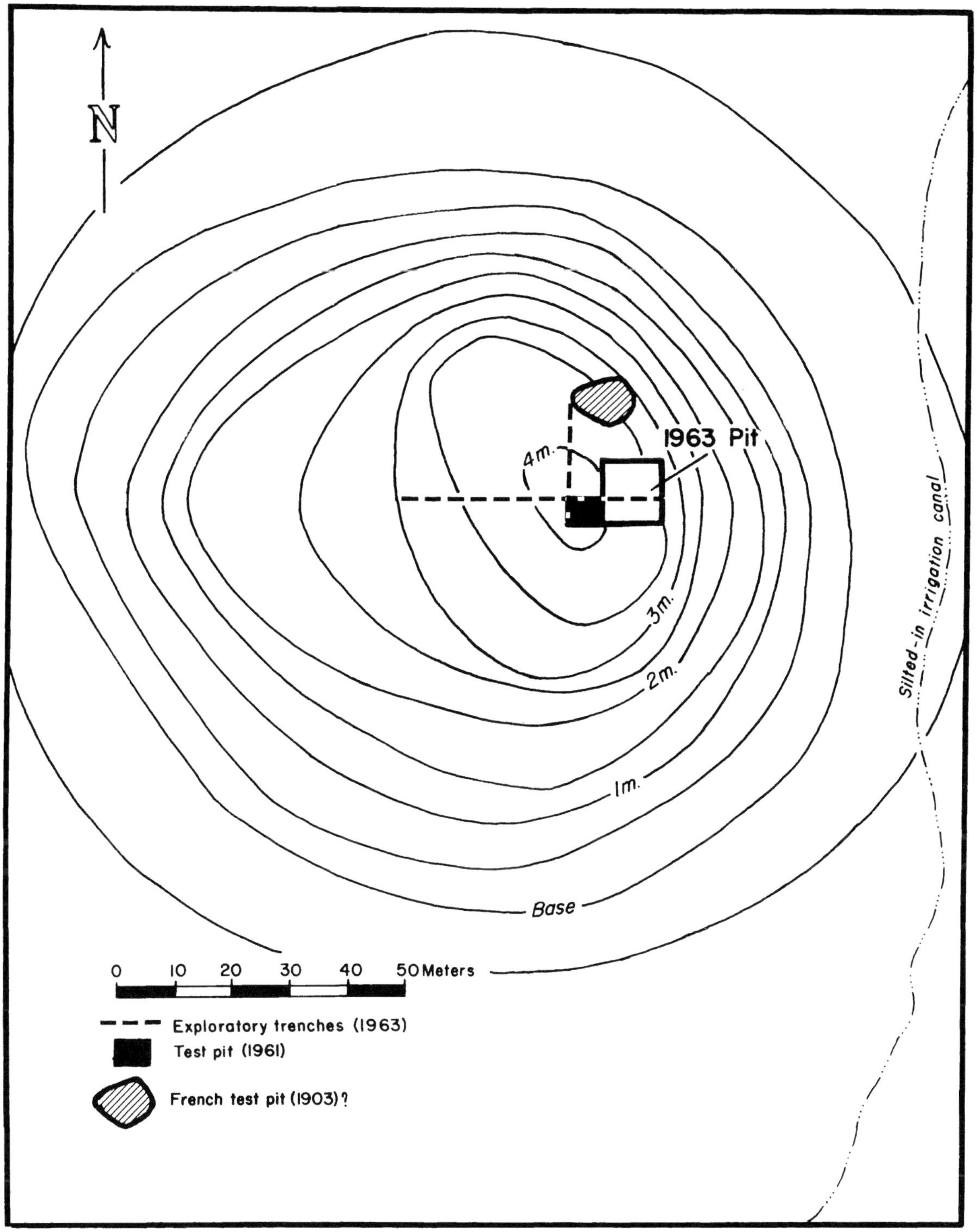

Fig. 4. Map of Tepe Ali Kosh.

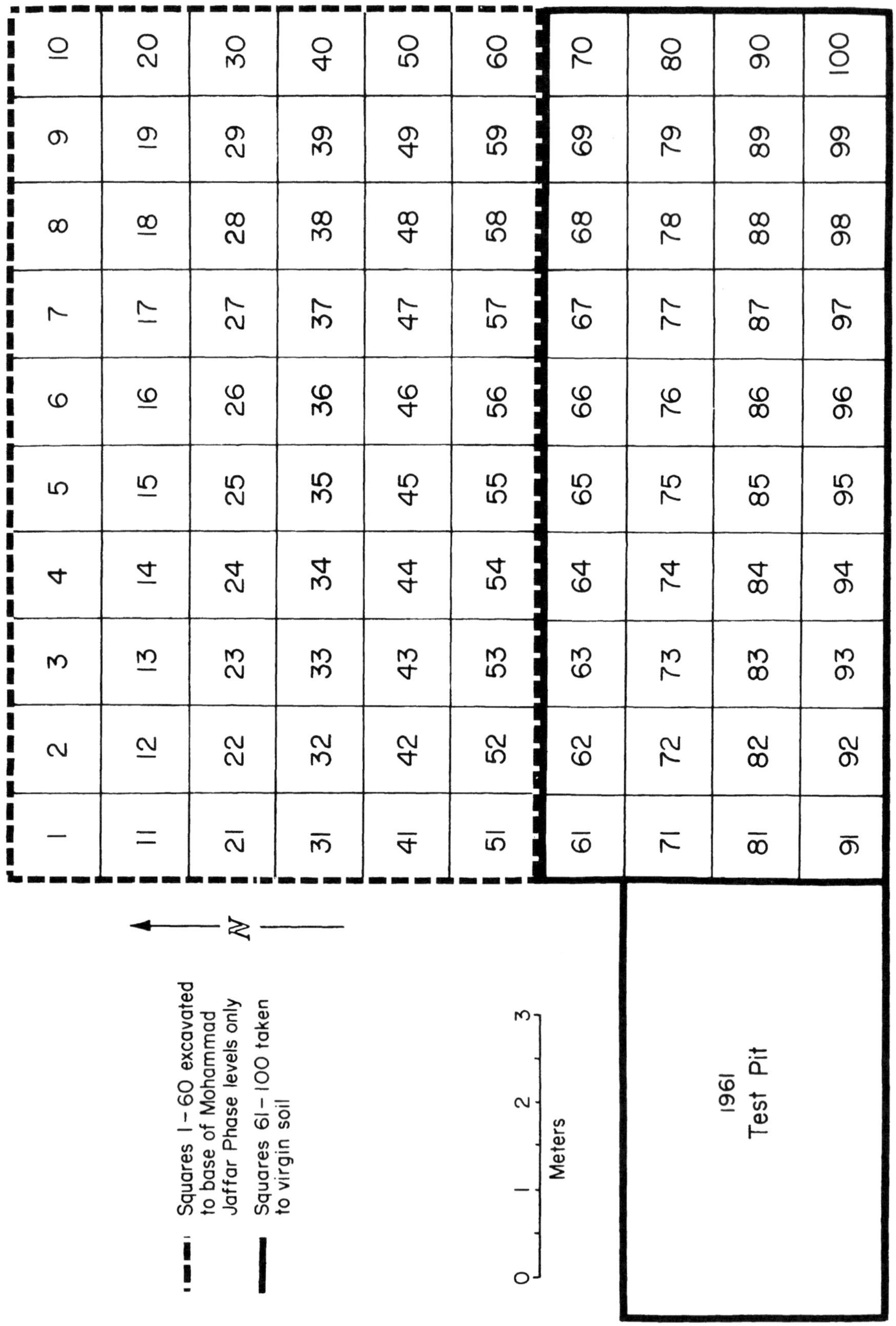

Fig. 5. Plan of one-meter squares at Tepe Ali Kosh, 1963.

task. Second in prestige was the role of the sieve operator, who prided himself on recovering small objects not discovered by his pickman. Some of our young sieve boys were astonishingly sharp-eyed, recovering such minute items as gerbil metapodials and tail vertebrae; one even caught a carbonized wheat grain in the small sieve. The lowest job on the prestige scale was that of the dirt carrier who, lacking both keen eyesight and manual dexterity, trudged back and forth between the pickman and his sieve crew.

Most of the pickmen became quite good at cleaning burials, calling for plastic bags when they uncovered radiocarbon samples, and recognizing seed-filled ash lenses. We can only conclude that their interest was genuine, for they were paid no more than the sieve men or dirt carriers, and we never resorted to the pernicious "baksheesh" system to spur them on. (It would simply have encouraged them to bring "small finds" in from the surface of other sites.) The archeologists in charge moved from man to man, often helping a pickman trowel out a particularly fragile bone or coat it with preservative; bagging up the materials from a ten-centimeter level within a one-meter square and labeling them; or showing a pickman how to bring out the color changes at the break between two natural strata by scraping with a sharp trowel. The idiosyncrasies and special skills of each pickman became clear, usually, by the end of the first few weeks.

The cultural period most shallowly represented, and consequently most poorly known at Ali Kosh, was the Mohammad Jaffar phase, which had been "mixed" in our 1961 test. In order to recover as large a sample of the materials of this period as possible, we excavated all one hundred squares until we were below deposits of Mohammad Jaffar type (stratigraphic zones A_1 and A_2). This occurred at a depth varying from 160 to 180 cm. below surface, depending on the natural stratigraphy. At this point, we discontinued work in our northernmost sixty squares and took the southernmost forty squares to virgin soil, which occurred at a depth of 7 meters below the surface. These squares passed through stratigraphic zones B_1 and B_2, belonging to the Ali Kosh phase, and C_1 and C_2, belonging to the Bus Mordeh phase. Had we attempted to expose 100 square meters of the latter two phases, we would never have reached the bottom of the site in the time at our disposal.

Hole, Flannery, and Neely began work at Ali Kosh September 22, 1963, using a crew of villagers from both Deh Luran and Musiyan. On October 15, Neely left to begin excavations at Tepe Sabz, taking the Deh Luran workmen with him, and Hole and Flannery continued at Ali Kosh with their crew augmented by new Musiyanis. On December 15, Flannery left to make a brief test at Tepe Musiyan, Area "E." Hole supervised the digging of the remainder of Ali Kosh to virgin soil on December 17, 1963.

THE DEPOSITIONAL HISTORY OF THE STRATIGRAPHIC COLUMN

Virgin Soil

The original surface on which the site of Ali Kosh was founded is a bed of white, sandy soil, which lies at a depth of 710 to 730 cm. below the summit of the present mound. This sandy soil is in turn underlain by a layer of sterile red clay at depths of 730 to 750 cm. A test of sterile soil at the bottom of Ali Kosh suggests that the red clay is again underlain by white sand at a depth of 770 cm., and that beds of clay and sand continue to alternate with each other as one digs deeper and deeper. Presumably these laminated beds represent the old land surface in this part of the Deh

Luran plain. Three meters of alluvium have covered that surface since the founding of Ali Kosh some nine thousand years ago.

The geologic origin of these sands and clays has not yet been determined. Whitish-buff sand dunes still occur at the nearby village of Bayat, where the Mehmeh River heads into the Jebel Hamrin. Red and green clays can still be detected in the swampy area in the center of the Deh Luran plain. The presence of carbonized swamp plants in basal levels at Ali Kosh (notably the bulrush, *Scirpus*), as well as remains of turtle, carp, catfish, and freshwater clam, suggests aquatic resources in the vicinity of the village similar to those available now. It may be that the geologic history of the Deh Luran plain, prior to the founding of Ali Kosh, was little different from today's pattern, one featuring seasonal swamps, blowing sand and dust, and gradual accumulation of alluvium from the many small intermittent streams in the area.

Zone C_2 —Bus Mordeh Phase

The oldest signs of human occupation, found resting on the white sand at the base of the site, are shown in the plain drawing of stratigraphic zone C_2 (Fig. 9). They consisted of the low wall stubs of two rooms, and a possible storage room or bin; an area of ash, compost, and midden debris dumped immediately to the east of the rooms; a "pavement" of small pebbles; and a heap of flint blades and chipping debris which underlay the ash and compost. Immediately superimposed on the heaped-up compost were the wall stubs of a second set of rooms which must have been built only slightly later than those resting on virgin soil; their bases overlapped slightly in depth with the tops of the wall stubs from the earliest rooms. The complex of features just enumerated made up our stratigraphic zone C_2, which began at virgin soil and rose to an average depth of 620 cm. below the surface of the mound, about one meter above sterile. (See section drawings, Figs. 6-8.)

The oldest rooms were two meters wide, and our one complete example about two-and-a-half meters long. The walls were built up of irregular, crude "bricks," 15 by 25 cm. in width and only 5 to 10 cm. thick, which appeared to be simply slabs of buff silt or mud with no tempering added. None had been fired; mud was the only mortar used between them, and no plaster of any kind could be detected on the bricks. The stubs of the walls were no more than 40 cm. thick and stood no more than 60 cm. high anywhere. No traces of matting were observed on the floors of the rooms, which seemed to be only stamped-down areas of earth. We found no ovens, hearths, or other features. Doorways were apparently a meter to a meter-and-a-half wide.

In the northwest corner of the excavation was a tiny cubicle, one meter by a meter-and-a-half in extent, with walls of small bricks which appeared to be slabs of the native red clay found underlying the site (see Virgin Soil). It is possible that this structure was a storage room of some kind.

A single wall stub from one of the larger rooms was constructed of packed buff mud rather than bricks. The mud was not chaff-tempered, nor did the small portion remaining appear to have been built up in courses as in tauf.

In the corner of one of these small rooms we found the crushed but still identifiable skull of a hornless sheep (see Figs. 119-120). This was our oldest concrete osteological evidence for animal domestication.

To the east of the rooms lay an extensive dump of gray ash, black ash, and compost which reached a depth of 40 cm. in places along the base of the brick walls. Besides numerous discarded figurine fragments, flint chips, and burnt animal bones, the ash contained literally thousands of carbonized seeds. The vast majority were

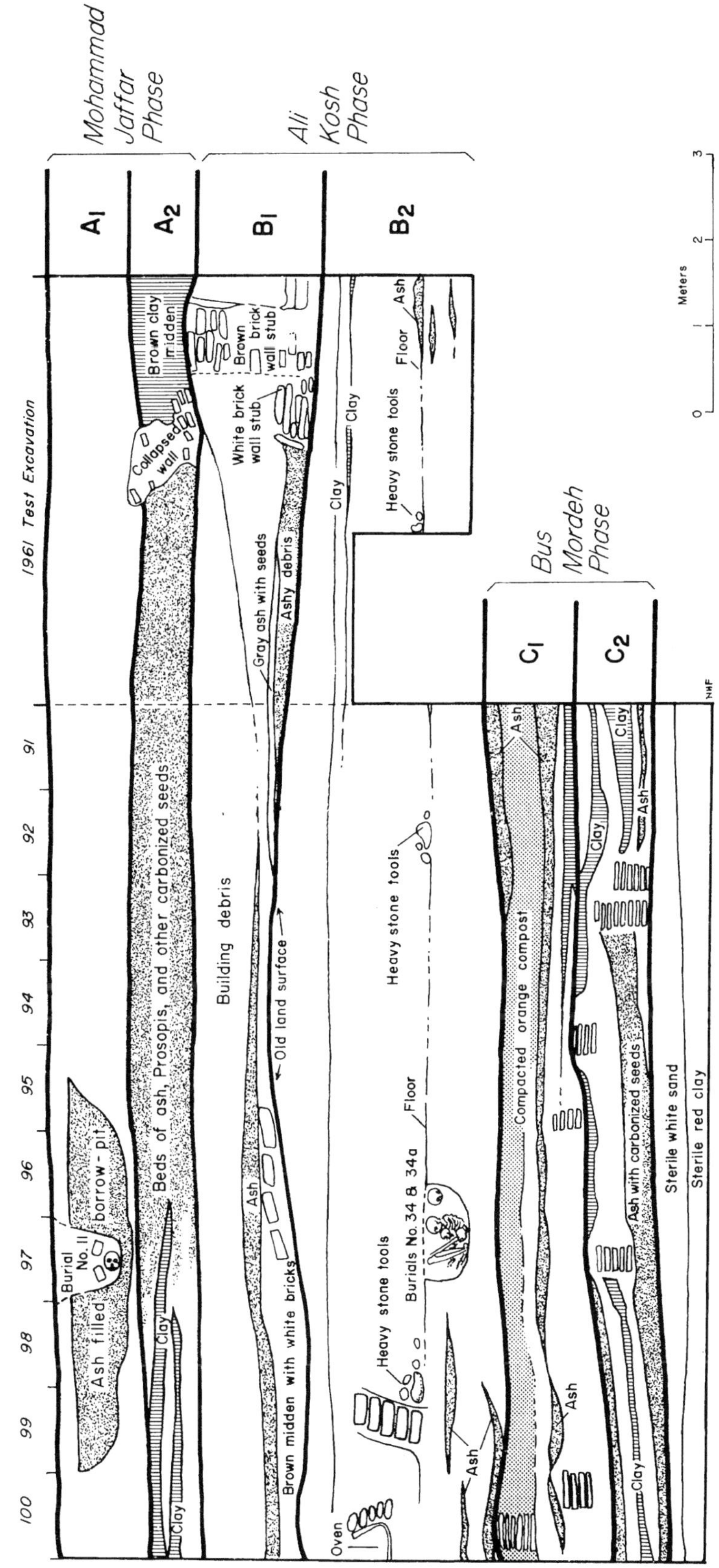

Fig. 6. Tepe Ali Kosh. East (left) to west (right) section drawing of the south wall of squares 91 to 100 after excavation.

the systematically-collected seeds of local wild legumes like *Astragalus* and *Trigonella,* but also included were coarsely-ground groats of grain and a few whole kernels of emmer wheat and two-row hulled barley. In Helbaek's opinion, these represented the leavings from hundreds of daily meals.

In the northeast corner of the excavation, our trench exposed a two-by-two-meter area of what appears to be a "pavement" of small river pebbles; we observed no walls in association with it. To the south lay a thick concentration of flint microblades and thousands of flint chips, covering an area one by three meters (in squares 87, 88, 97, 98, and 99). Both the pebble pavement and the area of chipping debris were partially overlain by the trailing edge of the ash and compost dump which extended out from the east wall of the rooms.

The second set of small rooms in zone C_2, whose brick wall stubs rested on the heaped-up compost, proved more difficult to trace.

Zone C_1 –Bus Mordeh Phase

In places, patches of gray ash and smears of green clay overlay the broken-down wall stubs of zone C_2. Disintegrated wall debris had filled and buried the rooms. Above this began the wall stubs of stratigraphic zone C_1, at an average depth of 620 cm.Zone C_1, which rose to 520 cm. below the surface of the mound, contained two sets of small brick buildings one above the other, separated in placed by an intervening ash layer 20 to 30 cm. thick.

The rooms of zone C_1, insofar as they could be traced, resembled those of zone C_2. Their walls were built up of unbaked, untempered slab "bricks" of green clay or buff silt, 15 by 25 cm. wide and 5 to 10 centimeters thick. One wall seemed to have been additionally reinforced with packed buff mud (Pl. 8*a*), but it is possible that this was only the base of a "bench" of some kind which rested against the bricks. Rooms in the eastern half of the excavation varied from one meter to two meters wide; no complete house plans were recovered, and once again no ovens, hearths, or floor mats were detected, although a few asphalt mat or basket impressions occurred in the refuse. The narrow, unplastered wall stubs stood only 30 to 40 cm. high.

Scattered through the debris outside these rooms were the bones of goat, gazelle, onager, wild ox and boar, fish and small game. The goats showed few osteological differences from the wild race, but the high percentage of young animals suggested that they were probably domestic during the Bus Mordeh phase. Patches of ashy compost, as in zone C_2, were filled with many carbonized wild legumes and some coarse groats of wheat and barley, as well as other plants. A few saddle-shaped grinding slabs and simple discoidal handstones suggested how the groats had been produced. Several figurines which appear to represent goats are interesting in the light of the evidence for domestication.

The presence of clams, catfish, carp, turtles, and carbonized swamp plants in the compost outside the Bus Mordeh rooms indicates that aquatic products were widely utilized in this phase.

Finally, the whole of stratigraphic zone C_1 was capped by a layer of jet black compost, gray ash, and compact orange organic debris some 30 to 40 cm. thick (see Figs. 6-8 and Pl. 5*b*). This layer effectively sealed off the Bus Mordeh rooms from zone B_2, and provided a nice natural stratum which could be used to define the upper limits of zone C_1, at an average depth of 520 cm. below the surface.

Included in this black compost (at a depth of 520 to 540 cm., in square 82) was a mass of human limb bones coated with red ochre (Pl. 13*a*). Three small turquoise beads and several strings of white stone beads were included in this badly-rotted bone deposit, which probably represented the reburial of the fleshless limbs of

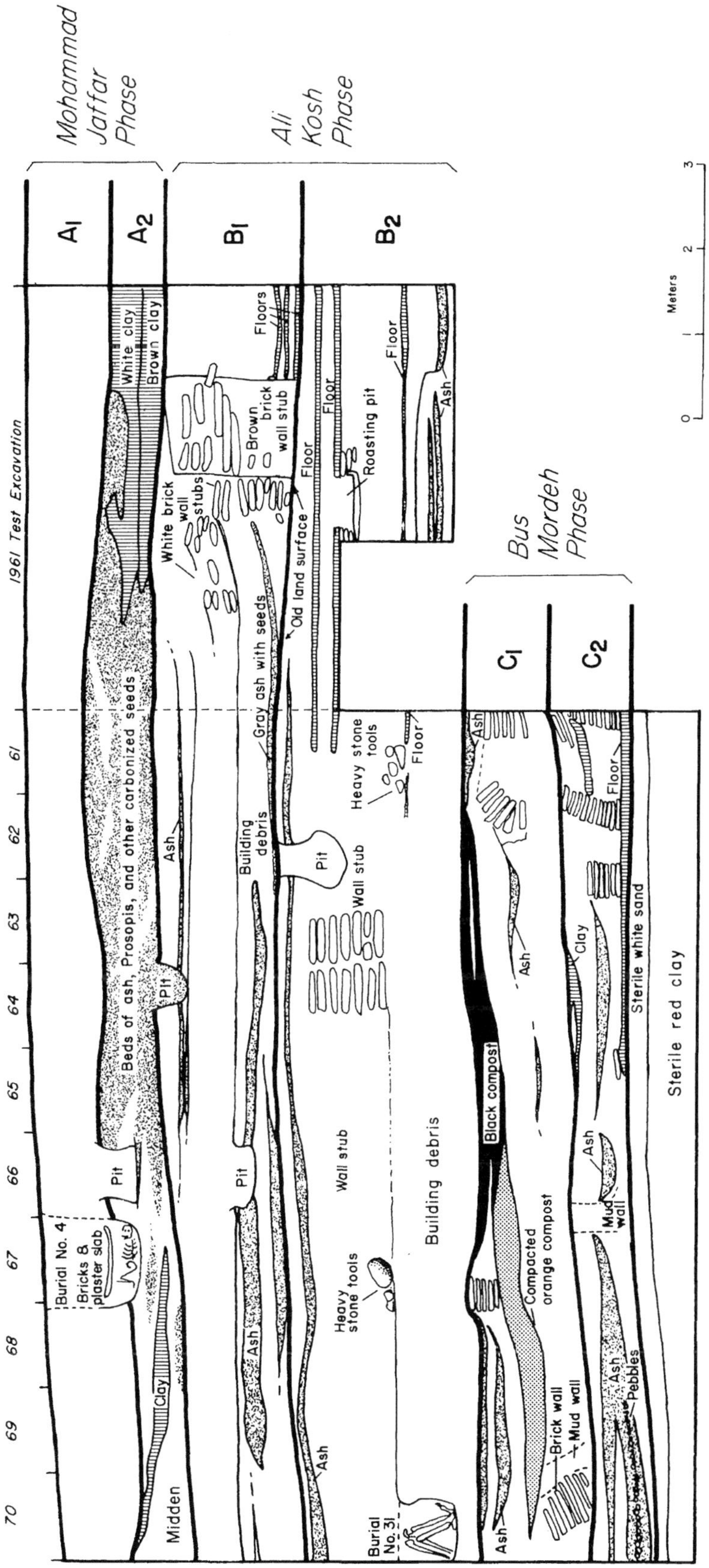

Fig. 7. Tepe Ali Kosh. East (left) to west (right) section drawing of the south wall of squares 61 to 70 after excavation.

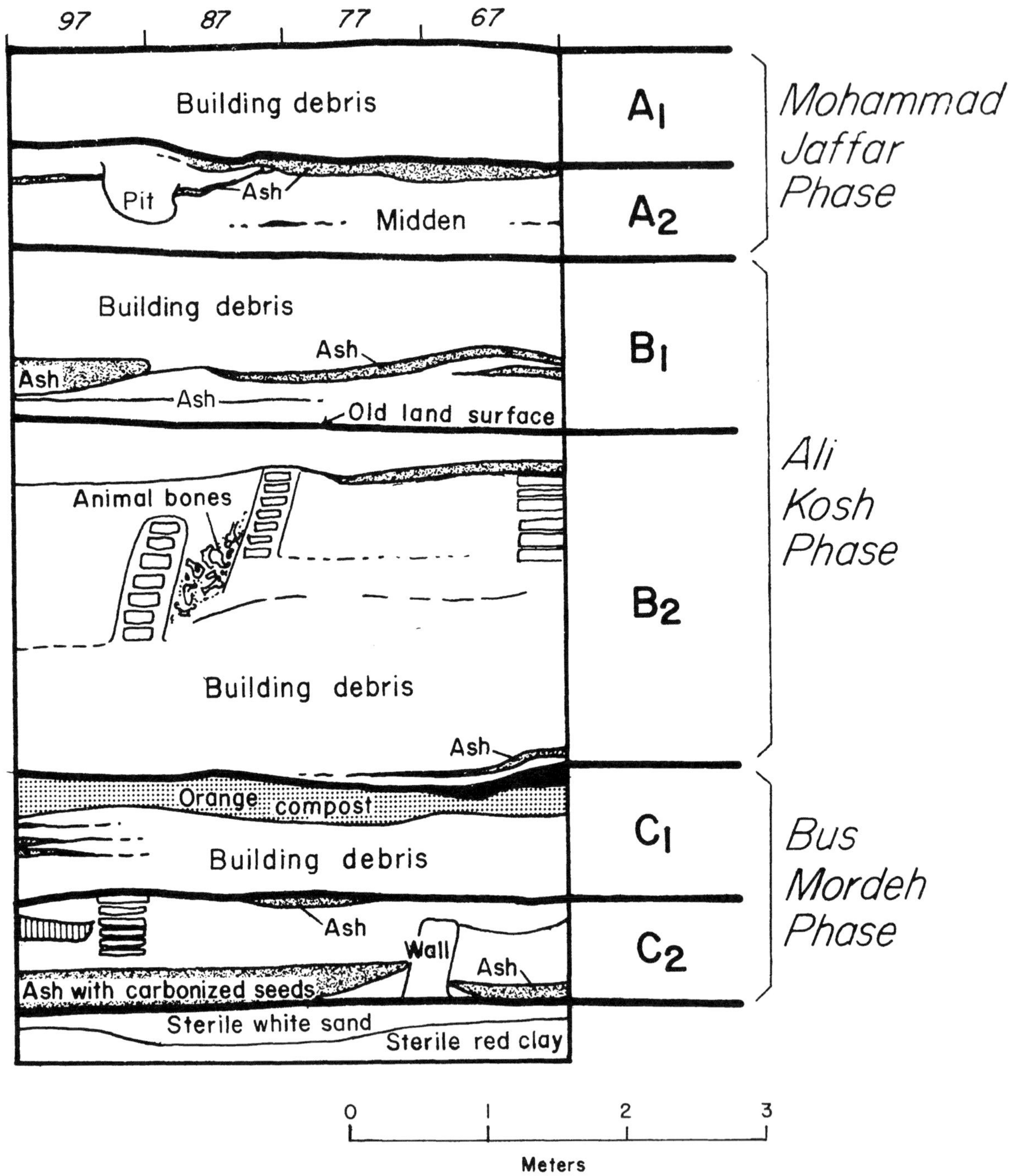

Fig. 8. Tepe Ali Kosh. Section drawings, 1963. Left, south (L.) to north (R.) drawing of west wall

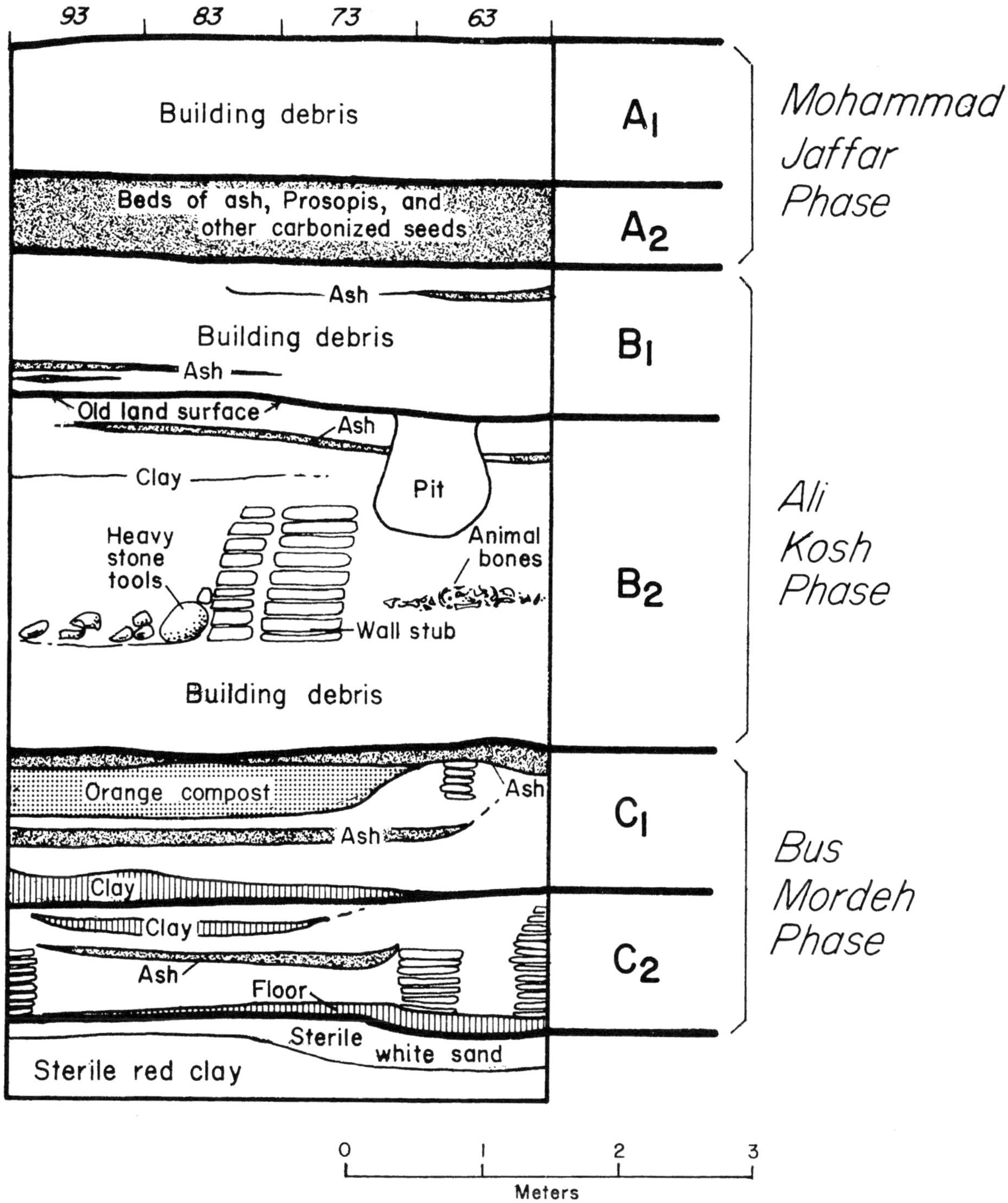

ıf squares 67 to 97. Right, south (L.) to north (R.) drawing of west wall of squares 63 to 93.

three adult individuals. We suspect this burial was intrusive from zone B_2.

Zone B_2—Ali Kosh Phase

A layer of nearly sterile mud-brick debris, interrupted by occasional lenses of ash, overlay zone C_1; it appeared that this debris had washed in from buildings which disintegrated just outside our excavation area. The oldest architectural features of zone B_2, appeared at a depth of 440 cm. below the surface of the mound, but walls were best preserved between 330 and 400 cm. At the latter depth, we uncovered portions of at least two houses, as well as hearths, ovens, and roasting pits. The contents of those houses represented the bulk of the material recovered from zone B_2, which ended at a depth varying between 260 and 300 cm. below the surface. At that point, it was overlain by a hard-packed white layer that appeared to be an old land surface which had formed over the houses once they collapsed (see section drawings, Figs. 6-8).

No great time need be allowed for the formation of this surface. After the houses collapsed this area was abandoned, while new houses were built on adjacent areas. The old land surface may have been a courtyard or just an unused area of the mound.

At a depth of 420 to 440 cm. in the eastern part of the excavation (squares 78-80, 88-90), we uncovered traces of the first room built within our excavated area during the Ali Kosh phase. This room had been so badly destroyed by later building operations that only the basal 20 cm. of one wall stub remained. The base of the stub was packed buff silt, like some of the wall stubs from the Bus Mordeh phase, but it differed from the latter in that one of its surfaces had been coated with mud plaster. The line of plaster was easily traced by scraping with a trowel, but the unplastered side of the low stub blended into the adjacent silty debris so well that parts of it were difficult to follow. We were immediately struck by the similarity of this feature to one we had found—at almost the same depth—in our 1961 test: this had been a very low, plastered stub which we tentatively interpreted as a possible pit house wall. It is now evident, from the feature found in 1963, that our "pit house wall" was probably only the badly-destroyed stub of a plastered mud wall. A carbon-14 sample taken from a hearth on the floor of that 1961 house, and resting against the plastered wall stub (Hole and Flannery, 1962:Fig. 11) yielded two dates of 6450 B.C. and 6465 B.C.; hence our suspicion that the Ali Kosh phase was underway by 6500 B.C.

Associated with the plastered wall stub found in 1963 was a patch of green clay floor, also badly destroyed by later building activities. Included in the floor was a hearth some 50 cm. in diameter and 10 cm. deep, found in square 89. The ash in this hearth contained many carbonized grains of emmer wheat and two-row hulled barley; some wild legumes were a smaller percentage of the total than they had been in the Bus Mordeh samples.

It was suggested by our 1963 excavations that, after its abandonment, the room just described above had not simply been allowed to collapse into a pile of building debris. Leveling operations seemed to have reduced it to the brief wall stub and section of partially destroyed floor we uncovered. These leveling operations probably were carried out in preparation for the building of the two houses which overlay the destroyed room at a depth of 330 to 420 cm. below mound surface.

We recovered only a portion of these two houses—parts of perhaps five rooms in all—but their architectural details were relatively clear, and their floors afforded us a very large sample of artifacts from the Ali Kosh phase. Relationship of the two houses to each other can be seen by refer-

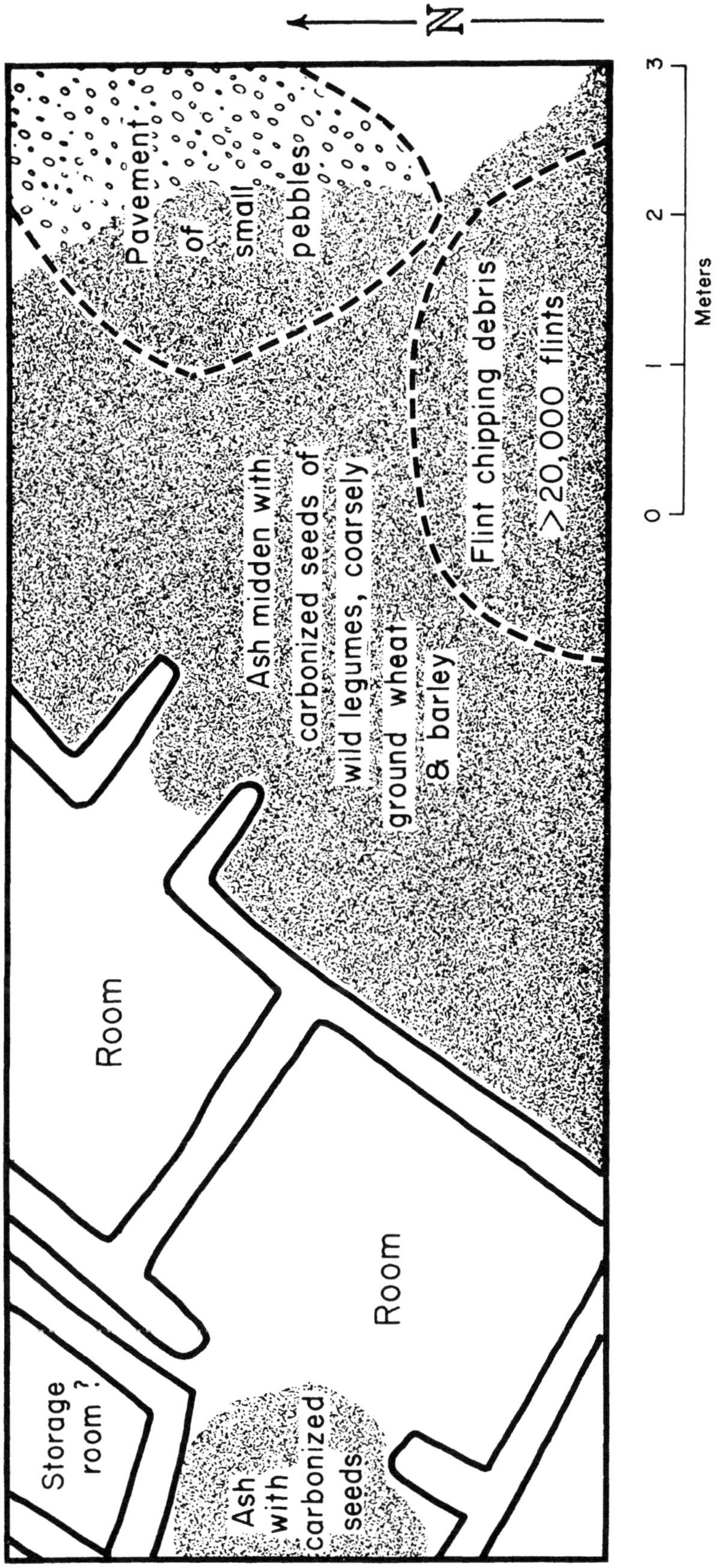

Fig. 9. Plan of zone C_2 (Bus Mordeh phase) at Tepe Ali Kosh. The hornless sheep skull (Fig. 119) came from the northeast corner of the southernmost room shown.

ence to the plot plan of zone B_2 (Fig. 10).

The walls of the early Ali Kosh phase buildings represented a technological improvement over the narrow, clay-slab constructions of zones C_1 and C_2, though their bricks were still unbaked and untempered with chaff. Most bricks were flat blocks of brown silt, averaging 40 cm. long, 20 to 25 cm. wide, and 6 to 10 cm. thick. They were usually laid in a single course with their long axes following the line of the wall; the evidence from our limited exposure suggests that where a wall made a corner, or two walls came together, they simply "butted" against each other, with no interlocking or "bonding" with bricks such as we found in later houses at Tepe Sabz (compare Figs. 11*a* and 18*b*). The mortar used between bricks was tan mud, and a layer of smooth mud plaster 2 to 3 cm. thick was applied to the side of the wall which faced the interior of the house. Floors were areas of stamped-down earth which might or might not have a thin coating of green clay. There were occasional suggestions (in the form of silica "ghosts," or more often impressions in asphalt) that twilled, over-two under-two reed mats had been laid on the floors (see Pl. 37*d,e*).

Two ovens were found in 1963, and a brick-lined "roasting pit" recovered in 1961 (Hole and Flannery, 1962:109 and Fig. 6) also belonged stratigraphically to zone B_2 (see section drawing, Fig. 7). None of these features occurred within a room; the ovens, in fact, were located just outside the rooms of the houses we uncovered at a depth of 330 to 420 cm. in our 1963 excavation. We are reminded that the ovens at Jarmo often opened into courtyards between buildings (Braidwood, Howe, *et al.*, 1960:42), and it is possible that the Ali Kosh ovens were located in such open areas rather than indoors.

Ovens were bell-shaped, 40 to 50 cm. deep, with an interior diameter of perhaps half a meter at the base. Their walls were of small bricks tightly set together, their inner surfaces coated with burned earth. None contained carbonized seeds, though ash was present (Fig. 11*b*). Our single "roasting pit," which was filled with goat bones and ash, may have been sunk into the clay surface of a courtyard or open area to the west of the houses in zone B_2; it was wider and shallower than either oven, having a diameter of nearly a meter and a depth of only 25 cm. (Fig. 11*c* and Pl. 10*d*).

Under the floors of the early Ali Kosh phase rooms were a number of seated, flexed burials of adults, and a few child burials—presumably former occupants of the house. A few of these burials were accompanied by ornaments of turquoise and shell, and five clearly showed traces of having been tightly wrapped in mats. The skulls of at least three adult females had been artificially deformed (see Pl. 12*b*). These burials are described in detail in Chapter XVIII.

After their abandonment, it appeared that the rooms in zone B_2 had served as dump or workshop areas, either for adjoining houses or for families living in other parts of the same house. Literally hundreds of heavy stone stools were found piled along the walls of the rooms, and we mapped these in place (see plan drawing, Fig. 10 and Pl. 10*c*). In the midden and drifted wall debris above this (in square 64, at a depth of 380 cm.) we found a bead hammered from native copper, one of the few such items known from the preceramic period.

The southernmost of the two houses, two rooms of which were exposed by our 1963 excavation, seemed to be oriented roughly northwest to southeast (290 degrees). In its west wall was a doorway opening into what may be a courtyard or an open area between buildings. Along the wall on either side of the doorway were piled dozens of saddle-shaped grinding slabs, discoidal handstones, "sashweight"

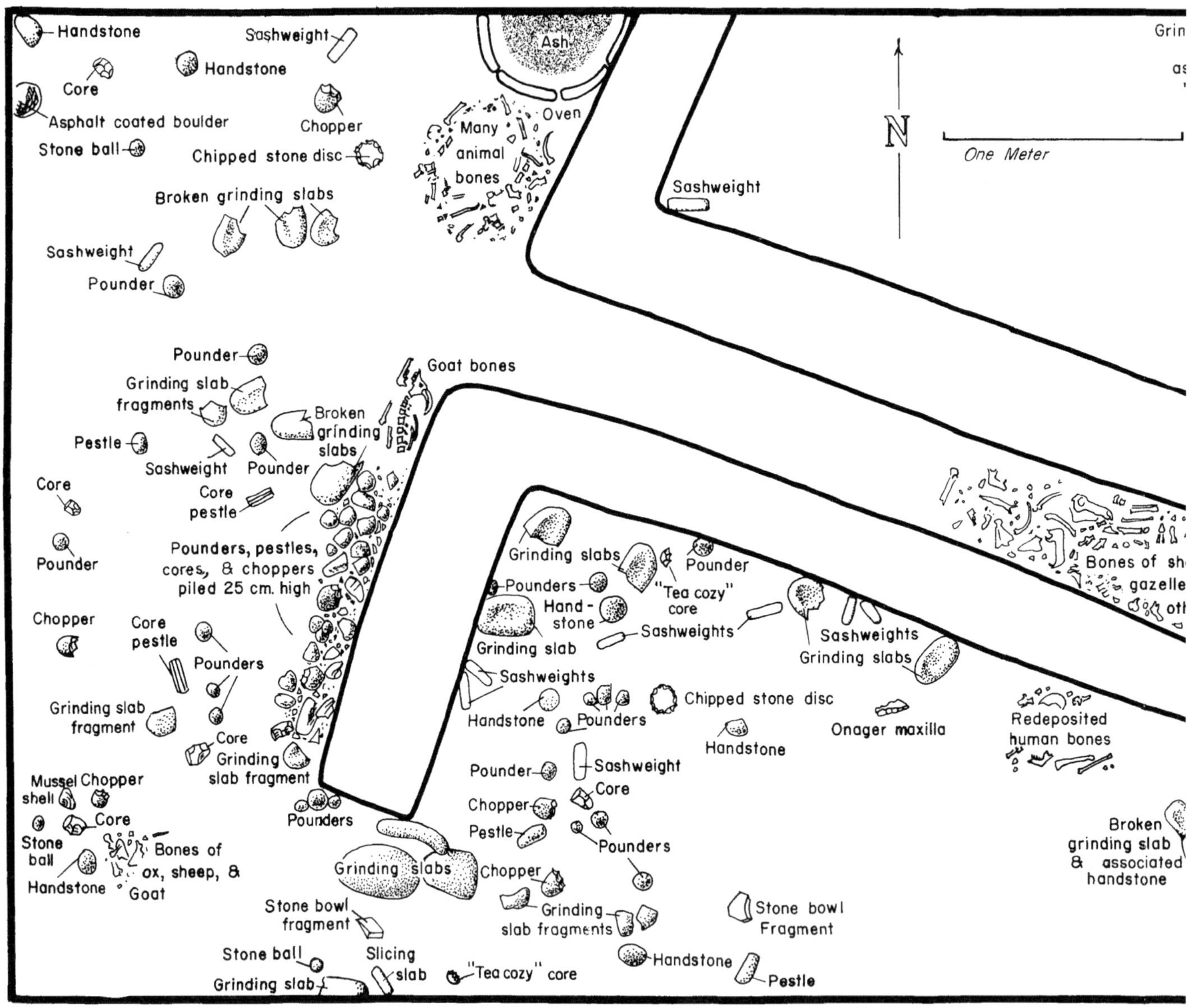

Fig. 10. Plan of zone B_2 (Ali Kosh phase) at Tepe Ali Kosh, with all to

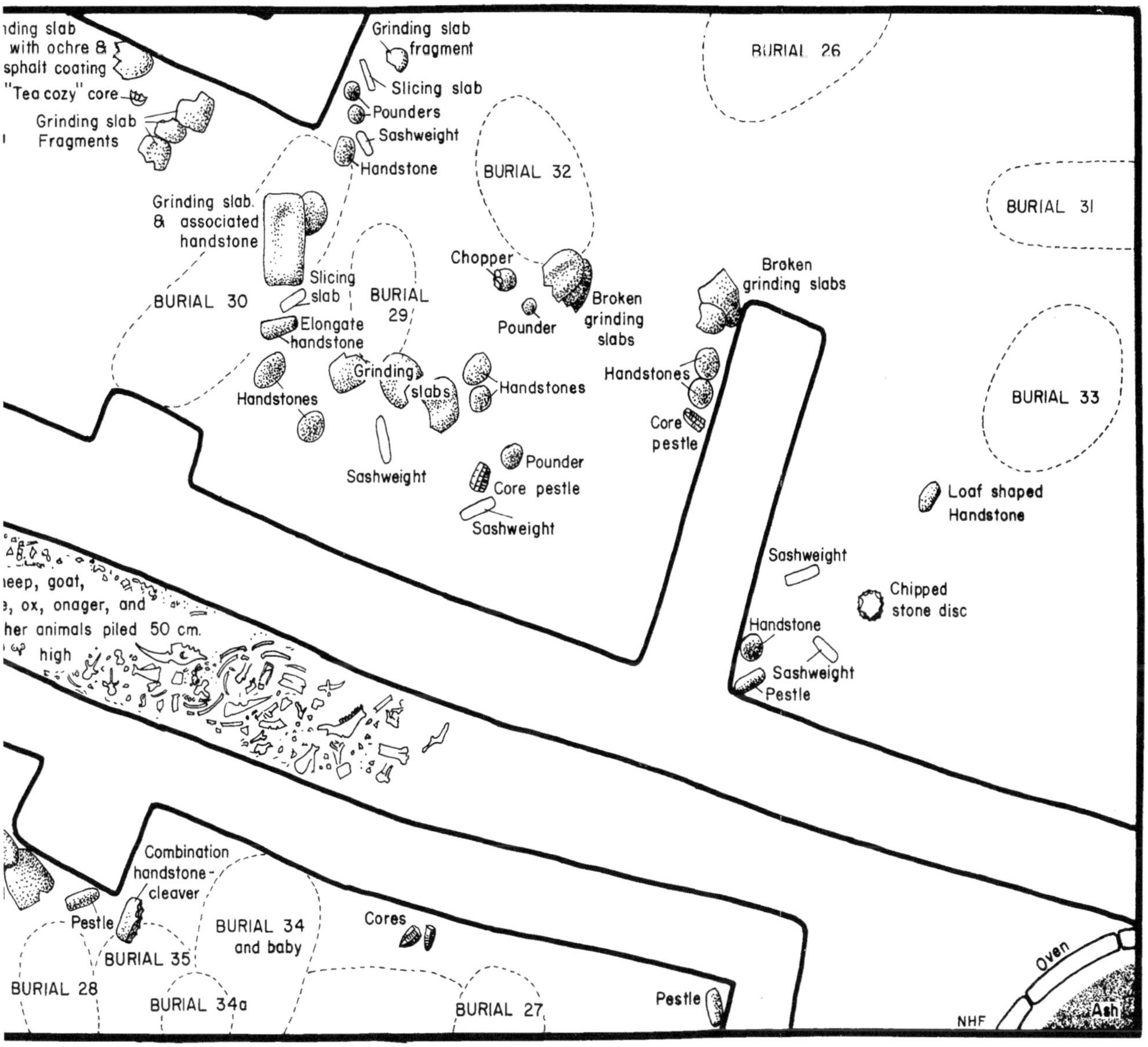

ools larger than a flint blade plotted *in situ*. Parts of two houses are shown.

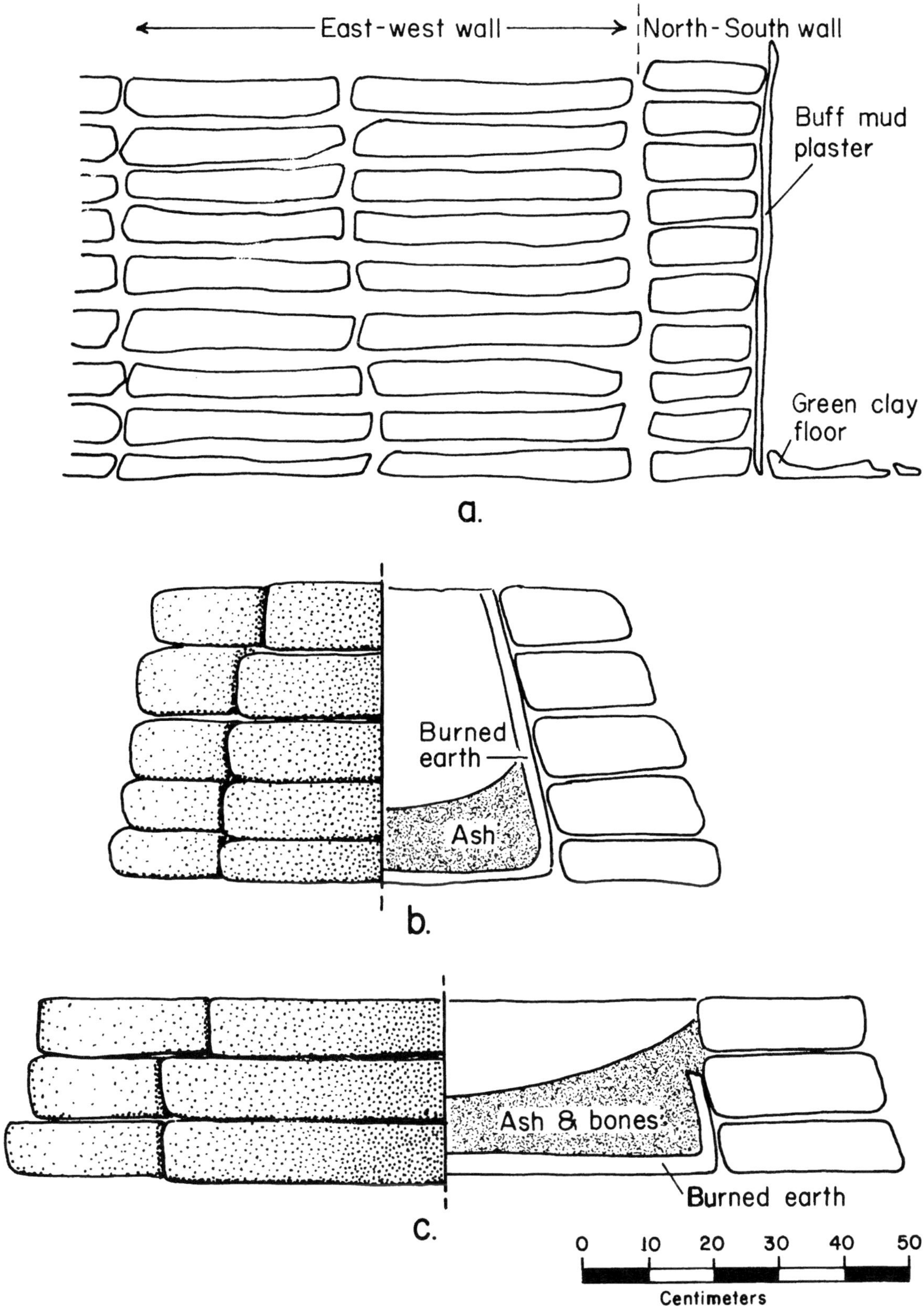

Fig. 11. Features of Ali Kosh phase houses, Tepe Ali Kosh: *a,* juncture of two brick walls in zone B_2, showing lack of bonding (southernmost house shown in Fig. 10); *b,* domed oven from zone B_2, 1963 (see Fig. 10); *c,* roasting pit, zone B_2, 1961.

asphalt-stirrers, flint nodule choppers, pounders or hammerstones, slicing slabs, flint core blanks and core pounders, pestles, scraper planes, chipped limestone discs and flint blades, intermixed with butchered animal bones. Included were goat horn cores which were medially flattened in cross-section, a genetic reflection of many generations of domestication (see Reed, 1960:130-131).

The northernmost house, three rooms of which were partially exposed by our excavation, ran parallel to the first house; the houses were separated by an alleyway half a meter wide, which contained a dump of animal bones piled up to a height of 50 cm. The partially-articulated limbs of butchered sheep and goats made up a portion of these, but also well represented were gazell, onager, wild ox, small mammals, fish and mussels.

Inside one room of the northernmost house was a smaller dump of grinding slabs, handstones, pounders, slicing slabs, core pestles, and other heavy stone tools. Many of the grinding implements were coated with asphalt and red ochre. Fragments of mat and basket impressions in asphalt were also present.

In the end, the walls of the abandoned houses in zone B_2 had crumbled down, and a layer of mud brick debris with occasional ash lenses had buried them. The top of this layer, which was quite irregular and varied in depth from 260 to 300 cm. below the surface, was extremely hard. It had the white, sun-baked, packed-down appearance of the present surface of the mound, and we suspect that it was produced sometime during the middle of the Ali Kosh phase, when occupation had temporarily moved off to one side of the mound, and the area of our excavation served as a yard or open area between houses. During the course of excavation, we scraped down to this old land surface carefully with trowels in all forty squares before proceeding deeper.

Zone B_1 –Ali Kosh Phase

After the formation of the old land surface which capped zone B_2, no additional house building took place in the area enclosed by the southernmost forty squares of our 1963 excavation; houses were built immediately to the west, in the area of our 1961 test pit. Middens and ash dumps associated with those houses, however, ran eastward through all the southernmost squares of our 1963 operation and therefore formed part of stratigraphic zone B_1 (see section drawing, Fig. 6).

Since the walls found at a depth of 180 to 300 cm. in our 1961 test pit have already been described (Hole and Flannery, 1962:108-14), we will repeat here only a few details of their construction, as well as their stratigraphic relationship to features in the 1963 excavation.

The two best-preserved walls were founded directly on the old land surface, in the western half of the 1961 pit. One of them ("Wall No. 2" of our 1962 report) was constructed of unbaked white silt bricks 40 by 25 cm. wide and 10 cm. thick; its stub stood half a meter high. The bricks resembled those used in zone B_2, but unlike the latter they were laid with their long axes at right angles to the line of the wall. Fragments of mud plaster clung to the east side of the bricks. One section of wall appeared to be packed mud rather than bricks, and had a small niche in it 30 by 30 cm. in extent.

Layers of midden, containing ash and carbonized sheep or goat dung, began at the base of this wall and ran eastward over the old land surface into squares 81, 82, 91, and 92 of our 1963 operation. Just above them rested a thin film of gray ash which spilled out over the midden and in places directly overlay the old mound surface. This ash, like other ash samples of the Ali Kosh phase, contained numerous carbonized seeds, internodes, and spikelet forks of cultivated emmer wheat and two-row hulled barley. Also included were a few grains of einkorn wheat, wild *Aegilops,* and ryegrass, as well as seeds of *Prosopis,* a wild legume which was destined to figure prominently in the diet of the succeeding Mohammad Jaffar phase.

A second wall ("Wall No. 1" of our 1962 report) stood immediately to the west of the one just described. It was built of unbaked brown, brownish-gray, or gray bricks which may have been slabs quarried out of a midden area somewhere on the mound. Some bricks were 25 by 25 cm. wide, others larger, and often the smaller bricks were laid in courses three bricks wide. This gave the wall an average width of nearly one meter. The structure had been rebuilt at least once, and had a number of possible green clay floors or floor resurfacings associated with it. Like the wall beside it, it had been coated with mud plaster, and there was a niche in it nearly a meter wide and half a meter from front to back. An apparent "doorway" only 70 cm. wide seemed to lead into the room.

Our 1961 test exposed very little of this late Ali Kosh phase room, but we did find asphalt impressions suggesting over-two under-two twilled floor mats, and a few stray chunks of wall plaster which may have been painted with red ochre. Just inside the doorway occurred a flexed, subfloor burial, in a pit which had been cut down from the level of the uppermost floor resurfacing. The burial pit yielded four pecked stone balls and a bell-shaped stone pendant.

After abandonment, this room had been used as a dump or working area in the manner of the zone B_2 houses. Piled along the wall were grinding slabs, discoidal handstones, pestles, pounders, flint nodule choppers, slicing slabs, fire-cracked rocks, and other debris. Several haunches of wild cattle and onager had been chopped up in the room, and their broken limb bones clustered around the discarded choppers and slicing slabs. Similar scatters of heavy stone tools appeared on some of the earlier floor resurfacings.

A few tiny fragments of pottery were recovered by sieving the dirt from zone B_1. Also discovered, however, were a few small fragments of modern bottle glass and iron nails, which had clearly come down by way of gerbil burrows (a few were even found in gerbil seed caches). In view of the latter—and in view of the rather dramatic appearance of pottery in some quantity in zone A_2—we regard the late Ali Kosh phase as probably preceramic, although our minds are not closed on the subject. According to Mellaart (1964*a*:81), digging at Çatal Hüyük, an early site in Anatolia, only a small proportion of rooms of the early ceramic period contained pottery. We regard the Ali Kosh phase as equivalent to lower Jarmo, however, which had no pottery.

With the collapse of the houses found in our 1961 test, a heavy layer of building debris formed over them and over the middens to the west. The upper limits of this semisterile debris lay some 160 to 180 cm. below the surface of the mound. Building activity then shifted somewhat to the north and west, and the Mohammad Jaffar phase was underway.

Zone A_2—Mohammad Jaffar Phase

Architectural traces of the Mohammad Jaffar phase were scarce and badly preserved in zone A_2. The small stub of a collapsed wall of red clay bricks was the only feature recovered in 1961. It was built on sloping wall debris which had covered the stubs of the Ali Kosh phase walls below it. To the west, a heavy mantle of brown clay and building debris filled the room associated with the red-brick wall of zone A_2; to the east began a thick layer of ash (see section drawing, Fig. 6).

This thick ash layer, which ran for more than nine meters to the east of the wall, was composed of lens after lens of white and black ash, piled half a meter deep in places. What it suggested most was a dump area just outside a house, where hearth contents had been thrown week after week for a considerable length of time.

The carbonized seeds from the ash samples had a somewhat different character from those of the Ali Kosh phase. Cultivated emmer wheat and two-row hulled barley were present, as well as *Aegilops* and a few wild einkorn grains, but they were far outnumbered by seeds from the fleshy pod of the thorny perennial legume *Prosopis,* congeneric with the mesquite plant of Mexico and the American southwest (whose pods and seeds were eaten by prehistoric American Indians). Some samples of ash were almost entirely *Prosopis*; others included cereals and tinier legumes. Adams (1965:5) points out that *Prosopis* is a plant which colonizes fallow land. It is also widely eaten by pastoral peoples of the Near East.

Also present in this deep ash midden were bones of sheep, goat, gazelle, wild ox, onager, small mammals, rodents, catfish, turtle, and fresh water mussel. Charred reeds, asphalt impressions of mats and simple twined baskets, flint sickles stained with asphalt used for hafting, bone awls and grooved rubbing stones all appeared in the rubbish. Most striking, however, was the first appearance of sherds in quantity, from pottery of three types: plain or lightly burnished bowls of light tan clay; bowls with a soft, lightly burnished red slip; and light tan bowls whose surface was decorated with fugitive red ochre paint in a variety of geometric designs (zigzags, simple checkerboards, chevrons, and others).

The deep ash beds faded out as they ran north, and five meters from the south wall of our 1963 excavation they were reduced to a series of lenses and wisps of charcoal. North of this, in squares 1 through 50, a few architectural features showed up, but all were difficult to trace. Part of a wall stub, running east-west for a meter or so, was recovered in squares 29 and 30. The wall was about half a meter wide, and composed of brown clay bricks 25 by 25 cm. across and 10 cm. thick; its mortar was green clay, and a strip of ochre-painted pinkish plaster covered its northern surface. Fragments of green clay floor ran west from it, and in squares 24 to 37 we uncovered a scatter of heavy tools that evidently lay on the floor. Included were several typical Mohammad Jaffar phase combination-mortar-and-grinding slabs; a bifacial boulder mortar; a shallow basin grinding slab; and an overturned asphalt-coated twined basket which was filled with carbonized seeds of *Prosopis*. Additional scatters of choppers, pounders, chipped discs, "sashweight" asphalt stirrers and other tools lay in the northwest corner of the excavation.

In squares 21 and 31 we discovered the first traces of stone architecture, the square end of what appeared to be a wall foundation of small river pebbles closely set together. The little we exposed of this foundation seemed to indicate its close similarity to the pebble structure more extensively recovered in zone A_1.

Although poor in architectural details, zone A_2 gave us a sample of seeds, bones, and artifacts which—combined with the evidence for stone wall foundations—greatly enlarged our picture of the Mohammad Jaffar phase. Zone A_2, including the deep ash midden and the house traces to its north, extended from 100 cm. below the surface of the mound to a varying depth of 160 to 180 cm. One hundred square meters of this zone were excavated.

Zone A_1—Mohammad Jaffar Phase

This uppermost and latest zone of the site comprised a stratum of buff building debris, extending from the present surface of the mound to a depth of 100 to 110 cm. It is clear that the source of this building debris was the collapse of a series of

Mohammad Jaffar phase houses on the north and west edges of our 1963 excavation, but the walls of the buildings themselves were difficult to trace at this depth owing to erosion, salt penetration, and leaching. As stated earlier, we removed the upper 50 cm. of this zone before beginning excavation by squares, since it was essentially featureless and the few artifacts it contained were mixed with those of later periods.

The most interesting trace of architecture recovered in zone A_1, was a pavement or wall foundation of smooth river pebbles set closely together. The pavement, which appeared at a depth of 60 to 80 cm., ran due north-south for a distance of 5 meters before disappearing into the north face of our excavation; its width averaged 60 to 65 cm. (see plot plan of zone A_1, Fig. 12, and Pl. 10*a*).

Immediately to the west of the pebble pavement was a north-south line of larger river boulders. Then came a gap of two meters, followed by what looked like the end of an east-west wall foundation of river boulders, which appeared in the west face of our excavation (square 11). The area enclosed by the two river-boulder foundations was apparently the floor of a room, for it was covered by scatters of the same kinds of heavy stone tools seen on the floors of abandoned Ali Kosh phase houses: flint nodule choppers and butchered wild ox bones, fragments of saddle-shaped grinding slabs, discoidal or sausage-shaped handstones, chipped limestone discs, pounders or hammerstones, pestles, "sashweights," and dozens of fire-cracked rocks. Bones of sheep and goat were very numerous, but they were accompanied by wild forms like gazelle, onager, and turtle. Broken bowls of Jaffar Painted pottery appeared at intervals in the debris.

East of the pebble pavement (in squares 19 to 20 and 26 to 28) we found five adult burials from the Mohammad Jaffar phase, some in whole but poorly preserved condition and others partially disturbed. All these burials were oriented north-south, and the positioning of the body was the same in every case: the individual lay on his left side with his head to the south, facing west, and his knees drawn up to the level of his hips. Some burials were accompanied by shell and turquoise jewelry, stone beads, and labrets (and one had the labret still in place on his lower jaw). The least disturbed wore G-strings or "loincloths" of small black disc beads, with a stone or clay bell pendant between the thighs. Adult males seemed to have the largest number of ornaments, but our sample of burials is too small to generalize from. We saw no evidence of the skull deformation noted in the Ali Kosh phase, nor were any of the individuals wrapped in mats. The burials are described in Chapter XVIII.

South of the burial area was a small patch of reddish-brown midden with flecks of ash and charcoal, animal bones, and fragments of mat and basket impressions in asphalt. To the east, near the edge of our excavation, we uncovered three more clusters of flint nodule choppers in association with butchered limb bones of onager and wild ox. Dumps of fire-cracked rocks accompanied some of them, and it appeared that one string of neck vertebrae had been cut apart with a large flint blade stained with red ochre.

The southeast corner of our excavation (squares 86 to 89 and 96 to 99) produced an ash-filled borrow-pit four meters in diameter and more than half a meter deep in places. The pit contained nothing but artifacts and debris typical of the Mohammad Jaffar phase, including dozens of sherds of Jaffar Plain, Jaffar Painted, and Khazineh Red pottery. Many of the sherds in the ash had been subjected to accidental refiring. Flint blades and flint cores, figurine fragments (including a number of "T-shaped" stalk figurines), and burned animal bones occurred in the pit. Included in the bones

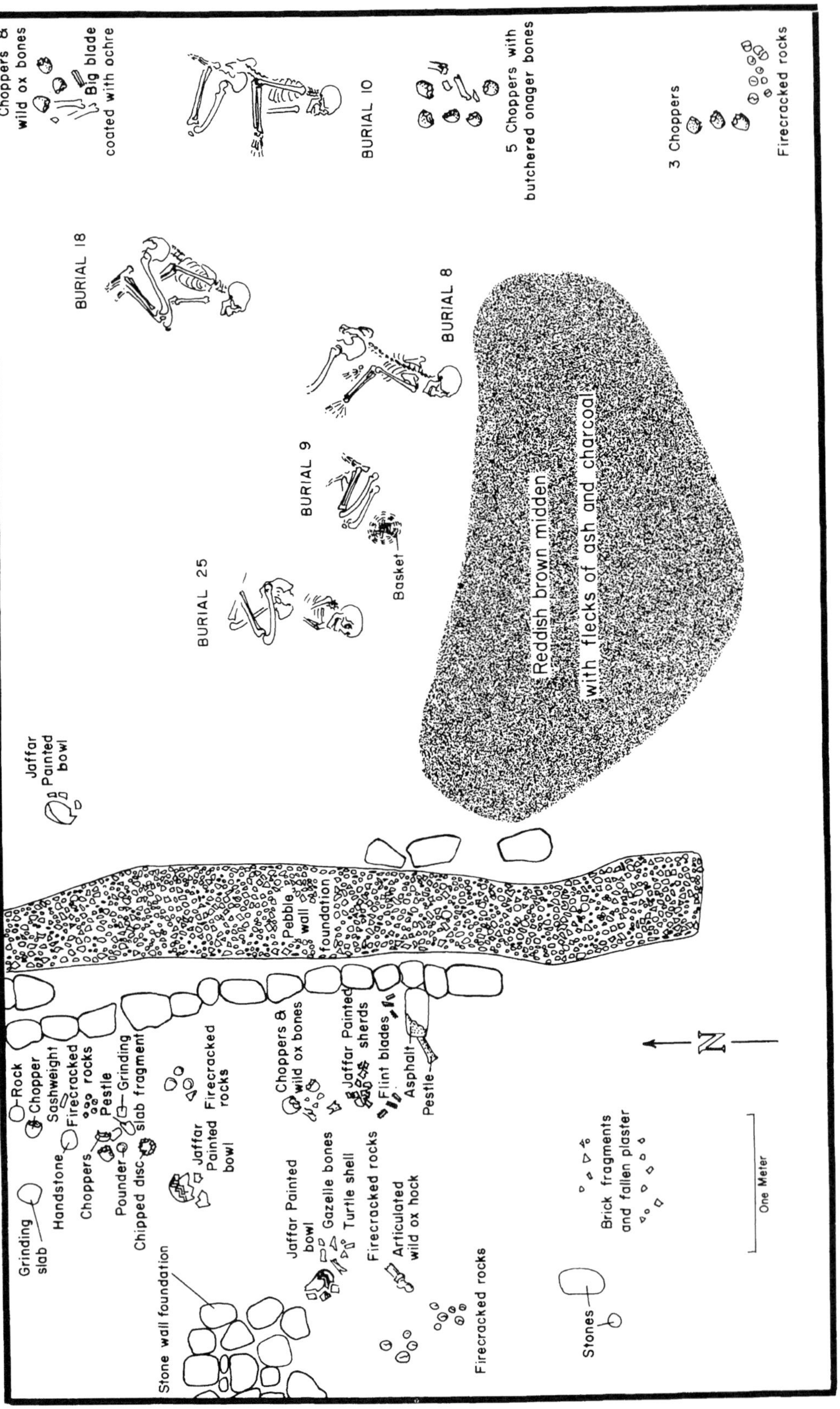

Fig. 12. Plan of zone A_1 (Mohammad Jaffar phase) at Tepe Ali Kosh (only area covered by squares 1 to 60 shown). To left, remains of a house with all tools larger than a flint blade plotted *in situ*. To right, burials outside house.

were goat horn cores which were not only medially-flattened (as in the Ali Kosh phase) but also had the spiral or helical twist characteristic of the later stages of goat domestication. Horns indistinguishable from those of wild goat appeared, as well as medially-flattened but non-twisted horns; so the phenotype of the Mohammad Jaffar goats was far from uniform.

Later Burials Intrusive into Zone A_1 – "Iron Age"

Our work in zone A_1 was considerably hampered by the presence of nearly twenty intrusive burials which had been placed in the site long after its abandoment. These burials were easily distinguished by their rotted condition, the chalky white color of their bones, their consistent east-west orientation, and the presence of such associated objects as copper earrings, copper pins and axes, and iron bracelets. Their burial pits were much softer and moister than the surrounding fill of zone A_1, and almost all the skelctons had chaff-tempered red bricks placed over them. A few were also overlain by stones or plaster slabs. Adult males and females, children and infants were included. The burials are described in Chapter XVIII.

V

THE EXCAVATIONS AT TEPE SABZ

DESCRIPTION OF THE SITE

Tepe Sabz lies 16 km. west-northwest of Ali Kosh and 7.5 km. south-southwest of the present village of Deh Luran. Seen from the east, the site is a large, squat mound whose lower slopes blend almost imperceptibly into the flat, barren plain. In the surrounding area grow scattered *Prosopis* and small wild melons; the lower slopes of the mound support small patches of similar vegetation. Tepe Sabz was apparently almost square in shape originally (measuring about 120 by 140 meters), but a third of the southwest portion of the site has been eroded away by undercutting during the winter rainy season, when the adjacent area is inundated (see Fig. 13 and Pl. 14). The small, flat-topped summit of the mound rises seven meters above the present alluvial plain, but our excavations revealed that the site is actually some 10.5 meters in depth, the lower 3.5 meters having been covered by alluvium.

DISCOVERY OF TEPE SABZ

The French, who surveyed the east side of the Deh Luran plain, evidently did not encounter Tepe Sabz, as the site is not indicated on their maps nor mentioned in the text of their report (Gautier and Lampre, 1905). The site was apparently first discovered and used as a geographic feature during map-making surveys by the British military prior to 1919.[1] The British map-makers used the name *Haft Chagha* ("seven forts") as a collective term referring to the seven archeological mounds located between the village of Deh Luran and Bayat. *Tepe Sabz* ("green mound") is the local name for the particular site we excavated. The Deh Luranis (some of whom are resettled Lurs) pronounce the name of the site *Tepe Sa'za* or *Su'za*. We have used the Farsi name to avoid confusion with the historic site of Susa, 100 km. to the southeast.

The first archeological surface collections were made at Tepe Sabz during a 1961 survey of the Deh Luran plain (Hole, 1961). The collection contained sherds belonging to all the early periods of the Susiana sequence as defined by Le Breton (1947, 1957).

EXCAVATIONS IN 1963

After a resurvey of several of the sites on the Deh Luran plain early in September of 1963, we decided that excavations at Tepe Sabz would offer our best opportunity to obtain a sequence of the prehistoric periods immediately following the Mohammad Jaffar phase. In fact, the presence of Khazineh Red pottery on the surface of

[1] See British Middle East Land Forces map, Iraq-Iran, 1:253, 440, Sheet I 38 X.

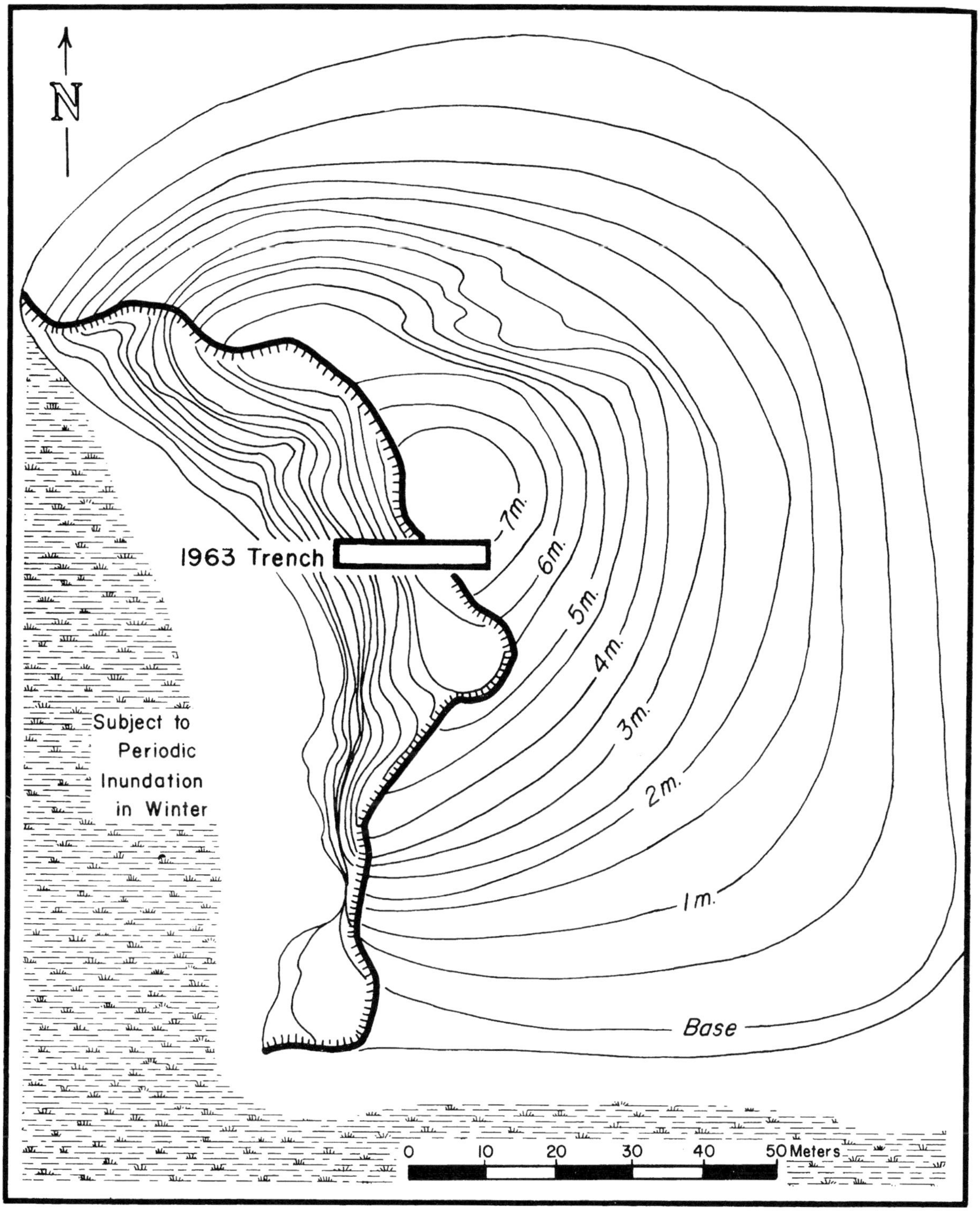

Fig. 13. Map of Tepe Sabz.

Tepe Sabz even led us to hope that basal levels of the site might date back to the Mohammad Jaffar phase. Although such was not the case, excavations at Tepe Sabz provided information on four periods of extreme interest in the prehistory of Khuzistan.

On October 15, 1963, a party composed of Deh Luran workmen trained at Ali Kosh began clearing a narrow portion of the eroded western face of Tepe Sabz in preparation for a stratigraphic trench. Because we know the trench would reach to a depth of at least seven meters, we decided that the most logical approach would be a step-trench, one which could be stepped toward the outer edge of the mound by gradual increments as work proceeded downward, thus facilitating entry and exit by workmen. Selecting the highest point on the site (and one which had yielded the most complete sequence of surface materials), we staked out a 3-by-5-meter trench in one-meter squares (Fig. 14). Running in a due east-west direction, the long axis of this trench was set at right angles to the west edge of the site in order to take advantage of the steep, eroded face on this side of the mound. This location permitted the most expeditious cutting of a step trench, since dirt could simply be carried out of the west end of the trench and down the eroded face. Our clearing operations, carried out in preparation for the step trench, also gave us a stratigraphic "preview" of the natural levels at the site before work on the one-meter squares began.

We carried out excavation of the fifteen one-meter squares in basically the same manner as described for Ali Kosh (see preceding chapter). After removing the uppermost 30 cm. from the first few squares by means of ten-centimeter levels, it became apparent that this part of the deposit was badly weathered and leached (much like the uppermost 50 cm. at Ali Kosh). Accordingly, we removed these upper 30 cm. at Tepe Sabz as a single unit from the remaining squares. Work then proceeded by means of ten-centimeter levels within one-meter squares.

In order to provide the longest "profiles" or cross-sections possible for drawing, we decided to leave the central east-west-running row of squares as a temporary balk (see Pl. 15). Thus we excavated the northernmost row of squares (Nos. 1,

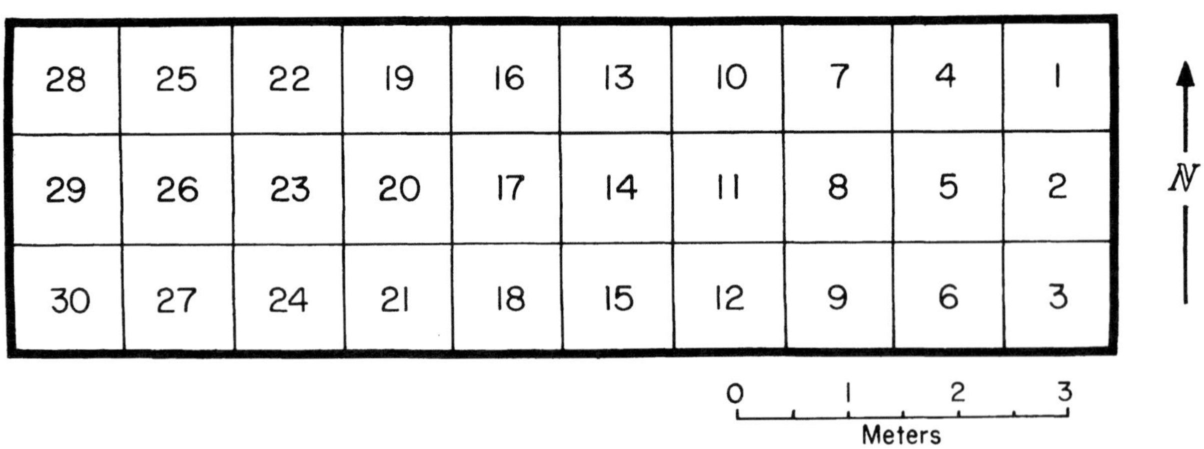

Fig. 14. Plan of first 30 one-meter squares in 1963 step-trench at Tepe Sabz. (The "clearing trench" occupied an area which could be designated "squares 31 to 52" by projecting the grid to the west.)

4, 7, 10, etc.) and the southernmost row of squares (Nos. 3, 6, 9, 12, etc.) to a depth of 1.5 meters before touching the central row (squares 2, 5, 8, 11, etc.) At this point, we drew the section presented by the north side of the excavated squares 3 through 12 (see Fig. 16), and followed this with excavation of the central row of squares. The north and south rows were always kept slightly deeper than the central row in order to provide a preview of coming strata. The north wall of the trench was also drawn (see Fig. 15), giving us an additional cross-section of the deposits at a point two meters farther to the north.

While the block of fifteen one-meter squares in the step trench was being excavated, we maintained a "clearing trench" three meters wide and immediately to the west of the step trench. This served as an access route from the eroded west face of the mound into the step trench proper. The clearing trench was not excavated by one-meter squares; it was dug rapidly with road-construction picks so that it would always be slightly deeper than the block of fifteen one-meter squares. It served, however, to lengthen the cross-section which could be drawn along the northernmost face of the excavation (Fig. 15), thus giving us additional stratigraphic information and architectural details. We mapped the brick walls which crossed the clearing trench, as most were in some way connected with the walls within the step-trench.

The first "step" of the step-trench was 1.5 meters. At this point, squares 1, 2, and 3 were discontinued, and three new squares (16, 17 and 18) were begun immediately to the west. This proved to be an awkward depth for our workmen (some of whom were under 1.5 meters in height), and henceforth steps of only one meter were made. In other words, with each successive descent of one meter in depth, the trench was stepped one meter to the west. In this manner, no more than three squares at a time were lost, enabling us to maintain as nearly a continuous and complete stratigraphic column as possible. Continuity was always maintained in twelve out of fifteen squares. And by stepping gradually to the west, we were able to keep the trench as close as possible to the eroded west face of the mound, which constituted our best means of entry and exist from the deepening step-trench.

After a few weeks of excavation at Tepe Sabz it became evident that the work was proceeding too slowly for completion of the sounding within our time limit. Without sacrificing the detail and accuracy for which we were striving, we found that the operation would proceed more rapidly by excavating each of the squares in the center row by twenty-centimeter levels rather than by the customary ten-centimeter levels. Shortly thereafter, as no features or materials requiring ten-centimeter levels of excavation were being encountered, we decided to dig all of the fifteen one-meter squares by twenty-centimeter levels. The changed procedures reduced the time it took to scrape the floor and the four walls of the square to bring out the stratigraphy, and to collect, label, and bag the artifacts and other materials recovered.

At a depth of six meters, we ceased to step the trench westward, and instead continued it straight downward to virgin soil, further increasing the rate of excavation by removing the twenty-centimeter levels as a unit from each row of five one-meter squares. The techniques and the units of excavation remained fine enough to permit us to note changes in soil texture and stratigraphy, recover seeds and other carbonized materials *in situ,* obtain the provenience of artifacts within a one-by-five-meter area 20 cm. in depth, and find even the faintest traces of architecture. At no time throughout the entire excavation was sieving with two sizes of screens abandoned. In short, as we learned more about the sites we were testing, our techniques of

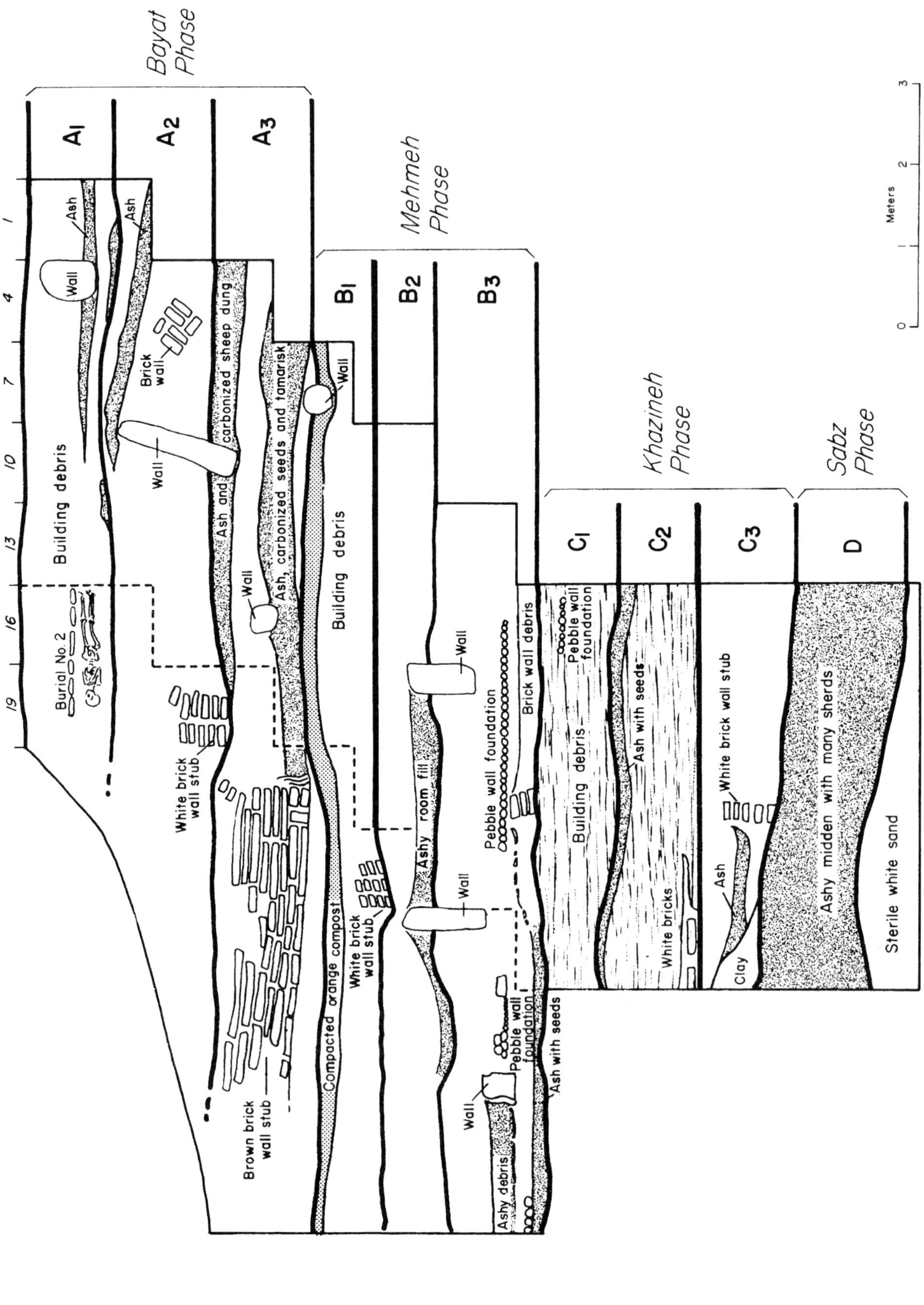

Fig. 15. Tepe Sabz. West (left) to east (right) section drawing of the north wall of squares 1 to 28 and adjacent part of the "clearing

excavation were modified to allow more rapid work without sacrificing accuracy and detail.

The entire step trench reached virgin soil on December 23, 1963, and the excavations at Tepe Sabz were terminated.

THE DEPOSITIONAL HISTORY OF THE STRATIGRAPHIC COLUMN

Virgin Soil

Tepe Sabz was founded on a surface of whitish-buff sandy soil. Sloping rather sharply downward from the southwest toward the northeast corner of the test, this surface was 990 to 1080 cm. below the present summit of the mound. No indication of a sterile red clay layer, as found below the sterile white sandy soil at Ali Kosh, was discovered at Tepe Sabz. It must be noted, however, that no actual attempt was made to carry the excavation below 1100 cm. in search of further changes in the stratigraphy of the undisturbed original land surface.

Zone D–Sabz Phase

The oldest evidence of human habitation discovered at Tepe Sabz, a deposit of ashy midden debris, lay on the sterile whitish-buff sandy soil at the base of the site (see section drawings, Figs. 15 and 16). A small conical pit and a lens-shaped concentration of sherds were the only features discovered within this midden. No architecture, as such, was found.

The dense, highly compacted deposit of greenish-gray midden was composed primarily of decayed and carbonized vegetal matter mixed with a fine, clay-like soil. Small lenses of a sterile buff clay, perhaps representing building debris, were found throughout the midden. Silica "ghosts" of plants, carbonized seeds, and actual "fossilized" seeds were collected.

The small conical pit was located at the juncture of squares 26 and 29. Approximately 40 cm. in diameter, the pit had been dug down through 20 cm. of refuse and extended an additional 20 cm. into virgin soil. In the pit were fragments of human bone and a great many almonds and flax seeds, fragments of asphalt with impressions from ovcr-two, under-two twilled matting and/or basketry, as well as remnants of decayed and carbonized plants. As little more than stains and silica "ghosts" of the decayed materials were found, it is unlikely that the almonds and flax seeds would have been preserved were it not for their fortuitous fossilization. This feature suggests an attempt to pack almonds and flax seeds in an asphalt-coated basket or mat, which was then placed in a pit.

It appears that the contents of the pit were forgotten or no longer wanted, for evidently not long after it was dug, the pit was covered with a lens-shaped concentration of sherds, which in turn was covered by an additional 60 to 70 cm. of trash. We can only guess whether the layer of sherds was purposefully placed over the pit, perhaps to protect its contents or mark its location, or if it merely represents the refuse from a nearby household. Because only one edge of the relatively large sherd deposit (about 1.0 by 2.0 meters in extent and 15 cm. in thickness) covered the pit, it seems likely that the latter of the two alternatives is correct. Pellets of carbonized sheep or goat dung were collected from throughout this midden as well as the remains of at least four dogs.

The midden also contained bone awls, spatulas and gouges, and star-shaped spindle whorls. Impressions in asphalt indicate that both the over-one, under-one plain plaiting and the over-two, under-two twilled plaiting techniques of mat and/or basket weaving were practiced at this time.

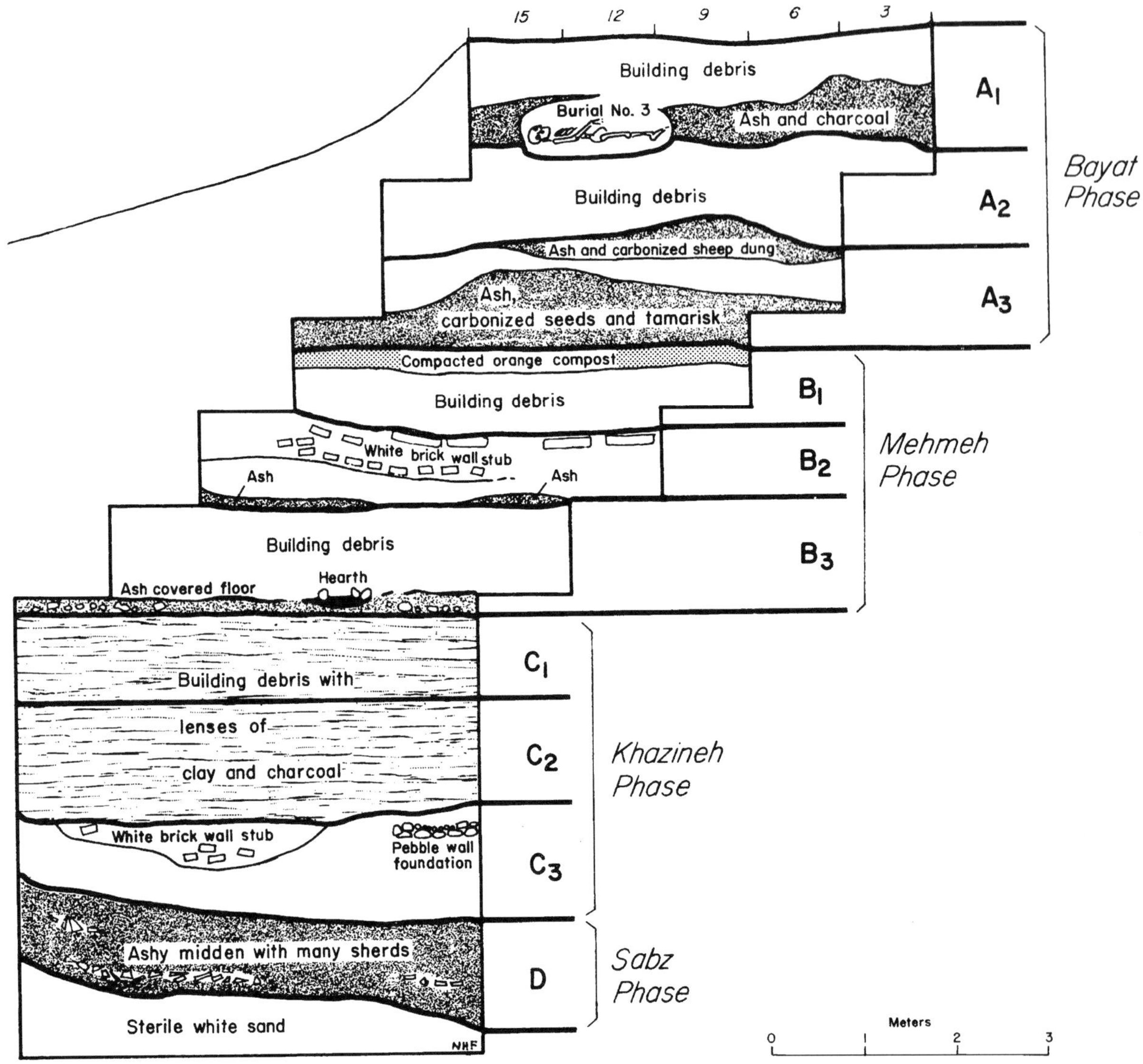

Fig. 16. Tepe Sabz. West (left) to east (right) section drawing of the north wall of squares 3 to 30 after excavation.

Parallel-line-incised stone bracelets and three types of labrets (cuff-link, T-shaped, and nail-shaped) were the only articles of personal adornment found. Flat topped boulder and saddle-shaped grinding slabs, combination-shallow-basin-and-mortar, and combination saddle-shaped-and-mortar types of grinding slabs also appeared in the refuse. Simple discoidal handstones and irregular sausage-shaped pestles were used on the various grinding slabs. One of the two chipped stone hoes recovered from Tepe Sabz came from this phase. Also found were perforated stones, some of which were probably sockets for door pivots; polished celts; spherical pounders or hammerstones; and an incised pebble, similar to the slicing slabs found at Ali Kosh.

Ceramics were the most numerous artifacts found in the Sabz phase, with Susiana Plain Buff by far the most abundant. Also present were Susiana Black-on-buff vessels with form and decoration related to Susiana *a* and Samarra.

Zone C_3 –Khazineh Phase

A deposit of highly-compacted, grayish-brown building debris with a few lenses of clay and ash, and the stub of a white mud-brick wall, overlay the midden of zone D. West of the wall stub was a layer of clay and another ash deposit, while in the southeast corner of the trench (on a level with the top of the stub) we found a wall foundation constructed of pebbles and cobbles.

The white brick wall stub was the oldest architectural remnant found in our trench at Tepe Sabz. Only 60 cm. in height, the stub was constructed of a single course of irregularly-shaped, untempered, sun-dried, white mud bricks which ranged from 22 to 28 cm. in width and 8 to 10 cm. in thickness. Although no mortar was distinguished as such, the uniform interstices between the bricks clearly indicated that they had been set into mud of the same composition as the bricks. The scatter of white mud bricks and crumbled wall debris in squares 20, 23, 26, and 29 appeared to be an upper part of the same wall, which fell toward the southwest. No other traces of architecture were found, and we were unable to detect the shape, dimensions, or orientation of the structure represented. The remainder of the fill in zone C_3 probably represents building debris from eroded architecture outside of the step trench.

The second level of construction in this zone consisted of a wall foundation made of unmodified water-worn cobbles, overlain by a second course of pebbles bordered by cobbles. Averaging only 15 cm. in thickness, this feature is similar to the more completely exposed wall foundation found in zone B_3 (Fig. 17*a*, Pl. 16) and the walls of the house mapped at Tepe Ashrafabad (Fig. 17*b*).

The wall in zone C_3 probably represents the northwest corner of a room.

Ten to 20 cm. above the wall foundation, at an average depth of 830 cm. below the surface of the site, the nature of the fill changed slightly, and it was at this break in the stratigraphy that we made the division between zones C_3 and C_2 of the Khazineh phase.

Our oldest example of coiled basketry appeared in zone C_3.

Zone C_2 –Khazineh Phase

Zone C_2 was characterized by a compacted, mottled-gray building debris which contained little more than fine lenses of clay and ash. In the northwest corner of the trench, a few white, sundried mud bricks, about 40 cm. wide by 8 cm. thick, were found lying just above the building debris of zone C_3, in a lens of greenish clay. These materials apparently had fallen from a structure to the north or west of the excavation. Capping this zone in the north half of the excavation was a deposit of gray ash, averaging about 10 cm. in thickness (see section drawing, Fig. 15).

Zone C_1 –Khazineh Phase

This meter-thick deposit, beginning at an average depth of 720 cm. and extending upward to within 620 cm. of the summit of the mound, consisted fundamentally of the same kind of fill found in zone C_2.

The only architectural feature appeared to be the edge of a wall-foundation, constructed of a single course of unmodified water-worn cobbles, each about 10 cm. in diameter. This was the last trace of architecture found in the Khazineh phase levels.

The artifacts recovered from the Khazineh phase levels showed many similarities with those of the Sabz phase, but a few changes and new trends were evident. Jaffar Plain pottery appeared in greatly reduced

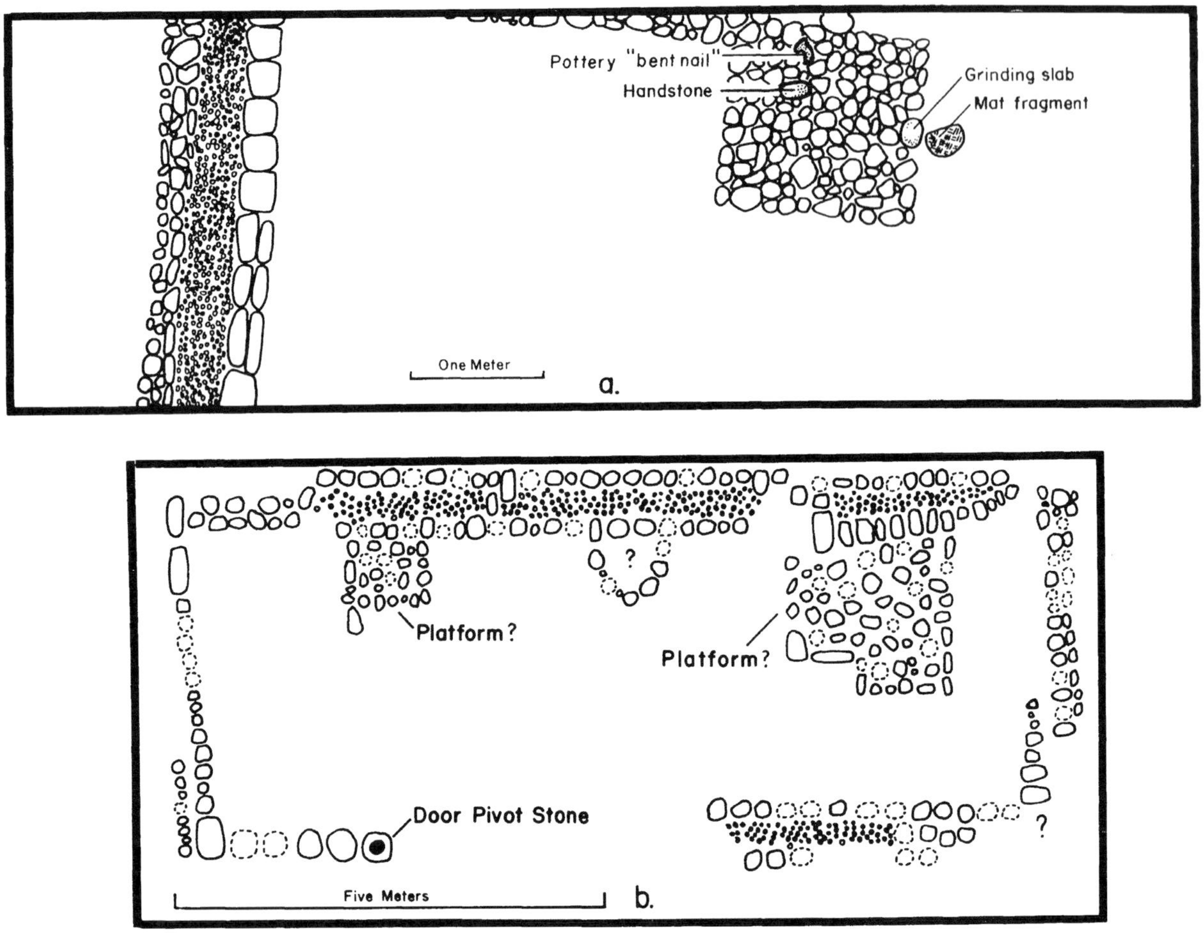

Fig. 17. Mehmeh phase houses: *a*, pebble and cobble wall foundations found in zone B_3 of step-trench at Tepe Sabz (see also Fig. 15 and Pl. 16); *b*, plan of stone house foundation at Tepe Ashrafabad (Chapter VII). North at top of drawing.

quantities, while Khazineh Red was the most abundant single type represented in the sherds from Khazineh phase levels. Many Susiana Black-on-buff vessel forms and designs were suggestive of Hajji Mohammad, Halaf, and Susiana *b*.

Previously-found types of matting and basketry continued, but coiled basketry had now joined them. Labrets declined in frequency. Flat-topped boulder grinding slabs, combination shallow-basin-and-mortar types, simple discoidal handstones, and irregular sausage-shaped pestles persisted, and cuboid pounder/rubbing-stones were added.

It should be noted that our 1963 step-trench passed through an area of dense building debris in the zones representing the Khazineh phase, and that artifacts other than pottery were not numerous. It is quite possible that discontinuities in the distribution of a number of artifact types would not have occurred had we dug through midden deposits of this phase.

Zone B_3 –Mehmeh Phase

At least five distinct levels of construction were found in the reddish-buff building debris in this zone. The architectural features gave us some of our best preserved examples of cobble wall-foundations, untempered mud brick walls, and untempered packed-mud walls.

1) A wall stub of white sun-dried mud bricks, each 35 to 38 cm. wide and 5 to 9 cm. thick, was the oldest evidence of construction in this zone. The wall had been founded directly on the mottled gray building debris of zone C_1, and its stub extended 20 cm. out from the north wall of the excavation into square 22, where it ended abruptly. Butting against this stub, and trailing off to either side, was a layer of whitish-buff mud brick wall debris which probably came from the upper portion of the wall as it was eroded away. Lying against the mud brick wall debris some 1.40 meters west of the white brick stub, and extending west into the area cleared for access to the trench, was a lens of dark gray ash containing a large number of carbonized seeds. Spanning the entire south half of the test, on the same stratigraphic level as the white mud brick wall and the dark gray ash lens, was a brown, ashy midden about 20 cm. thick. Perhaps the ash and the debris were refuse discarded by the occupants of the white brick structure.

2) The second level of construction, a cobble wall foundation, was built upon the dark gray ash lens and the brown ashy midden in the extreme northwest corner of the test. As only a few cobbles were visible in the north wall of the clearing trench, we were only able to determine that the feature had been constructed of a single course of unmodified river cobbles each about 10 cm. in diameter. In the south half of the step trench, on approximately the same stratigraphic level as the cobble wall-foundation, was the compacted surface of the brown midden. As illustrated in the profile of square 21 (Fig. 16), a hearth had been set into this floor. The hearth was about 75 cm. in diameter, 15 cm. deep, circular in plan, and filled with ash and fire-cracked rocks.

3) The third construction, extending in from the north wall of the clearing trench, was a packed-mud wall stub, made of whitish-buff, untempered mud. The stub was 48 cm. in maximum height and 30 cm. thick. The wall had been erected on the thin deposit of buff-colored fill and building debris covering the cobbles of the second construction level. No evidence of an opposing wall was found, but to the west a layer of dark ashy debris had been deposited to the height of the remaining stub. The ash butted against a single 3-to-5-cm. thick coating of clay plaster, so well-bonded to the stub (and similar in color) that only its finer texture betrayed its presence. Although the workmen opening the clearing trench had been cautioned to watch for indications of architecture, and we were constantly overseeing their work, this particular wall stub was not recognized until the north wall of the excavation had been scraped with our specially-made profiling shovel.

4) The fourth and most important level of construction in this zone was a stone-founded building, separated from the white-brick wall stub by a thin layer of buff building debris. The west portion of the foundation consisted of a layer of pebbles 5 cm. deep and 40 cm. wide, flanked on both sides by a row of unmodified cobbles and small boulders set in mud mortar (Pl. 16). As the excavation proceeded, it became apparent that it was somehow related to another wall, and a stone platform made from a single layer of water-worn pebbles and small cobbles. The plan and section of the structure (Fig. 17*a*) show the relationship between the platform and the wall.

It was only when we came across similar cobble wall foundations eroding out of nearby Tepe Ashrafabad that we could fully reconstruct the sort of house whose traces we found in zone B_3. The house we mapped at Ashrafabad (Fig. 17*b*) shows clearly that stone platforms occured within Mehmeh phase houses, whose walls were founded with a double row of cobbles and a layer of pebbles. We have no evidence for the upper wall construction.

The platforms inside the houses probably served to protect household goods against dirt and moisture. Some Deh Luran villagers regularly collect cobbles to put in the corner of their dwellings as platforms for their valuables. Perhaps the platforms were covered with matting and served as beds; fragments of mat-impressions found on the platform suggest this possible use. We also found grinding stones and a ceramic "bent nail" on the platform.

5) The fifth, and final, level of construction in zone B_3 was the southernmost portion of a structure with packed-mud walls. The structure was erected on a thin layer of buff building debris lying on the cobble wall-foundation of the previous level. This building provided the first set of opposing walls disclosed by our trench, and we were able to measure an interior dimension of 2.6 meters. The wall stubs were made of untempered whitish-buff mud like that used in the packed-mud wall of the third construction level. In this case, however, we were not able to find any trace of plaster. The three wall stubs stood from 80 to 95 cm. in height, with the southern and western walls 26 cm. thick and the eastern wall 40 cm. thick. No prepared floor could be distinguished in the uniformly-colored, compacted building debris filling the lower two-thirds of the structure.

Zone B_2—Mehmeh Phase

Capping the previous zone and beginning zone B_2 was a layer of dark gray ash. The head of a copper pin, (the only copper artifact found by us *in situ* at Tepe Sabz), came from this ash. The ash extended southwestward, over the tops of the wall stubs of the abandoned house of zone B_3, into the clearing trench.

Stratigraphically above and to the south of the packed mud-walls of zone B_3 were found the only architectural remains exposed in zone B_2. A white mud brick wall stub entered the trench from the south and ran north into square 20, where it ended abruptly. Surviving from 25 to 60 cm. in height, this wall was constructed of two sizes of sun dried mud bricks. The smaller ones, averaging 20 by 20 by 10 cm., were overlain by larger bricks averaging 20 by 50 by 10 cm. Other brick fragments from this wall were scattered throughout the reddish-buff building debris. The orientation and placement of the bricks seen in profile suggested the presence of an east-west wall, probably a room divider, butting against the white brick wall stub.

On a level with the base of the white mud brick wall stub was a lens of light gray ash and burned earth containing a concentration of sherds, the inverted fragments of two saddle-shaped grinding slabs, and two simple discoidal handstones. The remaining portions of the zone were composed of featureless reddish-buff building debris.

Zone B_1—Mehmeh Phase

Zone B_1 began immediately above the white and mud brick wall, at an average depth of 430 cm. below the surface of the mound. Characterized by highly compacted, reddish-buff building debris with a few lenses of black and gray ash, the zone was capped by a layer of what appeared to be compacted orange compost, which terminated at a depth of about 340 cm. The wall stubs of two widely-separated, different types of structures were contained within this zone.

About twenty cm. above the packed-mud walled structure of zone B_3, lay a wall stub consisting of three courses of sun dried, white mud bricks 15 to 20 cm. wide and 5 to 8 cm. thick. Although its bricks had been set into a buff mud mortar, the wall itself was not plastered. The stub was 40 cm. high, 60 cm. wide, and extended approximately 80 cm. out from the north wall of the excavation into the "clearing" trench. Its southern end terminated without a corner.

The compacted orange "compost" layer which marked the upper limits of zone B_1 covered the entire step trench and clearing area.

Throughout the debris of zones B_1, B_2, and B_3 occurred artifacts typical of the Mehmeh phase. These included ceramic "bent nails" (all but two of which came from the three zones mentioned above); Susiana Black-on-buff bowls with naturalistic designs such as "rows of goats" or "dancing men;" abundant vessels in Mehmeh Red-on-red; grooved mauls; and two new types of spindle whorls, the oval discoidal and punctate dome-shaped. Appearing for the last time in zone B_1 were star-shaped spindle whorls and ceramic "rings."

Matting and basketry continued essentially unchanged. The asphalt impression of one coiled basket bore on its inner surface impressions of seeds and spikelets, identified by Helbaek as six-row hulled barley and *Aegilops*. Bone awls, a fragmentary "needle" and a knife-like tool of bone were also found. Only one labret of the T-shaped type was unearthed in the Mehmeh phase levels.

Saddle-shaped slabs, combination-saddle-shaped-and-mortar-grinding slabs and simple discoidal handstones were abundant during this phase. The last examples of irregular sausage-shaped pestles and cuboid pounder/rubbing stones appeared in zone B_1. Two new distinctive handstone types, the loaf-shaped (faceted) handstone and the irregular sausage-shaped handstone, were present only during the Mehmeh phase. Polished celts, and perforated stone sockets for door pivots occurred in great quantity.

A comparison of the Tepe Sabz B_1 - B_2 artifacts with those found at Musiyan "E" (480 to 530 cm.) suggests that they were contemporary. Also after comparing artifacts, there is little doubt that the Mehmeh phase forms the major, if not the only component at Tepe Ashrafabad. Ties with the Mehmeh phase are widespread, including Susiana *c*, Ras al 'Amiya, and Eridu XII.

Zone A_3 – Bayat Phase

Three distinct levels of construction were found in zone A_3. Building debris and extensive ash layers containing carbonized plant remains, seeds, and sheep or goat dung comprised the fill surrounding the architectural features.

This zone began with the deposition of buff building debris above the orange compost layer which terminated the Mehmeh phase deposits. The first house pertaining to this zone was built in the area just to the west of our step trench. The section and plan drawings (Figs. 15 and 18*a*), show that the clearing area for the step trench coincided with the long axis of the building, providing the most nearly complete exposure of a room in our excavations at Tepe Sabz. The walls, perserved to a maximum of 1.10 meters in height, were constructed of two courses of dark reddish-brown bricks set into a buff mud mortar. These bricks, made of sun dried, untempered mud, were of two types: (1) a nearly square type averaging 50 by 50 by 10 cm., and (2) a type one-quarter that size, averaging 20 by 25 by 10 cm. The smaller bricks were apparently used to compensate for the variations in the length of the longer bricks and mortared joints, and served to even the length of each course. A simple sort of bonding may have been attempted in the one corner of the structure that was exposed (see section, Fig. 18*b*). The walls, averaging about 1.10 meters in thickness, were plastered on both surfaces. We were not able to ascertain the complete dimensions of this struc-

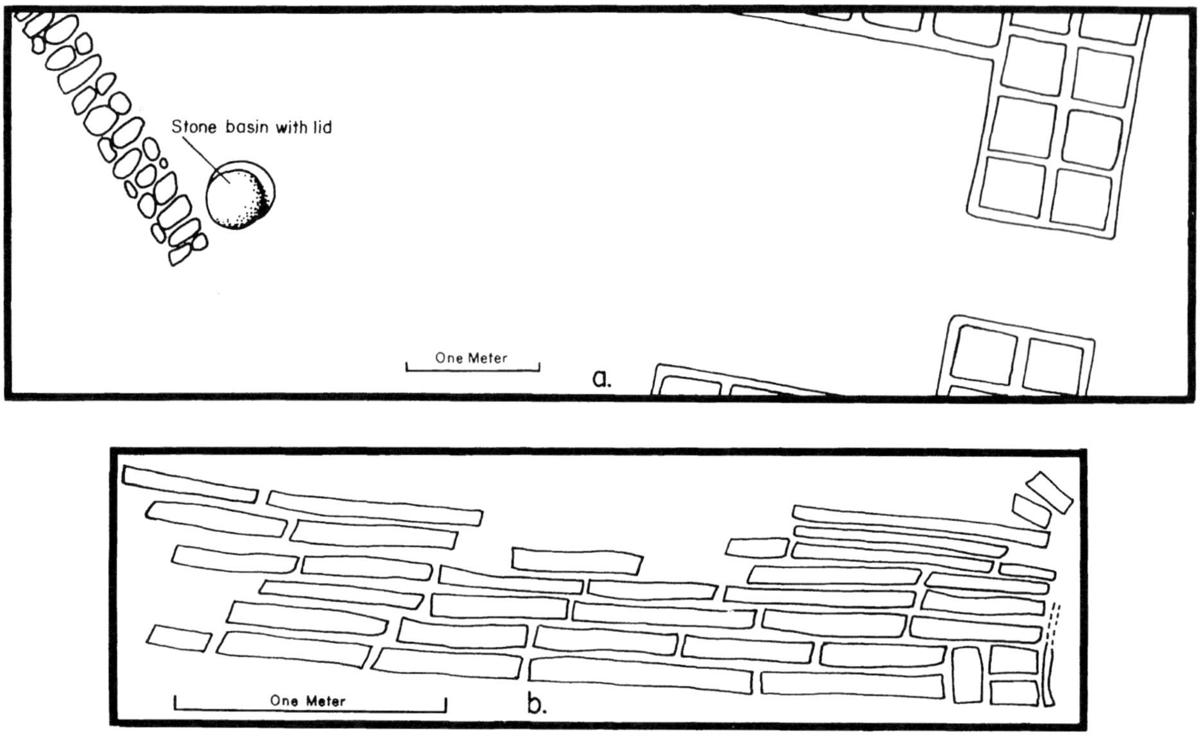

Fig. 18. Bayat phase house from zone A_3 at Tepe Sabz: *a,* plan view, showing wall stubs in "clearing trench," north at top of drawing. Walls to east are of clay-slab bricks; wall to west is stone-founded; *b,* cross-section of northeasternmost wall shown in *a,* showing technique of bonding at juncture between two walls (see also Fig. 15).

ture, but the north-south dimension of the room we exposed was about 2.75 meters, and there was a doorway 80 cm. wide in the eastern wall. There was no trace of the western wall.

While the building was occupied, or soon after it was abandoned, a layer of black and gray ash began to accumulate over the entire area exposed by our step trench. The ash collected against the east wall of the structure and spilled through the doorway onto its floor. This ash contained carbonized tamarisk wood and hundreds of carbonized seeds of 6-row barley, both hulled and naked. The radiocarbon samples of tamarisk have dated this zone of the Bayat phase to between 4100 B.C. and 3800 B.C.

Built atop this layer of ash, we found the second level of construction in zone B_3, a white, packed-mud wall stub, 30 cm. high by 35 cm. thick. No evidence of a corner, or of transverse and opposing walls, was found.

Covering the ash layer and the walls was a deposit of brownish-buff building debris. The last natural layer in this zone, a lens of dark gray ash containing carbonized sheep or goat dung, covered all but the southwest corner of the step trench.

Set into this layer of ash was a white, packed-mud wall averaging 1.60 meters in height and 35 cm. thick. This wall crossed the center of the step trench (see section drawing, Fig. 15). A presumed doorway, 80 to 100 cm. wide, was located in the wall. There was no evidence of a prepared floor or associated crosswalls.

Zone A_2—Bayat Phase

A nearly sterile deposit of reddish-buff building debris formed the bulk of the fill comprising this zone.

The oldest structure in A_2 was a mud-brick wall stub, averaging 75 cm. in height and 60 cm. thick, which spanned our clearing trench and rested on the west edge of the gray ash of zone A_3 (Fig. 15). The wall had a double course of unfired, untempered, white mud bricks set in buff mud mortar. The average brick was a uniform 30 by 50 by 10 cm.

The northeast portion of the step trench also cut through fragments of a collapsed brick wall. The average size of these scattered white bricks was about 30 by 35 by 12 cm. Figure 15 illustrates a cross-section of a fragment of this collapsed wall, showing a possible technique of bonding not found elsewhere in our excavations.

The corner of a trash-filled room represented the final architectural feature in this zone (Figs. 15 and 19). The wall stubs, 150 cm. in height and 40 cm. in thickness, were made of densely compacted, whitish-buff mud, and set into the level below. After the structure was abandoned, trash was thrown into the room to the height of the standing walls. This trash consisted of light gray ash with large quantities of sherds, charred seeds, and animal bones (which included the semiarticulared skeleton of a dog).

Burial No. 1 occurred in the featureless fill in the northwest portion of the excavation. It had been partially exposed by erosion on the west face of the mound, and the skull and scapulae were missing. Because of the erosion and leaching of most of the earth covering the burial, we were unable to determine if it was contemporary with zone A_2 or intrusive from zone A_1.

A lens of gray ash confined to the northeast portion of the step trench was the uppermost stratigraphic feature in this zone.

Zone A_1—Bayat Phase

The final and most recent zone of occupation at Tepe Sabz occupied the uppermost 150 cm. of the step trench. Although large ash lenses were present, the majority of the fill was featureless reddish-buff building debris. The zone contained four

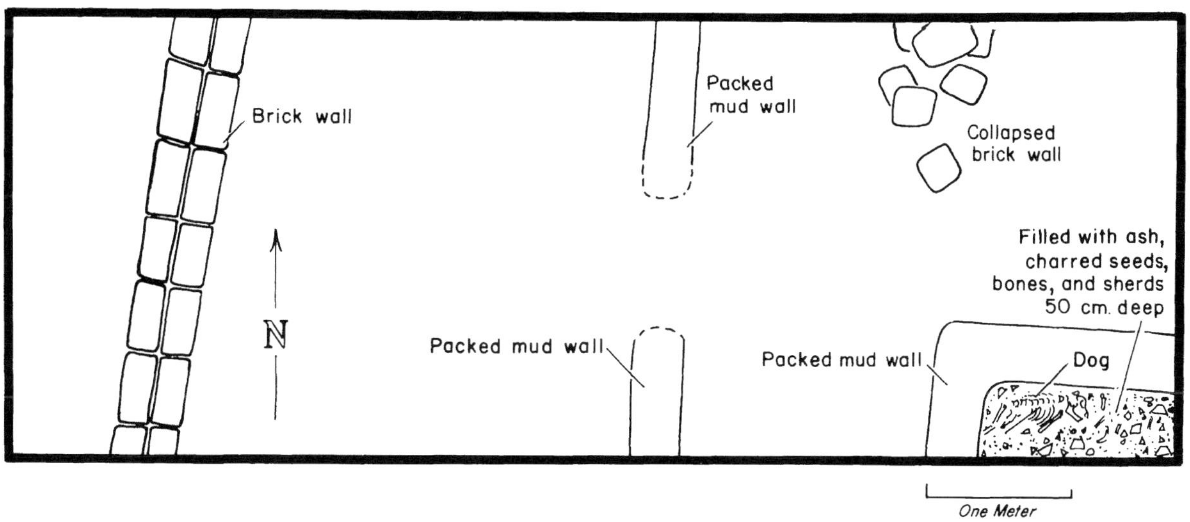

Fig. 19. Plan of zone A_2 (Bayat phase) at Tepe Sabz (See also Fig. 15.) The dog shown in the southeast corner of the drawing is the same illustrated in Fig. 130 *a,b*.

human burials and a single wall stub.

Throughout most of the trench, the base of zone A_1 was delimited by the lower edge of an ash bed that varied between 10 to 70 cm. in thickness. It appeared that while layer after layer of ash, charcoal and burned earth from the hearths of nearby houses were being thrown on the southern half of the exposed ash bed, a layer of building debris was trickling down over its northern end. Subsequently another layer of ash was thrown over the building debris.

A whitish-buff packed-mud wall was built on the ash bed. Now represented only by an eroded stub 70 cm. high by 35 to 45 cm. thick, the wall extended 30 cm. into the step trench, at which point it ended abruptly.

We found four primary burials (two adult females, one adolescent, and a newborn infant or foetus) in this zone. All were oriented east-west and lying on the right side (see Pl. 17). The newborn infant was semiflexed, while the two adults and the adolescent were extended. Artifacts were associated only with the two adult female burials, each of which had a saddle-shaped grinding slab and a simple discoidal handstone. Three of the four burials had coverings of stone slabs. To judge from present-day practice, the slab covers may indicate the level of the ground surface at the time of burial. Today shallow graves are usually capped with cement or stone slabs and boulders to prevent disturbance of the body by carnivores.

The upper 25 to 30 cm. of zone A_1 was powdery, grayish-buff fill having no observable stratigraphic features except the uppermost wall stub. The fill was similar to the upper 50 cm. at Ali Kosh, and is probably the result of the weathering and leaching of building debris.

Aside from pottery and flint, spindle whorls were the most numerous artifacts in the Bayat phase levels. Of these, the "chariot-wheel" type accounted for 49 out of 63 whorls. Only one fragment of matting or basketry (an over-two, under-two twilled plaited weave) was found. Awls, and a single example of a "spatulalike" tool, were the only implements of bone found. An incised bead seal made of amber, three labrets, and a chipped stone hoe were among the remaining small finds.

Saddle-shaped and combination saddle-shaped-and-mortar grinding slabs, and simple discoidal handstones, were the only grinding-implements recovered from Bayat phase levels. Remaining types of pecked and ground stone included sockets for door pivots, polished celts, spherical pounders, and a large stone basin with a lid.

Together, Susiana Plain Buff and Susiana Black-on-buff comprised about 95 per cent of the sherds recovered from Bayat phase levels. Susiana Plain Buff made an abrupt increase relative to the Black-on-buff. We may explain this by noting the trend to a more open "Late Ubaid" style, using less painted decoration. A new type, Bayat Red, occurred for the first time in significant amounts. Also occurring for the first time were three new rare ceramic types: a fine Black-on-tan, Bichrome Painted, and Burnished Black.

VI

THE TEST AT TEPE MUSIYAN "E"

DESCRIPTION OF THE SITE

By far the largest mound in the Deh Luran area—and one of the largest in Khuzistan—Tepe Musiyan lies in the southeast quadrant of the Deh Luran plain about two-and-a-half km. east of Ali Kosh. Musiyan is 450 meters long north to south and 300 meters east to west, with a circumference of nearly a kilometer-and-a-half; in places its summit exceeds 17 meters. Aerial photographs reveal the outlines of walls and fortifications on its north and west sides, and an early French expedition uncovered house complexes of baked bricks in the uppermost levels of the north-central part. Presumably these date to the latest occupation on the site, which may be contemporary with so-called "Elamite" levels at Susa. The French found not a single sherd of later Parthian and Sassanian material (Gautier and Lampre, 1905).

Surface materials, and the results of the French test cuts, however, reveal that much—if not most—of the accumulation of this large site took place in prehistoric times. They suggest, also, that Tepe Musiyan is not a single mound but an agglomeration of many smaller mounds, which grew together over the years. Heavy mantles of historic or photohistoric debris cover the prehistoric levels in many areas, and apparently fill the areas between some of the buried prehistoric mounds. At one place or another on the site, one finds surface evidence of virtually every prehistoric period in the area, back to and possibly including the Mohammad Jaffar phase.

EXCAVATIONS IN 1903

Gautier and Lampre (1905) excavated at Tepe Musiyan for three months in 1903, making a number of test cuts lettered from A to E. Their operation "E" was a 5 by 10 meter trench on the southwest corner of the mound, cut in the side of a slope where deposits stand 12 meters above the surrounding plain (see map, Fig. 20). They did not reach virgin soil, digging only to a depth of 2.5 meters above the plain. The lower levels reportedly contained "beautiful" painted pottery of "the most archaic" kind. At the lowest point to which they excavated, this pottery disappeared, "giving place to some specimens of worked flint" (Gautier and Lampre, 1905:69).

TESTING IN 1963

The description of the lower levels at Musiyan "E," discussed above, held out to us the intriguing possibility that Gautier and Lampre had indeed reached preceramic or Mohammad Jaffar phase materials at Tepe Musiyan. Since they did not illustrate the pottery, however, we could not be sure, and the bottom of their 1903

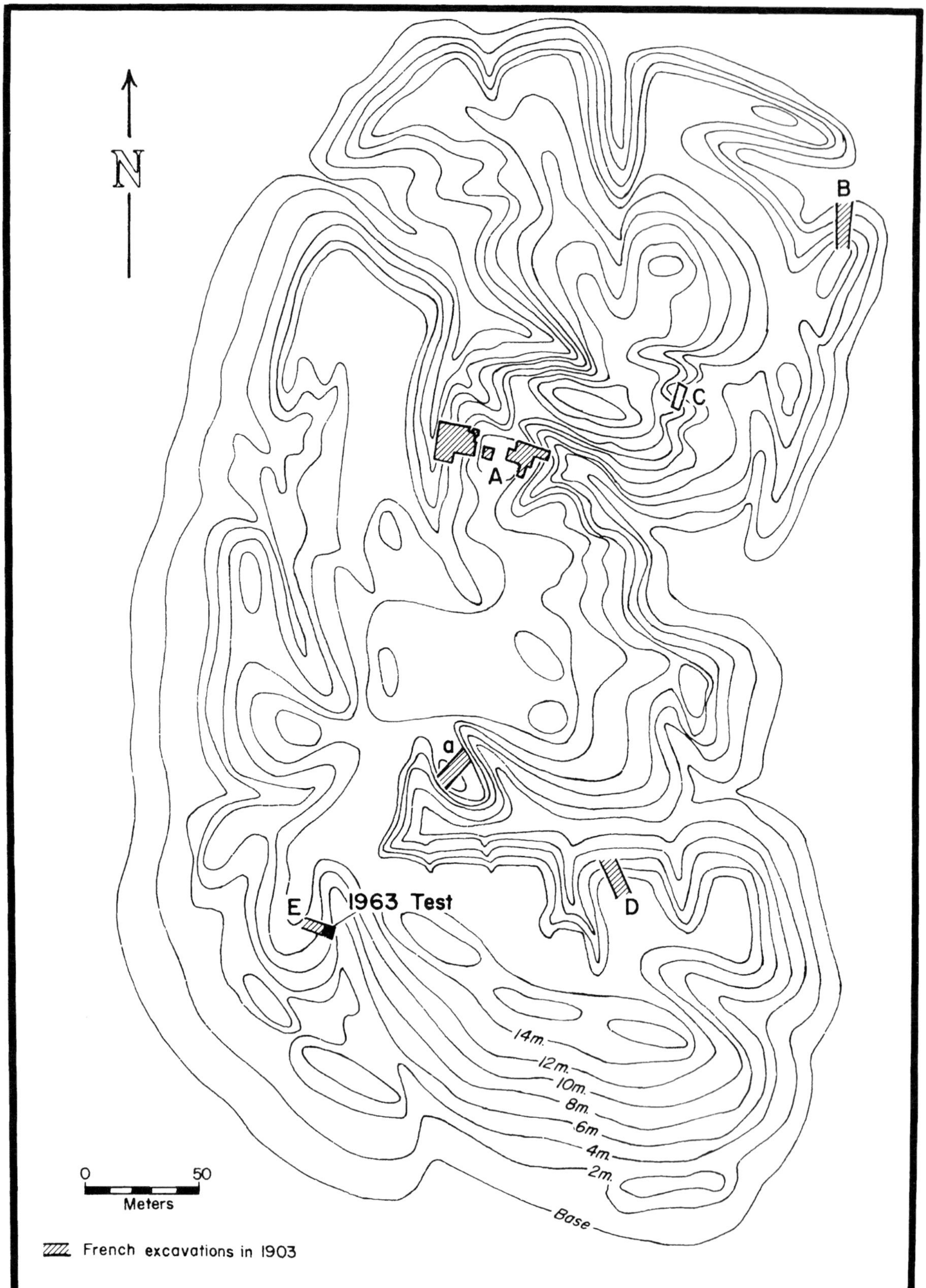

Fig. 20. Map of Tepe Musiyan.

excavation had long since been filled with mud washed down off the slopes of the mound.

In 1963, small flint blade cores similar to those found at Ali Kosh were discovered on the surface of Tepe Musiyan near operation E. We therefore decided to reopen the old French cut, in order to see first-hand the "most archaic" material recovered in the lowest levels by Gautier and Lampre.

To clear the debris from the west end of this cut, which had come down from 12 meters above the plain, seemed hopeless. The east end of the cut, which began at the base of the slope and therefore lay only 6 meters above the plain, looked more encouraging. On December 15, 1963, we put a crew of four Musiyan workmen to clearing a 4-by-6-meter area in the extreme east end of the old French cut. It proved convenient to cut 10 cm. beyond it to the north, so that the edge of the 1903 trench could be seen in the west face of our test and followed downward.

We cut 10 cm. below the floor of the 1903 trench, cleaned the faces of our test pit with sharp trowels, and examined the stratigraphy (see section drawing, Fig. 21; also Pl. 19*b*). Gautier and Lampre had cut through several meters of sherd beds with early historic or photohistoric material; below this were two more meters of featureless building debris. The last half-meter of their trench had cut through an ash layer and come down into the remains of a collapsed house of unbaked tan mud bricks similar to those at Tepe Sabz. Evidently it

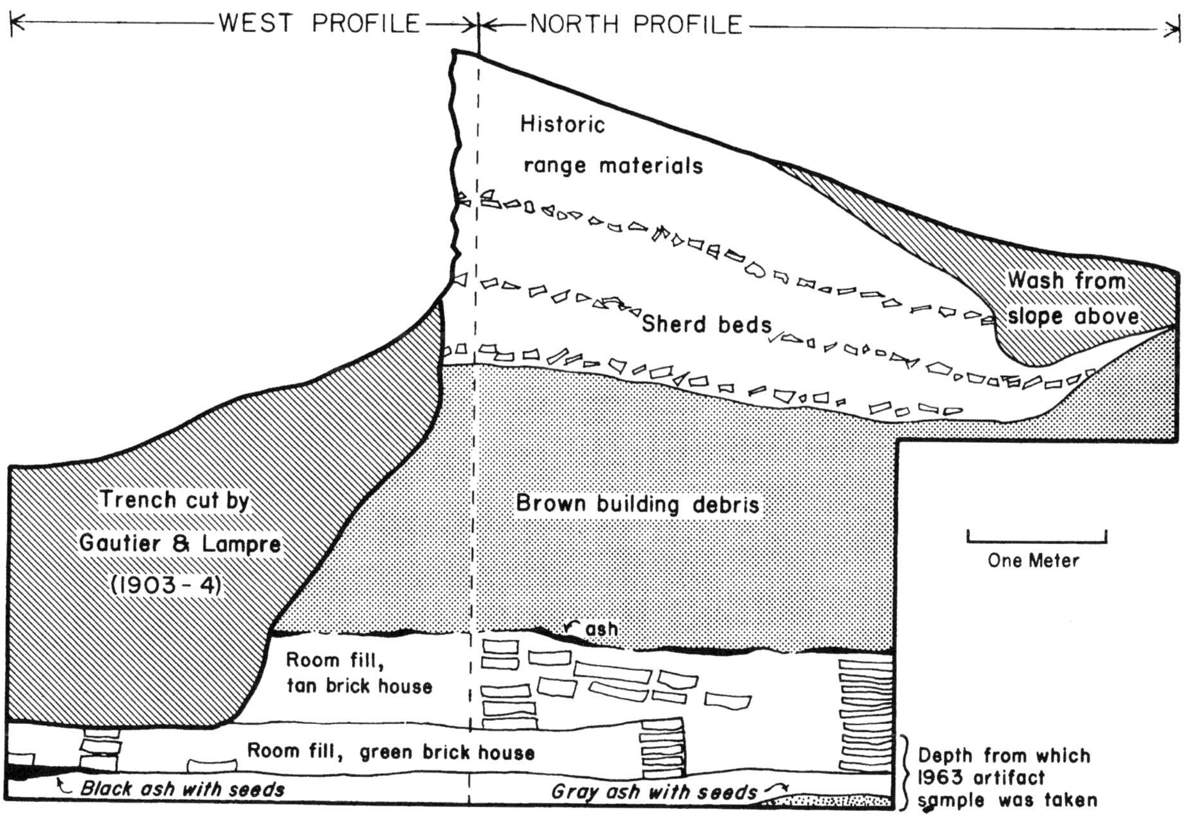

Fig. 21. Tepe Musiyan. West and north profiles of 1963 test pit in area "E," showing outline of Gautier and Lampre's 1903 excavation, and undisturbed building levels from which 1963 samples were taken.

was this level that had produced the "beautiful painted pottery" of which they spoke, for the house was filled with attractive Susiana Black-on-buff sherds.

In order to date the deposit, we took a sample of pottery and artifacts from undisturbed contex immediately below the old French cut. A square, 3 meters by 3 meters, was taken down to a depth of 50 cm. below the 1903 trench, using ten-centimeter levels. All artifacts, sherds, and bones were saved. If the French sightings are correct, this should be about 200 to 250 cm. above the surface of the surrounding plain. Examination of the stratigraphy (see Fig. 21) shows that our sample came from the room fill of a green brick house, one undisturbed corner of a superimposed tan brick building, and an ashy floor area just below. We back-filled the test on December 18.

The 1963 sample included 849 sherds, and a number of artifacts typical of the Mehmeh phase: "bent ceramic nails," sausage-shaped handstones, polished limestone celts, an oval-discoidal spindle whorl with notched edges, and other objects. Included in the Black-on-buff pottery were common Mehmeh phase designs like "rows of wild goats" and "dancing men."

Two small ash lenses were uncovered during our test. One, a patch of black ash, lay on the floor of the green brick house (see Fig. 21). The other, a patch of gray ash, underlay the floor. Carbonized seeds from these ash lenses were just as typical of the Mehmeh phase as were the artifacts. They included bread wheat, naked barley, lentils, vetch, almonds, and flax. Bones of domestic cattle accompanied them. Thus, the agricultural products during the Mehmeh phase seem to have been just as similar on both sides of the Deh Luran plain as were the artifacts.

Our brief test at Musiyan "E" yielded no evidence that Gautier and Lampre had reached preceramic levels, or even levels of the Mohammad Jaffar phase. A few more small flint blade cores turned up in the redeposited debris filling the old French cut, however, suggesting that somewhere on the southwest corner of Tepe Musiyan–perhaps deeply buried–there may be deposits of that age. It should be remembered that the floor of operation "E," even after our test, is still many meters above virgin soil.

Table 2

ARTIFACTS AND SHERDS RECOVERED AT TEPE MUSIYAN "E" AT A DEPTH OF 480-530 CM. (1963)

Pottery Types	No. Sherds	Per Cent of Sample
Susiana Plain Buff	452	53.2
Susiana Black-on-buff	302	33.6
Khazineh Red	59	7.0
Mehmeh Red-on-red	33	3.9
Bayat Red	1	0.1
Fine Black-on-tan	2	0.2
Totals	849	100.0

Clay artifacts: "Bent ceramic nail" (3); oval-discoidal spindle whorl with notched edges (1).

Ground-Stone Tools: Combination saddle-shaped grinding slab and mortar (1); nondescript grinding slab fragment (1); simple discoidal handstone (3); sausage-shaped handstone (2); cuboid pounder-rubbing stone (1); polished limestone celts (2); "blank" for polished celt (1); flint nodule chopper (1).

The following faunal remains were recovered from Tepe Musiyan, Operation "E" at a depth of 480 to 530 cm. in 1963 test excavations:

SHEEP OR GOAT
- 1 patella
- 1 fragment of metapodial shaft
- 1 splinter from a cheek tooth
- 1 unfused ulna from a tiny lamb or kid

DOMESTIC CATTLE
- 1 lower M_3
- 1 second phalanx

GAZELLE
- 1 distal left tibia

FRESH-WATER MUSSEL
- 2 valve fragments

CORRELATION OF MUSIYAN "E" (480 to 530) WITH THE TEPE SABZ SEQUENCE

The number of Susiana Black-on-buff bowls with "dancing men" and "rows of wild goats" motifs present at a depth of 480 to 530 cm. in Musiyan "E" led us to suspect, intuitively, that this building level dated to the Mehmeh phase. It remained, however, to verify this by means of statistical analyses of the ceramics. We also wanted to know where Musiyan "E" fit in the Mehmeh phase—early, middle, or late—and how it dated with regard to zones B_1, B_2, and B_3 at Tepe Sabz.

The technique we used was to submit the Musiyan "E" pottery sample to a Brainerd-Robinson matrix analysis. For a detailed explanation of the working of this technique, the reader is referred to the original publications by Robinson (1951) and Brainerd (1951). Briefly, the method works on the principle that most pottery types show a lenticular pattern of change through time: they start as a small percentage of the ceramic assemblage, grow to peak frequency, and then dwindle in popularity. Where many pottery types are present in a stratigraphic sequence, their relative proportions within the total assemblage make it possible to derive a quantitative chronology (Ford, 1962). That is, there will only be one moment in time when pottery type A constitutes 25 per cent of the sherd sample, while type B is 15 per cent and type C is 5 per cent. A few centuries later, for example, type B may have risen to 20 per cent and type C faded out of existence entirely, while a new type, D, now constitutes 3 per cent.

In the Brainerd-Robinson method, percentages of each pottery type are calculated for a series of levels at various adjacent sites. The figures are then placed in a matrix in which the percentages for every level are compared and contrasted with every other level. Resemblances are expressed as a figure which represents the sum of the differences between two levels, with 200.0 standing for the maximum in dissimilarity and 0.0 for the maximum in similarity (identical percentages for every pottery type observed in both levels). The matrix is then "ordered"—arranged so that every level appears next to the level it most resembles, and farthest from the level it least resembles. In theory, such an "ordering" should have the result of arranging all the levels in the chronological order in which they were deposited.

The calculations involved in the Brainerd-Robinson method, while demonstrably more accurate than an "intuitive" ordering of the various levels from broadly contemporaneous sites, is extremely time-consuming if the mathematics must be done by hand. Fortunately, an electronic computer can be programmed to take the raw data—actual sherd counts by level—and come up with the (theoretically) "best" chronological ordering within minutes. This was the technique we used with the data from Tepe Sabz and Musiyan "E." Using a program worked out with Mary Shaw of Carnegie Tech, Hole fed into the computer raw sherd counts from all stratigraphic zones at Tepe Sabz as well as from Musiyan "E," 480 to 530 cm.

Two approaches were tried by Hole and Shaw (1967). The first was to attempt to correlate Musiyan "E" with the Tepe Sabz sequence by means of calculating the percentages of the nine major pottery types present at both sites—Susiana Plain Buff, Susiana Black-on-buff, Khazineh Red, Bayat Red, and so on (see Chapter IX, "Pottery and Stone Vessels"). The second approach was to use only Susiana Black-on-buff pottery, calculating the percentages of each of the twenty-three most common vessel types in that ware for each level. The actual computer "print-outs" from both analyses are illustrated below

FINAL ORDER IS

K3	K9	K7	K6	K1	K5	K10	K8	K4	K2	K11
FINAL COEFFICIENT MATRIX										
200.0	194.2	193.7	141.8	166.4	145.8	125.4	117.4	98.3	89.6	81.7
194.2	200.0	192.9	143.4	168.3	147.3	127.4	119.3	100.3	91.5	83.7
193.7	192.9	200.0	148.0	172.7	151.9	131.7	123.7	104.6	95.9	88.0
141.8	143.4	148.0	200.0	159.5	159.5	143.1	134.4	122.2	109.5	107.7
166.4	168.3	172.7	159.5	200.0	178.9	158.9	151.0	129.6	121.6	114.3
145.8	147.3	151.9	159.5	178.9	200.0	179.5	171.0	145.5	134.4	130.2
125.4	127.4	131.7	143.1	158.9	179.5	200.0	189.5	156.3	138.2	136.4
117.4	119.3	123.7	134.4	151.0	171.0	189.5	200.0	156.2	138.3	136.3
98.3	100.3	104.6	122.2	129.6	145.5	156.3	156.2	200.0	177.4	178.8
89.6	91.5	95.9	109.5	121.6	134.4	138.2	138.3	177.4	200.0	187.9
81.7	83.7	88.0	107.7	114.3	130.2	136.4	136.3	178.8	187.9	200.0
COLUMN SUMS / 10										
155.4	156.8	160.3	156.9	172.1	174.4	168.6	163.7	156.9	148.4	144.5
A = SUM OF SQUARES OF NEGATIVE DIFFERENCES / 10										
60.5	62.0	61.1	0	17.6	0	0	0	0.2	0	0.0
B = SUM OF SQUARES OF ALL DIFFERENCES / 100										
47.3	45.6	47.7	50.3	33.2	21.9	27.9	35.1	31.9	27.2	27.8

SUM A / SUM B = 2014.188 / 39580.884 = 0.050888

Fig. 22. Final coefficient matrix from Brainerd-Robinson ordering of all stratigraphic levels at Tepe Sabz and Musiyan "E" (480 to 530 cm.), using nine major pottery types present at both sites. (K5 indicates Tepe Musiyan "E." All other zones indicated are from Tepe Sabz, as follows: K3=A_1, K9=A_2, K7=A_3, K6=D, K1=B_1, K10=B_3, K8=B_2, K4=C_3, K2=C_1, and K11=C_2.) This same matrix was run by Keith Dixon, California State College, Long Beach, with identical results (personal communication).

FINAL BRAINERD-ROBINSON CORRELATION MATRIX

SABZ	KHA3	KHA2	KHA1	MEH3	MUSE	MEH2	MEH1	BAY3	BAY2	BAY1
200.0	110.1	58.1	54.6	57.3	53.4	71.1	87.6	80.5	79.4	73.7
110.1	200.0	102.2	104.4	107.8	77.5	94.4	99.1	84.0	79.4	73.5
58.1	102.2	200.0	168.9	124.9	91.0	77.4	73.0	57.9	57.0	53.5
54.6	104.4	168.9	200.0	140.4	94.2	94.1	90.5	73.7	73.9	69.4
57.3	107.8	124.9	140.4	200.0	137.3	143.7	128.8	102.1	100.0	96.0
53.4	77.5	81.0	94.2	137.3	200.0	160.3	156.5	116.9	114.8	113.8
71.1	94.4	77.4	94.1	143.7	160.3	200.0	168.3	131.1	139.0	135.7
87.6	99.1	73.0	90.5	128.8	156.5	168.3	200.0	150.6	150.9	143.8
80.5	84.0	57.9	73.7	102.1	116.9	131.1	150.6	200.0	164.6	167.0
79.4	79.4	57.0	73.9	100.0	114.8	139.0	150.9	164.6	200.0	178.8
73.7	73.5	53.5	69.4	96.0	113.8	135.7	143.8	167.0	178.8	200.0
COLUMN ERRORS										
36.9	27.3	0	0.2	6.4	0	24.9	26.4	28.4	22.5	20.2
ERRORS BETWEEN COLUMNS										
0.2	111.6	2.2	6.2	0	40.9	21.3	0	8.4	2.4	

MATRIX NORM IS 193.1806966

Fig. 23. Final coefficient matrix from Brainerd-Robinson ordering of all stratigraphic levels at Tepe Sabz and Musiyan "E" (480 to 530 cm.), using 23 main vessel types in Susiana Black-on-buff pottery. (SABZ= zone D at Tepe Sabz, and MUSE= Musiyan "E." All other zones are those at Tepe Sabz, as follows: KHA3=C_3, KHA2=C_2, KHA1=C_1, MEH3=B_3, MEH2=B_2, MEH1=B_1, BAY3=A_3, BAY2=A_2, BAY1=A_1.)

(Fig. 22 and 23).

The matrix using the nine major pottery types from both sites placed Musiyan "E" squarely in the Mehmeh phase, but did not arrange the various zones at Tepe Sabz in their actual stratigraphic order. Final ordering achieved in that matrix was: Tepe Sabz A_1, A_2, A_3, D, B_1; then Musiyan "E," 480 to 530; then Tepe Sabz B_3, B_2, C_3, C_1, C_2. It is interesting to note that, while this matrix occasionally reversed the order of zones within a phase (e.g., inverting B_3 and B_2), it always kept all the zones of a given phase together: all B's, all A's, all C's, etc. This suggests that our assignment of zones to phases has some reality, and that Musiyan "E" truly belongs somewhere between zones B_1 and B_3 at Tepe Sabz. The one obvious defect of this matrix is its incorrect placement of zone D—it was placed adjacent to zone B_3 because both the Sabz and Bayat phases have a high frequency of unpainted buff ware and lack Mehmeh Red-on-red, among other things.

The matrix using the twenty-three most common vessel types within Susiana Black-on-buff achieved perfect stratigraphic ordering. All zones at Tepe Sabz appeared in proper order from A_1 to D. This suggests that the various vessels of Black-on-buff are very sensitive chronological indicators. The potential for establishing regional chronologies and correlating sites by means of matrix analyses based on the changing frequencies of these vessels would seem to be high. In this second matrix (Fig. 23), Musiyan "E," 480 to 530 cm., appears between zones B_2 and B_3 of the Mehmeh phase at Tepe Sabz. We conclude, therefore, on the basis of both matrices, that the houses at a depth of 480 to 530 cm. in Musiyan "E" were occupied some time between the abandonment of the houses in zone B_3 at Tepe Sabz and the construction of the houses in zone B_1 at that same site.

VII

A MEHMEH PHASE HOUSE PLAN FROM TEPE ASHRAFABAD

DESCRIPTION OF THE SITE

Tepe Ashrafabad is a mound only 2 meters high and 50 meters in diameter, which lies a km. and a half northwest of Tepe Sabz. Our surface collection from this small site indicates a Mehmeh phase village, with little evidence of preceding or succeeding phases. "Bent ceramic nails," Susiana Black-on-buff sherds with "rows of wild goats" or "dancing men" motifs, fragments of Mehmeh Red-on-red pottery, and many other items show strong relationship with the materials from zones B_1, B_2, and B_3 at Tepe Sabz.

A number of stone house foundations have been exposed by erosion around the base of the mound. We were struck by the similarity of some of the features of these houses to the stone foundations partially uncovered in zone B_3 of Tepe Sabz. Since the houses are presumably contemporary, we mapped the best preserved example at Tepe Ashrafabad in an effort to clarify the findings in our trench at Tepe Sabz. Mapping was carried out December 24, 1964.

THE HOUSE PLAN

The house is 4.5 meters wide and 10.5 meters long (see Fig. 17*b* and also Pl. 18*a*). A single door on one of the long sides (south) was equipped with a perforated stone to receive the lower end of the door pivot. Set against the back wall of the house were two pebble "platforms" like the one discovered at Tepe Sabz (zone B_3), as well as a semicircular enclosure of stones which may be the foundation for a storage bin.

At least seven meters of the back wall of the house had a foundation resembling the one exposed in Tepe Sabz, zone B_3: a layer of small river pebbles, forty cm. wide, flanked by two rows of river cobbles. It was clear that part of the front wall of the house had been founded in the same way, although many stones from the latter wall had been removed for use over modern graves.

The area enclosed by this Mehmeh phase house is about 29 square meters, of which roughly 4 square meters is taken up by platforms and storage bins. Two other houses of the same size lie to the west of it, each separated from the others by several meters of open space. The arrangement and limited floor space of the houses suggests that each was probably a unit for no more than one family.

The complete house plan from Tepe Ashrafabad (Fig. 17*b*) may be compared with the foundations partially exposed in Tepe Sabz B_3 (Fig. 17*a*).

VIII

FLINT AND OBSIDIAN ARTIFACTS

INTRODUCTION

Tools of flint and obsidian were the most numerous category of artifacts found in the Deh Luran excavations, but their sheer quantity (about 41,000) may simply be a testimony to their low value individually. Most of these tools are small blades which were recovered only after careful sieving. As an example of the concentrations in which such flints may occur, we can point to a layer a few centimeters thick at the base of zone C_2 at Ali Kosh (Bus Mordeh phase), in which we found more than 7,000 flint blades and 13,000 pieces of chipping debris: a knapper of flint had evidently worked in this particular spot. However, chipped stone was liberally distributed throughout all areas of midden in this and other phases as well.

Turning first to superficial features, one can divide our sequence of flint tools into three parts.

1) The deposits in the Bus Mordeh, Ali Kosh and Mohammad Jaffar phases can be considered together, as having a relatively similar chipped-stone industry both in regard to the types of tools present, and in regard to quantity. More than 87,000 of our total 92,000 pieces of chipped stone were found in levels dating to these three phases. Twenty-four types of tools, related to at least half a dozen kinds of activities, occur in these phases, indicating a sophistication and specialization in chipped stone technology not evident in the later phases.

2) We can isolate Sabz phase levels at Tepe Sabz because of the occurrence there of tools made almost exclusively on a poor quality, locally-available gray flint. A Sabz phase discontinuity in flint-chipping tradition is suggested by the fact that there are many fewer types of tools than in the earlier phases; crescent-shaped microliths and various kinds of backed blades and sickles are added; obsidian is relatively rare. Lost are varieties of microliths and piercing-reaming tools, and scrapers nearly disappear.

3) In the Khazineh, Mehmeh, and Bayat phases we see continuity with the Sabz phase in the use of local flint for many tools, but we also find the increasing use of better quality material for making blades (many of which may have been imported). Finally, we see a relative increase in the use of sickles in the later phases.

We cannot satisfactorily account for the abrupt change in quality and quantity of flint work between the Mohammad Jaffar and Sabz phases on the basis of information presently available. Comparing the number of flints per cubic meter of dirt removed, we find that there are eight times as many pieces of chipped stone in the Bus Mordeh, Ali Kosh and Mohammad Jaffar deposits as there are in any of the later phases. Therefore, unless we were unwittingly digging in quite different kinds of deposits in the earlier and later phases, we cannot explain the discripency in quantity by considering only the volume excavated.

A sociological explanation may be more satisfactory. Taking into account the change in source material, it seems likely that the knappers in the Sabz phase were either (1) newcomers to the area, and unfamiliar with the better sources of flint; or

(2) more sedentary, and therefore less likely to visit distant previous sources of material. Either alternative could be supported by the fact that in the Sabz phase we find the introduction of irrigation and new agricultural products. By way of comparison, we note that flint also occurs in great quantity at Jarmo and Tepe Sarab, but not at slightly later sites, such as Hassuna or Matarrah, which are equivalent in age to the Sabz phase (Braidwood and Howe, 1960:36).

The reduced number of types of chipped stone tools in the Sabz phase may relate to the adoption of new modes of food-getting and the consequent abandonment of some previous activities, or to the performance of tasks requiring less specialized tools. The introduction of backed and truncated sickles seems to point to a technological improvement in the hafting of tools.

OBSIDIAN

The distribution of obsidian is also interesting, in that it is virtually confined to the three early phases, and in no case does it ever exceed two per cent of the total chipped stone. There is no obsidian in our samples from the Sabz and Khazineh phases, and only three pieces and six pieces were recovered from Mehmeh and Bayat phase levels, respectively. Two per cent of total chipped stone in both the Mohammad Jaffar and Ali Kosh phases was obsidian, but there was less than one per cent obsidian in the Bus Mordeh phase. These figures are consistent with Hole's findings at Tepe Sarab (Hole, 1961), where there was less than one per cent obsidian; but they are quite different from the figures at Jarmo, where the preceramic portion of the site had 28 per cent obsidian and the pottery-bearing levels 45 per cent. These facts can be directly related to the distance of the sites from the sources of obsidian according to recent studies (Renfrew, Dixon, and Cann, 1966). All the obsidian seems to derive from sources near Lake Van in eastern Turkey and Armenia.

TERMS USED IN ANALYSIS

General

Flint: As used here, the term refers to a related series of crypto-crystalline quartz rocks for which flint, chert and chalcedony are common names.

Obsidian: A natural glass of volcanic origin, which can be chipped to make sharp but brittle edges.

Core: A prepared piece of flint or obsidian from which flakes were struck.

Flake: Any piece of stone which was struck from a core.

Blade: A flake which is parallel-sided, and at least twice as long as wide. Blades are relatively thin and have one or more ridges (scars from previously detached blades) running the length of the piece. (Note that this definition is quite a variance with the way American archeologists use the term "blade.")

Bladelet: An unusually small blade. Here, the term is used only if the piece has secondary chipping and falls into one of the geometric or microlith types.

Microlith: Here, the term "microlith" or "microlithic" is used to suggest small tools, but not with the object of distinguishing a type of tool. Microliths can be considered the small end of a size continuum which also includes large pieces.

Edge: On a blade, edges run parallel to the long axis of the piece, in the sense of a "knife edge." On a flake, edges are the margins of the piece.

End: Edges which are at right angles to the long axis. Most flakes have no clear long axis, so "end" is considered to be the extremity farthest from the bulb of percussion in that case.

Bulb of percussion: A characteristic convex bulb

on one end of a flake, at the point of conchoidal fracture where it was struck from a core.

Bulbar surface: The surface (for "surface," read "face" interchangeably) on which the bulb of percussion is found. The bulbar surface is plain, having no scars from previously struck flakes. It is also called the "reverse" or "ventral" side.

Upper surface: The surface which shows the scars of previously removed blades or flakes. It is opposite the bulbar face, and is sometimes called the "obverse" or "dorsal" side.

Types of Chipping

Squamous: Retouch which consists of broad, shallow, and irregular flake scars. It is ordinarily used to shape the edges of flakes to make them into scrapers.

Stepped or resolved: Overhanging flake scars which occur in a series, producing a steep or semisteep face. These merge typologically with steep and squamous retouch.

Steep: Concentrated stepped and squamous chipping from one or both faces to produce a surface which is nearly perpendicular to the adjoining plain surface. This type of retouch can be used to blunt the edge of a backed blade, shape the end of a broken blade so that it becomes truncated, or shape flakes into various forms of scrapers.

Nibbling: Tiny, usually uniform-sized flake scars occurring along an edge. Nibbling may be caused by use or by deliberate retouch.

Battering: Concentrated stepped or resolved flaking on a small scale, often ending in a notch, or at least a very dull edge.

Nicking: Deeply concave flake scars, often on alternate opposite (upper and bulbar) faces of the same edge.

Crushing: The process of producing a dulled, pulverized edge by continuous pressure rather than by a sharp blow.

TOOL TYPES

For convenience, the tool types which seem to be related by use are clustered into functional groups. The relationship of the tools in each group is based on the type and location of chipping, the shape of the finished piece, or the use which can be inferred from wear. Although the details of the grouping are slightly different, the principle involved is essentially the same as applied in the study of chipped stone tools from Jarmo and Sarab (Hole, 1961).

Functional Group: Geometrics and Other Microliths

The six types in this group were probably used as arrowheads, or as barbs set serially in the heads of spears. Abundant historical evidence, ethnographic parallels, and arrows preserved in archaeological sites (Clark, 1963: Fig. 13,14) testify to the way similar artifacts have been used, but we cannot be very specific as to the type of projectile used in Deh Luran. A drawing on a pot of the Mehmeh phase (Fig. 131*a*) attests to the use of bows and arrows in Khuzistan, and from murals we know they were used at Çatal Hüyük at a time contemporary with the Mohammad Jaffar and Sabz phases. (Mellaart, 1963, Part II: Fig. 6).

The specific types of microlithic elements change during the Deh Luran sequence. First to appear (and confined to the Bus Mordeh, Ali Kosh and Mohammad Jaffar phases) are the various backed and nibbled bladelets. Geometric forms—trapezes and crescents—appear first in the Sabz phase, and are found as late as the Bayat phase. This sequence is by no means universal, however, and may pertain strictly to the local scene. Although many of the bladelets have predecessors in the late Paleolithic of Iran (Hole, 1966), triangles and crescents are found in deposits contemporary with the Bus Mordeh phase and earlier periods in Iraq (e.g., Zawi Chemi Shanidar), and especially in the Levant (e.g., Natufian sites).

We suggested in an earlier study (Hole, 1961:126-28) that diagonal-ended bladelets may have been set serially on spears to hunt gregarious herd animals on the valley floors, while the trapezes and crescents were used as tranchet arrows to kill lighter game. This hypothesis cannot be supported by our evidence from Deh Luran. The same wild animals were hunted throughout the sequence, although perhaps in diminished numbers as time passes. The shift in type of microlith probably relates, therefore, to the use of different hunting tools and the customary habits of hafting them.

In our type descriptions, we refer to thc geographic distribution of our tool types within the general Zagros area; however, these artifacts have seldom been reported in sufficient detail to allow very precise comparisons. The only large body of data which is precisely comparable to that obtained from Deh Luran comes from Jarmo and Sarab, two sites whose flints were studied by the same methods used in the present report (Hole, 1961). Although these studies have not been published, we feel that it may be useful at least to indicate which tool types, out of those we found at Deh Luran, were present at Jarmo and Sarab. The analysis of the Jarmo flint is based only on those portions of the site in which there were stratigraphic excavations which spanned several levels of architecture. These areas, known as Operations I and II, seem to catch the early (aceramic, Ali Kosh phase-like) and the later (pottery-bearing, Mohammad Jaffar phase-like) portions of the site (Braidwood and Howe, 1960: Fig. 6). Likewise, the artifacts studied from Tepe Sarab came from the relatively undisturbed deposits in one of two major areas of excavation. Other collections of relevant age from the immediate area have not been fully studied or published, and permit of only limited comparisons based on verbal descriptions and selected illustrations.

Type: Trapezes (Fig. 24*a*)

Sample: 1

Description: Sections of blades broken and retouched in such a manner that the shape of the finished piece is trapezoidal. The edges of the parent blade remain sharp, but the ends are retouched diagonally to the long axis of the blade. The retouch is steep, and may be directed from either the upper or bulbar face.

Temporal distribution: Bayat phase

Geographic distribution: Jarmo (Braidwood and Howe, 1960:Pl. 18); Sarab (Hole, 1961); Kuhbanen (Huckriede, 1962:Fig. 4); and many other sites.

Type: Crescents (Fig. 24*b,c*)

Sample: 2

Description: Sections of blades broken and retouched in such a manner that the shape of the finished piece is crescentic. The two retouched ends merge along one edge to form an unbroken arc. These pieces are probably functional equivalents of trapezes.

Temporal distribution: Sabz phase

Geographic distribution: Zawi Chemi (R. L. Solecki, 1964:407); Jarmo (Braidwood and Howe, 1960:Pl. 18); Tepe Guran (Mortensen, personal communication); and many other sites.

Although they are not listed in this report, we found five more crescents at Ali Kosh in 1961 (Hole and Flannery, 1962:122). These came from near the surface, in the featureless mixed zone. We are still in doubt as to whether those crescents were associated with Mohammad Jaffar material or whether they may relate to the Sabz phase sherds we found on the surface at Ali Kosh; hence these five additional examples are not included here.

Type: Diagonal-ended bladelets (Fig. 24*e-h*)

Sample: 15

Description: Bladelets which have retouch, diagonal to the long axis of the piece, across one end. The edges have no retouch, and the overall shape is of a scalene triangle.

Temporal distribution: Bus Mordeh, Ali Kosh, and Mohammad Jaffar phases

Geographic distribution: Jarmo (Braidwood and Howe, 1960:Pl. 18); Sarab (Hole, 1961); other sites.

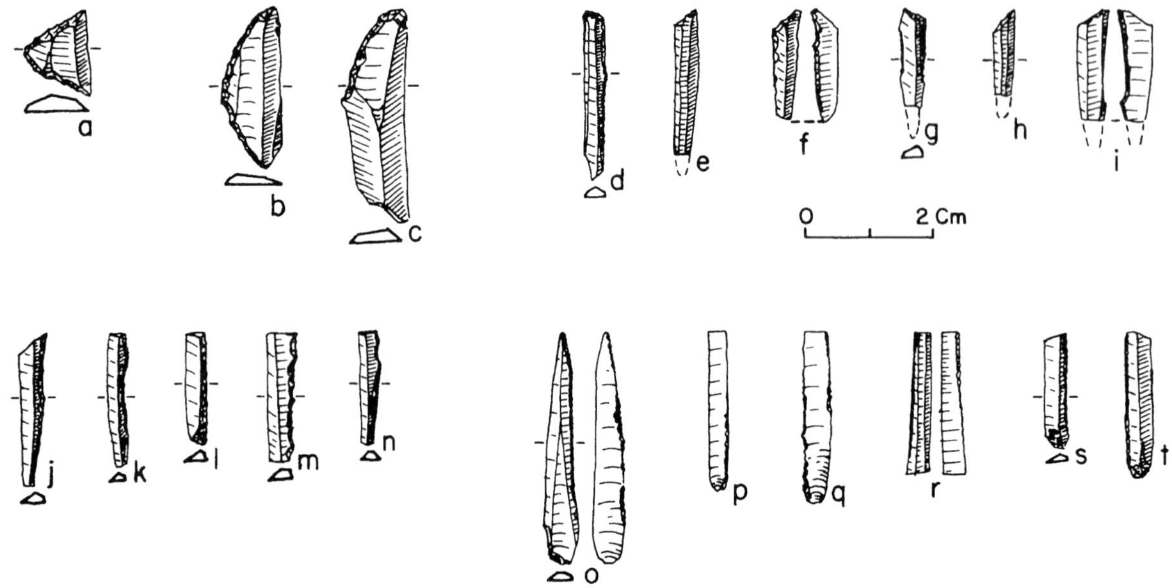

Fig. 24. Chipped stone tool types from Deh Luran: *a,* trapeze; *b,c,* crescents; *e,h,* diagonal-ended bladelets; *d,f,g,i,* diagonal-ended and backed bladelets; *j-n,* backed bladelets; *o-t,* nibbled bladelets (*d,m,n,* Tepe Ali Kosh, zone C_2, Bus Mordeh phase; *g,* Tepe Ali Kosh, zone C_1, Bus Mordeh phase; *k,s,t,* Tepe Ali Kosh, zone B_2, Ali Kosh phase; *h,p,r,* Tepe Ali Kosh, zone B_1, Ali Kosh phase; *e,i,j,l,o,q,* Tepe Ali Kosh, zone A_2, Mohammad Jaffar phase; *f,* Tepe Ali Kosh, zone A_1, Mohammad Jaffar phase; *b,c,* Tepe Sabz, zone D, Sabz phase; *a,* Tepe Sabz, zone A_3, Bayat phase).

Type: Diagonal-ended and backed bladelets (Fig. 24*d,f,g,i*)

Sample: 41

Description: Bladelets shaped like scalene triangles, which have steep retouch on an end and an edge. The backing on about half the pieces is from the upper face, and half is from the lower face. No piece in the Bus Mordeh phase has backing directed from the upper face.

Temporal distribution: Bus Mordeh, Ali Kosh, and Mohammad Jaffar phases

Geographic distribution: Zawi Chemi (R. L. Soleki, 1964:407); Karim Shahir (Braidwood and Howe, 1960:52); Jarmo (Braidwood and Howe, 1960:Pl. 18); Sarab (Hole, 1961).

Type: Backed bladelets (Fig. 24*j-n*)

Sample: 96

Description: Bladelets with backing along one edge. Most are broken, and some could be sections of geometrics.

Temporal distribution: Bus Mordeh, Ali Kosh and Mohammad Jaffar phases

Geographic distribution: Zawi Chemi (R. L. Solecki, 1964:407); Karim Shahir (Braidwood and Howe, 1960:52); Jarmo (Braidwood and Howe, 1960:Pl. 18); Sarab (Hole, 1961).

Type: Nibbled bladelets (Fig. 24*o-t*)

Sample: 391

Description: Bladelets with very shallow chipping along one or both edges. Nibbling is most common on the upper edge in the Bus Mordeh phase; on the lower edge in the Ali Kosh and Mohammad Jaffar phases; and on both edges alternately in the Mohammad Jaffar phase. Unremarkable as these pieces may look, chipping of this sort is confined to the microliths, and we suppose it must be related either to some specific use or to habits of hafting.

Temporal distribution: Bus Mordeh, Ali Kosh and Mohammad Jaffar phases

Geographic distribution: Kuhbanan (Huckriede, 1961:Fig. 3:7).

Functional Group: Piercing-Reaming Tools

The retouch on the four types included here is always on two edges, and done in such a manner that a point (or strong but blunt working shaft) is produced. Drills and "pointed pieces" have fairly sharp, thin tips which would have been suitable for drilling or piercing, whereas the reamers and flints with retouch on the bulbar side of one end seem too dull to puncture an object; they were probably used to enlarge holes already made. Any of these objects could have been used on hides, but there would have been no particular advantage in using stone tools over bone awls. We suggest, therefore, that these tools were probably used most often to drill stone (as in beads) and to work wood (of which we unfortunately have no trace). In this regard, we note that bone awls occur throughout the sequence.

Type: Drills (Fig. 25*a-h*)

Sample: 286

Description: Pieces on which steep retouch along both edges converges to form a point or tip. The tips are usually symmetrical, but in some cases one edge is straight and the other angles inward. The point is rarely at the bulbar end of the piece. Retouch may be directed from the upper face, the lower face, or from alternate faces (Fig. 15). A few pieces have the tip sharply delimited by shoulders (Fig. 25).

Temporal distribution: Throughout the sequence

Geographic distribution: Zawi Chemi (R. L. Solecki, 1964:407); Karim Shahir (Braidwood and Howe, 1960:53); Jarmo (Braidwood and Howe, 1960:Pl. 18); Kuhbanan (Huckriede, 1961:Fig. 3).

Type: Reamers (Fig. 25*k-p*)

Sample: 70

Description: Similar to drills in having steep bilaterial retouch, but reamers have essentially parallel rather than converging edges. Usually made on the bulbar end (which is normally the thickest), the tip tends to be squared off.

Temporal distribution: Bus Mordeh, Ali Kosh and Mohammad Jaffar phases

Geographic distribution: Zawi Chemi (R. L. Solecki, 1964:407); Jarmo, Sarab (Hole, 1961).

Type: Blades with end reduced on bulbar side (Fig. 25*q-s*)

Sample: 14

Description: One end has been reduced in thickness by squamous chipping on the bulbar side. Bulbar ends and broken ends are both treated this way, but not together on the same piece.

Temporal distribution: Bus Mordeh, Ali Kosh and Mohammad Jaffar phases

Geographic distribution: Jarmo, Sarab (Hole, 1961).

Type: Pointed pieces (Fig. 25*i,j*)

Sample: 14

Description: Blades and flakes which have limited retouch at one end, forming a point or tip. Perhaps functionally equivalent to drills, these may have accidentally resulted from the use of a conveniently-shaped piece of flint which had no prior preparation.

Temporal distributions: Bus Mordeh, Ali Kosh and Mohammad Jaffar phases

Geographic distribution: Jarmo, Sarab (Hole, 1961).

Functional Group: Sickles

Two types—plain sickles without secondary retouch, and sickles which have steep retouch on one edge or on the ends—are included in this group. Sickles by definition have glossy sheen on the cutting edge. The sheen was probably caused by prolonged rubbing against a fine abrasive—in this case the epidermis of plants whose cells contain silica. Although sheen has not been produced experimentally by reaping with flint sickles, this hypothesis is widely believed by archeologists. Discussions of sheen occur in Vayson (1919), Curwen (1930), and Steensberg (1943).

The most striking temporal difference in types of sickles is that the retouched varieties first become present in significant quantities with the Sabz phase, and they continue to be made through the Bayat phase. Breaking this down still finer, backed and truncated sickles are found

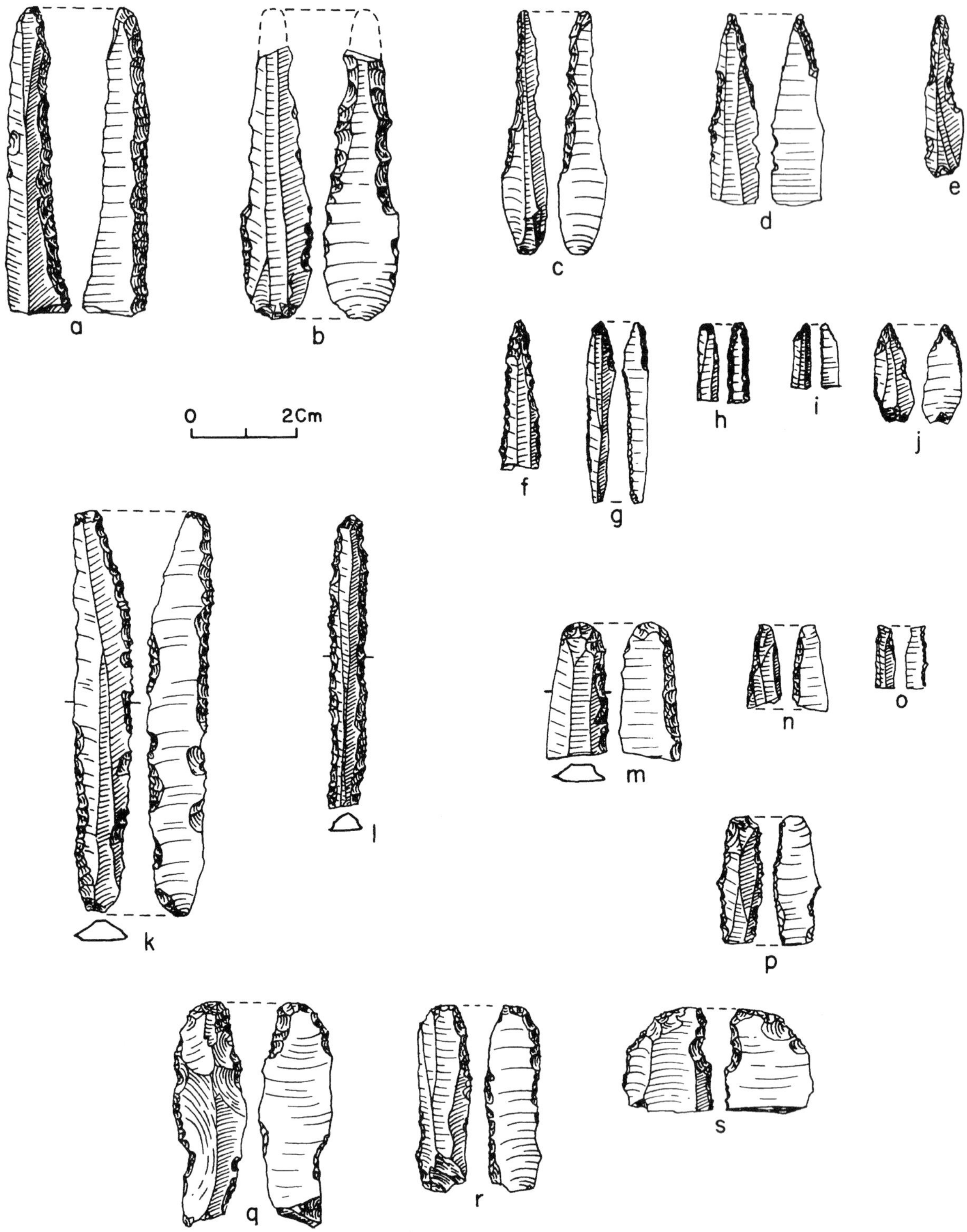

Fig. 25. Chipped stone tool types from Tepe Ali Kosh: *a-h,* drills; *i,j,* pointed pieces; *k-p,* reamers; *q-s,* blades with end reduced on bulbar side (*a,c,f,i,n,p,* zone C_2, Bus Mordeh phase; *d,e,* zone C_1, Bus Mordeh phase; *b,j,l,m,* zone B_2, Ali Kosh phase; *o,* zone B_1, Ali Kosh phase; *g,h,q,r,s,* zone A_2, Mohammad Jaffar phase; *k,* zone A_1, Mohammad Jaffar phase).

only in the Sabz and early Khazineh phases; backed sickles are found in the Sabz and Khazineh phases; and truncated sickles are found principally in the Ali Kosh, Mohammad Jaffar and Sabz phases. This distribution of truncated sickles is discontinuous, a fact made more apparent by the few examples in the Bayat phase having been made of a different flint from the ones in the Sabz phase. Finally, only in the Sabz phase are there more retouched sickles than plain sickles.

An interesting statistic, which has chronological implications, is that the percentage of sickles relative to other tools (omitting plain blades) increases with time. Table 3 shows that in the Bus Mordeh phase only 3.4 per cent of the tools were sickles, whereas by the Bayat phase 42.4 per cent of the tools were sickles.

Table 3

PERCENTAGE OF SICKLES TO TOTAL TOOLS IN EACH PHASE OF THE SEQUENCE AT ALI KOSH AND TEPE SABZ

Phase	Number of Sickles	Number of Tools*	Per cent Sickles
Bayat	87	205	42.4
Mehmeh	18	69	26.0
Khazineh	21	57	36.8
Sabz	24	104	23.0
Mohammad Jaffar	121	1575	7.6
Ali Kosh	114	1071	5.3
Bus Mordeh	42	1216	3.4

*Exclusive of plain, unretouched blades.

Type: Plain sickles (Fig. 26*a-f,n*)

Sample: 388

Description: Blades and elongated flakes which have sheen on one or both edges, but which are unaltered by deliberate chipping. Most of these implements have minor nicking on the edges, probably as a result of wear. The asphalt mastic used in setting sickles into a handle remains on many of these tools.

Temporal distribution: Throughout the sequence

Geographic distribution: Karim Shahir (Braidwood and Howe, 1960:53); Jarmo (Braidwood and Howe, 1960:Pl. 17); Sarab (Hole, 1961); reported from nearly every village site in Southwest Asia.

Type: Truncated and/or backed sickles (Fig. 26*f,g,h-m*)

Sample: 40

Description: Sickles with chipping on one or both ends (truncation) (Fig. 26), chipping on the ends and back (Fig. 26), or steep chipping along the back and none on the ends (Fig. 26). The retouching of the ends and backs presumably aids hafting by making a piece fit a predetermined spot in a handle which already contains other sickle elements. No sickles in the Bus Mordeh phase (and only a few in the early Bayat phase) have this sort of alteration.

Temporal distribution: Ali Kosh, Mohammad Jaffar, Sabz, Khazineh, Mehmeh, and Bayat phases

Geographic distribution: Unknown.

Functional Group: Scrapers

Scrapers are virtually confined to the Bus Mordeh, Ali Kosh, and Mohammad Jaffar phases. By far the most common of the four types is the round-ended scraper made on a blade. We find that there is little change throughout the three early phases, and that some continuity with the Sabz phase is indicated by the presence in the latter period of two types of scrapers. The only other scrapers in the later phases were two miscellaneous-ended blade scrapers in the Bayat phase.

Most of these tools, with their regular, smooth ends, were probably used either for skinning or for removing the fatty tissue which adheres to a freshly-skinned hide. Some may also have been used to work "tanning" material into the hides as they were treated, a possibility suggested by the fact that the ends of some of the scrapers are bevelled from use on a soft material. The absence of scrapers from the latter phases tends to support an inference that the use of woven cloth had replaced the use of skins for clothing and other artifacts.

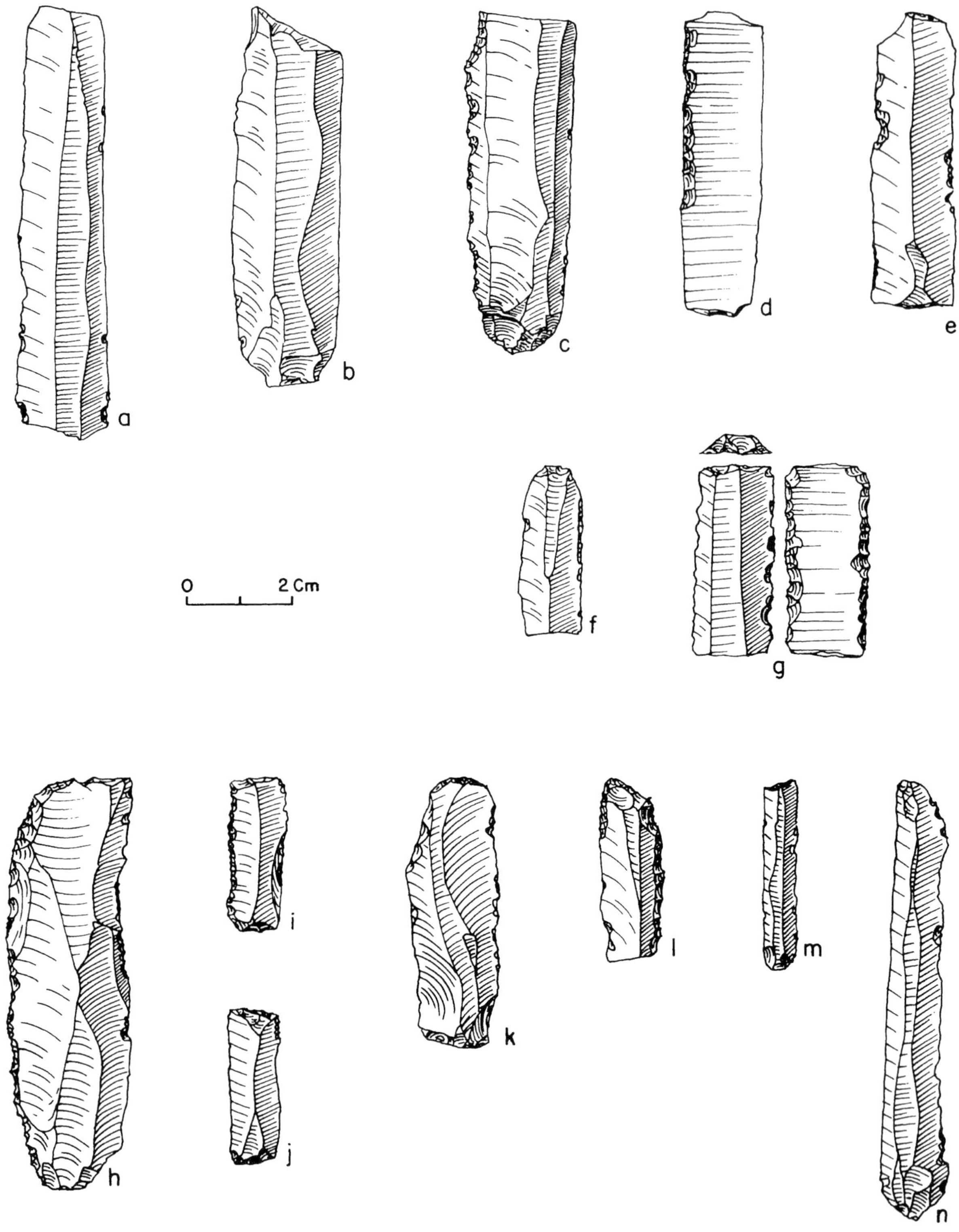

Fig. 26. Sickle blades from Deh Luran: *a-f,n,* plain sickles; *f,g,h-m,* truncated and/or backed sickles (*a,d,* Tepe Ali Kosh, zone B_2, Ali Kosh phase; *c,f,g,* Tepe Ali Kosh, zone B_1, Ali Kosh phase; *b,e,* Tepe Ali Kosh, zone A_1, Mohammad Jaffar phase; *h,j,k,l,* Tepe Sabz, zone D, Sabz phase; *i,* Tepe Sabz, zone C_2, Khazineh phase; *n,* Tepe Sabz, zone A_3, Bayat phase; *m,* Tepe Sabz, zone A_1, Bayat phase).

Table 4

OCCURRENCE OF CHIPPED STONE (BOTH FLINT AND OBSIDIAN) TOOL TYPES AT ALI KOSH, TEPE SABZ, AND TEPE MUSIYAN
(By Stratigraphic Zone)

Site and Zone	Geometrics and Other Microliths						Piercing-Reaming Tools				Sickles		Scrapers				Cutting-Scraping Tools							Misc. Tools			
	Trapezes	Crescents	Diagonal-ended	Diagonal-ended and Backed	Backed Bladelets	Nibbled Bladelets	Drills	Reamers	End Reduced on Bulbar Side	Pointed Pieces	Plain Sickles	Truncated and/or Backed Sickles	Blade, Round-end Scrapers	Flake, Round-end Scrapers	Blade, Misc. Ended Scrapers	Flakes with Bulbar End Retouch	Plain Blades	Backed Blades	Truncated and/or Backed Blades	Retouched or Used Blades	Notched Blades	Retouched or Used Flakes	Notched Flakes	Burins	Bifacially Chipped Flakes	Bifacially Chipped Point	Total Tools
TS - A_1	...	...	...	...	...	...	4	...	...	...	17	...	...	...	1	...	70	...	1	11	...	3	1	...	...	...	108
TS - A_2	...	...	...	...	...	...	...	...	...	...	15	...	...	...	1	...	76	...	4	13	4	2	1	...	...	...	116
TS - A_3	1	...	...	...	...	...	7	...	...	...	49	6	...	...	...	...	210	2	4	29	1	9	9	...	...	...	327
TS - B_1	...	...	...	...	...	...	6	...	...	...	13	...	...	...	...	...	51	1	1	11	...	6	2	...	1	...	92
MUS E	...	...	...	...	...	...	...	...	...	...	1	...	...	...	...	...	10	...	1	1	...	4	...	...	1	...	18
TS - B_2	...	...	...	...	...	...	1	...	...	...	2	1	...	...	...	...	16	...	2	5	1	2	1	...	...	...	31
TS - B_3	...	...	...	...	...	...	3	...	...	...	2	...	...	...	...	...	24	...	1	3	...	2	2	...	...	...	37
TS - C_1	...	...	...	...	...	...	...	...	...	...	3	1	...	...	...	...	17	1	...	2	1	4	3	...	1	...	33
TS - C_2	...	...	...	...	...	...	...	...	...	...	3	1	...	...	...	...	20	...	1	2	1	2	5	...	...	...	35
TS - C_3	...	...	...	...	...	...	1	...	...	...	6	7	...	...	...	...	13	...	...	4	...	6	2	...	...	...	39
TS - D	...	2	...	...	...	...	2	...	...	...	6	18	...	...	1	1	73	4	8	10	1	19	30	1	1	...	177
AK - A_1	...	...	3	7	4	63	21	12	3	...	44	2	12	2	4	...	3926	...	...	198	115	2	...	1	...	...	4419
AK - A_2	...	...	3	11	11	109	52	12	7	2	75	...	19	4	9	6	6590	...	...	405	348	9	...	...	...	...	7672
AK - B_1	...	...	2	2	2	64	37	3	2	1	63	2	19	3	14	5	7998	...	...	528	391	15	6	...	...	...	9157
AK - B_2	...	...	4	8	13	76	42	24	...	4	47	2	54	11	18	1	1791	...	...	298	292	11	3	2	2	...	2703
AK - C_1	...	...	...	5	11	23	33	4	...	1	18	...	45	1	8	...	2858	...	...	167	107	1	...	...	...	...	3282
AK - C_2	...	...	...	8	35	45	57	14	2	5	19	...	56	1	10	...	4913	...	...	221	173	2	2	2	...	...	5565
AK - C_2 Dump	...	...	3	...	20	11	20	1	...	1	5	...	2	...	2	...	7311	...	...	35	39	...	...	...	...	1	7451
Totals	1	2	15	41	96	391	286	70	14	14	388	40	207	22	68	13	35967	8	23	1943	1474	99	67	6	6	1	41262

Table 5

OCCURRENCE OF CHIPPED STONE (BOTH FLINT AND OBSIDIAN) TOOL TYPES AT ALI KOSH, TEPE SABZ, AND TEPE MUSIYAN
(By Cultural Phase)

	Geometrics and Other Microliths						Piercing-Reaming Tools				Sickles		Scrapers				Cutting-Scraping Tools							Misc. Tools			
Phase	Trapezes	Crescents	Diagonal-ended	Diagonal-ended and Backed	Backed Bladelets	Nibbled Bladelets	Drills	Reamers	End Reduced on Bulbar Side	Pointed Pieces	Plain Sickles	Truncated and/or Backed Sickles	Blade, Round-end Scrapers	Flake, Round-end Scrapers	Blade, Misc. End Scrapers	Flakes with Bulbar End Retouch	Plain Blades	Backed Blades	Truncated and/or Backed Blades	Retouched or Used Blades	Notched Blades	Retouched or Used Flakes	Notched Flakes	Burins	Bifacially Chipped Flakes	Bifacially Chipped Point	Total Tools
Bayat	1	. . .	. . .	. . .	. . .	. . .	11	. . .	. . .	. . .	81	6	. . .	. . .	2	. . .	356	2	9	53	5	14	11	. . .	. . .	. . .	551
Mehmeh	. . .	. . .	. . .	. . .	. . .	. . .	10	. . .	. . .	. . .	18	1	. . .	. . .	. . .	. . .	101	1	5	20	1	14	5	. . .	2	. . .	178
Khazineh	. . .	. . .	. . .	. . .	. . .	. . .	1	. . .	. . .	. . .	12	9	. . .	. . .	. . .	. . .	50	1	1	8	2	12	10	. . .	1	. . .	107
Sabz	. . .	2	. . .	. . .	. . .	. . .	2	. . .	. . .	. . .	6	18	. . .	. . .	1	1	73	4	8	10	1	19	30	1	1	. . .	177
Mohammad Jaffar. .	. . .	. . .	6	18	15	172	73	24	10	2	119	2	31	6	13	6	10516	. . .	. . .	603	463	11	. . .	1	. . .	. . .	12091
Ali Kosh	. . .	. . .	6	10	15	140	79	27	2	5	110	4	73	14	32	6	9789	. . .	. . .	826	683	26	9	2	2	. . .	11860
Bus Mordeh	. . .	. . .	3	13	66	79	110	19	2	7	42	. . .	103	2	20	. . .	15082	. . .	. . .	423	319	3	2	2	. . .	1	16298
Total	1	2	15	41	96	391	286	70	14	14	388	40	207	22	68	13	35967	8	23	1943	1474	99	67	6	6	1	41262

Type: Blade, round end scrapers (Fig. 27*a,b,e,f*)

Sample: 207

Description: Blades which have one or both ends convexly rounded, usually by steep retouch which extends to one or both of the edges (Fig. 27). A few are double-ended (Fig. 17). Some show traces of polishing from prolonged use on soft material. A few are made on sickles which had become too dull for cutting.

Temporal distribution: Bus Mordeh, Ali Kosh and Mohammad Jaffar phases

Geographic distribution: Zawi Chemi (R. L. Solecki, 1964:407); Jarmo (Braidwood and Howe, 1960:Pl. 17); Sarab (Hole, 1961); Kuhbanan (Huckriede, 1961:Fig. 3:22).

Type: Flake, round end scrapers (Fig. 28*a-c*)

Sample: 22

Description: Flakes with an edge or end convexly-shaped by relatively steep retouch. The thinner and narrower varieties grade into blade end scrapers. Most of these pieces have the retouch concentrated on an end, but a few are nearly discoidal, having retouch nearly all the way around. One group (eight examples), mainly found in the Ali Kosh phase (six examples), has rounded or irregular edges found

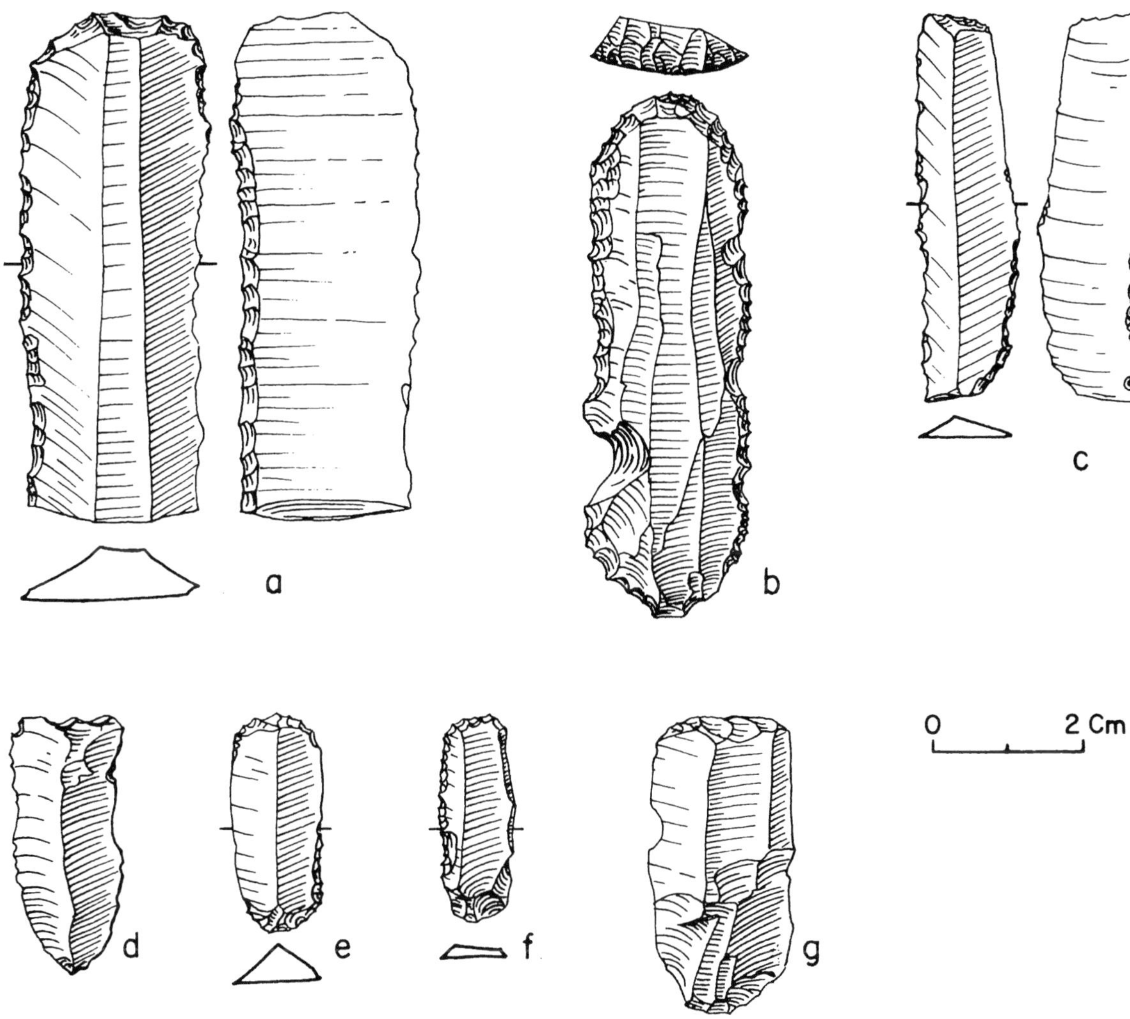

Fig. 27. End scraper types from Tepe Ali Kosh: *a,b,e,f,* blade, round end scrapers; *c,d,g,* blade, miscellaneous end scrapers (*b,f,* zone C_2, Bus Mordeh phase; *c,* zone C_1, Bus Mordeh phase; *e,g,* zone B_2, Ali Kosh phase; *d,* zone B_1, Ali Kosh phase; *a,* zone A_2, Mohammad Jaffar phase).

by steep step flaking. These pieces are somewhat rougher and chunkier than the others.

Temporal distribution: Bus Mordeh, Ali Kosh and Mohammad Jaffar phases

Geographic distribution: Karim Shahir, (Braidwood and Howe, 1960:53); Zawi Chemi (R. L. Solecki, 1964:407); Jarmo (Braidwood and Howe, 1960:Pl. 19); Sarab (Hole, 1961); Kuhbanan (Huckriede, 1961:Fig. 3:19,20,30).

Type: Blade, miscellaneous end scrapers (Fig. 27*c,d,g*)

Sample: 68

Description: Included are blades whose ends are retouched but not rounded (Fig. 27), and others that simply show signs of wear on an otherwise steeply-broken edge. The retouched ends are oriented from horizontal to, to diagonal to, the long axis of the blade.

Temporal distribution: Principally in the Bus Mordeh, Ali Kosh and Mohammad Jaffar phases

Geographic distribution: Karim Shahir (Braidwood and Howe, 1960:52); Jarmo (Braidwood and Howe, 1960:Pl. 17); Sarab (Hole, 1961).

Type: Flakes with bulbar end retouch (Fig. 28*d,e*)

Sample: 13

Description: These flakes have secondary retouch on the bulbar end, which resulted in a smooth edge suitable for scraping. They are thin in section and tend to be crescentic or subround in plan. Although the retouch on the bulbar end makes them look somewhat like flakes struck from a prepared core of Levallois type, the latter type of core is not found in our Deh Luran sequence.

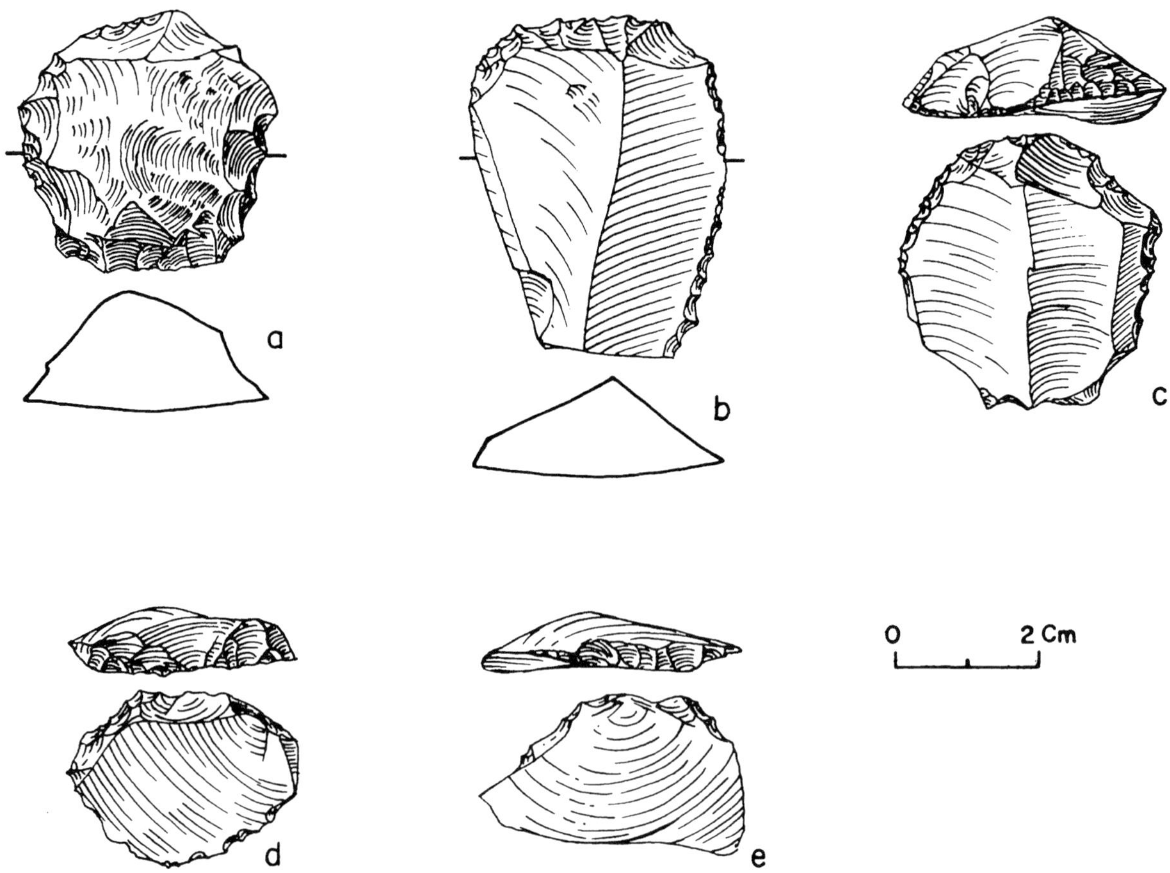

Fig. 28. Chipped stone tool types from Tepe Ali Kosh: *a-c,* flake, round end scrapers; *d-e,* flakes with bulbar end retouch (*c,* zone C_2, Bus Mordeh phase; *e,* zone B_1, Ali Kosh phase; *d,* zone A_2, Mohammad Jaffar phase; *a,b,* zone A_1, Mohammad Jaffar phase).

Temporal distribution: Late Ali Kosh, Mohammad Jaffar, and Sabz phases

Geographic distribution: Jarmo, Sarab (Hole, 1961).

Functional Group: Cutting-Scraping Tools

This is a varied group of seven types of tools, ranging from plain blades to notched flakes; but all the tools seem related principally to cutting and light-duty scraping. With the exception of the backed and truncated blades, none of these types was deliberately retouched to manufacture a stereotyped tool.

By far the most abundant type is the plain blade (some 35,000 out of the 41,000 tools recovered), which accounts for more than half of all tools in all phases except Sabz and Khazineh. The great quantity of blades is both a measure of the skill of the flint knappers and an indication of the cheap regard in which blades were held. It is also a testimony to the need for sharp cutting-edges, since very few of the blades show signs of having been seriously dulled before being discarded. Blades were probably used in handles, but may have been more often held in the hand, used for a short time until they had become greasy or nicked, and then discarded in favor of a fresh blade. Most of the blades must have been used on soft material, probably flesh or fiber, because they are not seriously damaged.

The chief chronological indicators in this functional group are the backed and truncated blades, which occur only in the Sabz, Khazineh, Mehmeh, and Bayat phases. Looking at the proportion of plain blades to all tools, we can also see clear differences between phases. During the Bus Mordeh, Ali Kosh, and Mohammad Jaffar phases, plain blades account for more than 80 per cent of the total tools. They drop to 41 per cent in the Sabz phase, but later increase in frequency in the following manner: Khazineh 47 per cent, Mehmeh 57 per cent, and Bayat 65 per cent. These data indicate a technological break between the Mohammad Jaffar and Sabz phases, and suggest a return toward the greater use of blades in the later phases. However, some skewing of these proportions may have resulted from the fact that the flint used in the Sabz phase was of poor quality, and did not lend itself well to the manufacture of blades. In the later phases there seems to have been an increase in the use of "foreign" flint, and it is even likely that finished blades were being imported.

Type: Plain blades

Sample: 35,967

Description: Blades which have no deliberate retouch, although the edges may have irregular chips and nicks.

Temporal distribution: Throughout the sequence

Geographic distribution: Throughout the Near East, but Jarmo and Sarab had large quantities similar to those of the three early phases at Ali Kosh.

Type: Backed blades (Fig. 29*a,b*)

Sample: 8

Description: Blades, or segments of blades, which have one edge blunted by steep retouch.

Temporal distribution: Sporadically during the Sabz, Khazineh, Mehmeh, and Bayat phases

Geographic distribution: Unknown (for this time period).

Type: Truncated and/or backed blades (Fig. 29)

Sample: 23

Description: Two varieties of retouched blades are included here: (1) truncated blades which have steep retouch on an end or ends, but none on the edges; and (2) blades which are both backed and truncated.

Temporal distribution: Sabz, Khazineh, Mehmeh, and Bayat phases

Geographic distribution: Unknown.

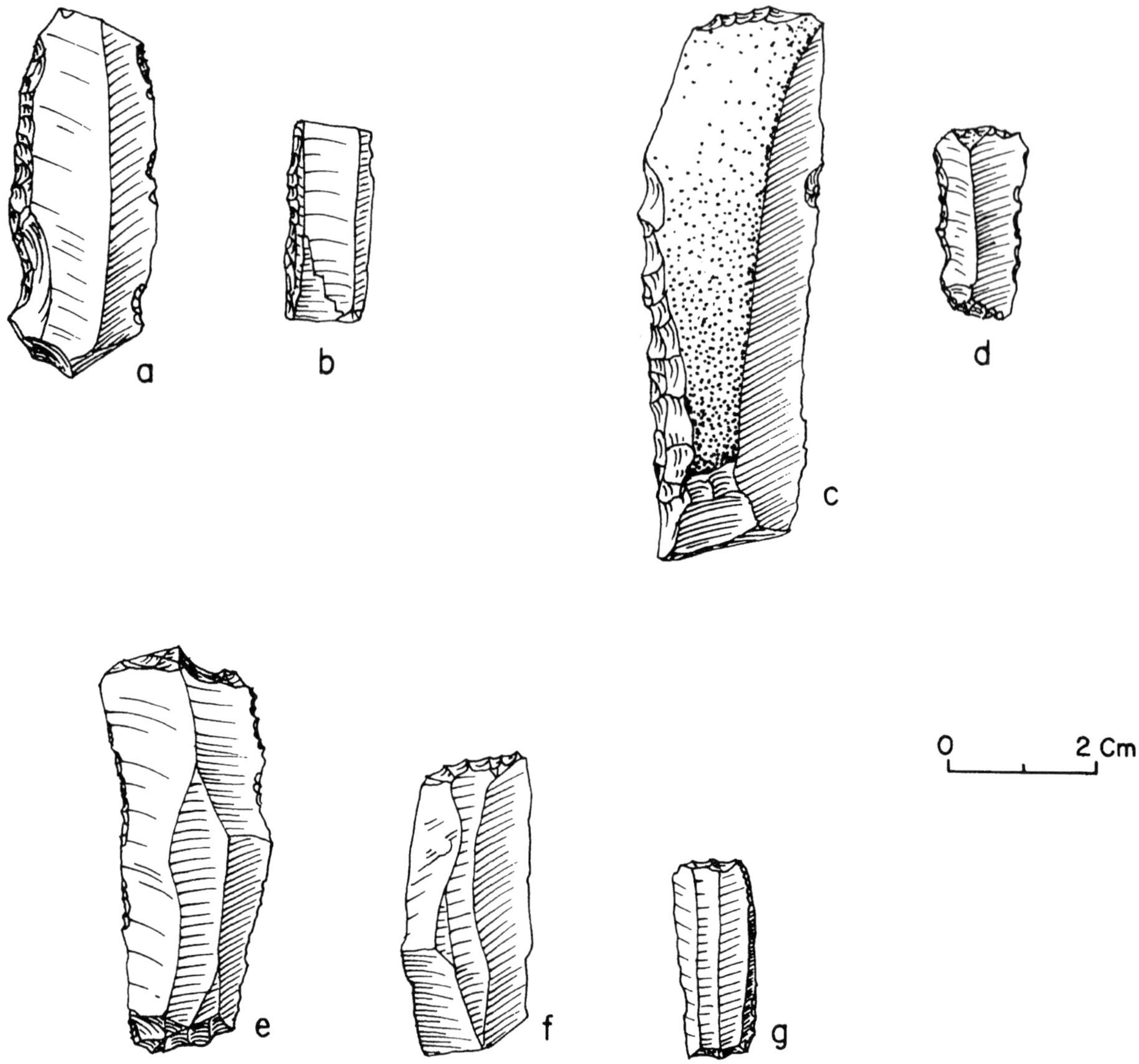

Fig. 29. Chipped stone tool types from Tepe Sabz: *a,b,* backed blades; *c-g,* truncated and/or backed blades (*c,d,f,* zone D, Sabz phase; *a,* zone C_1, Khazineh phase; *b,* zone B_1, Mehmeh phase; *g,* zone A_3, Bayat phase; *e,* zone A_1, Bayat phase).

Type: Retouched or used blades (Fig. 30*g-r*)

Sample: 1943

Description: Blades whose edge or edges have zones of chipping most which probably resulted from use. Arguments against their having been deliberately retouched include the fact that the chipping is localized, and it does not greatly alter the form of the blade. A small group, occurring sporadically through our three earliest phases, has zones of steep chipping on its edges, but the retouch is not extensive enough to be called "backing."

Temporal distribution: Throughout the sequence

Geographic distribution: Throughout the near East. See, for example, Jarmo (Braidwood and Howe, 1960:Pl. 17).

Type: Notched blades (Fig. 30*a-f*)

Sample: 1474

Description: Blades whose edges have been chipped to produce a notch or notches. Only rarely are the notches regularly enough spaced

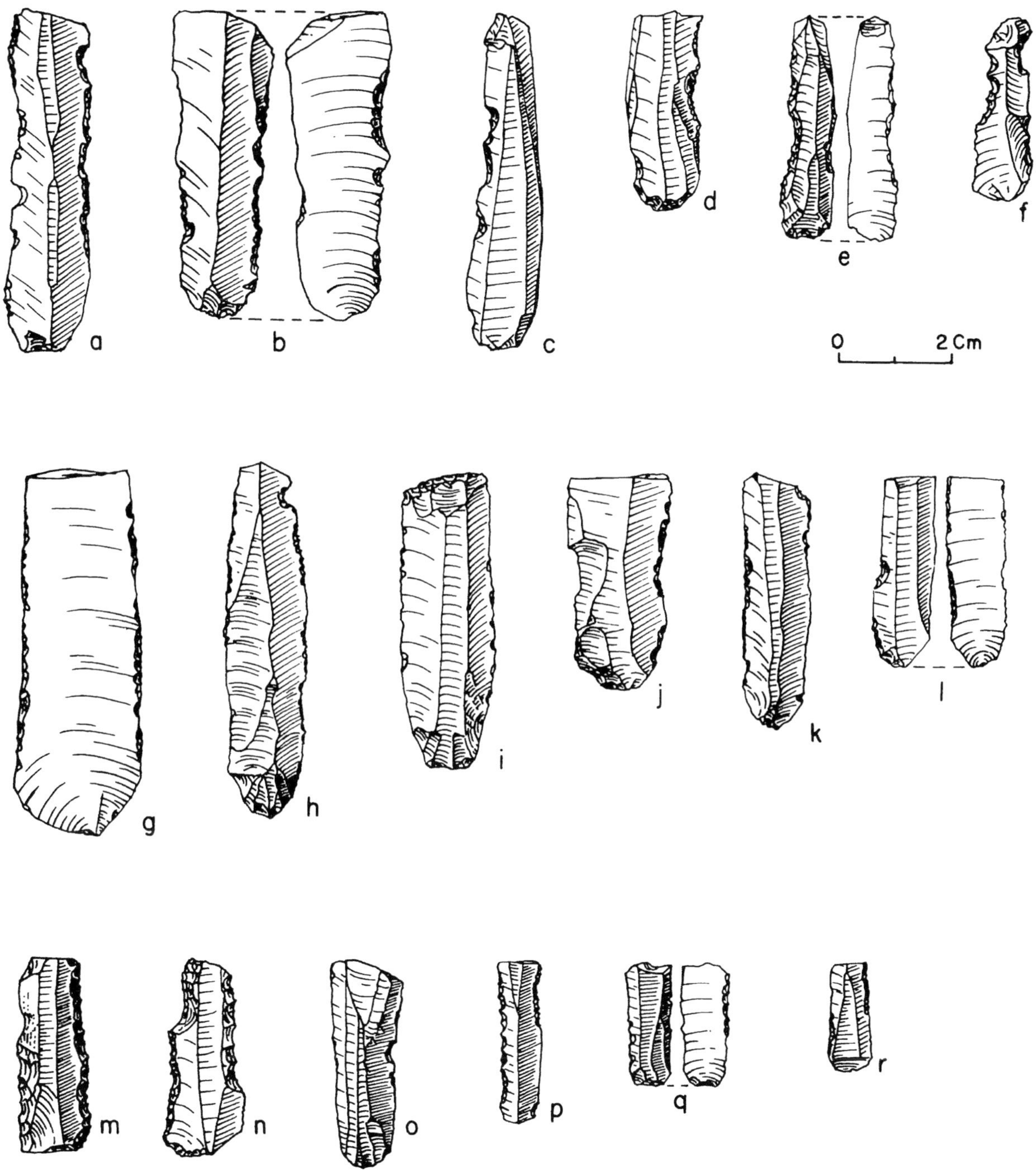

Fig. 30. Chipped stone tool types from Tepe Ali Kosh: *a-f,* notched blades; *g-r,* retouched or used blades (*m,* zone C_2, Bus Mordeh phase; *a-l, o-r,* zone B_2, Ali Kosh phase; *n,* zone B_1, Ali Kosh phase).

for them to be called "denticulated." Many of the notches probably were to prepare the flints as spokeshaves for wooden shafts.

Temporal distribution: Throughout the sequence

Geographic distribution: Throughout the Near East. See, for example, Jarmo (Braidwood and Howe, 1960:Pl. 17).

Type: Notched flakes (Fig. 31*e,f*)

Sample: 67

Description: Flakes whose edges have been chipped to produce a notch or series of irregularly-spaced notches.

Temporal distribution: All phases (except, so far, the Mohammad Jaffar phase)

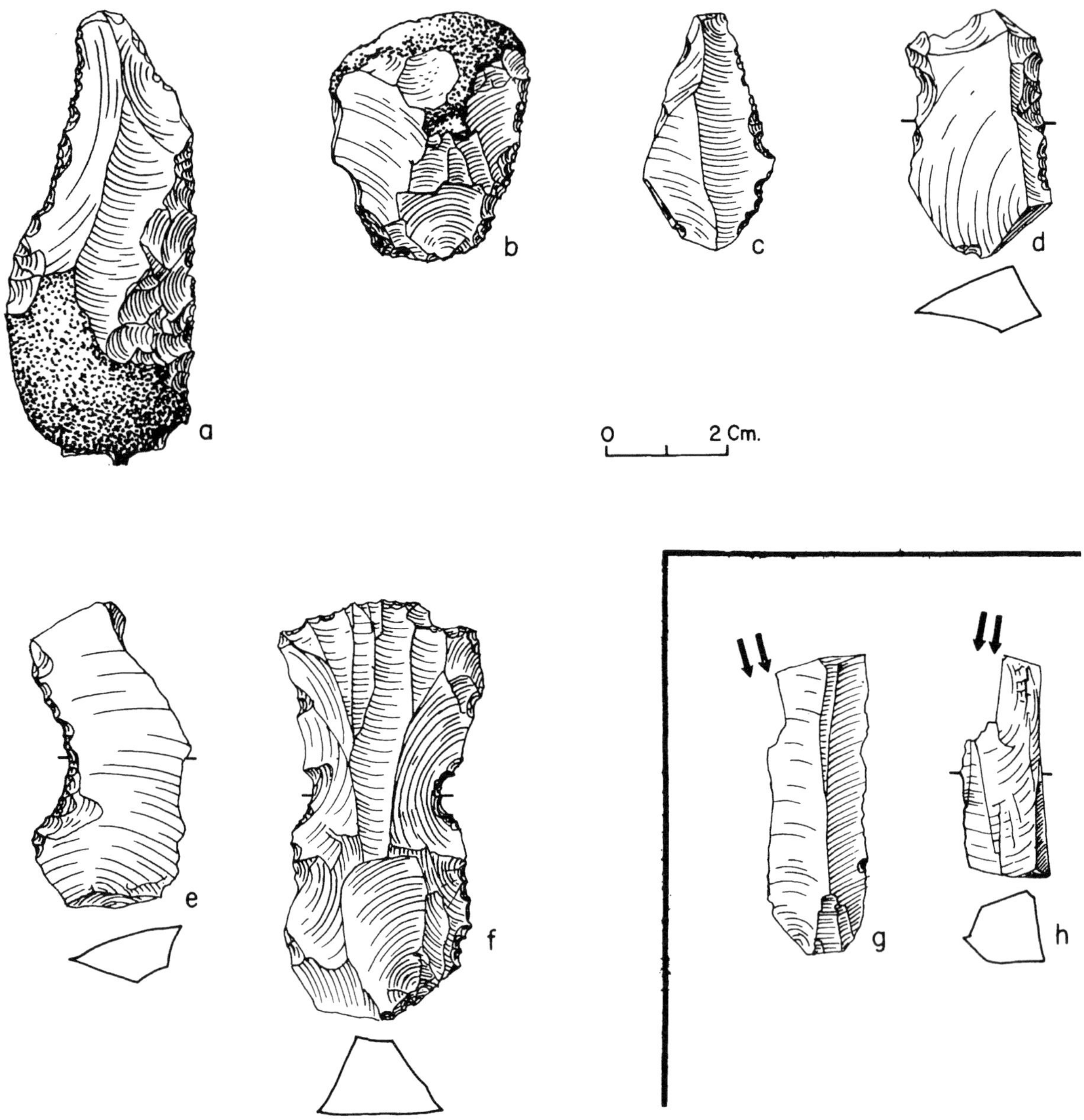

Fig. 31. Chipped stone tool types from Tepe Ali Kosh: *a-d,* retouched or used flakes; *e-f,* notched flakes; *g-h,* burins (*h,* zone C_2, Bus Mordeh phase; *e,f,* zone B_2, Ali Kosh phase; *a-c,g,* zone B_1, Ali Kosh phase; *d,* zone A_2, Mohammad Jaffar phase).

Geographic distribution: Karim Shahir (Braidwood and Howe, 1960:52); and probably throughout the Near East.

Type: Retouched or used flakes (Fig. 31*a-d*)

Sample: 99

Description: Flakes whose edges or edges have zones of chipping which probably resulted from use. The chipping is localized and does not greatly alter the form of the flake.

Temporal distribution: Throughout the sequence

Geographic distribution: Throughout the Near East.

Miscellaneous Tools

Type: Burins (Fig. 31*g,h*)

Sample: 6

Description: All are simple burins, with the burin blow having been struck on a broken end of a blade or flake to produce a sharp, strong chisel or graver edge. Burins were used to cut and engrave stone, bone and wood. These tools were most popular in the upper paleolithic, and occur in very low frequency in sites contemporary with our present sequence, except in the Levant. We have no examples of the engraving that may have been done with the burins.

Temporal distribution: Sporadically in the Bus Mordeh, Ali Kosh, Mohammad Jaffar, and Sabz phases

Geographic distribution: Zawi Chemi (R. L. Solecki, 1964:407); Jarmo, Sarab (Hole, 1961); probably at other sites of this age?

Type: Bifacially-chipped flakes (Fig. 32*a,b*)

Sample: 6

Description: Irregular flakes which have an edge roughly chipped from both faces. These tools were probably used for chopping or cutting, although they are not very large.

Temporal distribution: Sporadic. Examples in the Ali Kosh, Sabz, Khazineh, and Mehmeh phases

Geographic distribution: Unknown.

Type: Bifacially-chipped point (Fig. 32*c*)

Example: 1, from the Bus Mordeh phase, zone C_2 at Ali Kosh

Description: A broken implement with an oval cross-section and rough flaking on both faces. The edges merge to form a dull point.

Geographic distribution: Not reported from the Zagros area, but our specimen appears to be identical to a tool David French picked up on the surface of Pinarbasi-Bor, a site in Anatolia (French, 1964:Fig. 7-8). The age of this site is not specified, but it may be preceramic. The point is also similar to the "daggers" Bialor illustrates from Çatal Hüyük (Bialor, 1962:95-96, Fig. 9).

CHIPPING DEBRIS

Cores and other residue from the manufacture of tools vary from phase to phase, as one would expect, given the nature of the raw materials used and the differences in technique of chipping.

The finest chipping technique is found in the three early phases (Bus Mordeh through Mohammad Jaffar) and is exemplified by the production of blades from symmetrically-fluted, bullet-shaped cores. Only two such cores occur in the Sabz phase, and they seem distinctly out of character with the remainder of the flint in that period; no later examples are known. The other cores in the Sabz phase are crudely chipped from small nodules of locally-derived flint (probably from the bed of the Mehmeh River). A further reflection of the change in technique and material in the later phases may be seen in the fact that, from the Sabz phase on, flake cores far outnumber blade cores. In this connection, recall that many of the Mehmeh and Bayat phase blades could have been imported as finished tools, and not made locally. This was decidedly not

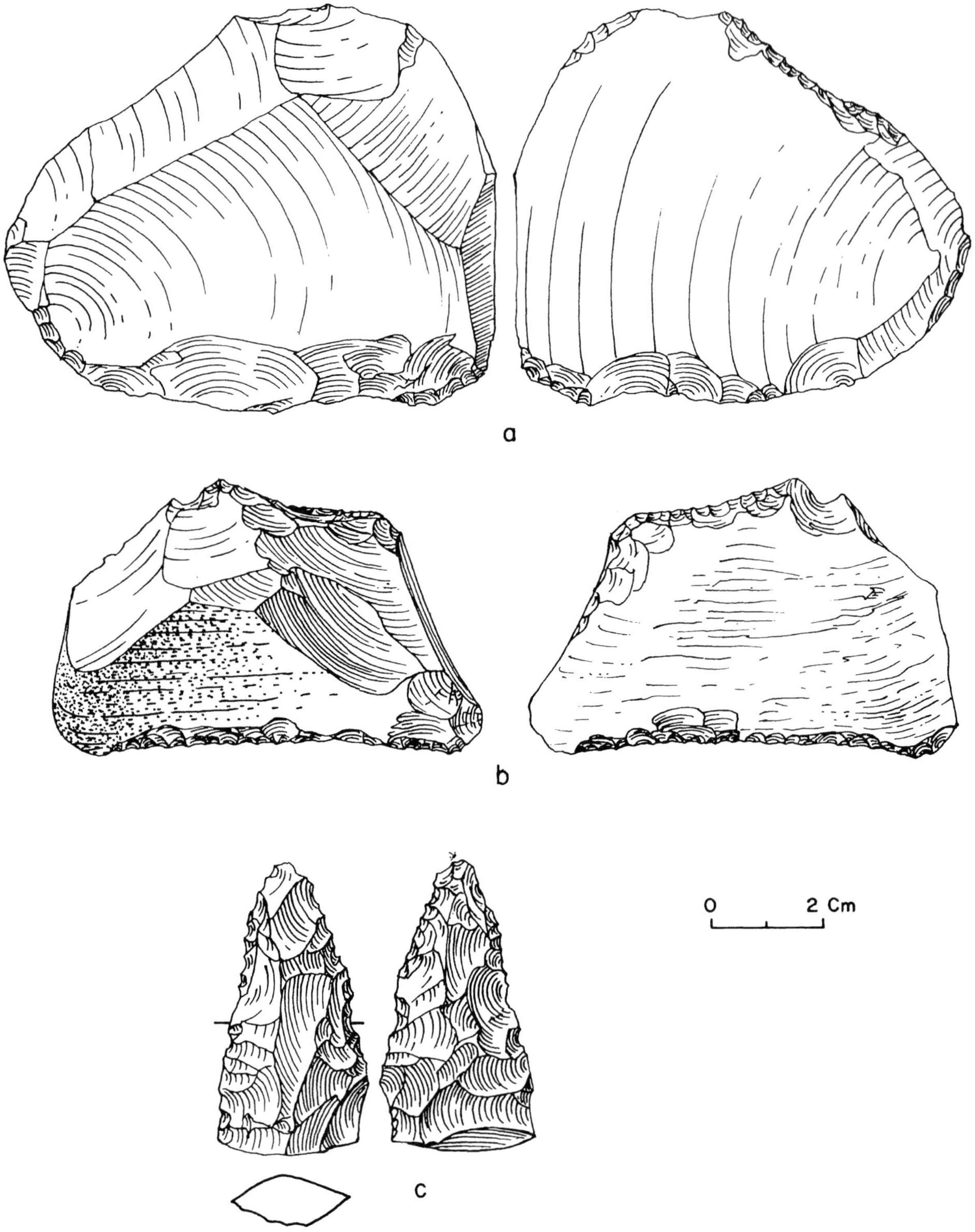

Fig. 32. Chipped stone tool types from Tepe Ali Kosh: *a,b,* bifacially-chipped flakes; *c,* bifacially-chipped point (*a,b,* zone B_2, Ali Kosh phase; *c,* zone C_2, Bus Mordeh phase).

the case in the early phases, where large quantities of chipping debris indicate local manufacture.

Many types of cores, both for blades and flakes, do not occur after the Mohammad Jaffar phase, a fact in harmony with the general reduction in variety of tool types at the same chronological point in our sequence.

Within the three earliest phases, we can see some changes in the types of cores. "Tongue-shaped" cores are found only in the Mohammad Jaffar and Ali Kosh phase levels, while very large blade cores are found only in the early part of the Ali Kosh phase. Since these unusual cores may not have been locally manufactured, it is probable that their occurrence reflects chance rather than chronological position.

Flake cores also show some changes. "Tea cozy" cores (perhaps intended to be scrapers) are found in the Ali Kosh and Mohammad Jaffar phases, but not continuously throughout the various strata. Although they are rare, "tea cozies" seem to be a horizon marker, since they are also found in contemporary deposits at Jarmo and Sarab (Hole, 1961).

To judge from the kinds of chipping debris and its abundance, it appears that in the early periods most chipping of flint was done in houses and courtyards on the site. We can only explain the trend toward relatively higher frequencies of finished tools in the Khazineh, Mehmeh, and Bayat phases by saying that less chipping seems to have been done *in situ*. For some purposes, these later peoples at Tepe Sabz no doubt made their own tools; but as mentioned above, it is unlikely they made their own blades. Many of the blades are of colored flint, as opposed to the uniform gray of the local material; and many of the large blades came from nodules which are larger than any observed in older levels in the Deh Luran excavations. Furthermore, we know that by Khazineh or Mehmeh phase times, there were specialized "flint knapperies" in existence in the Zagros, which probably exported blades over a wide area. We cite as an example Tepe Muriyan in the Kermanshah Valley, tested by Braidwood (1960:696).

Blade Cores

Type: Bullet-shaped blade cores (Fig. 33*b-g*)

Sample: 564

Description: Small, conical cores with round or slightly oval platforms. The platform, generally unfaceted, is perpendicular to the long axis. Blades were struck around the entire perimeter. The cores are ordinarily widest at the platform, and narrow to a point at the lower end. They range in length from 2 to 5.5 cm. and have a rim diameter from 0.3 to 2.5 cm. The majority of the cores have lengths of around 3 cm. and diameters between 1 and 1.5 cm.

Temporal distribution: Bus Mordeh, Ali Kosh, and Mohammad Jaffar phases; only two examples from the Sabz phase

Geographic distribution: Karim Shahir (Braidwood and Howe, 1960:53); Jarmo (Braidwood and Howe, 1960:Pl. 19); Sarab (Hole, 1961); Kuhbanan (Huckriede, 1961:Fig. 3:23-27); perhaps a few at Tepe Guran (collections of the Danish National Museum).

Type: Tongue-shaped blade cores (Fig. 34*c,d*)

Sample: 18

Description: Blade cores with an oval horizontal section which gives the piece the general shape of a human tongue. The size of these cores is about the same as for the bullet-shaped cores, although the platforms are oval rather than round. None occurred at Tepe Sabz.

Temporal distribution: Ali Kosh and Mohammad Jaffar phases, with one example from the Bus Mordeh phase

Geographic distribution: Jarmo (Braidwood and Howe, 1960:Pl. 19); Sarab (Hole, 1961).

Type: Semi-chipped blade cores (Fig. 38*a-c*)

Sample: 113

Description: Cores which are not chipped around the entire periphery, although in other respects they are like the bullet-shaped cores.

Since some of these are not trimmed completely, they may be only partially used; in other instances, it would appear that defects in the flint prevented the total use of the core. Most of the blade cores in the later phases of the sequence are of this type.

Temporal distribution: Throughout the sequence

Geographic distribution: Zawi Chemi (R. L. Solecki, 1964:408); Karim Shahir (Braidwood and Howe, 1960:53); Jarmo, Sarab (Hole, 1961); Tepe Guran (collections in the Danish National Museum).

Type: Very large blade cores (Fig. 34*a,b*)

Sample: 5

Description: A few cores from the Ali Kosh phase are extraordinarily large (7 to 11 cm. long and 2.5 to 4 cm. in diameter) and evidently made from a different source of flint from the majority of the Ali Kosh examples. The blades struck from these cores were some 0.5 to 1.2 cm. wide. After their use as cores, some of these were reused as pestles (Pl. 31*i-l*).

Temporal distribution: Ali Kosh phase

Geographic distribution: Unknown.

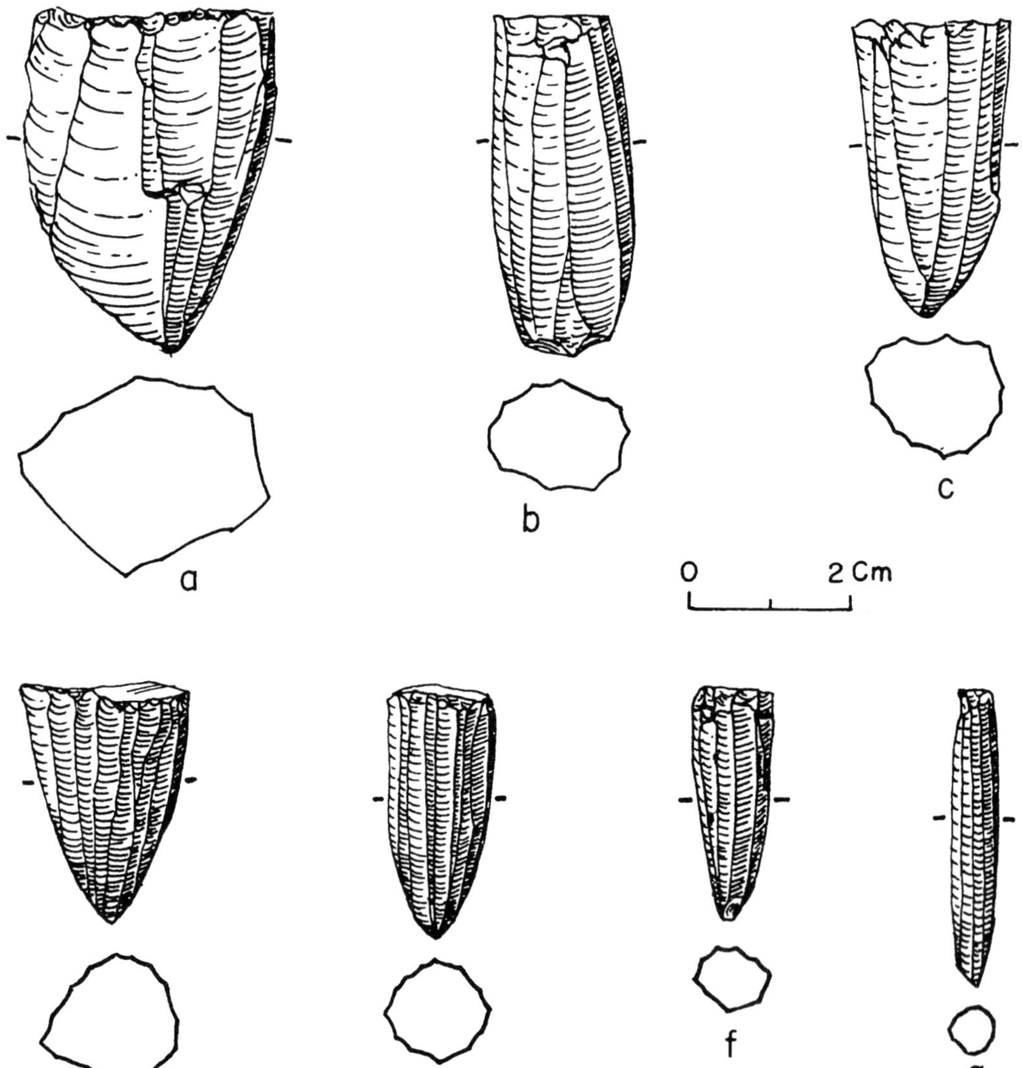

Fig. 33. Chipped stone cores from Tepe Ali Kosh: *a,* semi-chipped blade core; *b-g,* bullet-shaped blade cores (all from zone A_1, Mohammad Jaffar phase).

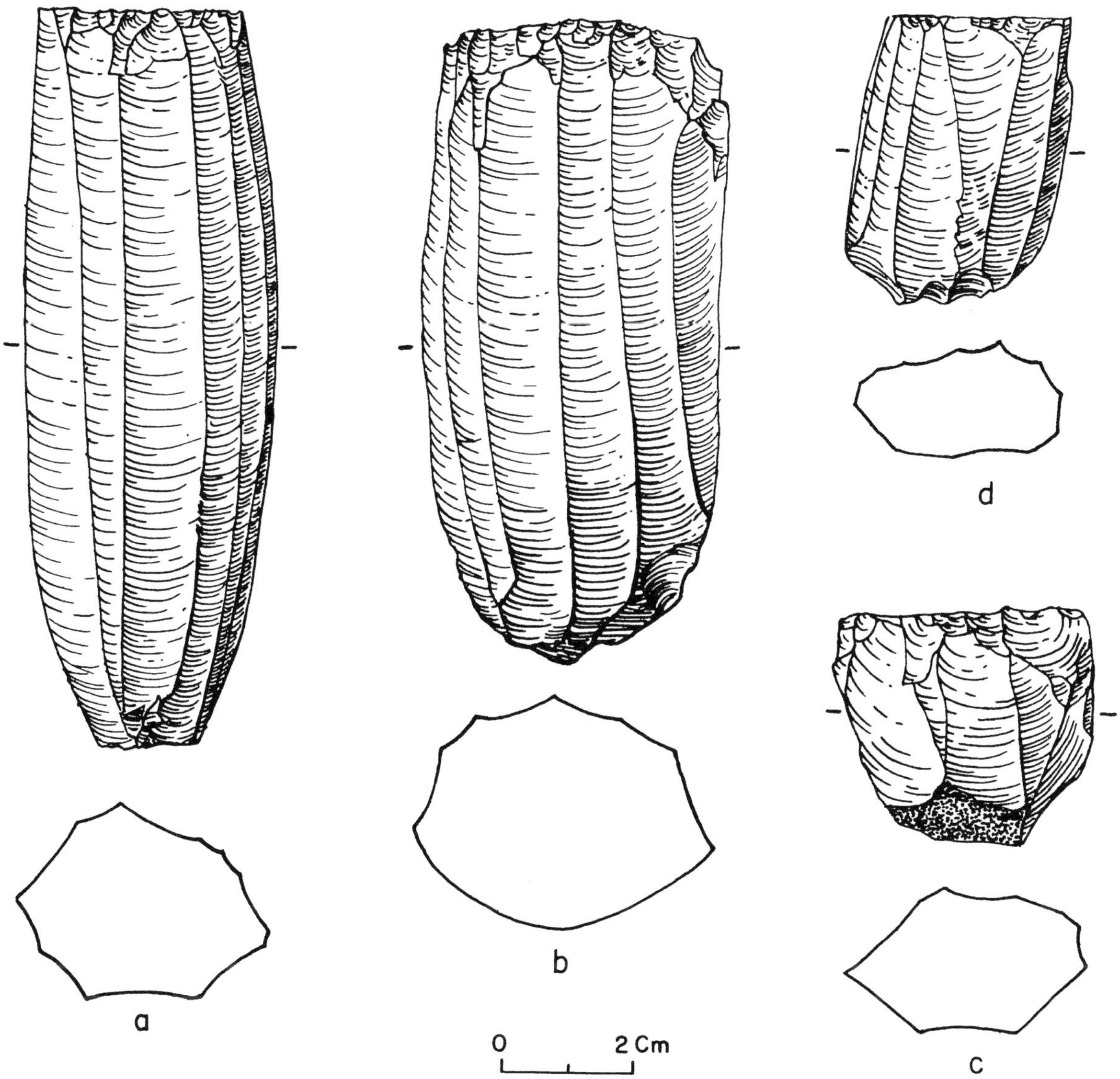

Fig. 34. Chipped stone cores from Tepe Ali Kosh: *a,b,* very large blade cores; *c-d,* tongue-shaped blade cores (*a,b,d,* zone B_2, Ali Kosh phase; *c,* zone B_1, Ali Kosh phase).

Flake Cores

Type: Whole-chipped flake cores (Fig. 35*a-c*)

Sample: 79

Description: Cores from which flakes were chipped, all from a single platform which is at right angles to the long axis of the core. The flakes were chipped around the entire periphery of the platform. Although these cores are ordinarily pyramidal in shape, they may also be chunky. Some of these, especially those found at Ali Kosh, may be roughed-out blanks from which blades were to be struck. Some show defects in the flint which probably caused the knapper to discard the core.

Temporal distribution: Bus Mordeh, Ali Kosh, and Mohammad Jaffar phases

Geographic distribution: Jarmo, Sarab (Hole, 1961).

Type: "Tea cozy" flake cores (Fig. 35*d,e*)

Sample: 14

Description: Flake cores which have an oval platform, and a height about equal to the

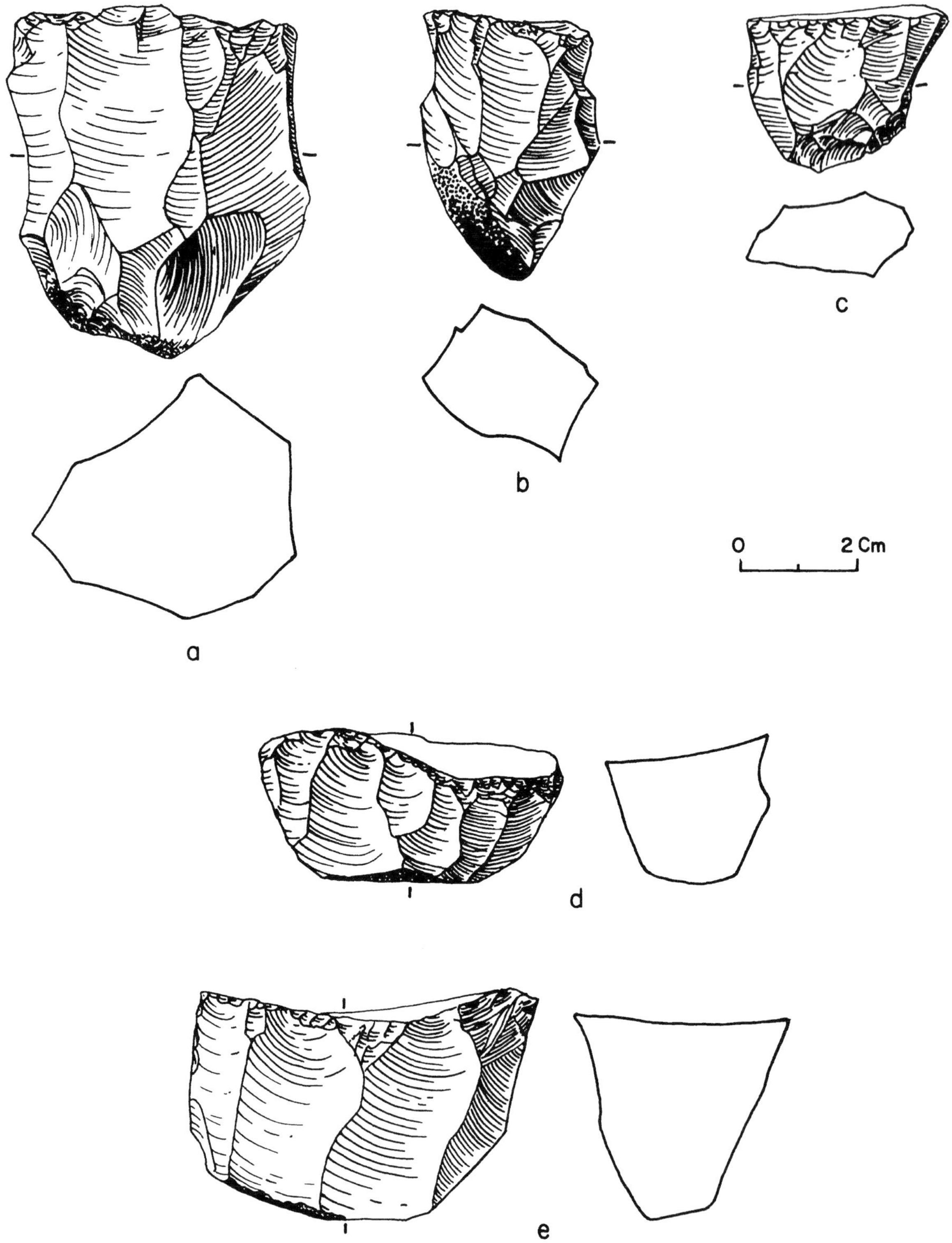

Fig. 35. Chipped stone cores from Tepe Ali Kosh: *a-c,* whole-chipped flake cores; *d,e,* "Tea cozy" flake cores (*d,e,* zone B_2, Ali Kosh phase; *b,c,* zone B_1, Ali Kosh phase; *a,* zone A_2, Mohammad Jaffar phase).

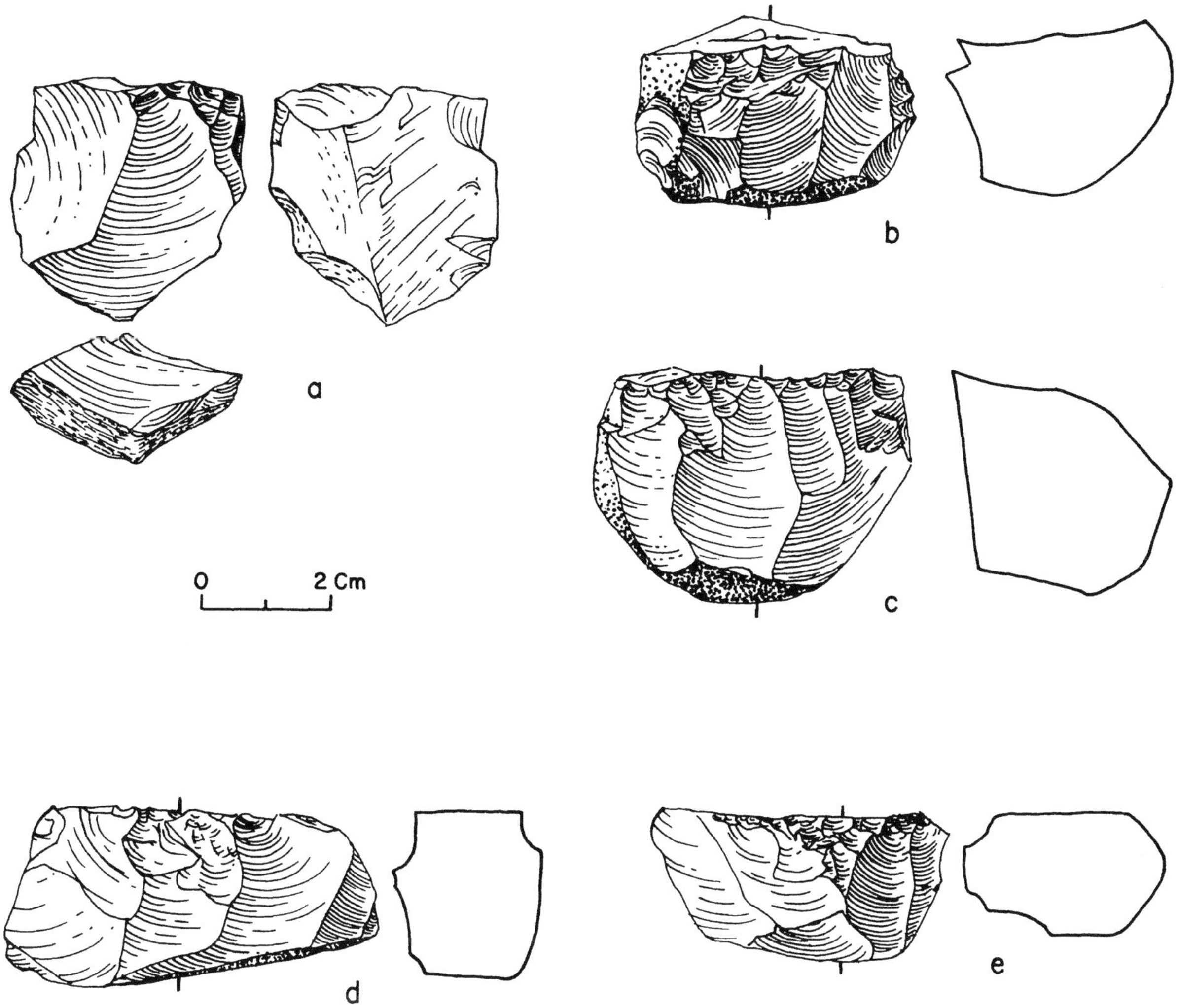

Fig. 36. Chipped stone cores from Tepe Sabz: *a-c,* semi-chipped flake cores; *d,e,* thin nodule flake cores (*a,c-e,* zone D, Sabz phase; *b,* zone B_3, Mehmeh phase).

width of the platform. No apparent attempt was made to strike fine blades from these, although some of the tongue-shaped cores may have begun like this. Characteristically, secondary chipping around the periphery of the platform has smoothed the rough edges left by the primary flaking. No examples had edges beveled from use, although these pieces may well have been used as scrapers. Similar pieces at Jarmo had edge-beveling, and nearly identical pieces in the New World—called "scraper-planes"—have been found with plant fibers adhering as a result of their having been used for shredding plants.

Temporal distribution: Ali Kosh and Mohammad Jaffar phases

Geographic distribution: Jarmo (Braidwood and Howe, 1960:Pl. 19), Sarab (Hole, 1961).

Type: Discoidal flake cores (Fig. 37*a,b*)

Sample: 4

Description: Cores which are roughly-chipped bifacially around their edges, resulting in a sinuous edge which recalls the manner in which hand-axes are flaked. There are no clear signs of battering on the edges, which one would expect it they had been used for chopping.

Temporal distribution: Sporadic. Bus Mordeh, Ali Kosh, and Khazineh phases

Geographic distribution: Jarmo, Sarab (Hole, 1961).

Type: Semichipped flake cores (Fig. 36*a-c*)

Sample: 164

Description: Nodules of flint which were roughly chipped from one platform, or from two opposed platforms, to produce flakes. In no case was the chipping entirely around the periphery of the piece. Some of these may represent the initial roughing-out of flint prior to making a blade core.

Temporal distribution: Throughout the sequence

Geographic distribution: Zawi Chemi (R. L. Solecki, 1964:408); Karim Shahir (Braidwood and Howe, 1960:53); Sarab, Jarmo (Hole, 1961).

Type: Amorphous flake cores (Fig. 40*a,b*)

Sample: 45

Description: These flake cores have several non-opposed platforms, and present a chunky,

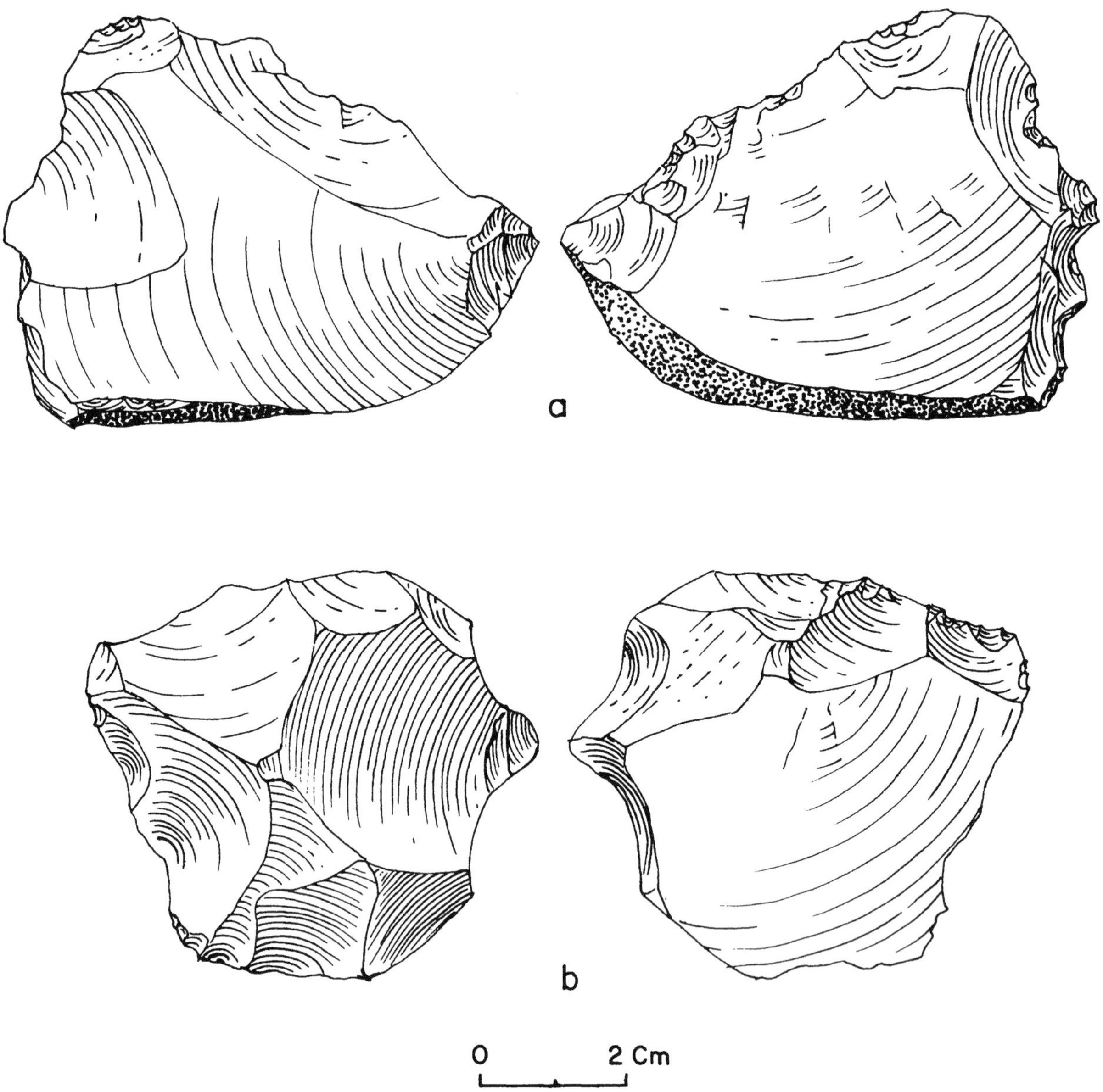

Fig. 37. Chipped stone cores from Tepe Sabz: *a,b,* discoidal flake cores (*b,* zone C_3, Khazineh phase; *a,* zone C_2, Khazineh phase).

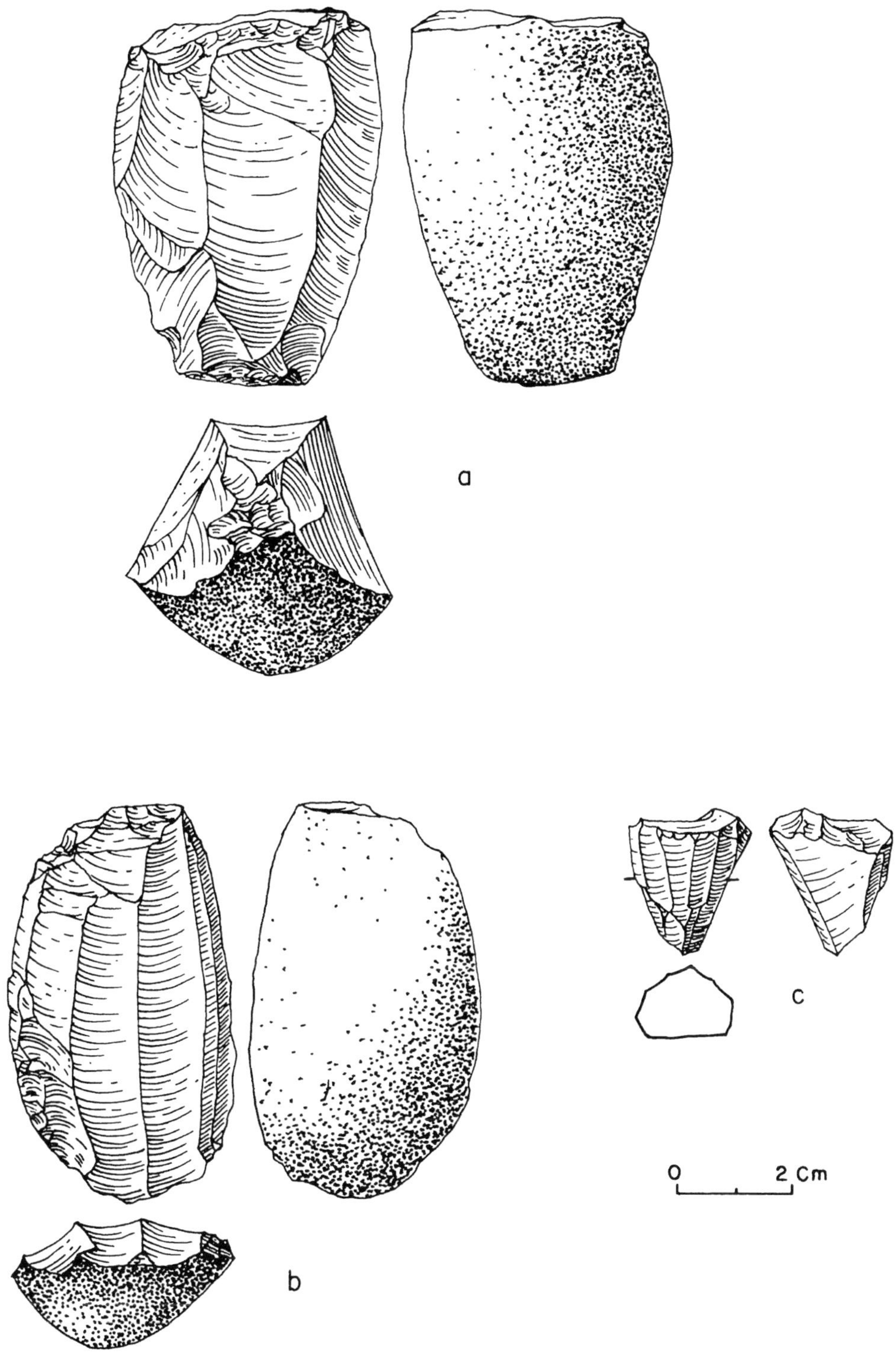

Fig. 38. Chipped stone cores from Tepe Sabz: *a-c,* semi-chipped blade cores (*c,* zone D, Sabz phase; *a,* zone B_3, Mehmeh phase; *b,* zone A_2, Bayat phase).

irregular appearance. The platforms are not flat or very extensive, as are those on the other types of flake cores.

Temporal distribution: Sporadically throughout the sequence

Geographic distribution: Zawi Chemi (R. L. Solecki, 1964:408); Jarmo, Sarab (Hole, 1961).

Type: Thin nodule flake cores (Fig. 36*d,e*)

Sample: 19

Description: Found only at Tepe Sabz, these cores result from the source of flint used by the knappers there; often they struck a few flakes off thin nodules of flint. There was no real effort to shape these into pyramidal cores; the intent was satisfied with the removal of a few rough flakes.

Temporal distribution: Sabz, Khazineh, and Mehmeh phases

Geographic distribution: Unknown.

Core Fragments

Tablets of Blade Cores (Fig. 41*i*)

Sample: 35

Description: Upper portions of blade cores which were removed by a blow parallel to the plane of the platform. Some of these may have been removed in order to renew a platform which had become too battered.

Temporal distribution: Bus Mordeh, Ali Kosh, and Mohammad Jaffar phases; only one example in the Sabz phase

Geographic distribution: Jarmo, Sarab (Hole, 1961).

Edges of Striking Platforms (Fig. 41*f-h*)

Sample: 242

Description: A slice off the top of a core, produced by blows struck at the edge of the platform and transverse to the long axis of the core. The resultant pieces are elongate and triangular-sectioned.

Temporal distribution: Throughout the sequence

Geographic distribution: Sarab (Hole, 1961).

Faces of Cores (Fig. 41*a-c*)

Sample: 433

Description: A blow, struck on the platform, removed an unusually wide flake from the face of the core. The flake includes scars from several blades or flakes, and should probably be regarded as an accident. A variety of core face

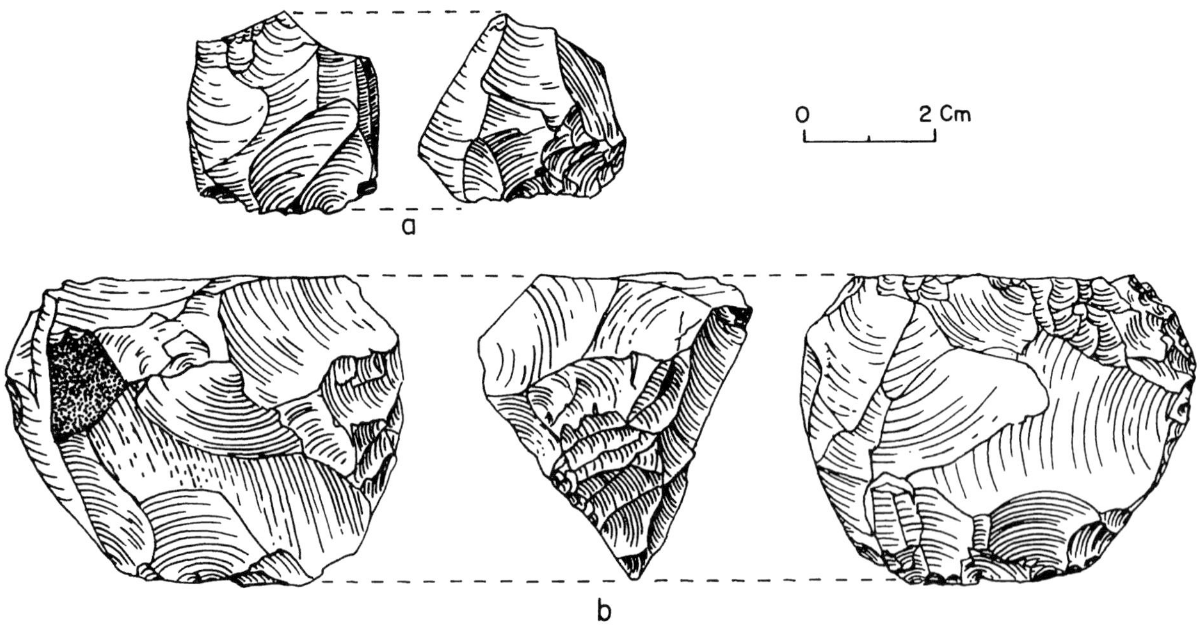

Fig. 39. Chipped stone cores from Tepe Ali Kosh: *a,b,* amorphous flake cores (both zone B_2, Ali Kosh phase).

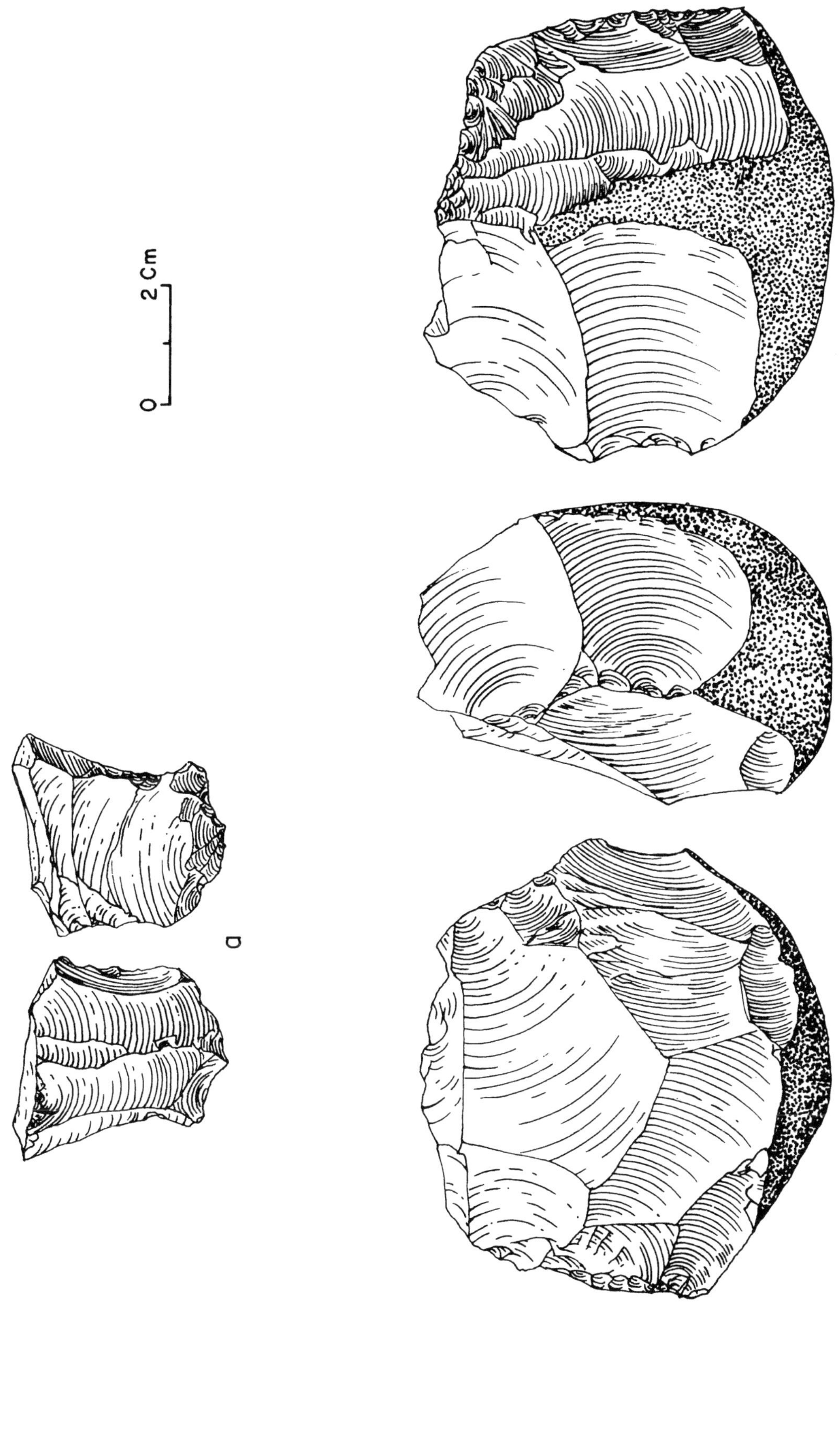

Fig. 40. Chipped stone cores from Tepe Sabz: *a,b*, amorphous flake cores (*a*, zone D, Sabz phase; *b*, zone B_2, Mehmeh phase).

is the "plunging flake," similar to the above but including a substantial portion of the bottom of the core along with the face (Fig. 41). A final group of fragments included here consists of midsections of bullet-shaped cores.

Temporal distribution: Throughout the sequence

Geographic distribution: Jarmo, Sarab (Hole, 1961).

Miscellaneous Core Fragments (Fig. 41*d*)

Sample: 209

Description: Pieces which show scars from several previously-removed flakes or blades, but which do not fall into one of the other categories. Any piece which is not a simple flake or blade, yet can be definitely related to a core as part of the trimming process.

Temporal distribution: Throughout the sequence.

Debitage

Sample: 48,746

Description: Flakes which have no signs of retouch. We regard these as analogous to sawdust—useless debris left over from the manufacture of tools.

Temporal distribution: Throughout the sequence.

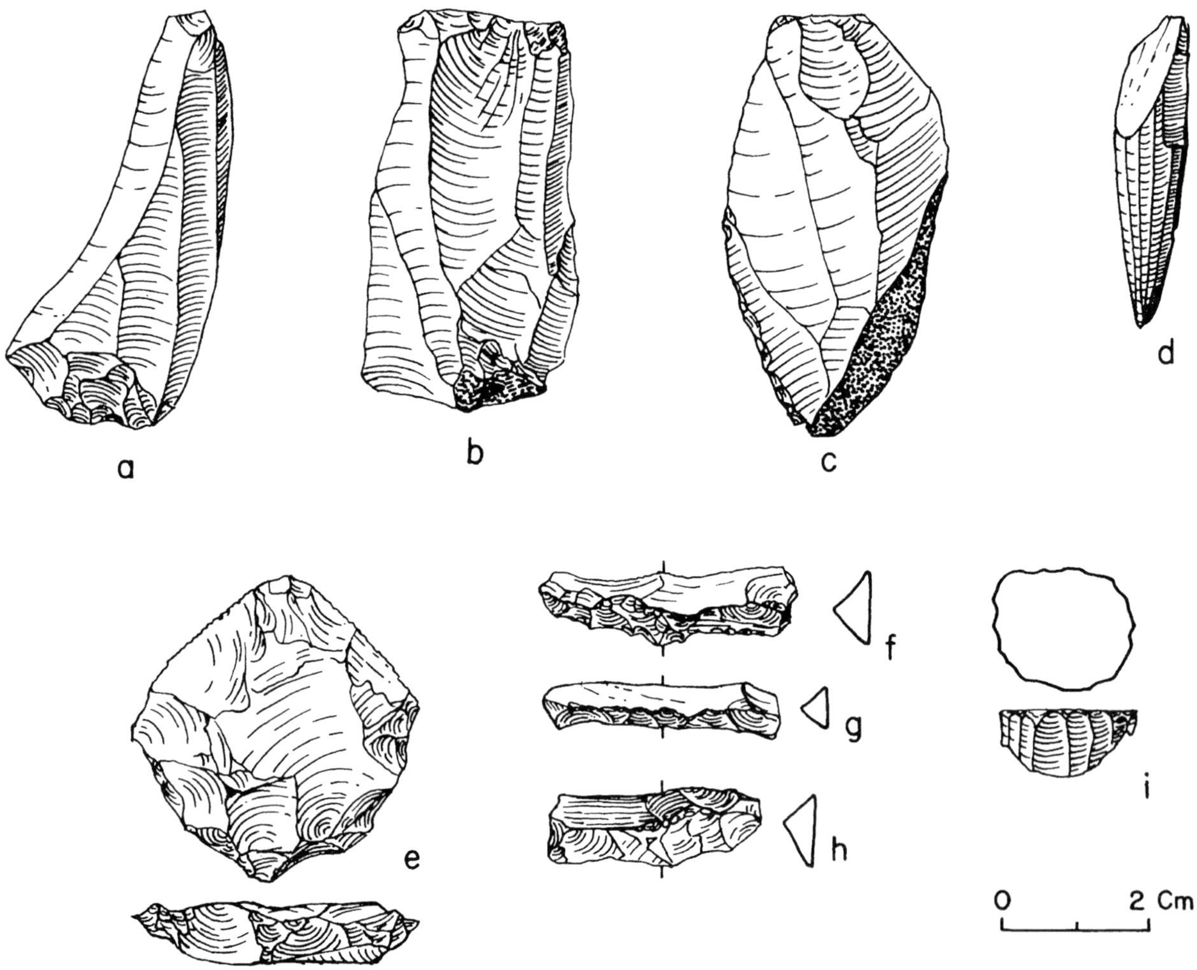

Fig. 41. Miscellaneous core fragments from Tepe Ali Kosh: *a-c,* faces of cores; *d,* miscellaneous core fragment; *e,* tablet of flake core; *f-h,* edges of striking platforms; *i,* tablet of blade core (*a-g,i,* zone A_2, Mohammad Jaffar phase; *h,* zone A_1, Mohammad Jaffar phase).

Table 6

OCCURRENCE OF CHIPPING DEBRIS (BOTH FLINT AND OBSIDIAN) AT ALI KOSH, TEPE SABZ, AND TEPE MUSIYAN
(By Stratigraphic Zone)

Site and Zone		Blade Cores			Flake Cores						Core Fragments						
	Bullet Cores	Tongue-shaped Cores	Semi-chipped Cores	Very Large Blade Cores	Whole-chipped Cores	Tea Cozy Cores	Discoidal Cores	Semi-chipped Cores	Amorphous Cores	Thin Nodule Cores	Tablets of Blade Cores	Edges, Platforms	Faces	Miscellaneous	Debitage	Total Chipping Debris	Total Chipped Stone (Tools and Debris)
TS - A_1	...	...	2	...	...	...	...	1	...	...	...	3	1	...	147	154	262
TS - A_2	...	...	2	...	...	...	...	...	...	...	...	2	...	...	126	130	246
TS - A_3	...	...	2	...	...	...	...	2	1	...	...	5	5	5	412	432	759
TS - B_1	...	...	1	...	...	...	...	5	...	1	...	2	5	2	230	246	338
MUS E	...	...	...	...	...	...	...	...	...	...	...	1	...	...	32	33	51
TS - B_2	...	...	2	...	...	...	...	...	1	...	...	2	...	2	89	96	127
TS - B_3	...	...	2	...	...	...	...	7	2	1	...	2	2	1	143	160	197
TS - C_1	...	...	1	...	...	...	...	11	1	2	...	1	1	2	171	190	223
TS - C_2	...	...	...	...	...	...	...	5	...	...	...	1	4	2	194	206	241
TS - C_3	...	...	1	...	...	...	2	6	...	2	...	4	5	2	295	317	356
TS - D	2	...	3	...	...	...	...	55	12	13	1	9	25	12	1564	1696	1873
AK - A_1	84	3	10	...	12	3	...	10	...	...	4	24	59	23	5451	5683	10102
AK - A_2	137	5	3	...	20	...	...	7	3	...	16	46	106	53	5764	6160	13832
AK - B_1	106	1	7	...	12	...	...	23	9	...	5	36	86	63	5348	5696	14853
AK - B_2	76	8	14	5	23	11	1	15	8	...	6	31	57	20	5400	5675	8378
AK - C_1	51	...	13	...	4	...	...	9	3	...	3	24	25	10	4305	4447	7729
AK - C_2	80	...	33	...	7	...	1	8	5	...	...	47	52	12	6035	6280	11845
AK - C_2 Dump	28	1	17	...	1	...	...	...	...	...	...	2	...	...	13040	13089	20540
Totals	564	18	113	5	79	14	4	164	45	19	35	242	433	209	48746	50690	91952

Table 7

OCCURRENCE OF CHIPPING DEBRIS (BOTH FLINT AND OBSIDIAN) AT ALI KOSH, TEPE SABZ, AND TEPE MUSIYAN
(By Cultural phase)

Phase	Blade Cores				Flake Cores						Core Fragments				Debitage	Total Chipping Debris	Total Chipped Stone (Tools and Debris)
	Bullet Cores	Tongue-shaped Cores	Semi-chipped Cores	Very Large Blade Cores	Whole-chipped Cores	Tea Cozy Cores	Discoidal Cores	Semi-chipped Cores	Amorphous Cores	Thin Nodule Cores	Tablets of Blade Cores	Edges, Platforms	Faces	Miscellaneous			
Bayat	...	...	6	...	...	...	...	3	1	...	...	10	6	5	685	716	1267
Mehmeh	...	...	5	...	...	...	...	12	3	2	...	7	7	5	494	535	713
Khazineh	...	...	2	...	...	...	2	22	1	4	...	6	10	6	660	713	820
Sabz	2	...	3	...	...	...	...	55	12	13	1	9	25	12	1564	1696	1873
Mohammad Jaffar	221	8	13	...	32	3	...	17	3	...	20	70	165	76	11215	11843	23934
Ali Kosh	182	9	21	5	35	11	1	38	17	...	11	67	143	83	10748	11371	23231
Bus Mordeh	159	1	63	...	12	...	1	17	8	...	3	73	77	22	23380	23816	40114
Totals	564	18	113	5	79	14	4	164	45	19	35	242	433	209	48746	50690	91952

Table 8

OCCURRENCE OF OBSIDIAN AT ALI KOSH, TEPE SABZ, AND TEPE MUSIYAN
(By Cultural Phase)

Phase	Piercing-reaming Tools	Blade, Round-end Scraper	Flakes with Bulbar End Retouch	Plain Blades	Retouched or Used Blades	Retouched or Used Flakes	Cores	Edges, Platforms	Miscellaneous Fragments	Debitage	Total Tools	Total Chipping Debris	Total Obsidian	Per Cent of Total Chipped Stone
Bayat	...	...	...	5	...	...	...	...	...	1	5	1	6	0.5
Mehmeh	...	...	...	3	...	...	...	...	...	...	3	...	3	0.4
Khazineh	...	...	...	...	...	...	...	...	...	...	...	...	...	...
Sabz	...	...	...	...	...	...	...	...	...	...	...	...	...	...
Mohammad Jaffar . .	...	1	1	239	14	7	4	4	2	145	262	155	417	2
Ali Kosh	1	...	...	257	9	4	2	3	1	197	271	203	474	2
Bus Mordeh	...	...	...	182	6	...	2	1	1	155	188	159	347	0.9
Totals	1	1	1	686	29	11	8	8	4	498	729	518	1247	...

IX

POTTERY AND STONE VESSELS

INTRODUCTION

From 1961 to 1963, we recovered some 30,000 pot sherds and 84 stone bowl fragments from stratigraphic excavations at Ali Kosh, Tepe Sabz, and Tepe Musiyan "E." Just as at Jarmo (Braidwood, Howe, *et al.*, 1960) and Tepe Guran (Mortensen, 1964), stone bowls preceded pottery in the chronological sequence, but their priority was not very impressive; only three stone bowl fragments appeared in Bus Mordeh phase levels, and stone bowls achieved their maximum abundance and diversity in levels just before and during the introduction of pottery.

All pot sherds recovered from the stratigraphic excavations were saved and shipped to the United States for study. During the course of analysis, we distinguished seven major (and a few minor) types of pottery which could be classified and described according to the binomial nomenclature system currently in use throughout the western hemisphere. The pottery types we distinguished are defined in this chapter.

For each stratigraphic zone, a count was made of the number of potsherds of each type, and on the basis of this we calculated the percentage which each type constituted in the total sherd count for that zone. Changes in per cent of each type from zone to zone constituted one more line of evidence for dividing our stratigraphic sequence into phases. These percentage changes are shown graphically in Figures 64 and 69.

Such percentages come from counts of sherds, not whole vessels. They should in no way be considered a reflection of the "real" proportion which certain types of pottery constituted in typical households of each cultural phase. To give only one example of the difficulties encountered, we know of no way to tell sherds of unpainted ("plain") vessels apart from sherds from unpainted areas on otherwise decorated ("black-on-buff") vessels. Hence many sherds from the unpainted bases of Susiana Black-on-buff bowls were undoubtedly classified as Susiana Plain Buff. Still another problem is that large bowls may break into more sherds than small bowls. We are not extremely concerned with such problems because, presumably, any archeologist working in the Deh Luran plain in the future will encounter the same difficulty; any percentages he calculates from sherds alone will be skewed in the same way ours are, which means that his results should be roughly comparable with ours. Mehmeh phase levels at Tepe Musiyan and Tepe Sabz, six km. apart, showed identical percentages of pottery types when the sherds were sorted according to the same criteria. It is entirely possible that if we were able to sort the sherd sample from Tepe Jowi, we would find much the same picture there during the Mehmeh phase (=Susiana *c*). Thus the trends of pottery changes which our study revealed should be useful in comparing pottery assemblages from sites all over Khuzistan.

STONE BOWLS

Sample: 84 fragments

Temporal distribution: 72 out of 84 occur in the Ali Kosh, Mohammad Jaffar and Sabz phases; others appear sporadically throughout the sequence.

Introduction

Sherds of stone bowls were relatively rare at Ali Kosh and Tepe Sabz, but considerable variety was indicated both in type of bowl and in the quality of manufacture. The stone used ranged in hardness from gypsum to marble. Some of the vessels were highly polished, while others were left rough, with the marks of manufacture still evident on their surfaces.

The shapes of the stone bowls are similar to many of our earliest pottery vessels, and in some cases may have been used for the same purposes. The discovery that stone bowls preceded pottery in the Zagros Mountain area (though not, perhaps, by a very long time span) led immediately to the hypothesis that early pottery was an imitation of these stone vessels. Alternatively, the stone bowls in the late preceramic period of the Zagros might simply be imitations of pottery which had already been invented elsewhere; the evidence to decide this issue is not yet at hand. Is the issue even crucial? Some authors maintain that pottery, after all, has no characteristic form: "the history of pottery is. . .largely moulded by the histories of other materials" like wood, basketry, skins, and gourds (Scott, 1954:377).

Stone Vessel Forms

Bowls with simple, direct rim (Fig. 42 *l-r*).–These low, open bowls have bases which are flat or slightly rounded, joining the walls either in a smooth curve (Fig. 24*l*) or a carination (Fig. 42*t-v*). Rim diameters range normally from 14 to 24 cm., although one aberrant has a diameter of 45 cm. Typical heights are between 7 and 8 cm. These bowls, which occur throughout the sequence (but with most examples coming from the Ali Kosh phase) resemble specimens from Jarmo (Braidwood, Howe, *et al.,* 1960:Pl. 21:12).

Bowls with out-turned or "beaded" rim (Fig. 42*a-h*).–These open bowls, usually with a flat base, also find analogies at Jarmo (Braidwood, Howe, *et al.,* 1960:Pl. 21:14). We note that beaded rims, whether on stone bowls or pottery, seem to be largely confined to the Ali Kosh, Mohammad Jaffar, and Sabz phases. Rim diameters range between 14 and 24 cm., and heights from 7 to perhaps 14 cm. The vessel walls are ordinarily about 5 mm. thick at the midsection, but bases may be as thick as 1 cm.

Large shallow "tray" (Fig. 42*s*).–This aberrant specimen stood 4 cm. high and had a rim diameter of 16 cm.

Oval bowl (Fig. 42*w*).–This example, from the Mohammad Jaffar phase, is a crudely-made vessel with a slightly-incurving simple rim and a flat base which is oval in plan. It is 10 cm. long, 8 cm. wide, and stands 5.5 cm. high.

Miniature vessels (Fig. 42*x*).–Several sherds of highly polished cups or miniature bowls were found in the Bus Mordeh, Ali Kosh, and Mohammad Jaffar phase deposits. Rim diameters are about 4 cm., and heights about 3 to 4 cm.

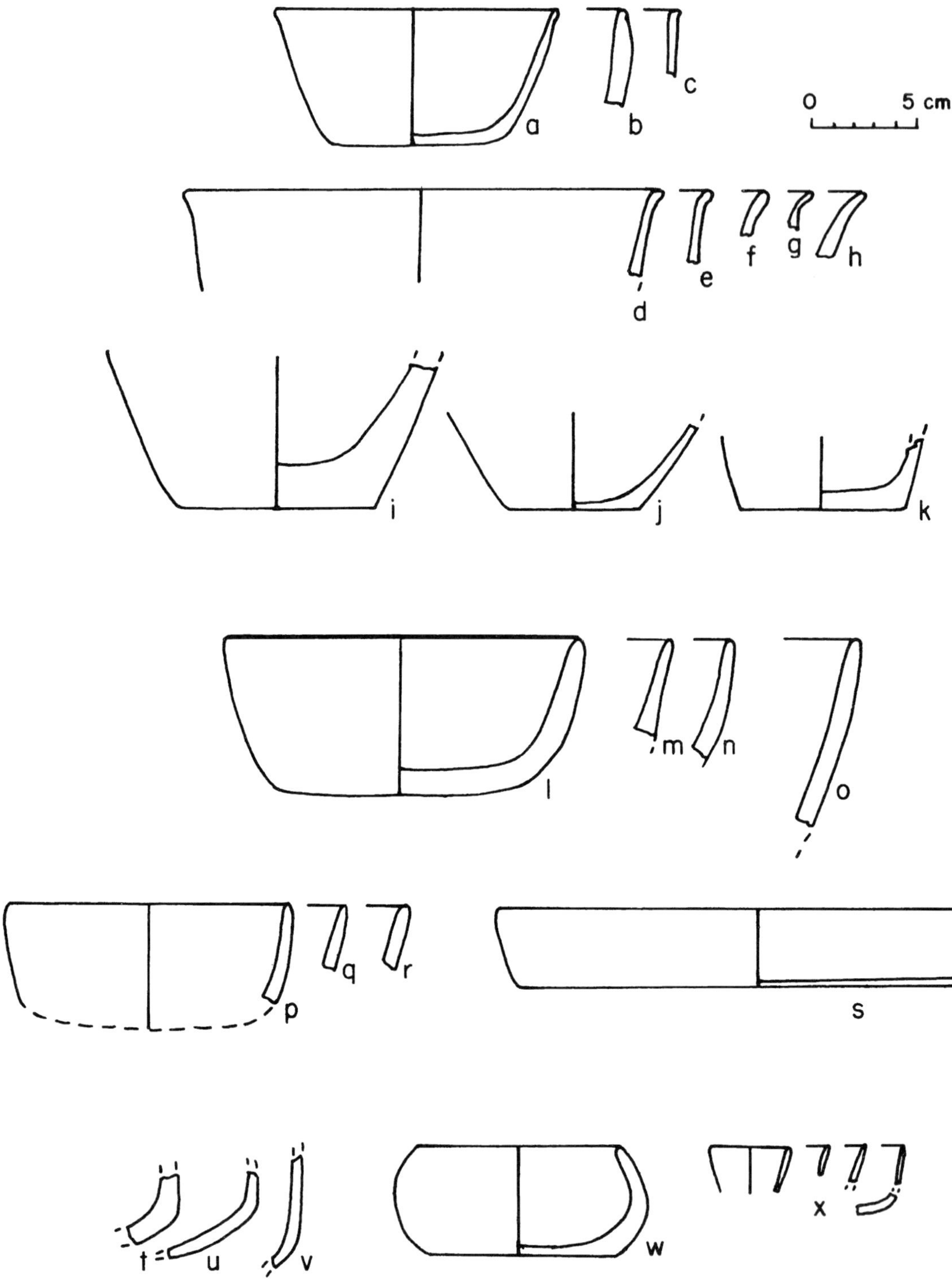

Fig. 42. Stone bowls from Deh Luran (reconstructed): *a-h,* bowls with "beaded" rim; *i-k,* flat bases; *l-r,* bowls with simple, direct rim; *s,* large shallow "tray"; *t-v,* carinated vessel wall sherds; *w,* oval bowl; *x,* miniature vessels (*a,i,k,l,n-q,s,u,* Ali Kosh phase; *b,d-h,j,r,t,w,x,* Mohammad Jaffar phase; *c,m,v,* Sabz phase).

Table 9

OCCURRENCE OF STONE BOWL FORMS AT ALI KOSH AND TEPE SABZ
(By Stratigraphic Zone)

Site and Zone	Bowls with Simple, Direct Rim	Bowls With Out-turned or Beaded Rim	Miscellaneous Flat Base Fragments	Large Shallow "Tray"	Oval Bowl	Miniature Vessels	Miscellaneous Fragments	Total
TS - A_1 ...	1	...	...	...	...	...	...	1
TS - A_2 ...	...	...	...	...	...	...	...	...
TS - A_3 ...	...	...	...	...	...	...	1	1
TS - B_1 ...	1	...	...	...	...	...	3	4
TS - B_2 ...	...	...	...	...	...	...	...	...
TS - B_3 ...	...	...	...	...	...	...	1	1
TS - C_1 ...	...	...	...	...	...	...	...	...
TS - C_2 ...	...	...	...	...	...	...	...	...
TS - C_3 ...	...	...	...	...	...	...	2	2
TS - D	2	2	...	...	...	...	6	10
AK - A_1 ..	2	3	...	...	...	1	8	14
AK - A_2 ..	...	3	...	...	1	2	8	14
AK - B_1 ..	3	4	1	...	...	1	6	15
AK - B_2 ..	6	5	2	1	...	...	5	19
AK - C_1 ..	...	...	...	...	...	...	1	1
AK - C_2 ..	1	...	...	...	...	1	...	2
Totals ..	16	17	3	1	1	5	41	84

Table 10

OCCURRENCE OF STONE BOWL FORMS AT ALI KOSH AND TEPE SABZ
(By Cultural Phase)

Phase	Bowls with Simple Direct Rim	Bowls With Out-turned or Beaded Rim	Miscellaneous Flat Base Fragments	Large Shallow "Tray"	Oval Bowl	Miniature Vessels	Miscellaneous Fragments	Total
Bayat	1	...	...	...	...	...	1	2
Mehmeh ...	1	...	...	...	...	...	4	5
Khazineh ..	...	...	...	...	...	...	2	2
Sabz	2	2	...	...	...	...	6	10
Mohammad Jaffar	2	6	...	...	1	3	16	28
Ali Kosh ...	9	9	3	1	...	1	11	34
Bus Mordeh ...	1	...	...	...	...	1	1	3
Totals ..	16	17	3	1	1	5	41	84

POTTERY

Typology

Students of Near Eastern archeology have used the word "type" in a multitude of ways, with little noticeable consistency from site to site. Each author has adapted the term to fit his particular problems and needs. For some, the "type" has been a painting style (e.g. "Eridu ware"); for others it has meant only a vessel shape (Oates, 1960:Pl. IV), or a combination of shape and painted design (Stronach, 1961).

As defined below, we use the term "pottery type" in yet another way. Our pottery analysis generally follows that of Ford (1962) and others. Each of our pottery types consists of vessels characterized by a particular paste, surface treatment, decoration, and range of shapes, which occurred during a specific period within a specific geographical area. We have given each of these types a two-part name—for example, "Susiana Black-on-buff"—one term of which is intended to be descriptive, and the other of which refers either to the region or period of its maximum distribution.

Each pottery type has a specifiable "life span," a fact which will be made clear by reference to the frequency polygon charts (Figs. 64 and 69). Let us take as a convenient example the type Khazineh Red, whose name indicates both its color and the fact that its maximum use occurred in the Khazineh phase. All Khazineh Red sherds show the same general paste, temper, and range of surface treatment, and virtually all come from a complex of four vessel shapes. Sherds of this type make up only a small percentage of the Mohammad Jaffar phase pottery (roughly 10 per cent), but they increase with time, reaching their statistical peak (about 35 per cent) in the Khazineh phase. Thereafter they decrease steadily, and by the Bayat phase have dwindled to only 2 per cent. In the Bayat phase a new type of red pottery—Bayat Red—rises to prominence. Every sherd of Bayat Red is clearly distinguishable from every sherd of Khazineh Red, not only because the paste and temper of each type differs strongly, but because each involves a different set of vessel shapes. Khazineh Red was made into hole-mouth jars, open bowls, hemispherical bowls, and necked jars; Bayat Red was made into large carinated bowls, hole-mouth jars, and necked jars of a somewhat different shape. Thus, although one might speak of a "red-ware tradition" in the Deh Luran plain in prehistoric time, the type of red ware involved is quite different depending on the period involved and there is no apparent continuity between them. Red sherds are present in all levels; but Khazineh Red and Bayat Red, as types, have distinct distributions in time.

As a further aid to understanding, brief definitions of the terms we will use in describing our pottery types are given below, but we do not intend to conduct an exhaustive discussion of pottery or pottery classification. Good papers on archeological pottery have already been published (e.g. Shepard, 1956; Colton, 1953). We wish only to define our terms because no standard terminology has yet been agreed upon by Near Eastern pottery analysts.

Terms Used in Analysis

Paste: The clay, along with any natural inclusions, from which the vessels were made. (Often referred to as "fabric" in Near East reports.)

Temper: Non-plastic particles added to the clay by the potter, usually in order to increase the porosity of the paste so that shrinking and warping during drying will be minimized.

Temper size: We follow Shepard (1956:118) in restricting "coarse temper" to particles over 0.5 mm. in diameter, and "fine temper" to particles under 0.25 mm. in diameter, with "medium temper" particles occupying the 0.25 to 0.5 mm. range.

Surface Treatment: The final touches applied to the outside of the vessel by the potter before firing.

Wet-smoothing: The wiping of the surface of the newly-made pot with wet hands or a piece of fabric before firing.

Burnishing: The rubbing of leather-hard pottery with a hard implement, such as stone, to close the surface pores of the clay.

Checking: The flaking-off of particles of the vessel surface.

Crazing: A network of fine cracks on the surface of a vessel,

Slip: A fine solution of well-cleaned clay applied to the surface of a vessel (See Colton, 1954:39-40; Shepard, 1956:191-93).

Wash: A very thin, watery slip.

Self-slip: If the paste is fine, wet-smoothing the surface will cause the finer particles to rise to the surface, and the result will be much the same as if a slip had been applied. The difficulty of telling the difference between a slip and self-slip has been discussed previously (See Braidwood and Braidwood, 1960:33-34).

Carbon streak: A dark line seen in the cross-section of sherds from a vessel which did not oxidize completely when fired. (Usually referred to as a "dark core" in American reports.)

Firing cloud: A discolored blotch on the vessel surface, caused by contact with burning fuel or another vessel during firing.

Smudging: A blackening of the vessel surface caused by carbon or tarry combustion products.

Hardness: We measured the hardness of the Deh Luran pottery by means of Moh's scale, which, although in common use, is at best a rough test. Moh's scale provides a set of ten minerals, ranked in hardness from 1 (talc) to 10 (diamond). For example, if a sherd can be scratched by fluorite (hardness of 4) but not by calcite (hardness of 3), and if the sherd itself will scratch calcite, its hardness must be between 3 and 4 (see Shepard, 1956:114 and Table 4).

Color: Color of the paste and surface of Deh Luran pottery was measured against 196 color chips provided by the Munsell Soil Color Charts, the standard most commonly in use throughout the United States and Europe (Munsell, 1961). The Munsell charts divide color into three attributes–hue, value, and chroma–so that any given color chip can be designated by a number (e.g., 5YR 6/4) and name (e.g., "reddish brown"). The charts have the advantage of standardizing color terms for pottery and facilitating comparisons.

Vessel Forms: Our pottery drawings are reconstructions of nearly all the shapes in which the prehistoric pottery of Deh Luran appeared. The illustrations should in turn make clear the definitions of vessel form used in the text of the report.

Decoration: "Reserve" decoration or "negative" painting–the application of dark paint in such quantity that the design appears in the light, unpainted areas, rather than vice versa. Such technique was common in the Sabz, Khazineh, and Mehmeh phases. "Ticked rim" painting–a row of small black triangles or similar marks running around the rim of a vessel (see Fig. 59*a*).

Techniques of Pottery Manufacture used in the Prehistoric Sequence

Chaff or straw and grit (principally sand) were the most commonly-used tempering materials in the Deh Luran sequence. During the Mohammad Jaffar phase, chaff was overwhelmingly the dominant temper. From the Sabz phase onward, the situation was somewhat different: although chaff continued as a common temper in the coarser cooking pots (principally Khazineh Red), both Susiana Plain Buff and Black-on-buff were largely grit-tempered (or untempered). By the time of the Bayat phase, nearly all the temper used was grit.

With some very fine clays, it is possible to make pots without the addition of nonplastic temper; discovery of such fine clay sources was apparently achieved by the Khazineh phase, to judge by sherd thin sections of some of the finer vessels of that period.

Burnishing was common on the chaff-tempered vessels of the Mohammad Jaffar and Sabz phases. Burnishing, by closing the pores of the vessel surface, helps to make vessels suitable for holding liquids, but there are other methods of achieving the same results: coating the inside of the pot with a waterproof substance is the chief alternative method. In Deh Luran, it appears that some vessels were coated with a thin layer of tar, but one cannot easily decide whether the asphalt is for waterproofing, or whether the vessels had simply been used for the boiling of asphalt.

Most of the vessels found in our sequence were hand-made–or so we infer from the uneveness of their sides, their assymmetry, their lack of complicated profiles, and the presence of rough marks of scraping. None of the pottery shows any sign of having been coiled, and in fact, at the present writing, the only area of the Near East where early coiled pottery has been reported is Anatolia (Mellaart, 1964*a*:82). A few badly shattered sherds from Tepe Sabz show separations which suggest that they may have been built up as successive laminae.

The technique of using an anvil inside the pot and a paddle outside to compact and shape the clay may have been applied at Deh Luran, although we have only circumstantial evidence. At least two artifacts found at Tepe Sabz–the "bent ceramic nails" and the "grooved mauls"–resemble pottery anvils used in other parts of the world (Scott, 1954:Fig. 228; Colton, 1953:Fig. 4). So far no universally acceptable theory for the function of the "bent nails" has appeared. None of ours showed signs of abrasion, so we doubt that they were mullers as some authors have suggested.

Flat bases are present on some of the oldest pottery in our sequence, as well as on most of the heavy vessels from all periods. Some of the larger flat-bottomed vessels in the Mohammed Jaffar and Sabz phases are oval in plan view, a trait they share with early vessels from parts of Kurdistan, for example Tepe Sarab (collections of the Museé Iran Bastan). The bases appear to have been made as flat slabs, to which nearly-vertical walls were added; often the junctures of wall and base are thick in outline, like a human heel. This would seem to have been one solution arrived at by the early potters when faced with the problem of joining the plastic sides with the base in such a way as to achieve a tight fit. Another solution is to make the joint into an oblique angle or carination which is somewhat thicker than the vessel walls, because of the overlapping of the two sections. Sherds from vessels which broke across the carination seem to show this type of layering at the joint, and some of them show that the potter pinched the clay at the joint to effect a tight bond.

The question of the use of the wheel in early periods is still a matter of some debate. Braidwood and Braidwood (1960:32) distinguished between hand-made and wheel-made according to the "absence or presence of horizontal striations and the degree of uniformity of wall thickness." In a further note they disclaim the ability to distinguish between wheels of various speeds (*Ibid*:232, footnote 9). It seems certain that intermediate stages, such as the use of a slow wheel or tournette (especially devices which turn the pot slowly around a non-fixed axis) will be very difficult to identify from the signs of the pots themselves. From the Mehmeh phase onward, however, our sequence includes vessels made with a degree of fineness, uniformity, and precision that is difficult to imagine unless some sort of wheel was in use.

Included in this category are fine bell-shaped bowls in Susiana Black-on-buff (Bowl type 11), whose walls are only a few millimeters thick, as well as vessels with sharply-everted and rolled rims; other examples are vessels with carinations sharply angled along a clearly horizontal plane around the entire body. It is only on certain of the less well-finished pieces that one sees the horizontal striations of which the Braidwoods speak, for on most fine vessels these striations have been removed by subsequent smoothing or slipping.

At opposite ends of our sequence we could line up pots that would perhaps convince all viewers that, on the one hand, Mohammad Jaffar phase vessels were all hand-made, while on the other hand, most Bayat phase vessels were wheel-made. In between, as our pottery descriptions will indicate, we believe we see evidence of both techniques. We are not prepared to announce the instant at which the effective wheel was put into use, and in any case we regard our evidence as suggestive rather than definite. One problem is that the break between hand-made and wheel-made pottery is not a temporal one: at one and the same time, the ancient Deh Luran villagers deemed it appropriate to make Khazineh Red and Mehmeh Red-on-red pottery by hand, while they made some Susiana Plain Buff and Susiana Black-on-buff vessels by wheel.

The paint used to decorate the surface of the pottery in our sequence also showed interesting changes through time. The oldest painted pottery type, Jaffar Painted, bore geometric designs made with somewhat fugitive red-ochre paint. Since all these vessels were fired at a rather low temperature, the ochre (which is an iron peroxide) remained red.

The prehistoric villagers of the Deh Luran plain continued to use iron oxide pigments for pottery decoration, but an interesting change had taken place by the time of the Sabz phase: vessels were now fired at sufficiently higher temperatures so that the paint turned black, tawny, or chocolate brown. The paint color seen on Susiana Black-on-buff is far from uniform, though the paint itself does not vary; laboratory analysis at Rice University in 1964 suggested that the pigment was an iron oxide whether the end result (after firing) was brown, black, reddish-black, or greenish-black. Other authors (e.g. Oates, 1960; Stronach, 1961) have noticed similar ranges of color in the early "painted buff wares" of the Mesopotamian and Khuzistan lowlands. Often they comment that the reddish or reddish-black varients can be smudged with a finger or partially washed off, and the same was true at Deh Luran throughout all phases.

All the early painted pottery of the Zagros Mountain area—whether from the Mohammad Jaffar phase or from Tepe Guran, Tepe Sarab, Jarmo, or Hajji Firuz —shares the common characteristic of fugitive reddish paint over a buff background. Painted pottery of the next phases—whether from Eridu, Hajji Muhammad, Jaffarabad, or Tepe Sabz—was a strikingly different appearance: black or chocolate paint over a cream or greenish-buff background. It is interesting to contemplate the possibility that this "striking difference" may be little more than the result of higher firing temperature for the iron oxide paint.

THE POTTERY SEQUENCE

The seven major pottery types we distinguished at Deh Luran appeared in the following order, from earliest to latest:

Jaffar Plain
Jaffar Painted
Khazineh Red
Susiana Plain Buff
Susiana Black-on-buff
Mehmeh Red-on-red
Bayat Red

Few of these types were restricted to a single phase of the sequence, but only two types of sherds appeared in all phases. Thus each phase was characterized by the percentages of each pottery type, rather than simple presence or absence (see Fig. 69).

1) Three types—Jaffar Plain, Jaffar Painted, and Khazineh Red— appeared together in the Mohammad Jaffar phase, the point at which pottery was introduced to our sequence.
2) In the Sabz phase, Jaffar Painted virtually disappeared, but Jaffar Plain and Khazineh Red continued. New types added in this phase were Susiana Plain Buff (abundant) and Susiana Black-on-buff (less common).
3) In the Khazineh phase, Khazineh Red reached its maximum frequency, while Jaffar Plain dwindled to a trace. The dominant plain type was Susiana Plain Buff. Susiana Black-on-buff, the major painted pottery type of the Susiana sequence, appeared to reach a peak in this phase, primarily because a greater proportion of the vessel surface was covered with intricate patterns than at any other time (and hence more painted sherds were recovered). Just at the end of the phase appeared significant traces of a new type, Mehmeh Red-on-red, which was to increase during the subsequent phase.
4) In the Mehmeh phase, Mehmeh Red-on-red achieved its maximum frequency. Khazineh Red continued, but was far less common than it had been in the previous phase. Susiana Plain Buff and Susiana Black-on-buff continued, but fewer sherds of Black-

on-buff were recognized because less of the vessel surface was covered with intricate patterns than during the Khazineh phase. Some of the finer vessels suggest the use of the wheel. Just at the end of the phase appeared sherds of a new type, Bayat Red.

5) In the Bayat phase, Bayat Red increased in frequency to become the dominant red pottery type. Painting on the Susiana Black-on-buff grew less careful and intricate, and covered still less of the vessel surface, the result being that "Plain Buff" sherds were overwhelmingly more common than any other type during the Bayat phase. Khazineh Red and Mehmeh Red-on-red were only a tiny percentage of the pottery at this point, having virtually run the course.

Just as significant as the pottery types themselves were vessel forms within them. Even when a pottery type had a relatively long life span—as, for example, Susiana Black-on-buff—certain of its vessel shapes appeared to be more rigidly restricted in time. Although Susiana Black-on-buff occurred throughout the Sabz, Khazineh, Mehmeh, and Bayat phases, black-on-buff pedestal bases with "windows" were virtually confined to the Sabz phase; open bowls with interior "Hajji Muhammad" designs appeared mainly in the Khazineh and early Mehmeh phases; and high-necked jars had their main distribution in the Bayat phase. Thus the vessel forms within each type made possible an even greater refinement of the sequence (see Fig. 64).

1) In the Mohammad Jaffar phase, the range of vessel shapes was rather limited, consisting mainly of deep bowls with slightly outturned rims. There were also flat-based bowls with thickened "heels" at the wall-base juncture, and (late in the phase) hole-mouth jars.
2) All three of the above shapes continued into the Sabz phase. They were joined by large oval basins, bowls with pedestal bases, and shallow hemispherical bowls with incurved rims.
3) In the Khazineh phase, most of the Mohammad Jaffar shapes faded out of the record, with the exception of the now-abundant hole-mouth jar. A proliferation of bowl forms took place: there were several varieties of small hemispherical bowls covered with complicated exterior decoration, and many varieties of large open bowls with complicated interior decoration. Pedestal bases disappeared. "Sauce-boats" and low-necked jars were numerous.
4) In the Mehmeh phase, hole-mouth jars and some of the highly-decorated small bowl forms were less numerous, and deep bowls with repetitive exterior motifs rose to prominence. Bell-shaped bowls of extreme thinness appeared, along with ledge-rim jars. Sauce-boats, and large open bowls continued.
5) In the Bayat phase, few of the small hemispherical bowls with exterior decoration remained, for they had been almost completely replaced by large coarse bowls with decoration limited to hanging loops or at most a few wavy vertical lines. High-necked jars and large carinated plain bowls were common. Gone were the open bowls with complex interior design, the sauce-boats, basins, and other early vessel shapes.

As can be readily seen from a close examination of the drawings of the characteristic vessels of each phase, certain design motifs are also restricted in time, and can be considered as characteristic of a phase as its percentages of pottery types or its vessel shapes. Moreover, certain combinations of vessel shape and painted design are of briefer duration than either shape or design taken alone.

The pottery sequence is thus based on differences in frequencies of each type, vessel form, and decoration. Together these comprise three independent lines of evidence that reinforce the chronological segments we distinguished by stratigraphic excavations. Perhaps more importantly, these data—when carefully plotted—constitute a set of horizon markers which allow us to fit surface collections, or sherds from brief soundings at other sites, into our relative chronology.

TYPE DESCRIPTIONS

Type: Jaffar Plain

Sample: 1620 sherds

Temporal distribution: Mohammad Jaffar, Sabz, and Khazineh phases, with eight stray sherds (presumably redeposited) in later levels.

Appearance: A hand-made, poorly-fired, friable undecorated ware. Like analogous plain wares from Jarmo, Sarab, and Tepe Guran, it is primarily chaff-tempered, with a dark unoxidized core and a buff surface blotched with reddish or grayish firing-clouds.

Paste: Porous, and pitted as a result of the burning-out of vegetal fibers.

Temper: During the Mohammad Jaffar phase, this type was almost wholly chaff-tempered, although small particles of grit could sometimes be found. The use of grit increased with time. Even Sabz phase examples, with a great deal of grit, are still loosely-compacted, with abundant holes from burned-out chaff. The grit varies from 0.3 to 0.7 mm. in diameter and is well-distributed throughout the paste.

Color: The paste is usually buff with a gray carbon streak, or gray throughout. The surface, where not covered by reddish or gray firing-clouds, varies from light brown (7.5 YR 6/4 on the Munsell scale) and light reddish brown (5 YR 6/4) to pink (5 YR 7/4), tan, or buff.

Surface treatment: All vessels were smoothed, and a few (especially in the Mohammad Jaffar phase) were burnished. A thin wash of the same clay as the paste may have been used, to judge from the cracking and peeling of some of the surfaces.

Decoration: None.

Vessel Forms

Small carinated bowls (Fig. 43*e-f*).—Restricted to the Mohammad Jaffar phase, these have a profile not unlike some of the Tepe Guran vessels (e.g. Mortensen, 1964:Fig. 16*d*). No measurable specimens were recovered.

Convex-walled bowls (Fig. 43*a-d*).—This was the most common vessel shape during the Mohammad Jaffar phase. These deep vessels have convex walls, slightly outturned rims, and rounded bases; close analogies can be seen in some of the undecorated buff bowls from Tepe Guran (Mortensen, 1964:16*h*). A few sherds of trough spouts were found in the Mohammad Jaffar phase (Fig. 43*o-r*). Rim diameters of these bowls range from 14 to 24 cm., with a mean of 17 cm. The vessels are between 6 and 15 cm. in height, with walls 6 to 9 mm. thick at the midsection.

Miniature vessels (Fig. 43*n*).—Tiny bowls with rim diameters of less than 6 cm. were a rare feature in the Mohammad Jaffar phase.

Deep bowls.—In both the Mohammad Jaffar and Sabz phases occurred a number of deep bowls which, because of their fragmentary nature, we were unable to reconstruct. The rims were simple (Fig. 43*g-i*) or sometimes slightly beveled interiorly (Fig. 43*j*), and some of the larger rim sherds made it appear that many of these vessels were oval in plan, like the deep basins of the Sabz phase (in Susiana Plain Buff). Bases were of several kinds: flat (Fig. 43*s-v*), rounded (Fig. 43*w-x*), or gently carinated (Fig. 43*k-m*). Unfortunately, it was impossible to match any of the rims with any of the bases directly, so their association is presumptive. Some of the bases also suggest oval bowls, and it is interesting to note in this regard that oval vessels occurred at Tepe Guran (Mortensen, 1964:114) and Tepe Sarab (collections in the Museé Iran Bastan).

It is difficult to estimate the rim diameter of these vessels, since few are truly round. Heights were generally greater than 12 to 14 cm., and the vessel walls at midsection were 6 to 10 mm. thick. Bases ranged from 9 to 30 cm., and some rim diameters may have been up to 40 cm. Some of the flat bases have a "heel" at the juncture between wall and base (Fig. 43*t*).

Hole-mouth jars.—Globular jars with a restricted orifice and a rounded base appeared in Jaffar Plain during the Sabz phase. Since they were identical in shape to Susiana Plain Buff examples, the reader

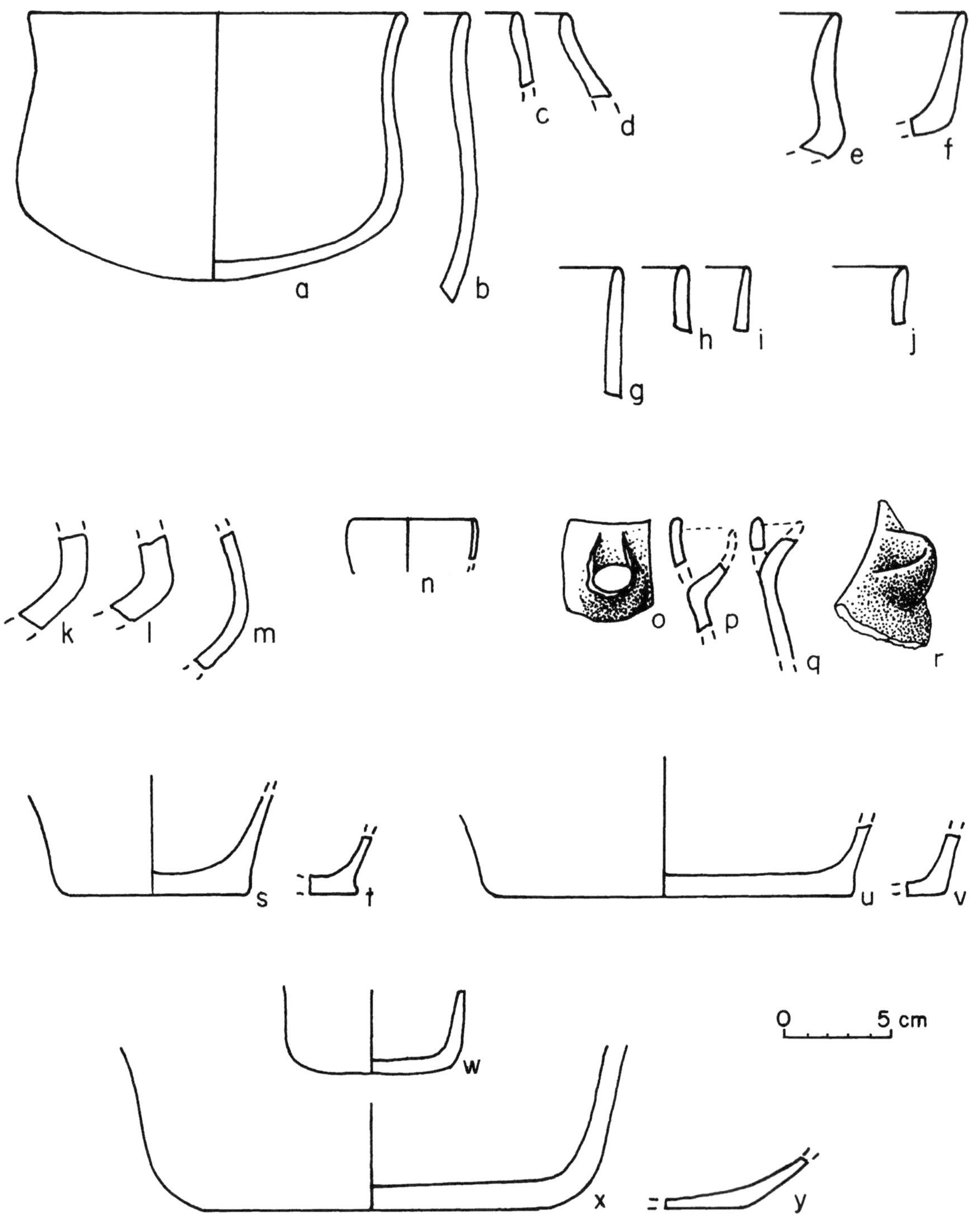

Fig. 43. Jaffar Plain pottery. Examples of vessel forms (reconstructed): *a-d,* convex-walled bowls; *e,f,* small carinated bowls; *g-i,* simple rims from deep bowls; *j,* beveled rim from deep bowl; *k-m,* carinated wall sherds; *n,* miniature vessel; *o,r,* rim sherds from convex-walled bowls, showing trough spouts; *p,q,* profiles of trough spouts; *s-v,* flat bases from deep bowls; *w,x,* rounded bases from deep bowls; *y,* flattened rounded base. Mohammad Jaffar and Sabz phase examples are shown.

is referred to Fig. 47*m* for an illustration. Some had "dimple" bases, recalling certain bowls from Tepe Guran, which had a rounded base "with a more or less concave bulb in the middle" (Mortensen, 1964:117). The rim diameters range between 15 and 33 cm.; we were unable to reconstruct a complete vertical profile, but judging from hole-mouth jars in some of the other pottery types (e.g. Khazineh Red, Susiana Plain Buff), the rim diameters were probably three-fourths the height of the vessel. Walls were 5 mm. thick at the midsection.

Type: Jaffar Painted

Sample: 844 sherds

Temporal distribution: Restricted to the Mohammad Jaffar phase. Eight stray sherds appeared in later levels at Tepe Sabz, but they are probably accidental, perhaps brought in in mud bricks? The absence of Jaffar Painted sherds in levels of the Sabz and early Khazineh phases indicates that the type actually went out of use after the Mohammad Jaffar phase.

Appearance: Jaffar Painted was merely produced by taking the common, convex-walled bowl of Jaffar Plain pottery and decorating it with geometric patterns in fugitive red-ochre paint. However, this combination of shape and design is so restricted in time and space when compared with Jaffar Plain that it seemed useful to regard it as a separate type.

Paste: Identical to the paste of Jaffar Plain during the Mohammad Jaffar phase.

Temper: Mainly chaff.

Color: Identical to Jaffar Plain.

Surface treatment: Identical to Jaffar Plain.

Decoration: Exterior designs in red ochre paint. A single sherd from Zone A_2 at Ali Kosh was painted with specular hematite. Lumps of red ochre occurred in the debris of the Mohammad Jaffar phase, and was the most widely-used pigment at Ali Kosh. For designs, see below.

Vessel Forms

Convex-walled bowls (Fig. 44).–Identical in shape to the convex-walled bowls of Jaffar Plain; only two bases were found which differed from the normal type (Fig. 44*r-s*). A few trough spouts occur, as on Jaffar Plain examples. These vessels are probably ancestral to the Sabz phase "Sabz Pots" (Bowl type 12*a* in Susiana Black-on-buff; see Fig. 50). The vessels range in height from 12 to 18 cm., and in rim diameter from 14 to 24 cm. Wall thickness at the midsection is 5 to 8 mm.

Decoration consists solely of geometric designs. Typically, the body of the vessel is treated as a unit; rows of zig-zags, chevrons, or open triangles encircle the bowl as a continuous horizontal band. Verticle panels are present, but rare. Usually the horizontal decorative band is delimited by a firm, thick line at top and bottom. The upper line runs just below the rim, while the lower line marks the juncture with the base, the latter never being painted.

By far the most common designs are horizontal zig-zags or chevrons (Fig. 44*a-c*). Occasional examples have the zig-zag rim band present at Tepe Guran and Sarab (Mortensen, 1964:Fig. 18), such as we illustrate in Figure 44*f*. Others have net-like patterns (Fig. 44*i*) like those on some of the later Guran pottery. Samarra-like "checkerboards" appear on other vessels (Fig. 44*d*).

"Tadpoles," or "blobbed lines," so common on the painted pottery at Sarab, Jarmo (Braidwood, Howe, *et al.,* 1960:Pl. 15: 12-17), and Guran (Mortensen, 1964:Fig. 17*a-e*) are totally absent at Ali Kosh. In spite of this, the surface color, paste, shape, and paint of the vessels is quite similar at all four sites. There are also similarities to the painted vessels of Hajji Firuz, an early site in the Solduz plain (Young, 1962:Fig. 6).

Precise draftsmanship is very rare at Ali Kosh, being confined to a single aberrant sherd which may not be of local manufacture (Fig. 44*m*). The design in that case is one which seems out of place in the Mohammad Jaffar phase, but not in later peri-

Table 11

OCCURRENCE OF VESSEL FORMS IN JAFFAR PLAIN POTTERY AT ALI KOSH AND TEPE SABZ
(By Stratigraphic Zone)

Site and Zone	Rims of Small Carinated Bowls	Rims and Bases of Convex-walled Bowls	Trough Spouts from Convex-walled bowls	Miniature Vessels	Rims of Deep Bowls (Some Oval)	Bases of Deep Bowls (Some Oval)	Rims of Hole-mouth Jars	Dimple Bases from Hole-mouth Jars	Unclassified Body Sherds	Totals
TS - A_1	...	...	...	...	...	...	...	...	...	...
TS - A_2	...	...	...	...	...	...	...	...	...	...
TS - A_3	...	...	...	...	...	...	...	...	4	4
TS - B_1	...	...	...	...	...	...	...	...	...	...
TS - B_2	...	...	...	...	...	...	...	...	1	1
TS - B_3	...	...	...	...	...	...	1	...	2	3
TS - C_1	...	...	...	...	...	3	...	...	21	24
TS - C_2	...	...	...	...	...	1	1	...	51	53
TS - C_3	...	...	...	...	...	...	1	...	13	14
TS - D	...	2	...	...	29	32	36	7	497	603
AK - A_1	...	38	7	4	16	21	...	...	610	696
AK - A_2	2	6	...	...	4	8	...	...	202	222
Totals........	2	46	7	4	49	65	39	7	1401	1620

Table 12

OCCURRENCE OF VESSEL FORMS IN JAFFAR PLAIN POTTERY AT ALI KOSH AND TEPE SABZ
(By Cultural Phase)

Phase	Rims of Small Carinated Bowls	Rims and Bases of Convex-walled Bowls	Trough Spouts from Convex-walled Bowls	Miniature Vessels	Rims of Deep Bowls (Some Oval)	Bases of Deep Bowls (Some Oval)	Rims of Hole-mouth Jars	Dimple Bases from Hole-mouth Jars	Unclassified Body Sherds	Totals
Bayat	...	...	...	...	...	...	...	...	4	4
Mehmeh	...	...	...	...	...	...	1	...	3	4
Khazineh..........	...	...	...	...	...	4	2	...	85	91
Sabz	...	2	...	...	29	32	36	7	497	603
Mohammad Jaffar....	2	44	7	4	20	29	...	...	812	918
Totals........	2	46	7	4	49	65	39	7	1401	1620

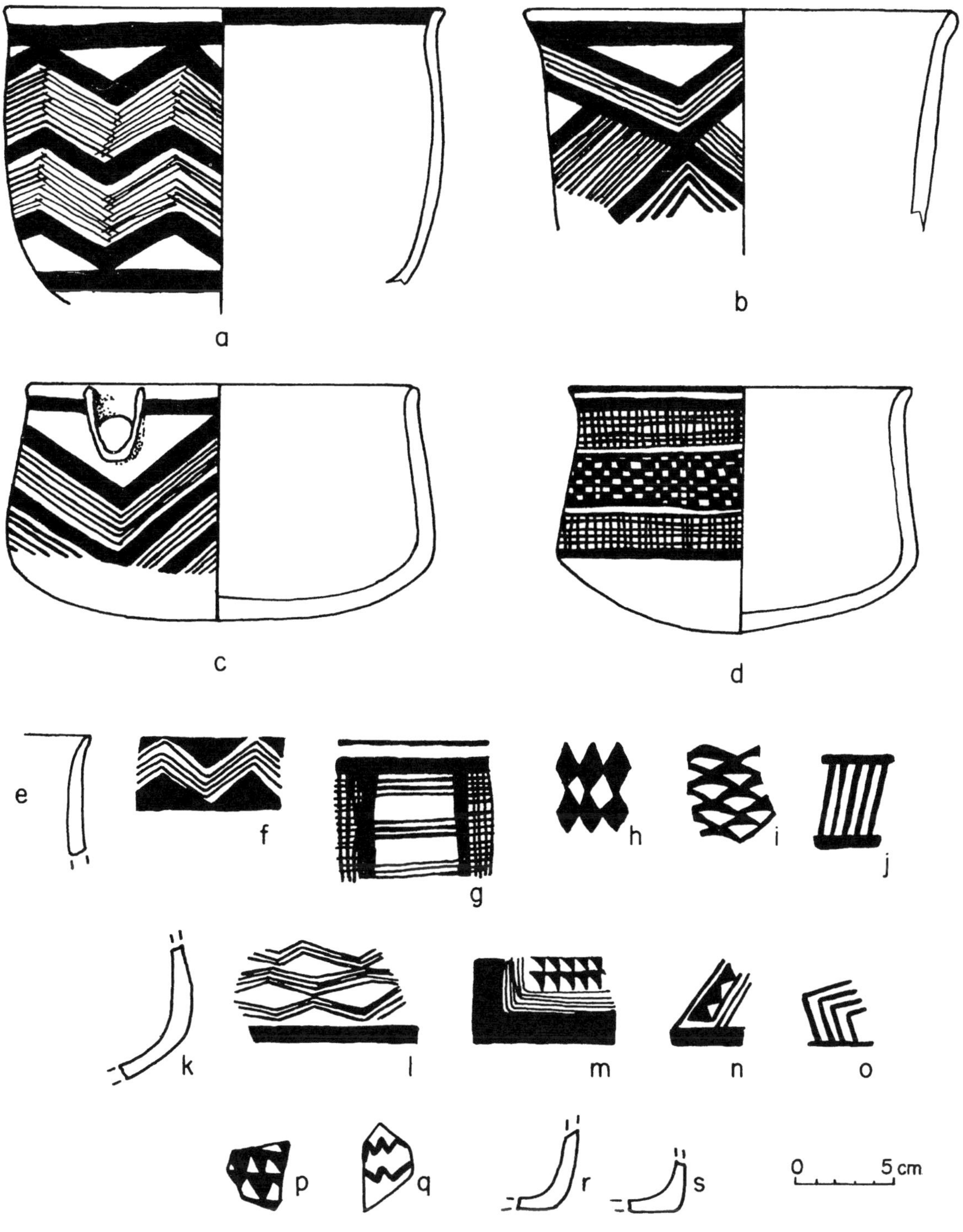

Fig. 44. Jaffar Painted Pottery. Examples of vessel forms (reconstructed) and full range of painted motifs: *a-d*, convex-walled bowls (*c* has fragmentary trough spout); *f-j*, designs found on exterior of rims of convex-walled bowls (*e*); *l-o*, designs found on exterior of lower vessel wall sherds (*k*); *p,q*, sherds with unique decoration; *r,s*, examples of abnormal bases. All examples from the Mohammad Jaffar phase.

ods; yet the paste, surface, and fugitive ochre decoration are similar to local pottery.

Table 13

OCCURRENCE OF VESSEL FORMS IN JAFFAR PAINTED POTTERY AT ALI KOSH AND TEPE SABZ
(By Stratigraphic Zone)

Site and Zone	Rims from Convex-walled Bowls	Bases from Convex-walled Bowls	Trough Spouts or Spout Fragments	Body Sherds	Total
TS - A_1	. . .	. . .	. . .	. . .	. . .
TS - A_2	. . .	. . .	. . .	. . .	. . .
TS - A_3	. . .	. . .	. . .	. . .	. . .
TS - B_1	. . .	. . .	. . .	2	2
TS - B_2	. . .	. . .	. . .	2	2
TS - B_3	. . .	. . .	. . .	. . .	. . .
TS - C_1	. . .	. . .	. . .	4	4
TS - C_2	. . .	. . .	. . .	. . .	. . .
TS - C_3	. . .	. . .	. . .	. . .	. . .
TS - D	. . .	. . .	. . .	. . .	. . .
AK - A_1 . . .	158	51	6	468	683
AK - A_2 . . .	31	11	4	107	153
Total . . .	189	62	10	583	844

Type: Khazineh Red

Sample: 2670 sherds

Temporal distribution: All phases, but reaching maximum frequency in the Khazineh phase.

Appearance: A relatively coarse red ware, hand-made, with a wide range of color variation due to inconsistent firing, or accidental refiring over cooking fires. Vessels are limited in range, and in some of the later phases are

Table 14

OCCURRENCE OF VESSEL FORMS IN JAFFAR PAINTED POTTERY AT ALI KOSH AND TEPE SABZ
(By Cultural Phase)

Phase	Rims from Convex-walled Bowls	Bases from Convex-walled Bowls	Trough Spouts or Spout Fragments	Body Sherds	Total
Bayat	. . .	. . .	. . .	. . .	. . .
Mehmeh . . .	. . .	. . .	. . .	4	4
Khazineh . . .	. . .	. . .	. . .	4	4
Sabz	. . .	. . .	. . .	. . .	. . .
Mohammad Jaffar	189	62	10	575	836
Total . . .	189	62	10	583	844

Table 15

OCCURRENCE OF DESIGNS ON CONVEX-WALLED BOWLS OF JAFFAR PAINTED POTTERY IN THE MOHAMMAD JAFFAR PHASE AT ALI KOSH
(By Stratigraphic Zone)

Site and Zone	Horizontal Zig-zags or Chevrons Encircling Body		Horizontal Bands of Cross-Hatch or Checkerboard		All Other Recognizable Designs		Total Sherds with Recognizable Design
	Rim Sherds	Body Sherds	Rim Sherds	Body Sherds	Rim Sherds	Body Sherds	
AK - A_1	42	148	5	16	7	3	221
AK - A_2	6	25	. . .	3	5	4	43
Total	48	173	5	19	12	7	264

irregularly shaped, even asymmetrical. Except in the Mohammad Jaffar phase, there is good evidence that most "cooking pots" were made of Khazineh Red.

Paste: May vary from medium to coarse on sherds from the same vessel. It is sandy and loosely-compacted.

Temper: Both grit and "chaff" tempering were used, with chaff comprising about 75 per cent in the Mohammad Jaffar phase and gradually giving way to grit tempering which, in the Bayat phase, accounts for about 75 per cent of the included material. The grit temper ranges in size from about 0.3 to 1.5 mm, with the mean size being about 0.6 mm. The temper is always abundant and fairly evenly-distributed throughout the paste. The hardness of this ware on Moh's scale ranges from 2 to 4, with the majority of the sherds being 2 to 3.

Color: Both the core and surface colors are highly variable; grey or purple firing clouds are common. Approximately half the sherds in all phases had a dark gray or black unoxidized core. This feature is relatively constant throughout the sequence. On the Munsell Scale, the surface color ranges from weak red to pink (10R 5/3 to 7.5YR 7/4) with the majority of the sherds falling within the light red range (2.5YR 6/6 to 5YR 6/6). Aside from the gray or black interior, the typical core color is reddish brown (5YR 6/4 or 6/6).

Surface treatment: Most of the Khazineh Red vessels in the Mohammad Jaffar phase were well-burnished, although some were simply wet-smoothed. By the Khazineh phase the proportions were reversed, and the majority of the vessels were only smoothed. During the Bayat phase, only rare vessels showed signs of burnishing. Both self-slip and applied slip seem to have been used throughout the sequence. The surfaces of slipped vessels may show signs of peeling or popping and the surface may be pitted where pieces of vegetal material burned out.

Decoration: Virtually none. A single sherd from the Khazineh phase had two small appliqué blobs (see "Hole-mouth jars," below).

Vessel Forms

Hemispherical bowls with beaded rims (Fig. 45*e-g*).—Rims on these vessels, which are restricted to the Mohammad Jaffar phase, resemble the beaded rims of some stone bowls. Rim diameters are 24 to 28 cm, and heights about 9 to 12 cm.

Hemispherical bowls with incurved rims (Fig. 45*a-d*).—Shallow bowls with a vertical to slightly-incurving simple rim; the rim diameters range from 11 to 34 cm., and we estimate the heights at about 6 to 12 cm. These occur sporadically throughout the sequence.

Open bowl rims (Fig. 45*n,o*).—The dominant bowl type in Khazineh Red after the end of the Mohammad Jaffar phase was a vessel with a simple or slightly-everted rim, and walls which ranged from slightly outslanting to greatly outslanting (45 degrees). Most sherds were too small to permit accurate measurement, but we estimate that the vessels were about the same size as Bowl Types 14 to 18 in Susiana Black-on-buff; that is, with a rim diameter of 16 to 36 cm. Some of the carinated wall/base junctures (below) found throughout the sequence may go with these rims, but some at least had flat bases.

Carinated bowls (Fig. 45*h-j*).—Examples of carinated wall/base junctures occurred throughout the sequence, but only in the Mohammad Jaffar phase did we find small, highly-burnished carinated bowls resembling those from Tepe Guran (Mortensen, 1964:Fig. 16*k*). Rim diameters of these were about 15 to 18 cm.

Flat-based bowls (Fig. 45*k-m*).—Fragments of flat bases occurred throughout the sequence. A single measurable flat-based bowl with concave sides came from the Mohammad Jaffar phase; its rim diameter was 10 cm. (Fig. 45*k*).

Hole-mouth jars (Fig. 46).—Hole-mouth jars with round, sometimes dimpled bases, and simple rims constituted the most common vessel shape in Khazineh Red. The mouths are asymmetrical, reflecting their crude hand-made construction. One small

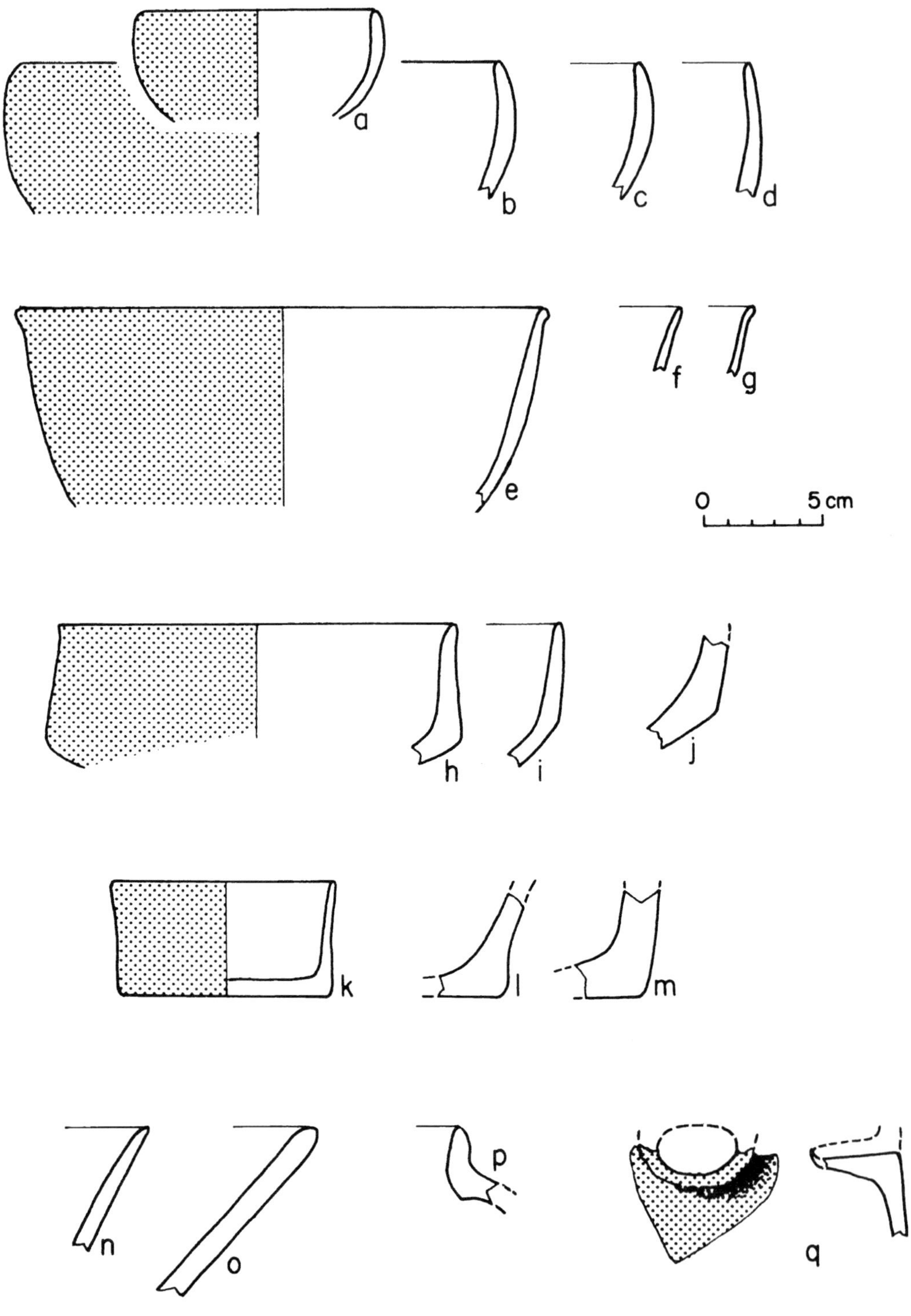

Fig. 45. Khazineh Red pottery. Examples of vessel forms (reconstructed): *a-d,* hemispherical bowls with incurved rims; *e-g,* hemispherical bowls with beaded rim; *h-j,* carinated bowls; *k-m,* flat-based bowls; *n,o,* open bowl rims; *p,* necked jar sherd; *q,* fragmentary trough spout.

(atypically coarse) vessel from the Bayat phase had a carinated side. The rims average about 17 cm. in diameter, and the heights about 25 cm. The smallest example, from the Bayat phase, had a rim diameter of 5 cm. and was 8 cm. high. Based on a small sample, we judge the typical rim diameter to be roughly three-fourths of the height. One rim sherd from the Khazineh phase had two small appliqué blobs arranged vertically below the rim. No other sherds showed any decoration. Hole-mouth jars began late in the Mohammad Jaffar phase and continued throughout the sequence, but dimple bases (Fig. 46*b*) are not known with certainty before the Khazineh phase. Many hole-mouth jars in Khazineh Red are crusted with carbon from cooking, or with asphalt from tar-boiling.

Trough spout (Fig. 45*q*).–A single example appeared in Khazineh phase levels. It resembles similar spouts in Mehmeh Red-on-red.

Necked Jars (Fig. 45*p*).–Only three examples, from the Mehmeh and Bayat phases, were recovered. A single measurable example is a neck only 1.5 cm. high; size of the vessel is unknown. These may simply be

Table 16

OCCURRENCE OF VESSEL FORMS IN KHAZINEH RED POTTERY AT ALI KOSH, TEPE SABZ, AND TEPE MUSIYAN "E"
(By Stratigraphic Zone)

Site and Zone	Rims from Hemispherical Bowls with Beaded Rim	Rims from Hemispherical Bowls with Incurved Rim	Open Bowl Rims	Carinated Wall/Base Junctures	Flat Bases	Hole-mouth Jar Rims	Dimple Bases from Hole-mouth Jars	Trough Spouts	Rims from Necked Jars	Unclassified Body Sherds	Total
TS - A_1	...	1	5	...	3	3	...	...	...	75	87
TS - A_2	...	...	1	1	...	2	1	...	...	103	108
TS - A_3	...	...	2	1	6	7	...	...	1	140	157
TS - B_1	...	3	7	2	1	6	3	...	2	196	220
MUS "E"..........	...	...	1	2	...	...	...	...	...	56	59
TS - B_2	...	2	2	3	...	2	1	...	...	166	176
TS - B_3	...	3	8	6	1	4	2	...	...	137	161
TS - C_1	...	...	18	11	12	61	12	1	...	690	805
TS - C_2	...	3	13	7	4	22	3	...	...	411	463
TS - C_3	...	1	1	3	1	5	1	...	...	110	122
TS - D	...	...	4	4	1	8	...	...	...	115	132
AK - A_1	4	11	6	1	1	12	...	...	...	100	135
AK - A_2	3	2	4	1	...	...	...	...	...	35	45
Total	7	26	72	42	30	132	23	1	3	2334	2670

Table 17

OCCURRENCE OF VESSEL FORMS IN KHAZINEH RED POTTERY AT ALI KOSH, TEPE SABZ, AND TEPE MUSIYAN "E"
(By Cultural Phase)

Phase	Rims from Hemispherical Bowls with Beaded Rim	Rims from Hemispherical Bowls with Incurved Rim	Open Bowl Rims	Carinated Wall/Base Junctures	Flat Bases	Hole-mouth Jar Rims	Dimple Bases from Hole-mouth Jars	Trough Spouts	Rims from Necked Jars	Unclassified Body Sherds	Total
Bayat	...	1	8	2	9	12	1	...	1	318	352
Mehmeh	...	8	18	13	2	12	6	...	2	555	616
Khazineh	...	4	32	21	17	88	16	1	...	1211	1390
Sabz	...	...	4	4	1	8	...	...	...	115	132
Mohammad Jaffar	7	13	10	2	1	12	...	...	...	135	180
Total	7	26	72	42	30	132	23	1	3	2334	2670

derived from hole-mouth jars (see below) in which the rim was turned up in an aberrant manner.

Type: Susiana Plain Buff

Sample: 17,920 sherds

Temporal distribution: Sabz through Bayat phases, and later.

Appearance: A hard, usually well-fired and sand-tempered pottery with a buff to greenish-buff color, which was one of the dominant ceramic types throughout the whole of the late prehistoric sequence. Together with its painted counterpart, Susiana Black-on-buff, this type makes up the classic "buff-ware complex" which served as the basis for McCown's "Buff Ware Culture" in southwest Iran (McCown, 1957). Susiana Plain Buff, as its name implies, is the "ceramique claire" which was a dominant feature of the "Susiana sequence" worked out at the mounds of Jaffarabad, Bandibal, Jowi, and Bouhallan (Le Breton, 1947, 1957). In many aspects it is nearly indistinguishable from the unpainted buff wares at contemporary sites in southern Mesopotamia, for example Eridu, Hajji Muhammad, al Ubaid, and Ras al Amiya (Lines, 1953; Stronach, 1961). Its interregional relationships are probably extremely wide, but due to a lack of esthetic appeal, it has not been as fully studied as has the painted buff ware.

Paste: Compact and, in the later phases of our sequence, made up of very well-cleaned clay. It is fired buff throughout, without gray carbon streaks. Hardness on Moh's scale ranges between 2 and 5, with most sherds falling between 2 and 4.

Temper: Changes through time can be detected. During the Sabz phase, nearly all sherds have a sandy texture caused by the inclusion of coarse grit or sand. Eroded sherds of this phase have surfaces liberally dotted with sand grains averaging 0.5 mm. in diameter. Through time, fine grit gradually replaces coarse grit, and during the Mehmeh and Bayat phases sandy-textured sherds are largely confined to large basins and deep bowls. In all sand-tempered sherds, the temper is well distributed throughout the paste.

In the Khazineh phase appear our first vessels (deep, bell-shaped bowls) made of well-cleaned clay which does not seem to contain any visible tempering material. Such fine vessels increase with time, but do not become dominant until the Bayat phase.

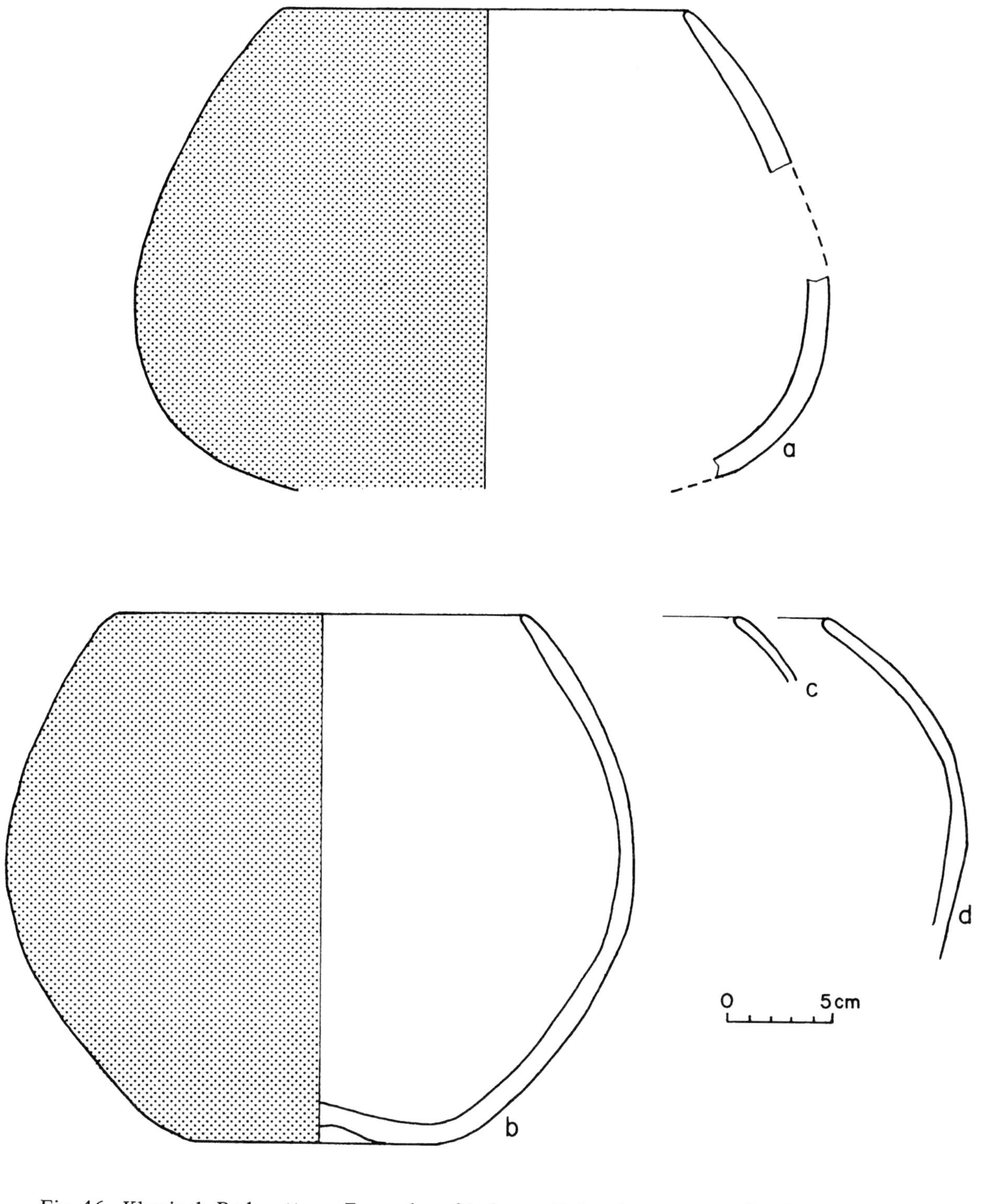

Fig. 46. Khazineh Red pottery. Examples of hole-mouth jars (reconstructed); *b* has dimpled base.

In the Bayat phase occur some rare and poorly-fired jars tempered with chaff as well as fine grit. By this time, in other words, Susiana Plain Buff had grown from a largely coarse-sand-tempered ware into a rather complex ceramic with vessels featuring coarse sand, fine sand, fine sand and chaff, or temperless clay. Attempts to divide Susiana Buff into subtypes along these lines disclosed a close correlation between vessel form and temper. The prehistoric potter evidently deemed it appropriate to make large basins with coarse temper, reserving his untempered finely-cleaned clay for delicate bell-shaped bowls. Rather than subdividing this type, therefore, we have regarded it as a single developing tradition which underwent numerous experiments and modifications as time went on.

Color: The surface color ranges from pale greenish-buff (the majority) to a pale green, pale yellow, and pale orange. The green, yellow, and orange sherds are confined to the well-fired, very finely-made bell-shaped bowls. On the Munsell scale, the range is from 2.5Y 4/2 to 10YR 8/6. All of the vessels are thoroughly fired, and the cores are essentially the same color as the exterior.

Surface treatment: All of the vessels have smoothed surfaces, but there is no evidence that they were slipped, polished, or burnished.

Decoration: Virtually none. A single vessel from the Khazineh phase had plastic "rope" decoration (Fig. 48*aa*). In the section that follows, we will describe the forms of all vessels in "buff ware" which had no painting. However, as noted in the introduction to this chapter, our counts of "unclassified body sherds with no paint" almost certainly include small, plain fragments from unpainted areas on Susiana Black-on-buff vessels.

Vessel Forms

Introduction.—The relationship between vessel forms in Susiana Plain Buff and Susiana Black-on-buff is rather interesting. Some forms, like hole-mouth jars with dimple bases, appeared only in Plain Buff. Most of the other forms appeared in both plain and painted variants. For the most part, however, the Plain Buff variants did not lend themselves well to typological "splitting," and hence were less useful as chronological markers than their Black-on-buff counterparts.

For example, let us examine the history of the large carinated bowl with slightly outleaning sides and a rim diameter of 30 to 40 cm. This kind of bowl was made throughout the Khazineh, Mehmeh, and Bayat phases. In the Khazineh phase, it was nearly always painted, with the result that only 3 rim sherds and 5 carinated base sherds of this shape appeared in our "Plain Buff" category. The number of unpainted bowls increased in the subsequent phases of the sequence, but all we are able to do is call them "bowls with outleaned walls, some carinated," without a division into finer categories. On the other hand, the painted versions of this bowl can be broken into a number of variants with chronological significance; most of these variants have been assigned numbers by Stronach (1961; and see our discussion of numbered Bowl Types in Susiana Black-on-buff). Exterior painting of such bowls, with a certain set of designs, had one distribution in time; interior painting of the same vessel form, with a different set of designs, had another temporal distribution.

Susiana Plain Buff is, therefore, not so useful chronologically as Black-on-buff. Its vessel form categories were broader, the shapes harder to reconstruct in some cases, and the mass of undecorated body sherds useful only as an indication of how much of the vessel surface was unpainted (vs. painted) for a given phase.

What we have done in our shape analysis is to distinguish three categories of vessel forms: (1) those which are useful for chronological purposes, (2) those which are less useful for chronological purposes, and (3) rare forms. It should be noted that those forms which we found less useful for chronology are not simply shapes which were made throughout the sequence; they are groups of closely-related shapes, each probably with temporal significance, but which we found difficult or impossible to separate on the basis of sherds alone.

Chronologically Useful Forms

Unpainted version of the "Sabz Pot" (Fig. 47*a*).—"Sabz Pots" in Susiana Black-on-buff are described on p. 136. The unpainted version is a small, deep bowl with a gently rounded base and a rim which is slightly outflaring above the midsection. The only measureable, reasonably-complete specimen stood 6 cm. high and had a rim diameter of 9 cm., with a wall thickness of 9 mm. at the midsection. Its period of maximum frequency was the Sabz phase, with a few sherds occurring also in Khazineh phase levels—the identical distribution of its painted counterpart.

A single rim sherd of this type of bowl appeared in zone A_1 at Ali Kosh, in the Mohammad Jaffar phase. It was one of six sherds of Susiana Plain Buff pottery which were found in that zone. Unless these small buff-ware sherds were intrusive (a possibility, given the nearness of zone A_1 to the surface, and the presence of rodent burrows), this may mean that the first production of Susiana Plain Buff took place late in the Mohammad Jaffar phase, and that the unpainted version of the "Sabz Pot" was one of the first shapes to appear in that ware. Certainly these small, deep bowls are similar enough to the convex-walled bowls in Jaffar Plain to represent a derivation from them. This question cannot be satisfactorily answered until we have excavated a site with Sabz phase levels clearly overlying materials of the Mohammad Jaffar phase.

Large basins, some oval (Fig. 47*b-k*).—These large, deep, relatively crude vessels were extremely troublesome subjects for analysis, because of their usually fragmentary condition and the difficulty of matching rim sherds with base sherds. Basins were made during all periods of the sequence at Tepe Sabz. Their sides varied from absolutely vertical to somewhat outleaned, with all angles of inclination in between. In most cases, given the extreme irregularity of the rim, it was difficult to determine the precise inclination; therefore, rather than presenting an impressionistic division into earlier and later variants, we have simply counted all the rim sherds of basins together (Tables 18, 19). It is obvious that this amounts to "lumping" several potentially distinct types of basins, but we did not feel secure enough to divide them on the basis of our sherd sample.

Study of the base sherds was only slightly less frustrating. Most showed walls which outleaned to at least a certain degree, and we simply counted all of these together. There was, however, one variant which seemed to be restricted to the Sabz phase (with the exception of two enigmatic fragments from Tepe Musiyan "E"). This was a flat base with an absolutely vertical wall rising from it, the two being joined in a smooth curve rather than a "kink" or carination (see Fig. 47*b*). Twenty-nine out of thirty-one examples came from the Sabz phase, and constituted the only really useful attribute (chronologically speaking) which we were able to distinguish in our sample of basin sherds.

Because many of the basins (including, perhaps, nearly all the Sabz phase examples) were oval rather than round, it is difficult to estimate rim diameters. Rim sherds from the narrow ends of the oval have curvatures indicating a diameter of 25 to 30 cm. Rim sherds from the broad sides of the oval have almost no curvature at all, or indicate an impossibly large vessel (over 50 cm.). Probably these vessels, like their Black-on-buff counterparts, were about 25 cm. wide and 30 to 40 cm. long.

Heights are easier to measure, because of the presence of rim-to-base sections. These are usually in the neighborhood of 13 to 20 cm. high, with a few taller or

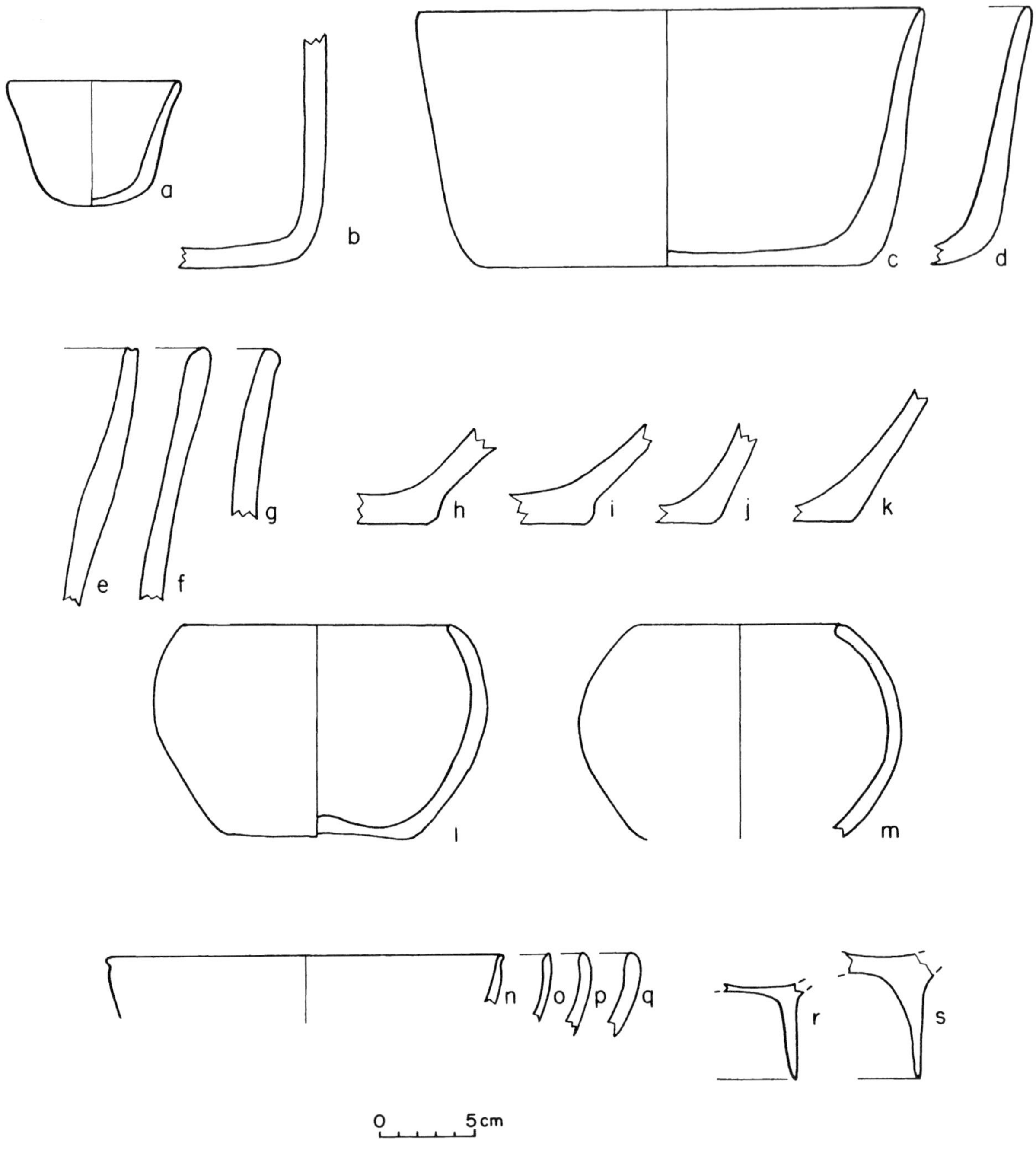

Fig. 47. Susiana Plain Buff pottery. Examples of vessel forms in common usage during the Sabz phase (reconstructed): *a,* unpainted version of "Sabz pot;" *b,* curved wall/base juncture from large basin; *c,d,* typical large basins; *e-g,* rims from large basins; *h-k,* angled wall/base junctures from large basins; *l,m,* hole-mouth jars (*l* has dimpled base); *n-q,* rims of hemispherical bowls; *r,s,* unpainted pedestal bases.

shorter examples. Wall thickness at the midsection is about 10 mm., though aberrant specimens may be as thick as 15 mm.

Oval basins are an early vessel form, showing linkages with the Mohammad Jaffar phase, and the oval bowls of Tepe Guran (Mortensen, 1964:114) and Tepe Sarab (collections in the Museé Iran Bastan). They occurred in "Susiana *a*" levels at Tepe Jaffarabad (Le Breton, 1947:Fig. 8:1).

Hole-mouth jars, some with dimple bases (Fig. 47*l,m*).—These are similar in shape and virtually identical in temporal distribution to the hole-mouth jars made in Jaffar Plain pottery. Twenty-nine out of thirty-five rim sherds appeared in the Sabz phase, with a few (possibly redeposited) fragments in later levels. The jars are crudely-made, asymmetrical, and globular, with bases which may be gently rounded or have a "concave bulb" or dimple. Restorable examples had rim diameters of 12 to 20 cm. and heights of 9.5 to 11 cm. The wall thickness at midsection was 6 to 9 mm. Frequently, the insides of these jars were coated with a thin wash of asphalt.

Hemispherical bowls, some with beaded rims (Fig. 47*n-q*).—The shape of these shallow vessels is reminiscent of Bowl Types 1 to 6 in Susiana Black-on-buff (see below). The walls (and presumably the bases) are gently curved, and the rims vertical, very slightly incurved, or very slightly outleaned. A few beaded rims suggest the red-burnished vessels and stone bowls of the preceding Mohammad Jaffar phase. Rim diameters vary between 14 and 20 cm. and heights probably were in the neighborhood of 4 to 10 cm.: no reconstructable examples were found. Wall thickness at the midsection was between 6 and 9 mm. Fifteen of twenty rim sherds appeared in the Sabz and Khazineh phases, a distribution which further indicates relationships with Bowl Types 1 through 6 in Susiana Black-on-buff.

Unpainted pedestal bases (Fig. 47*r,s*).—Since virtually all of these came from Sabz phase levels, they are probably related to the painted pedestal bases in Susiana Black-on-buff from the same phase. However, it was not possible to determine whether or not they were perforated by small "windows" as were the Black-on-buff pedestals (see p. 138). The only measurable examples stood about 5 cm. high and had a diameter of about 6 cm.

No reconstruction of the bowls (or basins?) supported by these pedestals was possible, but indications are that they were flat-based.

Pedestals are widespread in this period of Near Eastern prehistory (see discussion under Susiana Black-on-buff). Le Breton (1957:Fig. 5) illustrates pedestalled vessels from Hassuna, Samarrah, and Jaffarabad, and it would not be hard to find examples as far away as the Iranian plateau (for example, in Hissar IA; see Schmidt, 1937:Fig. 33).

Unpainted version of early ring base.—This appears to be merely a plain version of the early ring bases in Susiana Black-on-buff (see Fig. 52*h*). Probably related to the pedestals mentioned above, and found only in the Sabz phase, it was attached to some kind of carbinated cup or bowl (see Le Breton, 1957:Figs. 4 and 5 for relevant comparative material).

Sauce boat.—The "tail" portion of a sauce boat, identical to those in Susiana Black-on-buff, was found in the Sabz phase (see p. 141 for description of vessel form in Black-on-buff). Because of the concentration of Black-on-buff sauce boats in the Sabz and Khazineh phases, we have regarded this as a chronologically useful form in spite of the fact that only one Plain Buff specimen was found.

Bowls with outleaned walls, some carinated (Fig. 48*a-f*).—Large bowls with outleaned walls and simple, beveled, flat-topped, or concave rims were made during the Khazineh, Mehmeh, and Bayat phases. At least some of these bowls had carinated bases, but it was rarely possible to match up rim and base sherds. Rim diameters ranged from 25 to 40 cm., with most falling in the vicinity of 35 cm. A few reconstructed vessels have heights of 6 to 15 cm. Wall thickness at the midsection falls between 5 and 15 mm.

Rim sherds of these bowls may at times be hard to distinguish from those of basins with outleaned walls, but generally they lean outward at a greater angle, and are thinner and more finely made.

Large carinated bowls are common in ceramic periods *b* and *c* in Susiana proper (Le Breton, 1957:Fig. 4), at Ras al Amiya (Stronach, 1961:Pl. LII), and probably most lowland sites of this phase; although plain varieties are not as frequently illustrated as painted ones, it is clear that they are present.

Bell-shaped bowls (Fig. 48*g-h*).—This is the unpainted version of "Bowl Type 11" in Susiana Black-on-buff. It was by far the most common shape in Plain Buff during the Mehmeh and Bayat phases, with 663 rim sherds found in the Bayat phase alone. The bowls are thin, well-made (probably by wheel), and symmetrical, with no tempering material apparent in the clay even when examined with a binocular microscope.

Most bases are round, though a few have a slight carination. The walls lean or curve outward gently as they rise, ending in a simple rim which narrows almost to a knife-edge in some cases; a few rims are beaded. Rim diameters range from 12 to 20 cm. and heights from 8 to 13 cm. The walls are exceptionally thin, averaging 5 mm. at the midsection and often no more than 1 mm. at the rim.

Fine, unpainted bell-shaped bowls characterized by Susiana *d* ceramic complex (Le Breton, 1957:Fig. 7), which we regard as related to the Bayat phase. This may have been their point of maximum frequency, for they are much less common in the Mehmeh phase, and Stronach (1961:112) speaks of unpainted examples as being relatively rare at Ras al Amiya. In the Deh Luran plain, they began in the Khazineh phase and increased with time, their most explosive increase coming in the Bayat phase. This explosive increase is only partially the result of an increase in manufacture of bowls of this shape; it is also the result of a decrease in painting on such bowls.

Ledge-rim jars (Fig. 48*i,j*).—Globular jars with low necks, and a small projecting ledge inside the neck near its juncture with the body of the vessel; presumably, this ledge supported a lid. Like their Black-on-buff counterparts, these occur in the Mehmeh and Bayat phases.

The necks stand 1 to 2 cm. high, and the ledges project inward between 4 and 13 mm. Rim diameters are greater than 7 cm. Because of the fragmentary nature of our sample, we could not determine the diameter of the body of the vessel.

Unpainted version of later ring base (Fig. 48*k,l*).—Like their Black-on-buff counterparts, these bases were attached to large, round vessels which may have been either bowls or globular jars. No complete specimens were found. The rings stand 5 to 10 mm. high and have a diameter of 10 to 12 cm. All appeared in the Bayat phase. For comparable examples from Susiana *d* (both plain and painted), see Le Breton, 1957:Fig. 7.

Wide, shallow bowls (Fig. 48*m-o*).—Only three rim sherds of these low, saucerlike vessels were found, all in Bayat phase levels. The bases were presumably round; rims were simple or slightly beaded. Rim diameters are 24 to 34 cm. and heights about 4 to 6 cm. Wall thickness reached 1 cm. near the base. Similar unpainted buff ware vessels were found at Ras al Amiya (Stronach, 1961:Pl. LII:27).

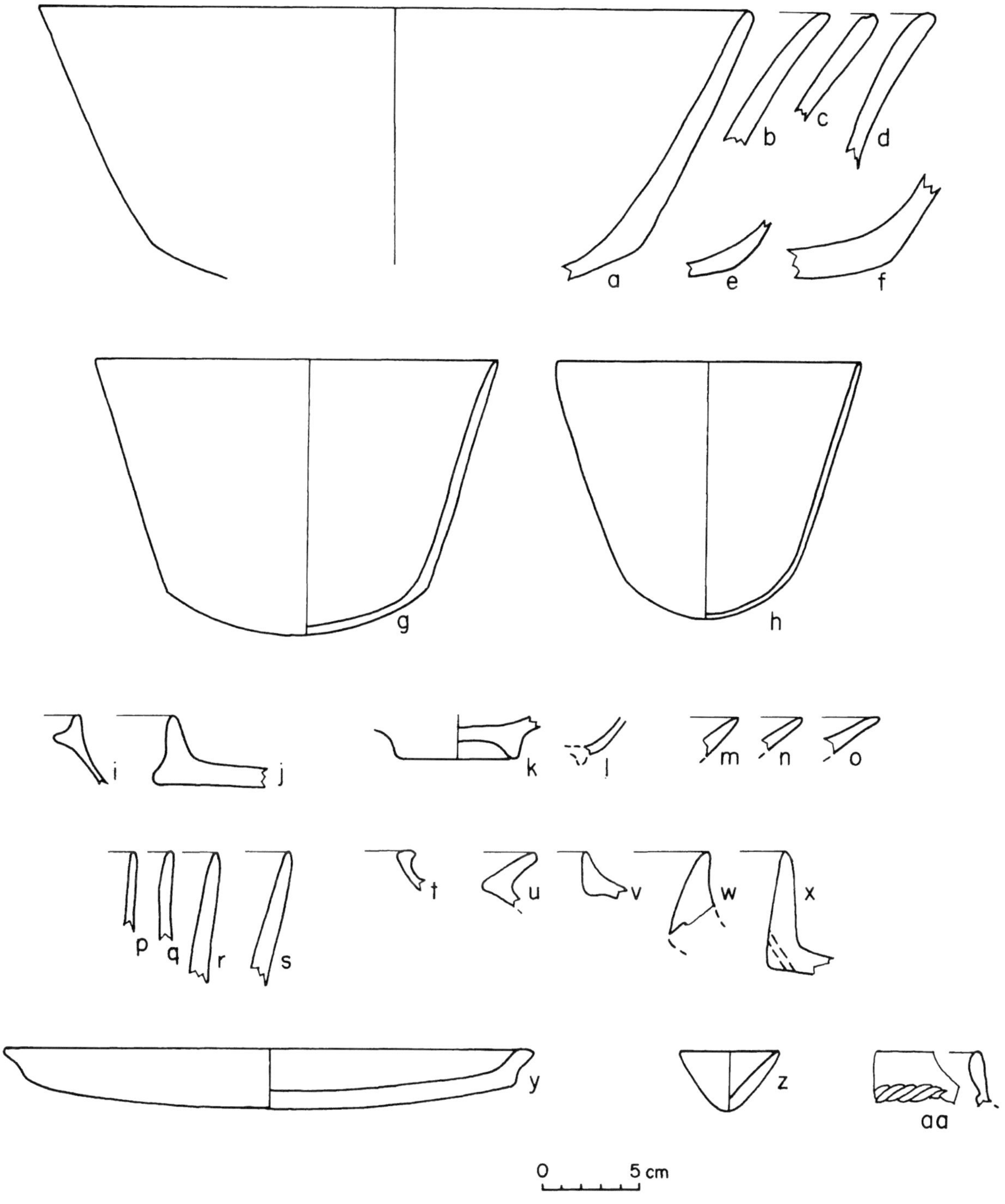

Fig. 48. Susiana Plain Buff pottery. Examples of vessel forms in use during the Khazineh, Mehmeh, and Bayat phases: *a,* bowl with outleaned wall, carinated; *b-d,* rims of bowls with outleaned walls; *e,f,* basal angle sherds of carinated bowls with outleaned walls; *g,h,* bell-shaped bowls; *i,j,* rims of ledge-rim jars; *k,l,* later type of ring base; *m-o,* wide, shallow bowls; *p-s,* rims of deep bowls with vertical to slightly flared walls; *t-x,* range of variation in jar necks; *y,* dish; *z,* small cup; *aa,* sherd with rope decoration.

Forms Chronologically Less Useful

Deep bowls with vertical to slightly flared walls (Fig. 48*p-s*).—These are the unpainted version of "Bowl Type 12" in Susiana Black-on-buff; and, like "Bowl Type 12," they almost certainly include a number of kinds of deep bowls, perhaps with chronological significance, which we were unable to divide on the basis of rim sherds alone. Rims of this type occur throughout the Tepe Sabz sequence, with high frequencies in the Sabz and Bayat phases. This bimodal distribution is further proof that we have "lumped" two (or more) kinds of bowls, which future investigators may be able to separate.

These deep bowls are finer than the basins of Plain Buff, but not nearly so fine as the bell-shaped ("Type 11") bowls. Rim diameters range from 10 to 20 cm., and heights must have been about 10 to 13 cm., although no complete examples were found.

Jars with necks (Fig. 48*t-x*).—Several varieties were found, but since only thirty-three sherds in all occurred in our excavation, we decided against trying to divide them into categories. Heights of the necks ranged from low (1.5 cm.) to high (5 cm.), with all gradations in between. Some had vertical necks, some slanted inward slightly, others slanted outward slightly, or were greatly everted. Rim diameters ranged from 4 to 17 cm. A few were perforated on the neck and shoulder, presumably for suspension cords. The difficulty of finding two necks just alike discouraged a finer typology on the basis of our limited sample. A few Bayat phase specimens had coarse chaff added to the grit temper.

Rare Forms

Dish (Fig. 48*y*).—The Mehmeh phase produced a shallow dish with concave walls and a gently rounded base. The dish stands 1 cm high and has a rim diameter of 26 cm.

Small cup (Fig. 48*z*).—A single sherd of a small cup with a rim diameter of 5 cm. was found in a Bayat phase level.

Rope decoration (Fig. 48*aa*).—A single rim sherd from the Khazineh phase, which may be part of an atypical jar neck, shows plastic decoration in the form of a modeled "rope" at the junction between jar neck and body.

Type: Susiana Black-on-buff

Sample: 7699 sherds

Temporal distribution: Sabz through Bayat phases, and later.

Appearance: Identical to Susiana Plain Buff with the addition of (1) painted designs and (2) in some cases, a wash or slip of the same clay as the paste, which provides a suitable background for the paint. This is the classic "ceramique peinte" of the Susiana sequence (Le Breton, 1947, 1957), and the "painted buff ware" of McCown (1957). Related buff wares, sharing a number of painted designs and vessel forms with Susiana Black-on-buff, dominated central Mesopotomia between 5500 and 3000 B.C. Sites linked to Tepe Sabz through shared forms and motifs in painted buff ware include Jaffarabad, Bandibal, Jowi, Bouhallan, Tall-i-Gazir, Eridu, Hajji Muhammad, al Ubaid, Ras al Amiya, and many others.

Paste: Identical to Susiana Plain Buff, with the same range of color and hardness.

Temper: Identical to Susiana Plain Buff, with the same changes through time: coarse sand, giving way to finer sand (except for certain vessels), or to temperless well-cleaned clay.

Color: Similar to Susiana Plain Buff. Some differences in surface color of the vessels can be detected between the Sabz phase and all later phases. Most sherds of the Sabz phase range between pale yellow-green (5Y 8/2 on the Munsell scale) and very pale brown (10YR 7/3). Sherds of the Khazineh, Mehmeh, and Bayat phases are usually buff or yellow (10YR 8/6) to dark grayish-green (2.5Y 4/2). Very hard-fired, well-made vessels in the latter phases may be pale green, yellow, or slightly orange (see Susiana Plain Buff).

Surface treatment: All vessels have smoothed surfaces (although some of the coarser vessels may feel gritty, due to the presence of sand

Table 18

OCCURRENCE OF VESSEL FORMS IN SUSIANA PLAIN BUFF POTTERY AT ALI KOSH, TEPE SABZ, and TEPE MUSIYAN "E"
(By Stratigraphic Zone)

	Chronologically Useful Forms														Less Useful Forms				Rare				
Site and Zone	Unpainted Version of "Sabz Pot"	Flat Bases from Vertical-walled Basins (Some Oval)	Rims of Hole-mouth Jars	Dimple Bases from Hole-mouth Jars	Rims of Hemispherical Bowls	Unpainted Pedestal Bases	Unpainted Version of Early Ring Base	Sauceboat "Tail"	Rims, Bowls with Outleaned Walls	Carinated Bases, Bowls with Outleaned Walls	Bell-shaped Bowls (Unpainted Version of Bowl Type 11)	Ledge-rim Jars	Unpainted Version of Later Ring Base	Wide, Shallow Bowls	Rims, Deep Bowls (Unpainted Version of Bowl Type 12)	Rims of Large Basins (Miscellaneous Varieties)	Bases from Large Basins (Outleaned Walls)	Miscellaneous Jars with Necks	Dish	Small Cup	Sherd with "Rope" Decoration	Unclassified Body Sherds with No Paint	Totals
TS - A_1	. . .	. . .	. . .	. . .	1	. . .	. . .	. . .	1	2	97	1	1	. . .	14	16	30	4	. . .	. . .	. . .	2,523	2,690
TS - A_2	. . .	. . .	4	. . .	2	. . .	. . .	. . .	2	. . .	193	. . .	4	. . .	18	14	26	6	. . .	1	. . .	2,924	3,194
TS - A_3	. . .	. . .	. . .	. . .	1	1	. . .	. . .	5	4	373	2	1	3	12	29	21	6	. . .	. . .	. . .	4,760	5,218
TS - B_1	. . .	. . .	1	. . .	1	. . .	. . .	. . .	11	6	42	1	. . .	. . .	7	8	15	6	1	. . .	. . .	2,201	2,300
Mus "E" . . .	. . .	2	. . .	. . .	. . .	. . .	. . .	. . .	1	1	2	1	. . .	. . .	1	. . .	14	1	. . .	. . .	. . .	429	452
TS - B_2	. . .	. . .	. . .	. . .	. . .	. . .	. . .	. . .	4	4	6	. . .	. . .	. . .	2	7	13	1	. . .	. . .	. . .	747	784
TS - B_3	. . .	. . .	. . .	. . .	. . .	. . .	. . .	. . .	1	5	17	. . .	. . .	. . .	1	4	8	4	. . .	. . .	. . .	763	803
TS - C_1	1	. . .	1	. . .	3	. . .	. . .	. . .	3	5	3	. . .	. . .	. . .	2	1	4	. . .	. . .	. . .	1	509	533
TS - C_2	1	. . .	. . .	. . .	. . .	. . .	. . .	. . .	. . .	. . .	3	. . .	. . .	. . .	3	1	7	1	. . .	. . .	. . .	257	273
TS - C_3	. . .	. . .	. . .	. . .	2	. . .	. . .	. . .	. . .	. . .	4	. . .	. . .	. . .	1	1	2	. . .	. . .	. . .	. . .	122	132
TS - D	7	29	29	5	10	4	1	1	. . .	. . .	. . .	. . .	. . .	. . .	14	52	39	4	. . .	. . .	. . .	1,340	1,535
AK - A_1 . . .	1	. . .	. . .	. . .	. . .	. . .	. . .	. . .	. . .	. . .	. . .	. . .	. . .	. . .	. . .	. . .	. . .	. . .	. . .	. . .	. . .	5	6
AK - A_2 . . .	. . .	. . .	. . .	. . .	. . .	. . .	. . .	. . .	. . .	. . .	. . .	. . .	. . .	. . .	. . .	. . .	. . .	. . .	. . .	. . .	. . .	. . .	. . .
Totals . . .	10	31	35	5	20	5	1	1	28	27	740	5	6	3	75	133	179	33	1	1	1	16,580	17,920

Table 19

OCCURRENCE OF VESSEL FORMS IN SUSIANA PLAIN BUFF POTTERY AT ALI KOSH, TEPE SABZ, AND TEPE MUSIYAN "E"
(By Cultural Phase)

	Chronologically Useful Forms														Less Useful Forms				Rare				
Phase	Unpainted Version of "Sabz Pot"	Flat Bases from Vertical-walled Basins (Some Oval)	Rims of Hole-mouth Jars	Dimple Bases from Hole-mouth Jars	Rims of Hemispherical Bowls	Unpainted Pedestal Bases	Unpainted Version of Early Ring Base	Sauceboat "Tail"	Rims, Bowls with Outleaned Walls	Carinated Bases, Bowls with Outleaned Walls	Bell-shaped Bowls (Unpainted Version of Bowl Type 11)	Ledge-rim Jars	Unpainted Version of Later Ring Base	Wide, Shallow Bowls	Rims, Deep Bowls (Unpainted Version of Bowl Type 12)	Rims of Large Basins (Miscellaneous Varieties)	Bases from Large Basins (Outleaned Walls)	Miscellaneous Jars with Necks	Dish	Small Cup	Sherd with "Rope" Decoration	Unclassified Body Sherds with No Paint	Totals
Bayat	...	...	4	...	4	1	...	...	8	6	663	3	6	3	44	59	77	16	...	1	...	10,207	11,102
Mehmeh	...	2	1	...	1	...	...	...	17	16	67	2	...	...	11	19	50	12	1	...	...	4,140	4,339
Khazineh ...	2	...	1	...	5	...	...	...	3	5	10	...	...	...	6	3	13	1	...	...	1	888	938
Sabz	7	29	29	5	10	4	1	1	...	...	...	...	...	...	14	52	39	4	...	...	...	1,340	1,535
Mohammad Jaffar	1	...	...	...	...	...	...	...	...	...	...	...	...	...	...	...	...	...	...	...	...	5	6
Totals ...	10	31	35	5	20	5	1	1	28	27	740	5	6	3	75	133	179	33	1	1	1	16,580	17,920

grains on the surface), and a few were given a wash or slip to produce the proper background for fine painting. The wash seems always to have been of the same clay as the paste.

Decoration: Designs in paint containing iron compounds. As several previous authors have pointed out, the paint has a fairly wide color range depending on (1) the thickness with which it is applied, and (2) the degree of firing. During the Sabz phase, this paint varied between gray (2.5Y N5/) and tawny or dark brown (7.5YR 4/4). It is interesting to note in this regard that the "Susiana *a*" pottery from basal Jaffarabad also had "tawny" paint (Le Breton, 1947).

From the Khazineh phase onward, the range in paint color is slightly different. Where applied heavily it is black or greenish-black, and sometimes even vitrified. When applied thinly, it may be (1) nonsmudging dark gray (5YR 4/1 to 7.5YR N4/) to dark reddish gray (5YR 4/2), or (2) easily-smudged weak red (2.5YR 4/2) to dark reddish-brown (2.5YR 2/4). The distinction between a reddish variant (which could be smeared with a wet finger) and a blacker variant which could not be smudged, had already been noticed at Ras al Amiya; there, "most of the red [shades] appear to be far from 'fast'" (Stronach, 1961:110). Stronach also noted a color range similar to ours, from purplish-black or greenish-black to weak red and brown (Stronach, 1961:109).

Presumably, this results from the fact that the iron paint used could turn either red or black, depending on how it was fired. Whether it was ultimately derived from ochre, or from some other iron peroxide or ore, remains to be established. In the following table we have attempted to show the percentage of reddish (smudging) to blackish (non-smudging) sherds by zone and cultural phase within our sequence.

Vessel Forms

Introduction:—In his analysis of the ceramics from Ras al Amiya, Stronach (1961:110) noted that "bowls of all shapes, merging into almost flat dishes,

Table 20

NUMBERS OF SHERDS WITH REDDISH (SMUDGING) PAINT AND BLACKISH (NON-SMUDGING) PAINT IN SUSIANA BLACK-ON-BUFF POTTERY AT TEPE SABZ AND TEPE MUSIYAN "E"
(By Stratigraphic Zone and Cultural Phase)

Phase	Site and Zone	Number of Sherds Reddish (Smudging)	Number of Sherds Blackish (Non-smudging)	Percentage of Sherds Reddish (Smudging): By Zone	Percentage of Sherds Reddish (Smudging): By Phase
Bayat	TS - A_1	31	559	6	7
	TS - A_2	59	785	8	. . .
	TS - A_3	86	1089	8	. . .
Mehmeh	TS - B_1	102	931	10	10
	MUS "E"	23	279	8	. . .
	TS - B_2	69	859	8	. . .
	TS - B_3	86	681	13	. . .
Khazineh	TS - C_1	109	606	18	17
	TS - C_2	66	401	16	. . .
	TS - C_3	20	153	13	. . .
Sabz	TS - D	13	692	2	2
Totals		664	7035	. . .	. . .

constitute much the most prolific form." There were wide-mouthed and hole-mouthed bowls, deep bowls with flaring sides, carinated bowls with both interior and exterior patterns, and shallow bowls or saucers, forming a continuum of shapes which were often difficult to divide or define. The solution hit upon by Stronach (*loc. cit.*) was to divide his main bowl forms into "21 different types, of which the first thirteen show only exterior decoration."

Most of Stronach's bowl types occurred at Tepe Sabz in Susiana Black-on-buff pottery. There, as at Ras al Amiya, we were faced with the same problem of dividing and defining shapes. Since Stronach's numbered bowl types were already in the literature—and presented in an extremely straightforward and orderly manner, which facilitated comparisons with our material—we decided to use his numbered types wherever possible. The alternative would have been twenty-one new numbers or different terminologies for bowls which differed negligibly from Stronach's, and this seemed highly inadvisable.

In a way, it is a pity Stronach's original numbering could not have been done on material from a sequence as long as that at Tepe Sabz. Ras al Amiya is apparently a one-period site; had Stronach been dealing with a long stratified sequence, he could have numbered the bowl types in the order of their appearance in time.

Despite this, we feel his "bowl types" are useful because, unlike previously numbered varieties of bowls seen in the literature of the Near East, they are not based on shape alone. All of Stronach's "bowl types" are based on a combination of vessel form with decoration. This in itself makes them useful horizon markers. A particular vessel form may last through several periods, but have exterior decoration with naturalistic motifs during only one of those periods. The combination of two characteristics isolates it further in time and space.

Although adhering to Stronach's numbering system, we will not present the "bowl types" in numerical order from 1 through 20 (his Type 21 did not appear at Tepe Sabz). Since we do have the advantage of a long sequence, we will present them in the order in which they made their appearance, by phase. Interdigitated with them the reader will find other vessel forms, not present at Ras al Amiya, which occurred in the stratigraphic sequence at Tepe Sabz. These will also be presented in order of their appearance.

Vessel Forms Typical of the Sabz Phase

Basins (Fig. 49).—These are similar in shape to the basins in Susiana Plain Buff, and like the latter are restricted to the Sabz phase. They may be round or oval in plan (and a few sherds even suggested rectangular ones) with vertical, slightly convex, or slightly outslanted walls and a simple rim. Bases are usually flat. Although oval specimens make measurements difficult, typical examples would seem to be 30 cm. long, 24 cm. wide, and about 15 cm. high. The body sherds are about 10 mm. thick.

Painting on these basins is usually widely-spaced and arranged vertically. Zigzags, straight lines, wavy lines, and checkerboards are all found in vertical columns. Some vessels have more closely-spaced painting, including chevrons within chevrons (Fig. 49*e*) and bird-like ("vulture") designs (Fig. 49*d*). A few sherds suggest that some of these more closely-painted vessels may have had pedestal bases (see below), but the evidence is inconclusive.

"Sabz Pots" (Fig. 50).—One of the most typical vessels of the Sabz phase, these are small, deep bowls with concave sides and gently rounded bases. They suggest a form which grew out of the convex-walled bowls of Jaffar Painted pottery (compare Figs. 44 and 50). Many of the designs

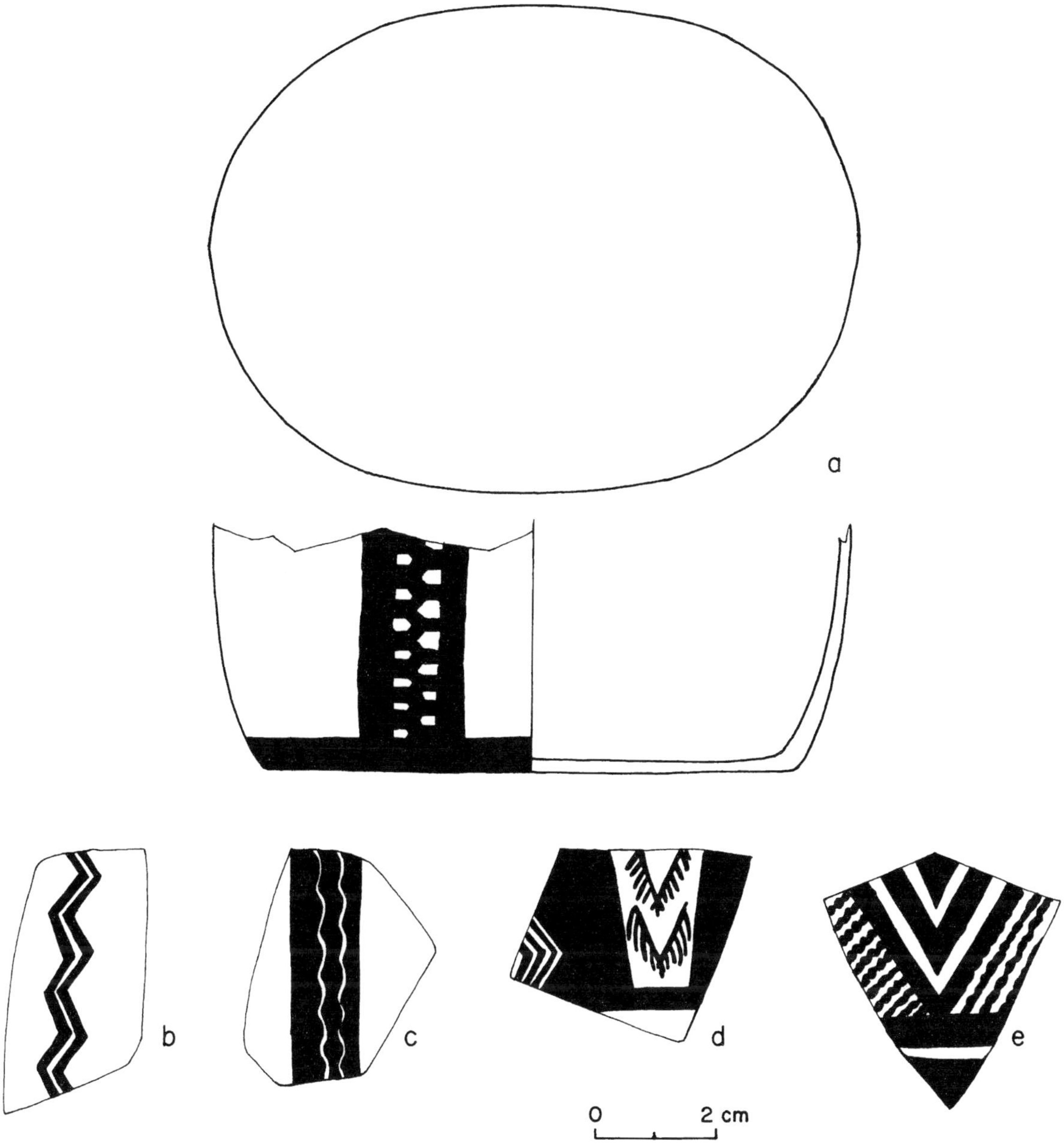

Fig. 49. Susiana Black-on-buff pottery: Large basins typical of the Sabz phase (reconstructed): *a*, plan (above) and section (below) of an oval specimen from zone D, Tepe Sabz; *b-e*, range of variation of external painted designs. Some of these bowls may have had pedestal bases as shown in Fig. 51*a-f*.

painted on them, however, are virtually unknown outside the Sabz phase (e.g. Fig. 50 *a,c,g,i,k,l*).

These small bowls have a gritty buff background, and the paint often has the "tawny" color characteristic of the Sabz phase. Typical examples have rim diameters of 14 to 16 cm., stand 7 to 10 cm. high, and have a wall thickness of 6 to 8 mm. at the midsection.

The most common designs are negative ("reserve") screens or checkerboards (Fig.

50*e*), with "fir trees" or vertical rows of pierced chevrons (Fig. 50*a*) second in frequency. A few pots have dogs with curly tails painted in the typically linear style of the Sabz phase (Fig. 50*g*). Other geometric motifs occur. Occasionally, a curious fork-like motif occurs on the interior (Fig. 50*a*).

It will be observed that the shallowest of these bowls begins to grade into Stronach's "Type 1" bowls (compare Fig. 50*d* and Fig. 55*f*). In this case, "Sabz pots" could be distinguished by their size, gritty texture, and tawny paint.

Bowls with pedestal bases (Fig. 51*a-g*).–Both bowls and basins occasionally had pedestal bases during the Sabz phase, but unfortunately we did not find any examples complete enough to allow a full reconstruction. However, very similar vessels appeared in basal Jaffarabad (Susiana *a*), and the reader may refer to Le Breton (1947:Fig. 11:9-13, and Fig. 46:11-12) for illustrations of more complete specimens. Particularly characteristic of the Sabz phase were pedestals with holes or "windows" cut in them, a trait shared by pedestals at basal Jaffarabad and Samarra (Hertzfeld, 1930:Chapter II).

It was clear that pedestals had been attached to at least ten shallow bowls, one large carinated bowl, and one straight-sided basin. The pedestals themselves expand as they extend downward from the vessel, so that the diameter is greater at the base of the pedestal than at its junction with the vessel. The "rim" of the base (i.e. the part in contact with the ground) may be slightly everted.

All pedestalled vessels are relatively coarse, the pedestals ranging in height from 4 cm. to more than 9 cm. Basal diameters are between 12 and 20 cm., and wall thicknesses between 7 and 9 mm. at the midsection. Designs painted on them are linear, and include horizontal, vertical, or diagonal parallel lines, wavy or zig-zag lines, or "ladder" motifs. Shallow bowls attached to pedestals may have interior designs as well as exterior ones, principally lines or open cross-hatching running vertically up the wall. Sometimes interior and exterior patterns were identical. In no case could the entire interior or exterior design be fully reconstructed.

Although most closely related to the pedestals of basal Jaffarabad and Samarra, both lowland sites, these pedestals find some parallels in the prehistoric villages of the Iranian plateau, notably Hissar (Schmidt, 1937:Figs. 32-34) and Sialk (Ghirshman, 1938:Pl. XLVI).

Early ring bases (Fig. 51*h*).–This early type of ring base may be no more than an extremely low pedestal; it is not related to the later ring bases of the Mehmeh and Bayat phases, which appear to be a new and different type. During the Khazineh phase there is a break in distribution of ring bases, further emphasizing the "bimodal" nature of this ceramic attribute through time.

Vessel Forms Typical of the Early Khazineh Phase

Stronach's "Bowl Types 2, 3, and 6" (Fig. 52).–We lumped together all of Stronach's small, incurved rim bowl types because we could find no real difference in temporal distribution among them. All began in the Sabz phase and reached their peak frequency during the early part of the Khazineh phase. The range of variation is shown in Fig. 52. For comparable examples, see Stronach, 1961:Pl. LXIV: 4, 6 and Pl. XLV: 4.

Rim diameters for the more hemispherical, open-mouthed end of the continuum average about 18 cm., and for the more close-mouthed examples, about 14 cm. Heights range from 4 to 9 cm. and wall thickness from 5 to 6 mm. at the midsection.

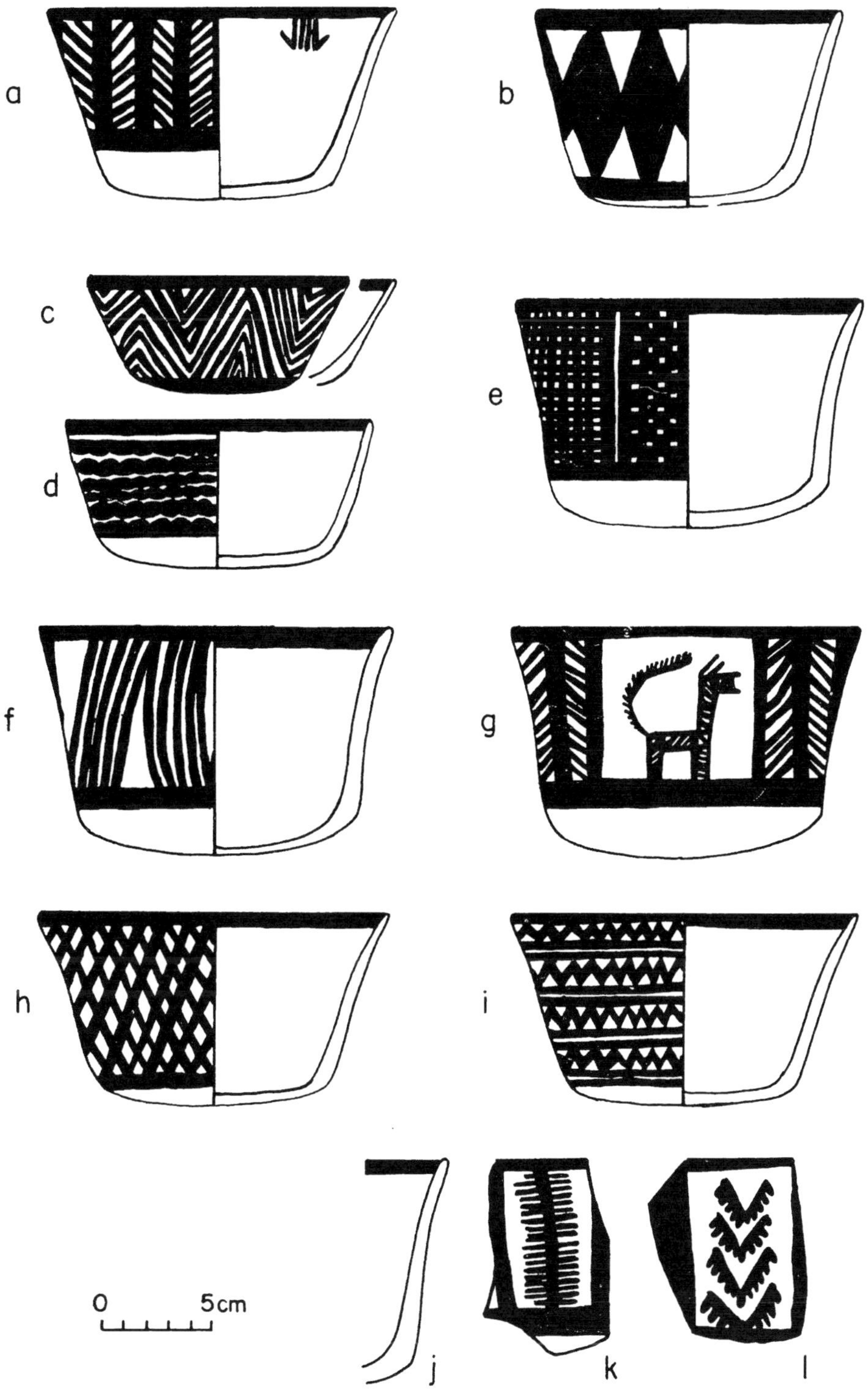

Fig. 50. Susiana Black-on-buff pottery. "Sabz Pots," typical of the Sabz phase (reconstructed): *a-i,* reconstructed examples of zone D at Tepe Sabz; *j-l,* more fragmentary examples. Full range of variation in exterior designs shown.

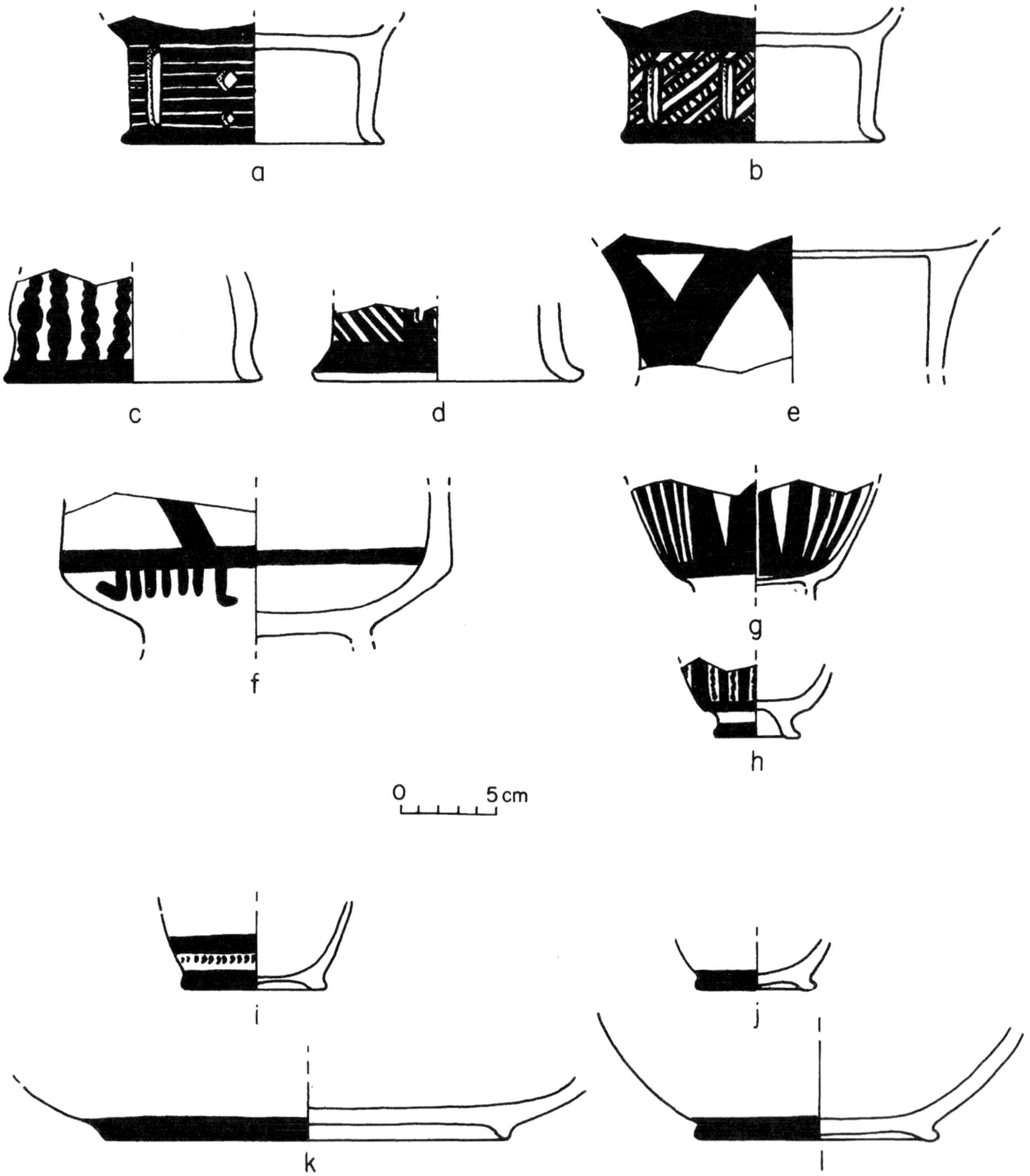

Fig. 51. Susiana Black-on-buff pottery. Examples of pedestal and ring bases (reconstructed): *a-g,* pedestal bases typical of the Sabz phase; *a,b,* and *d* have "windows" cut in them; *h,* early form of ring base (Sabz phase); *i-l,* later form of ring base (Mehmeh and Bayat phases).

Painted decoration is confined to the exterior, except for a simple band inside the rim on the more open variety. The upper part of the exterior is treated as a horizontal zone, with a repetitive pattern confined between solid bands at the top and bottom. The most frequent designs are wavy lines in reserve, but also common are reserve knotted-cord motifs (Fig. 52*h*), diamonds, or "bow ties" (Fig. 52*i*).

Bowls of this type appeared in Susiana *a* and *b* (Le Breton, 1957:Fig. 5: 18, Fig. 6: 5), at Hajji Muhammad (Ziegler, 1953:Pl. 28*d*), and Gird Banahilk (Watson, unpublished data). By the early Mehmeh phase they had nearly run their course.

"Sauce boats" (Fig. 53*a-f*).—These are small bowls with straight or slightly outflaring sides, each of which has a small "tail" or "handle" rising from the rim. Although they are only superficially similar to the "sauceboats" from early Eridu (Oates, 1960:Pl. IV: 2), the concept behind them seems to have been the same.

There are basically two types of handles on the Tepe Sabz examples, with overlap in time. Sabz and Khazineh phase examples usually have a simple erect tab, often perforated (Fig. 53*b*), while later Mehmeh phase examples often have a taller handle which curls over like a tongue (Fig. 53*e,f*).

Rim diameters vary from 5 to 15 cm., with heights in the 4 to 7 cm. range. Wall thickness at the midsection is 5 to 7 mm. Handles may be only 3 cm. high, or exceed 6 cm.

Decoration is mainly external, except for a black band on the rim interior, or a "fork" motif pendant from the rim. Exterior patterns during the Sabz and Khazineh phases are mostly reserve screens, crosshatch, or checkerboard. Later Mehmeh phase sauceboats with high, curled tails may have cursive zig-zag lines. Rim sherds from Sabz and Khazineh phase sauceboats, if they came from a part of the rim which did not preserve traces of the handle, could easily have been counted as fragments of "Sabz Pots," and some probably were. Variations in the upswing of the rim as it approached the handle made it easy to identify most sherds as coming from sauceboats, however.

Vessels of this peculiar type ran through the Eridu, Hajji Muhammad, and early Ubaid levels at Eridu (Oates, 1960), and appeared at Tepe Jowi in Susiana proper (Le Breton, 1947:Fig. 22: 1-2). They also can be found at Hajji Muhammad itself (Ziegler, 1953:Pl. 20*c,d*) and at Ras al Amiya (Stronach, 1961:Pl. LVII: 2-5). Obviously they are lowland items which occur rarely or never in the mountains to the east.

Vessel Forms Typical of the Late Khazineh Phase

Stronach's "Bowl Type 13" (Fig. 54).—These Stronach (1961:112) defines as "relatively small carinated bowls of fine to ordinary ware with finely drawn exterior patterns." Our carinated bowls show less variation than his do, approximating most closely the example he illustrates in Pl. XLVII: 9. Although similar in shape to his "Bowl Type 14," they have only exterior decoration, save for a solid band of black on the interior of the rim. Nevertheless, they would seem to have roughly the same temporal distribution as Bowl Type 14: beginning roughly at the start of the Khazineh phase, reaching their peak late in that phase, and lasting into the early Mehmeh phase.

The range of rim diameters is great, with extremes of 20 and 40 cm.; most vessels are in the 20 to 30 cm. span. Heights vary between 4 and 9 cm., and vessel walls at the midsection are 5 to 8 mm. thick.

Exterior decoration is confined to a horizontal panel running around the vessel, delimited by a solid band at the rim and another at (approximately) the point of carination. The most common design is a

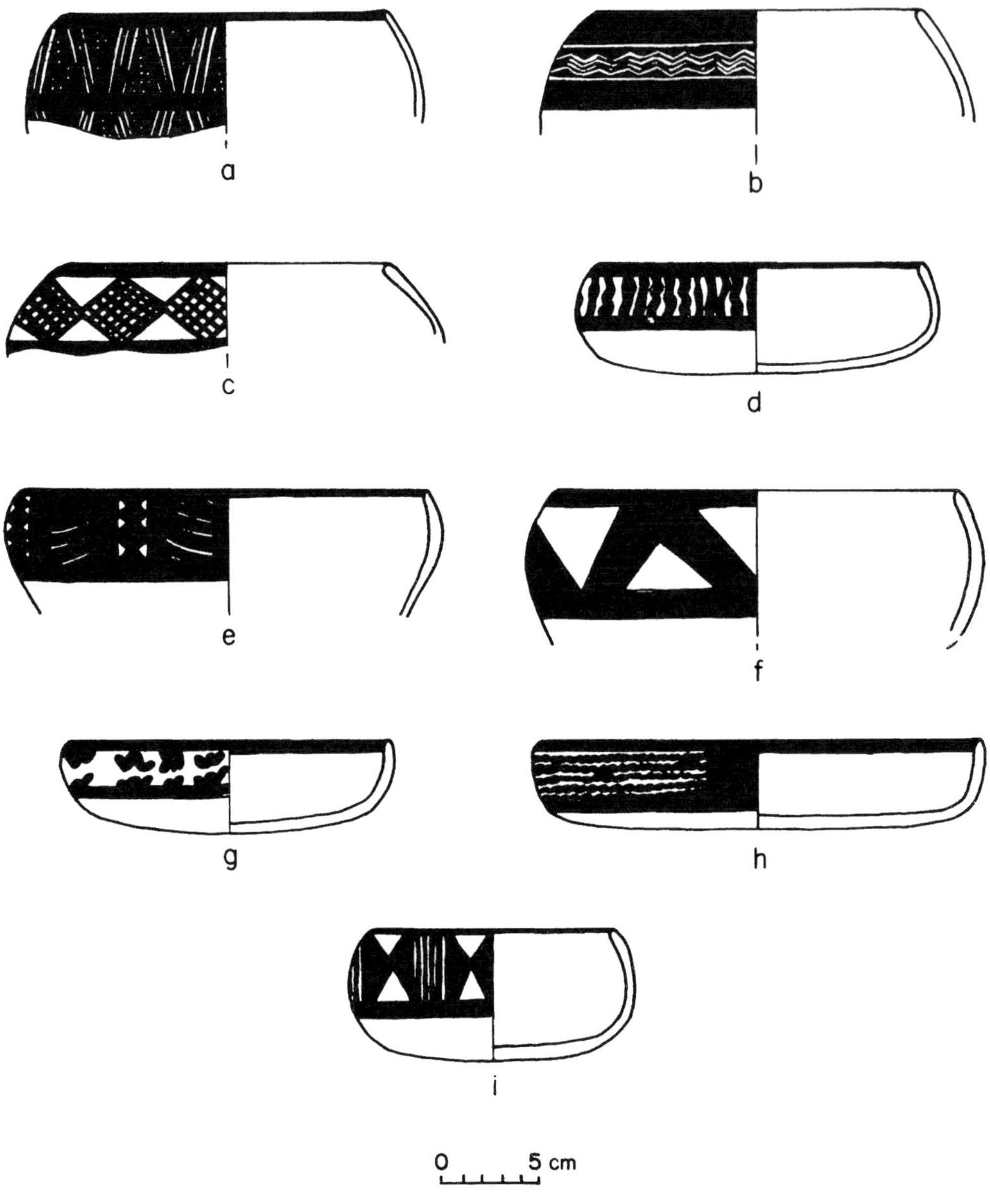

Fig. 52. Susiana Black-on-buff pottery. "Bowl types 2, 3, and 6" (reconstructed). All major variants shown.

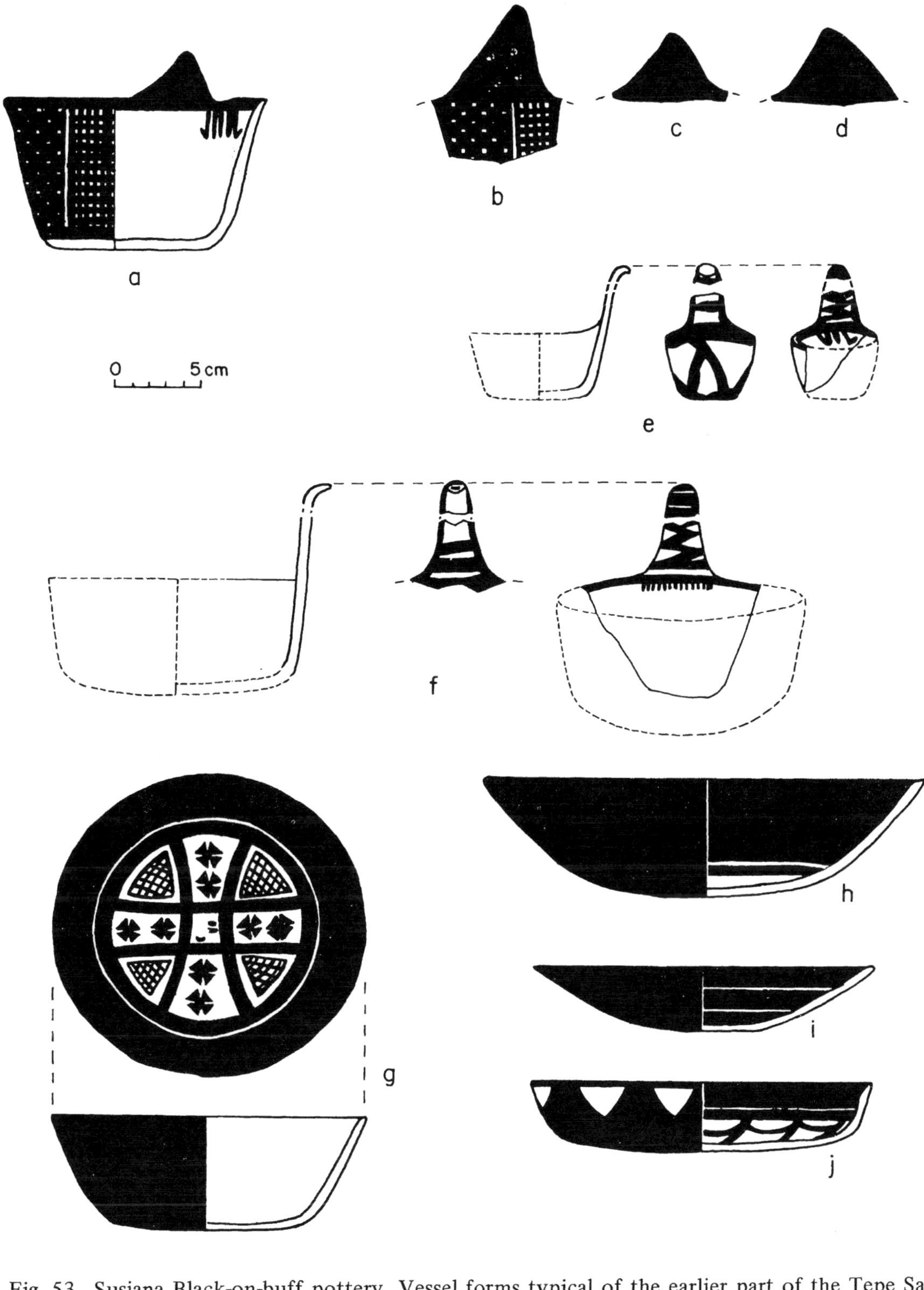

Fig. 53. Susiana Black-on-buff pottery. Vessel forms typical of the earlier part of the Tepe Sabz sequence (reconstructed): *a,* reconstructed "sauceboat" (Sabz phase); *b-d,* "handles" from "sauceboats" (Sabz and Khazineh phases); *e,f,* "sauceboats" with taller "handles" (Mehmeh phase); *g-j,* "Type 18" bowls. All major variants shown.

series of vertical lines interrupted by solid black "bow ties" (Fig. 54*d-f*), a style seen also on Bowl Type 13 at Ras al Amiya (Stronach, 1961:Pl. XLVII: 9). Rows of lozenges, wavy lines in reserve, or undulating bands of vertical lines are also frequent.

Bowl Type 13 is clearly related to Bowl Type 1 (below), both by shared designs and by similar temporal distribution. Sherds of Type 13 can easily be distinguished by the carination, but it will remain for future investigators to decide how useful it is to regard the two as separate. Type 13 Bowls appear as far to the north as Gird Banahilk (Watson, unpublished data) and early Tepe Gawra (Tobler, 1950:Pl. CXIII: 27).

Stronach's "Bowl Type 1" (Fig. 55).—These are small hemispherical bowls whose walls lean outward slightly (see also Stronach, 1961:Pl. XLIV: 1). All those recovered in reasonably complete condition had rounded bases, but for many the form of the base is uncertain. Rim diameters range from 10 to 20 cm., heights from 5.5 to 7.5 cm., and wall thicknesses are 2 to 5 mm. at the midsection. These bowls begin in the Sabz phase and last until the Mehmeh phase, with their major frequency falling in Khazineh times. Mehmeh phase examples tend to be slightly thinner and more finely made, and may have an out-turned lip (Fig. 55*k,l*).

Exterior designs may be arranged in horizontal bands, for example, of knotted cords in reserve (Fig. 55*f*) or less commonly, solid or hatched lozenges (Fig. 55*b,g,h*). Reserve designs in a black field (Fig. 55*a*), or panels of vertical or horizontal lines alternating with solid black panels also appear. Less common are open zig-zags and running ladders, typical Mehmeh phase motifs (Fig. 55*i,j*).

Type 1 bowls can be found at Tepe Jaffarabad (Le Breton, 1947:Fig. 10: 3) as well as Ras al Amiya during this period (Stronach, 1961).

Stronach's "Bowl Type 14" (Figs. 56 and 57).—These Stronach (1961:113) defines as "large carinated bowls with interior patterns" which "mostly share the shape and patterns of similar vessels from Hajji Muhammad." This bowl is one of the most characteristic and abundant vessels of the Khazineh and early Mehmeh phases; it is also widely distributed throughout the Near East. Bowl Type 14 appears as far to the south as Hajji Muhammad (Ziegler, 1953:Pl. 14,16) and Eridu (Oates, 1960:Pl. V: 17), and as far to the north as the Halafian levels at Arpachiyah (Mallowan and Rose, 1935:Fig. 61). Within Khuzistan itself, examples identical to ours can be found in Susiana *b,c* levels (Le Breton, 1957:Fig. 6: 7,10-14).

Bowl Type 14 is an open vessel with a flat or slightly rounded base, and an outleaned or outflaring wall which joins the base in a definite carination. Occasionally the carination shows a pronounced "kink" in the bowl profile, a feature common at Arpachiyah but less common at Ras al Amiya (Stronach, 1961:113). Rim diameters of our bowls range from 16 to 38 cm., in contrast to Ras al Amiya or Hajji Muhammad examples, which might have rim diameters up to 50 cm. (Stronach, 1961). Vessel heights are between 7 and 8.5 cm., and wall thickness at the midsection is 4 to 7 mm. These bowls are painted on both the exterior and interior, so densely (especially on the interior) that the design often appears in reserve.

Most characteristic of these bowls is the painting of the interior of the base, usually some variation of a "wheel" or "flower" design with spokes or petals radiating from a central hub. "Rosettes" or "sunbursts" are particularly common at all the sites mentioned above, and Tepe Sabz is no exception (see Fig. 56*b*). Another design, common at Tepe Jowi as well as Tepe Sabz during the Khazineh phase, is a field of interlocking "bow ties" (Fig. 57*f*). "Gears within gears" are also typical motifs.

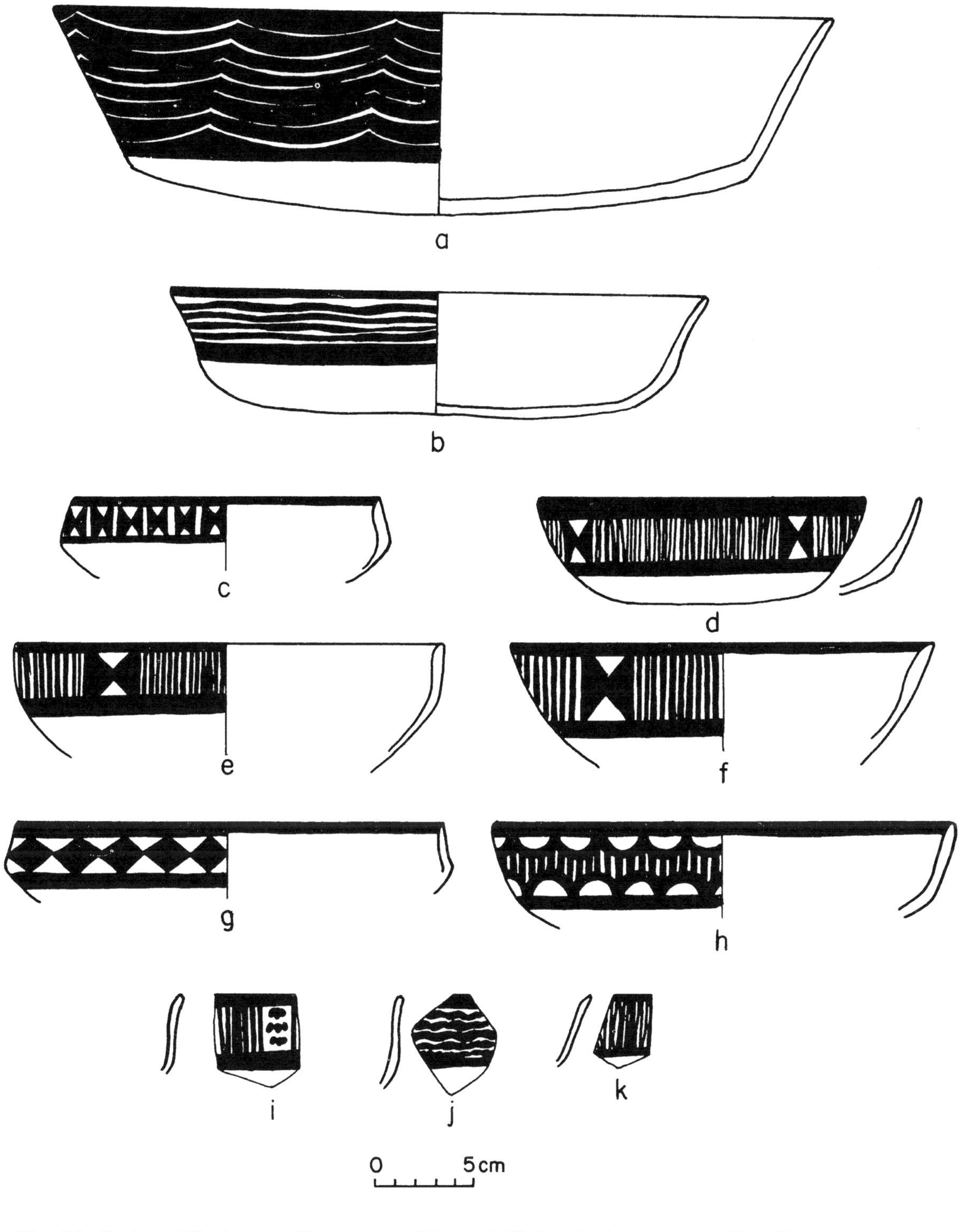

Fig. 54. Susiana Black-on-buff pottery. "Type 13" bowls (reconstructed). All major variants shown.

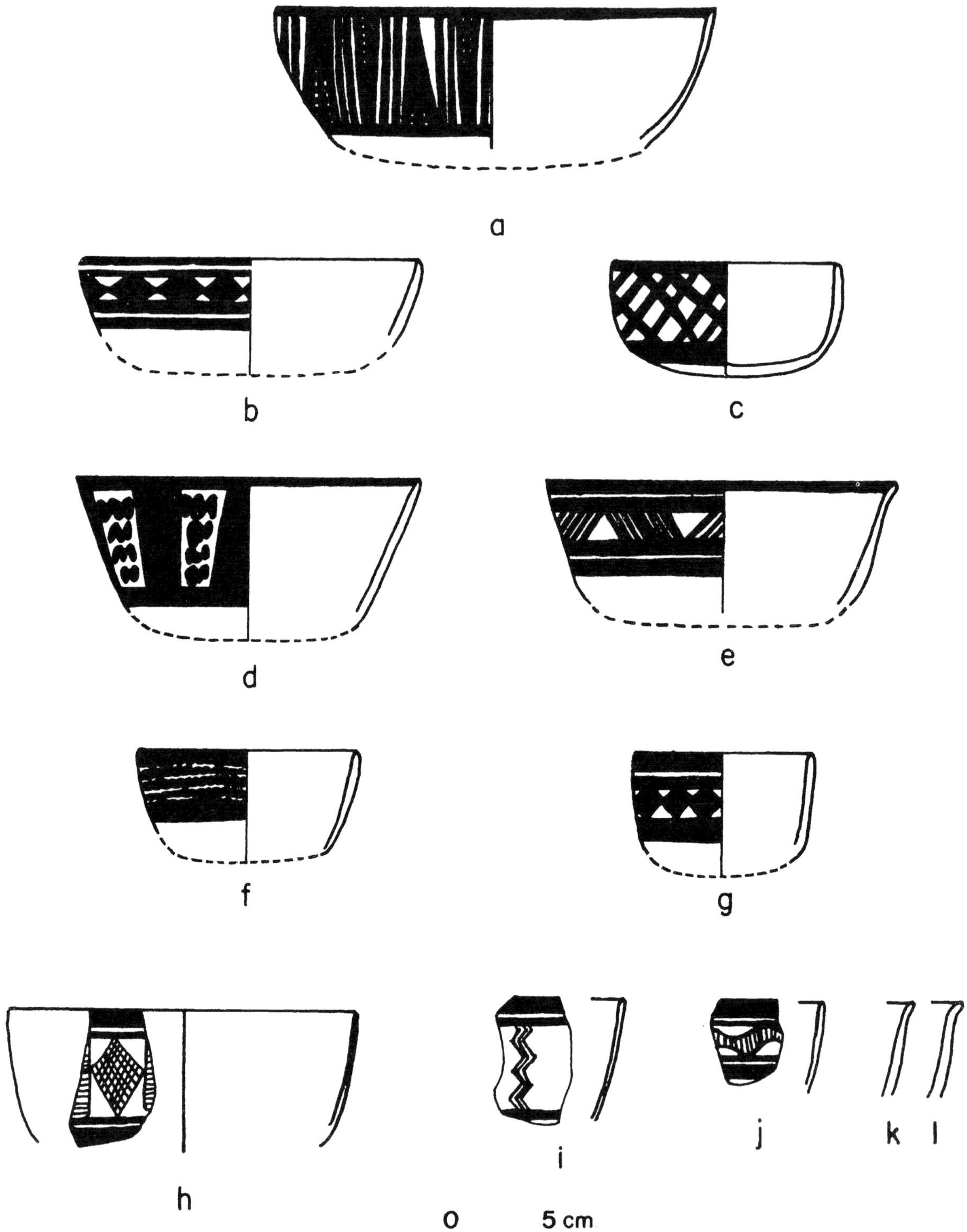

Fig. 55. Susiana Black-on-buff pottery. "Type 1" bowls (reconstructed). All major variants shown.

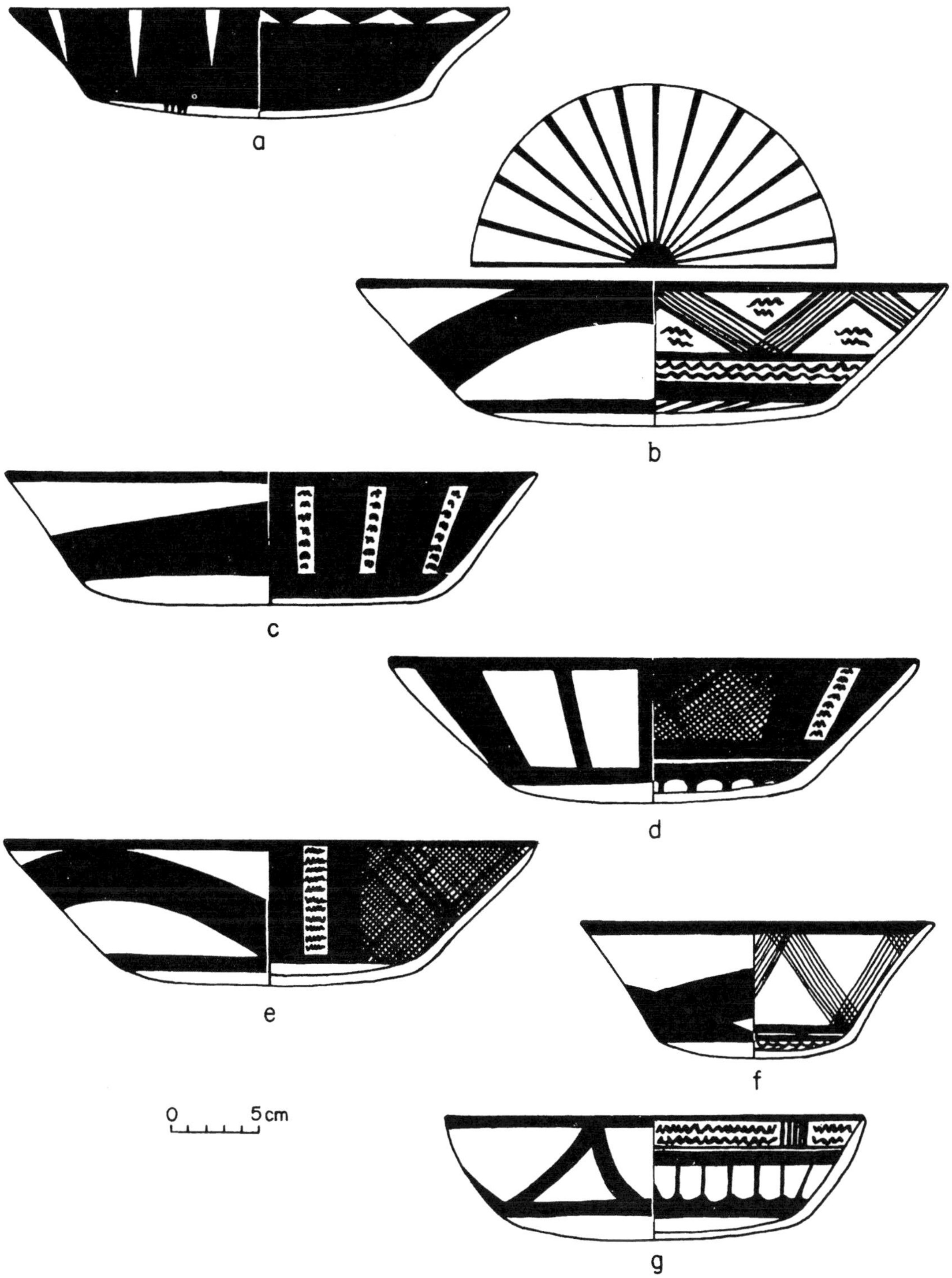

Fig. 56. Susiana Black-on-buff pottery. "Type 14" bowls (reconstructed), showing range of variation in vessel shapes. Exterior and interior patterns shown are most typical of the Khazineh phase, but occur in other phases as well; *b* shows a portion of the design painted on the inside of the floor of the bowl.

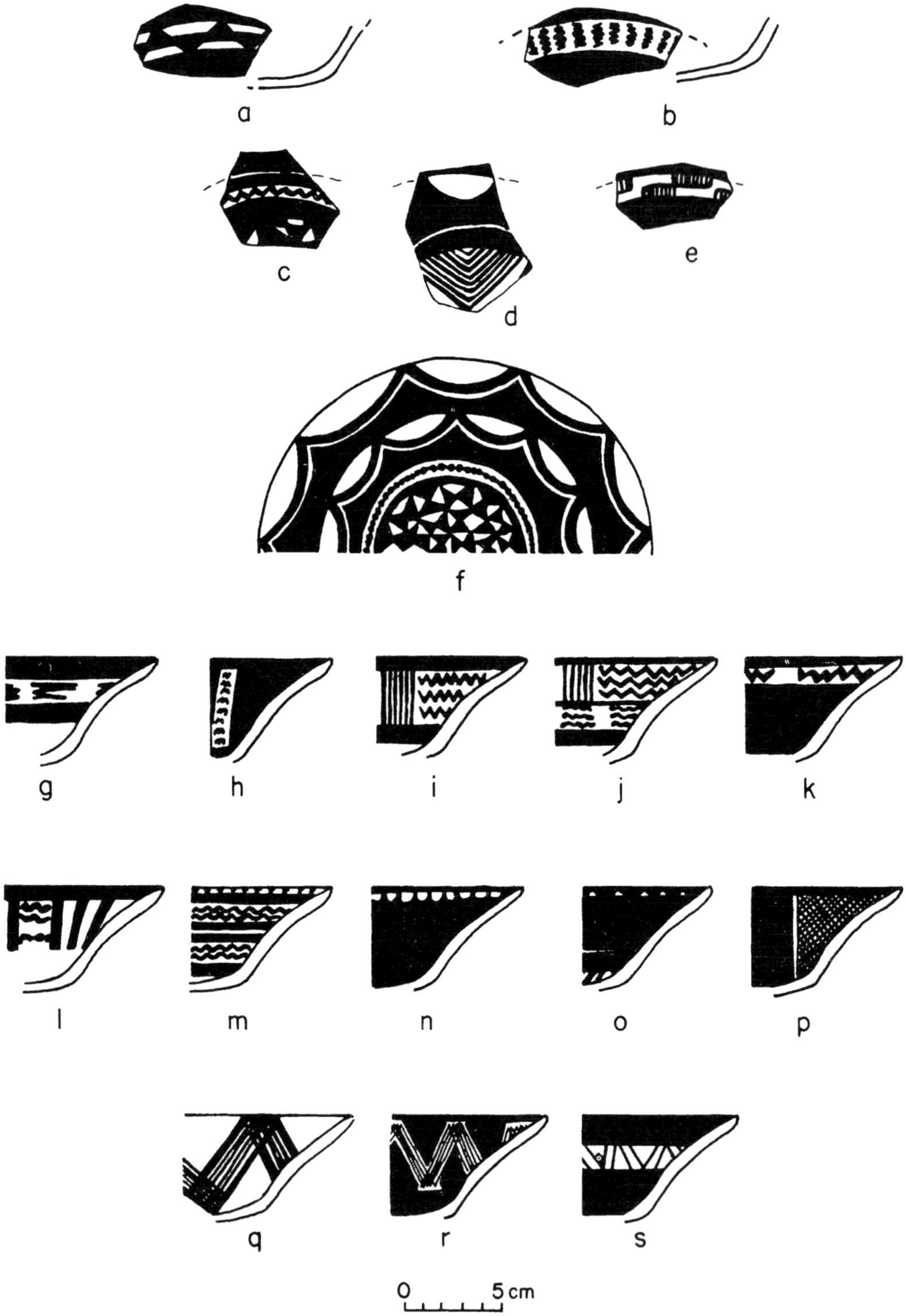

Fig. 57. Susiana Black-on-buff pottery. "Type 14" bowls (reconstructed): *a-f*, examples of designs painted in the inside of the floor of the bowl; *g-s*, additional range of variation in designs painted on the interior of the vessel wall.

The designs on the interior walls of Type 14 Bowls may have little to do with the designs on the interior of the base. The complete range of variation observed at Tepe Sabz is given in Fig. 57*g-s*. Vertical panels may rise out of the basal design and extend up the wall of the bowl, but just as frequent are horizontal bands with motifs not seen in the basal design. Included in the latter category are wiggly lines, sigmas, zig-zags and a few free-standing motifs. Also common on wall interiors are areas of negative cross-hatching, solid black panels, and a distinctive design (typical of Hajji Muhammad) which suggests railroad tracks crossing one another at regular intervals (Fig. 56*b,f*; Fig. 57*q,r*).

Exterior designs are quite different from interior designs, and it proved impossible to find interior and exterior motifs which were habitually associated. For the most part, exterior decoration was restricted to broad bands, open loops, or alternating black-and-white vertical panels.

In practice, it was impossible to separate small base sherds of Bowl Type 14 from base sherds of Bowl Type 18 (see below), unless the sherd preserved the carinated wall/base juncture. From their temporal distribution, however (see Fig. 64), it appears that most base sherds with interior painting belonged to Bowl Type 14.

Vessel Forms of the Mehmeh Phase

Stronach's "Bowl Type 18" (Fig. 53*g-j*).—Although beginning in the late Khazineh phase, these small hemispherical bowls with interior painted designs actually reach peak frequency in the Mehmeh phase. They range from shallow and saucerlike to medium depth, and have simple rims which may be slightly flattened on top. In their use of both interior and exterior painted designs, often with the reserve technique apparent, these resemble Bowl Type 14; however, they are never carinated and the range of designs is relatively limited.

These bowls have a rim diameter of 17 to 30 cm., a height of 4 to 7 cm., and a wall thickness of 4 to 5 mm. at the midsection. Most specimens are small, with rim diameters in the neighborhood of 19 to 20 cm.

Although a few Hajji Muhammad designs are found on Type 18 bowls, the local preference at Deh Luran was for solid black exteriors, and interiors which were also solid black except for a few concentric buff lines in reserve. Loops, parallel lines, and areas of cross-hatch are other motifs observed on vessels of this shape. Resemblances can be detected with vessels from Banahilk (Watson, unpublished data), Hajji Muhammad (Ziegler, 1953:Pl. 25*b*), and Susiana *b-c* (Le Breton, 1957:6:16).

Stronach's "Bowl Type 15" (Fig. 60*a-h*).—Large, carinated to flat-based bowls with outleaning walls, and rims which may be simple, flattened, or bevelled. These have, in the words of Stronach (1961:113), "only the minimum of painted decoration"—mainly, in the case of Tepe Sabz and Ras al Amiya, open or solid black loops hanging from the interior of the rim.

Most vessels have a rim diameter of 35 to 40 cm., although extremes of 28 cm. (Khazineh phase) and 60 cm. (Mehmeh phase) occurred. Height of this bowl type is about 8 to 13 cm., with a wall thickness of 5 to 10 mm. at the midsection.

The most sparsely-painted examples have only a "ticked" line around the rim, occasionally accompanied by a solid black line at the rim exterior. Others have only the interior loops mentioned above, of which the solid type is most common. Some exteriors may be solid black, or have broad zig-zags or triangles.

This bowl type occurred both at Hajji Muhammad and at Ras al Amiya (Stronach, 1961:113). In the Deh Luran sequence, it began in the Khazineh phase, reached peak frequency in early Mehmeh times, and lasted into the Bayat phase in small numbers.

Ledge-rim Jars (Fig. 58*a-e*).–Globular jars with short, vertical necks and an interior "ledge" at the base of the neck. The ledge usually projects inward at a 90 degree angle to the neck, although a few examples are slightly up-turned. The rim of the jar may be flat-topped, round or bevelled either internally or externally. The ledge may be perforated at intervals by small holes, where an instrument was pushed vertically through while the clay was still plastic.

Rim diameters of the jars vary from 14 to more than 40 cm. Because no complete vessels were found, it is difficult to estimate vessel size. The tops of the rims, as well as exterior of the neck, were painted solid black. Below this, on the exterior shoulder of the jar, are horizontal panels or bands of decoration. The uppermost is usually a row of X's, loops, sigmas, or some other fairly open design, which encircles the vessel at the point of contact between body and neck. Below this come wavy "ladder" designs, horizontal lines or bands, or rows of chevrons. Below the mid-body, the vessel may have been plain. A few aberrants are painted solidly black from rim to midsection.

Similar ledge-rim jars appeared in "Susiana *c*" levels at Tepe Jowi (Le Breton, 1947:Fig. 24:13), at Hajji Muhammad (Ziegler, 1953:Pl. 29*a,b*), and at Ras al Amiya (Stronach, 1961:Pl. LIV:1-3). Farther to the north they can be found also in strata XVI - XVII at Tepe Gawra (Tobler, 1950:Pl. LXXIV:20). We find no good parallels in the highlands.

"Goat bowls" (Fig. 59*b*).–Large, open, flat-based bowls whose outleaning walls have flat-topped or inwardly-beveled rims. Vessels have rim diameters of 35 to 45 cm., heights of up to 14 cm., and wall thicknesses of 6 to 9 mm. at the midsection. Although similar in shape to Stronach's "Bowl Type 15" (Fig. 59*a*), they can be readily distinguished by their unique designs, which did not occur at Ras al Amiya, Eridu, or Hajji Muhammad. These bowls are among the most characteristic vessels of the Mehmeh phase in the Deh Luran plain.

Rims of these vessels are always painted with a horizontal stripe on the inside, and the flattened upper surface of the rim bears a row of "ticking," usually in the form of small black triangles pointing toward the interior of the bowl. Decoration is restricted to the interior, and always involves some variation on the theme of wild goats following one another around the inside of the vessel wall (hence the name).

"Rows of wild goats" occur on pottery of Mehmeh phase sites in Susiana proper, though not on bowls of the same size and shape as the "Goat Bowls" of the Deh Luran sequence (see for example Le Breton, 1957:Fig. 6:31, 36, 37). Such naturalistic designs are virtually restricted to the Mehmeh phase, and provide a link with the Iranian Plateau rather than with the alluvium of Mesopotamia. Sialk (Ghirshman, 1938:Pl. LXXIV), Tepe Giyan (Conteneau and Ghirshman, 1935:Pl. 47), Tepe Hissar (Schmidt, 1937:Pl. VII), and Pisdeli Tepe (Dyson and Young, 1960:Fig. 3:3) all feature painted rows of goats during this period.

However, we failed to find in the literature any examples of large, open flat-based bowls with rows of goats painted on the interior, as seen at Tepe Sabz. That combination of shape and design may be unique to the Deh Luran region, although the style in which our goats are painted would seem to be well within the "Susiana" tradition (see Fig. 59*k-m*).

Vessel Forms Typical of the Bayat Phase

"Bowl Type 11-a" (Fig. 60*i,j*).–Although represented at Ras al Amiya (Stronach,

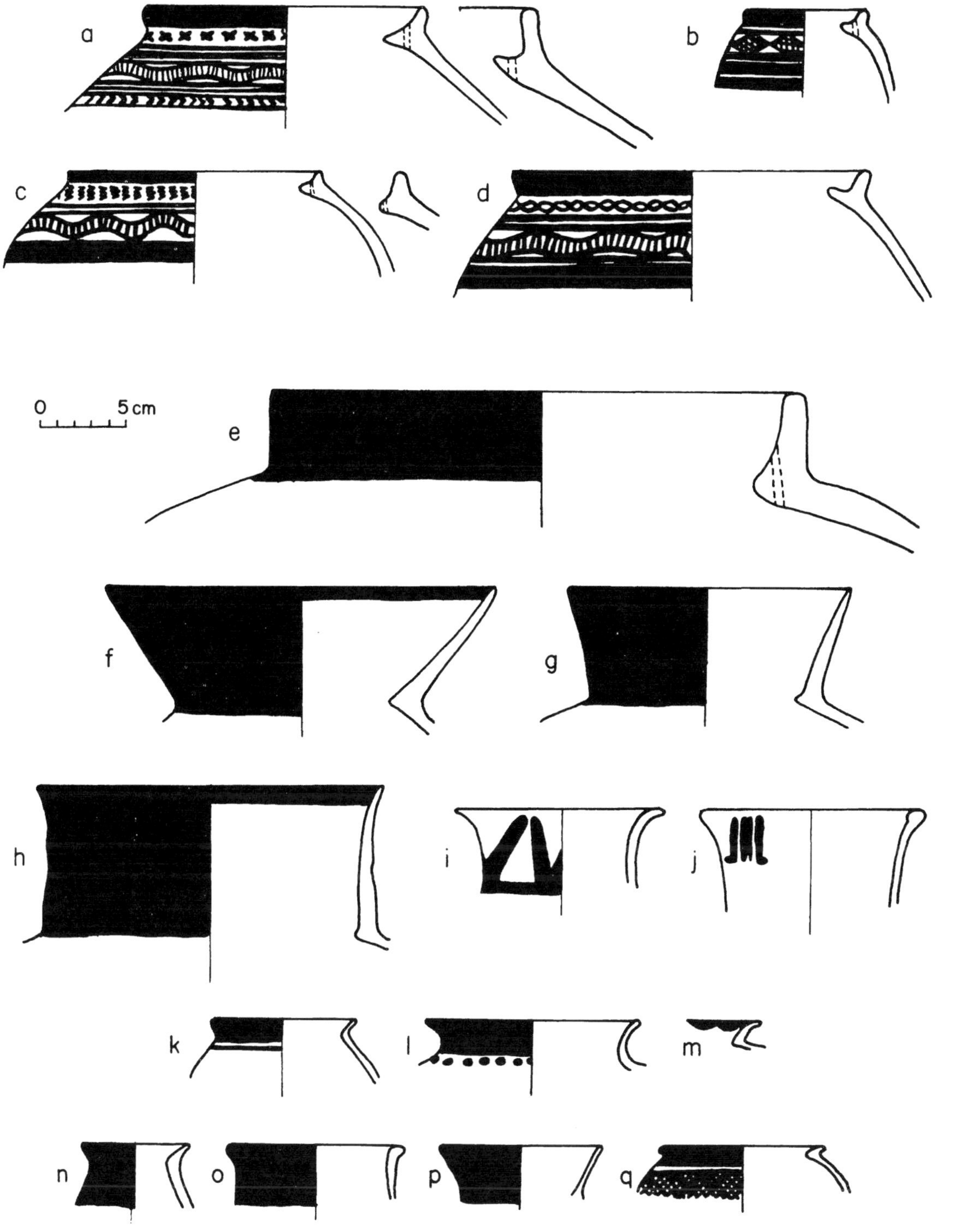

Fig. 58. Susiana Black-on-buff pottery. Examples of various types of jars (reconstructed): *a-d*, examples of ledge-rim jars, all from the Mehmeh phase, Tepe Sabz; *e*, large ledge-rim jar from Tepe Musiyan "E" (Mehmeh phase); *f-j*, high-necked jars (*f-h*, Bayat phase; *i,j*, Sabz phase); *k-q*, low-necked jars (*k,m,n,q*, Bayat phase; *p*, Mehmeh phase; *l,o*, Khazineh phase).

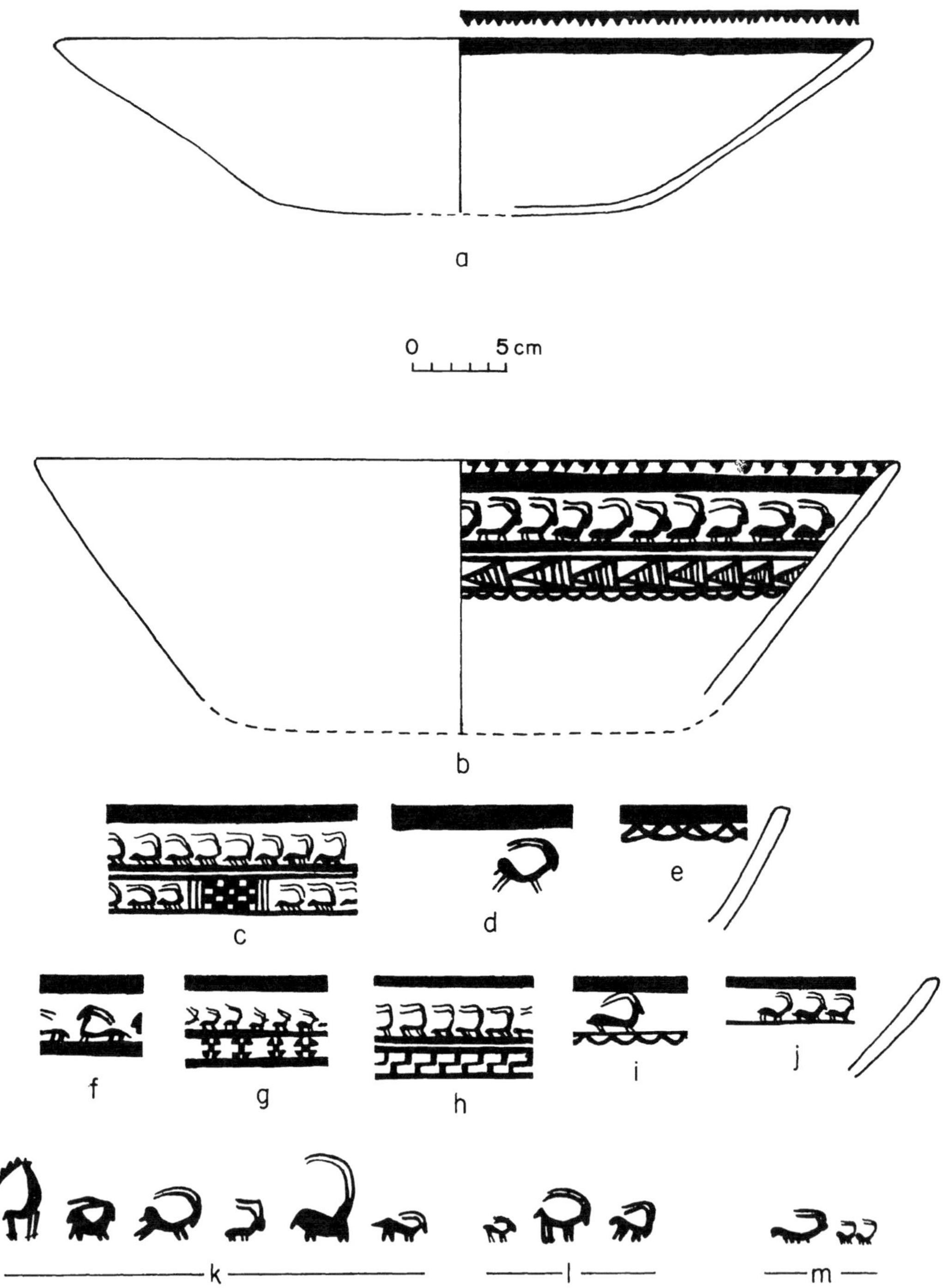

Fig. 59. Susiana Black-on-buff pottery. Examples of large bowls, including the "Goat Bowl" variant: *a*, "Type 15" bowl, Mehmeh phase; *b*, reconstructed "Goat Bowl" of the Mehmeh phase; *c-j*, examples of designs on the interior of the rim and upper vessel wall, all from Mehmeh phase levels at Tepe Sabz; *k*, examples of rendering of "goat" motif at Tepe Sabz (1963 excavations); *l*, examples of rendering of "goat" motif at Tepe Jowi (after Le Breton, 1947: Fig. 29: 7, 12, 3); *m*, examples of rendering of "goat" motif at Tepe Musiyan "E" (1963 excavations).

1961:Pl. LI:11), this type of bowl, with its very characteristic decoration, was not singled out as a separate entity. We have done so because of its usefulness as a horizon marker. "Type 11-*a*" is similar in general shape to Bowl Type 11, but it is less bell-shaped and its decoration is monotonously simple.

This bowl has a gently-rounded base and sides which are outleaned or slightly concave. The range in size is great (limits given in Fig. 60), as is the range in quality; small versions are as finely-made as Bowl Type 11, but the larger examples are fairly coarse. Rim diameter varies from 16 to 34 cm., the height from 10 to 21 cm., and wall thickness at the midsection from 3 to 7 mm. This range is bimodal, with 64 per cent of the sherds being from fine vessels clustered in the 16 cm. rim diameter category, and 35 per cent being coarse sherds from vessels in the 34 cm. rim diameter category. Few intermediate-sized examples occurred.

The most distinctive feature of Bowl Type 11-*a* is its decoration. There is only one motif, a wiggly vertical line enclosed between straight vertical lines. This same design appears at Ras al Amiya, but there it is always horizontal, not vertical (Stronach, 1961:Pl. LI:8-11). Examples like Stronach's also appeared at Hajji Muhammad (Ziegler, 1953:Pl. 23*b*). At Tepe Sabz, bowls of this type begin in the Mehmeh phase, but reach their maximum frequency in the Bayat phase.

It is Bowl Types 15 and 11-*a* which perhaps best exemplify what Stronach (1961:96) refers to as "the more sparsely decorated material of later Ubaid times." Such sparsity of decoration characterizes the Bayat phase and underscores its relatively late position in the "Susiana" sequence.

High-necked jars (Fig. 58*f-j*).—Nearly every phase of the Deh Luran sequence yielded some sherds of globular jars with necks exceeding 3 cm. in height; two crude Sabz phase examples are shown in Fig. 58*i-j*. However, jars with tall necks painted solid black on the exterior, such as shown in Fig. 58*e-h*, appeared mainly in the Bayat phase and were a useful horizon marker. The absence of high-necked jars in Khazineh phase levels further emphasizes the lack of relationship between the Bayat jars and the two unique Sabz phase examples (which could, conceivably, even be aberrant pedestals of some kind).

The typical Mehmeh or Bayat phase high-necked jar has a neck standing 3.5 to 8 cm. above the body of the vessel, and a rim diameter of 9 to 23 cm. Since no complete specimens were found, it is hard to specify the range in height. Similar specimens occurred at Ras al Amiya (Stronach, 1961:Pl. LIV-LV).

Later ring bases (Fig. 51*i-l*).—The Mehmeh and Bayat phases were also characterized by low ring bases, which were on the increase in the Bayat phase (Fig. 64). Painting on these bases was very simple, consisting mainly of a solid black line around the exterior. Since no complete vessels were found, we can only guess that the ring bases supported globular jars and perhaps deep bowls.

Heights of these bases vary from 8 to 15 mm., and their diameters range between 5 and 21 cm. Many are quite well made and uniform. They resemble contemporary ring bases from Susiana proper (Le Breton, 1957:Figs. 4, 7), which begin in Susiana *b* and last until Susa A. Similar bases appeared at Ras al Amiya (Stronach, 1961:Pl. LVII:12) and other lowland sites.

Vessels Forms Running Through Three or More Phases

Stronach's "Bowl Type 12" (Fig. 61).—Deep bowls with walls which are vertical, slightly outleaned, or slightly outcurved. Few of these could be fully reconstructed, and the rim profiles showed a continuum

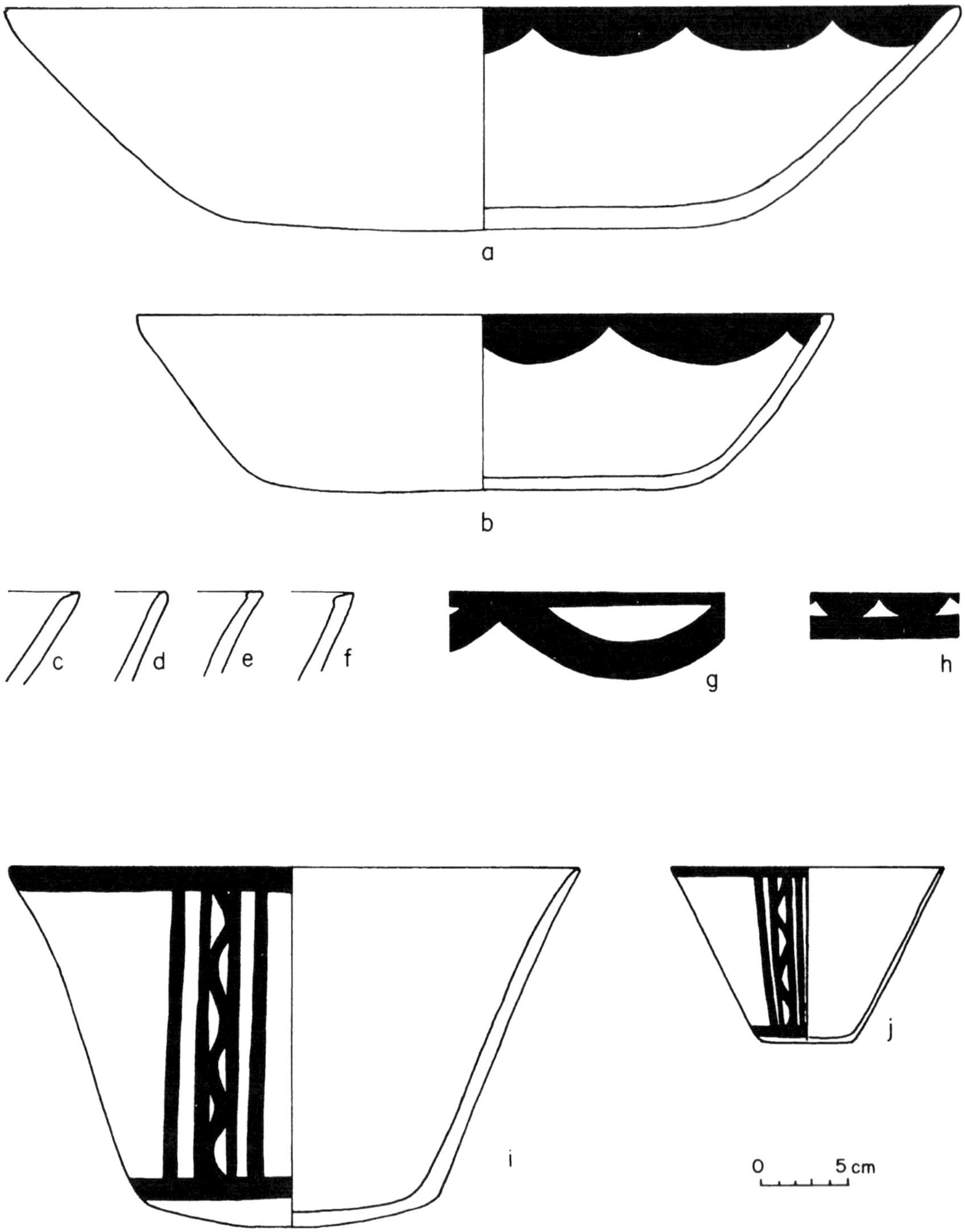

Fig. 60. Susiana Black-on-buff pottery. Bowl types common during the Mehmeh and Bayat phases (reconstructed); *a,b,* "Type 15" bowls, Mehmeh phase examples; *c-f,* rim profiles of "Type 15" bowls; *g,h,* painted motifs from interiors of rims of "Type 15" bowls; *i,j,* "Type 11-*a*" bowls, Bayat phase examples, showing size range.

which was extremely difficult to divide. The range of variation is shown in Fig. 61.

As at Ras al Amiya, these bowls were often not unlike Bowl Type 11 in general profile (see for example Fig. 61*h*), but they were considerably coarser and less bell-shaped. Rim diameters were on the order of 16 to 30 cm., with a wall thickness of 3 to 9 mm. at the midsection. Heights usually could not be determined, but some were at least 18 cm. tall.

It is clear from the bimodal distribution of this bowl, with one peak in the Sabz phase and the other in late Mehmeh–early Bayat phases (see Fig. 64), that we have actually lumped together two different bowl types. We were aware of this, but there seemed to be no way to separate the two types in practice, since we were dealing for the most part only with rim sherds. It is probable that many of the rims of this type found in the Sabz phase belong to the vessels which rested on pedestals. This cannot be told from the rim sherds alone, and therefore we are left in the unsatisfactory position of having one Bowl Type, No. 12, which runs through all periods, has two apparent "peaks," and is of less chronological value than it might be.

One can, however, distinguish a trend in design elements through time which may be useful. Beginning in the Sabz phase and continuing into the Khazineh phase, "reserve" screen or cross-hatch patterns are common on this type of bowl, often in combination with an interior "fork" motif (Fig. 61*a*). In the Mehmeh phase, horizontal bands of chevrons or running ladders, bands of geometrics, pierced zig-zags, and rim-ticking marks are typical (Fig. 61*e-j*). Designs of the Bayat phase are most often very simple ones like Fig. 61*l*. Future excavators in Khuzistan may, hopefully, be able to subdivide this bowl type into subtypes with temporal significance.

Similar bowls appeared in the Susiana *b* to *c* time range (Le Breton, 1957:Fig. 6:32).

Low-necked jars (Fig. 58*k-q*).—Jars with necks standing 3 cm. or less above the body occur through all phases, but reach peak frequency in the Sabz and Bayat phases. This bimodal distribution suggests that we are probably dealing with two types of low-necked jars which, if separated, might be useful horizon markers. Unfortunately, in our study we did not hit upon a convenient way of distinguishing the Sabz type from the Bayat type. Future investigators, preferably working with a larger sample (we had only thirty-seven diagnostic rim sherds), should aim at such a division.

Although the Sabz phase and Bayat phase jars overlap in size and decoration, certain tendencies can be detected according to phase. The Sabz phase examples tend to be larger (rim diameters mostly in the 14 cm. range) and more frequently exhibit widely-spaced vertical or diagonal lines. The Bayat phase examples are smaller (rim diameters mostly in the 8 to 10 cm. range), and most frequently exhibit only a black band or a row of loops at the rim. Mehmeh and Khazineh specimens (as well as some from the early Bayat phase) have close decoration over most of the body, often consisting of triangular or diamond-shaped areas filled with hachure, or solid grids of cross-hatching.

Low-necked, globular jars with bands of hachure-filled triangles or lozenges are one of the most widely-distributed items of the Ubaid ceramic complex, from Tepe Gawra (Tobler, 1950:Pl. CXXVIII:305) to al Ubaid itself (Woolley, 1955:Pl. 52: bottom row).

Stronach's "Bowl Type 11" (Fig. 62).—Deep, bell-shaped bowls of very fine quality, the thinnest and best-made of all vessels in our Deh Luran sequence. The simple, tapered rims are slightly everted, and the bases round. The extreme thinness and uniformity suggests that these vessels are wheel-made. Certainly they represent the

Fig. 61. Susiana Black-on-buff pottery. "Type 12" bowls (reconstructed): *a,* variant typical of the Sabz and Khazineh phases; *b-d,* exterior designs typical of the Sabz and Khazineh phases; *e-j,* variants and exterior designs more typical of the Mehmeh phase; *k,l,* variants and exterior designs more typical of the Bayat phase.

technical culmination of a deep-bowl sequence which began with the crude convex-walled bowls of the Mohammad Jaffar phase, progressed with the deep "Sabz Pots" of the Sabz phase, and reached its peak with these bell-shaped vessels in the Mehmeh and Bayat phases.

The temperless paste of these vessels is well levigated and the bowls hard fired, sometimes at a sufficiently high temperature to vitrify the paint and turn the vessel green. There is little range in size, almost all bowls having a rim diameter of about 21 cm., a height of 13.5 cm., and a wall thickness at midsection of about 5 mm. One unusually small example had a rim diameter of 16 cm. and a height of 10 cm. (Fig. 62*f*).

Except for a simple black band on the interior of the rim, all decoration of these bowls is external. Usually it is arranged in horizontal rows, delimited by bands of black paint at top and bottom. A few sherds show free-standing designs, and others suggest large areas of solid black, but these are exceptions.

Designs on this type of bowl change through time. During the Khazineh phase, most motifs were repetitive geometric patterns, while naturalistic designs (trees, boats, human beings) and free-standing motifs were virtually confined to the Mehmeh phase. During the Mehmeh and Bayat phases, a few bowls had only simple rim bands. Bayat phase examples often had only the simplest zig-zag lines (e.g., Fig. 62*e*).

Two designs particularly characteristic of the Mehmeh phase are the "rows of goats" (Fig. 62*b,d*), already discussed under "Goat Bowls" (above), and a motif which shows stylized human dancers standing on each others' shoulders (Fig. 62*c*). This design often occurs in conjunction with panels of white and black scalene triangles. Usually the "dancing men" are arranged as an almost geometric design, but a single Mehmeh phase sherd shows them rendered in more realistic style (Fig. 63*n*).

"Bowl Type 11" would seem to be widespread in the lowlands of Mesopotamia and Khuzistan. According to Stronach (1961:112), "This particular class of bowl . . .constitutes perhaps the finest product of the Ras al Amiya potter. It almost certainly represents a broad based version of the. . .bowl, which at Eridu itself developed into the superb offering bowls found in levels IX - VIII." Fine bell-shaped bowls with exterior patterns can also be found in Susiana *b* to *c* levels at Jaffarabad (Le Breton, 1947:Fig. 13:1-11), and in level XVIII at Tepe Gawra (Tobler, 1950:Pl. LXXIII*a*). At Tepe Sabz, they begin in the Khazineh phase and increase steadily with time, reaching their peak in the Bayat phase.

Rare Vessel Forms or Attributes

Small jars (Fig. 63*a-c*).—These three miniature vessels, with rim diameters of only 3 to 6 cm., came from Khazineh and early Mehmeh phase levels. Two of them resemble a "small painted jar" recovered at Ras al Amiya (Stronach, 1961:Pl. LIII:4). Decoration is limited to broad horizontal bands of black paint, or irregular vertical stripes.

Small cups (Fig. 63*d,e*).—These two vessels both came from the Bayat phase. Rim diameters are from 6 to 7.5 cm. and heights about 4.5 cm. Decoration in one case consists of a broad band of black on the upper half of the cup; in the other case, the exterior of the vessel is covered by broad cross-hatching.

Bird effigy (Fig. 63*j*).—A Mehmeh phase level produced this unique vessel, which must have been about 10 cm. long originally. "Bird track" designs are painted on the exterior, and the interior bears traces of red ochre. Bird effigies are not common at any site of this period, but comparable ex-

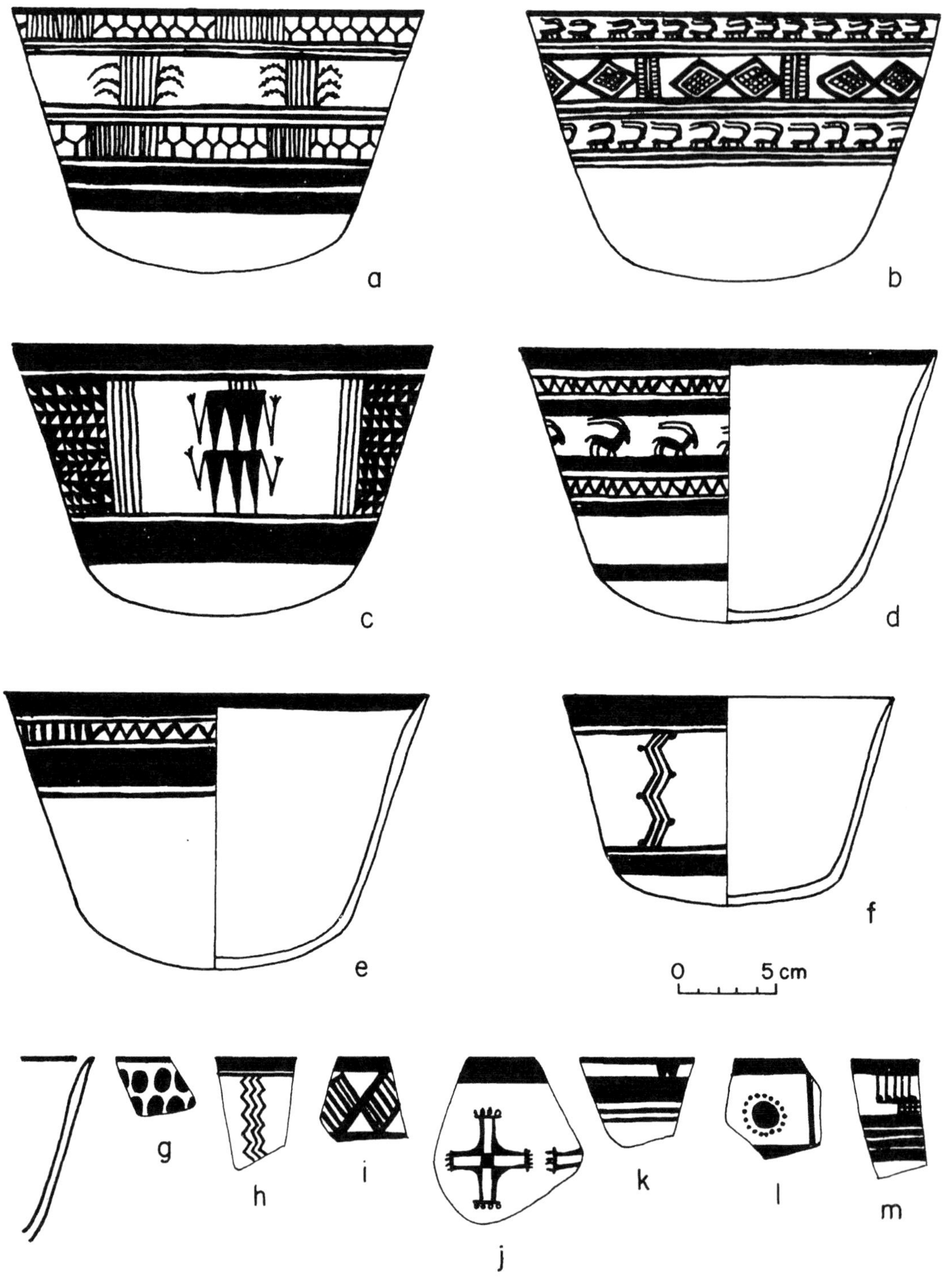

Fig. 62. Susiana Black-on-buff pottery. Examples of fine, bell-shaped bowls ("Type 11") from the Mehmeh and Bayat phases: *a-f,* reconstructions made from partially-restorable examples, showing range of variation in vessel form; *g-m,* examples of designs painted on exterior of rim and upper vessel wall. All major variants illustrated.

amples can be found at sites as far distant as Arpachiyah (Mallowan and Rose, 1935:72-75 and Pl. V:*b*).

Lip spouts (Fig. 63*f,g*).–Isolated small examples came from the Sabz and Bayat phases.

Strap handle (Fig. 63*h*).–One specimen came from the Bayat phase.

Perforated lug (Fig. 63*i*).–The Khazineh phase produced our only example of a vessel lug, some 3 cm. in diameter.

Rare but Significant Design Elements

"Bukrania" and "mouflon" designs (Fig. 63*k-m*).–The only three examples came from the Mehmeh phase, and two of those were found at Tepe Musiyan "E" rather than Tepe Sabz. Bukrania are typical of the Khabur region, occurring also at Tepe Gawra (Tobler, 1950:Pl. CX:10) and Gird Banahilk (Watson, unpublished data). Both bukrania and mouflon designs appeared at Ras al Amiya (Stronach, 1961:120).

Type: Mehmeh Red-on-red

Sample: 377 sherds

Temporal distribution: 320 out of 377 sherds come from the Mehmeh phase.

Appearance: Very much like Khazineh Red, with the addition of geometric designs in dark red paint. Vessels are hand-made, irregularly-shaped, and have a wide range of color due to uneven firing; the draftsmanship of the painting is careless but the designs are extremely varied. Mehmeh Red-on-red may be related to the "straw tempered ware" discovered by Stronach at Ras al Amiya, which is described as having "a pale red, straw-tempered core, a red-slipped surface, often burnished, and a matt form of paint, varying from dark purple to black" (Stronach, 1961:122). Stronach notes the "Iranian" characteristics of this ware, and places its origin somewhere to the east of Mesopotamia proper, with which we would agree; in fact, similarities can be seen with pottery from Tepe Hissar IA (Schmidt, 1937). This, coupled with the fact that painted "rows of wild goats" also occur at sites on the Iranian plateau during this period (see discussion under Susiana Black-on-buff, "Goat bowls"), suggests that during the Mehmeh phase the Deh Luran plain, and perhaps Khuzistan in general, received significant influence from the mountain areas to the east.

Paste: Loosely-compacted and crumbly, with a texture varying from medium to coarse on a single vessel. Hardness on Moh's scale varies between 2 and 5, with most sherds falling between 2 and 3.

Temper: Both chaff and grit (*cf.* Khazineh Red).

Color: The colors of the vessels themselves range from red (10R 5/6, 2.5YR 5/6), light red (2.5YR 6/6), reddish-brown (2.5YR 5/4), brown (7.5YR 5/4), pink (7.5YR 7/4), to pale brown (10YR 6/3).

Surface treatment: The vessels were all smoothed, and one sherd shows obvious use of a grayish wash. The surfaces are pitted from the burning-out of chaff.

Decoration: Geometric designs in a red or purple paint which is darker than the surface of the vessel (usually 7.5R 4/4, 10R 5/2, 10R 4/3, to 2.5 YR 5/2).

Vessel Forms

Hole-mouth jars (Fig. 65; Fig. 66*a*).–This was by far the most common form. These are squat, globular jars with dimple bases and simple, incurving rims. Occasionally, vessels might have trough spouts (Fig. 66*a*) or tubular spouts (Fig. 66*b*). These jars are crudely-made and often asymmetrical. Rim diameters range from 10 to 18 cm., and heights from 7 to 17 cm. The thickness of vessel walls at the midsection is 5 to 7 mm.

The range of variation in painted exterior designs on these hole-mouth jars is given in Fig. 65. A simple "net" design produced by cross-hatched lines crossing one another diagonally (see Fig. 65*m*; Fig. 66*a*) accounted for 70 per cent of the rim sherds of this shape. Also used were horizontal panels of tally marks, chevrons, zig-zag screens, dots, or wiggly lines. The hole-mouth jar covered by diagonal cross-hatch

Table 21

DISTRIBUTION OF VESSEL FORMS IN SUSIANA BLACK-ON-BUFF POTTERY AT TEPE SABZ AND TEPE MUSIYAN "E"
(By Stratigraphic Zone)

Site and Zone	Basins	"Sabz Pots"	Bowls with Pedestal Bases	Early Ring Bases	Bowl Types 2, 3, 6	"Sauce-boats"	Bowl Type 13	Bowl Type 1	Rims, Bowl Type 14	Bases, Bowl Type 14 (and 18)	Rims, Bowl Type 18	Bowl Type 15	Ledge-rim Jars	"Goat Bowls"	Bowl Type 11*a*	High-necked Jars	Later Ring Bases	Bowl Type 12	Low-necked Jars	Miscellaneous Jar Sherds	Bowl Type 11	Small Jars	Small Cups	Bird Effigy	Lip Spouts	Strap Handle	Perforated Lug	Unclassified Body Sherds	Totals
TS - A_1 . . .	. . .	. . .	. . .	. . .	1	. . .	. . .	1	. . .	. . .	. . .	2	. . .	. . .	31	13	6	48	. . .	3	55	. .	. .	. .	. .	. .	. .	430	590
TS - A_2 . . .	. . .	. . .	. . .	. . .	1	. . .	1	1	1	1	. . .	2	. . .	2	37	13	8	88	2	10	101	. .	2	. .	1	. .	. .	573	844
TS - A_3 . . .	. . .	. . .	. . .	. . .	2	1	. . .	3	6	2	2	5	2	4	118	7	4	150	10	5	127	. .	. .	. .	. .	1	. .	726	1175
TS - B_1 . . .	. . .	. . .	. . .	. . .	3	2	. . .	12	12	10	6	20	7	36	19	2	9	147	2	5	132	. .	. .	1	. .	. .	. .	608	1033
MUS "E". . .	. . .	. . .	. . .	. . .	1	1	. . .	1	4	2	3	6	3	10	2	. . .	1	13	. . .	1	20	. .	. .	. .	. .	. .	. .	234	302
TS - B_2 . . .	. . .	. . .	. . .	. . .	2	1	2	7	23	16	12	51	4	33	. . .	1	4	131	. . .	3	156	. .	. .	. .	. .	. .	. .	482	928
TS - B_3 . . .	. . .	. . .	. . .	. . .	2	4	20	16	55	32	2	47	6	13	. . .	2	. . .	80	. . .	11	81	1	. .	. .	. .	. .	. .	395	767
TS - C_1 . . .	. . .	. . .	. . .	. . .	4	1	18	27	105	80	6	10	2	. . .	. . .	. . .	. . .	78	1	15	40	. .	. .	. .	. .	. .	. .	328	715
TS - C_2 . . .	. . .	1	. . .	1	5	2	29	25	53	47	5	1	2	. . .	. . .	. . .	. . .	45	1	7	8	1	. .	. .	. .	. .	. .	234	467
TS - C_3 . . .	. . .	3	1	. . .	14	5	3	2	10	8	. . .	2	. . .	. . .	. . .	. . .	. . .	42	. . .	. . .	4	. .	. .	. .	. .	. .	1	78	173
TS - D	39	162	24	32	43	4	3	15	. . .	1	5	3	. . .	. . .	. . .	2	. . .	235	21	5	1	. .	. .	. .	1	. .	. .	109	705
Totals . . .	39	166	25	33	78	21	76	110	269	199	41	149	26	98	207	40	32	1057	37	65	725	2	2	1	2	1	1	4197	7699

Table 22

DISTRIBUTION OF VESSEL FORMS IN SUSIANA BLACK-ON-BUFF POTTERY AT TEPE SABZ AND TEPE MUSIYAN "E"
(By Cultural Phase)

Phase	Basins	"Sabz Pots"	Bowls with Pedestal Bases	Early Ring Bases	Bowl Types 2, 3, 6	"Sauce-boats"	Bowl Type 13	Bowl Type 1	Rims, Bowl Type 14	Bases, Bowl Type 14 (and 18)	Rims, Bowl Type 18	Bowl Type 15	Ledge-rim Jars	"Goat Bowls"	Bowl Type 11*a*	High-necked Jars	Later Ring Bases	Bowl Type 12	Low-necked Jars	Miscellaneous Jar Sherds	Bowl Type 11	Small Jars	Small Cups	Bird Effigy	Lip Spouts	Strap Handle	Perforated Lug	Unclassified Body Sherds	Totals
Bayat	. . .	. . .	. . .	. . .	4	1	1	5	7	3	2	9	2	6	186	33	18	286	12	18	283	. .	2	. .	1	1	. .	1729	2609
Mehmeh . . .	. . .	. . .	. . .	. . .	8	8	22	36	94	60	23	124	20	92	21	5	14	371	2	20	389	1	. .	1	. .	. .	. .	1719	3030
Khazineh . .	. . .	4	1	1	23	8	50	54	168	135	11	13	4	. . .	. . .	. . .	. . .	165	2	22	52	1	. .	. .	. .	. .	1	640	1355
Sabz	39	162	24	32	43	4	3	15	. . .	1	5	3	. . .	. . .	. . .	2	. . .	235	21	5	1	. .	. .	. .	1	. .	. .	109	705
Totals. . .	39	166	25	33	78	21	76	110	269	199	41	149	26	98	207	40	32	1057	37	65	725	2	2	1	2	1	1	4197	7699

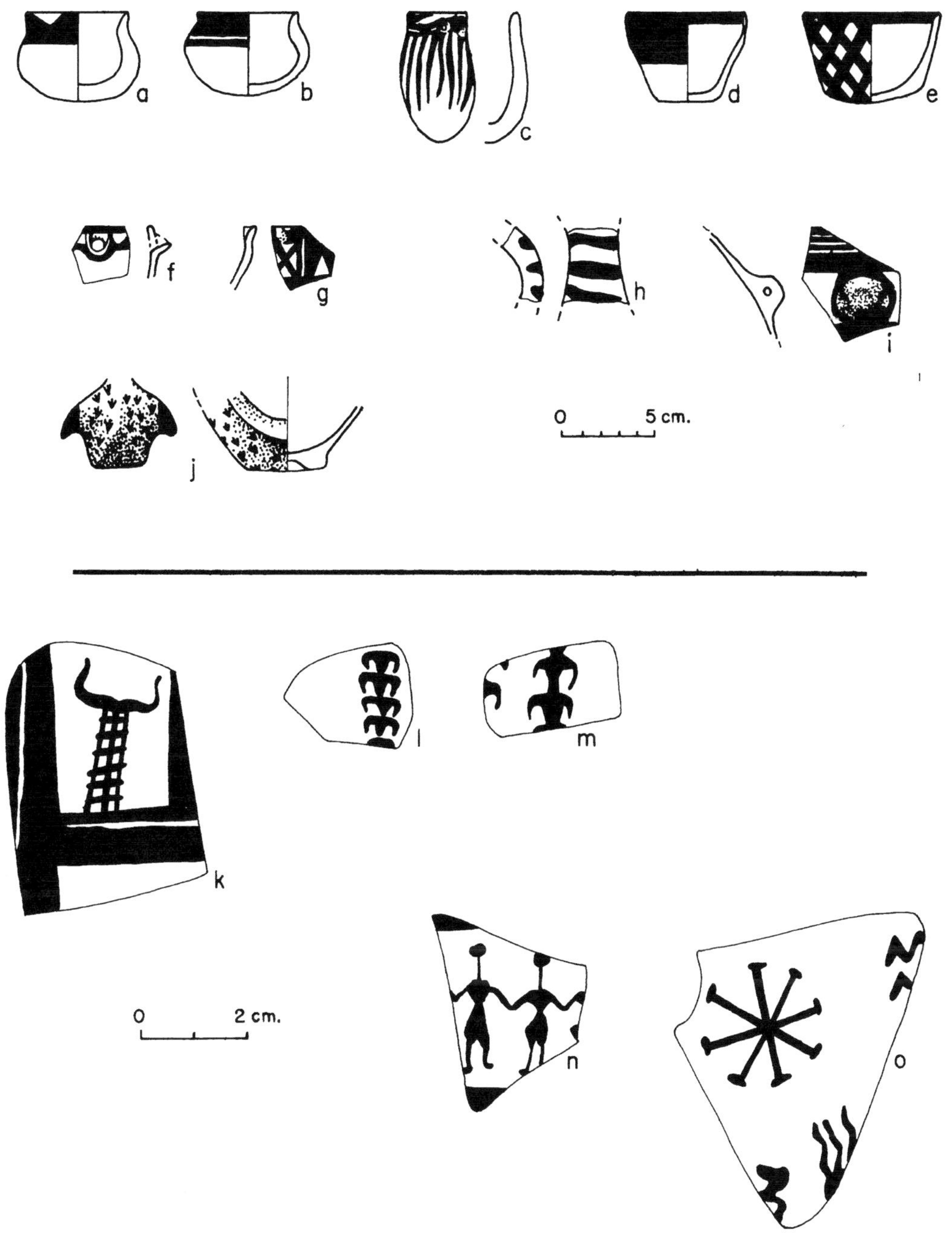

Fig. 63. Susiana Black-on-buff pottery. Miscellaneous rare items, mainly from Tepe Sabz: *a,* small jar, zone B_3 (Mehmeh phase); *b,* small jar, zone C_2 (Khazineh phase); *c,* small narrow jar, complete, from clearing trench (Khazineh phase levels); *d,e,* from zone A_2, Bayat phase; *f,g,* small lip spouts (*f,* Bayat phase; *g,* Sabz phase); *h,* small strap handle, zone A_3 (Bayat phase); *i,* small perforated lug, zone C_3 (Khazineh phase); *j,* bird effigy vessel, zone B_1 (Mehmeh phase); *k,* painted sherd showing *bukranium* motif, zone B_2, (Mehmeh phase); *l,* painted sherd showing *mouflon* motif, Tepe Musiyan "E" (Mehmeh phase); *m,* painted sherd showing *mouflon* motif, zone B_1 at Tepe Sabz (Mehmeh phase); *n,* sherd with "dancing men" painted motif, zone B_1 (Mehmeh phase); *o,* painted sherd from zone B_3 (Mehmeh phase).

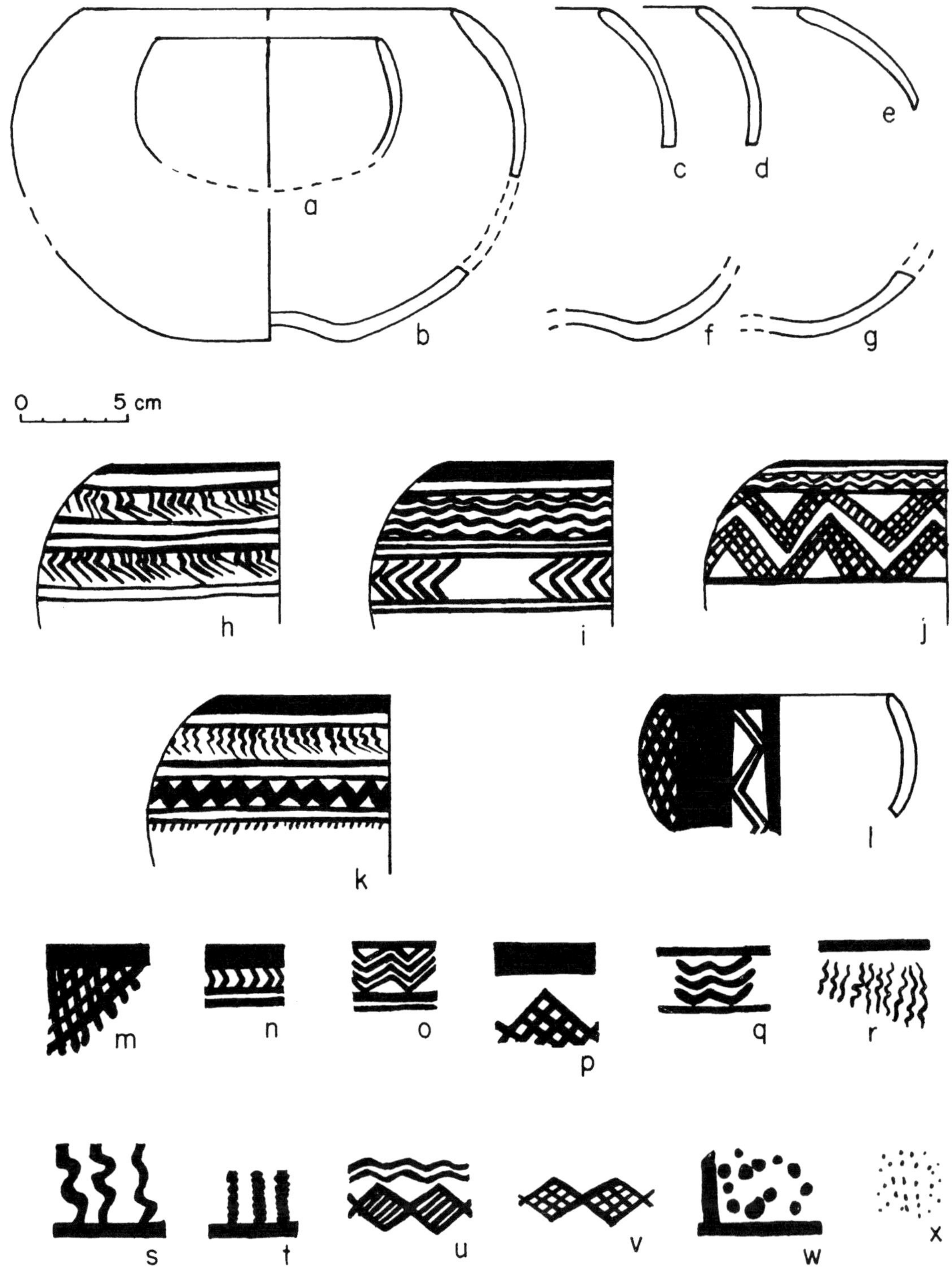

Fig. 65. Mehmeh Red-on-red pottery. Hole-mouth jars: *a,b,* reconstructed examples showing size range; *c-e,* variation in rim forms; *f,g,* dimpled bases; *h-l,* vessel exteriors showing typical motifs painted on rim and upper wall; *m-x,* additional range of variation in exterior painted designs, in decreasing order of frequency, from L. to R. (all Mehmeh phase examples).

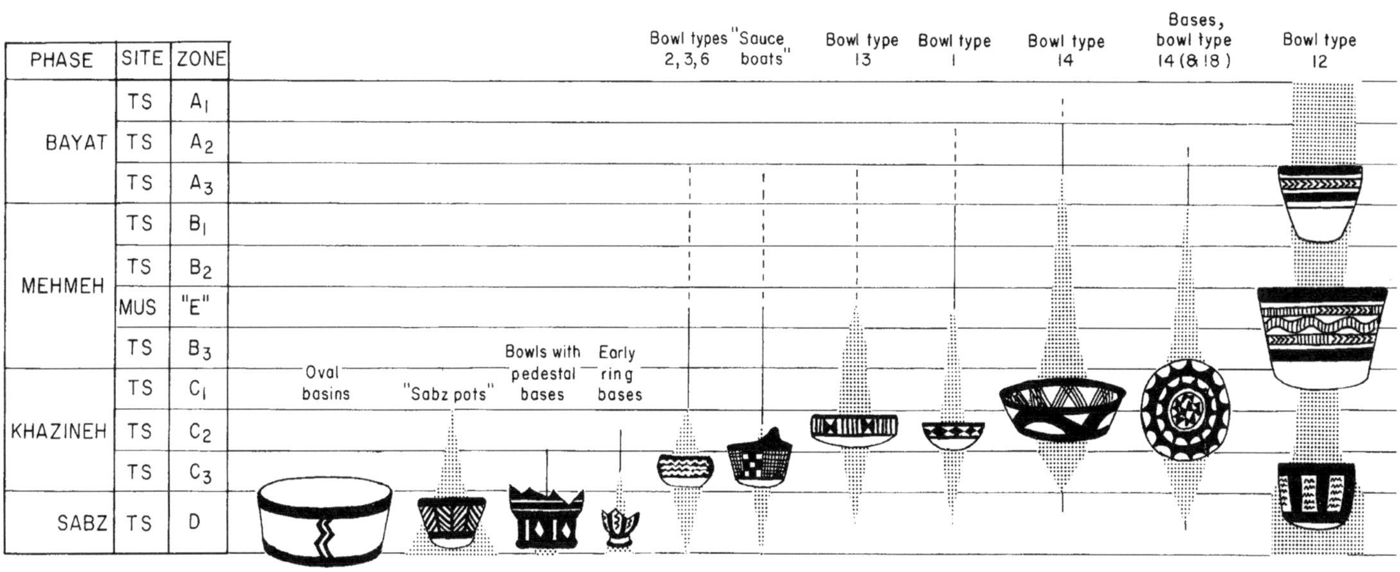

Fig. 64. Susiana Black-on-buff pottery: change
changes in percentage of 21 major vessel forms throu
Tepe Sabz and Tepe Musiyan "E." Frequency of each
the number of sherds of that type of vessel within the
levels were screened, and all sherds larger than 1 by
vessels of each period, but do not approach the full rang

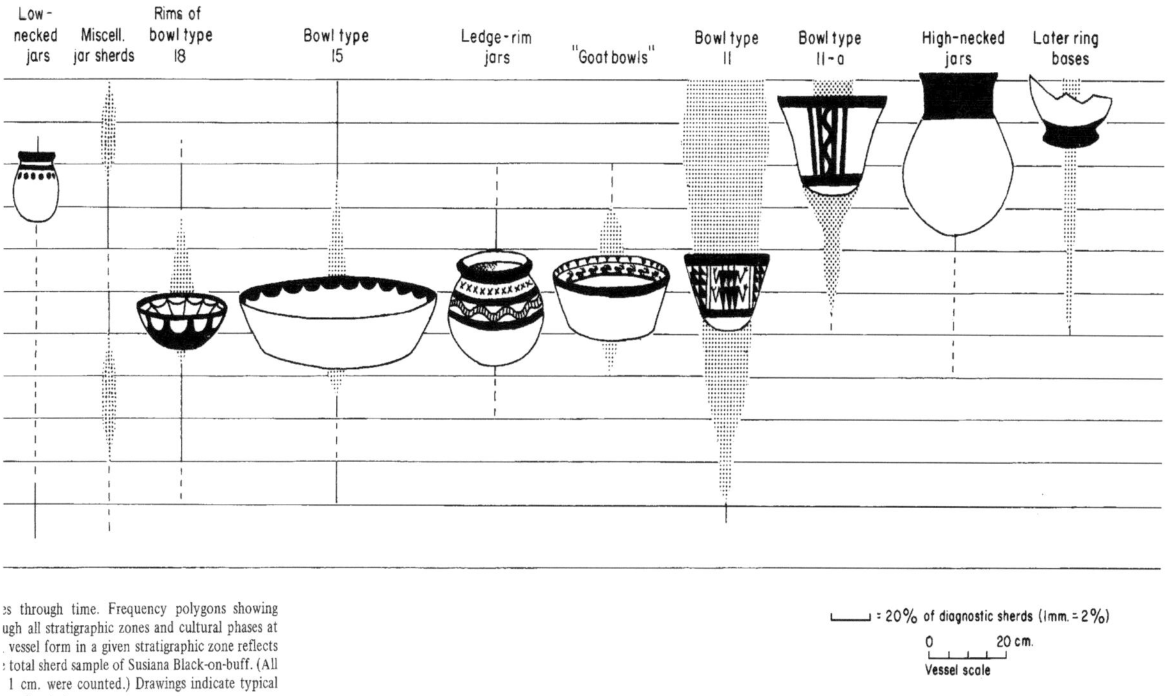

…s through time. Frequency polygons showing …ugh all stratigraphic zones and cultural phases at … vessel form in a given stratigraphic zone reflects … total sherd sample of Susiana Black-on-buff. (All … 1 cm. were counted.) Drawings indicate typical …ge of variation.

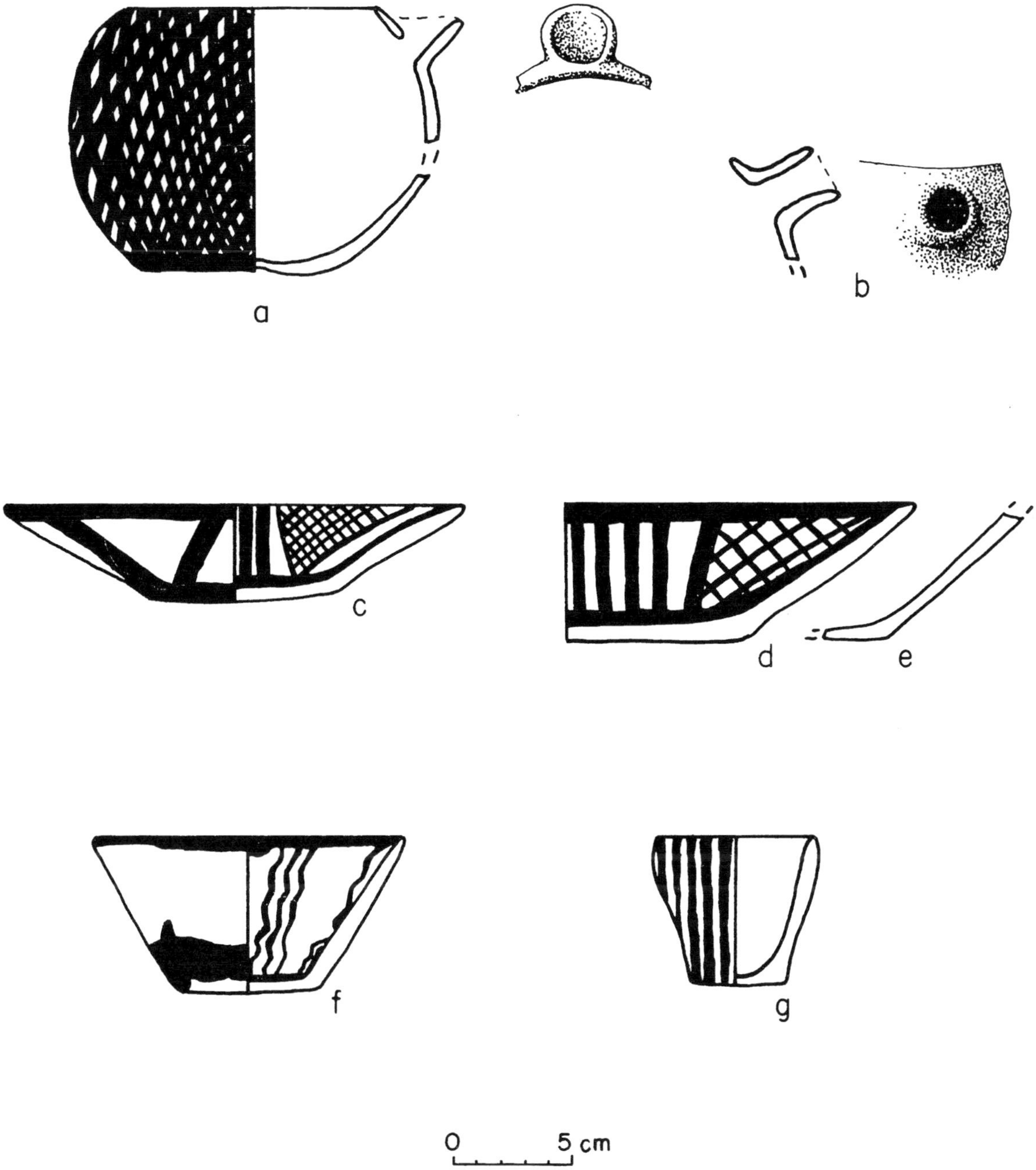

Fig. 66. Mehmeh Red-on-red pottery. Miscellaneous vessel forms (reconstructed): *a,* hole-mouth jar with trough spout: vessel form (L.) and drawing of spout as seen from above (R.); *b,* short tubular spout from hole-mouth jar: section (L.) and front view (R.); *c-e,* wide, shallow bowls with flaring walls; *f,* deep bowl with flaring wall; *g,* small cup. All Mehmeh phase examples.

was a real "horizon marker" for the Mehmeh phase, with only five sherds occuring in levels of the preceding and subsequent phases.

Wide, shallow bowls with flaring walls (Fig. 66*c-e*).–These have a rim diameter of 20 to 30 cm. and a height of only 4 to 6 cm. Wall thickness, about 6 mm. The exterior decoration consists of two horizontal bands encircling the vessel at rim and base, and occasionally joined by widely spaced diagonal lines. The interior decoration is predominantly rows of vertical lines, closely-spaced, separated by triangular areas filled with cross-hatch.

Deep bowls with flaring walls (Fig. 66*f*).–Small rim sherds of this vessel form could not always be distinguished from those of small cups (below), but the best-preserved examples indicate a rim diameter of about 14 cm. and a height of 7 cm. Wall thickness, about 6 mm. Decoration on the exterior includes horizontal lines at rim and base (often poorly drafted). On the interior, some vessels have wavy vertical lines in groups of three or four.

Small cups (Fig. 66*g*).–The few measurable examples are 6 cm. in height, with a rim diameter of about 7 cm. and a wall thickness of 6 mm. Decoration is limited to vertical lines on the exterior, fairly closely spaced, or else horizontal lines at rim and base which make it possible to confuse rims of cups and deep bowls.

Type: Bayat Red

Sample: 343 sherds

Temporal distribution: 309 out of 343 sherds occur in the Bayat phase. The type was increasing rapidly in frequency by the end of our sequence, and evidently went on to reach its peak at a later period. Dr. Robert H. Dyson Jr. informs us (orally) that red pottery of this type appears in the Susa *A* period in central Khuzistan, and furthermore, that it antedates (and can be readily distinguished from) the so-called "Uruk redware" of later times. Other Khuzistan sites where we have seen sherds of Bayat Red, indistinguishable from ours, include Chogha Mish.

Appearance: A hard, well-made red or salmon-colored pottery which is notable for its uniformity of color and texture. Vessels show the concentric striations thought to be characteristic of wheel-made pottery; on the average, they are larger than previous red-ware vessels made in the Deh Luran plain.

Paste: Compact and very dense, with few "pores" in the core. It has a fine to very fine sandy texture. Hardness ranges as high as 5 on Moh's scale, but most sherds fall between 2 and 3.

Temper: No vegetal material whatsoever was used. Most temper is quartz sand, but ground-up sherds were sometimes used along with the sand. The particles of temper range in size from 0.3 to 1.3 mm. It is difficult to judge whether the smaller particles were deliberately included in the paste, or whether they simply remained after imperfect cleaning of the clay.

Color: Ranges through pale red (10R 6/3), red (10R 5/6), light red (2.5YR 6/6), and pink (5YR 7/3 and 7.5YR 7/4), to brown (5YR 5/3). The color is usually homogeneous throughout the core and surface. No black unoxidized cores were seen, but on about one-fourth of the sherds a light gray streak remained in the center of the core.

Surface treatment: All the vessels are smoothed (although the interiors of jars are not as carefully treated), but none is burnished or polished with the care given to the Susiana Buff wares. Both added washes and "self slips" seem to occur. Any washes used are of the same clay as the paste, and they can only be detected when the surface peels or pops away. In a few instances a dark red (almost maroon) wash, or a lighter buff wash, were used over the red paste. The surface of the latter vessels are more carefully smoothed.

Decoration: None.

Vessel Forms

Large, carinated bowls (Fig. 67*a*).–Large bowls with relatively straight outleaning walls, simple rims, and slightly rounded bases which join the walls in a carination.

Table 23

OCCURRENCE OF VESSEL FORMS IN MEHMEH RED-ON-RED POTTERY AT ALI KOSH, TEPE SABZ, AND TEPE MUSIYAN "E"
(By Stratigraphic Zone)

Site and Zone	Rims from Hole-mouth Jars	Dimple Bases from Hole-mouth Jars	Trough Spouts from Hole-mouth Jars	Tubular Spouts from Hole-mouth Jars	Rims from Wide, Shallow Bowls with Flaring Walls	Rims from Deep Bowls and/or Cups	Bases from Shallow Bowls, Deep Bowls, and Cups	Miscellaneous Body Sherds	Totals
TS - A_1	...	...	...	...	...	...	...	2	2
TS - A_2	...	...	...	...	...	...	...	5	5
TS - A_3	3	...	...	...	1	1	...	13	18
TS - B_1	10	1	...	...	1	5	1	36	54
MUS "E".........	6	...	...	...	1	1	...	25	33
TS - B_2	10	11	1	2	7	2	5	74	112
TS - B_3	15	11	2	...	2	1	1	89	121
TS - C_1	1	...	...	...	...	...	...	14	15
TS - C_2	...	1	...	...	...	...	1	12	14
TS - C_3	...	...	...	...	...	...	...	2	2
TS - D..........	...	...	.....	....	.....	...	...	1	1
AK - A_1	...	...	...	...	...	...	...	...	...
AS - A_2	...	...	...	...	...	...	...	...	...
Totals.........	45	24	3	2	12	10	8	273	377

Table 24

OCCURRENCE OF VESSEL FORMS IN MEHMEH RED-ON-RED POTTERY AT ALI KOSH, TEPE SABZ, AND TEPE MUSIYAN "E"
(By Cultural Phase)

Phase	Rims from Hole-mouth Jars	Dimple Bases from Hole-mouth Jars	Trough Spouts from Hole-mouth Jars	Tubular Spouts from Hole-mouth Jars	Rims from Wide, Shallow Bowls with Flaring Walls	Rims from Deep Bowls and/or Cups	Bases from Shallow Bowls, Deep Bowls, and Cups	Miscellaneous Body Sherds	Totals
Bayat	3	...	...	...	1	1	...	20	25
Mehmeh	41	23	3	2	11	9	7	224	320
Khazineh.........	1	1	...	...	...	...	1	28	31
Sabz	...	...	...	...	...	...	...	1	1
Mohammad Jaffar	...	...	...	...	...	...	...	...	...
Totals.........	45	24	3	2	12	10	8	273	377

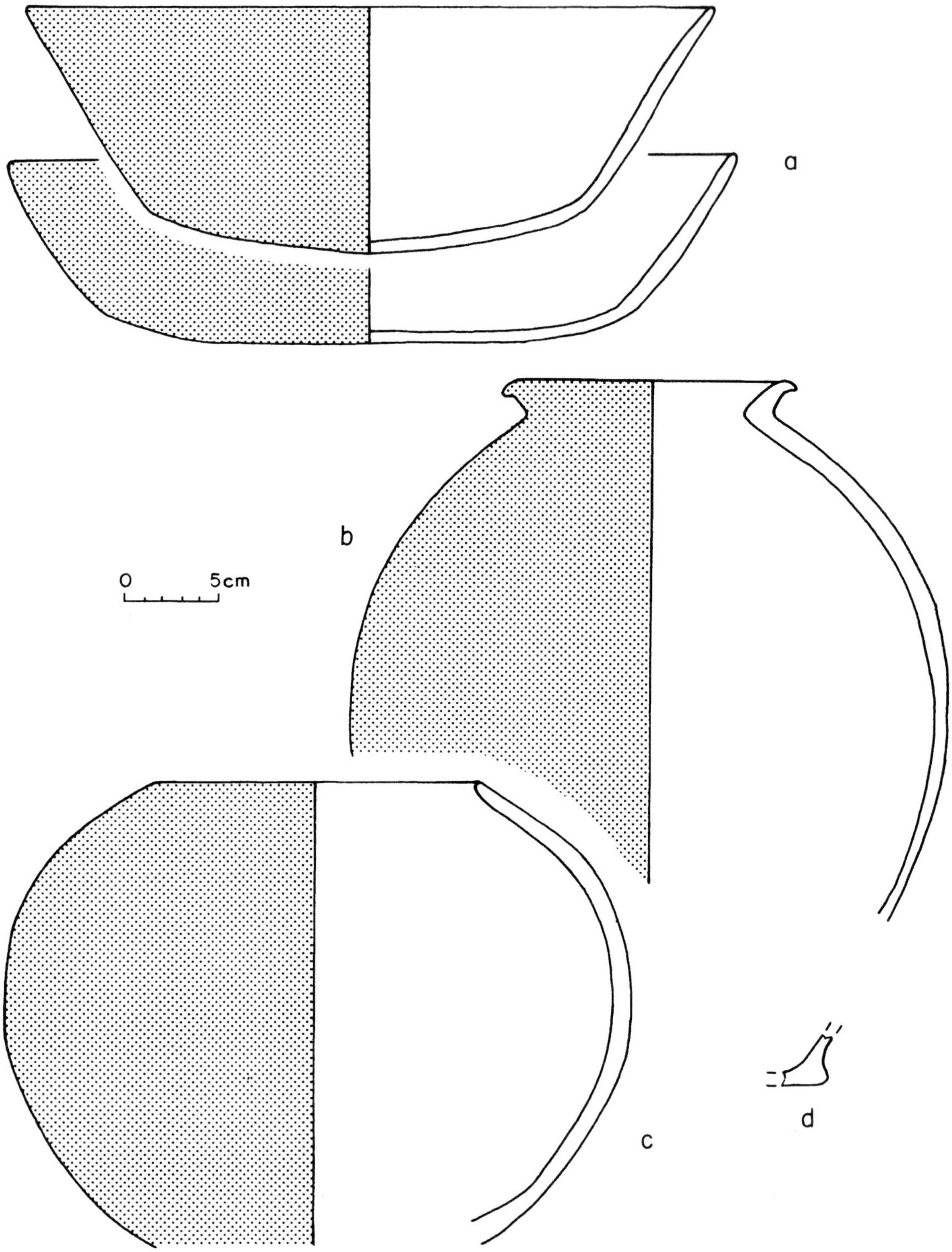

Fig. 67. Bayat Red pottery. Vessel forms typical of the Bayat phase (reconstructed): *a,* large carinated bowls; *b,* necked jar; *c,* hole-mouth jar; *d,* aberrant base.

The range in heights of reconstructed vessels is 10 to 13.5 cm., and in rim diameters, from 30 to 38 cm. The wall thickness at midsection is 7 to 8 mm. Confined to the Bayat phase, these vessels resemble large carinated bowls from the Susiana *c* to *d* periods (Le Breton, 1957:Fig. 4).

Hole-mouth jars (Fig. 67*c*).—Large globular jars with restricted orifices and (probably) rounded bottoms. Rim diameters are 12 to 26 cm., and the larger vessels stood about 25 cm. high. The walls are 8 to 9 mm. thick at midsection. The few sherds of this shape were found in the late Mehmeh and Bayat phases.

Necked jars (Fig. 67*b*).—Five rim sherds of large, globular, short-necked jars were found. The necks lean sharply outward, and the rims are rolled to the outside. The one measurable neck has a rim diameter of 15 cm. and stood 3 cm. high. At midsection, the vessel walls were 8 to 9 mm. thick. Found only in the Bayat phase.

Aberrant base (Fig. 67*d*).—A flat base with a "heel-shaped" wall/base juncture appeared in the Bayat phase. It could have belonged to an aberrant specimen of any of the shapes described above.

Table 25

OCCURRENCE OF VESSEL FORMS IN BAYAT RED POTTERY AT TEPE SABZ AND TEPE MUSIYAN "E"
(By Stratigraphic Zone)

Site and Zone	Sherds of Carinated Bowls	Rims of Hole-mouth Jars	Rims of Necked Jars	Miscellaneous Body Sherds	Totals
TS - A_1 . . .	17	4	. . .	111	132
TS - A_2 . . .	19	2	1	74	96
TS - A_3 . . .	21	. . .	2	58	81
TS - B_1 . . .	. . .	3	. . .	17	20
MUS "E" . . .	. . .	1	. . .	. . .	1
TS - B_2 . . .	. . .	. . .	. . .	11	11
TS - B_3 . . .	. . .	. . .	. . .	2	2
TS - C_1 . . .	. . .	. . .	. . .	. . .	. . .
TS - C_2 . . .	. . .	. . .	. . .	. . .	. . .
TS - C_3 . . .	. . .	. . .	. . .	. . .	. . .
TS - D	. . .	. . .	. . .	. . .	. . .
AK - A_1 . . .	. . .	. . .	. . .	. . .	. . .
AK - A_2 . . .	. . .	. . .	. . .	. . .	. . .
Totals . . .	57	10	3	273	343

Possibly Foreign Pottery Types

The following sherds represent types which may be derived from outside the Deh Luran area.

Fine Black-on-tan

General Description.—A fine, hard, wheel-made ware, with neatly-drafted designs, which compares in quality with bowls of Type 11 in Susiana Black-on-buff. The paste is very fine and well-compacted, with few pores; no tempering material was used.

Table 26

OCCURRENCE OF VESSEL FORMS IN BAYAT RED POTTERY AT TEPE SABZ AND TEPE MUSIYAN "E"
(By Cultural Phase)

Phase	Sherds of Carinated Bowls	Rims of Hole-mouth Jars	Rims of Necked Jars	Miscellaneous Body Sherds	Totals
Bayat	57	6	3	243	309
Mehmeh . . .	. . .	4	. . .	30	34
Khazineh . . .	. . .	. . .	. . .	. . .	. . .
Sabz	. . .	. . .	. . .	. . .	. . .
Mohammad Jaffar	. . .	. . .	. . .	. . .	. . .
Totals. . .	57	10	3	273	343

The surface color is light reddish-brown (5YR 6/4), and the paint is very dark gray (2.5YRN3). Hardness on Moh's scale is 4 to 5. The surfaces of the sherds are very well-smoothed, but striations remain as evidence of the potter's wheel. There is no evident use of a slip, and the sherd cores are the same color as the surfaces. Surfaces were not burnished or polished. The only vessel form present is like Bowl Type 11, deep bell-shaped bowls with slightly outflaring simple rims and rounded bases (Fig. 68*c-f*). At least four different bowls are represented by the ten sherds. All the sherds were found in the upper zones of the Bayat phase.

It is possible that this type is only an accidental product of the misfiring of the local Black-on-buff, but its occurrence, confined to one phase, and the details of some designs suggest that it is not of local origin. If so, it is more likely an import from Mesopotomia, to the west, than from the Iranian plateau area to the east. It is more suggestive of the fine bell-shaped bowls at Eridu (Oates, 1960:Pl. IV:17*b*) than of anything being made in interior Iran at the same time period.

Burnished Black

General Description.—Four sherds of hard, burnished black pottery occurred in the Bayat phase; they may all be from one vessel. The paste is fine-grained and well compacted, but it has some pores. Flakes of mica (possibly a natural occurrence in the clay?) are obvious to the eye. The whole sherd, core and surface, is a uniform black, suggesting that it was manufactured under different conditions from the usual Deh Luran wares. Both surfaces were highly burnished. One sherd has three parallel incised lines which were cut into the exterior surface following the burnishing. One rim sherd of a straight-sided open bowl, similar

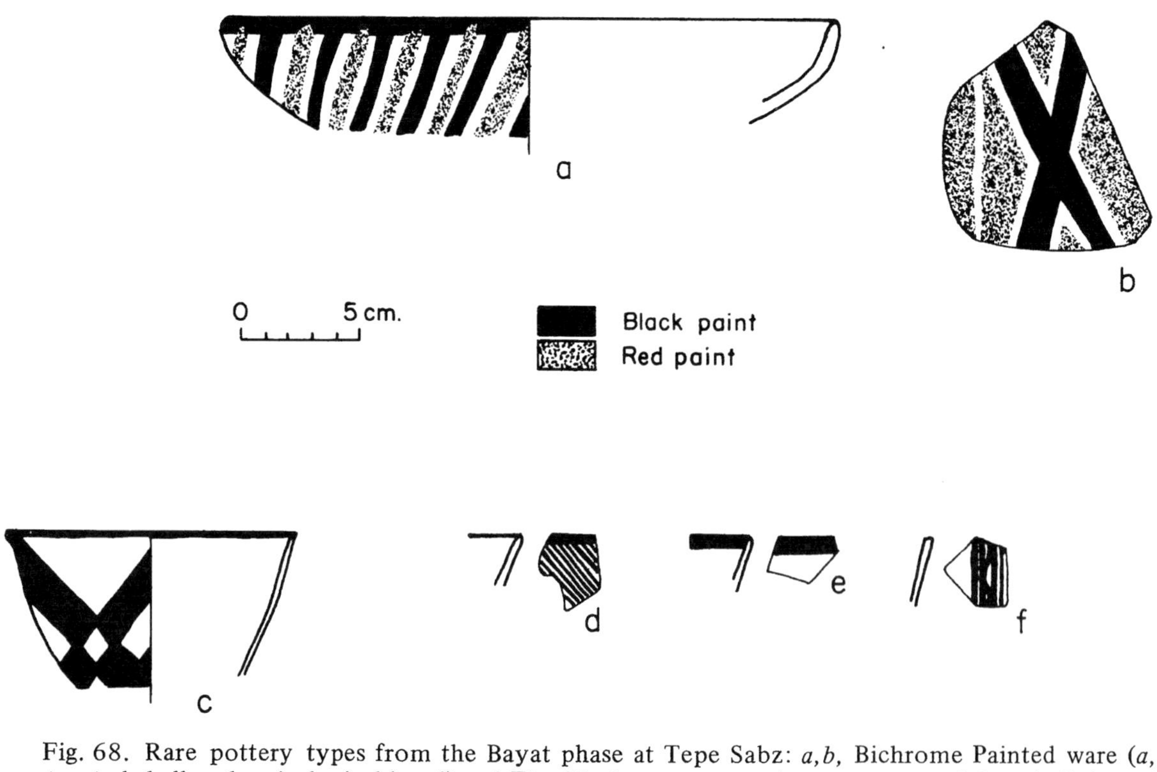

Fig. 68. Rare pottery types from the Bayat phase at Tepe Sabz: *a,b,* Bichrome Painted ware (*a,* reconstructed shallow hemispherical bowl); *c-f,* Fine Black-on-tan ware (*c,* reconstructed deep bell-shaped bowl, cf. "Type 11;" *d-f,* rim sherds from similar bowls).

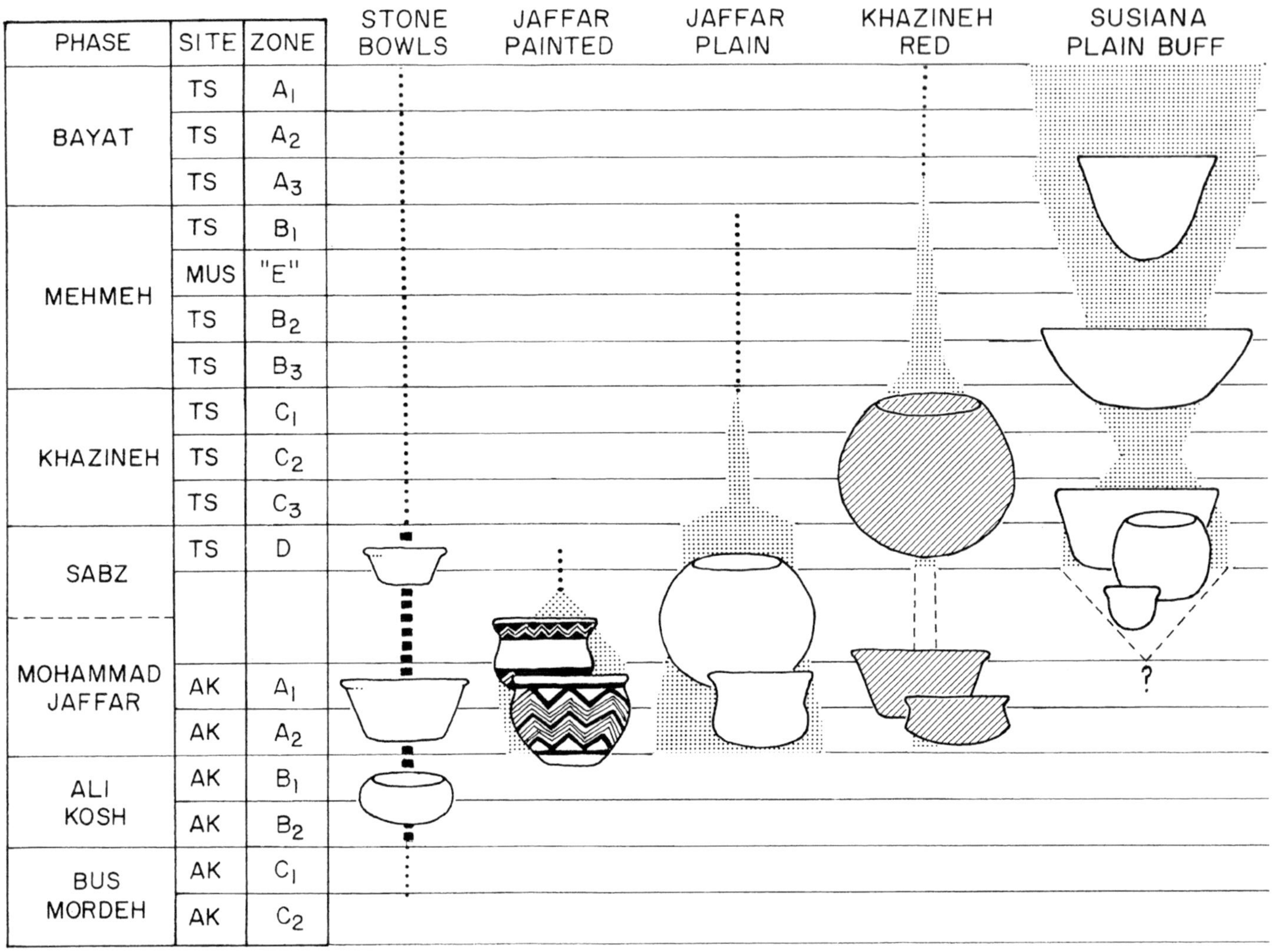

Fig. 69. Pottery types from the Deh Luran sequ
showing changes in percentage of all major pottery t
phases at Tepe Ali Kosh, Tepe Sabz, and Tepe Mu
stratigraphic zone reflects the number of sherds of th
were screened, and all sherds larger than 1 by 1 cm. wer
(indicated by the heavy black dashed line) is also shov
stone bowls *vs.* pottery were not calculated. Drawings i
approach the full range of variation.

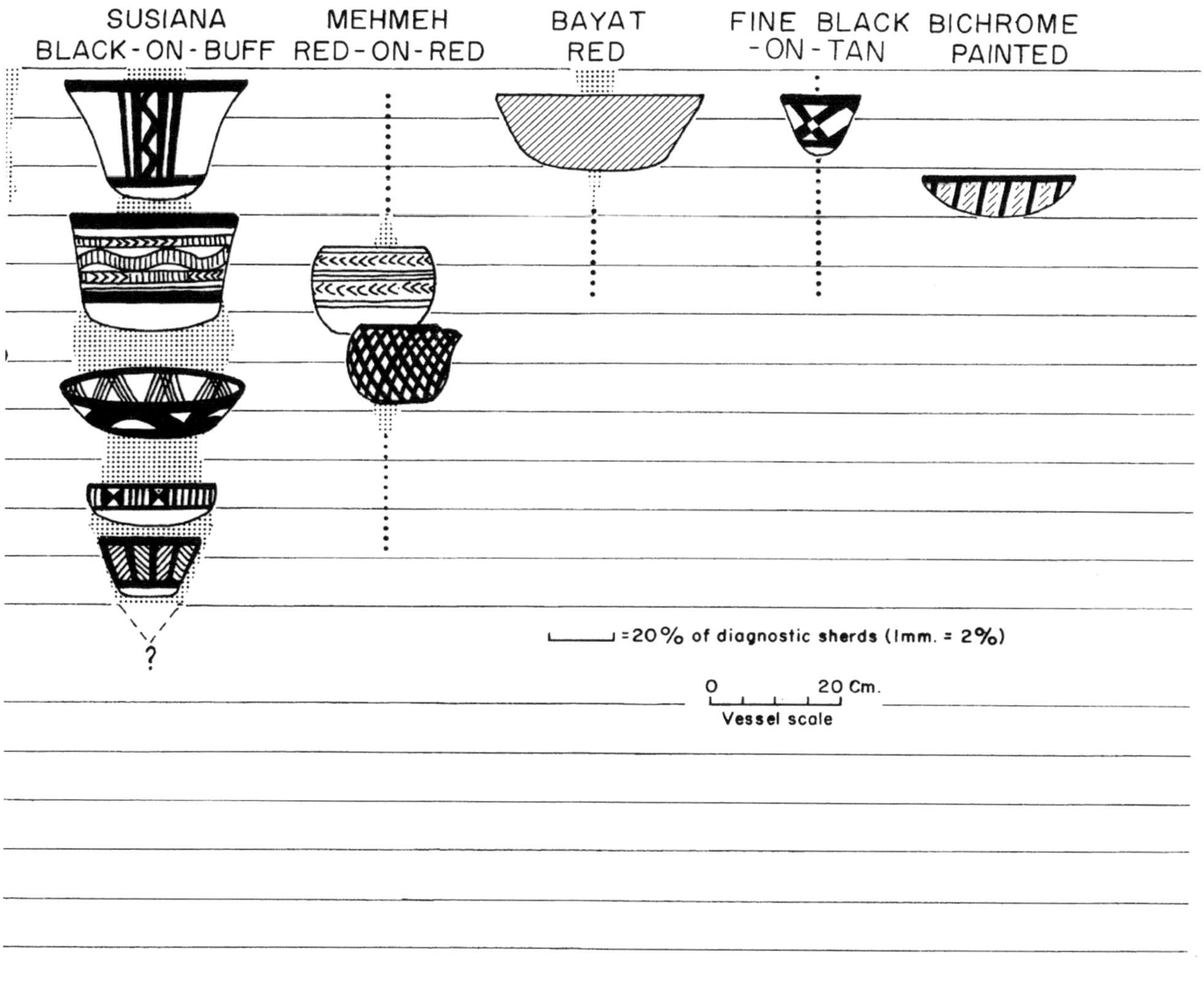

ɥuence: changes through time. Frequency polygons
types through all stratigraphic zones and cultural
[usiyan "E." Frequency of each type in a given
hat type within the total sherd sample. (All levels
ere counted.) Temporal distribution of stone bowls
own, for comparative purposes, but percentages of
s indicate typical vessels of each period, but do not

to Bowl Type 12 of Susiana Black-on-buff, was found. See Pl. 30*e,f*.

This type bears certain resemblances to some of the "dark-faced burnished wares" of the Syro-Cilician area (Braidwood and Braidwood, 1960).

Bichrome Painted

General Description.—Well-compacted buff ware with a sandy-textured paste which has rare pores or holes. No tempering material was observed. The vessels were coated inside and out with a thin light buff slip, and painted with linear and geometric designs (Fig. 68*a,b*). The sherds all appear to be hand-made. The surface of the vessels is off-white (2.5Y 8/2) and the paint is both dark red (7.5R 3/8) and black (2.5YR N2). The red and black are both chalky and somewhat fugitive. Some of the paint can be removed by rubbing with the finger. One sherd, 9 mm. thick, is from the midsection of a large bowl or basin (Fig. 68*b*). The remaining sherds are all from a shallow hemispherical bowl with a flattened rim (Fig. 68*a*). The rim diameter is 26 cm. and the vessel stands about 5 to 7 cm. high. All sherds were found in Bayat phase levels.

These unusual sherds are suggestive of the Bichrome Painted wares occurring in phases D and E of the Amuq sequence in Syro-Cilicia (Braidwood and Braidwood, 1960:Fig. 158:22), and the unique bichrome specimen from the lowest level at Khafajah (Delougaz, 1952:Pl. 4: Kh. IX 49). Coupled with the Black-on-tan and Black Burnished wares already described above, they may indicate that influences from culture areas to the west were reasonably strong during the Bayat phase.

Table 27

OCCURRENCE OF POSSIBLE FOREIGN POTTERY TYPES AT TEPE SABZ
(By Stratigraphic Zone)

Site and Zone	Fine Black-on-tan	Burnished Black	Bichrome Painted	Totals
TS - A_1	7	3	...	10
TS - A_2	4	...	...	4
TS - A_3	...	1	5	6
TS - B_1	...	...	...	...
TS - B_2	...	...	...	...
TS - B_3	...	...	...	...
TS - C_1	...	...	...	...
TS - C_2	...	...	...	...
TS - C_3	...	...	...	...
TS - D	...	...	...	...
Totals	11	4	5	20

Table 28

OCCURRENCE OF POSSIBLE FOREIGN POTTERY TYPES AT TEPE SABZ
(By Stratigraphic Zone)

Phase	Fine Black-on-tan	Burnished Black	Bichrome Painted	Totals
Bayat	11	4	5	20
Mehmeh	...	...	...	...
Khazineh	...	...	...	...
Sabz	...	...	...	...
Totals	11	4	5	20

X

GRINDING AND POUNDING TOOLS

TYPOLOGY AND TERMINOLOGY

The ancient occupants of Ali Kosh and Tepe Sabz used a variety of stone implements for grinding and pounding foods, pigments, and other substances, We recovered more than six hundred such implements in 1961 and 1963, and have divided them into five categories: grinding slabs, and the handstones which were rubbed over them; mortars, and the pestles which were used in them; and stone pounders of various kinds.

While reading through reports dealing with sites of the Ali Kosh - Tepe Sabz time range, we came across few attempts to establish a typology of grinding stones which would be of chronological significance. This came as a surprise to us, in view of the fact that our grinding-pounding implements lent themselves as well to typology as most of the other artifact categories.

Perhaps our biggest typological problem was one of nomenclature. Terms like mortar and pestle are sufficiently unambiguous, but we also needed a way of distinguishing between the "grinding stone" held in the hand and the "grinding stone" over which it is rubbed. A number of terms used in the literature, for example "quern" and "hand mill" proved inaccurate, for both technically refer to a pair of stones used as a team: the dictionary definition for "quern" is "an old form of handmill for grinding grain, the upper stone usually pierced and turned on a pin in the nether stone by means of a stick thrust into a notch in the edge." New World archeologists distinguish the upper stone by calling it mano, while the lower stone is referred to as a metate; but these Latin American terms are unfamiliar to the Near Eastern archeologist. We tentatively solved our problem with the following terms, used throughout this report:

Grinding slab: The lower stone of a pair of grinding stones, which rests on the ground.

Handstone: The upper stone of the pair, which is held in the hand(s).

THE CHRONOLOGICAL SEQUENCE

In many cases, the grinding implements were as characteristic of a phase (or group of phases) in our sequence as the pottery or flint. In the Bus Mordeh phase, only four grinding slabs were found. One was a simple type we refer to as a "flat-topped boulder," and the other three were saddle-shaped. Both types lasted into the Ali Kosh phase, at which point they were joined by pebble mortars and shallow basin grinding slabs; nearly one hundred slabs or mortars were found in levels of this phase. However, by far the greatest variety of grinding implements appeared in the succeeding Mohammad Jaffar phase. There were flat-topped-boulder and saddle-shaped slabs, shallow basin grinding slabs, pebble mortars and boulder mortars, and a number of "combination" tools: shallow basin grinding slabs which also had mortar sockets in them, and which seemed to be associated with the cylindrical objects which we call combination pestles and handstones.

By the time of the Sabz phase, shallow basin grinding slabs and pebble mortars had gone out of use, though saddle-shaped and flat-topped-boulder grinding slabs continued. In the Khazineh phase, flat-topped boulders and "combination" shallow-basin-and-mortar types made their last appearance in the sequence. Only a limited variety of grinding implements characterized the Mehmeh phase and the Bayat phase, with saddle-shaped grinding slabs (occasionally with added mortar sockets) predominating. Thus the saddle-shaped slab (along with its associated simple, discoidal handstone) was the only type occurring through all phases of the sequence.

A few of the minor grinding stone types were of highly-restricted stratigraphic occurrence; a convenient example is the type we call an "irregular sausage-shaped handstone." All four examples recovered at Tepe Sabz came from Mehmeh phase levels—and significantly enough, our test into Mehmeh phase levels at Tepe Musiyan "E" disclosed two more.

Grinding Slabs and Mortars

Type: Flat-topped boulder grinding slab (Fig. 70)

Sample: 11

Material: Limestone boulders

Description: These are river boulders which, in their natural state, had at least one relatively flat surface; that surface has been further flattened and smoothed by grinding. A feature which distinguishes them from other grinding slab types, however, is the fact that the grinding surface is never basin-shaped or saddle-shaped in cross-section, no matter which direction it is viewed from. Examples vary from 25 to 45 cm. in length.

Temporal distribution: Bus Mordeh through Khazineh phases.

Geographic distribution: A search of the archeological literature reveals no illustrated specimens of what we are calling "flat-topped boulder grinding slabs." We feel relatively confident that such must have existed at sites contemporary with Ali Kosh; however, it is possible that they have simply not been illustrated—or often, perhaps, not even recognized as tools.

Type: Saddle-shaped grinding slab (Figs. 71-73)

Sample: 172

Material: Limestone, often pitted

Description: These are slabs or boulders of limestone which have been ground until their upper surface presents a concave appearance. Most are about twice as long as they are wide, and such is the pattern of grinding that only the two ends of the long axis present unground "ridges" preserving the original surface of the rock. There are no ridges along the sides of the long axis, for the associated handstone (frequently our "simple discoidal" type) has been ground over these areas also. This lack of lateral ridges, besides giving the slab its "saddle-shaped" appearance, distinguishes it from our "shallow basin" type, which is completely enclosed by ridges. A few specimens were partially coated with asphalt, and many are stained with red ochre. They vary from 30 to 50 cm. in length.

Temporal distribution: Throughout the entire sequence, this was by far the most common type of grinding slab in use in the Deh Luran valley.

Geographic distribution: Similar saddle-shaped grinding slabs occurred at Jarmo (Braidwood, 1951:Fig. 11, lower right; Braidwood, 1952:Fig. 14, and possibly also the fragmentary specimen shown in Braidwood, Howe, *et al.* 1960:Plate 20, No. 6); at Hassuna (Braidwood, 1952:Fig. 7); in Sialk I (Braidwood, 1952:Fig. 6); and many other, later sites.

Type: Shallow basin grinding slabs (Fig. 74*c,d*)

Sample: 18

Material: Limestone

Description: These are shallow, roughly-circular basins, completely encircled by an unground ridge or lip, which preserves the original surface of the stone. The grinding action was clearly rotary, and confined to the center of the slab. It is evident from the wear that

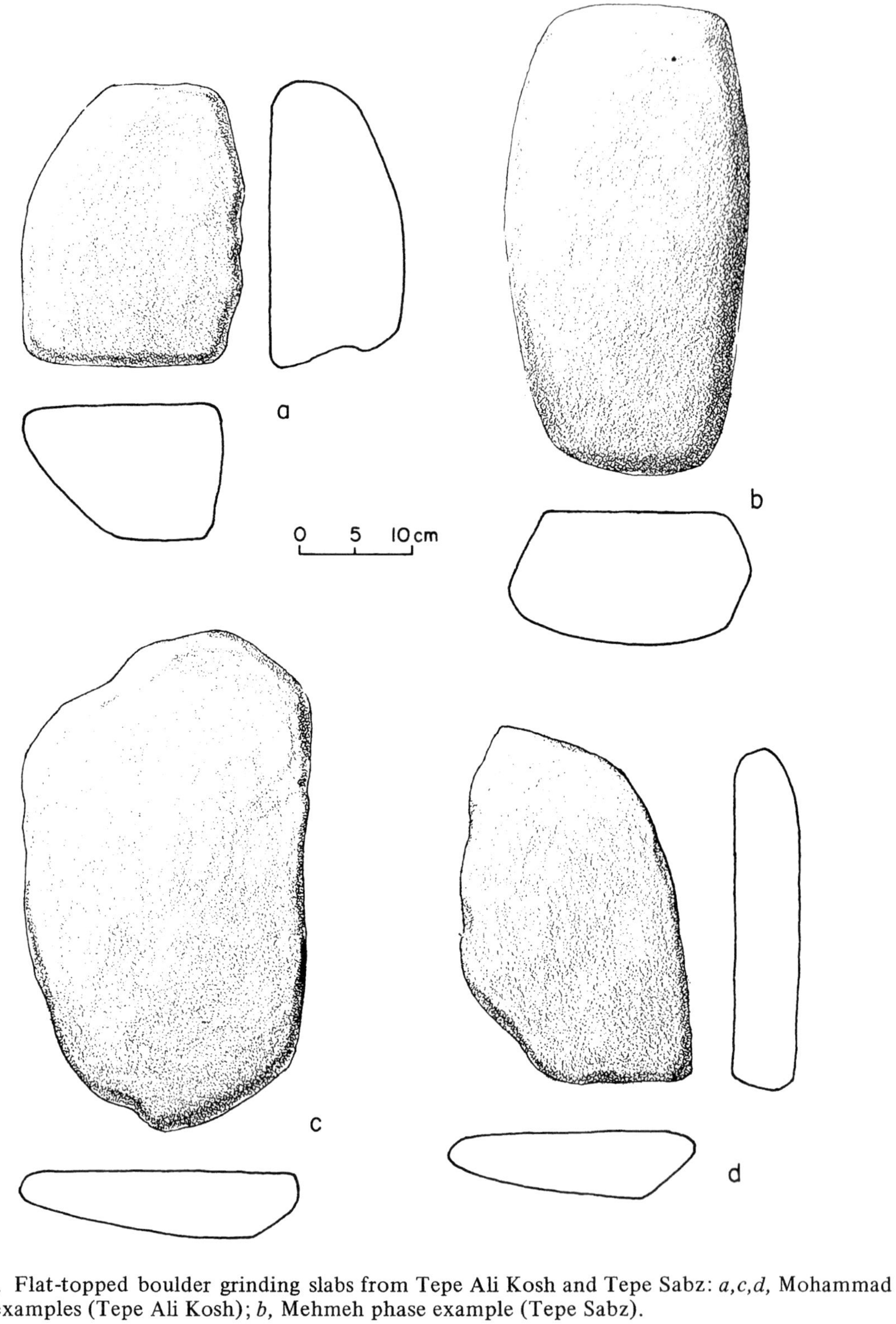

Fig. 70. Flat-topped boulder grinding slabs from Tepe Ali Kosh and Tepe Sabz: *a,c,d,* Mohammad Jaffar phase examples (Tepe Ali Kosh); *b,* Mehmeh phase example (Tepe Sabz).

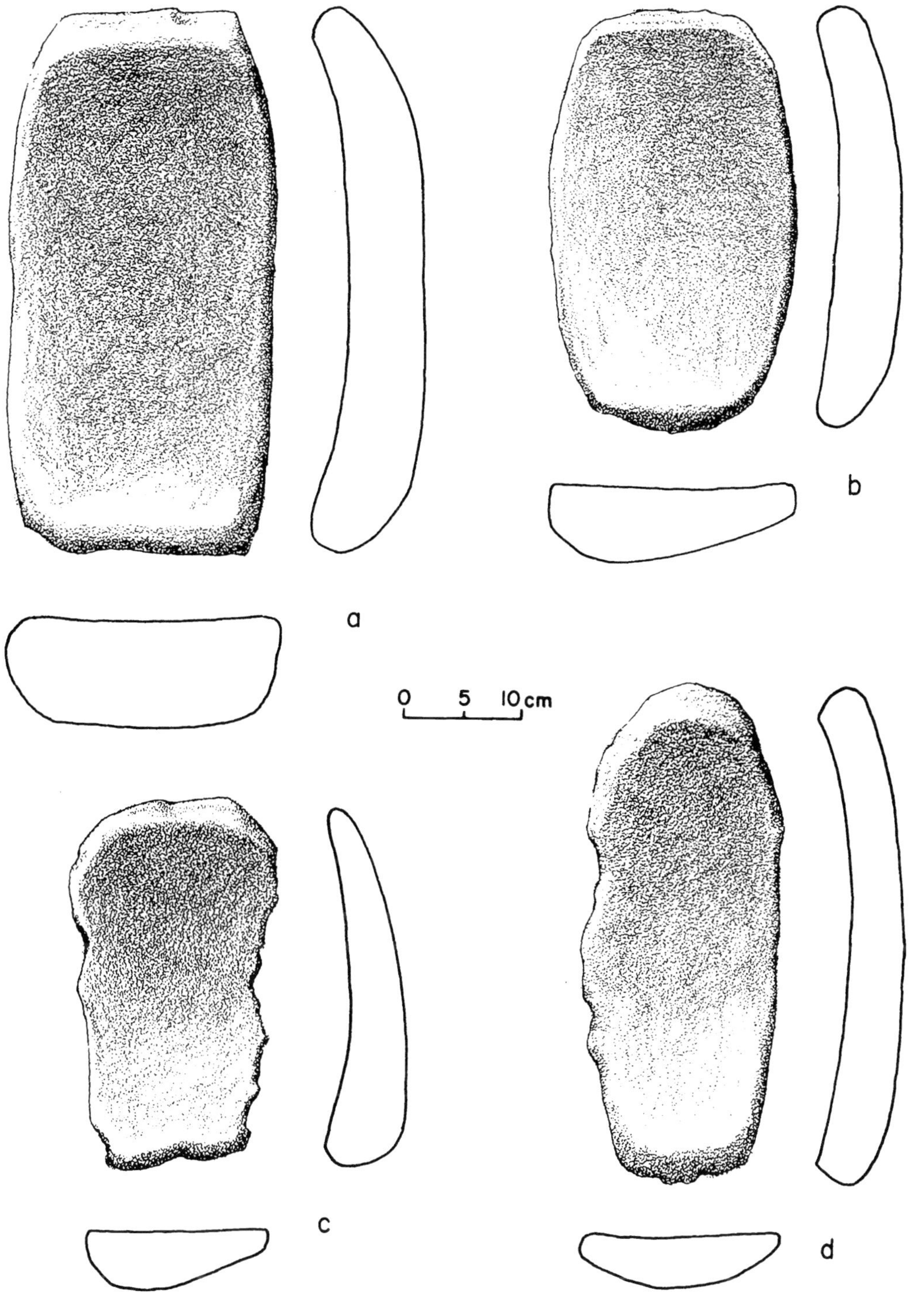

Fig. 71. Saddle-shaped grinding slabs from Tepe Ali Kosh and Tepe Sabz: *a,* slab associated with Burial 5, Tepe Sabz (Bayat phase); *b,* Tepe Ali Kosh (surface); *c,* Tepe Ali Kosh, zone B_2, house (Ali Kosh phase); *d,* Tepe Sabz, zone B_2 (Mehmeh phase).

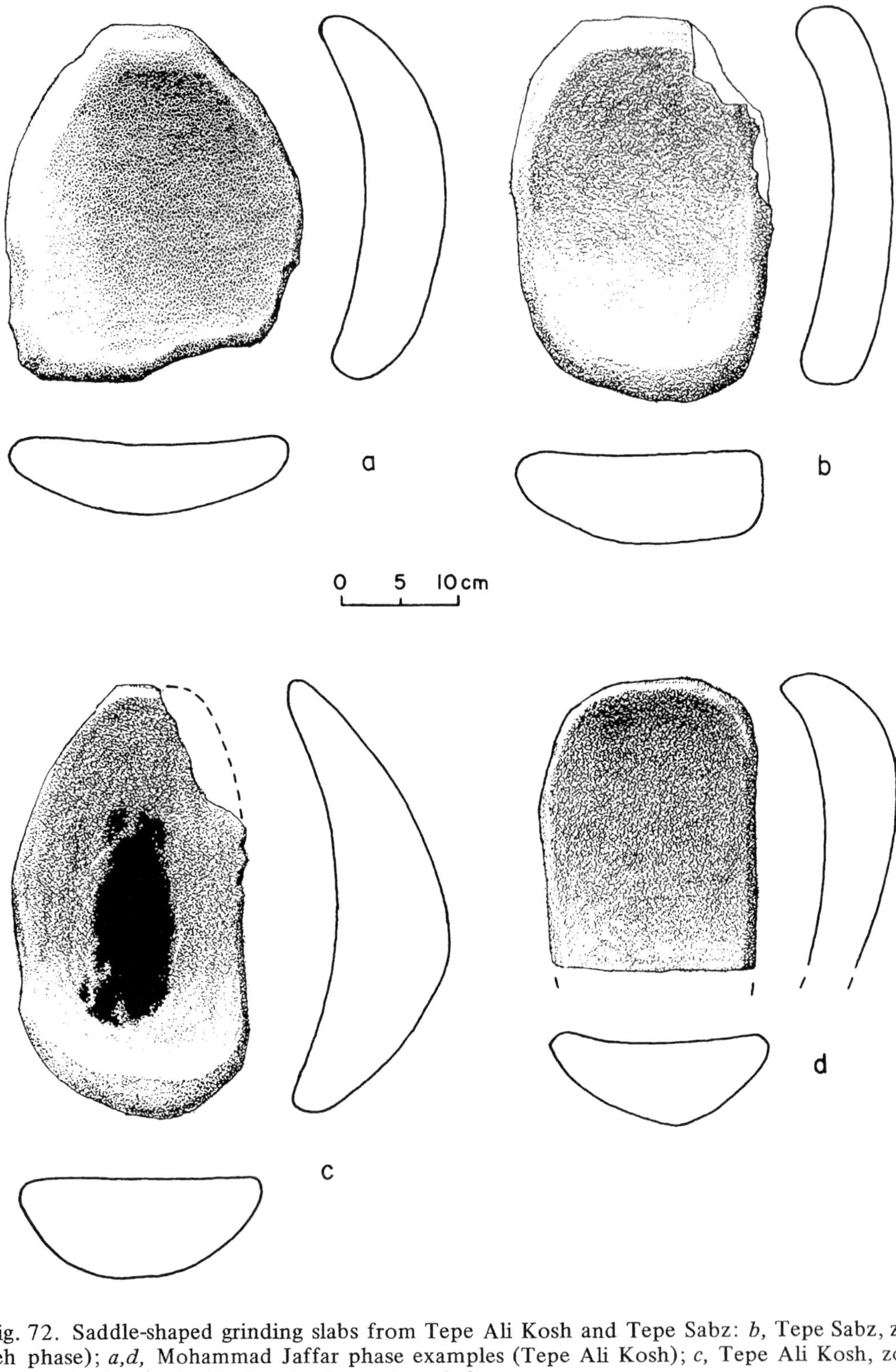

Fig. 72. Saddle-shaped grinding slabs from Tepe Ali Kosh and Tepe Sabz: *b,* Tepe Sabz, zone B_3 (Mehmeh phase); *a,d,* Mohammad Jaffar phase examples (Tepe Ali Kosh); *c,* Tepe Ali Kosh, zone B_2, house (Ali Kosh phase); the black stain shown is asphalt.

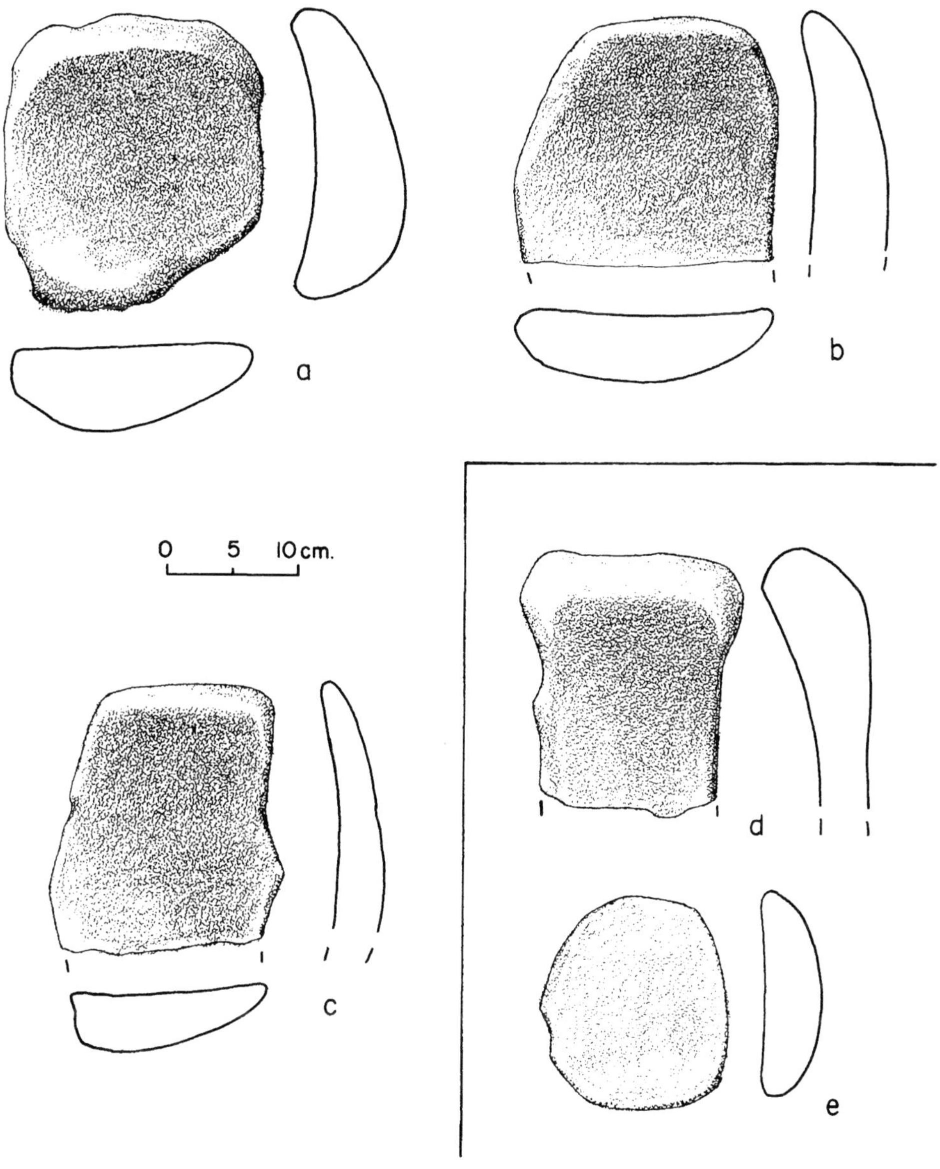

Fig. 73. Saddle-shaped grinding slabs from Tepe Ali Kosh and Tepe Sabz: *a-c*, Tepe Ali Kosh; *a*, zone A_1 (Mohammad Jaffar phase); *b*, (Ali Kosh phase); *c*, zone B_2 house (Ali Kosh phase); *d,e*, saddle-shaped grinding slab, (*d*) and its simple discoidal handstone (*e*), found in association at Tepe Sabz, zone C_1, square 29 (Khazineh phase).

these served as grinding slabs and not as mortars. A few contain smears of red ochre. They vary from 25 to 35 cm. in diameter.

Temporal distribution: These were used in small numbers in the Ali Kosh phase, but their major popularity was in Mohammad Jaffar times.

Geographic distribution: Similar shallow basins occurred at Jarmo (Braidwood, Howe, *et al.* 1960:Plate 20, No. 1).

Type: Combination shallow basin grinding slab and mortar (Figs. 74 *a,b*; 75*a-d*)

Sample: 15

Material: Limestone

Description: These are shallow basin grinding slabs, like those already described, with the addition of from one to two fairly deep and well-defined sockets which apparently served as mortars. The sockets are heavily worn from contact with pestles, while the surface of the basin has been ground down by rotary action with a handstone. These combination implements may be round, rectangular, or even pear-shaped in outline. Most are from 25 to 40 cm. in diameter, with an exceptional example reaching 50 cm.

Temporal distribution: With only two exceptions, these are confined to the Mohammad Jaffar phase. It would be interesting to know if they are similarly confined to pottery-bearing levels at contemporary sites, for example Jarmo.

Geographic distribution: This rather specialized type of combination mortar and grinding slab was found at Jarmo (Braidwood, 1951: Fig. 11 upper right; Braidwood, Howe, *et al.* 1960:Plate 20, No. 5) and perhaps at Zawi Chemi Shanidar (R. L. Solecki, 1964:406).

Type: Boulder mortar (Fig. 76)

Sample: 6

Material: Limestone boulders, most fairly round

Description: These are river boulders which are unmodified except for one–or sometimes two-deep, well-defined sockets which apparently served as mortars. They seem to have been selected for their weight and stability rather than conformation. Examples vary from 20 to 40 cm. in diameter.

Temporal distribution: Mohammad Jaffar through Khazineh phases.

Geographic distribution: Similar boulder mortars occurred at Jarmo (Braidwood, 1951:Fig. 11, upper left).

Type: Pebble mortar (Fig. 77*a-b*)

Sample: 7

Material: Limestone pebbles or cobbles, probably from the bed of the Dawairij River

Description: These tiny mortars are only 5 to 10 cm. in diameter, and consist of smooth river bed stones, each bearing a socket with evidence of grinding. One example contained red ochre, and it is not unreasonable to suppose that most may have been used for grinding pigment.

Temporal distribution: Our seven examples come from the Ali Kosh and Mohammad Jaffar phases.

Geographic distribution: Similar mortars were found at Jarmo (Braidwood, 1951:Fig. 11, lower center; Braidwood, Howe, *et al.* 1960:Plate 20, No. 3).

Type: Combination saddle-shaped grinding slab and mortar (Fig. 77*e*)

Sample: 8

Material: Limestone, often pitted

Description: These are saddle-shaped grinding slabs, like those already described, with the addition of one fairly deep and well-defined socket which apparently served as a mortar. The socket is heavily worn from contact with a pestle, while the surface of the slab has been ground down with a handstone just as are the plain saddle-shaped slabs. Their size range is the same as the latter.

Temporal distribution: Throughout the sequence at Tepe Sabz, though never in great numbers. They are probably the functional equivalents of the Mohammad Jaffar phase "combination shallow basin and mortar," but their temporal distribution is somewhat different, making them useful horizon markers.

Geographic distribution: Unknown.

Rare Type: Saddle-shaped slab with central depression (Fig. 77*d*)

Sample: 2

Material: Limestone, often pitted

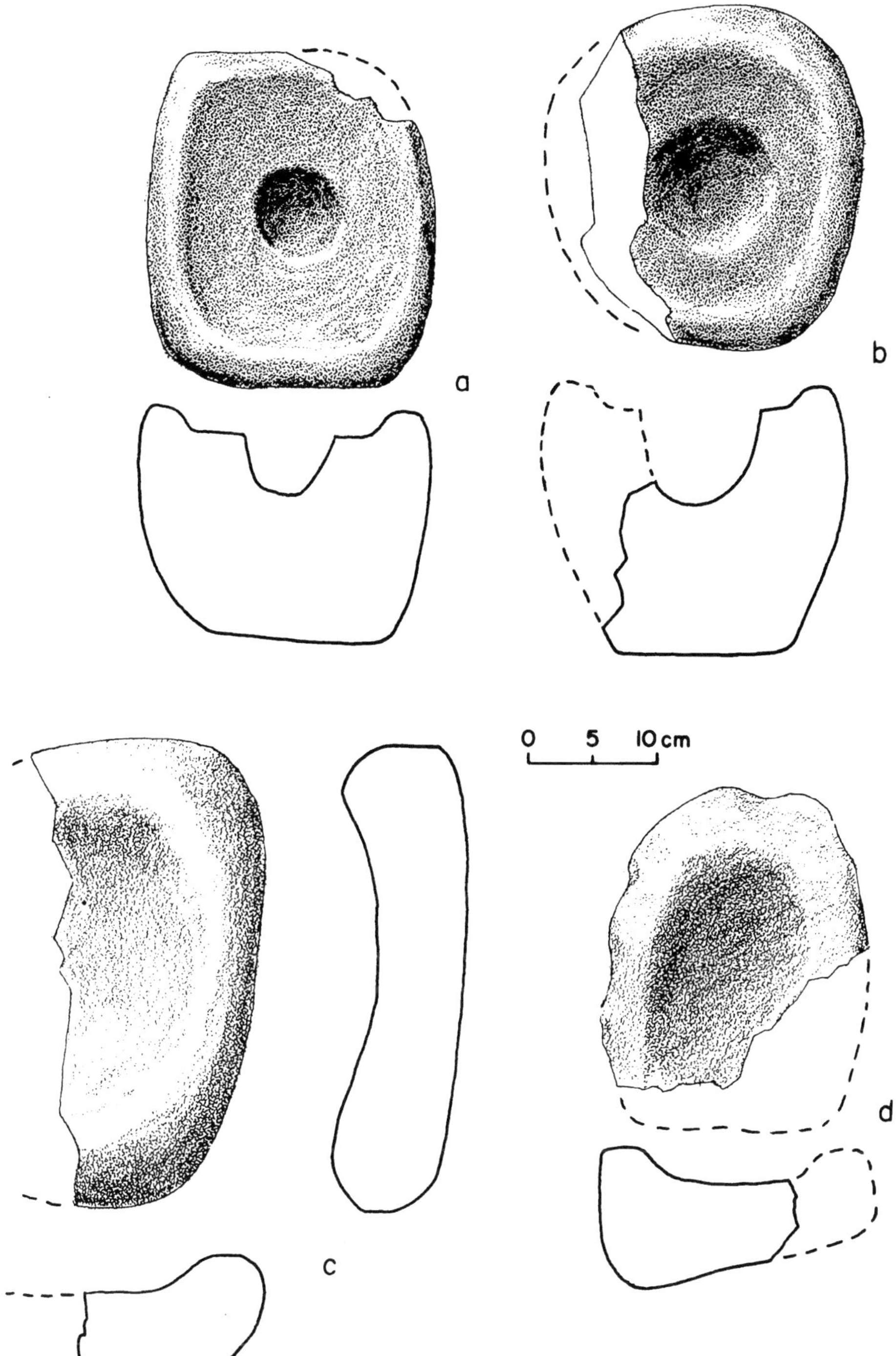

Fig. 74. Grinding stones from Tepe Ali Kosh and Tepe Sabz: *a,b,* combination shallow basin grinding slab and mortar type; *c,d,* shallow basin grinding slabs. *a,* Tepe Sabz, zone C_3 (Khazineh phase); *b,* Tepe Sabz, zone D (Sabz phase); *c,d,* Tepe Ali Kosh, zone A_2 (Mohammad Jaffar phase).

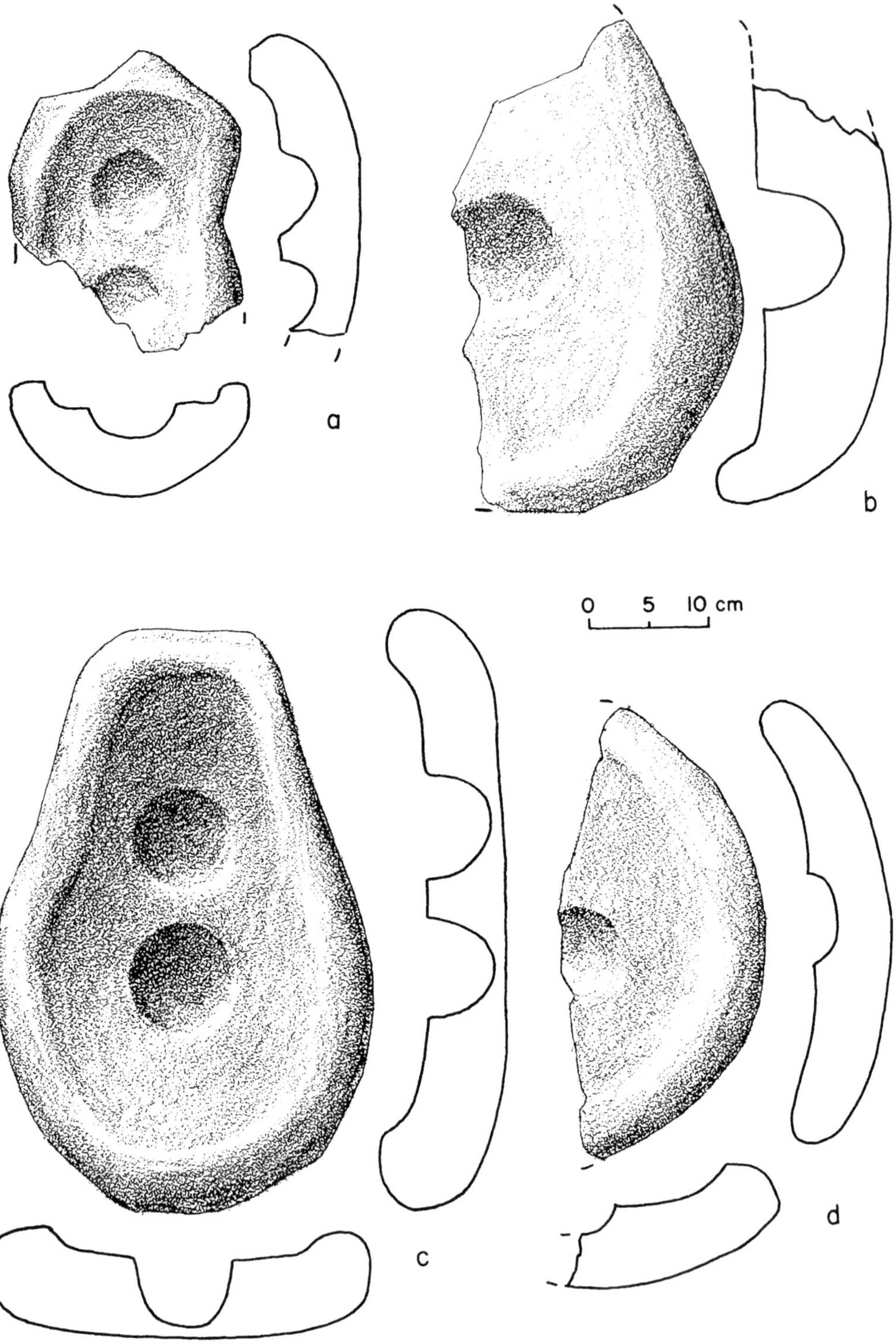

Fig. 75. Examples of combination shallow-basin-grinding-slab-and-mortar from the Mohammad Jaffar phase, Tepe Ali Kosh: *a,b,d,* zone A_1 ; *c,* zone A_2.

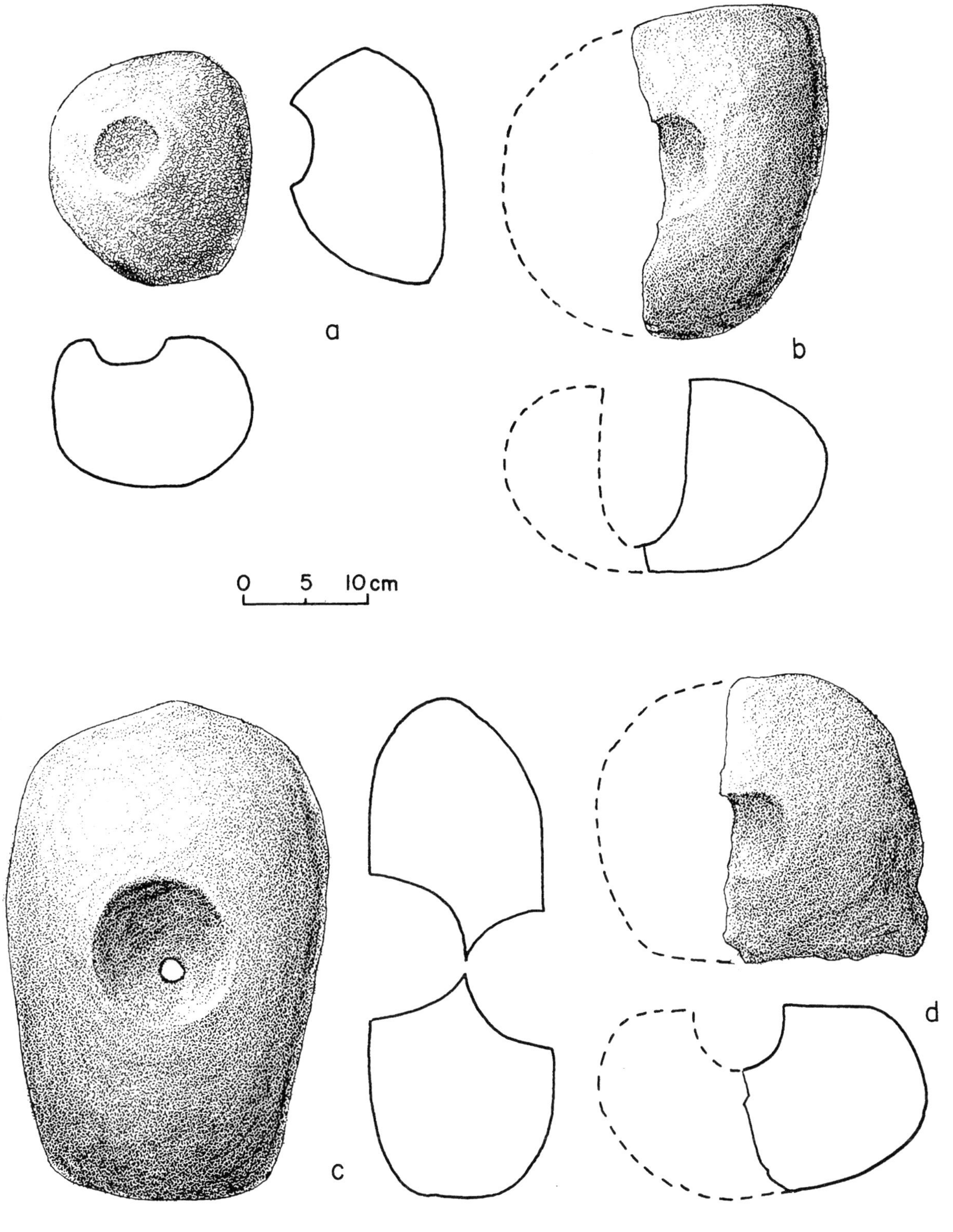

Fig. 76. Boulder mortars from Tepe Ali Kosh and Tepe Sabz: *a,* Tepe Sabz, zone C_3 (Khazineh phase); *b-d,* Mohammad Jaffar phase examples (Tepe Ali Kosh).

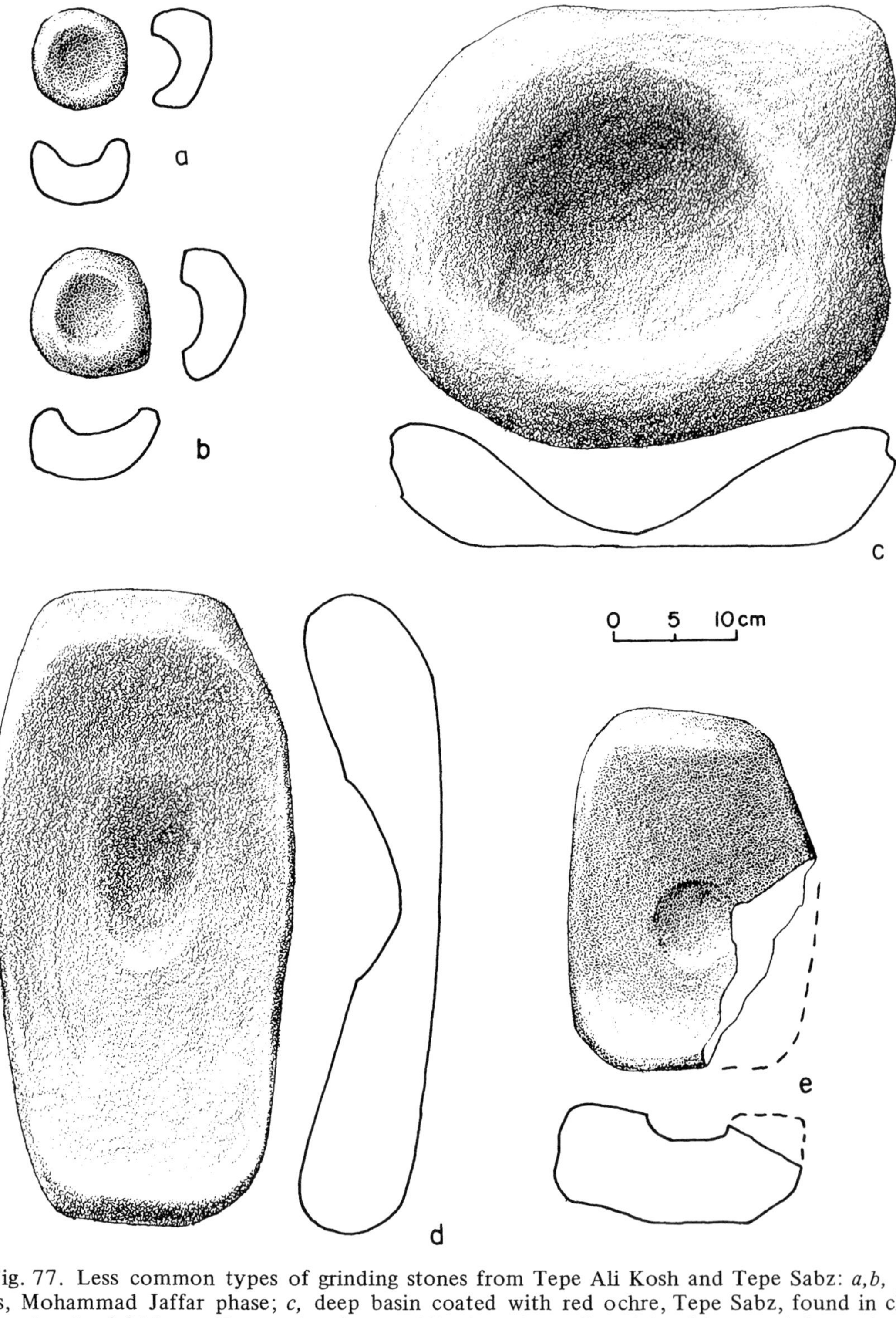

Fig. 77. Less common types of grinding stones from Tepe Ali Kosh and Tepe Sabz: *a,b,* pebble mortars, Mohammad Jaffar phase; *c,* deep basin coated with red ochre, Tepe Sabz, found in clearing trench at depth of 310 cm. (Bayat phase); *d,* saddle-shaped grinding slab with central depression, Tepe Sabz, zone B_1 (Mehmeh phase); *e,* combination saddle-shaped grinding slab and mortar, Tepe Sabz, zone B_3 (Mehmeh phase).

Description: An otherwise standard saddle-shaped grinding slab, bearing on its upper surface a poorly-defined depression which apparently did not serve as a mortar. The depression is somewhat longer than wide, following the long axis of the saddle-shaped slab, and its function is unknown.

Temporal distribution: Our only two examples came from the Khazineh and Mehmeh phases.

Geographic distribution: Unknown.

Aberrant deep basin (Fig. 77*c*)

Example: 1, from the Bayat phase

Material: Fine-grained gray limestone

Description: A heavy stone basin some 45 cm. in diameter, stained with red ochre over the whole of its interior depression. The raw material from which this basin is made is unlike that of the typical grinding stones from Tepe Sabz, and it probably did not function in food preparation.

Table 29

OCCURRENCE OF GRINDING SLAB TYPES AT ALI KOSH, TEPE SABZ, AND TEPE MUSIYAN
(By Stratigraphic Zone)

Site and Zone	Flat-topped Boulder	Saddle-shaped Slab	Shallow Basin	Combination Shallow Basin and Mortar	Pebble Mortar	Boulder Mortar	Combination Saddle-shaped Slab and Mortar	Saddle-shaped Slab with Central Depression	Miscellaneous Fragments and Abberants	Totals
TS - A_1	...	14	...	...	...	...	1	...	...	15
TS - A_2	...	...	...	...	...	...	...	...	...	...
TS - A_3	...	1	...	...	...	...	...	...	1	2
TS - B_1	...	3	...	...	...	...	1	1	...	5
Mus "E"	...	...	...	...	...	...	1	...	4	5
TS - B_2	...	22	...	...	...	...	...	...	...	22
TS - B_3	...	14	...	...	...	...	3	...	1	18
TS - C_1	1	5	...	...	...	...	...	1	1	8
TS - C_2	...	1	...	...	...	1	...	...	...	2
TS - C_3	1	3	...	1	...	1	...	...	...	6
TS - D	1	7	...	1	...	...	2	...	...	11
AK - A_1	3	16	8	9	2	3	...	...	3	44
AK - A_2	2	10	8	4	1	1	...	...	4	30
AK - B_1	...	23	1	...	3	...	...	...	7	34
AK - B_2	2	50	1	...	1	...	...	...	5	59
AK - C_1	...	2	...	...	...	...	...	...	...	2
AK - C_2	1	1	...	...	...	...	...	...	...	2
Totals.....	11	172	18	15	7	6	8	2	26	265

Table 30

OCCURRENCE OF GRINDING SLAB TYPES AT ALI KOSH, TEPE SABZ, AND TEPE MUSIYAN
(By Cultural Phase)

Phase	Flat-topped Boulder	Saddle-shaped Slab	Shallow Basin	Combination Shallow Basin and Mortar	Pebble Mortar	Boulder Mortar	Combination Saddle-shaped Slab and Mortar	Saddle-shaped Slab with Central Depression	Miscellaneous Fragments and Abberants	Totals
Bayat	...	15	...	...	...	...	1	...	1	17
Mehmeh	...	39	...	...	...	...	5	1	5	50
Khazineh	2	9	...	1	...	2	...	1	1	16
Sabz	1	7	...	1	...	...	2	...	...	11
Mohammad Jaffar	5	26	16	13	3	4	...	...	7	74
Ali Kosh	2	73	2	...	4	...	...	...	12	93
Bus Mordeh ...	1	3	...	...	...	...	...	...	...	4
Totals	11	172	18	15	7	6	8	2	26	265

Handstones

Type: Simple discoidal handstone (Fig. 78*a-f*)

Sample: 65

Material: Limestone cobbles, probably from the bed of the Dawairij River.

Description: As the name implies, these are symmetrical, disc-shaped cobbles which were used as handstones for the grinding slabs already described. In several instances, they were found in association with saddle-shaped grinding slabs, most frequently at Tepe Sabz (for example Fig. 73*d,e*). They have a lens-shaped cross-section, and no pronounced facets. They range from 5 to 19 cm. in diameter, and consequently some are as wide as or wider than the saddle-shaped grinding slabs with which they were used—a fact which helps explain the lack of unground lateral ridges on the latter. In most cases, these handstones are harder and more fine-grained than the slabs on which they were used. The handstones from Ali Kosh range between 5 and 16 cm. in diameter and average 10.6 cm, whereas those from Tepe Sabz range between 8 and 19 cm. and average 13 cm. There is no evidence for a regular increase in size phase by phase.

Temporal distribution: Throughout the entire sequence, from the Bus Mordeh phase to the Bayat phase, this type accounts for nearly half the handstones used by the prehistoric villagers in the Deh Luran plain.

Geographic distribution: Throughout Mesopotamia and the Zagros.

Type: Loaf-shaped (faceted) handstone (Fig. 78*q,r*)

Sample: 8

Material: Limestone cobbles, probably from the bed of the Dawairij River.

Description: These handstones are plano-convex, resembling bread loaves. The upper or convex surface has never been used, while the undersurface displays a very worn, level facet. Evidently these were rubbed back and forth over the grinding surface without ever being rolled or having their position shifted. The type of grinding slab with which they were used is unknown. All specimens are between

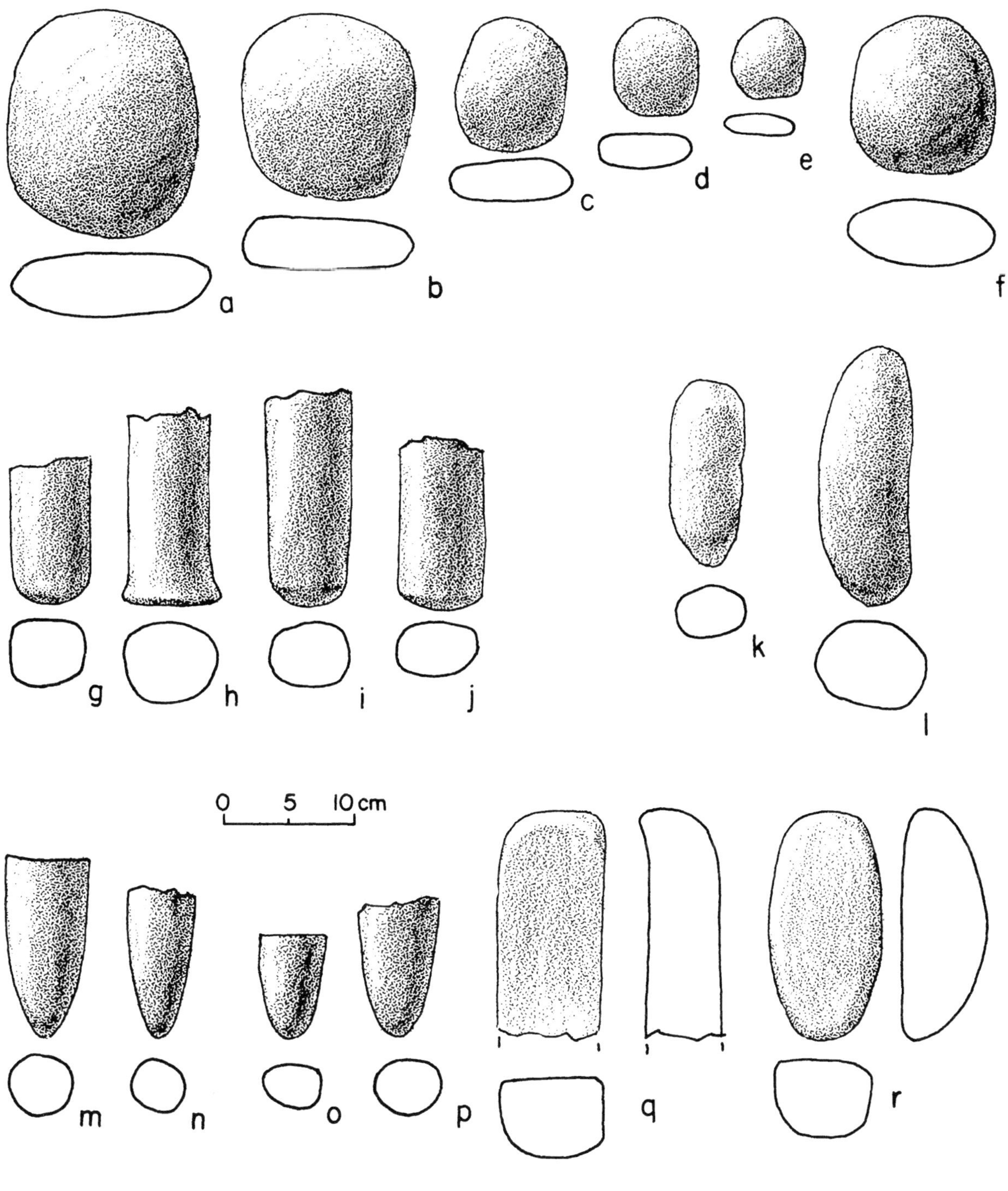

Fig. 78. Handstones and pestles from Tepe Ali Kosh, Tepe Sabz, and Tepe Musiyan "E": *a-f,* range of variation in simple discoidal handstones; *g-j,* combination cylindrical-pestle-and-rolling-handstone type; *k,l,* irregular sausage-shaped pestles; *m-p,* combination conical-pestle-and-rolling-handstone type; *q,r,* loaf-shaped (faceted) handstones (*c,p,* Bus Mordeh phase; *h,j,m,n,q,* Ali Kosh phase; *e,f,g,i,o,* Mohammad Jaffar phase; *l,* Sabz phase; *a,d,k,r,* Mehmeh phase, Tepe Sabz; *b,* Mehmeh phase, Tepe Musiyan "E").

15 and 20 cm. long, averaging about 18 to 19 cm.

Temporal distribution: With one exception, these are confined to the Ali Kosh and Mohammad Jaffar phases.

Geographic distribution: Unknown.

Type: Irregular elongate (faceted) handstone

Sample: 12

Material: Soft limestone cobbles

Description: These are long slender handstones which, in contrast to our "loaf-shaped type," bear several flat facets as a result of grinding. Thus, their position may have been shifted occasionally during the grinding process; but evidently they were never rolled. These pieces range between 10 and 15 cm. long with the exception of one aberrant specimen (22 cm.).

Temporal distribution: These were already in use during the Bus Mordeh phase, but most examples came from the Ali Kosh and Mohammad Jaffar phases.

Geographic distribution: Unknown.

Type: Small slab abrader

Example: 8

Material: Gritty gray tabular rock

Description: Palm-sized slabs which show signs of abrasion, as if they had been used for "sanding" wood or some other relatively soft material.

Temporal distribution: Sporadically throughout the sequence at Ali Kosh

Geographic distribution: Possibly related to the "rounded sandstone slabs" from Zawi Chemi Shanidar (R. L. Solecki, 1964:407).

Type: Irregular sausage-shaped handstone

Sample: 6

Temporal distribution: Mehmeh phase

Goegraphic distribution: Unknown.

Material: Limestone river cobbles

Description: Sausage-shaped cobbles 15 to 20 cm long and about half that in diameter, showing over their irregular surfaces considerable evidence of grinding. Evidently these were used as "rolling" handstones, for they never show facets; their ends never show use as pestles.

Pestles

Type: Combination conical pestle and rolling handstone (Fig. 78*m-p*)

Sample: 7

Material: Fine-grained limestone

Description: Limestone cones 6 to 7 cm. in diameter at their widest part, with definitely tapered ends which show pounding and grinding through use as a pestle. In addition, the sides of the implement show grinding all the way to the untapered end, which suggests that they were also used as "rolling" handstones; that is, handstones which were rotated as they moved over the surface of the grinding slab so that no facets developed on them anywhere. It is possible that these combination pestle-handstones may have been used with the combination mortar-grinding slabs found in the same levels.

These differ from the cylindrical pestle-handstones to be described next in that (*a*) their ends are clearly tapered, which probably suggests some functional difference, and (*b*) their temporal distribution is somewhat different.

Temporal distribution: Late Bus Mordeh through Ali Kosh phases

Geographic distribution: A possibly similar specimen is illustrated from Jarmo (Braidwood, Howe, *et al.*, 1960:Plate 20:2).

Type: Combination cylindrical pestle and "rolling" handstone (Fig. 78*g-j*)

Sample: 12

Material: Fine-grained limestone

Description: These are cylinders of limestone 6 to 7 cm. in diameter, one end of which shows pounding and grinding through use as a pestle. These ends are normally blunt, untapered, and gently rounded; only one specimen (Fig. 78*h*) has a slightly expanded or "bell-shaped" end. These pestles fit easily into the sockets of most of the mortars of the Ali Kosh and Mohammad Jaffar phases.

In addition to having served as pestles, these implements show grinding all the way up the cylinder which suggests they were also used as "rolling" handstones. The result is that the whole surface of the pestle-handstone is worn smooth, and on the finer-grained specimens this smoothness amounts to a high polish.

These combination tools may have been used with some of the combination mortar-grinding slabs.

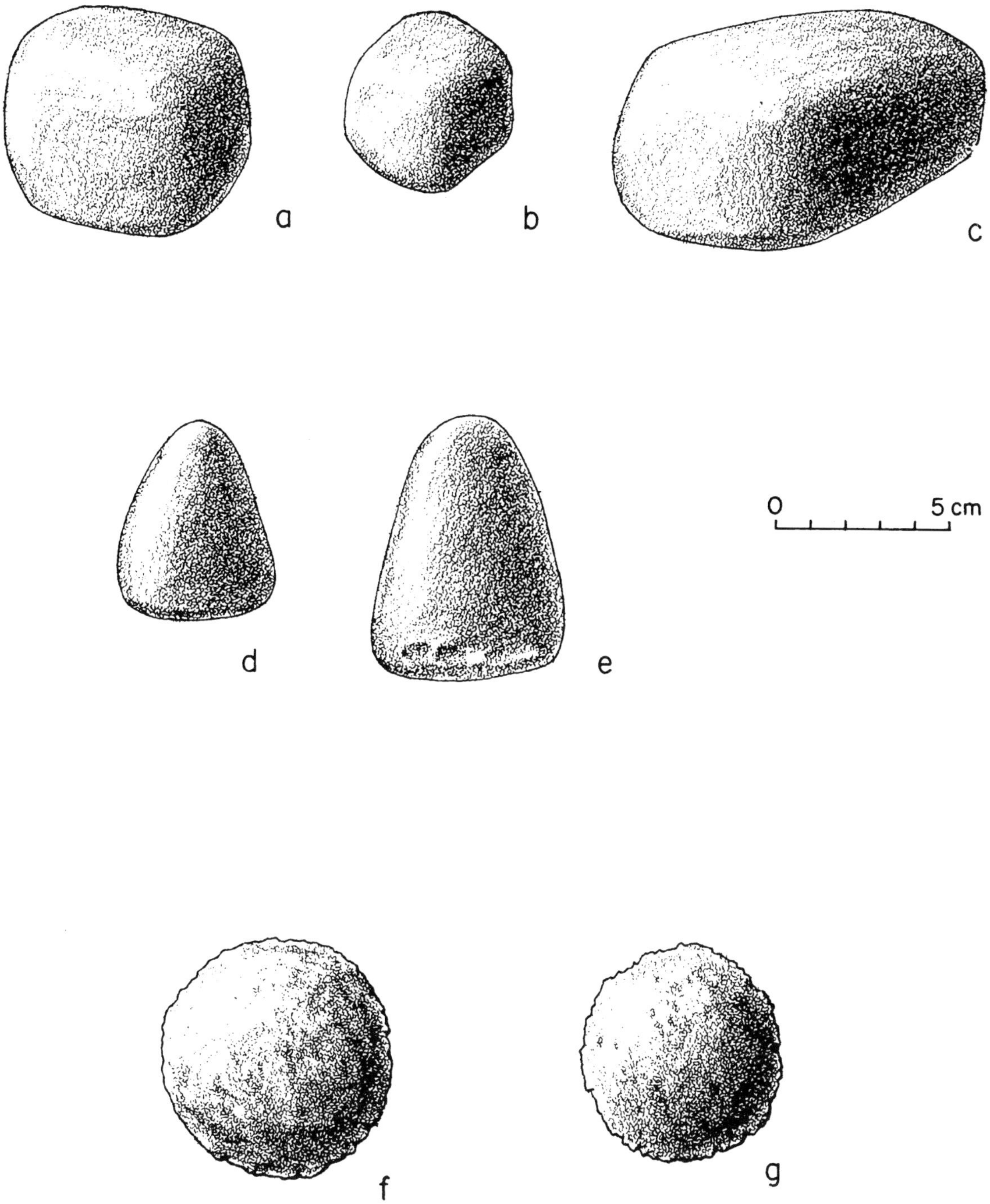

Fig. 79. Miscellaneous grinding and pounding implements from Tepe Ali Kosh, Tepe Sabz, and Tepe Musiyan "E": *a-c,* cuboid pounder/rubbing stones; *d,e,* stubby bell-shaped mullers; *f,g,* spherical pounders or hammerstones (*a,* Tepe Ali Kosh, zone B_2, Ali Kosh phase; *b,* Tepe Musiyan "E," Mehmeh phase; *c,* Tepe Sabz, zone C_3, Khazineh phase; *d,e,* Tepe Ali Kosh, zone A_1, Mohammad Jaffar phase; *f,g,* Tepe Ali Kosh, zone B_2, Ali Kosh phase).

Temporal distribution: These were first manufactured in the Ali Kosh phase, but were used in greatest numbers during Mohammad Jaffar times, a distribution somewhat different from that of the "conical" pestle-handstone.

Geographic distribution: Unknown.

Type: Stubby bell-shaped muller (Fig. 79*d-e*)

Sample: 2

Material: Hard, pitted gray rock

Description: Short, blunt mullers or pestles 6 to 8 cm. in length and 5 to 6 cm. in diameter at the maximum, with a gradual widening or "bell-shaped" effect at the end which was used for grinding. These stubby mullers fit comfortably in the palm of the hand.

Temporal distribution: Mohammad Jaffar phase.

Geographic distribution: Similar mullers are shown from as far away as Tepe Gawra (Tobler, 1950:Pl. XCVI:1-2) so they are undoubtedly of widespread occurrence.

Type: Irregular sausage-shaped pestle (Fig. 78*k-l*)

Sample: 15

Material: Limestone cobbles

Description: Sausage-shaped cobbles 11 to 20 cm. long and about half that in diameter, whose ends show pounding and grinding from use as pestles. There is no evidence that they were ever used as handstones.

Temporal distribution: Ali Kosh through Mehmeh phases

Geographic distribution: Unknown.

Type: Core pestle (Pl. 31*i-l*)

Sample: 8

Material: A fine-grained gray flint

Descritpion: These are large blade cores, similar in size and appearance to those occurring commonly at Tepe Sabz (but not common at Ali Kosh), whose ends have been battered in the manner of pestles. The sides of these pieces show no signs of pounding.

Temporal distribution: Early Ali Kosh phase

Geographic distribution: Unknown.

Pounders

Type: Spherical pounder or hammerstone (Fig. 79*f-g*)

Sample: 166

Material: River cobbles, often flint or quartz

Description: Stones averaging 6 cm. in diameter, battered into a spherical shape by heavy-duty pounding over all or most of their surfaces.

Temporal distribution: These were in use throughout the sequence but 130 out of 166 came from the Ali Kosh and Mohammad Jaffar phases, where they made up a large proportion of the debris on house floors.

Geographic distribution: This artifact may be widespread in early village sites, but is so nondescript that it has probably often been overlooked. Bruce Howe illustrates a "subcuboid hammer" from Karim Shahir which strongly resembles our pounders (Braidwood, Howe, *et al.*, 1960:Plate 23, No. 4), and Rose Solecki (1964:406) describes "chert hammer-stones" from Zawi Chemi Shanidar which may be similar. Another specimen is shown from Jarmo (Braidwood, 1952:Fig. 14).

Type: Core pounder

Sample: 81

Material: Flint blade and flake cores

Description: Chunky pieces of flint which began as cores and were later used as pounders. The edges of the platforms and distal ends are battered, and in some cases the piece is nearly round in shape as a result of the pounding. The use of blade cores for this purpose is rare, except for a small series found at Ali Kosh, where exceptionally large blade cores were reused as pounders. On all examples there are still traces of scars from the removal of flakes or blades.

Temporal distribution: Throughout the sequence; but the use of blade cores is confined to the Bus Mordeh and Ali Kosh phases.

Geographic distribution: Unknown.

Type: Cuboid pounder/rubbing stone (Fig. 79*a-c*)

Sample: 5

Material: Coarse, gritty limestone pebbles

Description: These are small irregular pebbles which (*a*) have been battered into a roughly cuboid shape by use as a pounder, and (*b*) bear several flat facets which indicate their use as grinding or rubbing stones (or abraders?) as well.

Temporal distribution: Scattered occurrences through the sequence

Geographic distribution: A possibly related object is illustrated from Jarmo (Braidwood, 1952:Fig. 14).

Table 31

OCCURRENCE OF HANDSTONES, PESTLES, AND POUNDERS AT ALI KOSH, TEPE SABZ, AND TEPE MUSIYAN
(By Stratigraphic Zone)

	Handstones					Pestles					Pounders			
Site and Zone	Simple Discoidal	Loaf-shaped	Irregular Elongate	Small Slab Abraders	Irregular Sausage-shaped	Combination Conical Pestle and Rolling Handstone	Combination Cylindrical Pestle and Rolling Handstone	Stubby Bell-shaped Muller	Irregular Sausage-shaped Pestles	Core Pestles	Spherical Pounder	Core Pounder	Cuboid Pounder-Rubbing Stone	Totals
TS - A_1	5	...	...	...	...	...	...	...	...	...	...	...	...	5
TS - A_2	...	...	...	...	...	...	...	...	...	...	2	...	...	2
TS - A_3	2	...	...	...	...	...	...	...	...	...	...	2	...	4
TS - B_1	4	1	...	...	...	...	...	...	1	...	1	2	1	10
Mus "E"	3	...	...	...	2	...	...	...	...	...	...	...	1	6
TS - B_2	7	...	...	...	3	...	...	...	...	...	...	3	...	13
TS - B_3	4	...	...	...	1	...	...	...	...	...	5	3	...	13
TS - C_1	5	...	...	...	...	...	...	...	1	...	2	2	...	10
TS - C_2	...	...	...	...	...	...	...	...	...	...	...	2	...	2
TS - C_3	2	...	...	...	...	...	...	...	1	...	1	3	1	8
TS - D	3	...	...	...	...	...	...	...	6	...	7	18	...	34
AK - A_1	3	1	3	...	...	...	7	2	...	...	13	8	...	37
AK - A_2	4	2	2	2	...	...	1	...	...	...	26	1	1	39
AK - B_1	13	1	...	1	...	1	1	...	6	...	5	5	...	33
AK - B_2	7	4	6	3	...	5	3	...	...	8	85	22	1	144
AK - C_1	2	...	1	...	...	2	...	...	...	...	12	4	...	21
AK - C_2	1	...	1	2	...	...	...	...	...	...	5	6	...	15
Total	65	9	13	8	6	8	12	2	15	8	164	81	5	396

Table 32

OCCURRENCE OF HANDSTONES, PESTLES, AND POUNDERS AT ALI KOSH, TEPE SABZ, AND TEPE MUSIYAN
(By Cultural Phase)

	Handstones					Pestles					Pounders			
Phase	Simple Discoidal	Loaf-shaped	Irregular Elongate	Small Slab Abraders	Irregular Sausage-shaped	Combination Conical Pestle and Rolling Handstone	Combination Cylindrical Pestle and Rolling Handstone	Stubby Bell-shaped Muller	Irregular Sausage-shaped Pestles	Core Pestles	Spherical Pounder	Core Pounder	Cuboid Pounder-Rubbing Stone	Totals
Bayat	7	. . .	. . .	. . .	. . .	. . .	. . .	. . .	. . .	. . .	2	2	. . .	11
Mehmeh	18	1	. . .	. . .	6	. . .	. . .	. . .	1	. . .	6	8	2	42
Khazineh	7	. . .	. . .	. . .	. . .	. . .	. . .	. . .	2	. . .	3	7	1	20
Sabz	3	. . .	. . .	. . .	. . .	. . .	. . .	. . .	6	. . .	7	18	. . .	34
Mohammad Jaffar	7	3	5	2	. . .	. . .	8	2	. . .	. . .	39	9	1	76
Ali Kosh	20	5	6	4	. . .	6	4	. . .	6	8	90	27	1	177
Bus Mordeh	3	. . .	2	2	. . .	2	. . .	. . .	. . .	. . .	17	10	. . .	36
Total	65	9	13	8	6	8	12	2	15	8	164	81	5	396

XI

MISCELLANEOUS STONE ARTIFACTS

PRESUMABLY UTILITARIAN

Type: Flint pebble choppers (Fig. 80; Pl. 31*e-h*)

Sample: 155

Material: River pebbles or cobbles of flint, probably from the bed of the Dawairij.

Description: These are pebbles or cobbles broken across one end and then chipped with two or three blows from one direction, so that a sharp edge at an angle of 60 degrees to the long axis of the pebble is produced. Most are 7 to 15 cm. in their longest dimension, with a few huge exceptions. The cutting edge is typically between 6 and 10 cm. in breadth.

Horizontal distribution: These are not randomly distributed throughout the site, but tend to occur in clusters of 4 to 8 in association with the chopped-up limb bones of large game such as onager and wild ox. They probably functioned much as a butcher's cleaver.

Temporal distribution: With few exceptions, these are confined to the Ali Kosh and Mohammad Jaffar phases; and most are concentrated in Late Ali Kosh-Early Mohammad Jaffar levels.

Geographic distribution: Similar choppers occur sporadically at contemporary sites like Tepe Sarab (Oriental Institute collections) and Tepe Guran (Mortensen, personal communication). Rose Solecki (1964:407) reports "numerous choppers" from Zawi Chemi Shanidar, but we are uncertain whether or not they are our flint-pebble type.

Type: Chipped-stone hoes (Fig. 81; Pl. 34*a-b*)

Sample: 4 from excavation (and some 2 dozen more from surface survey)

Material: Earlier examples (Ali Kosh-Mohammad Jaffar phases) are made from river cobbles of flint or sandstone; later examples (from Tepe Sabz) are made from standardized gray limestone cobbles.

Description: Large flakes struck from cobbles and rudely chipped into T-shaped or pear-shaped hoe blades (a few are more slender), whose bits are usually convex but not polished. The outer edge of the cobble usually forms one face of the blade, and the predominately unifacial chipping is directed from the bulbar face. The length ranges from 9 to 13 cm., the width of the shaft from 3 to 6 cm., and the bits from 4 to 14 cm. in width. In some instances, traces of asphalt remain on the shaft as evidence of hafting.

Temporal distribution: Sporadic occurrences throughout the sequence, from the late Ali Kosh phase on. Surface survey leads us to believe that we have not yet excavated the period of their maximum frequency, whatever that may be.

Geographic distribution: Throughout Susiana (Le Breton, 1947:Fig. 17, 1-3), Mesopotamia (see Stronach, 1961:105 for summary), and immediately adjacent areas from at least Hassunan times through the Ubaid.

Type: Polished celts (Fig. 82; Pl. 34*d-h*)

Sample: 75, if a few "roughed out" but incompletely polished specimens are included

Material: Limestone

Description: Flat, slender stone celts usually 8 to 18 cm. in length, with gradually-expanding bits which are often highly polished. The shortest examples have the form of an isosceles triangle, while in longer examples (which constitute the majority) the length is three times the width. A typical celt shows striations from grinding over all surfaces except the polished bit, and has squared-off edges, a square butt-end, and a gently-curved cutting edge. More than half the complete examples had traces of asphalt clinging to the butt, and several preserved so complete an asphalt jacket that the method of hafting was apparent (see Fig. 82*b*;

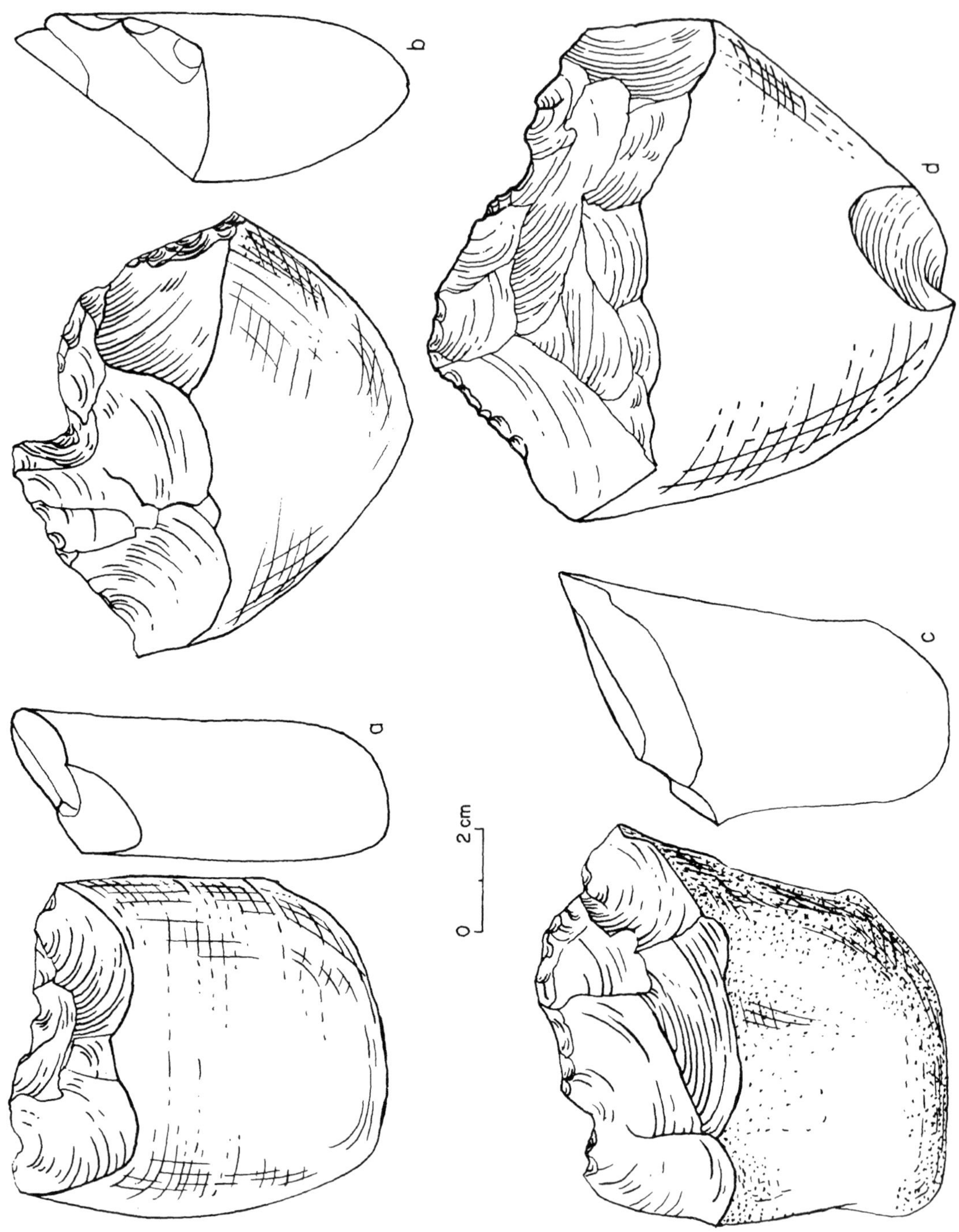

Fig. 80. Flint pebble choppers from Tepe Ali Kosh. All examples shown are from zone B_1, Ali Kosh phase.

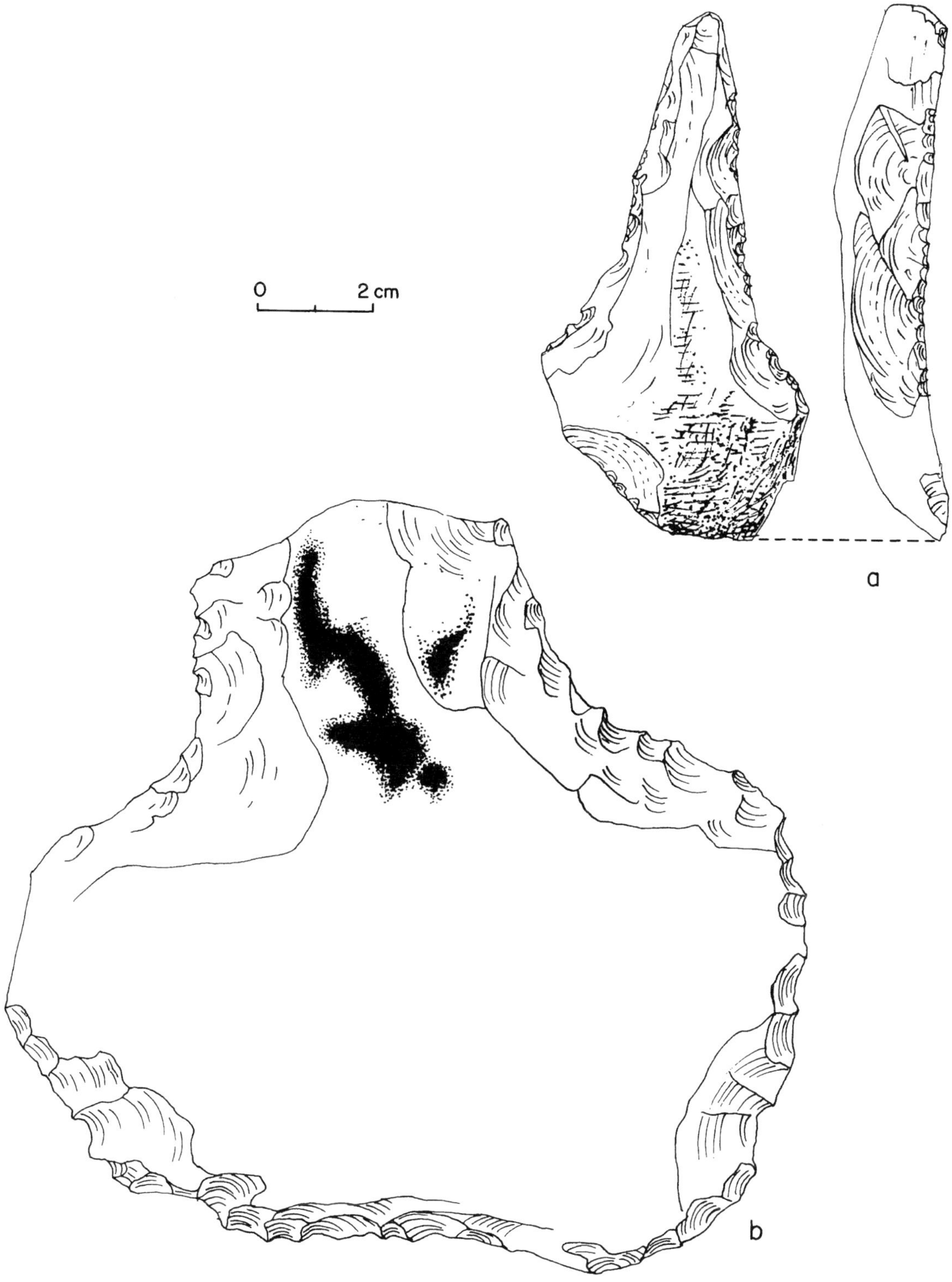

Fig. 81. Chipped stone hoes from Tepe Sabz: *a,* zone D (Sabz phase); *b,* zone A_3 (Bayat phase).

Pl. 34*h*). The bits are symmetrical in section, that is, none have the so-called "adze" type of bit.

Temporal distribution: Sabz through Bayat phases.

Geographic distribution: Throughout Khuzistan (Le Breton, 1947:Fig. 32, Nos. 1,2). Similar (but not identical) polished celts come from "buff-ware" sites in Mesopotamia, including Eridu, Hajji Muhammad, Ubaid, Ras al Amiya, and others (Perkins, 1949:85; Stronach, 1961:106). Our celts do not resemble those found in the Jarmo period of the Zagros Mountains (Braidwood, Howe, *et al.*, 1960:45), nor the chipped celts with polished bits from Karim Shahir (*Ibid*, Pl. 22B) or Zawi Chemi Shanidar (Rose Solecki, 1964:406-07).

Type: "Picks"

Sample: 4

Material: Gray flint

Description: Oblong, flattish nodules whose ends have been chipped to a thick triangular-shaped point. The butt ends are not altered, and retain the cortex. Judging by their blunted tips, two of the four have been heavily used. These pieces range between 7 and 11 cm. in length.

Temporal distribution: Found only in the Bus Mordeh phase

Geographic Distribution: A "possible pick" appeared at Zawi Chemi Shanidar (Rose Solecki, 1964:407).

Type: "Grooved mauls" (Fig. 83*g-h*)

Sample: 5 (four from excavation, one from surface collection at Tepe Sabz)

Material: Heavily pitted limestone

Description: These are possibly heavy hammer-heads or maul-heads of limestone, encircled by a groove 2 cm. wide which probably facilitated hafting. The battered undersurface is slightly rounded or convex in cross-section. Examples range from 8 to 12 cm. at their greatest diameter, and stand 8 cm. high. Our name is of convenience only.

Temporal distribution: Known so far only from the Mehmeh phase

Geographic distribution: Unknown.

Type: Small ground-stone chisels (Fig. 84*a-b*)

Sample: 3

Material: Fine-grained limestone

Description: Elongate, nearly parallel-sided chisels, which are thin and convex in cross-section. The tip is bevelled to a sharp edge, but in plan view it is convex-ended. The specimens, all broken, range from 7.5 to 10 cm. in length, 1.5 to 2 cm. in width, and 0.4 to 0.5 cm. in thickness.

Comment: Two examples were found in association with grooved rubbing-stones, on which they were probably whetted.

Temporal distribution: Known only from the Mohammad Jaffar phase.

Geographic distribution: Uncertain. Rose Solecki (1964:407) reports a "possible chisel" from Zawi Chemi Shanidar.

Type: "Sashweight" stirring rods or asphalt pounders (Pl. 32*a-e*)

Sample: 167

Material: Limestone river cobbles

Description: These rods are elongate, and rectangular in section like window sashweights, from whence their name is derived. Often the ends are split, broken, and reddened from heat, and smeared with asphalt. The asphalt is usually confined to the ends, as if the implements had been used to pound it, or to stir boiling asphalt as it was being prepared for use as a mastic. These objects range in length from 14 to 25 cm.

Temporal distribution: Through all phases, but 143 out of 167 occurred in Ali Kosh and Mohammad Jaffar phase levels.

Geographic distribution: Unknown.

Type: Slicing slabs (Pl. 33)

Sample: 50

Material: Limestone river pebbles

Description: Thin, elongate pebbles whose surfaces, and especially ends, are scarred with cut marks. Frequently the ends are considerably thinned as a result of the repeated cutting. (In some cases sashweight stirring rods were similarly scarred by cutting on their sides.) Lengths are generally in the 10 to 12 cm. range.

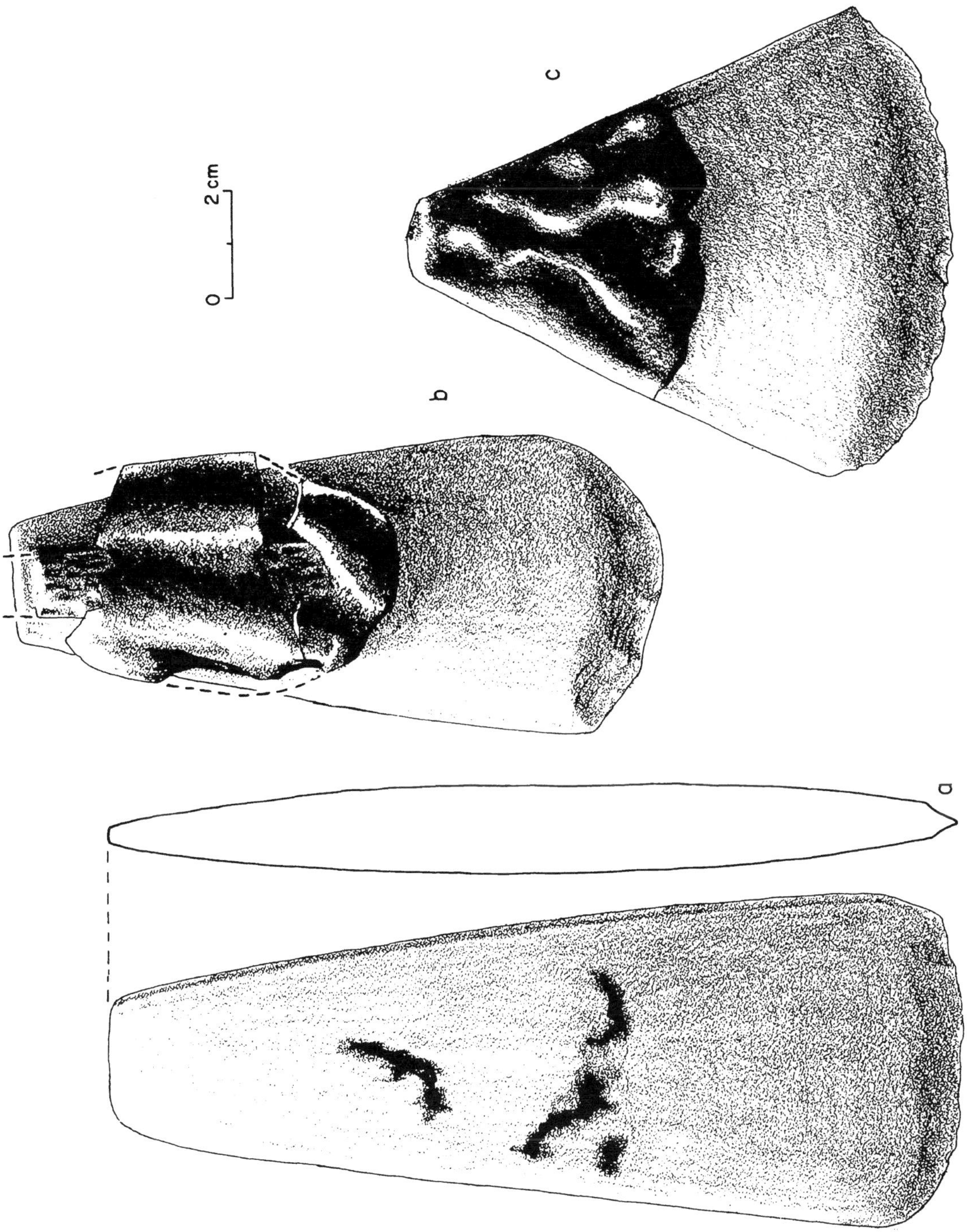

Fig. 82. Polished limestone celts from Tepe Sabz. All examples shown are from Mehmeh phase levels (zones B_2, B_3); all show traces of the asphalt used in hafting.

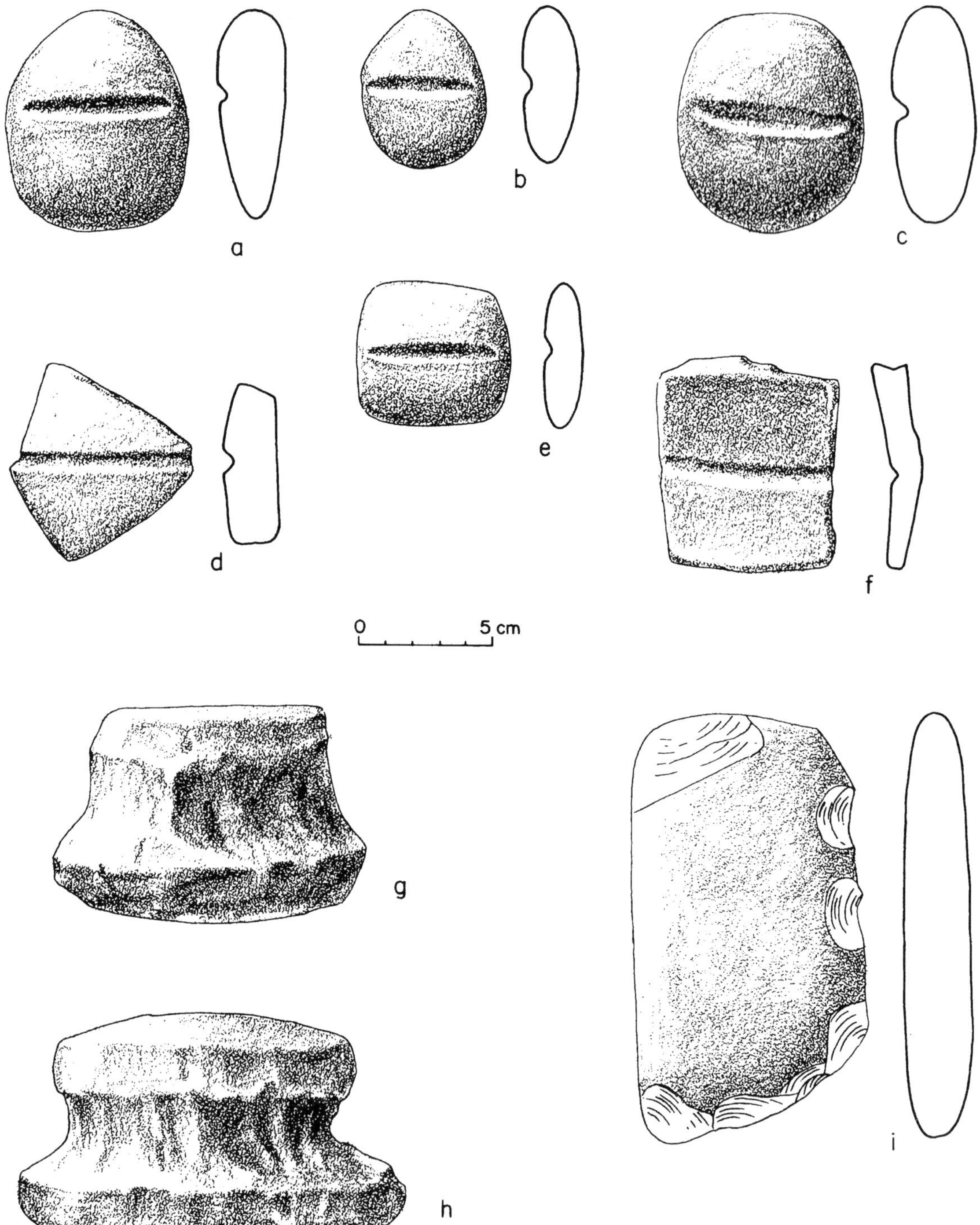

Fig. 83. Ground stone objects from Tepe Ali Kosh and Tepe Sabz: *a-f,* grooved rubbing stones; *g,h,* grooved mauls; *i,* limestone cleaver/rubbing stone (*a,* Tepe Sabz, zone D, Sabz phase; *b,* Tepe Ali Kosh, zone B_2, Ali Kosh phase; *c-f,* all from Mohammad Jaffar phase levels at Tepe Ali Kosh; *g,h,* Mehmeh phase levels at Tepe Sabz; *i,* Tepe Ali Kosh, zone B_2 Ali Kosh phase).

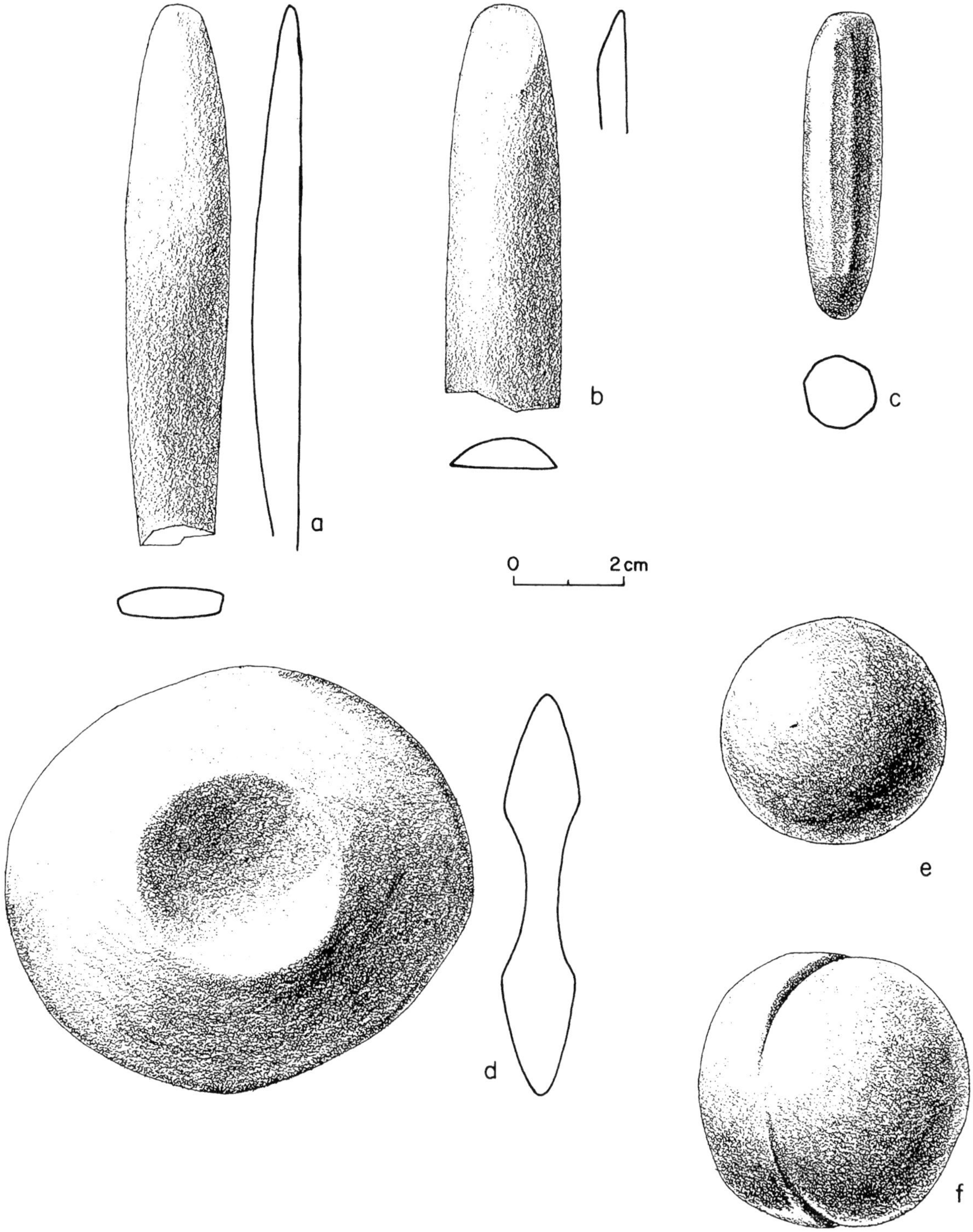

Fig. 84. Miscellaneous ground stone objects from Tepe Ali Kosh: *a,b,* small limestone chisels, zones A_1,A_2, Mohammad Jaffar phase; *c,* faceted rubbing stone, zone A_2, Mohammad Jaffar phase; *d,* limestone disc with pecked depression on either side, zone B_2, Ali Kosh phase; *e,* pecked stone ball, zone B_2, Ali Kosh phase; *f,* pecked stone ball with encircling groove, found with Burial 26, zone B_2, Ali Kosh phase.

Three aberrant examples which exhibit similar slice marks are included. These are irregular, flat pebbles with marks of slicing or abrasion. Two occur in the Sabz phase.

We suspect that these stones were slipped under sinews to provide a surface against which to cut with a flint knife. It is also possible that these were used as sharpening blocks for blade tools which were becoming hard to use because of adherent meat tissues.

Temporal distribution: Throughout Tepe Ali Kosh, with their maximum use coming in the Ali Kosh and early Mohammad Jaffar phases; and two unusual examples in the Sabz phase.

Geographic distribution: Known also from Hajii Firuz (specimens in University of Pennsylvania Museum collections) and Tepe Guran (Mortensen, personal communication). The Guran specimens are more frequently round than elongate, like the Sabz phase examples.

Type: Grooved rubbing stones (Fig. 83*a-f*; Pl. 35*d-f*)

Sample: 8

Material: Usually gray, gritty sandstone; a few are harder limestone pebbles

Description: Pebbles or tablets of stone varying from 4 to 7 cm. in diameter, each of which bears on its upper surface a centrally-placed groove some 3 to 5 mm. deep. These grooves may be U-shaped or V-shaped in cross-section, and give evidence of having been used for abrading; two limestone examples have grooves which even show high polish.

Comment: These stones have frequently been called "shaft-smoothers" or "arrowshaft straighteners," but obviously those whose groove is V-shaped in cross-section cannot have been used for that purpose. In the Mohammad Jaffar phase, two such "V-shaped" specimens were found in association with two small stone chisels in a way that suggested they had been used to sharpen the bits of the latter. Other specimens may have been used to sharpen bone or wooden awls, etc.

Temporal distribution: Mainly used during the Ali Kosh and Mohammad Jaffar phases, but their usage continued at least into the Mehmeh phase

Geographic distribution: Similar grooved rubbing stones are widely distributed in Kurdistan and Luristan, occurring at Jarmo (Braidwood, Howe, *et al.*, 1960:45), Zawi Chemi Shanidar (Solecki, 1963:Fig. 7*d,e*), Tepe Asiab (Braidwood, 1960:Fig. 4), Tepe Guran (Mortensen, personal communication), and Zarzi Cave (Garrod, 1930:Fig. 11).

Type: Small, faceted rubbing stones (Fig. 84*c*)

Sample: 2

Material: Limestone pebbles

Description: Pebbles less than 6 cm. in maximum diameter, which have facets on one or more faces, probably as a result of rubbing on a palette

Temporal distribution: Ali Kosh and Mohammad Jaffar phases

Geographic distribution: Widespread. Nearly identical examples occur at Tepe Guran, Luristan (Mortensen, personal communication).

Type: Chipped limestone discs (Pl. 32*f-h*)

Sample: 21

Material: Tabular fine-grained limestone

Description: Flat discs of limestone, bifacially chipped around the periphery to give them a round or oval outline. Diameters are in the 6 to 15 cm. range.

Temporal distribution: Twenty of the twenty-one occurred in the Ali Kosh and Mohammad Jaffar phases.

Geographic distribution: Widespread, occurring at such distant sites as Çayonü in Turkey (Braidwood, personal communication), Zawi Chemi Shanidar in Iraq (Rose Solecki, personal communication), and prehistoric sites near Seistan on the Indo-Iranian border (Fairservis, 1961:Fig. 3*e,f*). They are also present at Tepe Guran (Mortensen, personal communication).

Type: Perforated stones, including sockets for door pivots (Fig. 85*a-h*; Pl. 35*b-c*)

Sample: 26, if a few questionable specimens are included

Material: Roughly circular river cobbles

Description: Heavy, flat discs of stone with a lens-shaped cross-section which have been perforated in the center by drilling through from both sides. Some of the smaller specimens (approximately 5 cm. in diameter) are of uncertain use; but many of the larger examples (10 to 18 cm. in diameter) probably served as sockets, drilled to receive the lower ends of the vertical pivots on which the doors of the

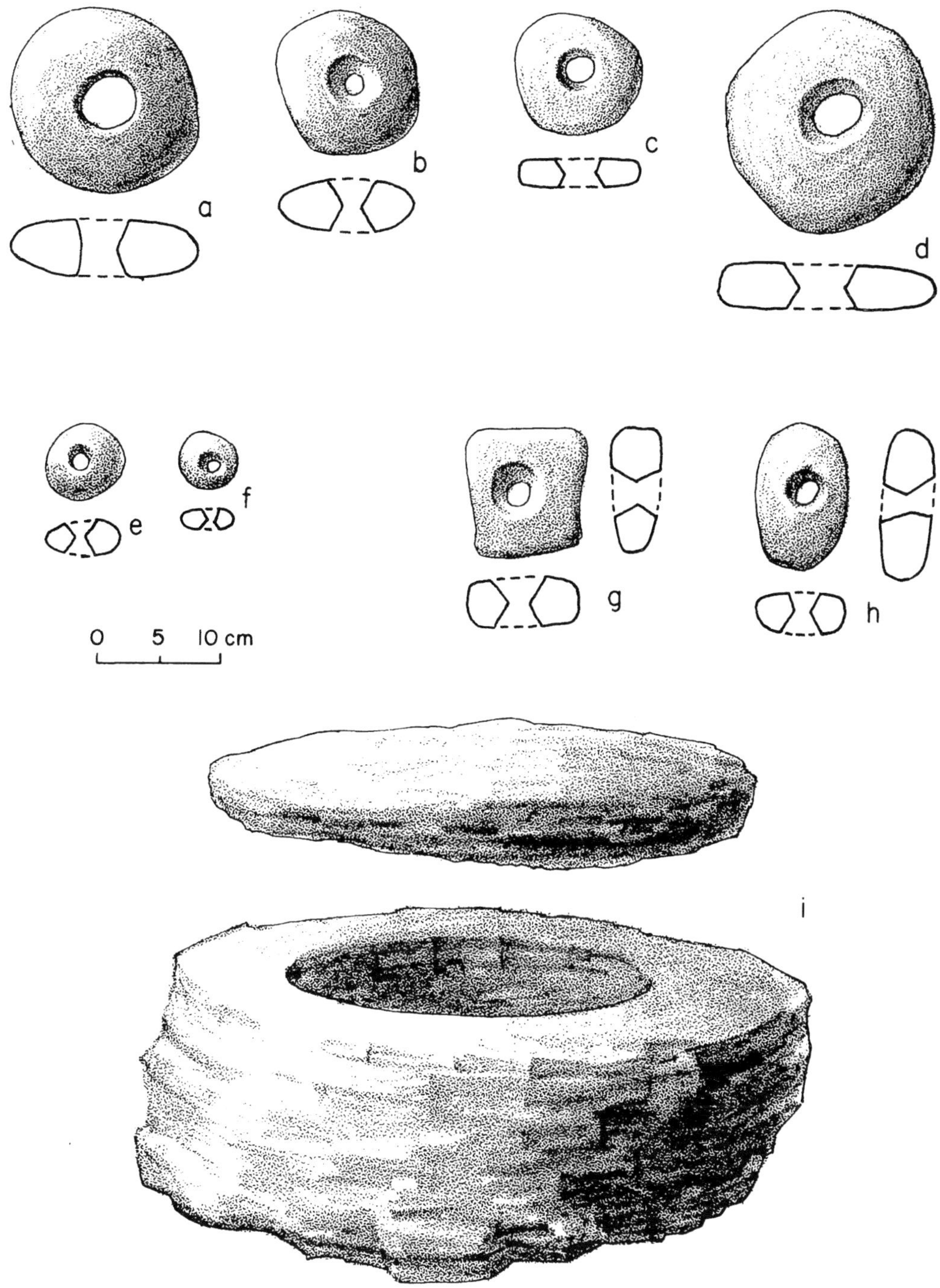

Fig. 85. Miscellaneous ground stone items from Tepe Sabz: *a-d,* perforated stones which probably served as sockets for door pivots (*a-c,* Mehmeh phase; *d,* surface); *g,* rectangular perforated stone from zone B_2 (Mehmeh phase); *h,* ellipsoidal perforated stone from Bayat phase levels in clearing trench; *i,* large stone basin with lid from Bayat phase levels in clearing trench (see Fig. 18*a*).

houses at Tepe Sabz swung. At Tepe Ashrafabad, we found the ground plan of a stone-founded house with one such door-pivot socket *in situ* (see Fig. 17*b*). Aberrant rectangular and ellipsoidal specimens occurred at Tepe Sabz (Fig. 85*g,h*), but most examples are shaped like doughnuts. None resemble the so-called "maceheads" found at some Near Eastern tells, which are spherical rather than flat in cross-section (see Tobler, 1950:Plate XCVII).

Temporal distribution: Throughout the sequence at Tepe Sabz. Apparently the Mohammad Jaffar phase antedates the use of such door construction at Deh Luran, and four of the five examples in the Sabz phase are atypical and hence questionable.

Geographic distribution: Such door-pivot sockets are common in the Mesopotamia-Zagros Mountain area, beginning as early as upper Jarmo (see Braidwood, Howe, *et al.*, 1960:43).

Limestone cleaver-rubbing stone (Fig. 83*i*; Pl. 35*a*)

Example: 1, from the Ali Kosh phase

Table 33

OCCURRENCE OF PRESUMABLY UTILITARIAN STONE ARTIFACTS AT ALI KOSH, TEPE SABZ, AND TEPE MUSIYAN
(By Stratigraphic Zone)

Site and Zone	Pebble Choppers	Chipped Stone Hoes	Polished Celts	Picks	Grooved Mauls	Chisels	Sashweights	Slicing Slabs	Grooved Rubbing Stones	Small, Facetted Rubbing Stones	Chipped Limestone Discs	Perforated Stones	Cleaver/rubbing Stone	Limestone Disc with Pecked Depressions	Large Basin with Lid	Total
TS - A_1	...	...	...	...	...	...	...	...	...	...	...	2	...	...	...	2
TS - A_2	...	...	3	...	...	...	...	...	...	...	...	2	...	...	...	5
TS - A_3	...	1	5	...	...	...	1	...	...	...	...	1	...	...	...	8
TS - B_1	1	...	11	...	3	...	1	...	...	...	...	7	...	...	1	24
Mus "E"	1	...	3	...	...	...	...	...	...	...	...	4	...	...	...	8
TS - B_2	...	...	13	...	1	...	1	...	...	...	...	4	...	...	...	19
TS - B_3	...	...	11	...	...	...	3	...	1	...	...	...	...	...	...	15
TS - C_1	...	...	3	...	...	...	2	...	...	...	...	...	...	...	...	5
TS - C_2	...	...	2	...	...	...	3	...	1	...	...	1	...	...	...	7
TS - C_3	...	...	3	...	...	...	1	...	...	...	...	...	...	...	...	4
TS - D.	2	1	21	...	...	...	4	2	...	...	...	5	...	...	...	35
AK - A_1	32	1	...	...	...	3	47	7	1	1	4	...	...	...	...	96
AK - A_2	63	...	...	...	...	...	38	12	3	...	2	...	...	...	...	118
AK - B_1	46	1	...	...	...	...	11	11	...	...	9	...	...	...	...	78
AK - B_2	13	...	...	...	...	...	47	15	2	1	5	...	1	1	...	85
AK - C_1	1	...	...	2	...	...	6	...	...	...	...	...	...	...	...	9
AK - C_2	...	...	...	2	...	...	2	3	...	...	1	...	...	...	...	8
Total	159	4	75	4	4	3	167	50	8	2	21	26	1	1	1	526

Material: A large, flat river cobble

Description: An oblong flat stone object, showing traces of rubbing or grinding on either side, which in addition had been unifacially-chipped around three-quarters of the periphery, producing a cleaver-like cutting edge. The implement is 16 cm. long and 8 cm. wide.

Geographic distribution: Unknown.

Limestone disc with pecked depression on either side (Fig. 84*d*)

Example: 1, from the Ali Kosh phase

Material: A limestone river cobble

Description: A flat stone disc 8 cm. in diameter, bearing on each face a centrally-placed pecked depression 5 mm. deep and some 2.5 cm. in diameter.

Geographic distribution: Similar pecked discs appeared at Jarmo (Braidwood, 1952:Fig. 14, center of page), and some "double-pitted stones" from Zawi Chemi Shanidar in Rose Solecki's collections at Columbia University appear similar.

Large stone basin with associated lid (Fig. 85*i*)

Example: 1, from the Bayat phase

Material: Heavy, laminated limestone

Description: This is a stone basin standing 20 cm. high and some 50 cm. in diameter, which was found during the clearing operations in front of the step trench at Tepe Sabz (see Fig. 18*a*). The carefully-prepared interior chamber contrasts with the rugged, unfinished outer surface. When found, the basin was upright, and covered by a lid manufactured from a limestone slab. This basin was obviously a container of some kind, and showed no evidence of ever having been used as a grinding stone.

Table 34

OCCURRENCE OF PRESUMABLY UTILITARIAN STONE ARTIFACTS AT ALI KOSH, TEPE SABZ, AND TEPE MUSIYAN
(By Cultural Phase)

Phase	Pebble Choppers	Chipped Stone Hoes	Polished Celts	Picks	Grooved Mauls	Chisels	Sashweights	Slicing Slabs	Grooved Rubbing Stones	Small, Facetted Rubbing Stones	Chipped Limestone Discs	Perforated Stones	Cleaver/rubbing Stone	Limestone Disc with Pecked Depressions	Large Basin with Lid	Total
Bayat	...	1	8	...	...	...	1	...	...	...	...	5	...	...	...	15
Mehmeh	2	...	38	...	4	...	5	...	1	...	...	15	...	...	1	66
Khazineh	...	...	8	...	...	...	6	...	1	...	...	1	...	...	...	16
Sabz	2	1	21	...	...	...	4	2	...	...	...	5	...	...	...	35
Mohammad Jaffar	95	1	...	...	...	3	85	19	4	1	6	...	...	...	...	214
Ali Kosh	59	1	...	...	...	...	58	26	2	1	14	...	1	1	...	163
Bus Mordeh	1	...	...	4	...	...	8	3	...	...	1	...	...	...	...	17
Total	159	4	75	4	4	3	167	50	8	2	21	26	1	1	1	526

POSSIBLY NON-UTILITARIAN

Type: Pecked stone balls (Fig. 84*e*)

Sample: 53

Material: Usually fine-grained limestone

Description: These spherical balls were carefully pecked from pebbles of irregular shape. When found in groups of two or three, they sometimes all have the same diameter (Hole and Flannery, 1962:120). The average diameter of these artifacts decreases with time from the Bus Mordeh phase, through the Ali Kosh phase, and into the Mohammad Jaffar phase (see Table 35).

Comment: No obvious function can be ascribed to these stones. Possible uses are as gaming pieces, light-duty pounders, weights, or even bolas stones.

Temporal distribution: Throughout the sequence at Ali Kosh, and sporadically in Tepe Sabz.

Geographic distribution: These occur at Jarmo (Braidwood and Howe, *et al.*, 1960:46) and other early village sites in the Zagros Mountains.

Pecked stone ball with encircling groove (Fig. 84*f*)

Example: 1, from the Ali Kosh phase

Material: Quartz

Description: A stone ball, 5 cm. in diameter, encircled by a shallow central groove after the manner of a "bolas stone."

Comment: Found adjacent to the knee of Burial 26 in zone B_2 at Tepe Ali Kosh. Possibly a unique object.

Geographic distribution: Unknown.

Incised pebbles (Fig. 86; Pl. 39*f*)

Sample: 4

Material: Fine-grained limestone pebbles

Description: From the Bus Mordeh phase at Ali Kosh comes a smooth, oval pebble with a lenticular cross-section, having on one face three parallel lines bisected at right angles by a single incised line, which completely encircles the pebble. The other side has two incised lines, the continuation of two from the reverse side, bisected by the single line (Fig. 86*a*).

A flat limestone pebble from the Mehmeh phase (Fig. 86*d*) has a design with four radiating branches incised in its center. The design resembles patterns commonly found on stamp seals (e.g., Tobler, 1950:Plate CLIX-16).

Two examples from the Khazineh and Sabz phases are limestone pebbles, roughly flaked along one edge, which have a zone of intersecting or criss-crossing incisions on one of their flat surfaces (Fig. 86*b-c*).

Comment: The examples from the Bus Mordeh and Mehmeh phases were clearly made deliberately; the others from Tepe Sabz may have been produced in somewhat the same manner as slicing slabs.

Geographic distribution: An incised pebble from Zawi Chemi Shanidar is illustrated by R.

Table 35

DIAMETERS OF PECKED STONE BALLS AT ALI KOSH (1963 DATA) AND TEPE SABZ
(In Centimeters)

Site and Zone	Number	Range	Average	Standard Deviation
TS*	6	3.42 - 4.88	4.29	.5
AK - A_1	12	1.92 - 4.17	3.19	.59
AK - A_2	14	2.27 - 5.02	3.57	.92
AK - B_1	2	3.85 - 4.03	3.94	. . .
AK - B_2†	14	3.41 - 5.97	4.32	.67
AK - C_1 AK - C_2	4	3.80 - 4.55	4.26	. . .

*The data from Tepe Sabz are lumped together, as no significant differences between zones could be seen

†One example from Ali Kosh, zone B_2 omitted because of its unusually small size—1.79 cm.

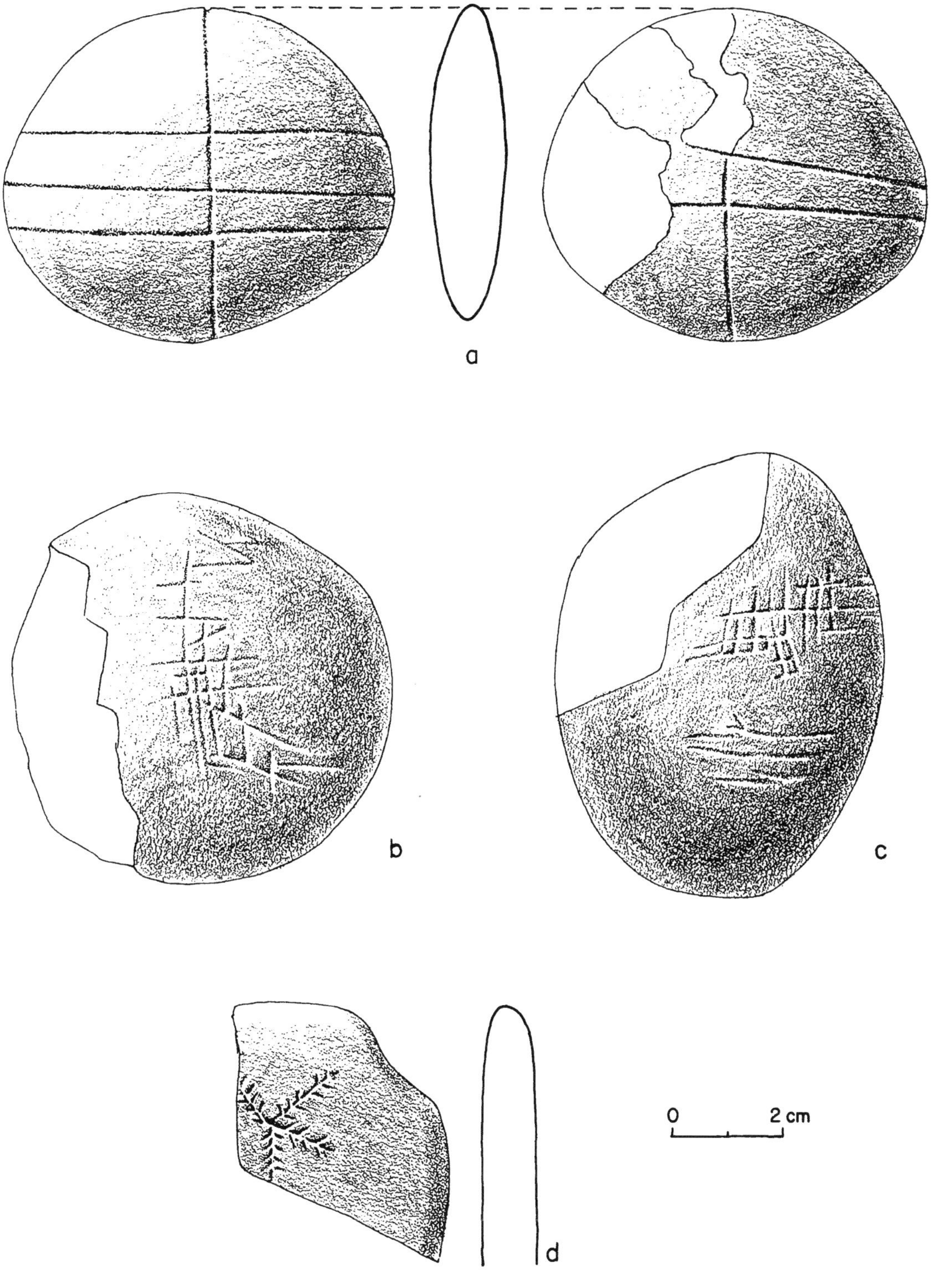

Fig. 86. Incised pebbles from Tepe Ali Kosh and Tepe Sabz: *a*, Tepe Ali Kosh, zone C_2, Bus Mordeh phase; *b*, Tepe Sabz, zone D, Sabz phase; *c*, Tepe Sabz, zone C_3, Khazineh phase; *d*, Tepe Sabz, zone B_2, Mehmeh phase.

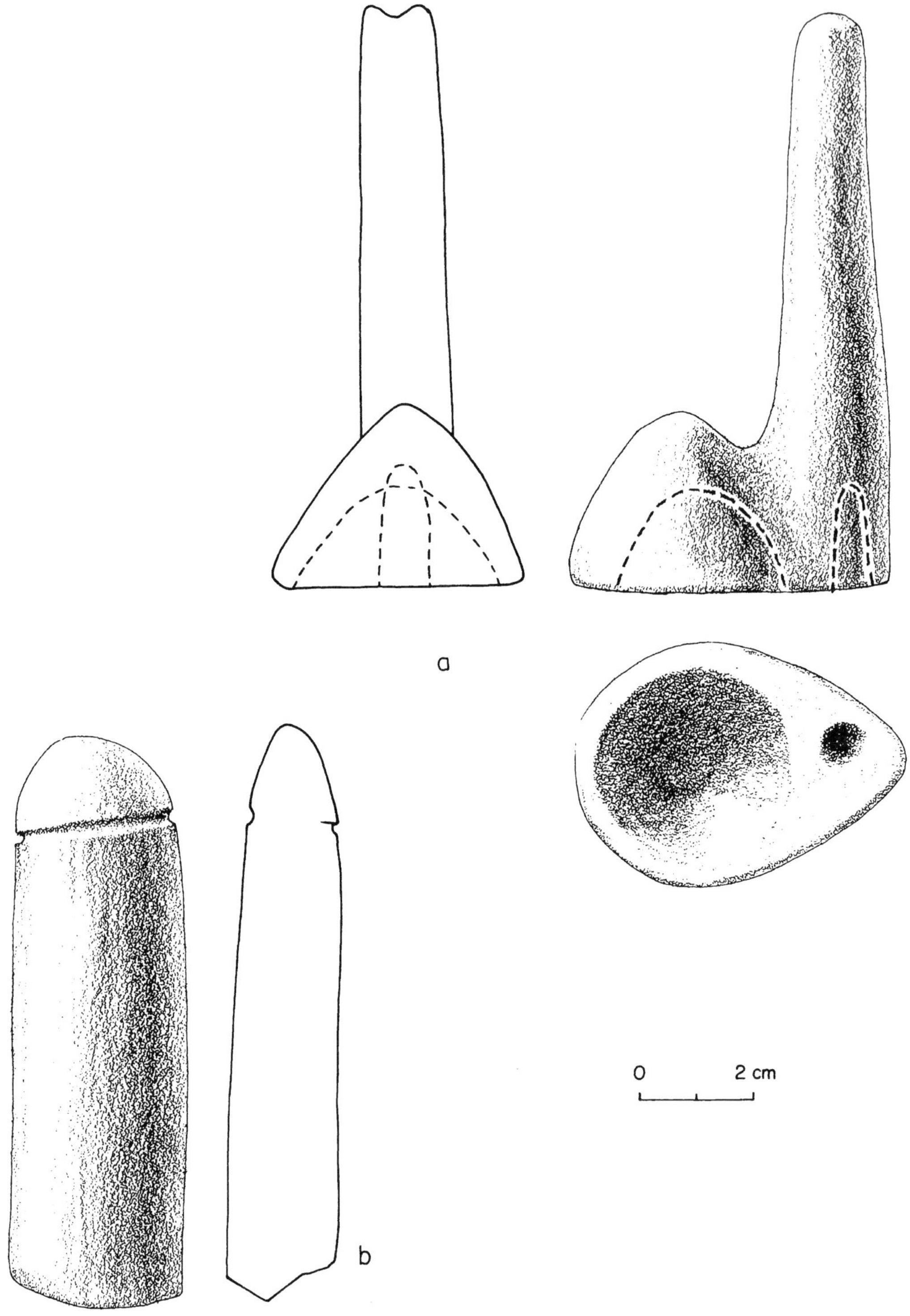

Fig. 87. Exotica from Tepe Ali Kosh: *a,* possible stone "phallus," zone A_2, Mohammad Jaffar phase; *b,* grooved elongate "amulet" (possibly a stone "phallus") zone C_1, Bus Mordeh phase.

S. Solecki (1963:Fig. 7*j*); stone pendants with incised decoration are mentioned at Jarmo (Braidwood, Howe, *et al.*, 1960:46).

Grooved, elongate phallic "amulet?" (Fig. 87*b*)

Example: 1, from the Bus Mordeh phase

Material: An elongate limestone river pebble

Description: This pebble, some 10 cm. long and 3 cm. wide, has been smoothed by grinding and has a shallow grove incised around it 1.5 cm. from one end.

Geographic distribution: This object is suggestive of some cruder examples of the ground stone "phalli" found at Jarmo (Braidwood, Howe, *et al.*, 1960:46) and Tepe Guran (Mortensen, 1964:Fig. 21). Our name is one of convenience only, however.

Table 36

OCCURRENCE OF POSSIBLY NON-UTILITARIAN STONE ARTIFACTS AT ALI KOSH AND TEPE SABZ
(By Stratigraphic Zone)

Site and Zone	Pecked Stone Balls	Grooved Stone Ball	Incised Pebbles	Grooved Amulet?	Possible Stone Phallus	Miscellaneous Fragments of Polished Stone	Total
TS - A_1	...	...	...	...	...	...	...
TS - A_2	...	...	...	...	...	...	...
TS - A_3	1	...	...	...	...	...	1
TS - B_1	...	...	...	...	...	...	...
TS - B_2	4	...	1	...	...	...	5
TS - B_3	2	...	...	...	...	1	3
TS - C_1	...	...	...	...	...	1	1
TS - C_2	...	...	...	...	...	...	...
TS - C_3	...	...	1	...	...	...	1
TS - D	...	...	1	...	...	2	3
AK - A_1....	12	...	...	...	...	1	13
AK - A_2....	14	...	...	...	1	...	15
AK - B_1....	2	...	...	...	...	1	3
AK - B_2....	14	1	...	...	...	...	15
AK - C_1....	2	...	...	1	...	...	3
AK - C_2....	2	...	1	...	...	1	4
Total....	53	1	4	1	1	7	67

Possible stone "phallus" (Fig. 87*a*; Pl. 38*a*)

Example: 1, from the Mohammad Jaffar phase

Material: Fine-grained metamorphosed limestone, perhaps white onyx or alabaster?

Description: See Figure 87*a*

Geographic distribution: Stone phalli occur at a number of early village sites (see Grooved, elongate "amulet"). Specimens nearly identical to ours were found with burials at Tell as-Sawwan (El-Wailly and Abu es-Soof, 1965:Fig. 66). The custom of including highly-polished stone exotica with male burials—'bells," stone phalli, etc.—seems to have been more widespread than is generally realized.

Miscellaneous fragments of polished stone

Examples: 7

Material: Alabaster or onyx

Table 37

OCCURRENCE OF POSSIBLY NON-UTILITARIAN STONE ARTIFACTS AT ALI KOSH AND TEPE SABZ
(By Cultural Phase)

Phase	Pecked Stone Balls	Grooved Stone Ball	Incised Pebbles	Grooved Amulet?	Possible Stone Phallus	Miscellaneous Fragments of Polished Stone	Total
Bayat	1	...	...	...	...	...	1
Mehmeh.....	6	...	1	...	...	1	8
Khazineh....	...	...	1	...	...	1	2
Sabz	...	...	1	...	...	2	3
Mohammad Jaffar.......	26	...	...	...	1	1	28
Ali Kosh.....	16	1	...	...	...	1	18
Bus Mordeh ..	4	...	1	1	...	1	7
Total.....	53	1	4	1	1	7	67

Description:
1) From the Bus Mordeh phase: the broken end of a polished stone rod with an encircling groove cut near one end
2) From the Ali Kosh and Mohammad Jaffar phases: two polished, broken cylinders of stone
3) From the Sabz phase: one fragment from round, highly-polished ball (originally 2.1 cm. in diameter) which had been drilled part-way through
4) From the Sabz and Mehmeh phases: two cylinders which may be "drill plugs," that is, the discarded cylinders produced when a larger stone was drilled through with a hollow tube and abrasive. Diameter about 2 cm.
5) From the Khazineh phase: a nondescript fragment.

XII

MISCELLANEOUS CERAMIC ARTIFACTS

SPINDLE WHORLS

Introduction

Our excavations at Ali Kosh and Tepe Sabz disclosed some ninety-six objects which are probably spindle whorls. Those from Tepe Sabz could easily be recognized as such, for they resemble spindle whorls used even today; and in fact, Neely's workmen from Deh Luran readily identified them as *sar-duq,* the local term.

As we moved back farther and farther in time, however, it became increasingly difficult to decide whether we were, or were not, dealing with true spindle whorls. The oldest ceramic specimens, understandably, came from the Mohammad Jaffar phase, where they were made from perforated sherds of early pottery. Below this, in the preceramic Ali Kosh and Bus Mordeh phases, occurred three stone specimens whose conformation sorely tempted us to regard them as early whorls. A decade ago, this would have been unthinkable. Today, with evidence of textiles at Çatal Hüyük (Mellaart, 1964*b*:99), we suspect there may already have been fiber to spin in the seventh millenium. Our "possible" stone whorls are therefore included here tentatively, for what they may be worth.

The spindle whorls of the Deh Luran plain seemed to be useful chronological horizon markers. Star-shaped whorls were largely concentrated in the Sabz and Khazineh phases while the painted "chariot wheel" type flourished in the Mehmeh and Bayat phases, to give only two examples. Further, our spindle whorl types often were of widespread occurrence at other Near Eastern tells.

Type: Perforated stone discs (Fig. 88*a-c*), possibly spindle whorls

Sample: 3

Material: Gray-brown limestone pebbles

Description: Biconically bored, perforated stone discs which may be flat or oval in cross-section, and which have at least a superficial resemblance to later, ceramic spindle whorls. Diameters vary from 3 to 5 cm.

Temporal distribution: Found only in the Ali Kosh and Bus Mordeh phases.

Geographic distribution: Pierced stone discs "of 'spindle-whorl' size" are reported from Jarmo (Braidwood, Howe, *et al.* 1960:45), and one centrally-pierced stone disc from Zawi Chemi Shanidar, illustrated with a group of stone pendants (R. S. Solecki, 1963:Fig. 7*k*) also reminds us of Bus Mordeh specimens.

Type: Perforated sherd discs (Fig. 88*d*), possibly spindle whorls

Sample: 7

Material: Body sherds of Khazineh Red or Susiana Plain Buff, depending on the cultural phase

Description: Chipped-sherd discs with ground-down edges, each perforated by a single central hole 5 to 6 mm. in diameter, biconically drilled. The discs are slightly concave in cross-section, and each has a diameter of about 5 cm.

Temporal distribution: Beginning in the Mohammad Jaffar phase and continuing sporadically throughout the sequence

Geographic distribution: "Pierced potsherd disks" which may be spindle whorls are present throughout the Near East by 5500-6000

B.C. (see for example Braidwood and Braidwood, 1960:55 or Fig. 58:2,3); we note also a "pierced disc of lightly baked clay" from preceramic Tepe Asiab which superficially resembles our specimens (Braidwood, 1960:Fig. 4).

Type: Star-shaped spindle whorl (Fig. 88*e-g*)

Sample: 13

Material: Susiana Plain Buff or Susiana Black-on-buff pottery

Description: These whorls have the shape of stars or asterisks with from 4 to 8 arms, and may be oval or plano-convex in cross-section. Most are from 4 to 5 cm. in diameter and have a thickness of 1 to 2 cm. Many have painted designs.

Temporal distribution: 10 out of 13 specimens were concentrated in Sabz and Khazineh phases at Tepe Sabz, but the type seems to have remained in use well into the Mehmeh phase.

Geographic distribution: These were common at Tepe Jowi in Susiana proper (Le Breton, 1947:Fig. 18, second row, and p. 149), but were not recorded by level; we are uncertain, therefore, whether they are most common in Susiana *a* levels in the Shaur River area, as they are at Deh Luran. They seem to have been present in prehistoric levels at Susa (de Mecquenem, 1928:Fig. 5, No. 8).

Type: "Chariot-wheel" spindle whorl (Fig. 89)

Sample: 59

Material: Susiana Black-on-buff pottery

Description: Large, highly convex ceramic discs, hemispherical in cross-section, the tallest of which almost resemble clapperless bells. All are painted on their upper surface with designs, no two of which are alike, and few of which correspond to designs on Susiana Black-on-buff vessels. One is left with the impression that the painting of these whorls was an individual affair with little or no standardization. Diameters of intact specimens range from 5.5 to 7.0 cm., and they often stand 2 to 3 cm. high. Le Breton called these miniature "chariot wheels" at Jowi (see below), although apparently there were no miniature "chariots" to go with them.

Temporal distribution: 54 of the 59 specimens were concentrated in the late Mehmeh and Bayat phases.

Geographic distribution: These were common at Tepes Jowi and Bandibal (Le Breton, 1947:Figs. 18 and 32:12-13), where they also showed great variety in painted designs. Once again, their stratigraphic position is unclear, but they evidently last into Susa A times (de Mecquenem, 1928:Fig. 9, No. 10).

Type: Oval-discoidal spindle whorl (Fig. 90*a-e*)

Sample: 12

Table 38

OCCURRENCE OF SPINDLE-WHORL TYPES (AND OBJECTS WHICH ARE POSSIBLE SPINDLE WHORLS) AT ALI KOSH, TEPE SABZ, AND TEPE MUSIYAN
(By Stratigraphic Zone)

Site and Zone	Perforated Stone Discs	Perforated Sherd Discs	Star-shaped Whorls	"Chariot-wheel" Whorls	Oval-discoidal Whorls	Punctate Dome-shaped Whorls	Totals
TS - A_1	...	1	...	12	1	1	15
TS - A_2	...	...	...	10	4	...	14
TS - A_3	...	4	...	27	3	...	34
TS - B_1	...	...	2	5	1	...	8
Mus "E" ...	...	...	...	...	1	...	1
TS - B_2	...	...	...	...	...	1	1
TS - B_3	...	...	1	1	2	...	4
TS - C_1	...	...	...	...	...	...	...
TS - C_2	...	...	2	...	...	...	2
TS - C_3	...	...	2	1	...	...	3
TS - D	...	...	6	3	...	...	9
AK - A_1	...	2	...	...	...	...	2
AK - A_2	...	...	...	...	...	...	...
AK - B_1	...	...	...	...	...	...	...
AK - B_2	1	...	...	...	...	...	1
AK - C_1	1	...	...	...	...	...	1
AK - C_2	1	...	...	...	...	...	1
Totals ...	3	7	13	59	12	2	96

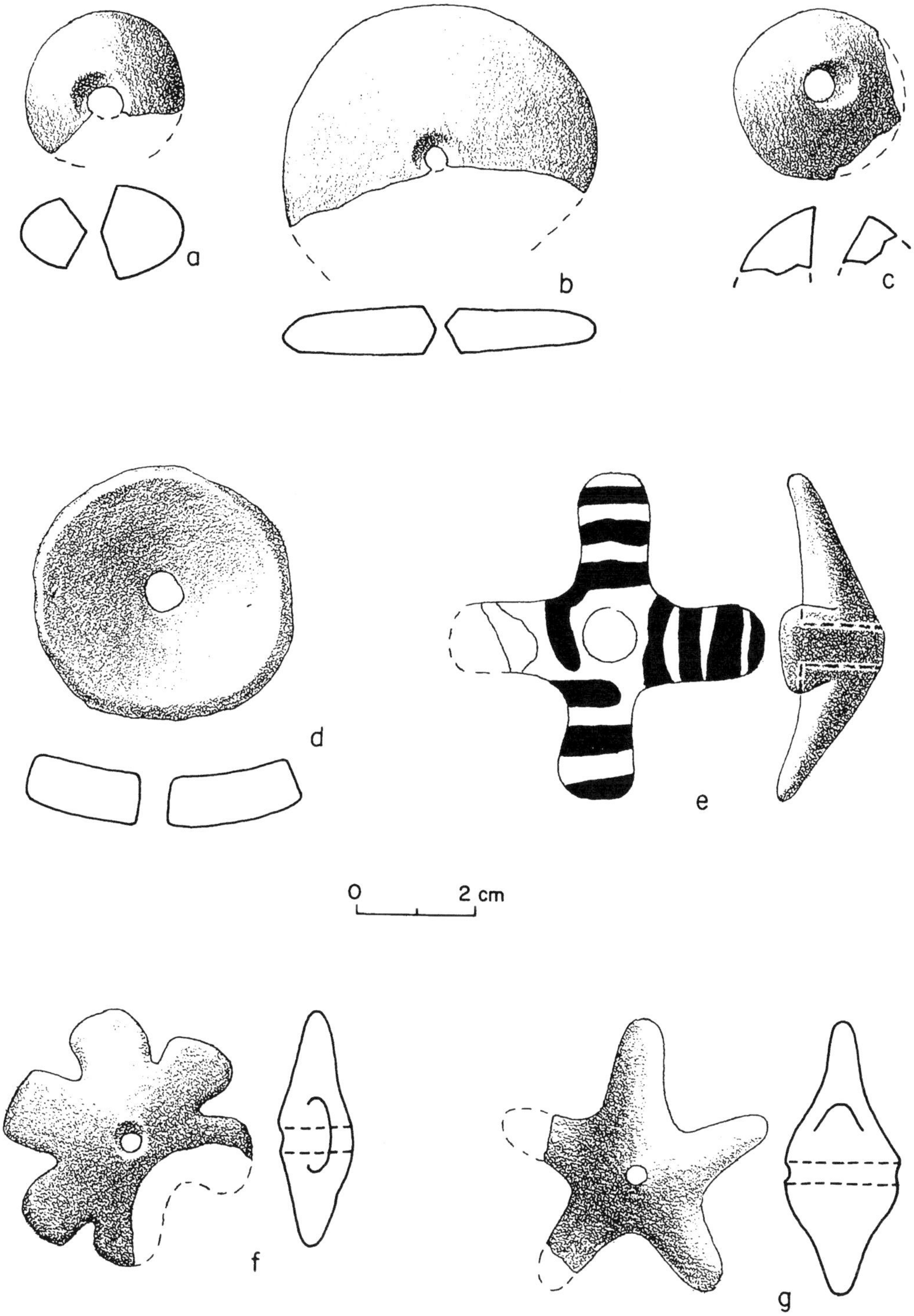

Fig. 88. Spindle whorls and pierced stone discs from Tepe Ali Kosh and Tepe Sabz: *a-c*, perforated stone discs (*a,b*, Bus Mordeh phase, *c*, Ali Kosh phase); *d*, potsherd disc whorl, Khazineh Red pottery, Mohammad Jaffar phase; *e-g*, star-shaped whorls, Susiana buff ware pottery (*e*, Sabz phase, *f,g*, Mehmeh phase).

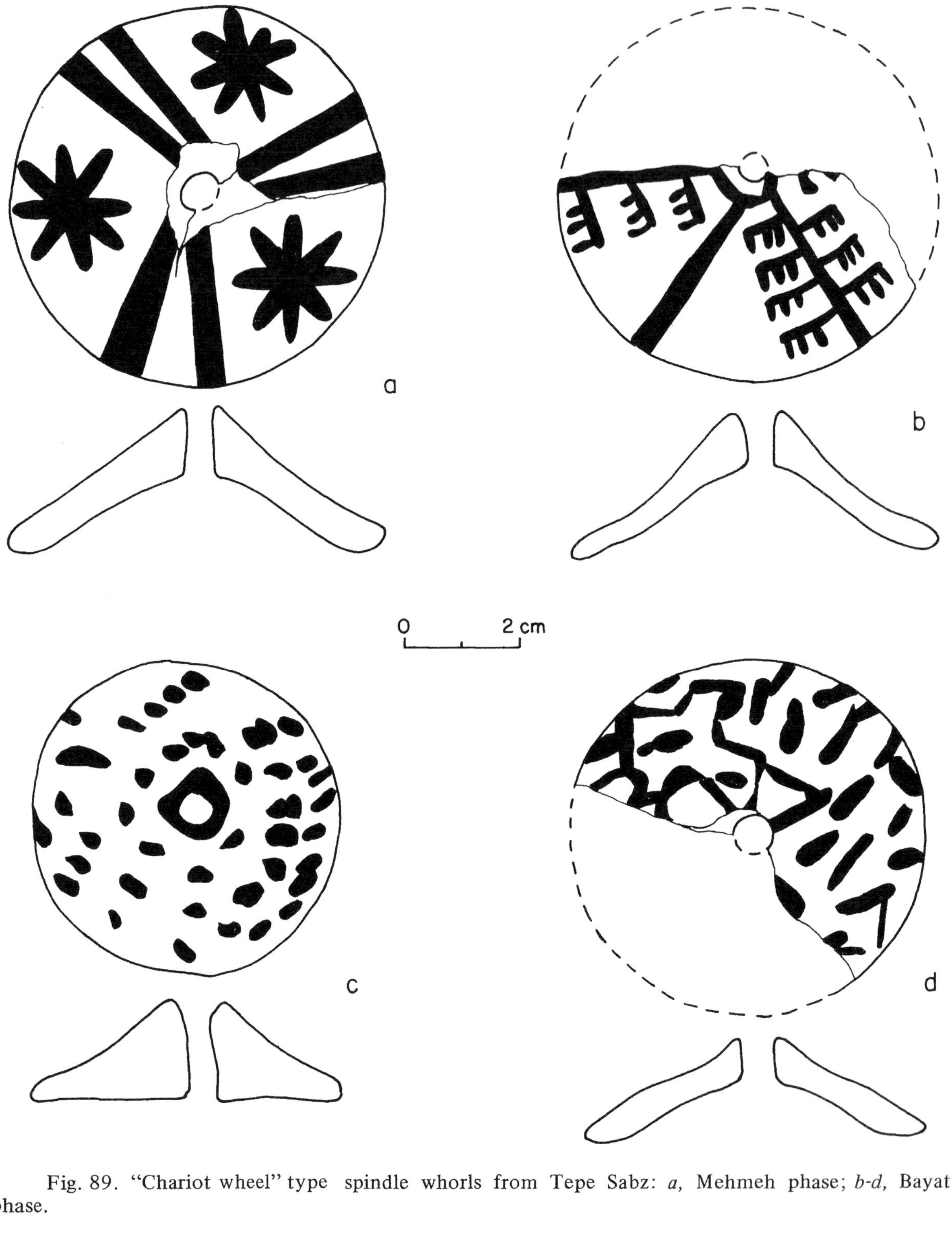

Fig. 89. "Chariot wheel" type spindle whorls from Tepe Sabz: *a*, Mehmeh phase; *b-d*, Bayat phase.

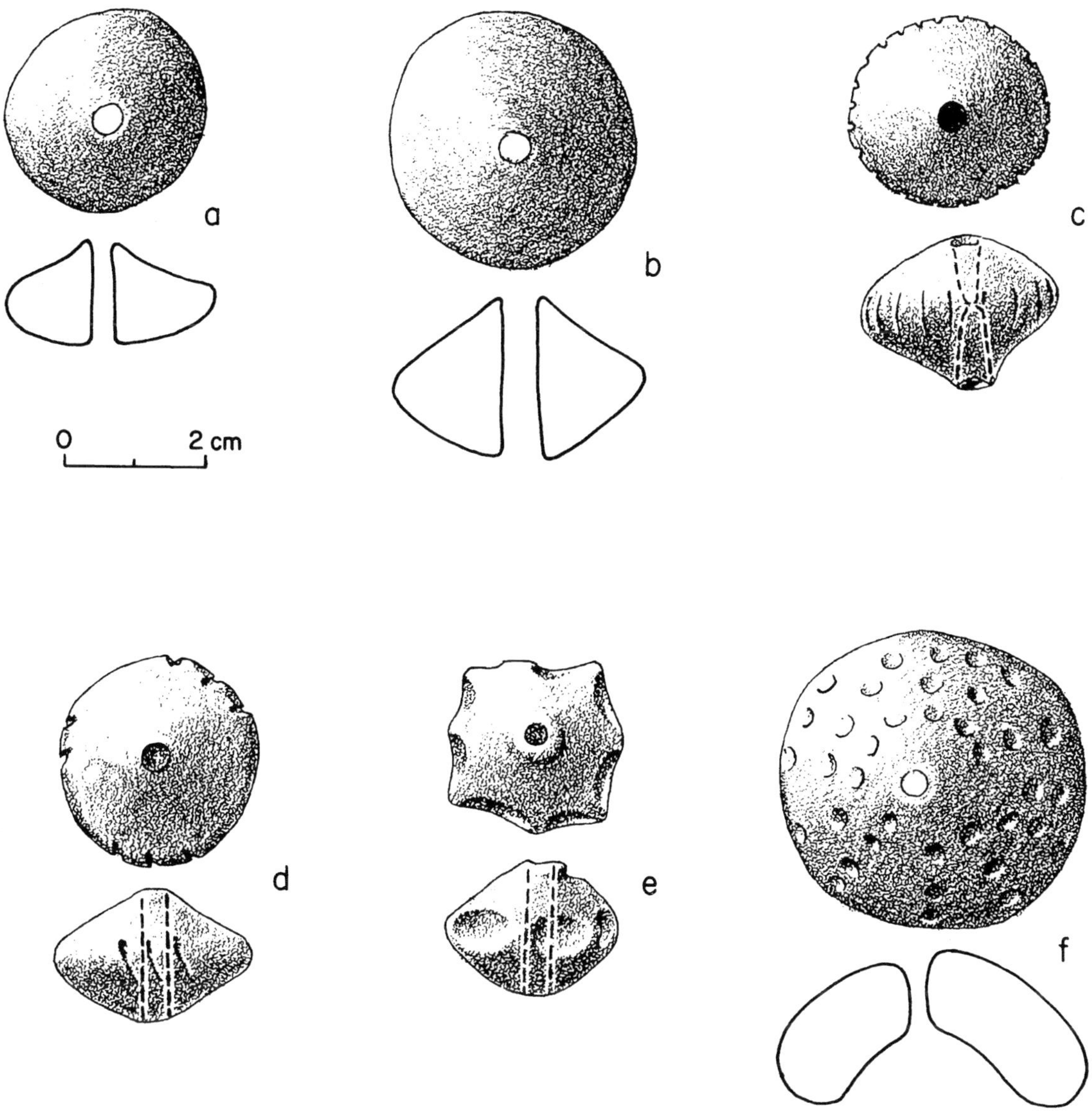

Fig. 90. Spindle whorls typical of the Mehmeh and Bayat phases, Tepe Sabz: *a-e,* range of variation in oval/discoidal type; *f,* punctate dome-shaped type (*a,b, d-f,* Bayat phase; *c,* surface).

Material: Susiana Plain Buff pottery, or lightly fired clay (terra cotta)

Description: Small, compact whorls which are discoidal in outline when viewed from above, but oval or lenticular in cross-section. Often a girdle of incised lines or notches encircles them at the point of their maximum diameter (Fig. 90*c*). The surface may also bear small clay fillets, thumb impressions, or other plastic decoration (Fig. 90*e*).

Temporal distribution: Mehmeh and Bayat phases

Table 39

OCCURRENCE OF SPINDLE-WHORL TYPES (AND OBJECTS WHICH ARE POSSIBLE SPINDLE WHORLS) AT ALI KOSH, TEPE SABZ, AND TEPE MUSIYAN
(By Cultural Phase)

Phase	Perforated Stone Discs	Perforated Sherd Discs	Star-shaped Whorls	"Chariot-wheel" Whorls	Oval-discoidal Whorls	Punctate Dome-shaped Whorls	Totals
Bayat	...	5	...	49	8	1	63
Mehmeh	...	...	3	6	4	1	14
Khazineh	...	...	4	1	...	...	5
Sabz	...	...	6	3	...	...	9
Mohammad Jaffar	...	2	...	...	...	...	2
Ali Kosh	1	...	...	...	...	...	1
Bus Mordeh	2	...	...	...	...	...	2
Totals	3	7	13	59	12	2	96

Geographic distribution: This type has a wide distribution in the Near East. It appears at Jaffarabad, Jowi, and Bandibal (Le Breton, 1947:Fig. 7:1, Fig. 18, top row, and Fig. 32:11); at Ras al Amiya (Stronach, 1961:Plate LXIII:2,3,4,6); at Tepe Gawra (Tobler, 1950:Plate CLV); and numerous other sites.

Type: Punctate dome-shaped spindle whorl (Fig. 90*f*)

Sample: 2

Material: Lightly fired clay (terra cotta)

Description: Small hemispheres of terra cotta, centrally perforated, whose shape is vaguely reminiscent of the "chariot wheel" spindle whorl. In contrast to the latter, however, these are only lightly fired, and never painted; the decoration consists of dozens of punctations made on the upper surface prior to firing. Specimens are 4 cm. in diameter and stand 2 cm. high.

Temporal distribution: Known only from the Mehmeh and Bayat phases

Geographic distribution: Unknown.

OTHER CERAMIC ARTIFACTS

Type: "Bent ceramic nails" (Fig. 91*a*)

Sample: 35

Material: Susiana Plain Buff pottery

Description: These are hornlike objects described in the Tepe Gawra report as "featured by a curved or sharply bent conical shaft, and a wide, convex head; a shape which altogether resembles a bent nail" (Tobler, 1950:169). They may be 10 to 12 cm. in length (bent).

Comment.—The name given this artifact is one of convenience only, and reflects the fact that their function is uncertain. Stronach (1961:107) feels that they may be mullers of some kind. Others have suggested that they may be temple decorations, but Tobler (*Ibid.*) states that their horizontal distribution at Gawra indicated that "they occur only in secular buildings." One might suggest their use as "anvils" for pottery making by the "paddle-and-anvil" technique.

Temporal distribution: These seem to serve as a dramatic horizon marker in the Deh Luran plain; 33 out of 35 occurred in Mehmeh phase levels.

Geographic distribution: Throughout Susiana (Le Breton, 1947:Fig. 32, No. 6), Mesopotamia (Tobler, *loc. cit.;* Stronach, *loc. cit.*) and immediately adjacent areas; they apparently were not used in the Syro-Cilician area, Kurdistan (?), or the Iranian high plateua.

Type: Chipped sherds (Fig. 91*b,c*)

Sample: 49

Material: Mostly Susiana Plain Buff pottery, with a few examples in Bayat Red and Khazineh Red

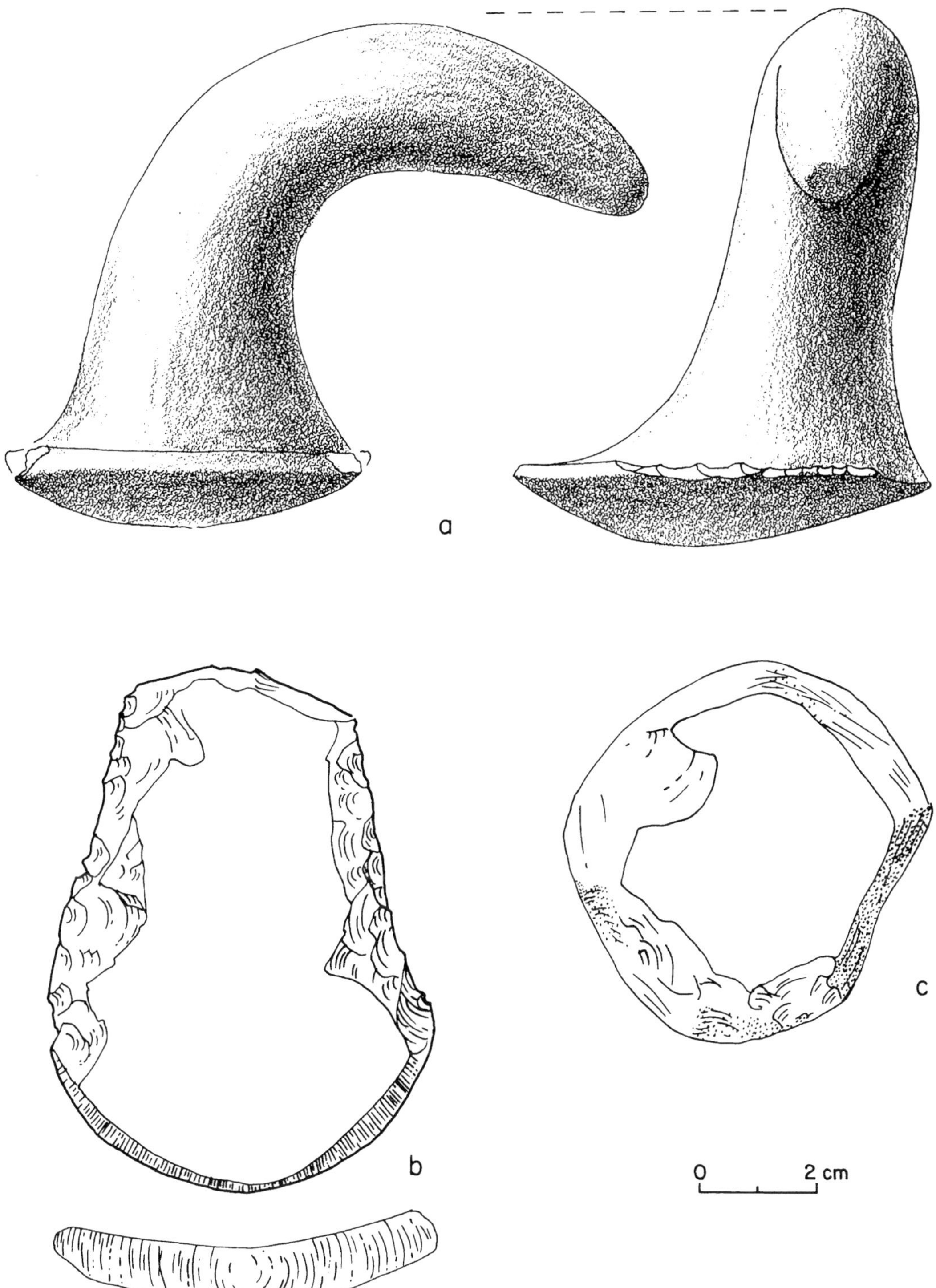

Fig. 91. Pottery objects typical of the Mehmeh phase, Tepe Sabz: *a*, "bent ceramic nail," zone B_2; *b*,*c*, chipped sherds, zones B_1 (*b*) and B_2 (*c*).

Description: Sherds which were deliberately chipped and/or ground on one or more of their edges. It is possible to divide these sherds into three subgroups, depending on the location and extent of retouch or grinding. They were probably used in the smoothing of pots and in other scraping, or even such tasks as light-duty chipping or hoeing.

a) Quadrangular or hoe-shaped (Fig. 91*b*). Sherds which are chipped or ground on three or more edges to produce a rough, rectangular or hoe-shaped object, sometimes with one smoothed convex edge. Some appear by their shape to have been suitable for hafting, but the majority were probably held in the hand.

b) Discoidal. Sherds chipped into a rough disc (Fig. 91*c*). Several were subsequently ground on the edges, probably as a result of use.

c) Miscellaneous. Sherds which are chipped or ground on one or more edges, but which either are fragmentary or have no over-all regular shape.

Table 40

OCCURRENCE OF VARIETIES OF CHIPPED SHERDS AT ALI KOSH, TEPE SABZ, AND TEPE MUSIYAN
(By Stratigraphic Zone)

Site and Zone	Quadrangular or Hoe-shaped	Discoidal	Miscellaneous	Totals
TS - A_1	...	...	...	...
TS - A_2	1	...	1	2
TS - A_3	2	...	3	5
TS - B_1	3	2	1	6
Mus "E"	...	1	...	1
TS - B_2	...	3	...	3
TS - B_3	2	2	1	5
TS - C_1	...	1	2	3
TS - C_2	...	...	1	1
TS - C_3	...	...	...	...
TS - D	10	1	12	23
AK - A_1	...	...	...	...
AK - A_2	...	...	...	...
Totals	18	10	21	49

Temporal distribution: Sabz through Bayat phases.

Geographic distribution: Chipped sherds have a wide distribution between 4000 and 6000 B.C. over most of Mesopotamia and the Zagros.

Type: "Pot lids" (Pl. 36*i*)

Sample: 7

Material: Susiana Plain Buff or Black-on-buff pottery

Description: Discoidal, saucer-shaped pieces of pottery with one or more holes for suspension. These somewhat irregular and asymmetrical pieces seem to have been tailored to particular pots. Most of them are chipped and ground from base sherds of Buff ware. In a few instances ring bases were used, and in only one instance was it evident that the lid was not made from a broken vessel. The wear of one side of these sherds may have occurred prior to their use as lids. The diameters range between 14 and 17 cm.

Temporal distribution: All but one occurred in Mehmeh phase levels.

Geographic distribution: Throughout the Mesopotamia-Khuzistan lowlands.

Ceramic Cone

Example: 1 from the Khazineh phase

Material: Susiana Plain Buff pottery

Description: A ceramic cone 7 cm. long, 13 cm. in diameter at the small round end and 1.8 cm. at the larger oval-section end. There is no apparent sign of wear on this object, nor any clue as to its use. It appears by shape, size, and stratigraphic occurrence to be different from the "bent nails." It is not a cone such as that used in cone mosaics in later periods.

Geographic distribution: Unknown.

Type: "Toy tops" (Pl. 36*e*)

Sample: 2 from the Bayat phase

Material: Lightly fired clay (terra cotta)

Description: Disc-shaped in plan, and of squat diamond-shaped form in section, these artifacts are 3.2 cm. in diameter and stand 3.1 cm. high. Their shape, as well as the polish occurring only about the areas receiving the greatest amounts of handling if spun (i.e., the points of the artifacts and around the edges of their disc-shaped center section), suggest their possible use as toy tops. We are unable to explain the presence of a thin coating of asphalt covering most of the upper surface of one of these artifacts.

Geographic distribution: Unknown.

Type: "Sling missiles" (Pl. 35*h-k*)

Sample: 16

Table 41

OCCURRENCE OF CERAMIC ARTIFACTS OTHER THAN SPINDLE WHORLS AT TEPE SABZ AND TEPE MUSIYAN
(By Stratigraphic Zone)

Site and Zone	"Bent Ceramic Nails"	Chipped Sherds	"Pot Lids"	Ceramic Cone	"Toy Tops"	"Sling Missiles"	Totals
TS - A_1	...	...	...	...	...	...	...
TS - A_2	1	2	...	...	...	4	7
TS - A_3	...	5	1	...	2	10	18
TS - B_1	7	6	3	...	...	...	16
Mus "E" ...	3	1	...	...	...	...	4
TS - B_2	12	3	2	...	...	...	17
TS - B_3	11	5	1	...	...	...	17
TS - C_1	1	3	...	...	...	1	5
TS - C_2	...	1	...	...	...	1	2
TS - C_3	...	...	...	1	...	...	1
TS - D	...	23	...	...	...	...	23
Totals ...	35	49	7	1	2	16	110

Material: Lightly baked clay

Description: Small objects, lenticular in cross-section, which are customarily referred to as "sling missiles" in the Near Eastern literature. Their name is of convenience only, since there is little evidence of their use as missiles. Most are between 4 and 5 cm. in length and 3 cm. wide.

Temporal distribution: Clusters occurred in the Khazineh and Bayat phases.

Geographic distribution: Throughout Mesopotamia, the Zagros, and the Iranian plateau. Specimens similar to ours are illustrated from Jaffarabad (Le Breton, 1947:Fig. 7:3), Matarrah (Braidwood, *et al.* 1952:Fig. 17:1-3), Sialk I-II (Ghirshman, 1938:Pl. LII:35-36), and many other sites.

Table 42

OCCURRENCE OF CERAMIC ARTIFACTS OTHER THAN SPINDLE WHORLS AT TEPE SABZ AND TEPE MUSIYAN
(By Cultural Phase)

Phase	"Bent Ceramic Nails"	Chipped Sherds	"Pot Lids"	Ceramic Cone	"Toy Tops"	"Sling Missiles"	Totals
Bayat	1	7	1	...	2	14	25
Mehmeh	33	15	6	...	...	...	54
Khazineh ...	1	4	...	1	...	2	8
Sabz	...	23	...	...	...	...	23
Totals ...	35	49	7	1	2	16	110

XIII

BONE ARTIFACTS

INTRODUCTION

We recovered eighty-three artifacts of animal bone during excavations at Ali Kosh and Tepe Sabz in 1961 and 1963. Included were awls, needles, spatulas, handles for compound tools, and many other items.

We counted all our bone artifacts in the field, and drawings of each category were made at the same time. It was planned that at our first opportunity, some of the larger functional categories (like awls) might be broken down into stylistic types which would have chronological significance within our sequence. However, the time for division of artifacts with the Iranian government came before we had an opportunity to accomplish this, so that in most cases our raw counts list the artifacts only as "gouges," "needles," or "awls," without subdivision into "metapodial awls" or "splinter awls."

Awls (Fig. 92)

Sample: 48, of various styles

Description: It is obvious that there are at least three main styles of bone awls in our sequence, but since roughly half our sample remained in Iran and could not be studied in detail, we have no counts on each of the styles by level. All were counted, however, simply as "awls." In general, nipple-like perforators and metapodial awls seem to be more common in the early part of the sequence, while awls made on long-bone splinters are particularly common at Tepe Sabz.

a) Metapodial awls (Fig. 92*a,b*)
Long, slender piercing tools made from either the proximal or distal end of the metacarpal or metatarsal bone of sheep, goat, or gazelle. They range from 5 to 7 cm. in length.

b) Small, nipple-like perforators (Fig. 92*c,d*)
These are short, stubby sections of worked bone, each bearing at its tip a sharp, projecting nipple some 3 to 5 mm. in length. The tools themselves are usually no more than 4 cm. long.

c) Long-bone splinter awls (Fig. 92*e,f*)
These are piercing or perforating tools made by carefully chipping and polishing a long splinter of limb bone from one of the local ungulates. Unbroken specimens range from 8 to 12 cm. in length.

Temporal distribution: Bone awls of one type or another occurred throughout the sequence.

Geographic distribution: Throughout the Near East.

Needles (Fig. 93*a-c*)

Sample: 6

Distribution: Carefully polished, slender long-bone splinters some 3 to 4 mm. in diameter, with an eye drilled in one end and the other end worked to a point. Complete specimens are 8 to 10 cm. in length, and may be round or lenticular in cross-section.

Temporal distribution: Four of our 6 specimens came from the Mohammad Jaffar phase, with one fragmentary and questionable specimen showing up as late as the Mehmeh phase.

Geographic distribution: Widespread. Needles occurred at Jarmo, with holes drilled "at the very end and sometimes a centimeter or so below the end" (Braidwood, Howe, *et al.* 1960:46); in Phase B of the Amuq (Braidwood and Braidwood, 1960:97); and at many other contemporary sites.

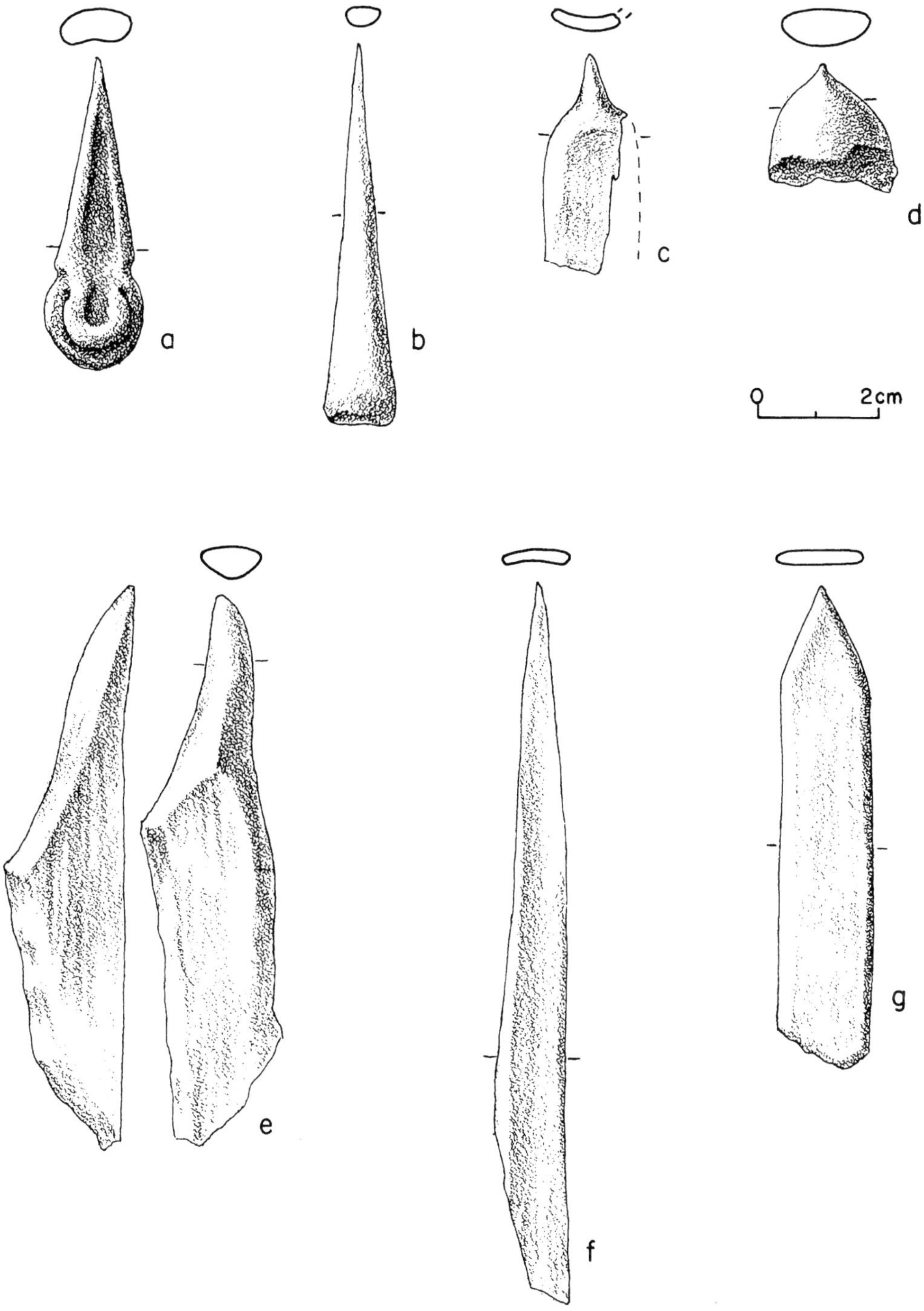

Fig. 92. Bone awls and perforators from Tepe Ali Kosh and Tepe Sabz: *a,* metapodial awl, made from distal end of sheep or goat metapodial, Tepe Ali Kosh, zone A_2 (Mohammad Jaffar phase); *b,* metapodial awl, made from proximal end of sheep or goat metapodial, Tepe Ali Kosh, zone A_1 (Mohammad Jaffar phase); *c,d,* nipple-like perforators from Tepe Ali Kosh (*c,* zone B_1, Ali Kosh phase; *d,* zone A_2, Mohammad Jaffar phase); *e,f,* splinter awls, made from slivers of ungulate limb bone (*e,* Tepe Sabz, zone A_3, Bayat phase; *f,* Tepe Ali Kosh, zone B_1, Ali Kosh phase); *g,* flat perforator, Tepe Sabz, zone A_2 (Bayat phase).

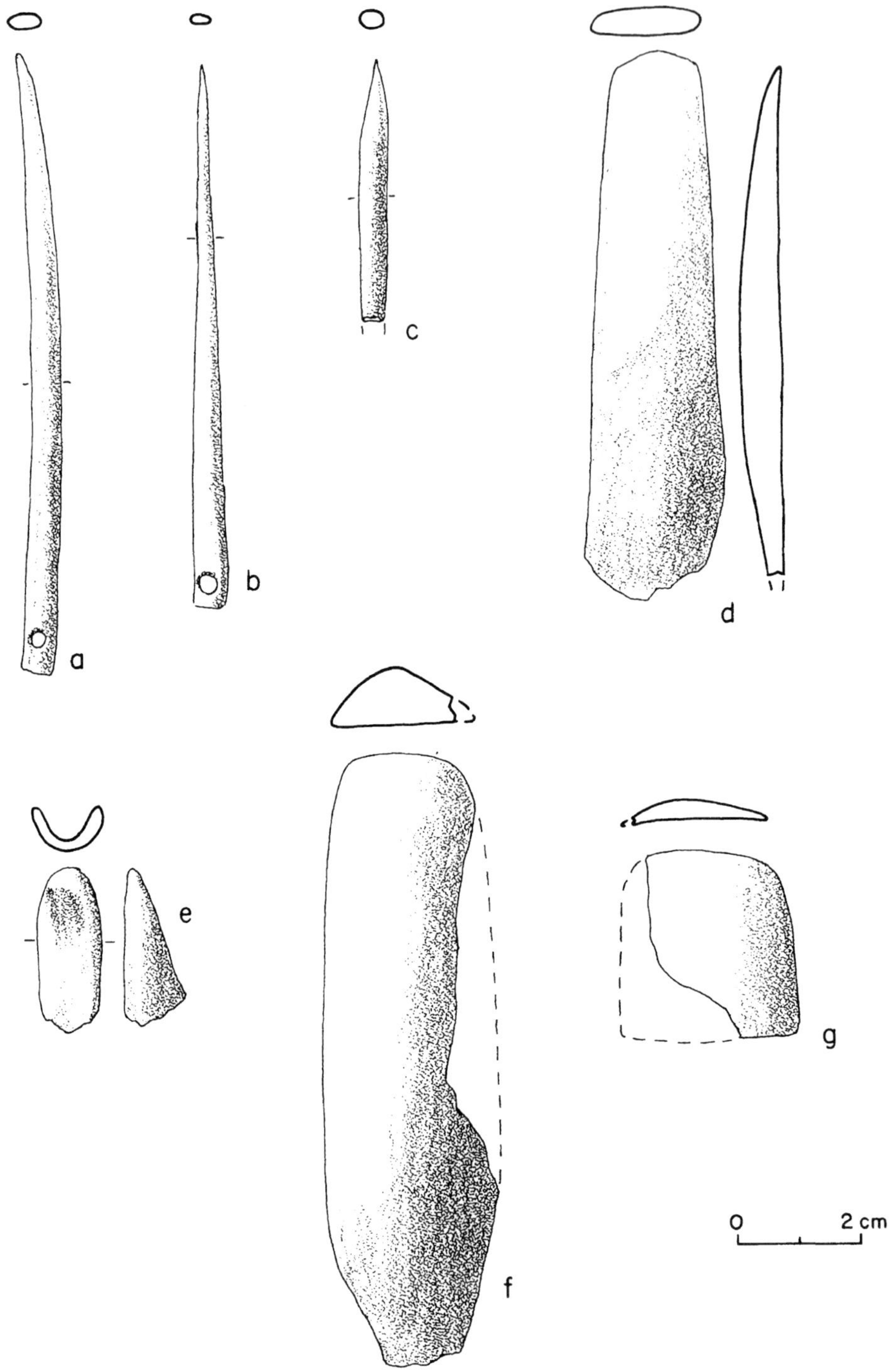

Fig. 93. Miscellaneous bone tools from Tepe Ali Kosh and Tepe Sabz: *a,b,* needles, Tepe Ali Kosh, zones A_1,A_2 (Mohammad Jaffar phase); *c,* needle (?), Tepe Sabz, zone B_3 (Mehmeh phase); *d,* spatula, Tepe Sabz, zone A_2 (Bayat phase); *e,* gouge, Tepe Sabz, zone D (Sabz phase); *f,* chisel, Tepe Ali Kosh, zone A_1 (Mohammad Jaffar phase); *g,* spatula, Tepe Ali Kosh, zone A_2 (Mohammad Jaffar phase).

Spatulas (Fig. 93*d,g*)

Sample: 6

Description: Long slats of polished bone which resemble a physician's tongue depressor. Complete specimens are 8 to 10 cm. long and usually no more than 3 to 4 mm. in thickness.

Temporal distribution: Sporadically, throughout the sequence.

Geographic distribution: Widespread. Similar spatulas were found in Amuq A and B (Braidwood and Braidwood, 1960:67 and 99); at Tepe Guran (Mortensen, 1964:119) and many other sites in the same time range.

Chisel (Fig. 93*f*)

Example: 1, from the Mohammad Jaffar phase

Description: A slat of long bone, worked in the manner of a spatula, but plano-convex in cross-section and beveled at one end to produce a chisel blade. It is 10 cm. in length.

Geographic distribution: Unknown.

Gouge (Fig. 93*e*)

Example: 1, from the Sabz phase

Description: A trough-shaped section of bone from an ungulate metapodial (preserving the ridges of the medullar canal), with one end sharpened as a gouge. The object is U-shaped in cross-section, and too fragmentary to measure.

Geographic distribution: Apparently similar bone gouges appeared in Phase A of the Amuq (Braidwood and Braidwood, 1960:Fig. 38-44);

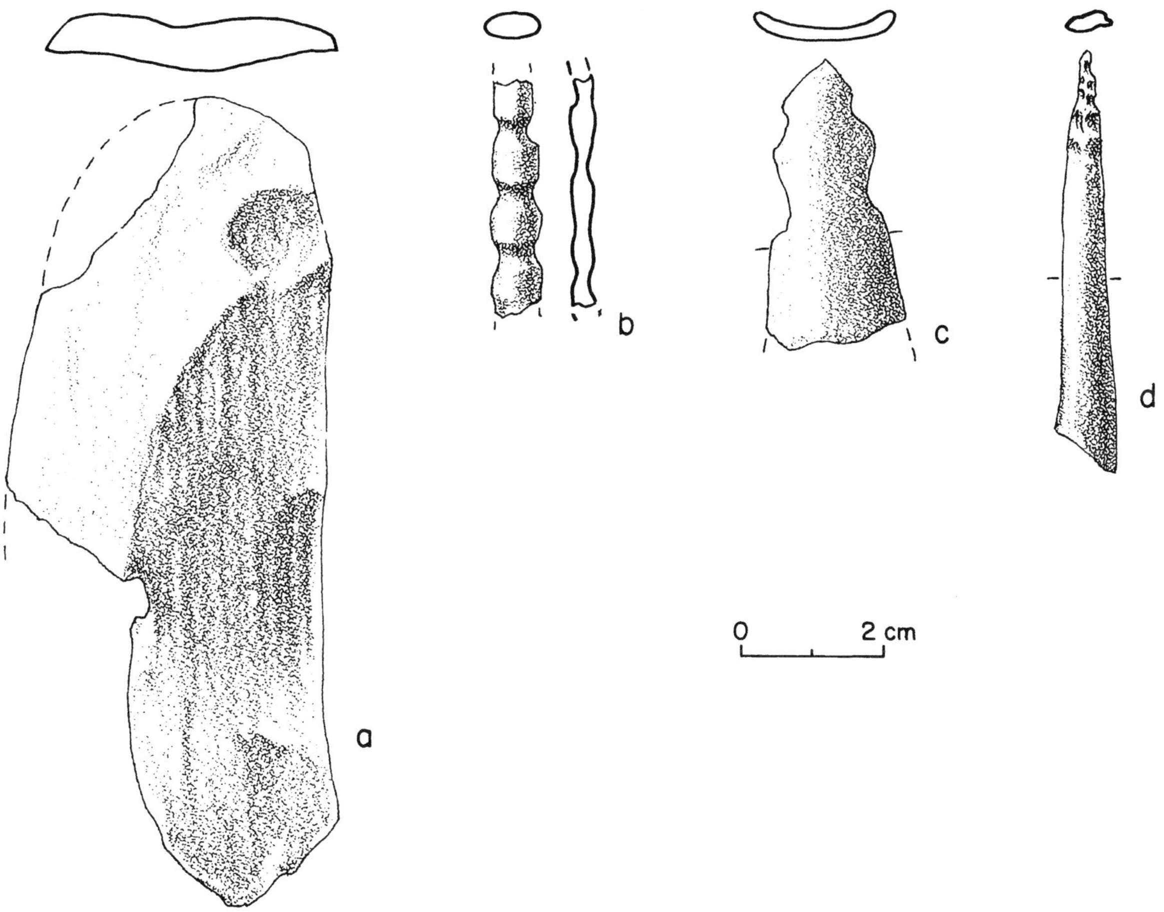

Fig. 94. Miscellaneous bone tools from Tepe Ali Kosh and Tepe Sabz: *a*, "knife," Tepe Sabz, zone B_2 (Mehmeh phase); *b*, bone handle, Tepe Ali Kosh, zone B_2 (Ali Kosh phase); *c*, bone handle, Tepe Ali Kosh, zone A_2 (Mohammad Jaffar phase); *d*, pressure-flaker, Tepe Ali Kosh, zone C_1 (Bus Mordeh phase).

and at Tepe Gawra in all strata (Tobler, 1950:214).

Pressure-flaker (Fig. 94*d*)

Sample: 2, one from the Bus Mordeh phase and one from the Khazineh phase

Description: A splinter of worked long bone, whose pointed end is covered with scars and nibble-marks which suggest its use as a pressure-flaking tool for flint.

Geographic distribution: Unknown.

"Handles" (Fig. 94*b,c*)

Sample: 3

Description: One, from the Ali Kosh phase, is a slender rod of bone (6 mm. in diameter), lenticular in cross-section, and ringed with shallow grooves at intervals of half a centimeter (Fig. 94*b*). A second, from the Mohammad Jaffar phase, is a flat, carved section of long bone whose incomplete condition precludes useful measurement (Fig. 94*c*). The third example, from the Sabz phase, is a mammal long bone into whose narrow canal a bone "awl" had been inserted. The haft and awl are both broken.

Geographic distribution: Bone handles are common at Near Eastern sites contemporary with our Ali Kosh and Mohammad Jaffar phases, but none of the illustrated examples are exactly like ours.

Cast of Bone Haft

Example: 1, from the Khazineh phase

Material: Asphalt

Table 43

OCCURRENCE OF BONE ARTIFACTS AT ALI KOSH AND TEPE SABZ
(By Stratigraphic Zone)

Site and Zone	Awls	Needles	Spatulas	Chisel	Gouge	Pressure-flaker	"Handles"	Cast of Bone Haft	"Knife"	Fragments of Polished Bone	Cut Long Bones	Totals
TS - A_1	...	...	...	...	...	...	...	...	...	...	...	...
TS - A_2	1	...	1	...	...	...	...	...	...	...	...	2
TS - A_3	3	...	...	...	...	...	...	...	...	...	...	3
TS - B_1	1	...	...	...	...	...	...	...	...	...	...	1
TS - B_2	...	...	...	...	...	...	...	...	1	...	...	1
TS - B_3	1	1	...	...	...	...	...	...	...	...	...	2
TS - C_1	...	...	...	...	...	...	...	...	...	...	...	...
TS - C_2	2	...	...	...	...	...	...	1	...	1	...	4
TS - C_3	2	...	...	...	...	1	...	...	...	...	...	3
TS - D	3	...	1	...	1	...	1	...	...	1	...	7
AK - A_1	6	1	...	1	...	...	...	...	...	1	1	10
AK - A_2	5	3	3	...	...	...	1	...	...	2	1	15
AK - B_1	4	1	...	...	...	...	...	...	...	1	...	6
AK - B_2	5	...	...	...	...	...	1	...	...	...	1	7
AK - C_1	4	...	1	...	...	1	...	...	...	3	...	9
AK - C_2	11	...	...	...	...	...	...	...	...	1	1	13
Totals.....	48	6	6	1	1	2	3	1	1	10	4	83

Description: Asphalt which apparently filled the inside of a bone that had been slotted to receive flint blades. The structure of the inside of the bone shows clearly on the cast, as does the width of the slot and its approximate depth. The 2 mm.-wide slot was cut through the bone and penetrated to the marrow cavity, a depth of some 2 mm. The bone itself had an internal diameter of about 7 mm.

"Knife" (Fig. 94*a*)

Example: 1, from the Mehmeh phase

Description: A large section from the long bone of an ox or onager carefully worked into the shape of a spatula, but with one lateral edge sharpened like the blade of a knife.

Geographic distribution: Unknown

Miscellaneous Worked Bone

a) Fragments of smoothed or polished bone occurred throughout the sequence at Tepe Ali Kosh (two were found in 1961).

b) Sections cut from ungulate long bone, but not further modified, also were found in all phases at Tepe Ali Kosh.

Table 44

OCCURRENCE OF BONE ARTIFACTS AT ALI KOSH AND TEPE SABZ
(By Cultural Phase)

Phase	Awls	Needles	Spatulas	Chisel	Gouge	Pressure-flaker	"Handles"	Cast of Bone Haft	"Knife"	Fragments of Polished Bone	Cut Long Bones	Totals
Bayat	4	. . .	1	. . .	. . .	. . .	. . .	. . .	. . .	. . .	. . .	5
Mehmeh	2	1	. . .	. . .	. . .	. . .	. . .	. . .	1	. . .	. . .	4
Khazineh	4	. . .	. . .	. . .	. . .	1	. . .	1	. . .	1	. . .	7
Sabz	3	. . .	1	. . .	1	. . .	1	. . .	. . .	1	. . .	7
Mohammad Jaffar	11	4	3	1	. . .	. . .	1	. . .	. . .	3	2	25
Ali Kosh	9	1	. . .	. . .	. . .	. . .	1	. . .	. . .	1	1	13
Bus Mordeh . . .	15	. . .	1	. . .	. . .	1	. . .	. . .	. . .	4	1	22
Totals	48	6	6	1	1	2	3	1	1	10	4	83

XIV

MATTING, BASKETRY, AND TEXTILES

INTRODUCTION

Patches of asphalt which bore impressions of matting or basketry were common at Ali Kosh and Tepe Sabz; in 1963, we found some ninety-five fragments which were large enough to permit identification of the weave. This was done by making "positive" plasticene impressions from the asphalt "negatives." A single textile impression in lightly baked clay was also found.

Most common were impressions of what appeared to be reed mats, of the kind often found as silica "ghosts" on the floors of prehistoric houses in the Mesopotamia-Zagros Mountain area. Also present were evidences of basketry of three types. The raw material used was probably the sea club-rush (*Scirpus*), which grows in the area, but this has not been botanically verified.

It is interesting, from the standpoint of chronology and culture history, that the early baskets at Deh Luran are twilled or twined; coiled baskets do not seem to make their appearance until the lower levels at Tepe Sabz. Apparently the techniques of coiled basketry entered the Deh Luran area about 5500 to 5000 B.C.

We note, in this regard, that coiled basketry appeared earlier than this in Anatolia (Helbaek, 1963:46). It may be that there were two somewhat different weaving traditions extant in southwestern Asia during the early village period: coiled basketry in Anatolia and twined basketry in the Zagros. By 5000 B.C. their distribution overlapped.

Matting

Over-one, Under-one Twilled Mat or Basket-wall Fragments

Sample: 23 fragments

Material: Reeds or club-rushes (?) varying from 4 mm. to 1 cm. in width

Comment: Because of the way the Ali Kosh baskets were made, it is often difficult to tell which of these fragments are from twilled mats and which are from the walls of shallow, tray-like baskets.

Temporal distribution: This type of weave appears in the Bus Mordeh phase, and lasts until the Mehmeh phase. It seems to have been most popular in Ali Kosh-Mohammad Jaffar times.

Geographic distribution: Unknown.

Over-two, Under-two Twilled Mats Fig. 95; Pl. 37*d,e*)

Sample: 60 fragments

Material: Reeds or club-rushes (?) ranging from 2 mm. to 2.5 cm. in width

Comment: This is the most common type of weave in our sequence. Most of the fragments are clearly from mats, and we suspect the larger weaves (rushes 2 cm. in width) were from floor mats like those at Jarmo, Hassuna, and similar sites.

Temporal distribution: Beginning in the Ali Kosh phase, these are common throughout the remainder of the sequence.

Geographic distribution: Over-two, under-two mats appear on the floors of prehistoric villages in Mesopotamia and Kurdistan (Braidwood, 1952:Figs. 7 and 14). Asphalt impressions identical to ours were observed by Neely and Flannery in the walls of the old French cut at Tepe Jowi in Susiana proper (1963).

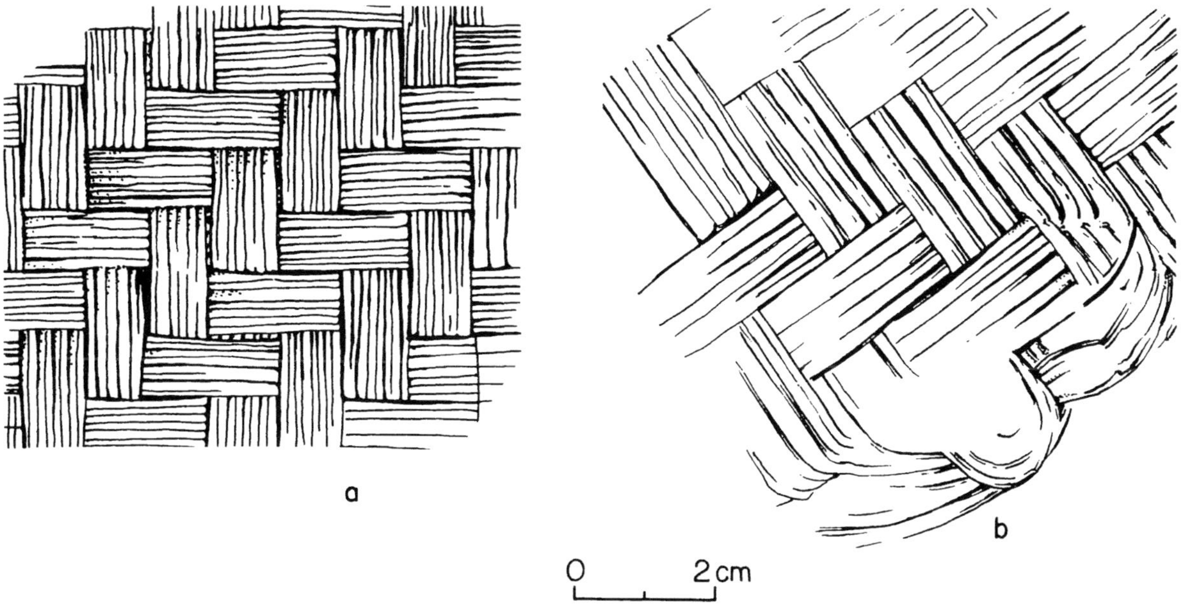

Fig. 95. Over-two, under-two twilled reed or club-rush mats from Tepe Ali Kosh and Tepe Sabz. Drawings are of "positive" modeling-clay impressions made from "negative" casts in spilled asphalt: *a,* Tepe Ali Kosh, zone A_2 (Mohammad Jaffar phase); *b,* Tepe Sabz, zone B_3 (Mehmeh phase).

Twined Baskets

Over-one, Under-one Twined Baskets with Floors (Pl. 37*b,c*)

Sample: 5 (fragmentary)

Material: Reeds or club-rushes (?) in the following widths:

a) Warps of 4 mm. by wefts of 2 mm.
b) Warps of 6 mm. by wefts of 6 mm.
c) Warps of 1 cm. by wefts of 1 cm.

Description: These are actually composite baskets or "carrying trays." The floor of the basket is twilled matting (over-two, under-two), and has a diameter of about 7 cm.; near the edges, this gives way to a different construction. Some of the reeds from the floor extend upright like radii, forming the warps of the basket wall, and wefts are interwoven through them in the over-one, under-one style called "randing" by Hodges (1964:Fig. 38, No. 1). What results is a wide, shallow basket perhaps 40 cm. in diameter. It is worth noting that all the examples we found which clearly showed both walls and floor, appeared to have been purposely coated with asphalt as if to strengthen the juncture between wall and floor.

Temporal distribution: Four of 5 examples are from the Ali Kosh and Mohammad Jaffar phases. Apparently these were replaced by coiled baskets later in the sequence.

Geographic distribution: Unknown.

Coiled Baskets

Coiled Baskets (Fig. 96; Pl. 37*a*; Pl. 39*h*)

Sample: 7 fragments

Material: The coils or "foundations" are bundles of grass, or rods (sticks or reeds), 0.5 to 1.0 cm in diameter; they are sewn together with pliable "splints" of wood or grass that range from 0.1 to 0.2 cm. in width.

Description: Two techniques of construction were evident in the examples recovered: (1) Close coiling using a simple, uninterlocked stitch over a grass bundle foundation (Fig. 96*a*). (2) A single specimen from the early Mehmeh phase illustrated close coiling using a simple, uninterlocked stitch over what appears to be a one-rod foundation (Fig. 96*b*). The direction of work in construction was uniformly right to left. The more complete specimens had "normal" or circular centers (Fig. 96*d*), and therefore, were circular in form.

Temporal distribution: These baskets are as characteristic of the Khazineh and Mehmeh phases as Susiana Black-on-buff pottery, but apparently were unknown in the Deh Luran area before about 5000 B.C.

Geographic distribution: Coiled baskets appear at Çatal Hüyük in Anatolia (Helbaek, 1963:46).

Textile

Plain-weave Textile (Pl. 39*g*)

Example: 1, from the Bayat phase

Material: Unknown.

Description: A small (2.5 by 4.2 cm.) fragment of lightly baked clay contained the impression of a plain-weave textile, woven in an over-one, under-one technique. A single instance of an over-two, under-two variation was noted upon close inspection of this fragment. Although able to identify the construction as being of S-spun, single-ply thread (0.6 to 1.0 cm. in diameter) we could not identify the material from which the threads were made.

Geographic distribution: Dyson (1964:121) states that the only actual preserved archeological textiles so far known from Iran are from Hasanlu (700 - 800 B.C.) and Susa (6th century B.C.). He also notes some "impressions in verdigris found on a few pieces of prehistoric copper at Susa and Tepe Sialk." We suspect that textile impressions in clay, like ours, might be more common than one would gather from the archeological literature.

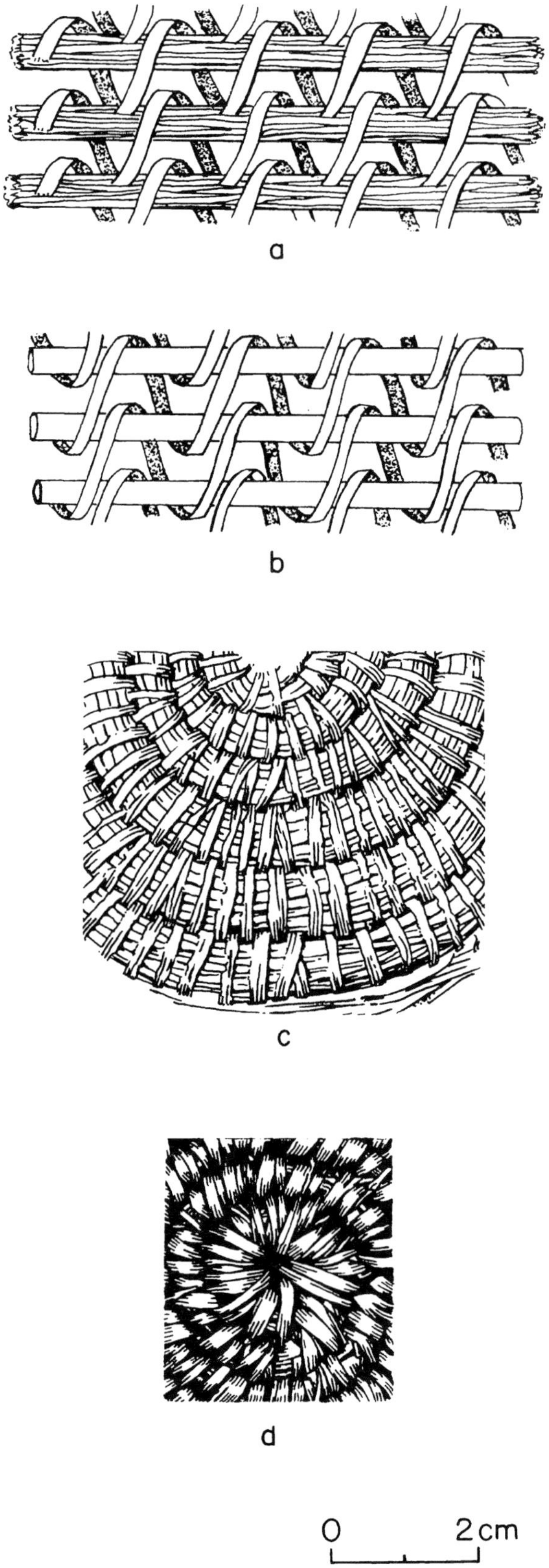

Fig. 96. Coiled basketry from Tepe Sabz, with diagrams indicating method of manufacture: *a,* simple uninterlocked stitch over grass bundle foundation (zone B_2, Mehmeh phase); *b,* same stitch over one-rod foundation (zone B_3, Mehmeh phase); *c,* drawing of "positive" modeling-clay impression made from "negative" cast in spilled asphalt (zone B_2, Mehmeh phase). Opposite side of asphalt cast had impressions of hulled barley from inside basket; *d,* "normal" circular basket center (reconstructed from several fragmentary Khazineh phase specimens). See also Pl. 37 and 39. (Technique of illustration follows Morris and Burgh, 1941.)

Table 45

OCCURRENCE OF MAT, BASKETRY AND TEXTILE IMPRESSIONS AT ALI KOSH AND TEPE SABZ
(By Stratigraphic Zone)

Site and Zone	Over-one, Under-one Fragments	Over-two, Under-two Matting Fragments	Over-one, Under-one Baskets with Floors	Coiled Baskets	Plain Weave Textile	Totals
TS - A_1	...	1	...	...	...	1
TS - A_2	...	...	...	...	...	...
TS - A_3	...	...	...	...	1	1
TS - B_1	...	2	...	...	...	2
TS - B_2	...	2	...	1	...	3
TS - B_3	1	4	...	2	...	7
TS - C_1	1	4	...	1	...	6
TS - C_2	...	4	...	2	...	6
TS - C_3	...	3	1	1	...	5
TS - D	2	12	...	...	...	14
AK - A_1	2	5	1	...	...	8
AK - A_2	5	10	1	...	...	16
AK - B_1	7	12	2	...	...	21
AK - B_2	1	1	...	...	...	2
AK - C_1	1	...	...	...	...	1
AK - C_2	3	...	...	...	...	3
Totals	23	60	5	7	1	96

Table 46

OCCURRENCE OF MAT, BASKETRY AND TEXTILE IMPRESSIONS AT ALI KOSH AND TEPE SABZ
(By Cultural Phase)

Phase	Over-one, Under-one Fragments	Over-two, Under-two Matting Fragments	Over-one, Under-one Baskets with Floors	Coiled Baskets	Plain Weave Textile	Totals
Bayat	...	1	...	...	1	2
Mehmeh	1	8	...	3	...	12
Khazineh	1	11	1	4	...	17
Sabz	2	12	...	...	...	14
Mohammad Jaffar	7	15	2	...	...	24
Ali Kosh	8	13	2	...	...	23
Bus Mordeh ...	4	...	...	...	...	4
Totals	23	60	5	7	1	96

XV

FIGURINES AND OBJECTS OF LIGHTLY-BAKED CLAY

INTRODUCTION

Small, lightly-baked clay figurines are common at early village sites throughout Mesopotamia and Kurdistan. In our sequence, they were virtually restricted to the Bus Mordeh, Ali Kosh, Mohammad Jaffar, and Sabz phases. Nearly all animal figurines appeared in the Bus Mordeh and Ali Kosh phases, while human figurines were concentrated in the Mohammad Jaffar phase. Abstract "T-shaped" figurines similarly clustered in Mohammad Jaffar levels, though one appeared in the Sabz phase as well. In all, we found some fifty-three figurines, a rather modest number when compared with sites like Tepe Sarab (Braidwood, 1960:Figs. 5-8). "Fired" pottery figurines did not appear until the Sabz phase.

Figurines

Type: Animal figurines (Fig.97*b-h*)

Example: 28

Material: Clay

Description: Stylized figurines of animals, showing general form rather than the details of anatomy. Heads lack eyes, nose, ears, and mouth, but horns were evidently present on some pieces. On one example, it is clear that horns were present but have been broken off (Fig. 97*e*). Bodies and legs are modeled with a minimum of detail and no suggestion of hair, wool, or hooves. One example has a short pendant tail (Fig. 97*b*). From the form of the body, one can guess that sheep or goats are most commonly represented. The horns do not clarify the identification further. One probable pig from the Bus Mordeh phase was recovered. There were no obvious dogs or cattle.

The body and legs of an unidentified animal, whose head and tail have been broken, came from the Bayat phase. It may not be at all related to the earlier figurines.

Temporal distribution: Twenty-seven out of 28 occurred in the Bus Mordeh and early Ali Kosh phases.

Geographic distribution: Throughout Kurdistan (see Braidwood, Howe, *et al.* 1960:Plate 16), Luristan (Mortensen, 1964) and Khuzistan.

Type: Human figurines (Fig. 97*a*; Pl. 38*i*)

Sample: 5

Material: Clay

Description: Lumpy, headless, seated representations of humans of undeterminable sex. The best-preserved examples show the arms embracing drawn-up knees. Clothing may be suggested by punctations encircling the waist. Another example, of the same general conformation but with less detail, has a concave base.

Temporal distribution: Four of the 5 are from the Mohammad Jaffar phase, with one example from the late Ali Kosh phase.

Geographic distribution: Seated human figurines are widespread in Kurdistan, appearing at Jarmo (Braidwood, Howe, *et al.* 1960:Pl. 16) Sarab (Braidwood, 1960:Fig. 8), and Tepe Guran (Mortensen, 1964); none of those illustrated closely resemble ours, however.

Horn-shaped Figurine Fragments?

Sample: 5

Material: Clay

Description: Slightly curved clay horns, round to oval in cross-section, which may possibly have been attached to animal figurines. Their shape suggests that they were meant to represent sheep or goat horns.

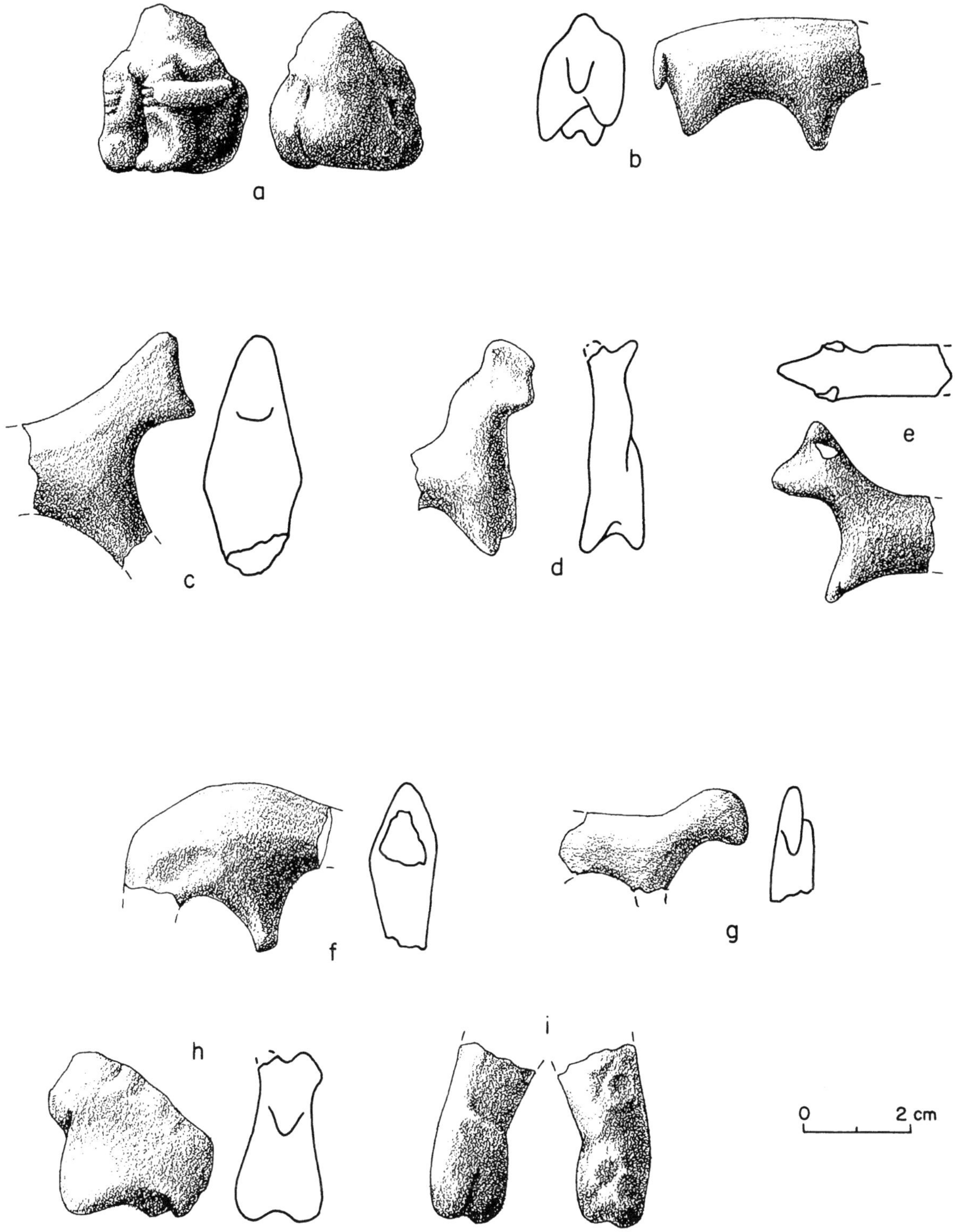

Fig. 97. Human and animal figurines from Tepe Ali Kosh: *a,* seated human figure with hands clasping knees (zone A_2, Mohammad Jaffar phase); *b-h,* animals (*c,d, f-h,* zone C_1, Bus Mordeh phase; *b,e,* zone B_2, Ali Kosh phase); *i,* possible fragment of animal, zone B_1 (Ali Kosh phase).

Temporal distribution: Unlike our animal figurines, these horns are concentrated in the late Ali Kosh and Mohammad Jaffar phases, suggesting that we may not correctly have discerned their purpose.

Geographic distribution: Unknown.

Type: T-shaped "figurines" (Fig. 98; Pl. 38*j*)

Sample: 12

Material: Clay

Description: Clay stalks centered on an elongate, and often slightly upcurving base. Few specimens are complete enough to allow an adequate description of all their details. The upright stalk was apparently pinched on the end, or had a small round blob applied to its upper end. One example, with an appliqued "button" has a vertical incised line just below that button; the base of the piece is encircled with a line of incised zigzags (Fig. 98*d*; Pl. 38*j*).

Temporal distribution: Ten of the twelve examples came from the Mohammad Jaffar phase.

Geographic distribution: In the upper part of Jarmo, similar objects with "double-wing bases" were found. (Braidwood, Howe, *et al.* 1960:44 and Plate 16:14, 15).

Clay Hand

Example: 1, from the late Ali Kosh phase

Description: A hand and part of a forearm made from lightly-baked clay. The fingers are only suggested by indentations where the finger tips should be.

Geographic distribution: Unknown.

Other Fragments

Examples: 2

Material: Buff ware pottery

Description: One is a T-shaped fragment which looks like a human torso. The other fragment consists of two clay cylinders joined like a pair of legs, each "leg" being about 2 cm. in diameter. It is possible that the clay cone described on page 212 was part of a similar object; its size, shape, and provenience suggest this.

Temporal distribution: Both examples are from the Sabz phase.

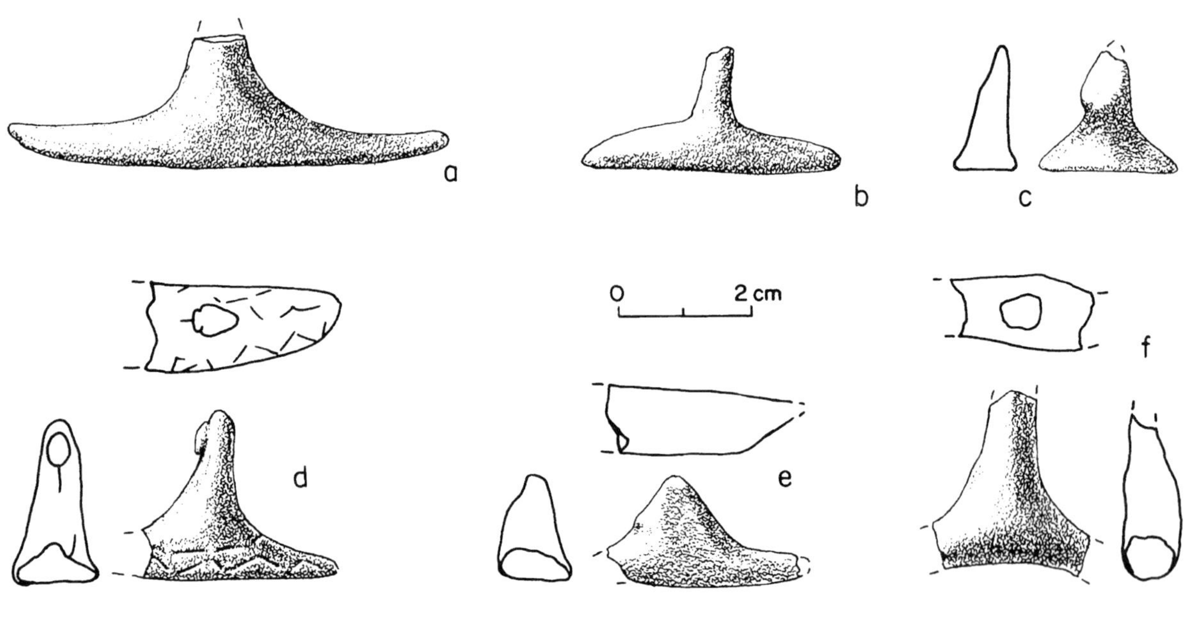

Fig. 98. T-shaped or "stalk" figurines from Tepe Ali Kosh: *a,b,f,* zone A_2 (Mohammad Jaffar phase); *c,* zone B_1 (Ali Kosh phase); *d,e,* zone A_1 (Mohammad Jaffar phase) (*d* was found in ash-filled borrow-pit in square 98, zone A_1).

Table 47

OCCURRENCE OF FIGURINE TYPES AT ALI KOSH AND TEPE SABZ (By Stratigraphic Zone)

Site and Zone	Animal Figurines	Human Figurines	Horn-shaped Figurine Fragments	T-shaped "Figurines"	Clay Hand	Other Fragments (Fired)	Totals
TS - A_1 . . .	1	. . .	. . .	. . .	. . .	. . .	1
TS - A_2 . . .	. . .	. . .	. . .	. . .	. . .	. . .	. . .
TS - A_3 . . .	. . .	. . .	. . .	. . .	. . .	. . .	. . .
TS - B_1 . . .	. . .	. . .	. . .	. . .	. . .	. . .	. . .
TS - B_2 . . .	. . .	. . .	. . .	. . .	. . .	. . .	. . .
TS - B_3 . . .	. . .	. . .	. . .	. . .	. . .	. . .	. . .
TS - C_1 . . .	. . .	. . .	. . .	. . .	. . .	. . .	. . .
TS - C_2 . . .	. . .	. . .	. . .	. . .	. . .	. . .	. . .
TS - C_3 . . .	. . .	. . .	. . .	. . .	. . .	. . .	. . .
TS - D	. . .	. . .	. . .	1	. . .	2	3
AK - A_1 . . .	. . .	1	1	5	. . .	. . .	7
AK - A_2 . . .	. . .	3	3	5	. . .	. . .	11
AK - B_1 . . .	. . .	1	1	1	1	. . .	4
AK - B_2 . . .	7	. . .	. . .	. . .	. . .	. . .	7
AK - C_1 . . .	16	. . .	. . .	. . .	. . .	. . .	16
AK - C_2 . . .	4	. . .	. . .	. . .	. . .	. . .	4
Totals . . .	28	5	5	12	1	2	53

Table 48

OCCURRENCE OF FIGURINE TYPES AT ALI KOSH AND TEPE SABZ (By Cultural Phase)

Phase	Animal Figurines	Human Figurines	Horn-shaped Figurine Fragments	T-shaped "Figurines"	Clay Hand	Other Fragments (Fired)	Totals
Bayat	1	. . .	. . .	. . .	. . .	. . .	1
Mehmeh . . .	. . .	. . .	. . .	. . .	. . .	. . .	. . .
Khazineh . . .	. . .	. . .	. . .	. . .	. . .	. . .	. . .
Sabz	. . .	. . .	. . .	1	. . .	2	3
Mohammad Jaffar	. . .	4	4	10	. . .	. . .	18
Ali Kosh . . .	7	1	1	1	1	. . .	11
Bus Mordeh .	20	. . .	. . .	. . .	. . .	. . .	20
Totals . . .	28	5	5	12	1	2	53

Miscellaneous Objects of Lightly-Baked Clay

Introduction

A great many clay objects, of unknown use but standardized form, were made during the occupation of Ali Kosh. Some of these may be parts of figurines or other representations in clay, but no examples were found which would allow such a definite conclusion. Since we have little evidence for the temporal or spatial distribution of these outside the Deh Luran plain, our typology remains largely descriptive. The largest proportion of the clay cylinders occurred in the Bus Mordeh and Ali Kosh phases. It is not clear to what extent the various "types" may be different fragments from the same object.

Type: Clay cylinders with pinched ends (Fig. 99*a-d*)

Sample: 78

Description: Cylinders which were asymmetrically pinched at one end, causing an outpouching on one side only. The other ends of these pieces are invariably broken. They range in length from 1.7 to 3.7 cm. and in diameter from .5 to 1.8 cm.

Temporal distribution: These cylinders are most frequent in the Bus Mordeh and Ali Kosh phases.

Geographic distribution: A "clay figurine" from Karim Shahir resembles our clay cylinders with pinched ends (Braidwood, Howe, *et al.* 1960:Pl. 23:8).

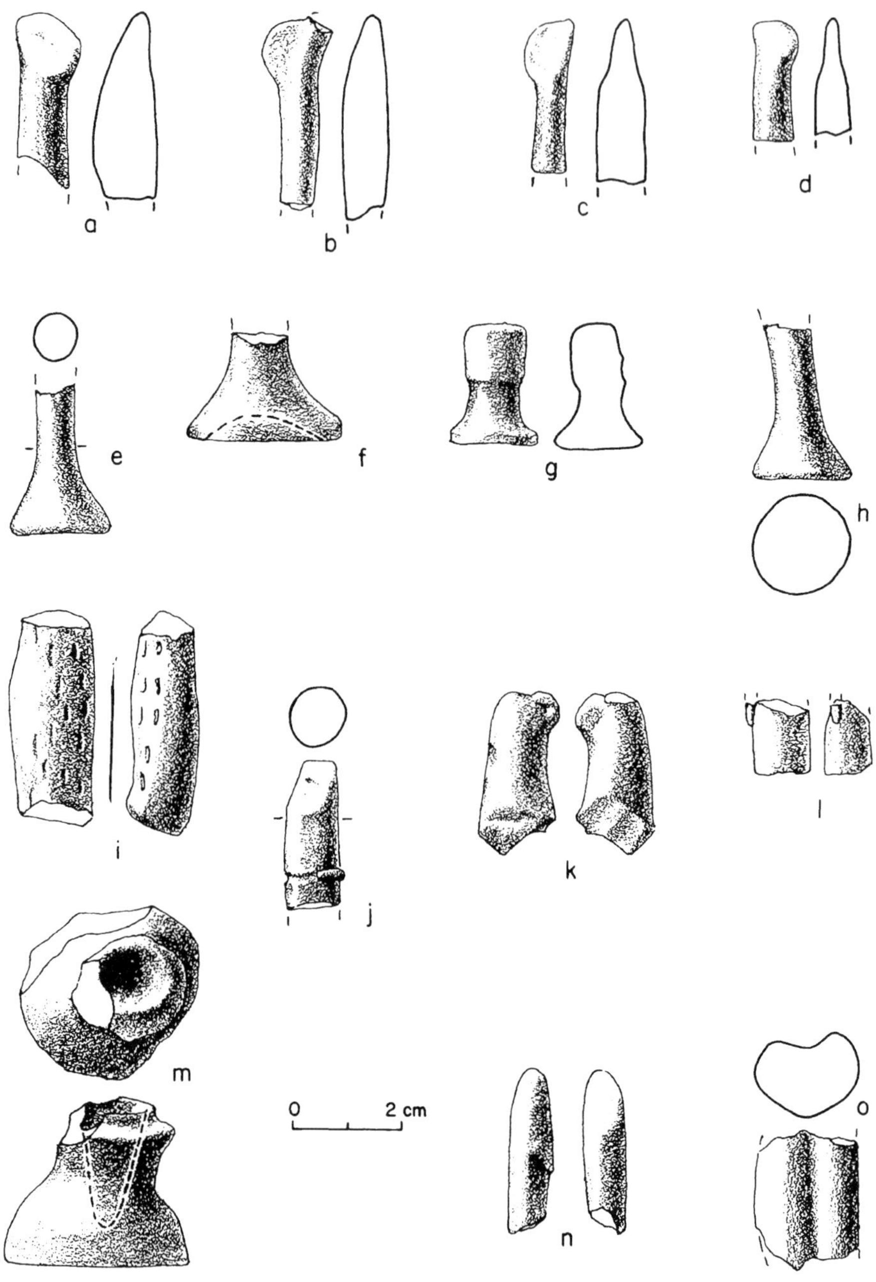

Fig. 99. Miscellaneous objects of lightly-baked clay from Tepe Ali Kosh: *a,b,* clay cylinders with pinched ends (Ali Kosh phase examples); *c,d,* clay cylinders with pinched ends (Mohammad Jaffar phase examples); *e-h,* clay cylinders with flared ends (Ali Kosh phase examples); *i,* clay cylinder with punctations, zone A_2 (Mohammad Jaffar phase); *j-l,* clay cylinders with applique-blobs or fillets, zone B_2 (Ali Kosh phase); *m,* clay "base," zone A_2 (Mohammad Jaffar phase); *n,* clay polisher? zone B_1 (Ali Kosh phase); *o,* enigmatic fragment, zone B_1 (Ali Kosh phase).

Type: Clay cylinders with a flared or bell-shaped end (Fig. 99*e-h*)

Sample: 181

Description: The bell-shaped examples (110 in all) have a slight concavity in the end; otherwise their distribution, size, and shape are identical to that of the seventy specimens with flared ends. Invariably the proximal ends of these pieces are broken, suggesting that they were only a part of some larger object. Their lengths range from 2.0 to 3.5 cm. and the diameters of the expanded ends from 1.5 to 2.7 cm. The body of the cylinder is round in cross-section.

Temporal distribution: Seventy per cent occur in the late Bus Mordeh and early Ali Kosh phases.

Geographic distribution: Unknown.

Type: Clay cylinders with plastic applications or punctations (Fig. 99*i-l*)

Sample: 31

Description: These are clay cylinders whose surfaces have been altered by plastic applications or punctations, perhaps to suggest anatomical details. One variety resembles our "cylinders with pinched ends," except that a clay blob has been applied to the side opposite the pinched-out area. In a few instances, the plastic application resembles human hair,

Table 49

OCCURRENCE OF MISCELLANEOUS OBJECTS OF UNFIRED CLAY AT ALI KOSH AND TEPE SABZ
(By Stratigraphic Zone)

Site and Zone	Clay Cylinders with Pinched Ends	Clay Cylinders with Flared or Bell-shaped Ends	Clay Cylinders with Applications or Punctations	Clay Cylinders with Both Ends Broken	Clay Stalks	Clay Balls	Clay Bases	Ovoid Clay Lumps	Clay Polisher?	Grooved Clay Polisher?	Totals
TS - A_1	...	...	...	...	...	...	...	...	...	...	...
TS - A_2	...	...	...	...	...	...	...	...	...	...	...
TS - A_3	...	...	...	...	...	...	...	...	...	...	...
TS - B_1	...	...	...	...	...	...	...	...	...	...	...
TS - B_2	...	...	...	...	...	...	...	...	...	...	...
TS - B_3	...	...	...	...	...	...	...	...	...	...	...
TS - C_1	...	...	...	...	...	...	...	...	...	...	...
TS - C_2	...	...	...	...	...	...	...	...	...	...	...
TS - C_3	...	...	...	...	...	...	...	...	...	...	...
TS - D.	...	...	...	...	...	...	...	...	...	...	...
AK - A_1	3	7	...	8	...	1	...	...	...	...	19
AK - A_2	4	9	1	4	...	1	2	...	...	...	21
AK - B_1	4	7	6	10	...	2	...	...	1	1	31
AK - B_2	17	40	3	43	...	4	...	...	...	...	107
AK - C_1	35	86	19	76	3	10	...	4	...	...	233
AK - C_2	15	32	2	34	2	2	...	...	...	...	87
Totals	78	181	31	175	5	20	2	4	1	1	498

which suggests that these may be highly stylized human figures. Other cylinders have lumps or blobs whose application suggests no obvious purpose. Still others are encircled by a plastic ring. A few cylinders are scarred by punctations, as if tatooing were being depicted (Fig. 99*i*).

Temporal distribution: Throughout the sequence at Ali Kosh, with their greatest frequency in the late Bus Mordeh phase.

Geographic distribution: Unknown.

Clay Cylinders with Both Ends Broken

Sample: 175

Comment: These are probably fragments of one of the preceding types.

Temporal distribution: Sporadically throughout the sequence at Ali Kosh, with their greatest frequency in the late Bus Mordeh and early Ali Kosh phases.

Type: Clay stalks

Sample: 5

Description: Drawn-out cylinders of clay, with both ends intact. The base is slightly flared, and the distal end tapers to a point.

Temporal distribution: Apparently confined to the Bus Mordeh phase.

Geographic distribution: Clay stalks appeared at Jarmo and Sarab (Oriental Institute collections in Chicago).

Type: Clay balls

Sample: 20

Description: Spherical balls of clay whose average diameter is 1.5 cm.

Temporal distribution: These balls were found throughout the sequence at Ali Kosh, with their greatest frequency in the late Bus Mordeh phase.

Geographic distribution: Unknown.

Type: Clay bases (Fig. 99*m*)

Sample: 2

Description: Objects of clay, resembling bases for miniature flag staffs. They are round in plan, and flat-bottomed, with a central cavity

Table 50

OCCURRENCE OF MISCELLANEOUS OBJECTS OF UNFIRED CLAY AT ALI KOSH AND TEPE SABZ

(By Cultural Phase)

Phase	Clay Cylinders with Pinched Ends	Clay Cylinders with Flared or Bell-shaped Ends	Clay Cylinders with Applications or Punctations	Clay Cylinders with Both Ends Broken	Clay Stalks	Clay Balls	Clay Bases	Ovoid Clay Lumps	Clay Polisher?	Grooved Clay Polisher?	Totals
Bayat	. . .	. . .	. . .	. . .	. . .	. . .	. . .	. . .	. . .	. . .	. . .
Mehmeh	. . .	. . .	. . .	. . .	. . .	. . .	. . .	. . .	. . .	. . .	. . .
Khazineh	. . .	. . .	. . .	. . .	. . .	. . .	. . .	. . .	. . .	. . .	. . .
Sabz	. . .	. . .	. . .	. . .	. . .	. . .	. . .	. . .	. . .	. . .	. . .
Mohammad Jaffar	7	16	1	12	. . .	2	2	. . .	. . .	. . .	40
Ali Kosh	21	47	9	53	. . .	6	. . .	. . .	1	1	138
Bus Mordeh . . .	50	118	21	110	5	12	. . .	4	. . .	. . .	320
Totals	78	181	31	175	5	20	2	4	1	1	498

perhaps formed by the insertion of a stick. In profile, the objects have a beveled rim, a constricted neck and an expanding base. One complete example is 3.5 cm. in diameter and 3.2 cm. high, with a central cavity 2.4 cm. deep.

Temporal distribution: Known only from the Mohammad Jaffar phase.

Geographic distribution: Unknown.

Type: Ovoid clay lumps

Sample: 4

Description: Small, football-shaped or oval-shaped lumps of clay, three of which were pierced, probably by a stick of small diameter.

Temporal distribution: All from the late Bus Mordeh phase.

Geographic distribution: Unknown.

Clay Polishers? (Fig. 99*n*)

Example: 2, from the late Ali Kosh phase

Description: Cylinders of lightly-fired clay, one end of which is beveled from abrasion. One is grooved.

XVI

ORNAMENTS

INTRODUCTION

Ornaments appeared in all levels at Ali Kosh and Tepe Sabz, but were more often found with burials than in midden deposits. They included pendants, labrets or "lip-plugs," bracelets, buttons, rings, and strings of beads. Ornament styles and raw materials varied from phase to phase during the sequence, providing us with another chronological tool.

In the Bus Mordeh phase, pendants and buttons were made of clam shell and boar tusk. Buttons were not found in Ali Kosh phase levels, but shell and tusk pendants continued; they were joined by plummet-shaped and bell-shaped pendants of stone. In the Mohammad Jaffar phase, crab claw pendants joined the stone bells and shell ornaments.

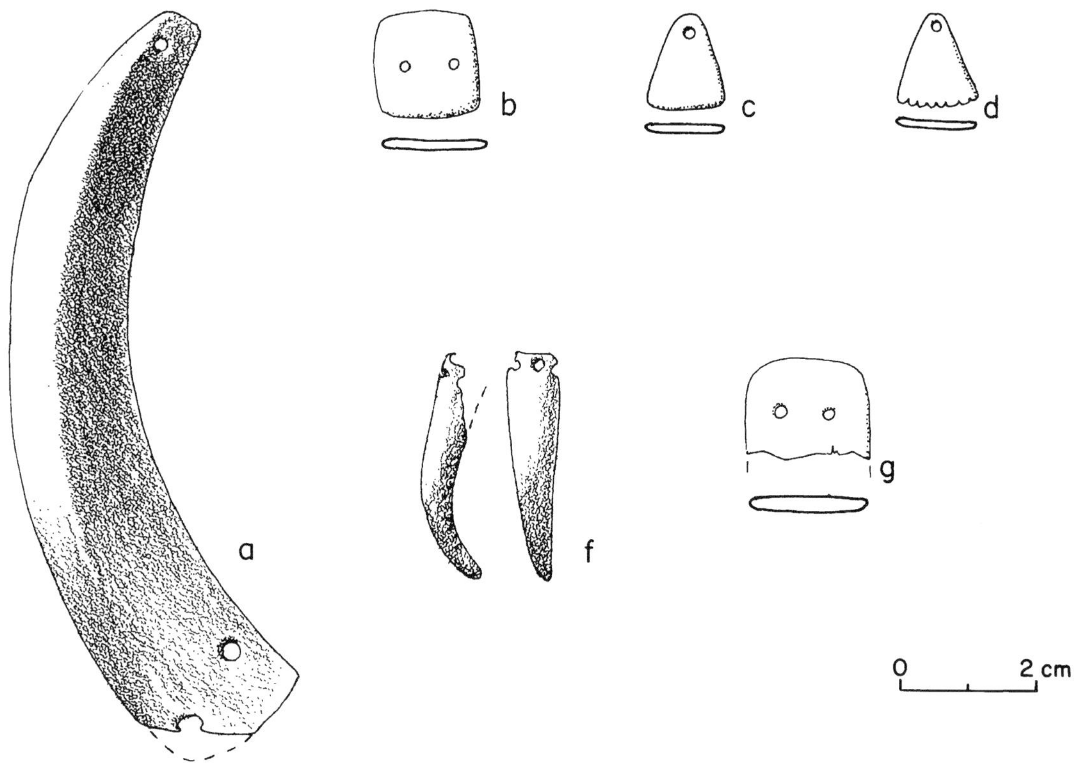

Fig. 100. Bone and shell ornaments from Tepe Ali Kosh: *a,* boar's tusk pendant, zone B_2 (Ali Kosh phase); *b,* mussel shell "button," zone C_2 (Bus Mordeh phase); *c,d,* triangular mussel shell pendants (Bus Mordeh and Ali Kosh phases); *e,* plummet-shaped mussel shell pendant found with mass of secondarily-buried limb bones near Burial 34, zone B_2 (Ali Kosh phase); *f,* crab claw pendant, zone A_1 (Mohammad Jaffar phase); *g,* bone pendant, zone B_2 (Ali Kosh phase).

Lip-plugs of stone, asphalt, or clay appeared in the Ali Kosh and Mohammad Jaffar phases, and lasted through the sequence at Tepe Sabz; their peak use was in Mohammad Jaffar - Sabz phase levels. These two phases also saw maximum use of stone bracelets of two kinds, plain and incised. A new ornament type appearing in the Khazineh, Mehmeh, and Bayat phases was the small ceramic "ring."

Although ornaments of all raw materials occurred in most phases, one could detect a general trend from bone and shell, to polished stone, to pottery, through time. Two raw materials foreign to Khuzistan—copper and turquoise—appeared at Ali Kosh. Turquoise beads were found with Ali Kosh - Mohammad Jaffar burials, and a single bead of hammered copper appeared in the Ali Kosh phase.

Pendants

Type: Boar tusk pendant (Fig. 100*a*)

Sample: 7 (including fragmentary specimens)

Material: The lower canine tooth of wild boar, *Sus scrofa*

Description: A cut and polished section of tusk (complete specimens average 10 cm. long) with holes drilled at one or both ends for suspension. One specimen from Ali Kosh phase has one hole drilled at the distal end and two at the proximal end.

Temporal distribution: Known only from the Bus Mordeh-early Ali Kosh phases

Geographic distribution: Unknown.

Type: Bell-shaped pendants (Fig. 101*g-i*; Pl. 38*b,c*)

Sample: 6

Material: Lightly fired pink clay; asphalt; or finely polished marble or alabasterlike stone

Description: These objects resemble small, clapperless bells, 2.5 to 5.0 cm. in diameter at the base, each of which has been perforated for suspension.

Associations: Four of these six "bells" were found with burials, as follows: alabaster or marble examples with Burial 8 (1963) and with an Ali Kosh phase burial in 1961 (Hole and Flannery, 1962:111); clay or asphalt bells with Burials 10 and 25 (1963). When the burials were undisturbed, the bells were found resting between the thighs of the individual, near the pelvis; and an occasional bead lodged in the perforation in the bell (Fig. 101*i*; Pl. 38*b*) suggests that they were worn as some part of the pubic covering of fine beads (see page 243). Only two fragmentary clay bells were found in midden context (Mohammad Jaffar and Khazineh phases). The fragment from the Khazineh phase is of asphalt, and has three parallel lines incised around its base.

Temporal distribution: Most frequent with burials of the late Ali Kosh and Mohammad Jaffar phases

Geographic distribution: Previously unreported from southwest Asia.

Type: Flat pebble pendants (Fig. 101*a,b*)

Sample: 3

Material: Fine-grained river pebbles

Description: These polished pebbles may be round, oval, or ellipsoidal in plan view, and all are about 5 cm. at their greatest diameter. Each is biconically drilled through at a point 2 to 3 mm. from one edge, so that the object could be suspended.

Temporal distribution: Bus Mordeh, Ali Kosh, and Mohammad Jaffar phases.

Geographic distribution: Similar perforated flat pebble pendants are known from the late preceramic of Kurdistan, including Zawi Chemi Shanidar (Solecki, 1963:Fig. 7*m,n,o*), Tepe Asiab (Braidwood, 1960:Fig. 4), and Karim Shahir (Braidwood, 1952:Fig. 13, top row center).

Mussel Shell Pendants (Fig. 100*c-e*; Pl. 39*a*)

Sample: 5

Material: Shells of river mussel (*Unio, Pseudodontopsis*)

Description: Two types were discovered. (*a*) The first consists of triangular sections of shell 1.5 cm. on a side, some with the base of the triangle having a denticulate edge. The apex is perforated for suspension (Fig. 100*c,d*). (*b*)

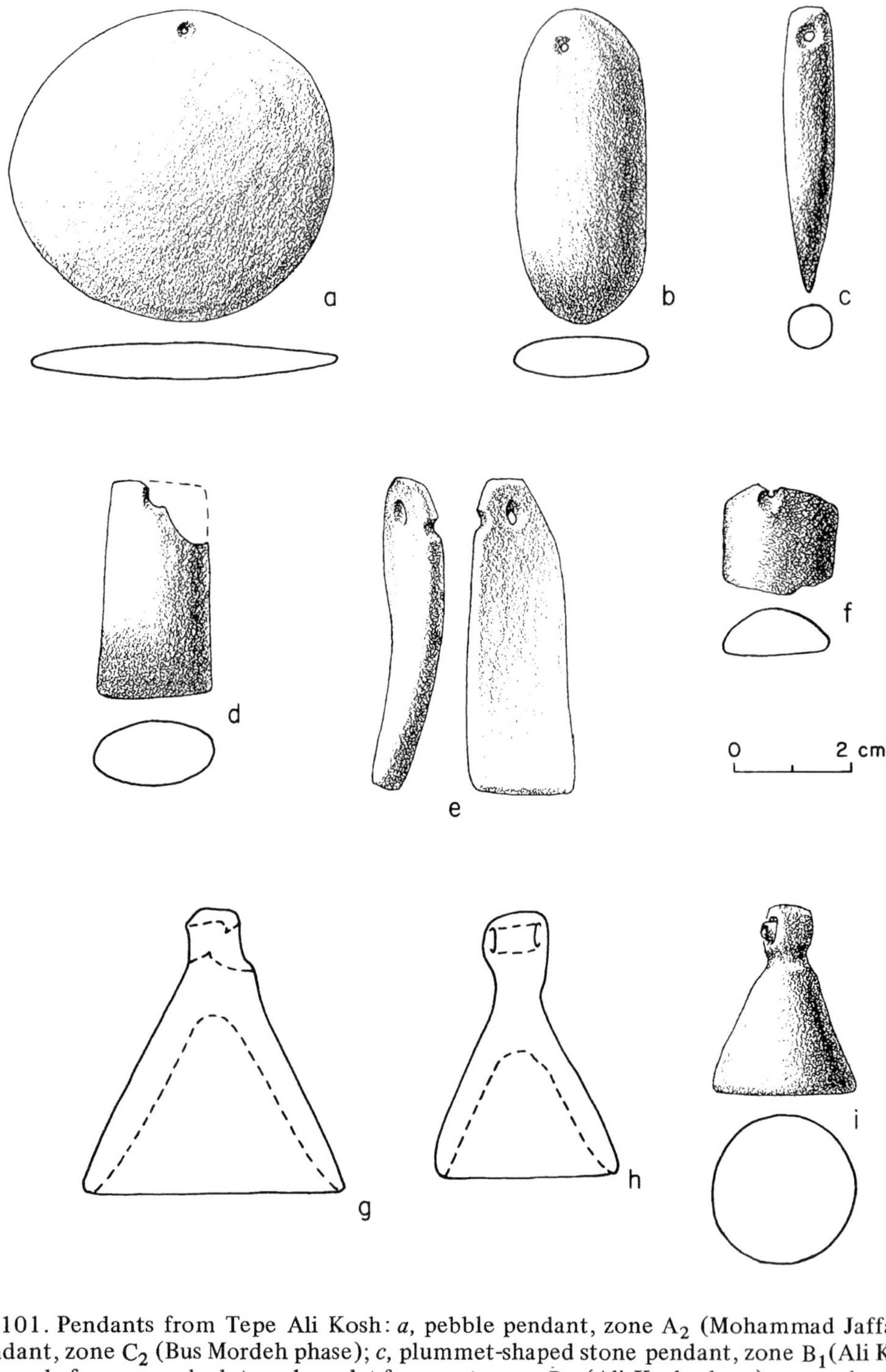

Fig. 101. Pendants from Tepe Ali Kosh: *a*, pebble pendant, zone A_2 (Mohammad Jaffar phase); *b*, pebble pendant, zone C_2 (Bus Mordeh phase); *c*, plummet-shaped stone pendant, zone B_1(Ali Kosh phase); *d*, pendant made from reworked stone bracelet fragment, zone B_2 (Ali Kosh phase); *e*, pendant made from reworked stone bowl sherd, zone B_2 (Ali Kosh phase); *f*, pendant made from reworked stone bracelet fragment, zone A_2 (Mohammad Jaffar phase); *g*, stone bell-shaped pendant, found with Burial 8, zone A_1 (Mohammad Jaffar phase); *h*, clay bell-shaped pendant, found near Burial 25 and possibly once associated with it (see text), zone A_1 (Mohammad Jaffar phase); *i*, clay bell-shaped pendant, with small bead lodged in perforation in proximal end, zone A_2 (Mohammad Jaffar phase).

The second is plummet-shaped, 6.5 cm. long, perforated at one end and pointed at the other (Fig. 100*e;* Pl. 39*a*).

Temporal distribution: The triangular-shaped examples were found in the Bus Mordeh, Ali Kosh, and Mohammad Jaffar phases. One plummet-shaped pendant came from the mass of secondarily-buried limb bones near Burial 34*a* in zone B_2, Tepe Ali Kosh. A fragment of the tip of another came from the area of the flint dump in zone C_2, Tepe Ali Kosh.

Geographic distribution: Unknown.

Type: Plummet-shaped pendants (Fig. 101*c*)

Sample: 2

Material: Fine-grained gray stone

Description: A slender, pointed, elongated cone of polished stone some 5 cm. in length; round in cross-section, with a maximum diameter of 8 mm; biconically drilled at the thick end so that it hung point down, in the manner of a slender plumb bob (cf. the "plummet stones" of New World archeological sites).

Temporal distribution: Known so far only from the Ali Kosh phase.

Geographic distribution: Pendants shaped like slender stone plummets seem to characterize the late preceramic of Kurdistan. Examples from Zawi Chemi Shanidar (Solecki, 1963:Fig. 7:1), and a possibly broken example from Karim Shahir (Braidwood, Howe, *et al.* 1960:Plate 23, No. 14) might be cited.

Miscellaneous Stone Pendants (Fig. 101*d-f*)

Examples: 3

Description: Villagers at Ali Kosh occasionally made pendants by reworking fragments of broken bracelets and stone bowls.

a) Fragments of stone bracelets which have been smoothed at the broken edges and biconically drilled some 2 mm. from one edge (Fig. 101*d,f*).

b) One body sherd from the curved wall of a pink stone bowl which had its broken edges smoothed and a hole drilled biconically 4 mm. from one end. The pendant is 5 cm. long. (Fig. 101*e*).

Temporal distribution: Ali Kosh and Mohammad Jaffar phases

Geographic distribution: Unknown.

Bone Pendant (Fig. 100*g*)

Example: 1, from the Ali Kosh phase

Material: A flat silver from an ungulate limb bone.

Description: This resembles a broken fragment of bone spatula, but one end has two perforations for suspension.

Geographic distribution: Unknown.

Crab Claw Pendants (Fig. 100*f*)

Sample: 2

Material: Pincers of an inland river crab, *Potamon* sp.

Description: These have been made by polishing the crab pincer and drilling a small hole through the proximal end for suspension.

Temporal distribution: Known only from the Mohammad Jaffar phase

Geographic distribution: Unknown.

Labrets

Introduction

Archeological sites from the period 6000 to 5000 B.C. in Khuzistan, Kurdistan, and Mesopotamia contain repeated references to small objects of bitumen (natural asphalt) or lightly baked clay, which have been called "studs," "toggles," "buttons," "terracotta pegs" and a variety of other names. For several years there has been a suspicion that some of these objects might be labrets or lip-ornaments, because of their resemblance to lip plugs worn by various peoples of the world. The lack of ethnographic data for such practices in the Mesopotamian area encouraged caution on this point, however.

In 1963, excavations in Mohammad Jaffar phase levels at Ali Kosh finally produced evidence that some of these artifacts were, in fact, labrets. Burial No. 10 in zone A_1 (squares 20 and 30), apparently an adult male, was equipped not only with a clay bell between his thighs but also had, resting *in situ* against the symphysis of the mandible, a labret of the type we have called "cuff-link shaped" (see Fig. 109). The lower central incisors of this burial showed a polish on their outer surfaces that apparently had come from contact with the flanges of the labret.

These labrets are ornaments inserted through a hole cut in the lower lip, and held in place by flanges which rest between the lip and the incisor teeth. Those found in the Deh Luran plain have been

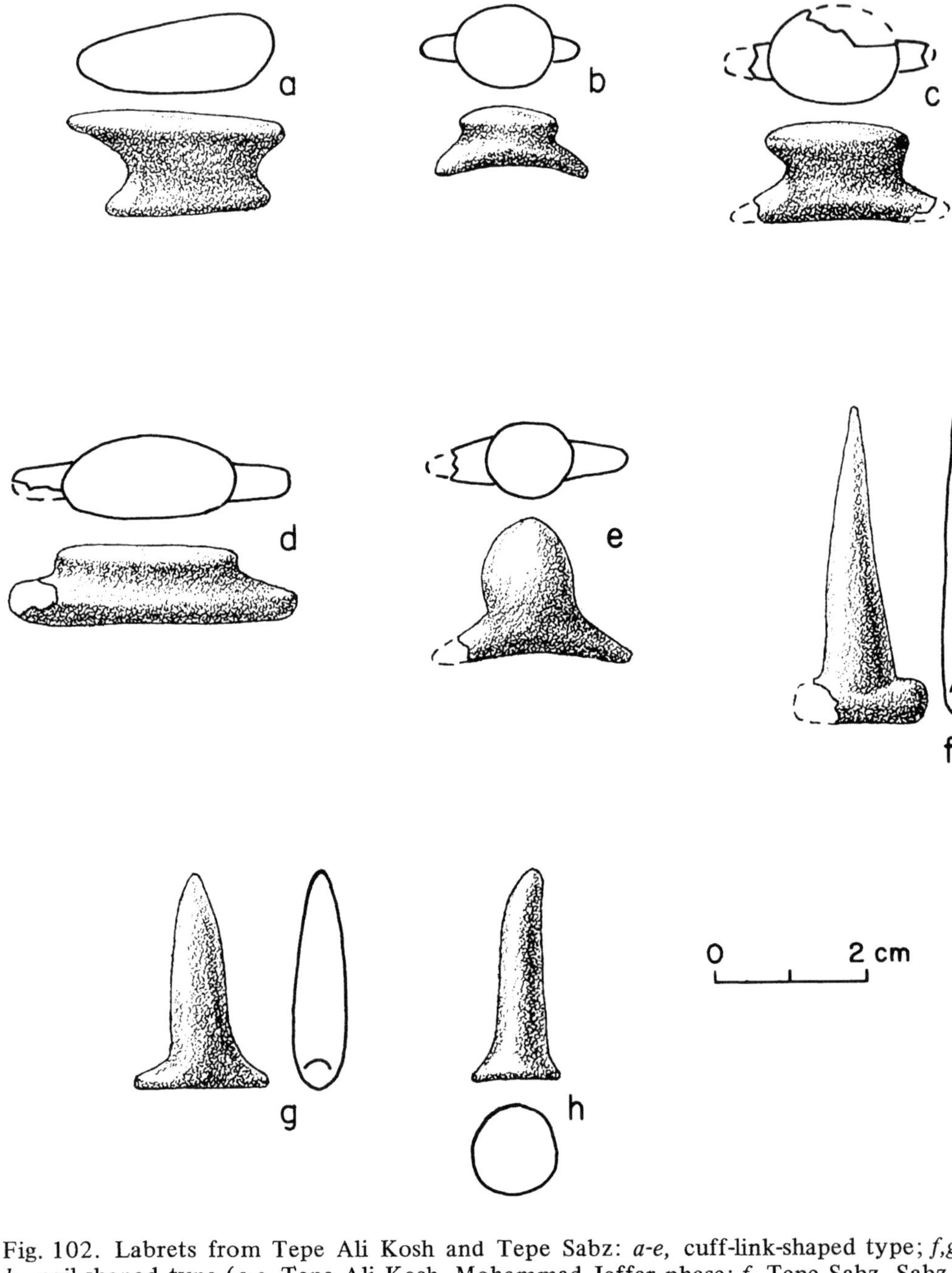

Fig. 102. Labrets from Tepe Ali Kosh and Tepe Sabz: *a-e*, cuff-link-shaped type; *f,g*, T-shaped type; *h*, nail-shaped type (*c-e*, Tepe Ali Kosh, Mohammad Jaffar phase; *f*, Tepe Sabz, Sabz phase; *a,h*, Tepe Sabz, Khazineh phase; *g*, Tepe Sabz, Mehmeh phase; *b*, Tepe Sabz, Bayat phase).

classified into three basic types which have some chronological significance. As a general rule, labrets seem to be more characteristic of the Mohammad Jaffar, Sabz, and Khazineh phases than of any other period; in all, we recovered thirty-two, including one turquoise example.

Type: "Cuff-link shaped" labret (Fig. 102*a-e*; Pl. 39*b*)

Sample: 15

Material: Either asphalt or fine-grained limestone

Description: These are shaped like squat, spherical, or oval "buttons" backed by a two-pronged flange, after the manner of a cuff-link. The top surface of the button is usually flat, but a few examples are slightly domed or convex. The flanges may be parallel to the plane of the face of the button, or may swing back away from it. The width (from face to flange) ranges from 0.6 to 1.3 cm. and the length from 0.8 to 2.2 cm.

Temporal distribution: 13 of our 15 examples come from the Mohammad Jaffar-early Khazineh time range.

Geographic distribution: Known from Bandibal in Susiana proper (Le Breton 1947:Fig. 32, No. 10) and from Tepe Sarab in Iranian Kurdistan (collection in the Museé Iran Bastan, Tehran). A more pointed version was found at Tepe Guran (Mortensen, 1964:Fig. 20:C).

Type: T-shaped labret (Fig. 102*f-g*; Pl. 39*c*)

Sample: 8

Material: Either fine-grained limestone or Susiana Plain Buff pottery

Description: Long, narrow, pointed labrets with a sharply defined T-shaped flange. They range in length from 2.5 to 4.0 cm. The shafts, which have their maximum diameter at the junction with the flange, taper gradually to a point.

Temporal distribution: Late Ali Kosh through early Bayat phases

Geographic distribution: Unknown.

Type: Nail-shaped labrets (Fig. 102*h*)

Sample: 8

Material: Either asphalt, clay, or fine-grained limestone

Description: These labrets have a long conical shaft, with the base of the cone expanding into a discoidal flange (like the head of a nail). The shaft may be either round or oval in cross-section. Their length varies from 1.7 to 3.0 cm., and their diameter from 1.0 to 1.3 cm. (at the base).

Temporal distribution: Known only from the Sabz and Khazineh phases

Geographic distribution: Scattered occurrences in Khuzistan and Mesopotamia (Stronach, 1961:Plate XLIII, Nos. 8,9; Tobler, 1950:Fig. XCII*a*, Nos. 11, 12) and the Iranian plateau (Ghirshman, 1938:Pl. LII:28-30).

Turquoise Labret (Fig. 103*a*; Pl. 38*e*)

Example: 1, from the Mohammad Jaffar phase (accompanying Burial No. 8)

Material: Mottled greenish-blue turquoise

Description: Shaped like a blunt variant of our "nail-shaped" labrets, with an expanded discoidal base, and a nipple-like projection on the distal end.

Geographic distribution: Unknown.

Bracelets

Type: Smooth-surfaced Stone Bracelets (Fig. 104*a-d*)

Sample: 5, all fragmentary

Material: Fine-grained limestone

Description: Rings of polished limestone with diameters of 7 cm. or larger. They may be round or plano-convex in cross-section. The surfaces are smooth and unstriated.

Temporal distribution: Most come from the Mohammad Jaffar phase; two bracelet fragments, however (reworked as pendants) were found in the Ali Kosh phase.

Geographic distribution: Widespread in the 7th and 8th millennia B.C. in Kurdistan. Examples come from Karim Shahir and Jarmo (Braidwood, Howe, *et al.* 1960:Plate 21, No. 1; Plate 23, Nos. 15, 16), Tepe Sarab (Braidwood, 1960:696), and other sites. Sialk I also had such bracelets (Braidwood, 1952:Fig. 6, lower right), as did Çayonü in Turkey (Braidwood, personal communication).

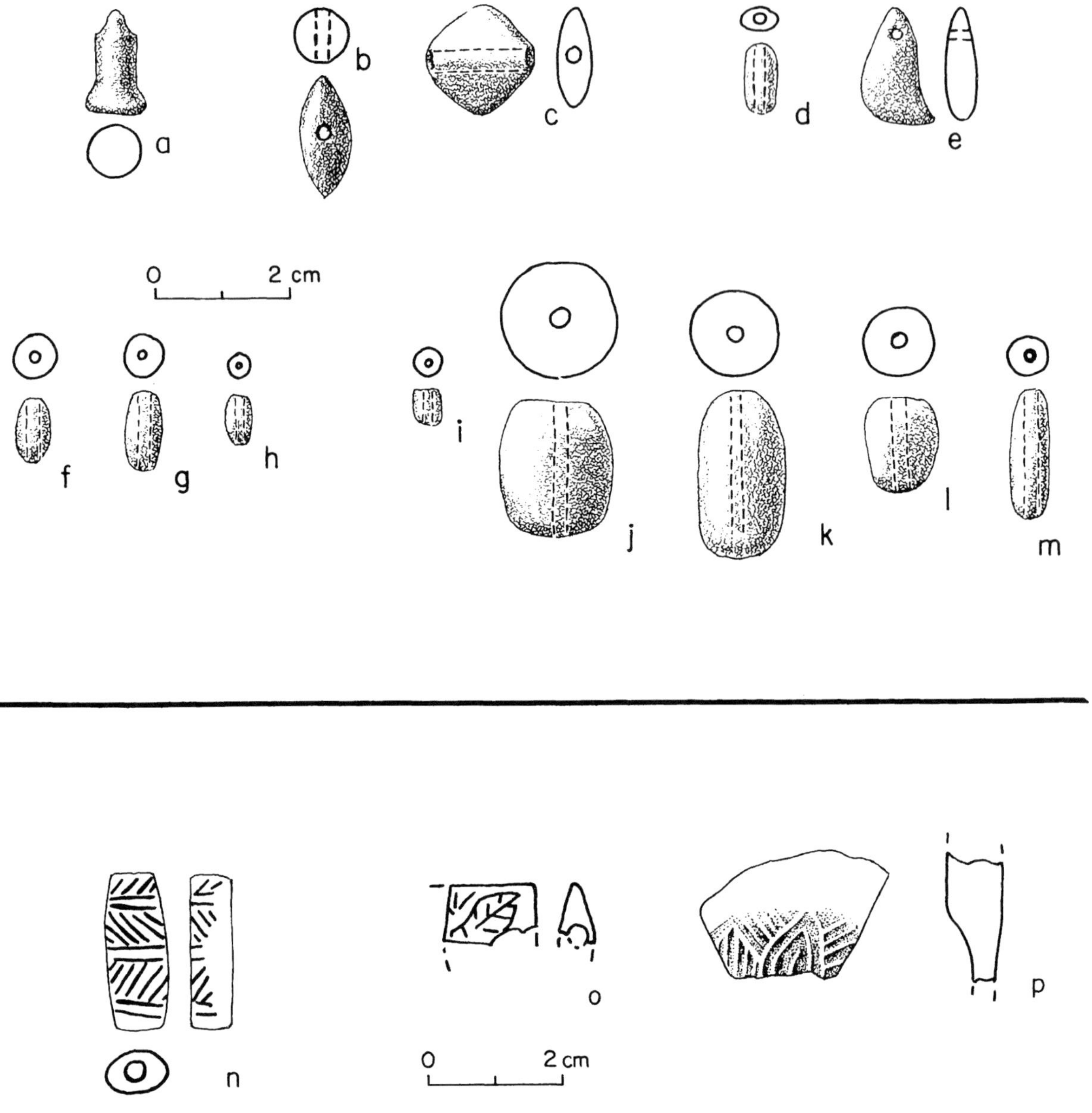

Fig. 103. Ornaments, bead seals, and seal impressions from the Deh Luran sites: *a-m,* turquoise ornaments from Tepe Ali Kosh; *a,* labret, Burial 8, zone A_1 (Mohammad Jaffar phase); *b,* bead, Burial 8, zone A_1 (Mohammad Jaffar phase); *c,* bead, Burial 8, zone A_1 (Mohammad Jaffar phase); *d,* bead, Burial 25, zone A_1 (Mohammad Jaffar phase); *e,* pendant, Burial 25, zone A_1 (Mohammad Jaffar phase); *f-h,* miscellaneous beads from zone A_1 (Mohammad Jaffar phase); *i,j,* beads, found with mass of bones, secondary burial, square 82, zone C_1, probably intrusive from zone B_2 (Ali Kosh phase); *k-m,* miscellaneous beads from zone B_2 (Ali Kosh phase); *n-p,* bead seals and seal impressions from the Bayat phase, Tepe Sabz; *n,* bead seal made of amber-like substance, zone A_3; *o,* fragment of bead seal made of soft stone, zone A_2, *p,* fragment of seal impression in lightly-baked clay, zone A_1.

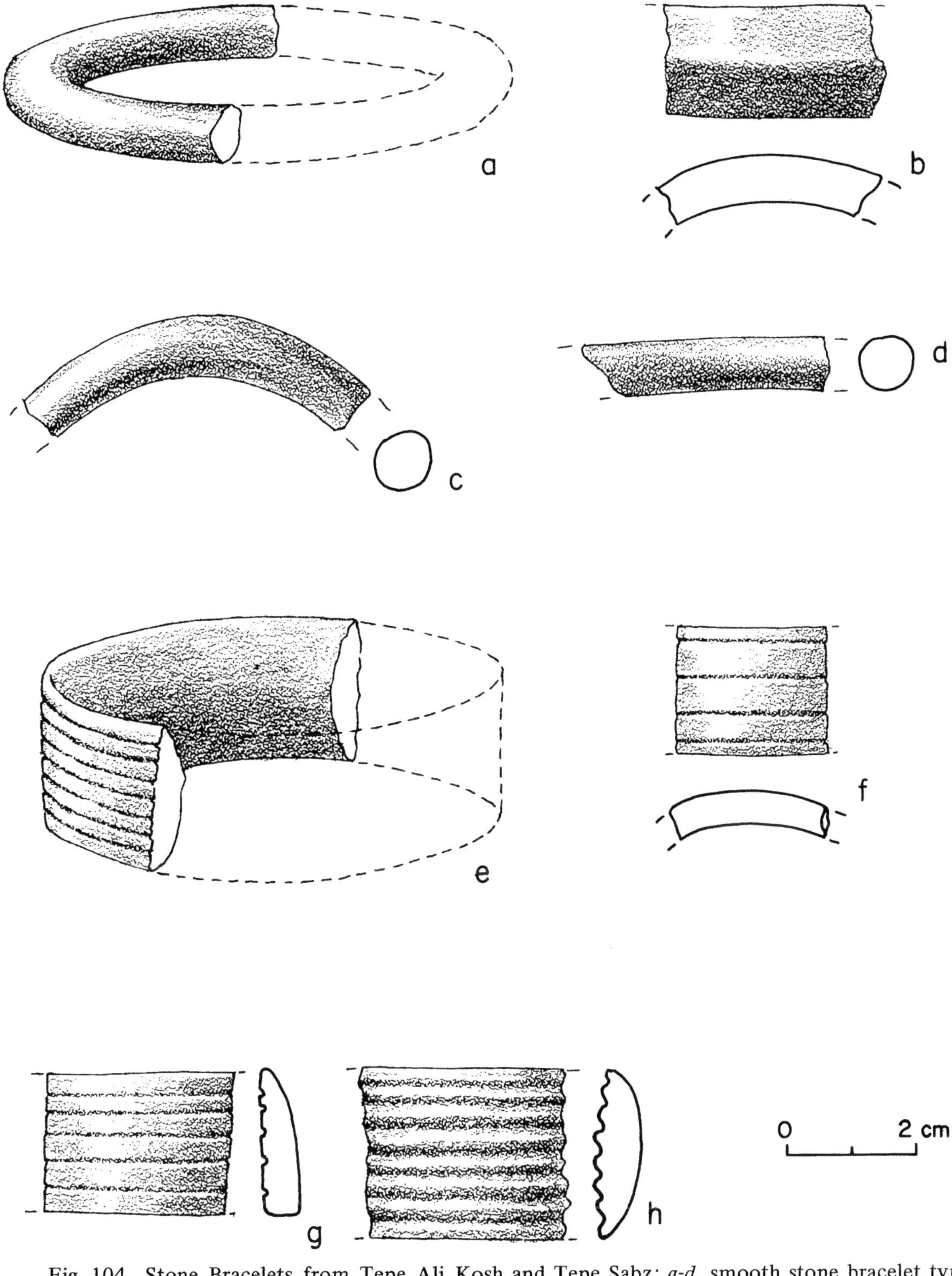

Fig. 104. Stone Bracelets from Tepe Ali Kosh and Tepe Sabz: *a-d,* smooth stone bracelet type; *e-h,* parallel-line-incised stone bracelet type (*a,* reconstruction from Mohammad Jaffar phase fragments; *b,d,* Mohammad Jaffar phase fragments; *c,* Ali Kosh phase fragment, Tepe Ali Kosh, zone B_2; *e,* reconstruction from Sabz phase examples; *f,* Bayat phase fragment, Tepe Sabz, zone A_3; *g,h,* Sabz phase fragments).

Type: Parallel-line-incised stone bracelets (Fig. 104*e-h*)

Sample: 7

Material: Fine-grained limestone

Description: Rings of polished limestone with a diameter of 7 cm. They may be flat, oval, or ellipsoidal in cross-section. The distinguishing characteristic of this type of ornament is that the outer surface bears from 4 to 6 shallowly-incised parallel lines which encircle the object, following the curve of the bracelet.

Temporal distribution: Six out of 7 came from the Sabz phase.

Geographic distribution: Identical specimens come from Tepe Sialk I-II (Ghirshman, 1938:Pl. LII:15,22).

Other Ornaments

Mussel Shell Buttons (Fig. 100*b*)

Sample: 3

Material: Shells of river mussel (*Unio, Pseudodontopsis*).

Description: Small discs or squares of shell, each with two perforations for suspension. These objects are 1.5 cm. in diameter, and resemble mother-of-pearl buttons.

Temporal distribution: Bus Mordeh phase

Geographic distribution: Doubly-perforated shell "buttons" resembling our occurred at Karim Shahir (Braidwood, 1952:Fig. 13, lower right).

Boar Tusk Button

Example: 1, from the Bus Mordeh phase

Description: One half of a round button cut from a boar's tusk and partly drilled. The button evidently broke during drilling.

Geographic distribution: Unknown.

Type: Ceramic rings and ring "blanks" (Pl. 36*a-d*)

Samples: 11

Material: Susiana Plain Buff pottery

Description: These are finger-ring size. Teardrop-shaped in cross-section, they are thickest near their inside edge and taper to a thin edge on the outside (Pl. 36*c,d*). Some were evidently made from thin sherds chipped into a roughly round shape, whose interior was reamed and scraped to the desired size. A number of roughly-chipped sherds with holes drilled in the center (Pl. 36*a,b*) may illustrate the beginning of this process. In other cases, the center seems to have been removed from a small domed patty of clay prepared for the purpose.

Temporal distribution: Sporadically throughout the sequence at Tepe Sabz

Geographic distribution: Unknown.

Stone Spool (Pl. 39*d*)

Example: 1

Material: Fine-grained gray stone

Description: Roughly round, 1.3 cm. in diameter. The disc is 7 mm. thick, has a groove about 1 mm. deep encircling the body, and each end is concave. (The depth of the concavity is about 1 mm.) The stone is polished, but scratches from the shaping tool remain. By analogy with the use of similar objects elsewhere, this may possibly be an ear spool, designed to be placed in the pierced lobe of the ear for decorative purposes.

Temporal distribution: Ali Kosh phase

Geographic distribution: Unknown.

Head of Copper Pin (Pl. 39*e*)

Example: 1, from the Mehmeh phase

Material: Copper

Description: Oval in plan and section, this pin head is 9 mm. by 11 mm. in size. The pin shaft is 3 mm. in diameter at its juncture with the head, and has been broken just below this point.

Geographic distribution: Copper pins with similar heads appear at Sialk in Periods I and II (Ghirshman, 1938:Pl. LII:49, 55, 59).

Beads

Introduction

Beads occurred throughout the Bus Mordeh, Ali Kosh, and Mohammad Jaffar phases, but by far the majority we found

Table 51

OCCURRENCE OF MISCELLANEOUS ORNAMENTS AT ALI KOSH AND TEPE SABZ
(By Stratigraphic Zone)

	Pendants								Labrets				Bracelets		Buttons		Rings		Spool	Pin
Site and Zone	Boar's Tusk	Bell-shaped	Flat Pebble	Mussel Shell	Plummet-shaped	Miscellaneous Stone	Bone	Crab Claw	Cuff-link	T-shaped	Nail-shaped	Turquoise	Smooth Surface	Incised	Mussel Shell	Boar's Tusk	Ceramic	Ring "Blanks"	Stone	Head of Copper Pin
TS - A_1	...	...	...	...	...	...	...	...	...	...	...	...	...	...	...	...	...	...	...	...
TS - A_2	...	...	...	...	...	...	...	...	...	...	...	...	...	...	...	...	...	...	...	...
TS - A_3	...	...	...	...	...	...	...	...	1	2	...	...	...	1	...	...	1	4	...	...
TS - B_1	...	...	...	...	...	...	...	...	...	1	...	...	...	...	...	...	1	1	...	...
TS - B_2	...	...	...	...	...	...	...	...	...	...	...	...	...	...	...	...	...	...	...	1
TS - B_3	...	...	...	...	...	...	...	...	...	...	...	...	...	...	...	...	...	...	...	...
TS - C_1	...	...	...	...	...	...	...	...	...	...	...	...	...	...	...	...	1	...	...	...
TS - C_2	...	...	...	...	...	...	...	...	...	...	1	...	...	...	...	...	1	...	...	...
TS - C_3	...	...	...	...	...	...	...	...	2	...	2	...	...	...	...	...	1	...	...	...
TS - D	...	...	...	...	...	...	...	...	1	3	5	...	...	6	...	...	1	...	...	...
AK - A_1	...	2	...	1	...	...	...	2	7	1	...	1	1	...	...	...	...	...	...	...
AK - A_2	...	1	1	...	...	1	...	...	3	...	...	...	4	...	...	...	...	...	...	...
AK - B_1	...	3	...	...	1	...	...	...	...	1	...	...	...	...	...	...	...	...	...	...
AK - B_2	2	...	1	2	1	2	1	...	1	...	...	...	...	...	...	...	...	...	1	...
AK - C_1	1	...	...	...	...	...	...	...	...	...	...	...	...	...	1	1	...	...	...	...
AK - C_2	4	...	1	2	...	...	...	...	...	...	...	...	...	...	2	...	...	...	...	...
Total	7	6	3	5	2	3	1	2	15	8	8	1	5	7	3	1	6	5	1	1

Table 52

OCCURRENCE OF MISCELLANEOUS ORNAMENTS AT ALI KOSH AND TEPE SABZ
(By Cultural Phase)

Phase	Pendants								Labrets				Bracelets		Buttons		Rings		Spool	Pin
	Boar's Tusk	Bell-shaped	Flat Pebble	Mussel Shell	Plummet-shaped	Miscellaneous Stone	Bone	Crab Claw	Cuff-link	T-shaped	Nail-shaped	Turquoise	Smooth Surface	Incised	Mussel Shell	Boar's Tusk	Ceramic	Ring "Blanks"	Stone	Head of Copper Pin
Bayat	. . .	. . .	. . .	. . .	. . .	. . .	. . .	. . .	1	2	. . .	. . .	. . .	1	. . .	. . .	1	4	. . .	. . .
Mehmeh	. . .	. . .	. . .	. . .	. . .	. . .	. . .	. . .	. . .	1	. . .	. . .	. . .	. . .	. . .	. . .	1	1	. . .	1
Khazineh	. . .	. . .	. . .	. . .	. . .	. . .	. . .	. . .	2	. . .	3	. . .	. . .	. . .	. . .	. . .	3	. . .	. . .	. . .
Sabz	. . .	. . .	. . .	. . .	. . .	. . .	. . .	. . .	1	3	5	. . .	. . .	6	. . .	. . .	1	. . .	. . .	. . .
Mohammad Jaffar	. . .	3	1	1	. . .	1	. . .	2	10	1	. . .	1	5	. . .	. . .	. . .	. . .	. . .	. . .	. . .
Ali Kosh	2	3	1	2	2	2	1	. . .	1	1	. . .	. . .	. . .	. . .	. . .	. . .	. . .	. . .	1	. . .
Bus Mordeh . . .	5	. . .	1	2	. . .	. . .	. . .	. . .	. . .	. . .	. . .	. . .	. . .	. . .	3	1	. . .	. . .	. . .	. . .
Total	7	6	3	5	2	3	1	2	15	8	8	1	5	7	3	1	6	5	1	1

were associated with burials. A few stray beads must have been accidentally lost by their wearers.

Beads were made of various materials, ranging from asphalt to shell to stone, and these categories include both locally available and imported raw material.

Where possible we shall describe the beads as they were worn, but a study of the distribution of various types also suggests that they may have some value as chronological indicators. The villagers at Ali Kosh seem most often to have used beads in necklaces, bracelets, and as tassels or fringes to the garments they wore around their waists.

Flat Black Disc Beads

Material: Soft black stone or asphalt

Description: Between about 3 and 7 mm. in diameter and ranging from paper-thinness to 2.5 mm. thick. The larger sizes are rare. These beads were used both as spacers in predominantly white strings, and alone in girdle fringes or tassels.

Temporal distribution: Bus Mordeh through Mohammad Jaffar phases

Geographic distribution: Similar beads occurred at the hips of burials at Tepe Sarab (unpublished data). They were also present at Tepe Guran (Mortensen, 1964:Fig. 20*g*).

Flat White Disc Beads

Material: Soft white stone

Description: Identical in size range to the flat black disc beads, with which they were generally used.

Temporal distribution: Bus Mordeh through Mohammad Jaffar phases.

Geographic distribution: Flat white disc beads appeared at Zawi Chemi Shanidar (Solecki, 1963:Fig. 7*u,y*) and Tepe Guran (Mortensen, 1964:Fig. 20*h*).

White Cylinder Beads

Material: Soft white stone

Description: The diameters are 6 to 7 mm. and the lengths range between 3 and 7 mm. long. The holes are bored straight through, and are between 2 to 3 mm. in diameter. These beads were used both alone and with flat blank disc beads of the same diameter.

Temporal distribution: Ali Kosh and Mohammad Jaffar phases

Geographic distribution: Unknown.

Tubular Beads

Example: 8

Material: Soft white stone

Description: About 15 mm. long and 3 mm. in diameter. We suspect these beads were probably used as spacers in necklaces, although none were found associated with a string. These beads all remain in Iran, and positive identification of the material could not be made.

Temporal distribution: Bus Mordeh through Mohammad Jaffar phases.

Geographic distribution: Similar beads were found at Zawi Chemi Shanidar (Solecki, 1963:Fig. 7*v*).

Red Disc Beads

Description: Two red stone disc beads were found in midden deposits in Bus Mordeh and Mohammad Jaffar contexts. Since neither bead was included in the division of antiquities, we are not able to identify the stones.

Bead Blanks?

Example: 3, from the Bus Mordeh and Ali Kosh phases

Material: Alabaster or marble?

Description: Flat, unperforated, bead-size discs. These were the only sign that bead-making may have been a local activity; that is, rods of raw material were not found.

Sea Shell Beads

Example: One 5-shell bracelet (see Burial 26) and two stray beads

Description: Red-and-white-striped sea shells (unidentified to species) which average about 1.5 cm. long. The shells were pierced by one or two holes; sometimes the natural opening was used as a second hole.

Temporal distribution: The bracelet was possibly originally associated with Burial 26 at Ali Kosh, which had been disturbed. The stray beads were found in Bus Mordeh and Ali Kosh phase levels.

Geographic distribution: Uncertain for this time range.

Small White Shell Beads

Example: 5

Material: Segments of a tubular shell

Description: Very fragile beads whose exteriors show parallel horizontal ribbing. None could be brought back to the United States, and the species of shell cannot be determined.

Temporal distribution: All were found in a Mohammad Jaffar phase midden. One group occurred in a string, and others were possibly elements in strings consisting chiefly of stone beads.

Geographic distribution: Unknown.

Cowrie Shell Beads

Example: 2, from the Mohammad Jaffar and Ali Kosh phases

Description: A cowrie shell with a single perforation for suspension

Geographic distribution: We are uncertain how widespread cowries are in the Mohammad Jaffar phase; certainly, they are abundant in later periods.

Turquoise Beads (Fig. 103*b-m*; Pl. 38*d,f-h*)

Example: 15

Material: Turquoise

Description: Less uniformity is seen in this group than in any other group of beads. The lack of standardization suggests that turquoise was regarded as a rare and precious material which was too valuable to cut extensively; rather, the natural shapes of the pieces were exploited. It is appropriate to consider these beads as they occurred.

1) The oldest set of beads was found with the decomposed mass of reburied human bones in the top of zone C_1 at Tepe Ali Kosh. Three small, polished, tubular beads, essentially like their white stone counterparts, and one large (2 by 1.5 cm.) roughly-shaped bead were found among these bones. All were drilled along the long axis (Fig. 103*i,j*).

2) Found under Ali Kosh phase house floors (and probably originally associated with burials) were three other roughly-shaped and fairly large turquoise beads, which measured 2.5 by 1.2, 1.4 by 1, and 1.9 by 0.6 cm. (Fig. 103*k-m*).

3) The most interesting group of turquoise beads was associated with Burial 8 (Mohammad Jaffar phase). There, two beads and a labret were found (Fig. 103*a-c*; Pl. 38*d-f*). The highly-polished beads occurred near the neck, and the labret lay near the breastbone, where it may have fallen from the region of the lip when the flesh decomposed (Fig. 108; Pl. 12*c*). The association of these beads with this relatively richly-decorated person was perhaps significant.

4) Another pair of turquoise ornaments was associated with Burial 25, Mohammad Jaffar phase (Fig. 103*d,e*; Pl. 38*g,h*). A tubular bead lay between the left shoulder and face, and a pendant lay near the top of the sternum (Fig. 108).

5) Three isolated, tubular beads, from a Mohammad Jaffar phase midden, had the following dimensions: 0.8 by 0.6, 1.2 by 0.6, and 0.8 by 0.4 cm. (Fig. 103*f-h*).

Geographical distribution: We know of no other turquoise beads in sites of this time period, but turquoise occurs with burials at the slightly later site of Tell es-Sawwan (El-Wailly and Abu es-Soof 1965:25).

Copper Bead (Pl. 42, 43)

Example: 1, from Tepe Ali Kosh, zone B_2 (Ali Kosh phase)

Material: Native copper

Description: A tubular bead made from a sheet of hammered native copper, somewhat laminated, which had been cut with a chisel-edged tool. The sheet was rolled so that the ends just overlapped. The piece is about 1.4 cm. long and 0.5 cm. in diameter. The bead was so oxidized that no metal remained, although it was possible, through microscopic examination, to see the laminations that resulted from hammering, as well as the fact that it had been cut with a chisel (see Cyril S. Smith, Appendix II). It was not possible to analyze the residue to determine its source, but one possibility would be the Anarak lode on the Iranian plateau (see below).

GEOGRAPHIC DISTRIBUTION AND DISCUSSION

It would once have been startling to find copper artifacts in a preceramic period such as the Ali Kosh phase. Today a number of copper items have been found in early village deposits, and it is generally accepted that the hammering of native copper preceded ceramics in the Near East. Copper is known from Çatal Hüyük (Mellaart, 1963:196; 1964*a*:113-14) and Çayonü (personal communication, R. J. Braidwood), both in Anatolia, and will undoubtedly be found at other pre-pottery village sites as time goes on. A good review of man's early encounters with metals in the Near East can be found in Wertime, 1964.

As Wertime points out, prehistoric peoples probably first visited copper sources to obtain malachite pigment, and later began cold-hammering the metal itself. The technology involved is no more sophisticated than flint-knapping, and is analogous to the working of copper by hunting-gathering Indian groups in northern North America at 3000 B.C. (Griffin, 1964:233).

Two locations, Ergani-Ma'aden in the Taurus Mountains and Anarak-Nachlak on the Iranian plateau, some 80 miles southeast of Sialk, are the most likely sources from which the prehistoric artisans of Turkey and Iran would have obtained their raw material. In each instance, native copper occurred in outcrops that were readily available to the curious passerby (Wertime, 1964:1258). Of these two sources, the Anarak location is certainly the closest to Ali Kosh. Given the presumed pattern of settlement and economic activities during that phase, one would expect some trade to have followed the normal route of transhumance–from Ali Kosh, east into the Zagros mountains and perhaps as far as the edge of the *kavir* where Sialk is situated (although there is no evidence that the latter site was occupied during the Ali Kosh phase).

Other finds of early copper artifacts, although not so early as those mentioned above, are at Sialk (Ghirshman, 1938:16, Pl. LII, 49, 53-56, 58-59), where one would expect to find them since the site is the nearest large settlement to the Anarak lode; at Arpachiyah (Mallowan and Rose, 1935:104) and Chagar Bazar (Mallowan, 1936:26) in Iraq; and Mersin in Turkey (Garstang, 1953:76, Fig. 50). The villagers at the latter three sites probably got their copper from Ergani-Ma'aden, a surmise that can be checked in the future following adequate technical analyses.

Strings of Beads at Tepe Ali Kosh

Strings of black and white beads were found in the following associations, beginning with the oldest:

1) Ali Kosh phase

a) At least two strings of beads were found with the sets of bones in the secondary burials which appear to be intrusive into zone C_1. In one instance, there was approximately one flat black bead for every three large flat white beads, and in the other instance the white and black beads alternated. Since only reburied limb bones are present in the deposit, we can only guess that the beads were once part of necklaces.

b) The seated skeleton designated Burial 26 in zone B_2 had a string of alternate flat black disc and flat white disc beads around his neck (Fig. 106).

2) Mohammad Jaffar phase

In the Mohammad Jaffar phase deposits, zone A_1, two strings of beads were associated with burials, and two strings were found without association. Because several burials in zone A_1 were badly disturbed by later intrusive Iron Age burials, it is possible that the beads were all originally associated with burials.

Burial 9 had a girdle of flat white shell beads around his waist. This badly-disturbed burial had no other artifacts.

Burial 8, the most complete and richest of the lot, had a bracelet of white stone disc beads on the left forearm near the elbow, and strings of black disc beads hanging from the hips. The latter, made of asphalt, are 3 to 4 mm. in diameter and were found literally by the hundreds. This burial was apparently a middle-aged male, who also had a bell-shaped pendant and three turquoise beads as ornaments.

The remaining strings of beads in the Mohammad Jaffar levels were of two different types. One string included amber-colored beads in every fourth position, with small white beads and occasionally a larger, barrel-shaped, fluted, white bead in between. The other string consisted of fragile, cylindrical white shell beads.

Table 53

OCCURRENCE OF ISOLATED BEADS AND STRINGS OF BEADS AT ALI KOSH
(By Stratigraphic Zone)

Site and Zone	Turquoise	Sea Shell	White Disc	Black Disc	Red Disc	White Cylinder	Tubular	White Shell	Cowrie Shell	Bead Blanks	Copper Bead
AK - A_1	+	...	S+	S+	+	+	+	S+	...	...	...
AK - A_2	...	...	+	...	...	+	+	+	+	...	...
AK - B_1	...	...	+	+	...	...	...	...	...	...	...
AK - B_2	+	S+	S+	S+	...	+	+	...	+	+	+
AK - C_1	+	+	S+	S+	+	...	+	...	...	...	...
AK - C_2	...	...	...	...	...	...	+	...	...	+	...

Note–S = string; + = isolated beads.

Table 54

OCCURRENCE OF ISOLATED BEADS AND STRINGS OF BEADS AT ALI KOSH
(By Cultural Phase)

Phase	Turquoise	Sea Shell	White Disc	Black Disc	Red Disc	White Cylinder	Tubular	White Shell	Cowrie Shell	Bead Blanks	Copper Bead
Mohammad Jaffar	+	...	S+	S+	+	+	+	S+	+	...	...
Ali Kosh	+	S+	S+	S+	...	+	+	...	+	+	+
Bus Mordeh	+	+	S+	S+	+	...	+	...	...	+	...

Note–S = string; + = isolated beads.

XVII

MISCELLANEOUS FINDS

Bead Seals (Fig. 103*n,o*)

Examples: 2

Material: Polished stone or amber

Description: One example is a cylindrical bead, incised with parallel lines (Fig. 103*n*). The other example, broken, was originally rectangular in plan and lenticular in section, with an incised leaf design on one face (Fig. 103*o*). Both examples were pierced longitudinally, and were probably stamped or rolled in wet clay.

Temporal distribution: The examples are from the Bayat phase, the same distribution we found for the seal impressions in lumps of clay (see below). In the Deh Luran plain as elsewhere, seals and their impressions seem to occur only in the later part of the prehistoric village sequence (Ubaid-Susiana *d,e*).

Geographic distribution: Beads with the designs similar to ours can easily be found in Susiana proper (Le Breton, 1947:Fig. 32 No. 17), as well as in southern Mesopotamia (cf. Ann L. Perkins, 1949:87).

Seal Impressions (Fig. 103*p*)

Example: 4

Material: Lightly-fired clay

Description: These were probably "ownership" impressions made in clay plugs which served to seal shut pottery containers. Some of the plugs show the shape of the vessel mouth. Impressions were made with incised beads such as those described above.

Temporal distribution: These apparently do not appear before the Bayat phase.

Geographic distribution: Throughout Khuzistan (and, to a lesser extent, Mesopotamia and the Zagros Mountain area) seal impressions occur whose designs resemble ours. Seal-impressed clay "jar labels" are common in the Ubaid period (see for example Mallowan and Rose, 1935:Pl. IX), but most of the seals involved were round, rather than lenticular like ours.

Shell Pressure Flakers

Example: 3, from the Ali Kosh phase

Material: River mussel shells (*Unio, Pseudodontopsis*)

Description: Fragments of mussel shell whose edges have been worn by use. The designation of these as tools for pressure flaking is suggested by the fact that similar objects were used for this purpose in the eastern woodlands of the United States. (When they saw them, Dr. and Mrs. Joseph R. Caldwell immediately suggested that our pieces were identical to pressure flakers they had found in their own excavations in that area.)

Geographic distribution: Previously unreported from southwest Asia.

Asphalted Stone Slabs

Examples: 3 whole, 4 fragmentary

Material: Tabular limestone

Description: All are rectangular and have asphalt along their edges (and also, in some cases, on the ends). The three whole examples were each about the same size, the average dimension being 27 by 15 by 4.5 cm. Where necessary to produce a good rectangular shape, the makers chipped the edges and ends. The location of the asphalt, along the edges and on one or both of the flat surfaces, suggests that the asphalt was used to bond these pieces to other objects, perhaps wood. There is no evidence that the stones were fastened to one another. In fact, our pieces were evidently out of their original context, for we found many of them re-used in the row of stones that formed the edges and base of the pebble wall foundation in zone A_1 at Ali Kosh (Mohammad Jaffar phase).

Temporal distribution: Mohammad Jaffar phase.

XVIII

BURIALS

EARLY ALI KOSH PHASE?

The only burial uncovered in Bus Mordeh phase deposits at the site of Ali Kosh was a secondary interment, containing the limb bones of at least three adult individuals. The heap of long bones lay in the black compost at the top of zone C_1 (Pl. 13*a*). Included were several strings of white stone beads and three ornaments of turquoise, and the whole burial had been coated with red ochre. This burial was probably intrusive from zone B_2 (Ali Kosh phase), but no pit could be detected in the black compost.

ALI KOSH PHASE

Thirteen primary burials and one secondary burial were discovered under house floors in zone B_2 at Ali Kosh (Figs. 105-107). Primary burials included nine adults, two children or infants, and two very young babies or foetuses. Three adults (probably all female) showed intentional skull deformation, and it is possible that some of the other skeletons did also, but the skulls were usually poorly preserved and badly crushed. With one exception, the adults were seated in a tightly-flexed position, and since "silica ghost" traces of reed or club-rush matting could be detected encircling at least four of them, it is probable that most were "bundle" burials–that is, individuals tightly flexed and sewed or rolled up in a mat before interment under the house floor. Personal ornamentation might be necklaces of white and black stone beads, or an occasional bracelet of sea shells.

The secondary burial was a re-interment of the limb bones of at least three individuals, accompanied by one turquoise bead, one bead of green stone, and a shell pendant; it resembled the secondary burial of limb bones found in zone C_1.

Burial 26

Location: Under house floor in squares 59 and 69, depth 385 to 400 cm., zone B_2 (Tepe Ali Kosh)

Orientation: Seated, tightly flexed

Vital statistics: Adult of indeterminant sex

Features: Wrapped in over-two, under-two twilled mat

Ornaments: Necklace of black and white stone beads around neck (and a nearby bracelet of red and white striped sea shells, possibly associated)

Offerings: Grooved stone ball at left knee (Fig. 84*f*)

Preservation: Poor; many bones crushed, hands and feet missing.

Burial 27

Location: Under house floor in square 98, depth 435 to 465 cm., zone B_2 (Tepe Ali Kosh)

Orientation: Legs and pelvis run north-south

Vital statistics: Adult of indeterminate sex

Features: None

Ornaments: None

Offerings: None

Preservation: Poor; upper part of body missing. Disturbed.

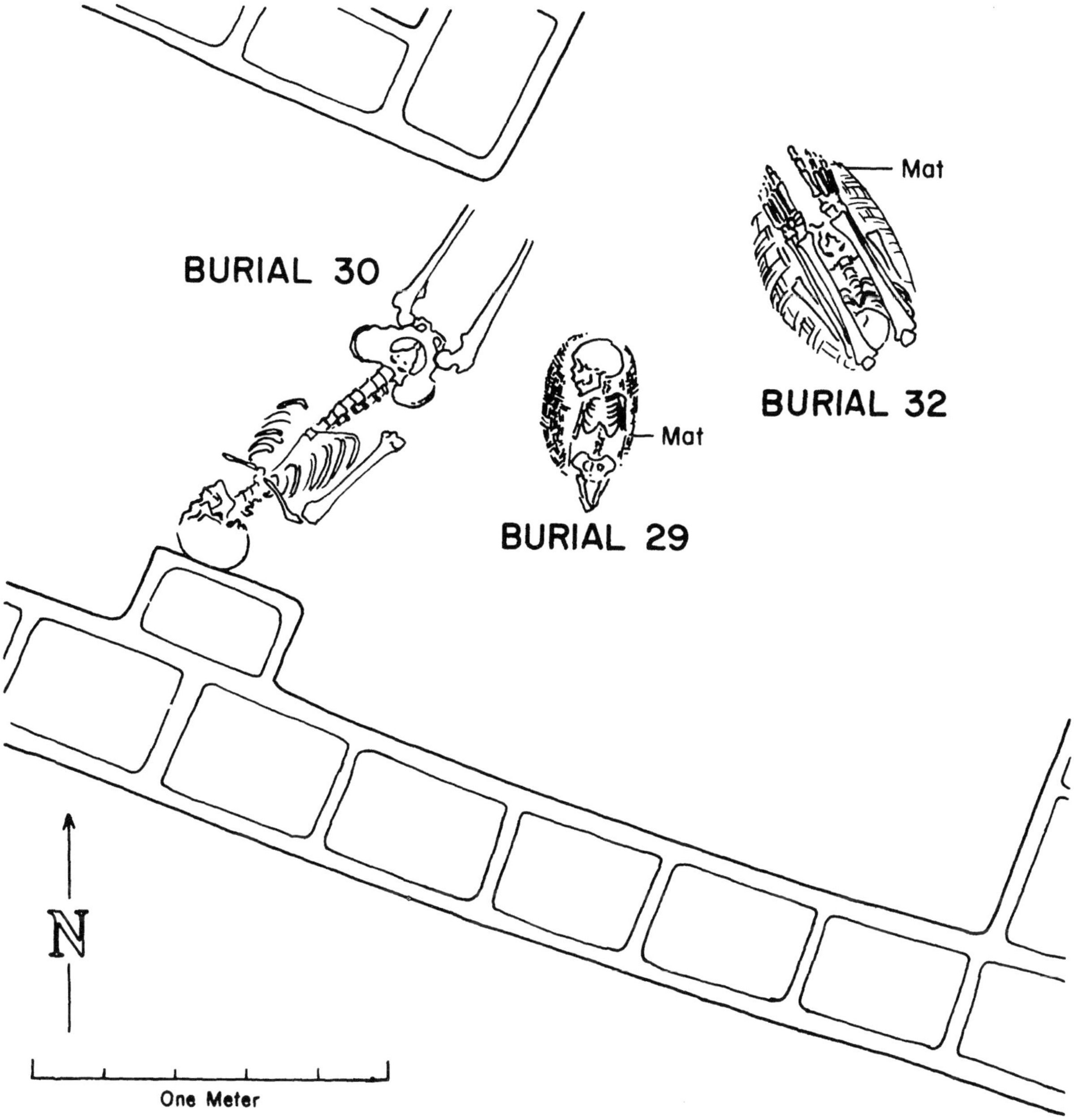

Fig. 105. Sub-floor burials in zone B_2, Tepe Ali Kosh (Ali Kosh phase): Burials 29, 30, 32. For location in house, see Fig. 10.

Table 55

THE BURIALS UNDER HOUSE FLOORS IN ZONE B_2 AT ALI KOSH

Type of Burial	Number	Number Showing Traces of Mat	Number with Clear Skull Deformation	Ornaments	Offerings
Adults (Primary)........	9	4	3	1 necklace 1 shell bracelet(?)	1 grooved-stone ball
Children or Infants......	2	1	...	1 shell bead	1 polished stone (facetted)
Newborn Baby or Foetus .	2	...	...	...	...
Secondary Burial (3 individuals)	1	...	...	1 turquoise bead 1 green stone bead 1 shell pendant	...
Totals...........	14	5	3	6	2

Burial 28

Location: Under house floor in square 96, depth 435 to 465 cm., zone B_2 (Tepe Ali Kosh)

Orientation: Supine, north-south (head north)

Vital statistics: Child, with premolars and permanent incisors present in jaws but unerupted (7 to 10 years?)

Features: None

Ornaments: Seashell bead near right mastoid

Offerings: Polished oval stone under right shoulder

Preservation: Poor

Burial 29

Location: Under house floor in square 77, depth 410 to 430 cm., zone B_2 (Tepe Ali Kosh)

Orientation: Supine, north-south (head north)

Vital statistics: Infant

Features: Wrapped in over-two, under-two twilled mat

Ornaments: None

Offerings: None

Preservation: Fair.

Burial 30

Location: Under house floor in squares 67 and 76, depth 410 to 430 cm., zone B_2 (Tepe Ali Kosh)

Orientation: Supine, northeast-southwest (head southwest)

Vital statistics: Adult of indeterminate sex

Features: None

Ornaments: None

Offerings: None

Preservation: Fair. Disturbed: left arm, lower jaw, both tibiae, and right radius and ulna missing.

Burial 31

Location: Under house floor in square 70, depth 435 to 465 cm., zone B_2 (Tepe Ali Kosh)

Orientation: Apparently seated, tightly flexed, originally; lower legs collapsed later

Vital statistics: Adult of indeterminate sex

Features: None

Ornaments: None

Offerings: None

Preservation: Good.

Burial 32

Location: Under house floor in square 68, depth 410 to 430 cm., zone B_1 (Tepe Ali Kosh)

Orientation: Seated, tightly flexed

Vital statistics: Adult of indeterminate sex

Features: Wrapped in over-two, under-two twilled mat

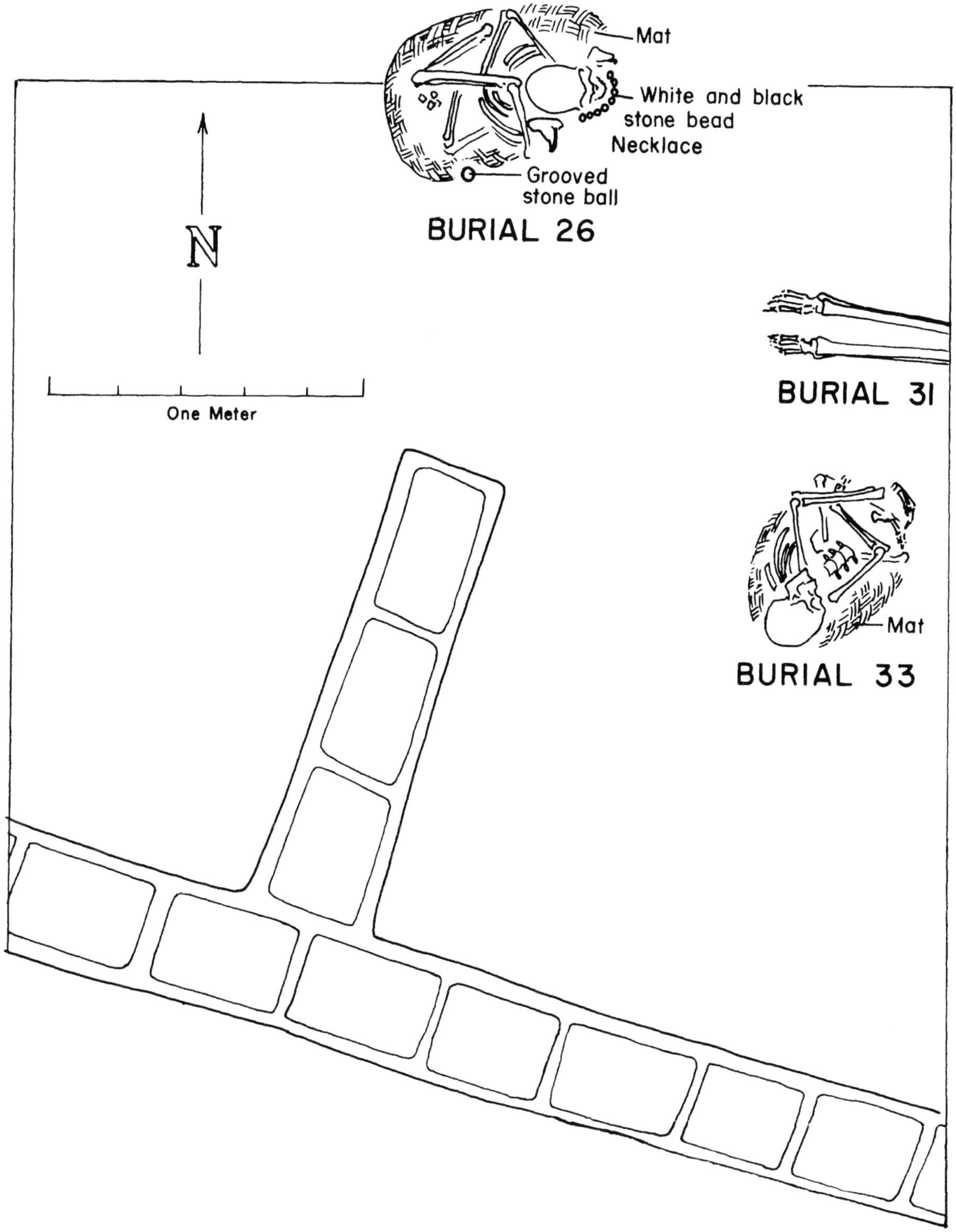

Fig. 106. Sub-floor burials in zone B_2, Tepe Ali Kosh (Ali Kosh phase): Burials 26, 31, 33. For location in house, see Fig. 10. A series of 5 sea shell beads found near Burial 26, possibly forming an associated bracelet, are not shown because they were not clearly *in situ*.

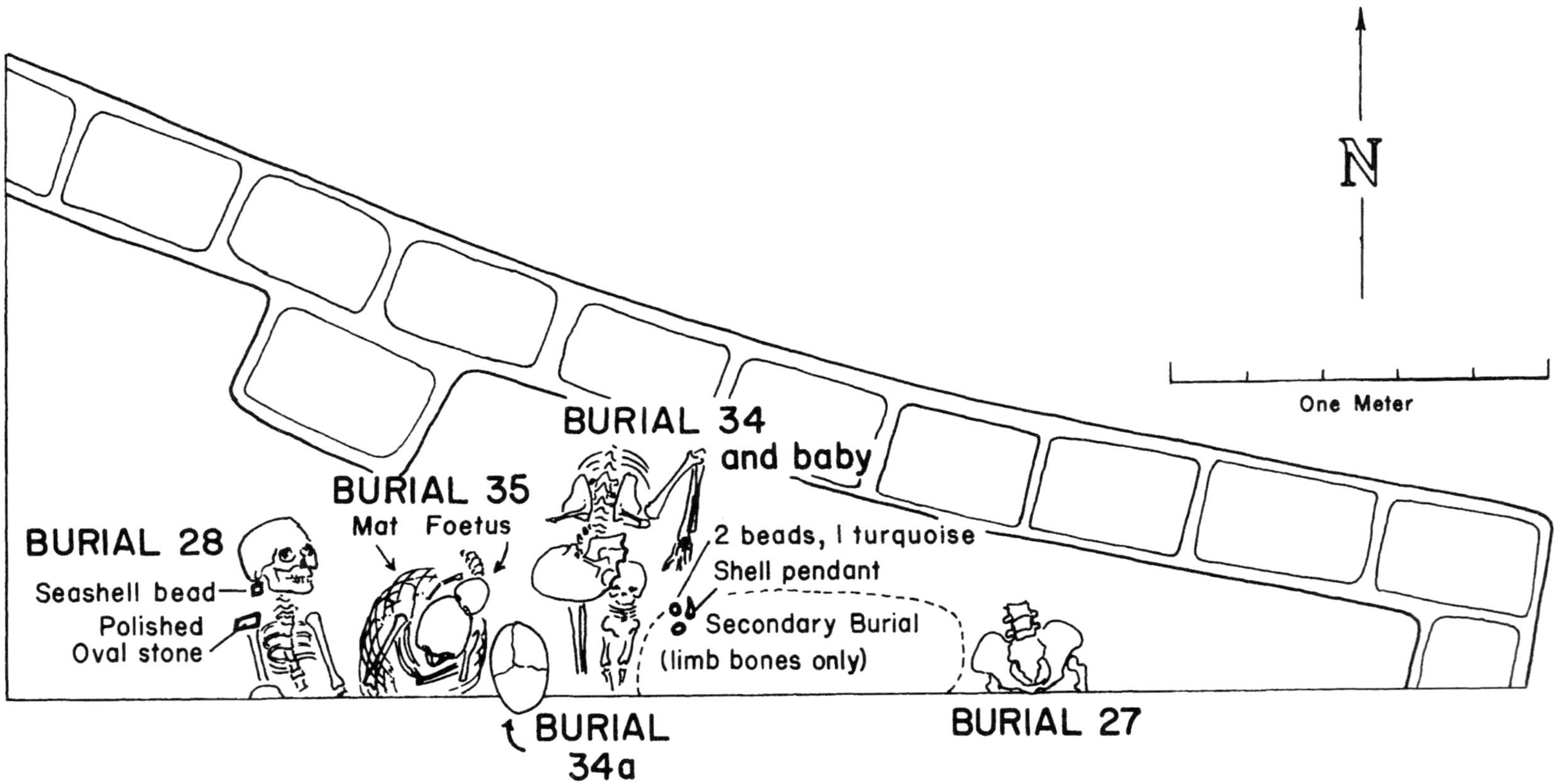

Fig. 107. Sub-floor burials in zone B_2, Tepe Ali Kosh (Ali Kosh phase): Burials 27; 28; 34 (and baby); 34*a*; 35 (and foetus); and secondarily-buried limb bones overlying Burial 34. For location in house, see Fig. 10.

Ornaments: None

Offerings: None

Preservation: Poor. Badly crushed.

Burial 33

Location: Under house floor in square 80, depth 428 to 450 cm., zone B_2 (Tepe Ali Kosh)

Orientation: Seated, tightly flexed

Vital statistics: Adult, perhaps female

Features: Wrapped in over-two, under-two twilled mat; skull deformation

Ornaments: None

Offerings: None

Preservation: Fair.

Burial 34 and Baby

Location: Under house floor in square 97, depth 438 to 465 cm., zone B_2 (Tepe Ali Kosh)

Orientation: Seated, flexed

Vital statistics: Adult female

Features: Newborn baby or foetus in lap; skull deformation

Ornaments: None

Offerings: None

Preservation: Fair.

Burial 34*a*

Location: Under house floor in square 96, depth 465 to 475 cm., zone B_2 (Tepe Ali Kosh)

Orientation: Unknown, as only skull extends into the excavation area

Vital statistics: Adult, probably female

Features: Skull deformation.

Burial 35 and Foetus

Location: Under house floor in square 96, depth 440 to 474 cm., zone B_2 (Tepe Ali Kosh)

Orientation: Seated, tightly flexed

Vital statistics: Adult, probably female

Features: Wrapped in over-two, under-two twilled mat; foetus found directly above it

Ornaments: None

Offerings: None

Preservation: Poor. A few limbs missing.

Secondary Burial

Location: Under house floor in square 97, depth 435 to 465 cm., zone B_2 (Tepe Ali Kosh)

Orientation: Long bones were piled together, running east-west

Vital statistics: At least 3 adults represented

Features: None

Ornaments: 1 turquoise bead; 1 green stone bead; 1 pendant of mussel shell

Offerings: None

Preservation: Poor, included are 5 femora, 4 tibiae, 4 fibulae, 1 humerus, 2 radii, 2 ulnae.

LATE ALI KOSH PHASE?

A single burial found in our 1961 test pit at Ali Kosh (zone B_1) was located beneath a house floor associated with "Wall No. 1" at a depth of 300 cm. The burial was tightly flexed and only partially included within our test pit. Associated with it was a stone bell pendant like those found with later Mohammad Jaffar phase burials, and four pecked stone balls a little over 3 cm. in diameter, which lay near the feet (Hole and Flannery, 1962:111).

MOHAMMAD JAFFAR PHASE

Five primary burials were discovered in the area to the east of the pebble wall foundation in zone A_1 at Ali Kosh (see plot plan, Fig. 12). All were oriented north-south (with the head south), and each lay on its left side, facing west, with the legs partially flexed. No evidence of mat-wrapping was detected. Ornaments included labrets; shell bracelets; and stone or clay bell pendants between the thighs. Two burials were accompanied by turquoise ornaments, and one had an asphalt-coated basket near his hips. None had deformed skulls.

The most elaborately equipped burial was Number 8, a middle-aged man. Two turquoise beads and a possible labret of turquoise lay between his skull and shoulder; his right forearm had a bracelet of white shell beads. A patch of red ochre stained the ground near his right shoulder, possibly indicating where some perishable offering had disintegrated. He wore a "G-string" or loin-cloth on which small disc beads had evidently been sewn, and from which a number of strings or fringes of black disc beads hung down over both legs and his pelvis. Resting against the pubic bone and between the thighs was a bell-shaped pendant of polished stone (see Fig. 108 and Pl. 12*c*).

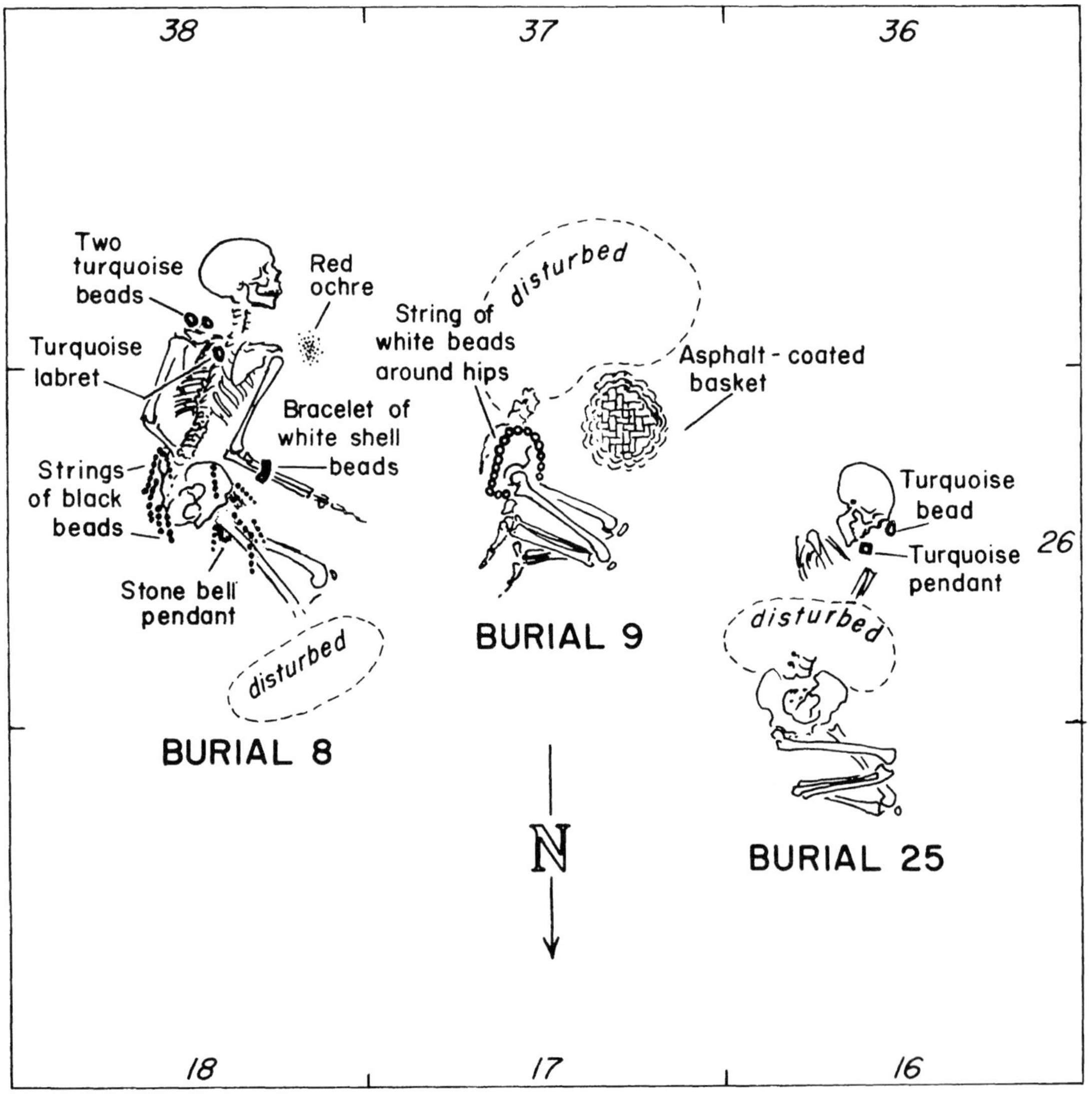

Fig. 108. Burials outside house in zone A_1, Tepe Ali Kosh (Mohammad Jaffar phase): Burials 8, 9, 25. For location with regard to house, see Fig. 12. The clay bell pendant found near Burial 25 (Fig. 101*h*) is not shown because it was not clearly *in situ*.

Burial 8

Location: Squares 28 and 38, depth 50 to 80 cm., zone A_1 (Tepe Ali Kosh)

Orientation: Semiflexed on left side, north-south (head south)

Vital statistics: Middle-aged male

Features: Stain of red ochre (4 by 8 cm.) near right shoulder

Ornaments: Stone bell pendant between thighs; bracelet of white stone beads on right forearm; turquoise beads at neck; turquoise labret or ear plug fallen between scapulae; strings of black disc beads at hips

Preservation: Fair. Lower legs disturbed by later pit.

Burial 9

Location: Square 27, depth 60 to 73 cm., zone A_1 (Tepe Ali Kosh)

Orientation: Semiflexed on left side, north-south (head south)

Vital statistics: Adult of indeterminate sex

Ornaments: Girdle of white beads around waist

Offering(?): Twined basket (in asphalt) near pelvis

Preservation: Poor. Disturbed; upper half of body missing.

Burial 10

Location: Squares 20 and 30, depth 55 to 80 cm., zone A_1 (Tepe Ali Kosh)

Orientation: Semiflexed on left side, north-south (head south)

Vital statistics: Middle-aged male

Ornaments: Clay bell pendant between thighs; bitumen labret *in situ* resting against lower incisors and front of mandible; a stray labret near the hips may possibly be associated

Preservation: Fair.

Burial 18

Location: Squares 18 and 19, depth 25 to 40 cm., zone A_1 (Tepe Ali Kosh)

Orientation: Semiflexed on left side, north-south (head south)

Vital statistics: Adult of indeterminate sex

Ornaments: 1 bone bead near feet may possibly be associated (?)

Preservation: Poor; some digits and ribs missing.

Burial 25

Location: Squares 16 and 26, depth 80 to 100 cm., zone A_1 (Tepe Ali Kosh)

Orientation: Semiflexed on left side, north-south (head south)

Vital statistics: Middle-aged (?) adult of indeterminate sex, possibly male

Ornaments: One turquoise pendant near top of sternum; 1 turquoise bead between left shoulder and face. A broken clay bell pendant, found nearby, perhaps came from the pelvic area, and was removed when the burial was disturbed by a later pit.

Preservation: Poor. Disturbed by a pit which carried away the mid-section, plus the lower arms.

SABZ, KHAZINEH, AND MEHMEH PHASES

No burials found.

BAYAT PHASE

Five primary burials were encountered in zones A_1 and A_2 at Tepe Sabz—three adults, one adolescent, and an infant. All but the infant were extended, and each lay on its right side, oriented east-west. Two skeletons (both probably females) were accompanied by grinding implements, and three burials, including one of the females, were covered with stone slabs. No ornaments were observed, and the graves were simple pits in the fill between houses (see Fig. 110 and Pl. 17).

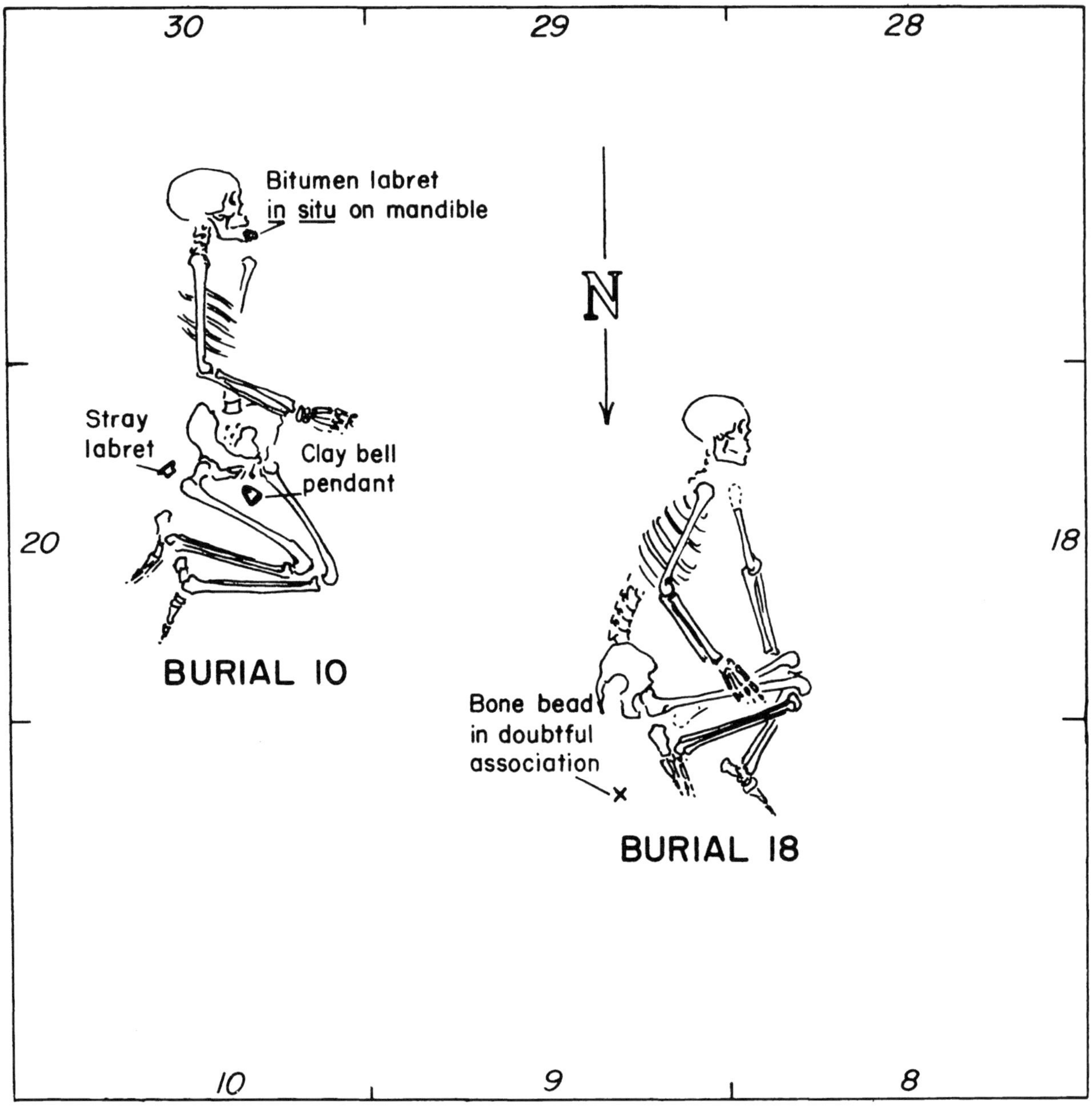

Fig. 109. Burials outside house in zone A_1, Tepe Ali Kosh (Mohammad Jaffar phase): Burials 10, 18. For location with regard to house, see Fig. 12.

Burial 1

Location: Squares 22 and 25, depth 122 to 136 cm., zone A_2 (Tepe Sabz)

Orientation: Extended east-west (head west), on right side

Vital statistics: Adult, possibly male (?)

Features: None

Ornaments: None

Offerings: None

Preservation: Poor; partly eroded out of ravine where step trench began; skull and scapulae missing.

Burial 2

Location: Squares 16 and 19, depth 78 to 100 cm., zone A_1 (Tepe Sabz)

Orientation: Extended east-west (head west), on right side

Vital statistics: Adult female

Features: 6 stone slabs overlay the grave

Ornaments: None

Offerings: 1 saddle-shaped grinding slab and 1 discoidal handstone placed at her shoulder and hips

Preservation: Fair.

Burial 3

Location: Squares 11, 12, and 14, depth 107 to 128 cm., on border between zones A_1 and A_2 (Tepe Sabz)

Orientation: Extended east-west (head west), on right side

Vital statistics: Adolescent, probably female

Features: None

Ornaments: None

Offerings: 1 saddle-shaped grinding slab and 1 discoidal handstone placed at back and hips

Preservation: Good.

Burial 4

Location: Squares 2 and 5, depth 72 to 80 cm., zone A_1 (Tepe Sabz) near Burial 5

Orientation: Semiflexed east-west (head west), on right side

Vital statistics: Newborn infant or foetus

Features: Covered by stone slabs, including several broken grinding stones

Ornaments: None

Offerings: None

Preservation: Good.

Burial 5

Location: Squares 2 and 5, depth 75 to 100 cm., zone A_1 (Tepe Sabz), near Burial 4

Orientation: Extended east-west (head west), on right side

Vital statistics: Adult (possibly male?)

Features: Covered by a dozen stone slabs, including grinding stones

Ornaments: None

Offerings: None

Preservation: Fair.

INTRUSIVE "IRON AGE" BURIALS

Long after the abandonment of Ali Kosh, a series of twenty graves had been dug into zone A_1 of the area we excavated in 1963. Each grave contained a primary burial, oriented east-west or nearly east-west (see grave plan, Fig. 111). The skeletons were characterized by a pale white color, brittle condition, and consistent orientation; the graves were much softer than the surrounding mound fill, and twelve out of twenty contained chaff-tempered red clay bricks which had been heaped over the body. A few even had boulders or slabs of lime plaster covering the skeleton.

We have no way of dating these burials precisely, but since some were wearing iron bracelets, they come from a period considerably more recent than our range of interests. Copper earrings, copper "shroud pins," or copper axes accompanied a few skeletons (see Fig. 112).

All ages and both sexes seemed to be represented in this cemetery. There were fourteen adults (some aged), six children or infants (and one foetus or newborn baby between the legs of its mother). Twelve of the fourteen adults were supine and extended, with one or both arms folded over the chest. Copper earrings and iron bracelets seemed to occur mainly on female skeletons, but one of the most elaborately equipped burials was a child of 6 to 8 years.

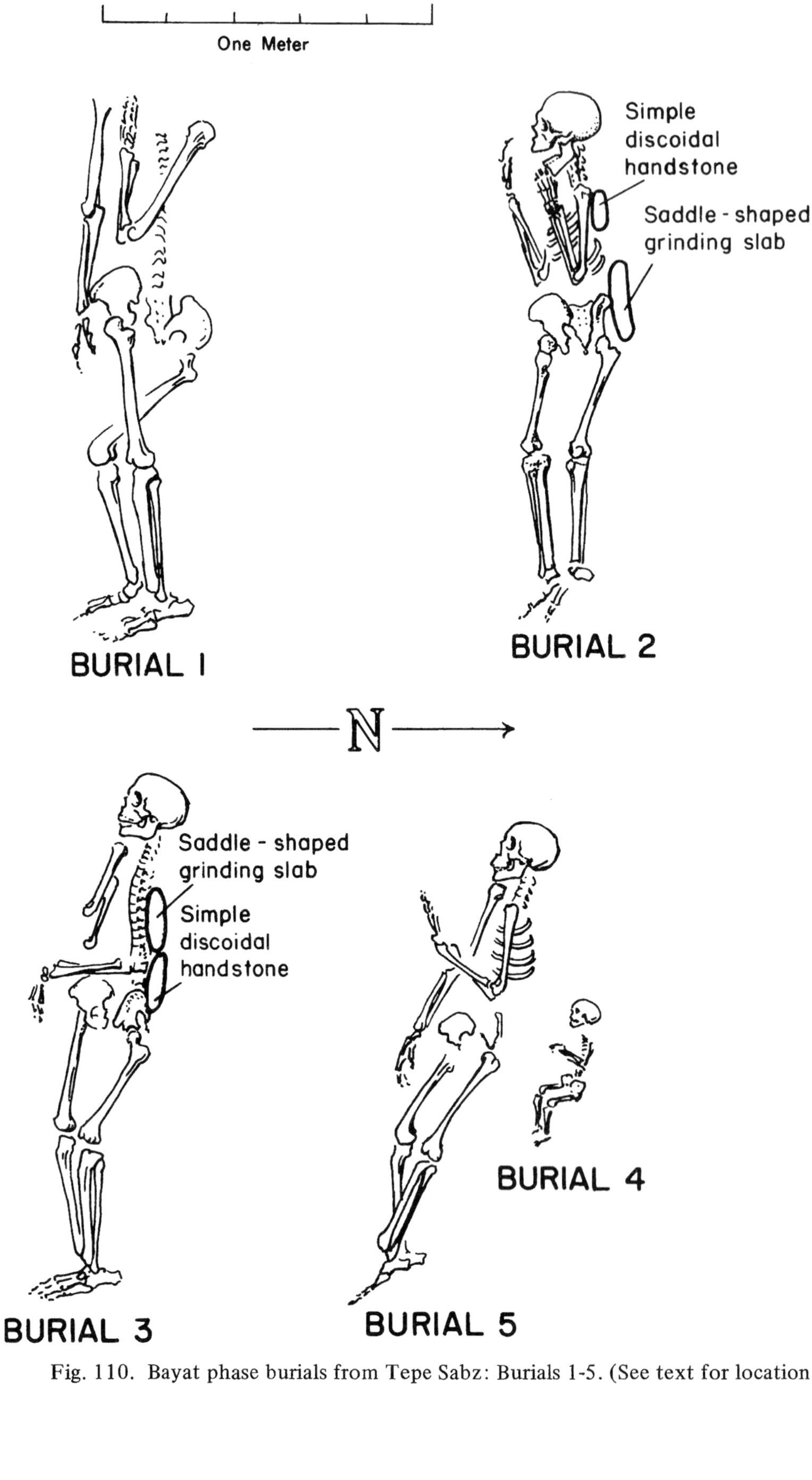

Fig. 110. Bayat phase burials from Tepe Sabz: Burials 1-5. (See text for location.)

Table 56

INTRUSIVE "IRON AGE" BURIALS IN ZONE A_1 OF ALI KOSH

Burial Number	Orientation	Head To	Legs	Arms	Age	Probable Sex	Features	Ornaments	Offerings
1....	NW-SE Supine	NW	Extended	Folded on chest	Adult	?	Covered by red bricks and plaster	None	Copper axe
2....	E-W Supine	W	Extended	One folded over chest	Adult	?	None	None	None
3....	E-W Supine	W	Extended	One folded	Adult	?	Covered by red bricks	None	None
4....	E-W on R side	W	Semi-flexed	At sides	Child 3-5 years	?	Covered by red bricks and plaster	None	None
5....	E-W Supine	W	Extended	At sides	Infant	?	None	None	None
6....	E-W Supine	W	Extended	Not found	Adult	?	Covered by red bricks	None	None
7....	NW-SE Supine	NW	Extended	At sides	Child 3-5 years	?	None	None	None
11....	NW-SE?	NW	Not found	Not found	Child	?	Covered by red bricks	None	None
12....	NW-SE Supine	NW	Extended	Folded on chest	Middle Aged	Male	Covered by red bricks and stones	None	None
13...	E-W Supine	W	Extended	Folded	Adult	?	Covered by red bricks and stones	None	None
14....	E-W Supine	W	Extended	At sides	Aged	Female	Covered by red bricks	None	None
15....	NW-SE Supine	NW	Extended	Folded	Adult	Female	Foetus or newborn baby between thighs	Copper earrings at left mastoid; iron bracelet on left forearm	None
16....	NW-SE Supine	NW	Extended	One folded	Aged	Female	Covered by red bricks	None	None
17....	E-W Supine	W	Extended	Folded on chest	Adult	Female?	None	None	None
19....	Unknown (body disturbed)	?	?	?	Adult	?	None	None	None
20....	NW-SE Supine	NW	Extended	Folded on chest	Adult	Female	None	Iron bracelet on left forearm	None
21....	E-W Prone	W	Extended	At sides	Child 5-8 years	?	Covered by 5 stones	None	None
22....	E-W Supine	W	Extended	Folded on chest	Child 6-8 years	?	Covered by red bricks	Copper earrings	Copper axe, copper pin
23....	NW-SE Supine	NW	Extended	Folded on chest	Adult	?	Covered by red bricks	None	None
24....	E-W	W	Extended	Folded	Adult	Female	Covered by red bricks	Copper earring on right mastoid; necklace of white and red beads	None

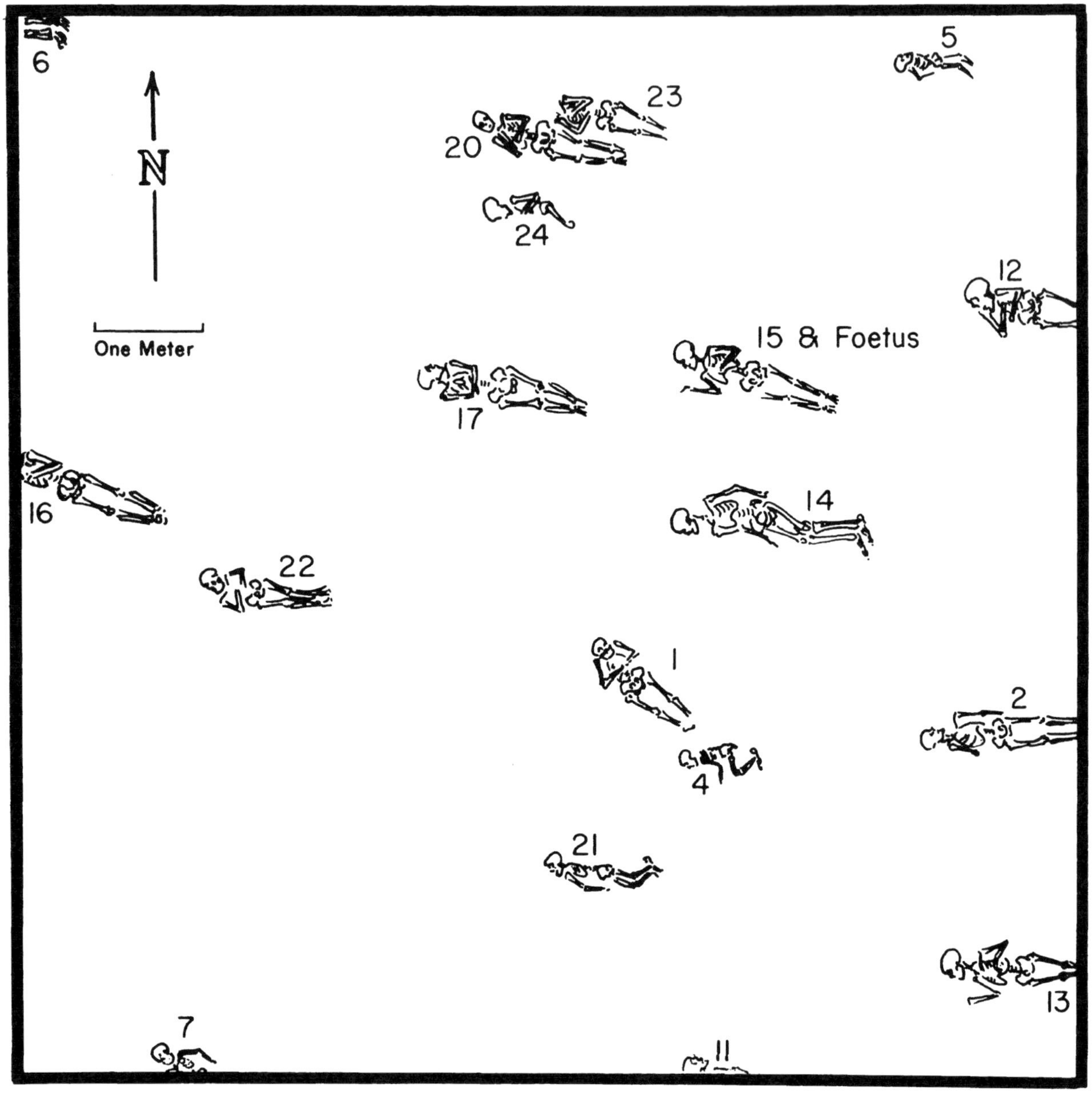

Fig. 111. Intrusive "Iron Age" burials in zone A_1, Tepe Ali Kosh. Area shown is that of squares 1 to 100, excavated in 1963.

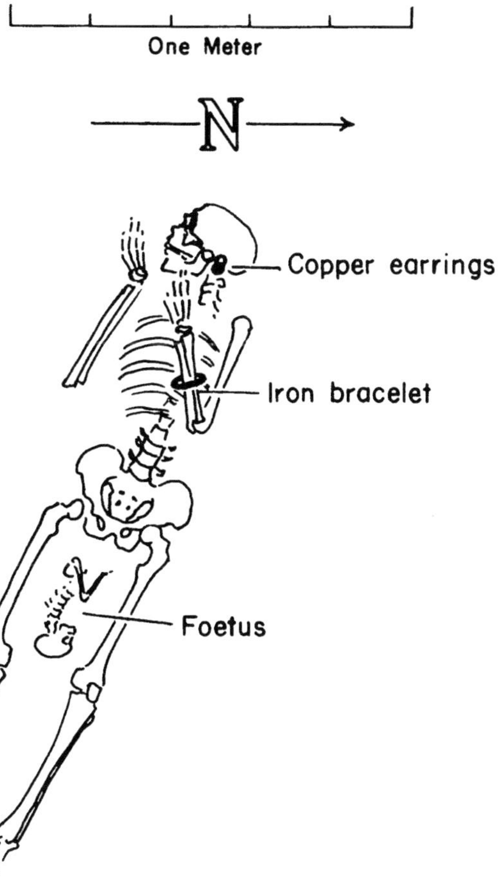

Fig. 112. Burial 15 at Tepe Ali Kosh (intrusive, "Iron Age," zone A_1). See text.

XIX

THE ANIMAL BONES

In the course of our 1961 and 1963 excavations in the Deh Luran plain, we recovered some 100,000 broken animal bones, teeth, horns, and fragments of shell. Through the courtesy of the Department of Antiquities, Museé Iran Bastan, we were allowed to transport all this material to the United States for study; half was eventually returned to Iran. Thus it was possible to study the total screened samples from all levels of all sites excavated: Ali Kosh, Tepe Sabz, and Tepe Musiyan "E."

As is customary in sites of this time period, about 85 per cent of the faunal remains were splinters from the midsection of the limb bones of ungulates. Since these included no trace of either articular end, nor any other diagnostic character, they could not be further identified. The number of fragments which could be more specifically keyed out was 13,599 (see Table 57). About 4000 of these were broken vertebrae, ribs, and splinters from the cheek teeth of sheep, goat, and gazelle, which by reason of their fragmentary nature could not be separated by genus with any reliability. The broken ribs and vertebrae of these small bovids, except for the atlas and axis, are really frustratingly similar, and sheep and goat teeth cannot be distinguished.

Of the remaining bones and teeth, 5000 were definitely those of sheep and goats; 2000 were definitely identified as gazelle. These three animals constituted the majority of ungulates eaten in the Deh Luran plain during all periods investigated by us.

Other ungulates eaten with some frequency at Deh Luran were the onager (500 fragments) and wild ox (200 fragments). Fish (275 fragments) and freshwater mussels (400 valves) were also popular foods in the early periods of the sequence.

THE FAUNAL ASSEMBLAGE

The animal bones from Ali Kosh, Tepe Sabz, and Musiyan "E" provide clues not only to subsistence practices but also local environment. They are clearly the debris of a goat- and sheep-herding group who lived in a steppe or plains environment with abundant wild ungulates. There were bodies of fresh water in the vicinity of the site which provided fish, mussels, and winter water fowl. And the villages served as burrowing grounds for hundreds of small plains-adapted wild rodents and lizards.

The full roster of species identified from the Deh Luran sites is as follows:

Large Mammals
- Wild goat (*Capra hircus aegagrus*)
- Domestic goat (*Capra hircus hircus*)
- Domestic sheep (*Ovis aries*)
- Gazelle (*Gazella subgutturosa*)
- Onager (*Equus hemionus*)
- Wild ox (*Bos primigenius*)
- Domestic cattle (*Bos taurus*)
- Pig (*Sus scrofa*)

Small Mammals
- Large Canids
- Domestic dog (*Canis familiaris*)
- Red fox (*Vulpes vulpes*)
- Hyena (*Hyaena hyaena*)
- Wild cat (*Felis* cf. *libyca*)

Beech marten (*Martes foina*)
Weasel (*Mustela* cf. *nivalis*)
Hedgehog (*Hemiechinus auritus*)
Indian gerbil (*Tatera indica*)
Karun desert gerbil (*Meriones crassus*)
Bandicoot-rat (*Nesokia indica*)
House mouse (*Mus musculus*)

Birds
Gray goose (*Anser anser*)
White-fronted goose (*Anser albifrons*)
Mallard duck (*Anas platyrhynchos*)
Diving duck (*Aythya* sp.)
Crane (*Grus grus*)
White stork (*Ciconia ciconia*)
Heron (*Ardea cinerea*)
Eagle (*Aquila* sp.)
Hawk or kite, unidentified
Black partridge (*Francolinus francolinus*)
See-see partridge (*Ammoperdix griseogularis*)
Hooded crow (*Corvus corone*)
Songbirds, unidentified

Reptiles
Water turtle (*Clemmys caspica*)
Lizard (*Varanus* cf. *griseus*)
Lizard (*Uromastix* cf. *hardwickii*)

Fish
Carp family, unidentified
Catfish, unidentified

Invertebrates
Freshwater mussel (*Pseudodontopsis euphraticus*)
Freshwater mussel (*Unio tigridis*)
Freshwater mussel (*Leguminaia wheatleyi*)
Freshwater snail (*Melanoides tuberculatus*)
Freshwater snail (*Melanopsis* spp.)
River crab (*Potamon* sp.)

While Flannery is responsible for the mammalian and avian identifications, he would like to express his thanks to several zoological colleagues at the Smithsonian Institution, who either identified, or aided in the identification of, non-mammalian remains. These include Drs. George Watson (birds), James Peters (reptiles), William Taylor (fishes), Joseph Morrison (mollusks), and Fenner Chace (crustacea). In addition, we owe thanks to a number of mammalogists, especially Drs. Henry Setzer (Smithsonian Institution), Charles Reed (University of Illinois), Dexter Perkins, Jr. (Harvard, Mass.), and Sándor Bökönyi (Hungarian National Museum), for their advice and criticism.

EARLY ANIMAL DOMESTICATION AT DEH LURAN: A SYNOPSIS

Detailed studies of the fauna from Ali Kosh and Tepe Sabz, summarized in the pages which follow, produced some data bearing on all five of the earliest animal domesticates: sheep, goat, cattle, dog, and pig.

Before 7000 B.C., the Bus Mordeh villagers already had sheep who were hornless (females?), a sure sign of domestication. However, they kept goats in far greater numbers. These goats show only slight osteological evidence of domestication, but a study of the age-profile of the population indicates they could not have been a random sample of a wild goat population. Only two-thirds reached an age of 1 year, and less than a third reached 3.5 years.

During the Ali Kosh phase, these goats began to show clearly the medially-flattened horn core typical of early domestic *Capra hircus*. Male sheep, however, retained the wild-type horn core. This was a time when populations of early domestic sheep and goats exhibited a variety of phenotypes from wild to domestic, with many transitional and intermediate forms present.

By the Mohammad Jaffar phase, male sheep had begun to exhibit domestic horn characters, and at least a few goats had the helically-twisted horn typical of modern domesticates. These "modern" characters were eventually fully stabilized by the Sabz phase, perhaps around 5500 B.C.

Table 57

TOTAL COUNTS OF IDENTIFIED ANIMAL BONES FROM ALI KOSH AND TEPE SABZ
(By Stratigraphic Zone)

Phase	Site	Zone	Ribs, vertebrae, Teeth of Goat, Sheep and/or Gazelle	Ungulates						Smaller Mammals									Other Vertebrates				Invertebrates			Totals
				Goat and/or Sheep	Gazelle	Onager	Aurochs	Domestic Cattle	Pig	Domestic Dog	*Canis* sp.	Red Fox	Hyaena	Wild Cat	Marten	Weasel	Hedgehog	Small Rodents	Birds	Turtle	Lizard	Fish	Crab	Mussel	Water Snail	
Bayat	TS	A_1	23	16	10	4	. . .	5	3	. . .	. . .	. . .	. . .	. . .	. . .	. . .	. . .	1	. . .	. . .	. . .	. . .	. . .	2	. . .	64
	TS	A_2	55	30	15	1	. . .	9	. . .	12	. . .	1	. . .	. . .	. . .	. . .	. . .	3	1	5	. . .	. . .	. . .	1	. . .	133
	TS	A_3	173	62	16	8	. . .	5	1	6	. . .	8	. . .	. . .	. . .	. . .	. . .	7	. . .	3	7	1	. . .	2	. . .	299
Mehmeh	TS	B_1	23	14	2	1	. . .	3	1	. . .	. . .	. . .	. . .	. . .	. . .	. . .	. . .	3	. . .	. . .	3	. . .	. . .	. . .	. . .	50
	TS	B_2	22	23	2	1	. . .	2	. . .	. . .	. . .	. . .	. . .	. . .	. . .	. . .	. . .	3	. . .	. . .	. . .	. . .	. . .	. . .	. . .	53
	TS	B_3	11	19	5	. . .	. . .	2	. . .	. . .	. . .	1	. . .	. . .	. . .	. . .	. . .	8	3	3	. . .	. . .	. . .	. . .	. . .	52
Khazineh	TS	C_1	24	7	2	2	. . .	1	. . .	3	. . .	. . .	. . .	. . .	. . .	. . .	. . .	1	3	. . .	. . .	. . .	. . .	. . .	. . .	43
	TS	C_2	23	10	4	. . .	. . .	. . .	. . .	4	. . .	. . .	. . .	. . .	. . .	. . .	. . .	. . .	. . .	. . .	. . .	. . .	. . .	. . .	. . .	41
	TS	C_3	13	17	4	. . .	. . .	. . .	. . .	. . .	. . .	. . .	. . .	. . .	. . .	. . .	. . .	1	1	. . .	. . .	. . .	. . .	. . .	. . .	36
Sabz	TS	D	101	98	15	2	. . .	16	8	50	. . .	2	. . .	1	5	. . .	1	3	1	1	. . .	7	. . .	3	2	316
Mohammad Jaffar	AK	A_1	362	359	177	44	17	. . .	3	. . .	4	4	. . .	. . .	. . .	. . .	. . .	33	4	4	53	35	3	43	1	1,146
	AK	A_2	317	344	245	99	15	. . .	2	. . .	5	15	1	8	. . .	1	1	40	6	6	84	73	. . .	68	1	1,331
Ali Kosh	AK	B_1	292	335	259	84	37	. . .	. . .	. . .	2	1	. . .	1	. . .	. . .	1	12	3	9	22	24	3	70	2	1,157
	AK	B_2	1760	2333	1002	199	139	. . .	18	. . .	2	15	. . .	1	. . .	. . .	1	130	5	8	79	81	. . .	96	8	5,877
Bus Mordeh	AK	C_1	461	879	224	30	16	. . .	2	. . .	. . .	6	. . .	. . .	. . .	. . .	. . .	76	2	12	80	29	. . .	58	1	1,876
	AK	C_2	248	455	215	20	8	. . .	2	. . .	. . .	1	. . .	. . .	. . .	. . .	. . .	31	1	23	31	25	. . .	65	. . .	1,125
Totals. . . .			3908	5001	2197	495	232	43	40	75	13	54	1	11	5	1	4	352	30	74	359	275	6	408	15	13,599

In the Sabz phase appeared domestic cattle which were significantly smaller than the ancestral *Bos primigenius*. Domestic dogs, represented not only by partially-articulated skeletons but also by paintings on pottery vessels, were now present in the villages of the plain. The pottery motifs show them to have fluffy tails curled up over the back like the modern Kurdish guard dog.

Sheep increased steadily with time (and were destined to become Khuzistan's most abundant domesticate in Early Dynastic times). Finally, in the Bayat phase, *ca.* 3800 B.C., appeared a single pig whose tooth measurements suggest it might have been domestic. Pigs could hardly have played much of a role in the local diet, however.

CHANGES IN HUNTING PATTERN: A SYNOPSIS

One of the most striking changes taking place during the course of the Deh Luran sequence was a dwindling of interest in aquatic resources–fish, mussels, freshwater turtles and crabs. Literally hundreds of fragments of these animals occurred in Bus Mordeh, Ali Kosh, and Mohammad Jaffar levels, while they appeared only sporadically at Tepe Sabz. Since carbonized seeds of bulrush or sea clubrush (*Scirpus maritimus*) also disappear in later phases of the sequence, it may be that the depressed central portion of the Deh Luran plain was a shallow slough which shrank late in the Mohammad Jaffar phase, making aquatic food sources less obtainable. Whatever the case, it appears that the first sedentary peoples on the Khuzistan steppe made use of the various marsh or slough habitats of that environmental zone.

The prehistoric Deh Luranis were hunters of gazelle, and onager or wild ass, and they maintained this activity through all periods of the sequence. Design motifs on sherds of the Mehmeh phase (and/or Susiana *c*) suggest that they may have hunted gazelle with bow and arrow along known gazelle trails (see below). They also obtained a few wild goats during trips to the nearby mountains.

Early in our sequence, the inhabitants of the plain also hunted the wild ox or aurochs, *Bos primigenius,* but there is no evidence for this animal after the end of the Mohammad Jaffar phase. The increasing amount of land under cultivation at Deh Luran, plus the spread of domestic sheep and goat herds, must have reduced the area available for wild ungulates, and *Bos primigenius* seems to have been the first to disappear. Possibly the gazelle and onager survived because they could utilize the very saline portions of the steppe which were of only marginal value to sheep and goats.

Another change in wild resource exploitation which characterized the Deh Luran sequence was a decreased use of migratory water fowl. Villagers of the Bus Mordeh, Ali Kosh, and Mohammad Jaffar phases ate numbers of the wild ducks, geese, herons, cranes, and storks which visit the marshes of Khuzistan during the winter months. In later periods, bird remains are few. It may be that the shrinking of our postulated Deh Luran slough reduced the availability of water fowl; or alternatively, increased agricultural activity, after the beginnings of irrigation during the Sabz phase, left less time for fowling.

LIFE BEFORE HERDING

No sites of the food-collecting era have so far been discovered in Khuzistan, but the animal bones from early village levels at Ali Kosh allow us to speculate on hunting practices in that region before animal domestication began. If we ignore all evidence of domestic sheep and goats in the refuse, we might suggest the following hypothesis: late food-collecting peoples in Khuzistan probably lived by exploiting the permanent resources of the rivers and reed marshes, where they fished, collected mollusks, turtles, and crabs, and harvested quantities of water fowl in the winter. They also stalked the wild ungulates of the plain: principally gazelles, because of the size and number of their herds, but also aurochs and wild ass. Wild pigs, foxes, hedgehogs, partridges, and other small fauna probably rounded out the meat diet.

CAPRINES: GOATS AND SHEEP

Sample: 5001 fragments (not counting ribs, stray teeth, and lower vertebrae, see Table 57)

Temporal distribution: All phases

Introduction

Two small bovids, members of the subfamily Caprinae, accounted for half the animal bones at Ali Kosh and Tepe Sabz.

All domestic goats (*Capra hircus*) are believed to be descendents of the Persian wild goat (*Capra hircus aegagrus*), the "bezoar" or "pasang" of Asia Minor, the Zagros and Elburz Mountains, and the Caucasus (Reed, 1960:130). In the Deh Luran area, these wild goats can still be found on the rocky slopes of the mountains to the north (Kuh-i-Siah) and even on some of the more rugged low ridges of the Jebel Hamrin. The roofs of a number of houses at Deh Luran and Musiyan are decorated with sets of horns, up to a meter in length, from male wild goats shot in one or the other of these ranges. Goats do not inhabit the plain. On level ground they are poor runners, fair game for the nearest man or wolf. Their best defense is great climbing ability, which more or less restricts them to the cliffs high above the plain. They could only have been obtained by prehistoric villagers after many kilometers of walking, followed by a long climb into the mountains. The average Deh Lurani sees hundreds of gazelle for every wild goat he runs across in his lifetime. The high proportion of goats at Ali Kosh, from the very beginning of the sequence, reflects the fact that these animals were domesticated captives, not hunted wild animals (see below).

All domestic sheep of the Near East (*Ovis aries*) are believed to be descendents of the Asiatic mouflon or wild red sheep, *Ovis orientalis* (Reed, 1960:135). This animal is known from Cyprus and Asia Minor to Iran and Afghanistan, and today in the Luristan and Kermanshah districts of Iran herds of up to fifteen or twenty individuals can be sighted. However, we know of no herds in the Deh Luran area today, and in fact there is little suitable terrain for them. Unlike goats (which prefer steep cliffs and rockslides) and gazelles (which prefer flat open plains), the wild red sheep are most frequently encountered in rolling country with round-top hills and less precipitous topography. There is little of such country in the immediate vicinity of Ali Kosh, and it is therefore no surprise that only domestic sheep remains were found in the lower levels of the site. By 2000 B.C., domestic sheep were of prime economic importance in Khuzistan (Adams, 1962:115).

Osteological Problems

As the Old Testament suggests, it is not always easy to separate the sheep from the goats. The horn cores are different enough, but once past the skull the Near Eastern faunal analyst is in trouble. Perkins (1964:1565), who has spent much time on the problem as anyone, sums it up thus: "The postcranial skeletons of sheep and goats are remarkably similar, and the separation of sheep and goat skeletal material is notoriously difficult unless there is a size difference between the two forms; this is not the case in the Near East. Differences reported in the literature have been based on small samples or on comparison with modern domestic races, and are not reliable."

Our gross bone fragment counts on the Caprinae, therefore, list goats and sheep as if they were one animal (Table 57). It will be apparent from the table cited that Caprines were the most commonly eaten animals throughout our sequence. Their bones constituted 67 per cent of the faunal remains from the Bus Mordeh phase. During the succeeding Ali Kosh and Mohammad Jaffar phases, increased hunting of gazelle, onager, and wild ox lowered the Caprine percentage, but it never fell below 49 per cent. In the later portion of the sequence, Sabz through Bayat phases, Caprines surged ahead of all other animals to reach frequencies as high as 75 per cent.

How many of these Caprines were goats, and how many were sheep? To determine this we had to turn to a small number of key skeletal elements whose reliability so far seems relatively secure:

The Horn Core.—The bony core which supports the sheath of the horn is significantly different in the two species involved. The goat (*Capra hircus*) has hollow cores with a keeled front surface, while the wild sheep (*Ovis orientalis*) has cores which are solid except for a few small sinuses, and flat or gently rounded on their front surface. We recovered 126 horn cores or fragments of cores which could be classified. Of these, 117 were *Capra*, and eight were *Ovis*.

Tables 58 and 59 show the temporal distribution of this horn material. Horn cores of goat appeared in every zone of the sequence except zone C_2 of Tepe Sabz (which had no cores at all). Horn cores of sheep did not appear until the Ali Kosh phase, and only occasionally thereafter. On the basis of horn cores alone, one might guess that goats represented nearly 100 per cent of the Caprines in the Bus Mordeh phase, and the majority of the Caprines in the rest of the sequence. However, this is because some sheep were hornless (see below).

The Distal Metapodial.—A major breakthrough in sheep and goat identification was the discovery of diagnostic characters in the distal metapodial, made by a Russian osteologist, Vera Gromova (1953). These characters have since been checked by Dexter Perkins (personal communication) and Flannery, using Caprine material in the Chicago Natural History Museum, the U. S. National Museum, the Zoological Museum of the University of Copenhagen, and other collections. In contrast to some of the characters proposed by Gromova and others, the metapodial characters seem to work reliably on both wild and domestic *Ovis* and *Capra*. We are grateful to Dr. Sophie D. Coe for translating sections of Gromova's monograph from the Russian.

The distal end of the metapodial has two identical condyles, separated by a sagittal notch (Fig. 113). Each is shaped somewhat like a small gear or wheel with an inner (medial) articular surface and an outer (lateral) articular surface. Gromova calculated the diameters of each of these articular surfaces and found that in goats,

Table 58

DISTRIBUTION OF HORN CORES OF GOAT (*CAPRA*) AND SHEEP (*OVIS*) AT ALI KOSH AND TEPE SABZ
(By Stratigraphic Zone and Cultural Phase)

Phase	Site	Zone	Goat Horn Cores	Sheep Horn Cores	Total Cores
Bayat	TS	A_1	1	...	1
	TS	A_2	1	...	1
	TS	A_3	5	1	6
Mehmeh	TS	B_1	1	...	1
	TS	B_2	2	...	2
	TS	B_3	1	...	1
Khazineh	TS	C_1	1	...	1
	TS	C_2	...	...	...
	TS	C_3	3	...	3
Sabz	TS	D	9	...	9
Mohammad Jaffar	AK	A_1	13	2	15
	AK	A_2	8	...	8
Ali Kosh	AK	B_1	6	...	6
	AK	B_2	56	5	61
Bus Mordeh	AK	C_1	3	...	3
	AK	C_2	9	...	9
Totals			117	8	126

the outer one is smaller (relative to the inner) than in sheep. To be precise, she found that in *Ovis aries* and *Ovis orientalis* the outer articular surface had a diameter which varied between 62.9 and 62.2 per cent of the inner; while in *Capra hircus hircus* and *Capra hircus aegagrus* the outer surface had a diameter which varied between 55 and 60.2 per cent of the inner. Small as this distinction may seem, it has so far held up. "Clear and absolute generic distinctions are visible in these indices. Here we have a trait which is apparently not changed in the direction of the genus *Capra* among domestic sheep, a change which is found with most traits" (Gromova, 1953:78). It also works regardless of whether the metacarpal or metatarsal is involved. One possible explanation of the difference is that it gives goats a wider range of rotation at the metapodial-first phalanx joint, which they need in climbing.

Excavations at Ali Kosh and Tepe Sabz produced 386 distal metapodials of Caprines. Because many had been chipped or battered, however, only 241 could be reliably measured. Of these, 210 were in the *"Capra hircus"* range, and 17 in the *"Ovis"* range, with 14 falling in the "gap" in between (outer surface between 60.2 and 62.9 per cent of the inner). Gromova's figures for other species of *Capra* (e.g., *C. siberica)* suggest that most specimens in the "gap" are goats also.

The temporal distribution of measurable metapodials almost exactly parallels that of horn cores. Goat metapodials appeared in every cultural phase in the sequence, and constituted 100 per cent of the specimens in the Bus Mordeh phase; sheep metapodials did not appear until the Ali

Table 59

REMAINS OF CAPRINES (GOATS AND SHEEP) FROM ALI KOSH AND TEPE SABZ
(By Stratigraphic Zone)

Phase	Site	Zone	Number of Identified Fragments	Minimum Number of Individuals	Individual Fragments Recovered: Horn Cores	Skull Fragments	Petrous Bones	Maxilla	Mandible	Atlas/Axis	Scapula	Humerus	Radius	Ulna	Innominate	Femur	Patella	Tibia	Carpal	Tarsal	Calcaneum	Astragalus	Metapodial	1st Phalanx	2nd Phalanx	3rd Phalanx	Other Postcranial
Bayat	TS	A_1	16	(2)	1	...	...	...	1	...	1	1	1	...	...	...	...	1	1	...	...	1	4	1	3	...	...
	TS	A_2	30	(6)	1	...	...	1	8	1	2	7	2	1	...	...	...	1	...	...	...	3	...	3	...	...	...
	TS	A_3	62	(15)	6	2	...	1	14	2	1	1	3	1	4	2	...	2	...	1	3	3	8	7	1	...	...
Mehmeh	TS	B_1	14	(2)	1	...	...	1	2	1	...	1	...	1	...	1	...	1	1	...	...	2	1	1	...	...	...
	TS	B_2	23	(3)	2	...	...	...	...	...	...	3	1	4	2	1	...	...	...	...	2	3	2	1	1	1	...
	TS	B_3	19	(3)	1	...	...	...	1	1	...	1	1	...	...	...	...	2	1	...	...	2	3	2	2	2	...
Khazineh	TS	C_1	7	(1)	1	...	1	...	...	...	...	...	1	...	...	...	...	1	1	...	...	...	...	1	...	...	1
	TS	C_2	10	(2)	...	...	...	...	2	...	...	...	...	1	1	1	...	...	...	...	...	...	4	1	...	...	...
	TS	C_3	17	(3)	3	...	1	...	...	1	...	...	...	2	1	2	...	1	...	...	1	2	2	1	...	...	...
Sabz	TS	D	98	(7)	9	...	1	1	9	1	1	9	7	4	3	5	...	7	...	1	1	3	18	12	6	...	...
Mohammad Jaffar	AK	A_1	359	(19)	15	6	20	5	11	4	11	34	18	12	24	13	4	22	35	5	10	31	31	22	15	9	2
	AK	A_2	344	(21)	8	...	17	7	17	7	18	25	13	12	12	13	11	8	21	2	11	39	36	34	20	11	2
Ali Kosh	AK	B_1	355	(17)	6	3	6	6	27	4	20	36	22	12	19	12	3	24	14	5	10	27	31	28	15	3	2
	AK	B_2	2333	(85)	61	47	58	20	48	93	71	170	167	67	102	156	21	119	186	65	83	113	260	172	154	95	5
Bus Mordeh	AK	C_1	879	(32)	3	7	29	7	19	18	15	42	41	23	22	26	6	35	85	34	27	59	138	105	73	61	4
	AK	C_2	455	(17)	9	6	14	4	7	3	12	23	22	15	10	16	5	28	30	12	21	33	54	64	41	21	5
Totals			5001	(235)	127	71	147	53	166	136	152	353	299	155	200	248	50	252	375	125	169	321	592	455	331	203	21

Kosh phase. Our large metapodial sample, however, shows sheep increasing with time. In the Ali Kosh phase they were only 1 to 17 per cent of the Caprines, but by the later part of the Mohammad Jaffar phase they had increased to 40 per cent. Throughout the sequence at Tepe Sabz, where our sample is smaller, sheep fluctuated from zone to zone; but from the early Khazineh phase on, they constituted about 50 per cent of the Caprines (see Figs. 114, 115).

The Third Phalanx.—Another character worked out by Gromova and tested extensively by Perkins is the profile of the plantar surface of the third phalanx (Gromova, 1953:Fig. 28; Perkins, personal communication). In goats, this under surface appears as a tall but rather straight-sided triangle, while in sheep it is more "slipper-shaped," with concave sides (Fig. 113). This may be functionally related to the goat's ability to spread its hooves apart and grip, while climbing over rough terrain with few footholds.

This is a qualitative character which is a bit more difficult to apply than the metapodial ratio. Our sequence produced 117 third phalanges (mostly from the early phases) which were sufficiently undamaged to evaluate. Only 5 of these had the "slipper shape" of Gromova's *Ovis* specimens, and these occurred in the Ali Kosh, Mohammad Jaffar, and Mehmeh phases. All 50 of the intact third phalanges from the Bus Mordeh phase had the shape Gromova assigned to Capra. Thus the phalanx data more or less parallels that of the horn cores and metapodials.

Other Criteria.—Several other criteria are occasionally used for distinguishing the postcranial bones of sheep and goat, but we felt uncomfortable about using them.[1] Some, like the different contour of the proximal first phalanx (where it fits against the distal metapodial) may be reliable, but we did not trust our own ability to detect the subtle difference involved. Rather than make subjective decisions, we decided to rely on the horn cores, metapodials, and third phalanges described above, all three of which seemed to tell us the same story: mainly goats in the Bus Mordeh phase, more sheep added in Ali Kosh and Mohammad Jaffar times, and an average of 50 per cent goats and 50 per cent sheep in the upper levels at Tepe Sabz.

Evidence of Domestication

Goats.—Conclusions about goat domestication at Ali Kosh and Tepe Sabz depended to a large extent on the shape of the horn core. In the male wild goat of Iran, *Capra hircus aegagrus,* the horn is scimitar-shaped, often with a sharp keel on the anterior surface, and a basal cross-section which is usually "irregularly quadrangular" or doubly convex (Reed, 1960:130; Braidwood, Howe, *et al.* 1960:Plate 29). We say "usually" because the final word has not been said yet about the range of variability in wild goat horn cores; we have seen wild goats from the Jebel Hamrin whose cross-section was more lens-shaped than quadrangular. The essential point is that, even a third of the way up from the base, the medial surface of the horn core is convex, and although the horn may curve gently to the outside it is in no way twisted like a corkscrew. Near the tip, the medial surface of the core begins to flatten as it diminishes in size.

Early villages in the Near East frequently contain goats whose horn cores (one-third of the way up from the base) are

[1]See, for example, the other criteria used by Gromova (1953) and Boessneck, Müller, and Teichert (1964). These seem to work on European Neolithic breeds, but we have not yet had time to check them adequately on Near Eastern material. Recently, Dexter Perkins and Barbara Lawrence have reported (personal communication) that it appears that many of them will, indeed, work for the Near Eastern races.

Phase	Site	Zone	DISTAL ARTICULAR SURFACE OF METAPODIAL: m = less than 63 % n (GOAT)	DISTAL ARTICULAR SURFACE OF METAPODIAL: m = more than 63% n (SHEEP)	THIRD PHALANX: Plantar surface elongated triangle (GOAT)	THIRD PHALANX: Plantar surface slipper-shaped (SHEEP)
			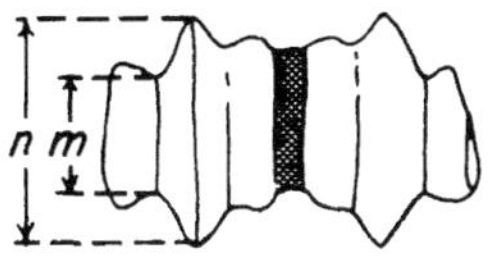	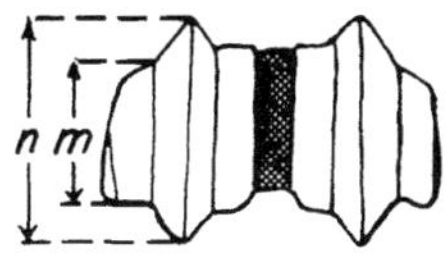		
BAYAT	TS	A_1		2		
BAYAT	TS	A_2				
BAYAT	TS	A_3	1	1		
MEHMEH	TS	B_1				
MEHMEH	TS	B_2	1		1	
MEHMEH	TS	B_3	2	1		2
KHAZINEH	TS	C_1				
KHAZINEH	TS	C_2	1	1		
KHAZINEH	TS	C_3	1	1		
SABZ	TS	D	6	1		
MOHAMMAD JAFFAR	AK	A_1	9	6	5	1
MOHAMMAD JAFFAR	AK	A_2	9	1	2	
ALI KOSH	AK	B_1	10	2	2	
ALI KOSH	AK	B_2	117	1	52	2
BUS MORDEH	AK	C_1	47		38	
BUS MORDEH	AK	C_2	19		12	

Fig. 113. Statistics on distal metapodials and third phalanges of Caprines (goats and sheep) from Tepe Ali Kosh and Tepe Sabz. Diagnostic characters of each bone according to Gromova (1953) and Boessneck, Müller, and Teichert (1964) are given at the top of the diagram. Specimens are listed by stratigraphic zone and cultural phase. (See also Fig. 114 and text.)

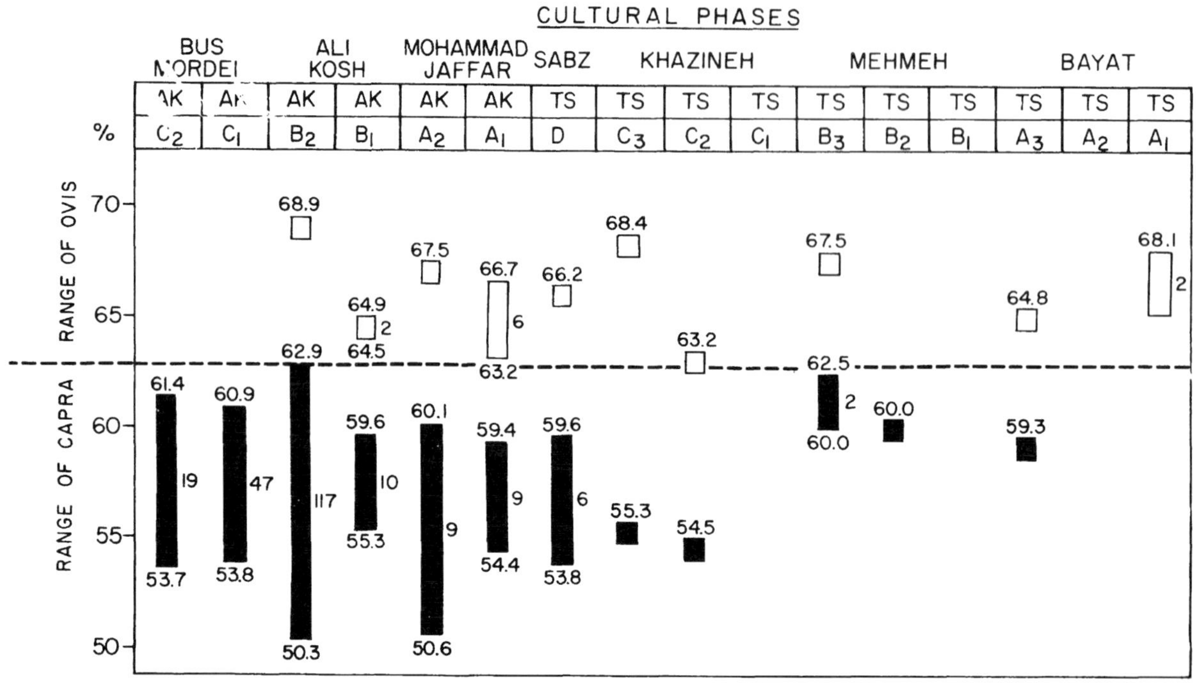

Fig. 114. Statistics on distal metapodials of Caprines (goats and sheep) at Tepe Ali Kosh and Tepe Sabz. Following Gromova (1953), the diameters of the lateral condyle (*m*) and the medial condyle (*n*) were taken and *m*/*n* expressed as a percentage (see Fig. 115 and text). Where *m* was less than 63 percent *n*, the metapodial was diagnosed as goat (*Capra*); where *m* was more than 63 percent *n*, it was diagnosed as sheep (*Ovis*). The horizontal dashed line indicates Gromova's dividing line between the two genera. Black bars indicate goat metapodials; white bars those of sheep. Number to the right of each bar indicates size of sample; numbers at the ends of each bar indicate extremes of *m*/*n* in each sample, expressed as a percentage. Where only one number is given, only one measurable metapodial was present. Samples are listed by stratigraphic zone and cultural phase. Note relative increase in sheep through time.

almond-shaped or lozenge-shaped in cross-section, presumably from genetic changes that followed domestication. This change in shape is apparently caused by a flattening of the medial surface, for in the next "stage" of domestication occur horn cores which are truly plano-convex (Reed, *loc. cit;* Braidwood, Howe, *et al.* 1960:Plate 29*c*,*d*). Still later, the horn begins to exhibit the helical or "corkscrew" twist characteristic of modern domestic goats; the right horn (seen from above) twists counter-clockwise, the left horn clockwise. Such horn cores may have a medial surface which is not merely flattened, but even concave.

Fig. 115 shows the distribution of goat horn cores with all these characteristics at Ali Kosh and Tepe Sabz, and typical examples are illustrated in Figs. 116 to 118. We recovered a total of 117 horn cores or fragments from both sites, but only 52 were sufficiently well-preserved and fully-grown to evaluate. The "wild" quadrilateral or *"aegagrus"* cross-section appeared only in the Bus Mordeh, Ali Kosh, and Mohammad Jaffar phases. In those same levels appeared slightly lozenge-shaped or almond-shaped examples, like those from Jarmo which Reed calls "presumably domestic" (Braidwood, Howe, *et al.*, 1960:Plate 29, caption). Most of these are present in the Ali Kosh phase. Are they early domesticates, or within the range of variation for wild *Capra hircus ageagrus?* Their distribution in time closely parallels

TYPE OF HORN CORE

Phase	Site	Zone	Cross-section quadrilateral 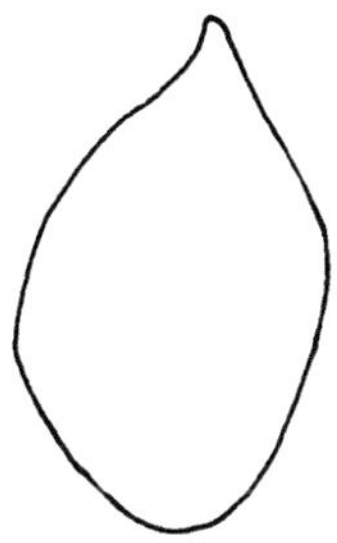	Cross-section lozenge-shaped 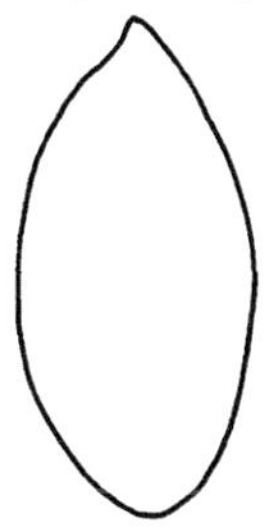	Medially flat, but untwisted 	Medially concave, helical twist 	Too young or too broken to diagnose
BAYAT	TS	A_1				1	
	TS	A_2				1	
	TS	A_3			1	3	1
MEHMEH	TS	B_1			1		
	TS	B_2				1	1
	TS	B_3					1
KHAZINEH	TS	C_1					1
	TS	C_2					
	TS	C_3					3
SABZ	TS	D			2	1	6
MOHAMMAD JAFFAR	AK	A_1	4	1		1	7
	AK	A_2					8
ALI KOSH	AK	B_1		1	2		3
	AK	B_2	11	7	8		27
BUS MORDEH	AK	C_1	2?	2			
	AK	C_2		2			7

Fig. 115. Statistics on goat horn cores from Tepe Ali Kosh and Tepe Sabz. Cores are classified by type of cross-section, and listed by stratigraphic zone and cultural phase. All drawings show medial surface to the right.

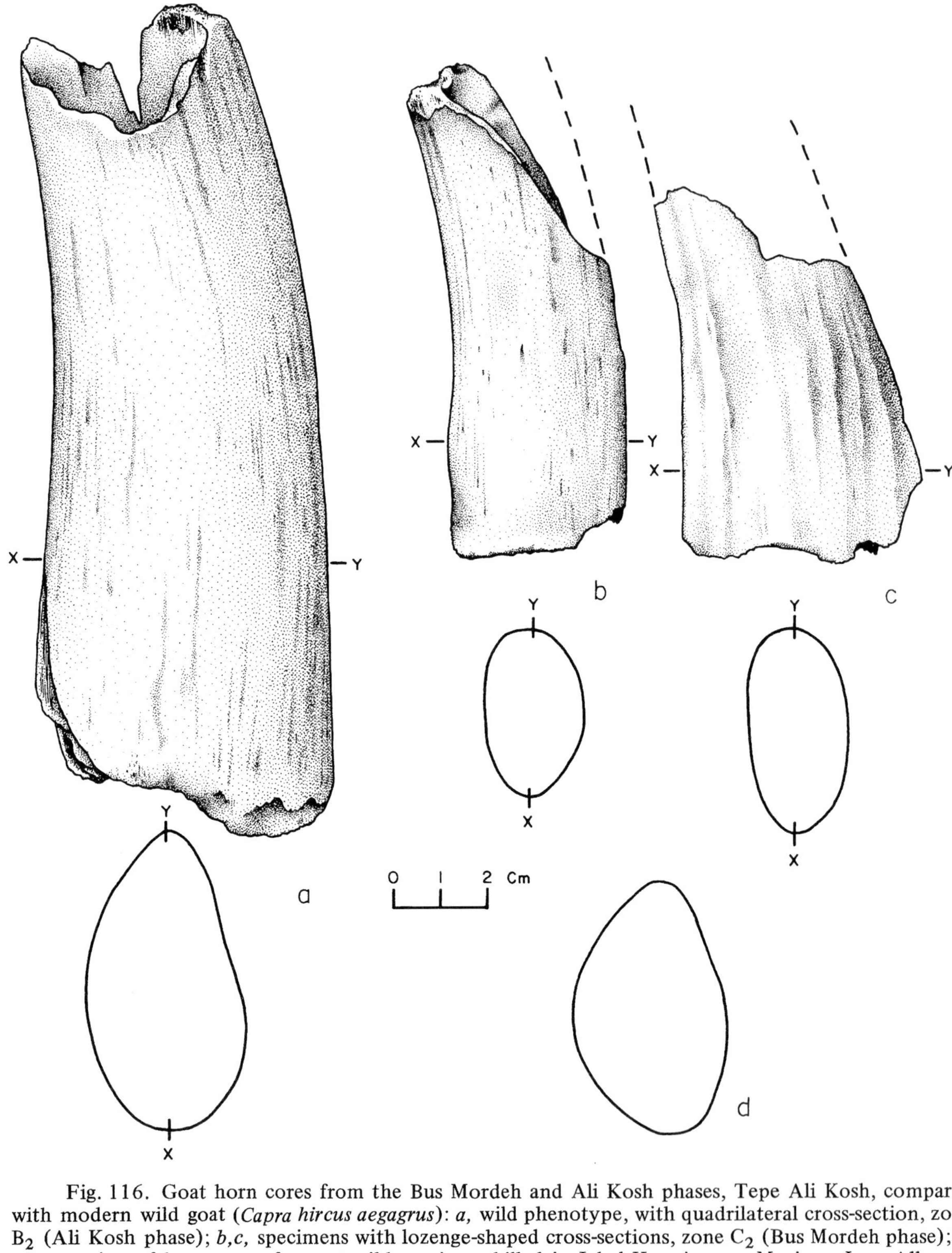

Fig. 116. Goat horn cores from the Bus Mordeh and Ali Kosh phases, Tepe Ali Kosh, compared with modern wild goat (*Capra hircus aegagrus*): *a,* wild phenotype, with quadrilateral cross-section, zone B_2 (Ali Kosh phase); *b,c,* specimens with lozenge-shaped cross-sections, zone C_2 (Bus Mordeh phase); *d,* cross-section of horn core of recent wild specimen killed in Jebel Hamrin near Musiyan, Iran. All cores drawn as if from the right side, to facilitate comparison. All cross-sections have medial surface to the right.

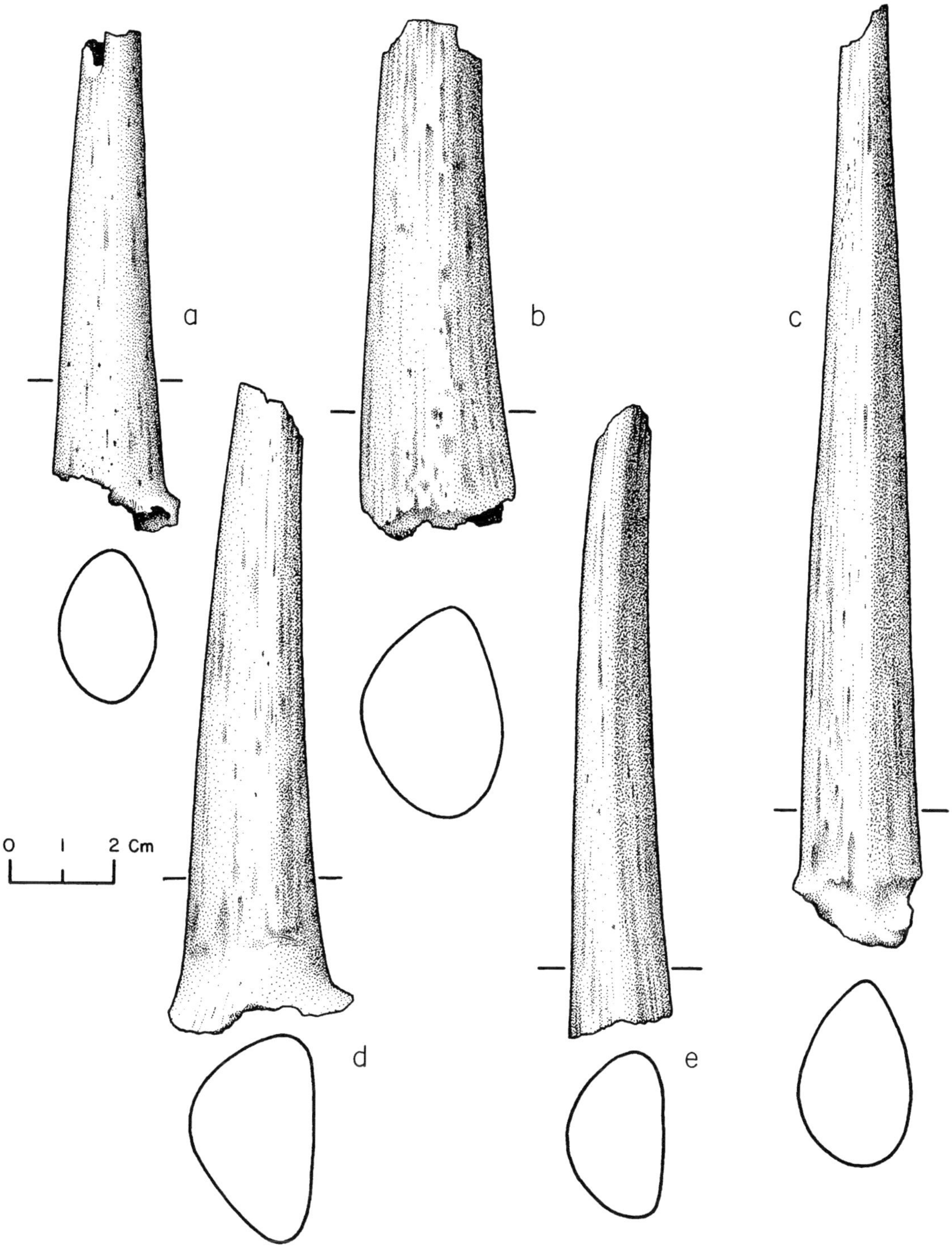

Fig. 117. Goat horn cores from Tepe Ali Kosh: *a,c,* specimens with lozenge-shaped cross-section; *b,* wild phenotype, with quadrilateral cross-section; *d,e,* primitive domestic specimens with medially-flattened cross-section (*a,* zone C_1, Bus Mordeh phase; *b,d,e,* zone B_2, Ali Kosh phase; *c,* zone A_1, Mohammad Jaffar phase). All cores drawn with anterior surface facing reader, to facilitate comparison. All cross-sections have medial surface to the right.

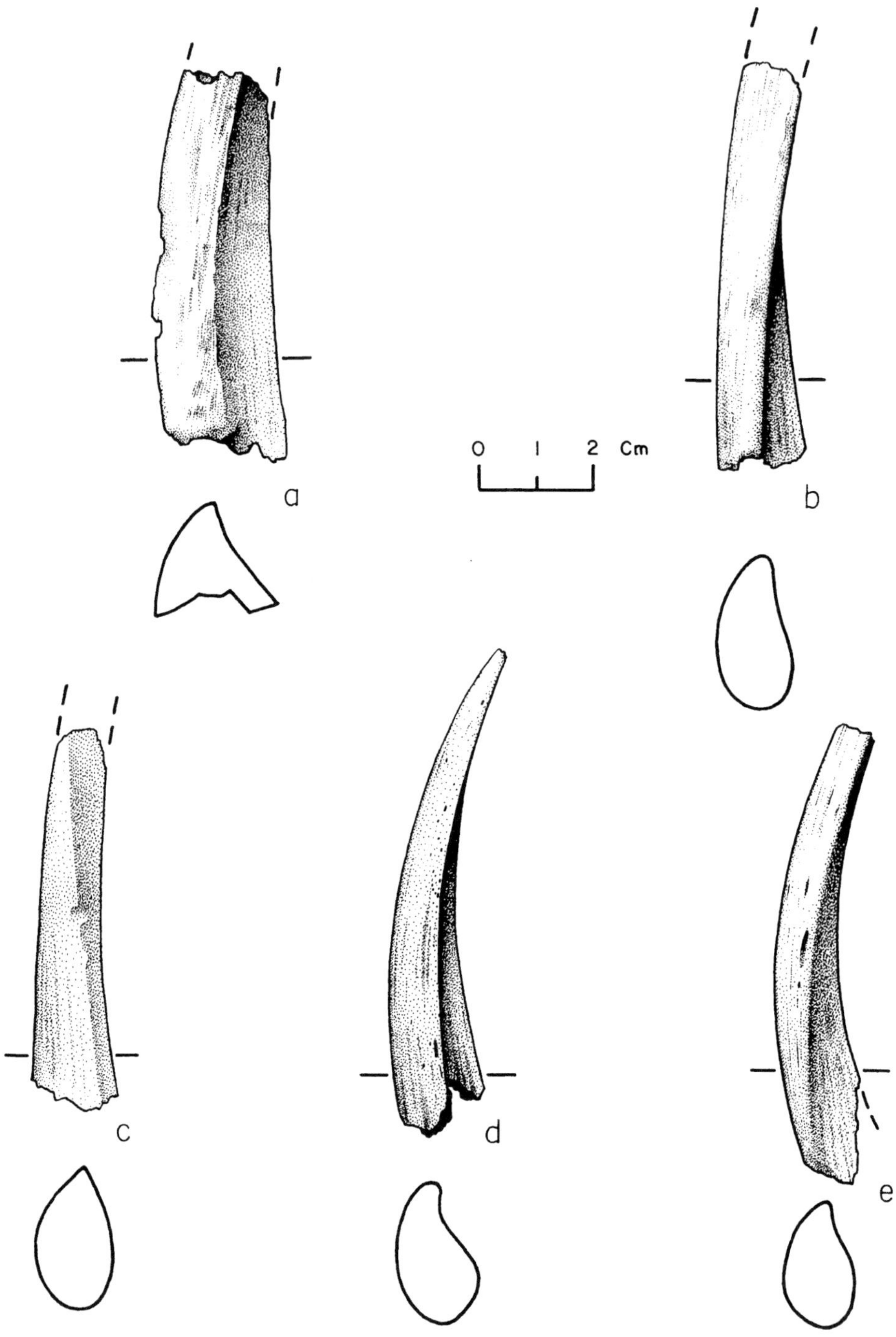

Fig. 118. Domestic goat horn cores from Tepe Ali Kosh and Tepe Sabz. All specimens shown have concave medial surface and helical twist. All are drawn with the anterior surface facing the reader, to facilitate comparison, and all cross-sections have the medial surface to the right: *a,* primitive helically-twisted specimen, found in ash-filled borrow pit in square 98, zone A_1 at Tepe Ali Kosh (Mohammad Jaffar phase); *b,* Tepe Sabz, zone D (Sabz phase); *c,* Tepe Sabz, zone B_2 (Mehmeh phase); *d,e,* Bayat phase specimens, Tepe Sabz.

that of the "quadrilateral" horn cores, but they clearly differ from what Reed calls the "typical" *aegagrus* horn core cross-section.

Quadrilateral and lozenge-shaped horn cores were the only kind discovered in Bus Mordeh phase levels (Fig. 115). Those goats, in other words, showed little if any deviation from the wild phenotype. On the basis of horn cores alone, one could only say that the evidence was "suggestive" of domestication. Other lines of evidence, however, contribute further evidence that the Bus Mordeh goats were in fact domestic. First, given the environmental situation of the broad, flat Deh Luran plain, it is extremely unlikely that goats would constitute 73 per cent of the hoofed-mammal remains (which they do in the Bus Mordeh phase) if they were obtained only by hunting. Second, it is extremely unlikely that so many immature goats would have been eaten unless domestication was in effect. Less than a third of the Bus Mordeh phase goats ever reached maturity (see pp. 281-286).

Clearly and unquestionably medially-flattened horn cores made their first appearance in the Ali Kosh phase. These cores, whose cross-section is truly plano-convex rather than almond-shaped, were most abundant in that period, but lasted into the early Bayat phase in some cases. Although medially flat, they showed no trace of a helical twist (Fig. 117*d,e*). They resemble the early domestic horn cores which typified the Jarmo goats (Reed, 1960:131). We note that in our sample from the Ali Kosh phase, medially flat and lozenge-shaped cores outnumbered quadrilateral ones by nearly 2 to 1.

The first helically-twisted horn core appeared in the Mohammad Jaffar phase. It was found in an ashy borrow pit in zone A_1 at Ali Kosh, in association with T-shaped "stalk figurines," Jaffar Plain and Khazineh Red pottery, and typical bullet-shaped flint blade cores of that phase. The horn is not as extremely twisted as are those of modern domestic goats (see Fig. 118*a*), but rather, like some of the goat horns from Jarmo, shows "some tendency towards twisting" (Reed, 1960:131).

Ali Kosh, like Jarmo, shows not only clear evidence of domestic goat but also "the simultaneous presence of numerous transitional stages between the wild-type morphology and that of later times" (Reed, *op. cit.*). In addition, its oldest phase, the Bus Mordeh, reaches back into a period when morphological differences from the wild type are barely (if at all) detectable, and other lines of evidence must be called into play to demonstrate domestication. The clear stratigraphy at Ali Kosh makes it possible to see the order and timing of each successive morphological change: lozenge-shaped cores, then plano-convex cores, then helically-twisted ones. It would be interesting to know whether the same sequence pertained at Jarmo, with helically-twisted horn cores restricted to the levels with pottery, but almond-shaped cross-sections appearing already in preceramic levels.

The "corkscrew" horn core increased with time, to become the typical horn core of the Bayat phase by a ratio of 5 to 1. From the Mehmeh phase onward, these cores are indistinguishable from those of modern domestic goats in Khuzistan. Their medial surface is virtually concave, the horn small and highly twisted (Fig. 118*b-e*). By the time of the Bayat phase, screwhorn goats were widespread throughout the Near East.

Why did their horns become flattened and twisted? No answer is yet forthcoming. Reed points out that the numerous transitional stages involved imply that "flattening" and "twisting" are mutually independent characters, each of which is probably controlled by numerous genes, and he suggests that neither was consciously selected for by the early herders (Reed, 1960, 131-32). Is it not possible, however, that these characters are somehow genetically linked to other attributes which were selected for? Was it purely by chance that the screwhorn goat arose, or were his horns a byproduct of selection for a longer coat of hair, increased fertility, milk production on a scale useful for man, or some factor increasing survival? We may never know.

Sheep.—Little has been published about osteological characters useful for distinguishing wild and early domestic sheep in the Near East. As in goats, most discussion has centered around the horn core.

The horns of wild *Ovis orientalis* sweep back and to the side in an incomplete circle, with the tip of the horn resting at the animal's withers (not at his cheek, as in the Bighorn sheep of America). Zeuner comments that "a fairly general difference between large domesticated and wild horns is that the latter rise much more steeply. One might say that domestication has caused a weakening of the horn base so that it tends to drop away to the side, instead of rising steeply. . . . Since it is a universal rule in the males that very strong horns develop an outer frontal angle in addition to the inner which is always present, weakening of the horns implies a flattening of the curvature corresponding to the outer frontal angle. In other words, weak horns tend to resemble those of goats, in which the inner frontal angle only is developed" (Zeuner, 1963:166). Female *Ovis orientalis* horns are much smaller, and in some domestic breeds females have no horns at all. This is the case in Iran today.

In the Ali Kosh phase appear sheep horn cores indistinguishable from those of wild *Ovis orientalis* at Tepe Guran and in the collections of the U. S. National Museum (see Fig. 121*a*). The male horn leaves the frontal bone at a 45° angle from the long axis of the skull, and its cross-section (near the base) has strongly developed inner and outer angles. Even half-way to the tip, these angles are maintained. Consequently, the cross-section is like an irregular, inverted almond, with its sharp point downward, and its upper surface rounded, bulging to the outside.

However, in the Mohammad Jaffar phase appears a type of sheep horn core which has the weakened, "goat-like" cross-section described by Zeuner. A clearly male horn core from zone A_1 at Ali Kosh (Fig. 121*b*) has only the inner angle (or front edge) of the horn developed. This upper surface has a knife-edge, with the lower surface rounded—the cross-section literally appears to be the reverse of that seen in the wild sheep, for now the sharp point of the "almond" points *upward.*

The Hornless Female Sheep, Bus Mordeh Phase

On the floor of one of the Bus Mordeh phase houses, resting literally just above sterile soil at a depth of 730 to 750 cm., appeared the badly crushed and twisted skull of a small Bovid. Included were parts of both frontal bones, the occipital, both parietals (squamosals), and the rim of the orbit. Although from an adult, the skull is hornless; only two small vestigial nodes appear on the upper part of the frontal where the horns should have been (Fig. 119).

At first we regarded this skull with great apprehension. It appeared to be that of a Caprine, but Ellerman and Morrison-Scott (1966:389) also point out that the Persian gazelle (*G. subgutturosa*) is characterized by hornless females.[2] After the specimen had been carefully cleaned, however, it became clear that it was not a gazelle. Where the sagittal suture meets the anterior edge of the occipital, the juncture has the shape of a "Y," a feature which is diagnostic of

[2]For example, female gazelles at Deh Luran are hornless (see Plate 3*a*).

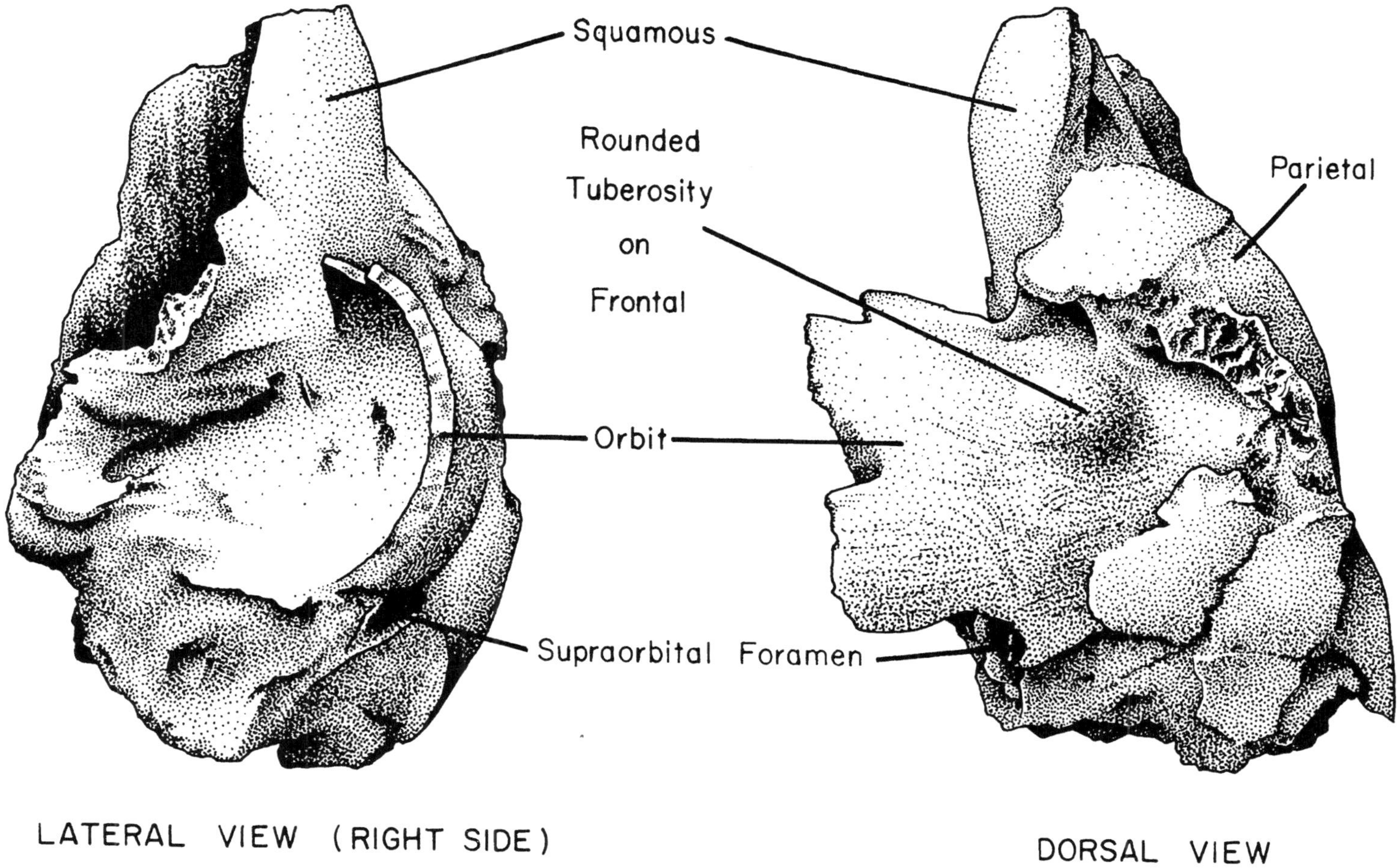

Fig. 119. Badly crushed skull of hornless sheep from zone C_2 at Tepe Ali Kosh (Bus Mordeh phase), with major landmarks indicated. Rounded tuberosity on frontal indicates where horn would appear in a normal wild specimen.

sheep; in goats, this juncture is "T"-shaped (Boessneck, Müller, and Tiechert, 1964: Figure 7).

Prior to this, the oldest known hornless sheep were from the Neolithic of Hungary (Bökönyi, 1964:Figs 1 and 2). In November of 1966, Dr. Sándor Bökönyi of the Hungarian National Museum was able to examine our specimen and pronounced it unquestionably a female hornless sheep, with many resemblances to European Neolithic examples he had studied. Bökönyi's identification, in view of his considerable experience with early Neolithic faunal remains, finally overcame our apprehension.

Hornless wild sheep are unknown from the Zagros area. This small, crushed skull from the Bus Mordeh phase presently stands as the oldest osteological evidence for animal domestication in the world. Its date must lie between 7900 and 7000 B.C.

The appearance of hornless domestic sheep before 7000 B.C. lends support to Dexter Perkins' arguments for sheep domestication at Zawi Chemi Shanidar (Perkins, 1964). The Zawi Chemi sheep show no osteological difference from the wild form, but Perkins noted an extremely high frequency of immature animals—far higher than the expected frequency in a herd of wild sheep. Many zoologists have regarded this as inadequate evidence for domestication, since it is known that immature wild sheep (especially those under a year in age) are more susceptible to predation than sheep in the prime of life (Buechner, 1960). It is for this reason that we have presented a full "survivorship curve" for the Ali Kosh sheep and goats, rather than simply dividing them into "mature" and "immature" specimens (see below).

However, if female sheep had begun to lose their horns before 7000 B.C., presumably through genetic changes following domestication, we assume they must have been first domesticated at a still-earlier date. Zawi Chemi, with its radiocarbon date of about 8900 B.C., is not too ancient to have been one of the first sheep-herding sites.

The problem is not a simple one. Despite our evidence for hornless sheep, remains of *Ovis* are extremely rare in the Bus Mordeh phase; goats probably outnumbered them by more than 10 to 1. And even as late as the Ali Kosh phase, male sheep still had the wild-type horn core; it was not until Mohammad Jaffar times that male sheep began to exhibit the horn core typical of domestic (*Ovis aries*) breeds.

Table 60

DISTRIBUTION OF SHEEP HORN CORES WITHIN THE SEQUENCE FROM ALI KOSH AND TEPE SABZ

Phase	*Orientalis* Type	*Aries* Type	Fragment of Hornless Skull	Too Broken to Diagnose
Bayat	...	1	...	...
Mehmeh	...	...	...	...
Khazineh	...	...	...	...
Sabz	...	...	...	...
Mohammad Jaffar	...	1	...	1
Ali Kosh	3	...	...	2
Bus Mordeh	...	...	1	...
Total	3	2	1	3

However, sheep increased steadily with time, constituting half the domestic Caprines in the upper levels at Tepe Sabz.

The identification of hornless sheep in Bus Mordeh phase levels clears up one other problem which troubled us as we analyzed the fauna from Tepe Sabz. It was clear from our examination of metapodials and phalanges that sheep and goats were present in about equal numbers, yet there were far fewer sheep horn cores than goat horn cores. This difference between the "observed" and "expected" proportions of horn cores becomes understandable now that we know that only male sheep had horns, while both male and female goats were horned.

In 1959, Reed pointed out that whereas we do have definite evidence for many domestic goats prior to 6500 B.C., the records for sheep are extremely meager for the succeeding 2000 years, "if all unverified claims are discounted" (Reed, 1959:1634). Our find of a hornless sheep in the Bus Mordeh phase suggests that one reason domestic sheep have so rarely been identified from early village sites is because of a lack of horn core material. When Caprine skulls are hornless, they are much more easily crushed into unidentifiable fragments by the weight of the overlying earth. It may be for that reason that no domestic sheep were identified from Banahilk (Reed, 1960:135-36) or Tepe Guran (Flannery, unpublished data). Sándor Bökönyi (personal communication) has recently identified numerous hornless sheep from Tepe Sarab, however, and awareness of the possibility of such specimens in the future may help fill out the picture of early sheep domestication considerably.

Summary

In the Deh Luran plain, hornless domestic sheep were present in very small numbers as early as the Bus Mordeh phase; presumably, these were females. Sheep increased through time, and by the Mohammad Jaffar phase, males had begun to show evidence of the domestic-type horn core. By the end of the occupation of Tepe Sabz (Bayat phase, *ca.* 3800 B.C.), sheep were as numerous as (or more numerous than) goats, and still increasing. Two thousand years after the abandonment of Tepe Sabz, the most numerous category of livestock in Khuzistan seems to have been sheep, some of which were fed on barley (Adams, 1962:115). Over the long run of prehistory, therefore, sheep proved to be better adapted to the lowland steppe than goats—possibly because of a panting mechanism which enables them to survive the high summer temperatures better (Schmidt-Nielsen, 1964:99).

The Ages of the Caprines at Ali Kosh

Reed (1963:211) has suggested that "where the yield of bones from a site has been large, detailed study may yield evidence not only on the kind of animals present but also on the relative numbers of each, and the ages represented. . . . For each kind of domestic animal, what proportions were killed at what ages? (That is, what was the population structure of the herd?) Was the age at death the same for both sexes or was one sex preserved preferentially?" He further suggests that such studies be based on the rate of fusion of the epiphyses of the animals involved, as well as their rate of tooth eruption and wear.

An example of such a study is the work of Ewbank, Phillipson, Whitehouse, and Higgs (1964), who studied sheep mandibles from an Iron Age site in England. The authors were able to place 181 mandibles into a series of 26 "steps" or stages of maturity from 3 months of age to 2 years.

Our sample of mandibles of goat and sheep from Ali Kosh was too small and too fragmentary for such a study. Since our

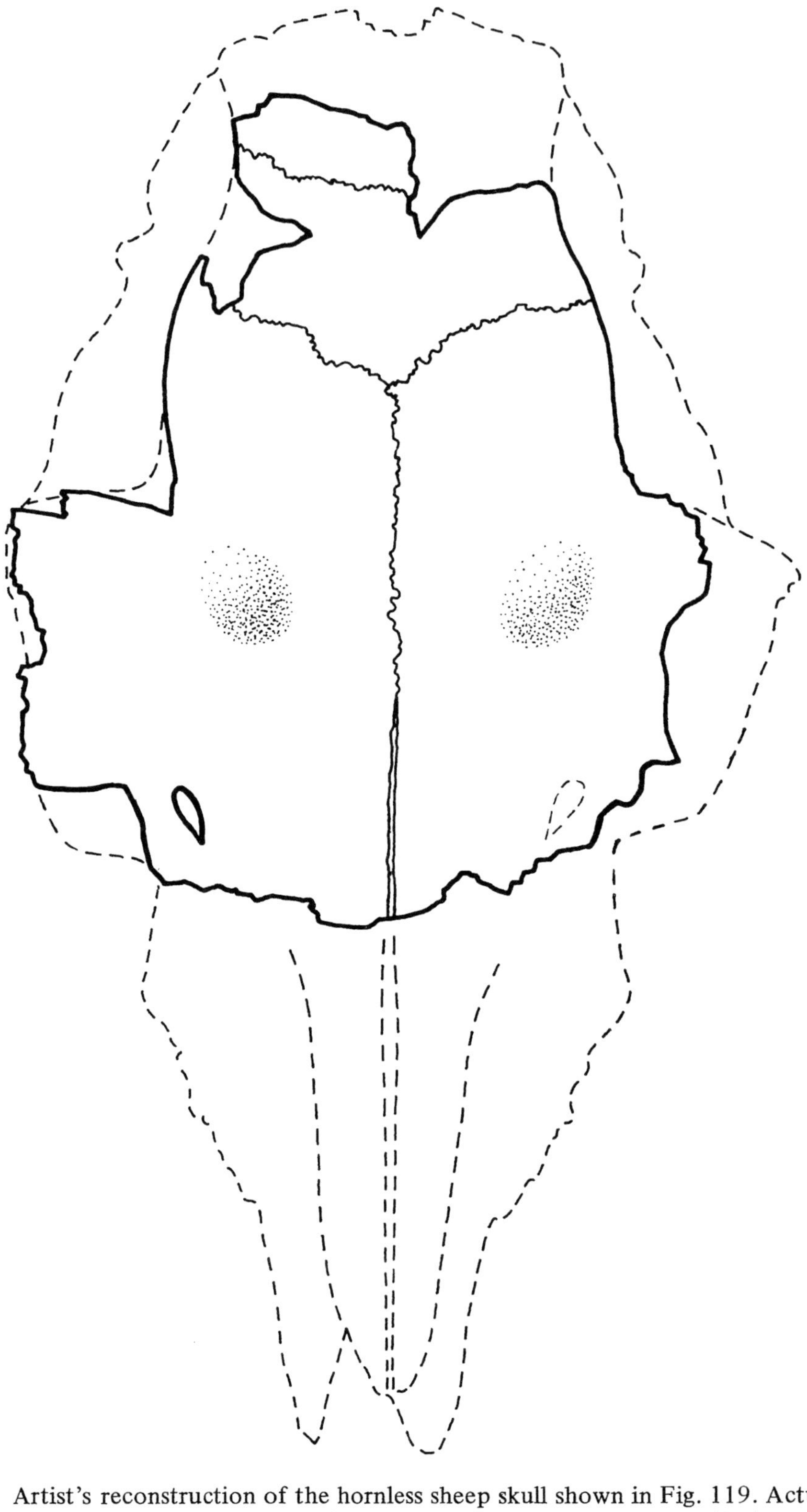

Fig. 120. Artist's reconstruction of the hornless sheep skull shown in Fig. 119. Actual specimen as it would have looked in life (heavy solid line) has been superimposed on the skull of a modern domestic sheep (dashed line).

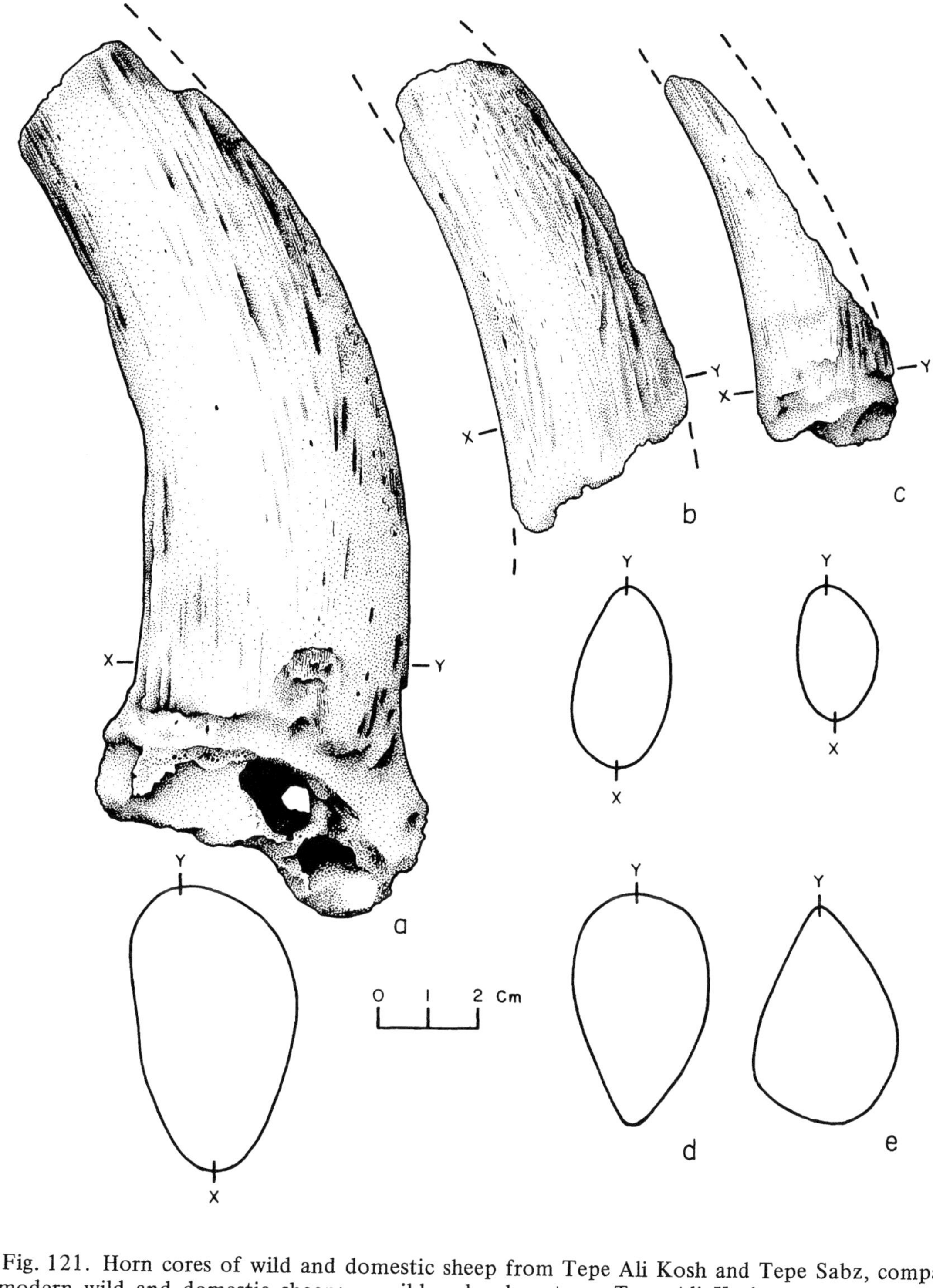

Fig. 121. Horn cores of wild and domestic sheep from Tepe Ali Kosh and Tepe Sabz, compared with modern wild and domestic sheep: *a,* wild male phenotype, Tepe Ali Kosh, zone B_2 (Ali Kosh phase); *b,* early domestic specimen, Tepe Ali Kosh, zone A_1 (Mohammad Jaffar phase); *c,* later domestic specimen, Tepe Sabz, zone A_3 (Bayat phase); *d,* cross-section of horn core of modern wild *Ovis orientalis* from Iran, male, U.S. National Museum specimen no. 32710; *e,* cross-section of horn core of modern domestic ram, Khorramabad, Iran. All specimens shown as if from the right side, to facilitate comparison. All cross-sections have the medial surface to the right.

sample of limb bones numbered in the thousands, however, we have attempted to determine the age at which goats and sheep were usually killed, based on fusion of epiphyses. Not all articular ends were complete enough that we could determine whether they were fused or not; but large samples were available from the Bus Mordeh, Ali Kosh, and Mohammad Jaffar phases.

There are a number of pitfalls in the aging of early domestic animals. As pointed out by Silver (1963:264), "sheep vary widely in the age at which they reach maturity, the so-called improved breeds maturing much earlier than hill breeds. Figures published by authors in the late eighteenth and early nineteenth centuries suggest that at that time sheep were regarded as having similar tooth eruption dates to cattle, but modern authorities, referring to modern breeds of sheep, give eruption dates which are considerably younger." One aspect of domestication is that it has greatly accelerated the growth cycle in some animals.

A number of authors have given dates of fusion for the epiphyses of sheep and/or goats. The most recent studies, like those of Smith (1956) have relied on X-rays taken at regular intervals on modern domesticates. Although done with the latest techniques and equipment, these researches have often been avoided by faunal analysts on two grounds: (1) modern breeds may have a more rapid rate of fusion than wild sheep and early prehistoric domestic sheep, and (2) X-rays would tend to show the bone as "fused" as soon as no light could be detected between the shaft and the epiphysis, when in reality it might not be fully fused until months later. For the prehistoric analyst, the question is: at what point is the epiphysis so solidly fused that it will not separate in the ground even after the cartilage has rotted away? And at what point will even the line of fusion have disappeared?

As Table 61 will indicate, the youngest dates for fusion are given by authors dealing with modern breeds; figures compiled by Silver (1963) on semi-wild European hill sheep of the late eighteenth century are the oldest. In our reconstruction of the herds at Ali Kosh, we have followed the figures for semi-wild rather than modern breeds.[3] We can only hope that those figures hold for Caprines in general, for we have no fusion dates for goats.

Table 62 gives the raw data on epiphysis fusion for Ali Kosh and Tepe Sabz by cultural phase. We have divided the bones into five groups, numbered A through E, according to the nearest half-year at which the epiphysis fuses.

Bones of Group A (proximal radius, distal humerus, tubercle of the scapula, and the main bones of the innominate) all fuse within the first year of life. Bones of Group B (the first and second phalanges), fuse between one year and a year-and-a-half. Group C (the distal tibia) fuses at about two years. Group D (the distal metapodials) fuses at a point between two and two-and-a-half years. Bones of Group E (the proximal and distal femur, distal radius, and proximal tibia) are all fused by approximately three years of age. For each cultural phase, we calculated the percentage of fused *vs.* unfused epiphyses in each of the five groups. On the basis of these percentages, we have constructed "survivorship curves" for each phase (Fig. 122).

Bus Mordeh Phase

Of the bones fusing within the first year (Group A), 68 per cent showed fusion. Of

[3]Silver's figures give substantially later fusion dates for all bones than do Smith (1965) or Todd and Todd (1938) as will be seen in Table 61. For this reason they are by no means universally accepted. As we learn more about rates of fusion it may be necessary to revise our figures, which can be easily done from the raw data on fusion presented in the present work. All that can be said at the moment is that, if a case for domestication can be made using Silver's more conservative figures, then the case will be stronger should Smith's fusion dates prove to be applicable.

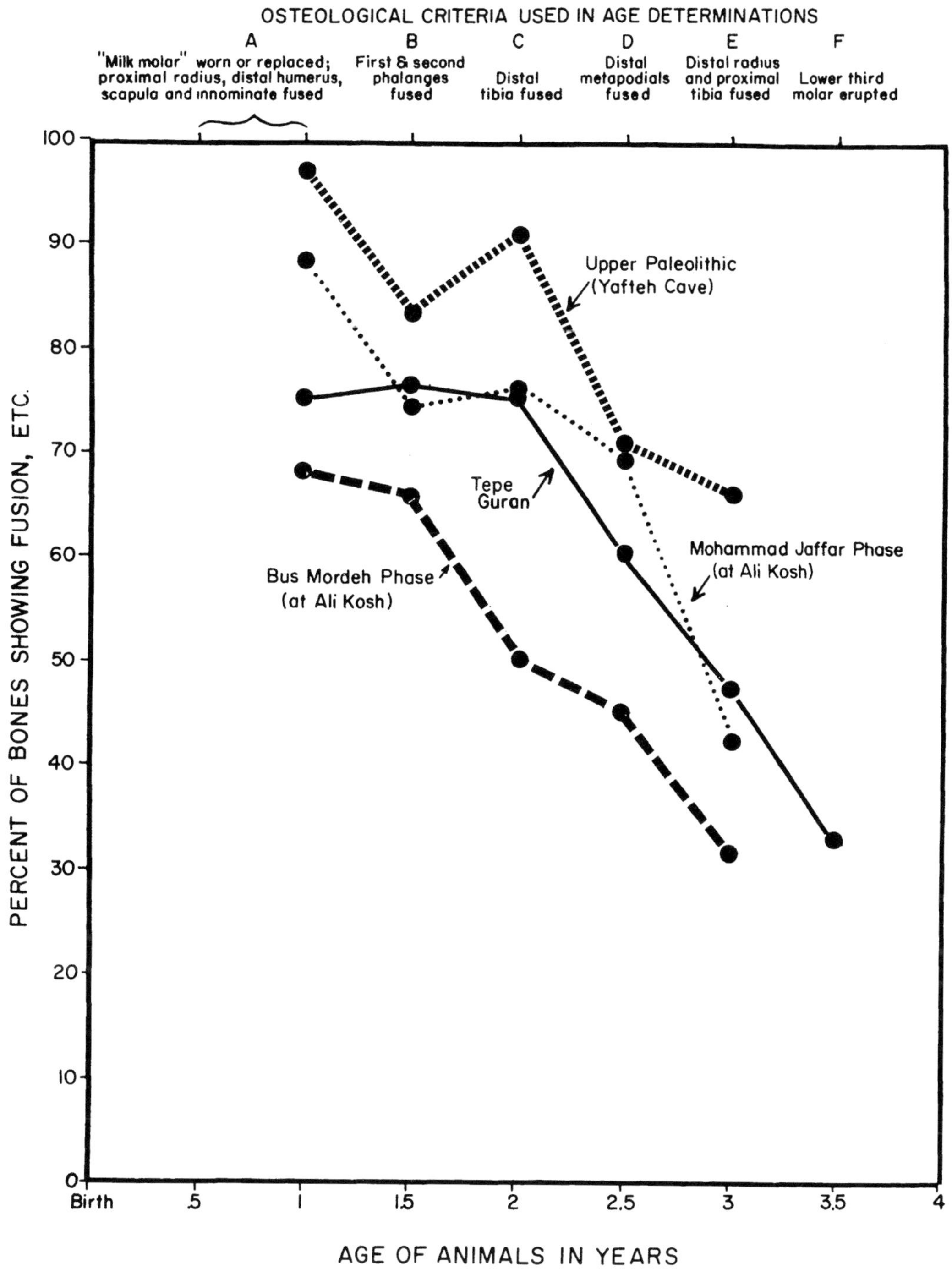

Fig. 122. "Survivorship curves" for wild and domestic populations of Caprines from archeological sites in Iran. Criteria for ageing included fusion of the epiphyses of the limb bones, and eruption of molar teeth. Raw data are given in Table 62 (see text). Ages at fusion follow figures given by Silver (1963) for semi-wild hill sheep. Sites represented include Yafteh Cave, Upper Paleolithic (wild goats and sheep); Tepe Guran, ca. 5800 to 6500 B.C. (domestic goats); and Bus Mordeh phase and Mohammad Jaffar phase samples from Tepe Ali Kosh (domestic goats and sheep).

those fusing about the first year-and-a-half (Group B), 66 per cent were fused. We conclude that about two-thirds of each generation of Caprines reached the age of a year-and-a-half without having been eaten.

Thereafter, the percentage dropped rapidly. Only half the Caprines survived until the end of their second year (Group C), and only 45 per cent were still uneaten at the age of two-and-a-half years (Group D). By the time of fusion of the distal radius, proximal tibia, and both ends of the femur (*ca.* 3 years), only 32 per cent of the animals were still uneaten. Less than a third, in other words, had any chance of reaching full maturity.

Ali Kosh Phase

Life expectancy was greater in the Ali Kosh phase. About 91 per cent of the Caprines reached one year of age without having been eaten, and three-quarters survived to a year-and-a-half. At the end of the second year, two-thirds were still alive. Some 42 per cent reached three or three-and-a-half years of age. This increase in longevity between the Bus Mordeh and Ali Kosh phases is clearly shown on the graph (Fig. 122).

Mohammad Jaffar Phase

Statistics for the Mohammad Jaffar phase were very similar to those of the Ali Kosh phase. Of the bones fusing within one year, about 88 per cent show fusion. At the one-and-a-half year mark, about three-quarters of the Caprines were still alive. Precisely the same number as in the Ali Kosh phase reached three years of age (42 per cent). The only difference is an increase in the numbers of Caprines which reached two or two-and-a-half years. Nearly 70 per cent of the Mohammad Jaffar phase distal metapodials showed the fusion characteristic of two-and-a-half-year-old Caprines.

Tepe Sabz

The sample of fused and unfused bones from Tepe Sabz is too small to be treated statistically with any confidence. However, aside from an improbably high frequency of fused distal tibiae (probably due to sampling error), the percentages for the site as a whole roughly follow those of the Ali Kosh and Mohammad Jaffar phases. About 90 per cent of the Caprines reached one year of age, and three-quarters survived to a year-and-a-half. About 60 per cent reached two-and-a-half years, and some 40 per cent lasted to the age of three years.

Expected Frequency for Wild Caprines

How closely do the "survivorship curves" for the goats and sheep at Ali Kosh compare with that of a wild herd? There are very few reports on wild Caprines which could serve as a basis for comparison. One of the best is Adolph Murie's study of wild sheep (*Ovis dalli*) in Alaska under conditions of predation by wolves (Murie, 1944:123).

Working with a sample of 575 sheep which had died within a circumscribed range area, Murie calculated the numbers of individuals who had died at each age interval from 1 to 14 years. Subyearling lambs were not counted, because the mortality rate was extremely erratic, and many carcasses had undoubtedly been dragged off by wolves. Buechner (1960:85), in reworking the data of Murie and others, described the life pattern in wild *Ovis* as "characterized by very high mortality among lambs, extremely low mortality in the age groups between 1 and 9 years of age and high mortality in the older age groups beyond approximately 10 years" (see Buechner, 1960: Table 22 for survivorship curve). This is because certain age groups, specifically the very young and the very old, are more vulnerable to disease and predators than animals in the prime of life.

Murie's study showed that once a wild sheep reached one year of age, his chances greatly improved. Of every 1000 sheep reaching that age, 847 would still be alive the following year; 835 would reach three years; 821 would reach four years; and so on (Buechner, *Ibid.*). This allowed us some comparison with the Caprines from Ali Kosh.

We compared the Mohammad Jaffar phase "survivorship curve" with (1) the expected curve for a wild sheep population, based on Buechner's graph of Murie's data, and (2) the curve for the Caprines at the contemporary site of Tepe Guran, Luristan (Mortensen, 1964). The percentages of fused and unfused bones from Guran were calculated by precisely the same methods used at Ali Kosh (Flannery, unpublished data).

About 88 per cent of the Mohammad Jaffar goats and sheep reached one year of age. According to Murie's figures, 84.7 per cent of those (or 75 per cent of the herd) should have reached two years of age. This is close to the actual figure (76 per cent) which did so. After this, however, the two curves diverge. At three years of age, 73 per cent of the Caprines should still have been alive, whereas only 42 per cent were. And at four years of age, there still should have been 72 per cent alive. At this point, there is no similarity between the curve for wild *Ovis* and the curve for the Mohammad Jaffar domesticates.

On the other hand, the Mohammad Jaffar curve rather closely follows that for Tepe Guran. Both plunge steeply after two years of age, a time when most wild sheep would be enjoying the prime of life. Such survivorship curves would thus seem to be typical of domestic Caprines in early sixth millenium villages, where most goats (and/ or sheep) were eaten while still less than three-and-a-half years old.

Perhaps more significant is a comparison of the age profiles of the Ali Kosh and Guran Caprines with those from the site of Yafteh Cave near Khorramabad, in Luristan. Yafteh Cave was occupied during the upper Paleolithic period known as the Baradostian (30,000 - 20,000 B.C.), and many wild goats (and a few sheep) were hunted during the occupation there. The cave was excavated by Hole (1966), and the fauna (unpublished) was analyzed by Flannery and Jane C. Wheeler. Wheeler calculated the percentages of fused to unfused epiphyses among the Yafteh Cave goats and sheep, using the same criteria Flannery had employed at Ali Kosh and Tepe Guran. The curves for all three sites are compared in Figure 122.

Note that while there is close agreement between the curves for Tepe Guran and the Mohammad Jaffar phase at Ali Kosh, the curve for Yafteh Cave is quite dissimilar. Some 97 per cent of the Yafteh Cave Caprines showed fusion of bones of Group A, those fusing at about one year. More than 300 bones of Group B (one-and-a-half years) were available for measurement, and nearly 83 per cent were fused. Ninety per cent of the Group C bones were fused, but the sample in this case was somewhat smaller.

From here on, the curves diverge more widely. About 68 per cent of the hunted Caprines from Yafteh Cave had reached two-and-a-half years of age, and more than 65 per cent were over three or three-and-a-half years old. Given all the possible sources of error in this type of calculation, it is striking that this figure is within seven percentage points of the expected frequency based on Buechner's graph of Murie's data. It is equally striking that the fusion percentage for Group E bones at Yafteh is twice the percentage in the Bus Mordeh phase.

We suggest that, where a large bone sample is present, calculation of these survivorship curves may be a useful method of comparing and contrasting Caprines at different sites. Especially in cases where there is no *osteological* evidence of domestication (e.g., medially flat horn cores), the mortality curve might be helpful. Should it differ drastically from the "expected" curve, domestication might be inferred. In the past, such inferences have involved a single bone (e.g., the distal metapodial), or a few bones at best (e.g., metapodials and phalanges). Given the highly erratic fluctuations of subyearling death rates in wild Caprine population (Buechner, *op. cit.*), single-bone age-determinations could be dangerous; since wild sheep or goats often give birth to twins, the percentage of young animals in a wild herd could be quite high during a year of unusually low lamb mortality. Buechner's figures also indicate that high frequencies of *very* young lambs may not be proof of domestication at all. A better indicator might be the strikingly small numbers of yearlings who go on to reach four years of age in a domestic herd.

Before such population curves can be a truly useful tool, we need more and better data on the rates of epiphysis fusion in wild goats and sheep, specifically on those races inhabiting the Near East. We hope we have presented our raw data on fusion in the Ali Kosh-Tepe Sabz Caprines (Table 62) in such a way that they can be reworked when more reliable figures are available. At the moment, we can only present a suggested blueprint for future studies.

Butchering Technique

The numbers of cut, sliced, split, and roasted bones of Caprines at Ali Kosh and Tepe Sabz enabled us to reconstruct the butchering process in greater detail for these animals than for any other. The bulk of our information comes from the Bus Mordeh and Ali Kosh phases.

The early villagers skinned the animal first, and evidently the last few tail vertebrae were carried away with the hide, for they were virtually never found. Then they

Table 61

RATES OF FUSION OF THE EPIPHYSES OF SHEEP LONG BONES ACCORDING TO VARIOUS AUTHORS

Skeletal Component	Time of Fusion—To Nearest Month		
	Modern Sheep Smith (1956)	Modern Sheep Todd and Todd (1938)	Semi-wild Hill Sheep Silver (1963)
Proximal radius	4	6	10
Distal humerus	4	8	10
Scapula (tubercle)	5	8	6-8
Innominate	...	...	6-10
Second phalanx	6-8	...	13-16
First phalanx	9-10	...	13-16
Distal tibia	15	12	18-24
Distal metapodial	15-16	12	18-28
Proximal femur	17-18	33	30-36
Distal femur	18-20	33	36-42
Distal radius	21	33	36
Proximal tibia	25	33	36-42

Table 62

RAW DATA ON COUNTS OF FUSED *VS.* UNFUSED EPIPHYSES AMONG THE CAPRINES FROM ALI KOSH AND TEPE SABZ

	Group A Bones Fusing Within 1 Year								Group B About 1.5 Years				Group C 2 Years		Group D 2.5 Years		Group E Fuse About 3 - 3.5 Years							
	Proximal Radius		Distal Humerus		Scapula (tuber.)		Innominate		2nd Phalanx		1st Phalanx		Distal Tibia		Distal Metapodial		Proximal Femur		Distal Femur		Distal Radius		Proximal Tibia	
Phase	F	U	F	U	F	U	F	U	F	U	F	U	F	U	F	U	F	U	F	U	F	U	F	U
Bayat.	5	. . .	9	. . .	4	. . .	2	2	3	1	7	4	3	. . .	2	4	. . .	1	. . .	1	1	. . .	. . .	1
Mehmeh	1	. . .	3	. . .	. . .	. . .	2	. . .	1	1	1	2	2	1	2	3	. . .	1	. . .	1	. . .	. . .	. . .	. . .
Khazineh	. . .	. . .	. . .	. . .	. . .	. . .	1	1	. . .	. . .	3	1	1	1	4	1	. . .	2	1	. . .	1	. . .	. . .	. . .
Sabz	4	. . .	9	. . .	1	. . .	3	. . .	6	. . .	9	3	7	. . .	8	2	1	1	2	1	. . .	3	. . .	. . .
Mohammad Jaffar.	19	. . .	53	6	28	1	27	9	29	6	38	18	19	6	34	15	11	9	2	4	3	9	2	3
Ali Kosh.	100	6	167	26	85	6	110	11	134	35	141	59	61	30	113	77	45	46	32	46	27	56	24	28
Bus Mordeh . . .	22	9	44	19	16	11	21	11	85	29	101	68	23	23	54	67	9	12	9	12	7	25	4	13

Note:–Ages of fusion follow Silver (1963); Smith (1956) and Todd and Todd (1938) give generally younger fusion dates. F = fused; U = unfused.

separated the head from the neck by cutting between the occipital condyles and the atlas with flint blades. Blade marks on at least three different atlases from zone B_2 at Ali Kosh show that this was done with the ventral or "throat" side upward. The lower jaw and tongue were removed, probably while in this same position, and the villagers smashed open the skull to remove the brains. The occipital region remained intact, but the palate and underside of the skull were usually damaged beyond recognition. Skull fragments never showed roasting, and neck vertebrae rarely did.

The Bus Mordeh-Ali Kosh villagers removed the forelimb as a unit, by some process which nearly always destroyed the blade of the scapula. They occasionally discarded the elbow joint (distal humerus-proximal radius and ulna) in a state of articulation, but one rare example from the Ali Kosh phase shows that someone tried to cut through the elbow with a flint pebble chopper. Such choppers do not normally appear to have been used on animals as small as a goat or gazelle; more common were flint blade marks. From the Bayat phase at Tepe Sabz, we recovered distal humeri with up to twenty blade marks on the ventral surface, about a centimeter above the condyle. From the location of the horizontal blade scars, it appears that the villagers were cutting away the biceps or brachialis muscle as a whole, rather than attempting to disjoint the elbows.

One other task for which the Ali Kosh villagers occasionally used a pebble chopper was in separating the hind limb from the pelvis. Four pelves from zone B_2 show an identical pattern of butchering marks: chopper scars on the shaft of the ilium near the origin of the rectus femoris, knife marks on the blade of the ilium at the origin of the gluteus maximus, slices on the shaft of the ischium, and knife marks just below the acetabulum. Another pelvis from B_1 shows a similar pattern—attempts to free the head of the femur from the acetabulum with a flint blade, and to sever the ilium with a chopper blow. Obviously, so long as the femur came away from the trunk, the villagers didn't care whether bits of fractured pelvis were attached or not. The result is that there are many more blade marks on the pelvis than on the head of the femur. In contrast, butchers at Tepe Guran often left a great many cut marks on the femur head because they preferred to cut it out of the acetabulum, rather than break the pelvis (Flannery, unpublished data).

The rest of the lower limb was usually disjointed with flint blades. A distal tibia from the Bus Mordeh phase has three blade marks just behind the medial malleolus, evidently where the long medial ligament was cut to free the distal tibia from the metatarsal. Proximal ends of metapodials from the same phase have blade marks on the underside of the shaft, and one goat metacarpal even has a few cleaver marks at this point. However, numerous groups of carpals and tarsals from these lower levels remained in articulation. We conclude that the femur and tibia were the prized portions of the hind limb, and that once the distal tibia had been freed by flint blades (or occasionally by a chopper), the metapodial and its attached tarsals might be discarded as a unit. There is very little meat on the limb below this point.

Many of the lower extremities, in fact, were found in articulation. Obviously the hooves were discarded in this condition, for we frequently found first, second, and third phalanges in articulation. Occasionally, first phalanges were still attached to the distal metapodial, and carpals or tarsals still attached to the proximal metapodial. The astragalus occasionally remained articulated with the distal tibia when that bone was freed from the metatarsal. Such occurrences lasted into the later phases of the sequence as well. From the Sabz to the

Bayat phases, some distal metapodials of goat were found articulated with the first phalanges.

There was an even higher frequency of articulations in lambs and kids than in adult Caprines. In the Mehmeh and Bayat phases, whole forelimbs or hind limbs of very young animals (4 to 6 months) were occasionally discarded as a unit. Their metapodials identify them as both sheep and goat.

Considering the number of Caprine bones recovered from Ali Kosh and Tepe Sabz, the number of burned or carbonized bones is relatively small: only 103 out of 5000, or about 2 per cent. Most carbonized bones, however, are from lower limb extremities where there would be little meat to protect them from fire. Phalanges, carpals and tarsals, astragali and calcanea were the most frequently burned. If a haunch of goat is roasted, it is not the tibia and femur which would be burned, for they are protected by several pounds of meat. The area from the astragalus to the phalanges, which is covered only by tough tendons and skin, might well be carbonized. We suggest that goats and sheep were occasionally "barbecued" or roasted directly over hot coals. The Ali Kosh phase produced at least one "roasting pit" which contained goat bones and ash, situated just outside a brick-walled building (see Fig. 11*c* and Hole and Flannery, 1962:109).

More common than roasting, however, was some technique which did not scorch the bones. Blade marks (see above) indicate that most, if not all of the major muscles were cut off the bone. A large number of unfused bones were found still in contact with (though easily detachable from) their epiphyses. This suggests that boiling of meat on-the-bone was not particularly common, for prolonged boiling would have melted the cartilage and separated the shaft from the epihysis. Much of the meat must have been cut off before cooking or roasting, therefore (cf. the boneless "kabab" which is still a favorite Iranian dish).

When the Caprine bones had been stripped of flesh, they were broken open so that the marrow could be extracted. In order to shake the marrow out of the shaft of the bone, the villagers seem to have tapped the broken end against a hard surface. The broken edges of some limb bones show a resultant chipping which (although irregular) almost resembles percussion technique on flint. Dr. Junius Bird of the American Museum of Natural History reports (personal communication) that he observed the Indians of Patagonia using the technique for marrow removal when he visited them in the 1930's. At that time he noted the scale-like "retouch" produced on the broken edges of the bone. This "retouch" also occurs on gazelle bones from Ali Kosh (see Fig. 123*c,e*).

Bones were broken open in a variety of ways. Some were "notched" with a flint blade and then snapped at the point of the notch, but the frequency of this was not so high as we thought on the basis of our 1961 sample (Hole and Flannery 1962:132). A few were chopped open with pebble choppers, but most were probably just hit with a heavy rock, like one of the pounders common in the Ali Kosh and Mohammad Jaffar phases. Most bones were not simply snapped in half, but literally smashed to pieces, with little remaining to identify them but the articular end.

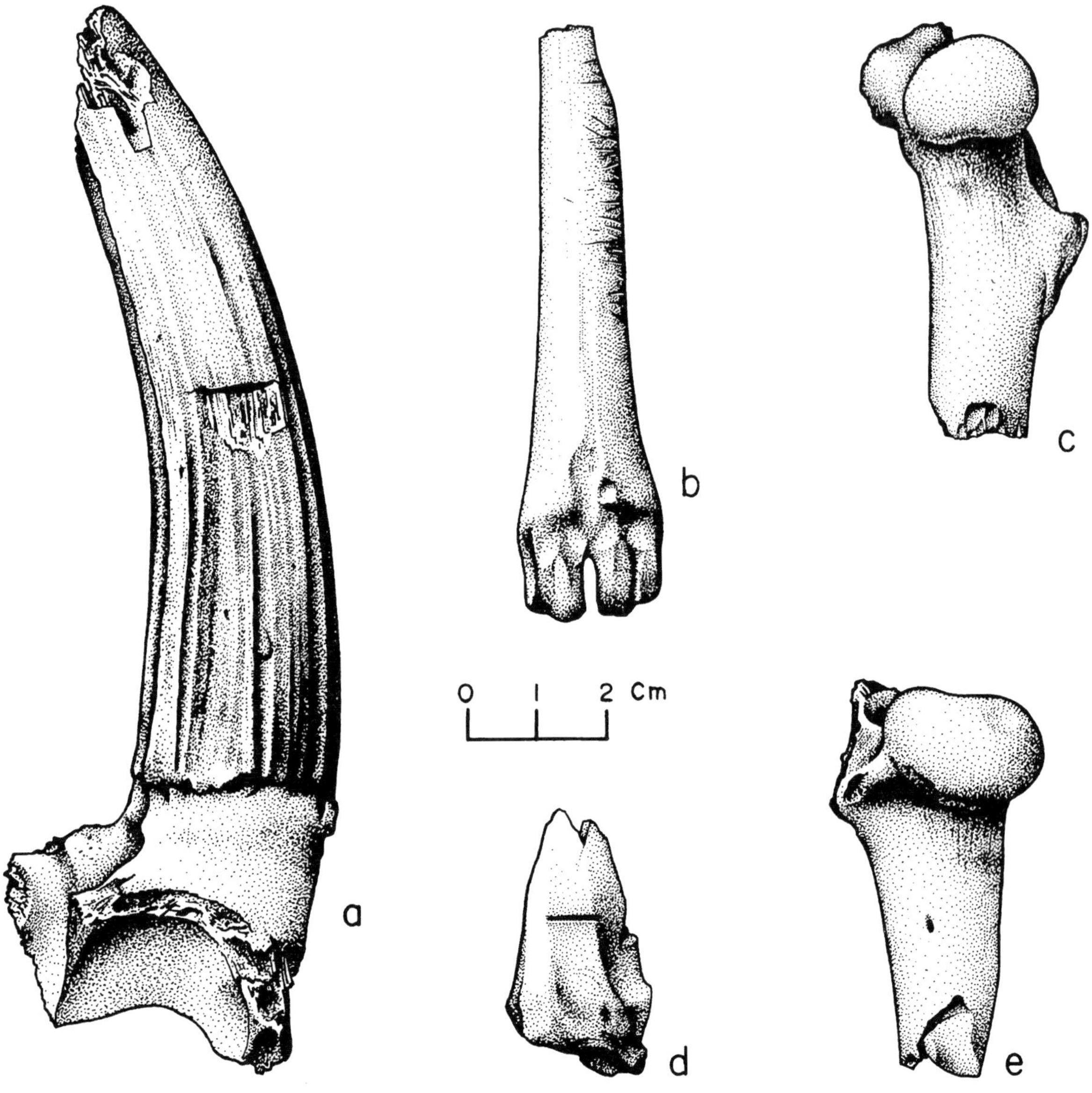

Fig. 123. Bones of gazelle (*Gazella subgutturosa*) from Tepe Ali Kosh: *a,* horn core, male, zone A_2 (Mohammad Jaffar phase); *b,* distal metapodial, showing wear on the articular surface and many flint blade marks on the shaft (zone C_2, Bus Mordeh phase); *d,* distal radius, showing flint blade mark on dorsal surface (zone C_2, Bus Mordeh phase); *c,e,* broken proximal femora from zone B_1 (Ali Kosh phase), showing scale-like "retouch" on the lower edge which results from tapping the bone against a hard surface to extract marrow (see text).

Table 63

REMAINS OF GAZELLE (*GAZELLA SUBGUTTUROSA*) FROM ALI KOSH AND TEPE SABZ
(By Stratigraphic Zone)

Phase	Site	Zone	Number of Identified Fragments	Minimum Number of Individuals	Individual Fragments Recovered																					
					Horn Core	Skull Fragment	Petrous Bone	Maxilla	Mandible	Atlas/Axis	Scapula	Humerus	Radius	Ulna	Innominate	Femur	Patella	Tibia	Carpal	Tarsal	Calcaneum	Astragalus	Metapodial	1st Phalanx	2nd Phalanx	3rd Phalanx
Bayat	TS	A_1	10	(2)	...	...	...	1	1	1	2	2	1	...	...	...	...	...	...	...	...	...	...	1	1	...
	TS	A_2	15	(2)	3	...	...	...	2	1	...	2	1	1	1	...	...	1	...	...	...	...	1	2	...	...
	TS	A_3	16	(4)	2	...	...	...	2	...	...	4	1	...	...	...	...	1	...	...	...	...	2	3	1	...
Mehmeh	TS	B_1	2	(1)	1	...	...	...	...	...	...	...	...	...	...	...	...	...	...	...	...	...	...	1	...	...
	TS	B_2	2	(1)	...	...	...	...	1	...	...	1	...	...	...	...	...	...	...	...	...	...	...	...	...	...
	TS	B_3	5	(1)	2	...	...	...	...	1	...	...	...	...	...	...	...	1	...	...	...	1	...	...	...	...
Khazineh	TS	C_1	2	(1)	...	...	...	...	...	1	...	...	...	...	...	...	...	...	...	...	...	...	1	...	...	...
	TS	C_2	4	(1)	1	...	...	...	1	...	1	...	...	...	...	...	...	...	...	...	...	...	1	...	...	...
	TS	C_3	4	(2)	2	1	...	...	...	...	...	...	...	...	...	...	...	...	...	...	...	...	1	...	...	...
Sabz	TS	D	15	(3)	2	...	...	...	3	...	2	...	1	2	...	2	...	...	...	...	...	...	2	1	...	...
Mohammad Jaffar	AK	A_1	177	(7)	8	3	2	3	13	4	9	8	3	2	10	8	6	8	6	3	2	10	11	24	18	16
	AK	A_2	245	(11)	15	...	4	5	13	5	11	18	8	3	14	12	8	9	9	3	7	19	31	23	22	6
Ali Kosh	AK	B_1	259	(15)	9	1	4	5	19	3	20	26	5	8	13	13	2	22	2	4	3	11	27	29	22	11
	AK	B_2	1002	(44)	43	20	16	7	23	41	43	102	34	24	30	113	4	78	57	17	34	25	84	91	75	41
Bus Mordeh	AK	C_1	224	(10)	7	3	7	6	7	7	6	18	4	6	9	17	4	10	11	9	4	8	13	32	20	16
	AK	C_2	215	(6)	11	1	4	3	4	6	3	8	8	6	5	14	2	5	10	4	2	4	16	44	35	20
Totals			2197	(111)	106	29	37	30	89	70	97	189	66	52	134	179	26	135	95	40	52	78	190	251	194	110

GAZELLE

Sample: 2197 fragments (not counting ribs, stray teeth, and lower vertebrae; see Table 63 and Fig. 123)

Temporal distribution: All phases

Introduction

The Persian gazelle, *Gazella subgutturosa,* was the most common single wild animal hunted by the ancient villagers of Deh Luran. It was the only species whose bones approached in number those of domestic goat at Ali Kosh and Tepe Sabz. Gazelles constituted 24 per cent of the ungulate remains in the Bus Mordeh phase, and they increased during the Ali Kosh phase to about 30 per cent. Some 34 per cent of the ungulates eaten during the Mohammad Jaffar phase were *G. subgutturosa.* With the advent of irrigation agriculture and cattle domestication in the Sabz phase, hunting became less important in the local economy; gazelles dwindled to 12 per cent, but remained the wild animal most abundantly relied upon. As late in the sequence as the Bayat phase, they were still 25 per cent of the ungulate remains.

Gazelles are still common on the Deh Luran plain, and we passed herds of from 3 to 20 nearly every evening on our return to camp from Tepe Sabz. During the winter of 1961, we found them congregated by rain-filled depressions north of Ali Kosh just at daybreak. They are harder to find during the heat of the day, when they retreat to the shelter of ravines and wadis along the margins of the plain. The Iranian border police, who hunt them at night with Jeeps and shotguns, presented us with two males in the autumn of 1963, and we suspect we could have had as many more as we wanted.

The local gazelles are small, fawn-colored creatures measuring 60 to 70 cm. at the shoulder, and considered better eating than either sheep or goat. They are capable of tremendous bursts of speed, which make it clear that they could only have been hunted in prehistoric times by some kind of ambush technique, by drives or "surrounds," or by some rather sophisticated stalking procedure. Once alerted they are off and running, but they have one habit which has been noted and used by Jeep-equipped hunters: they tend to run in a wide circle, and by estimating their speed and the circumference of the circle it is often possible to intercept them at a prearranged spot. Experimenting with this technique, Neely came near running over gazelles on several occasions during his daily trip across the plain.

For the later periods of our sequence, we have some suggestions of hunting technique. A Mehmeh phase ("Susiana *c*?") sherd from Tepe Jowi, illustrated by Le Breton, shows a hunter with a bow and arrow (Fig. 131*a*). Another Mehmeh phase sherd, this time from our test at Tepe Musiyan "E," shows a wild goat (or gazelle) accompanied by what may be a series of cloven hoofprints, resembling a trail (Fig. 131*b*). The wadis of the Tepe Sabz area today are filled with gazelle trails of this sort, along which a hunter could lie in wait for the herd. Finally, a probable Mehmeh phase sherd from Tepe Bandibal shows what appear to be a pair of male gazelles; the tall, ridged horn covers are characteristic of *G. gutturosa* (Fig. 131*c*). There may be grounds to suspect, therefore, that gazelle hunting in Khuzistan was done with bow and arrow along known gazelle trails. Unfortunately, we have no evidence for the hunting pattern during the early phases of our sequence, save for the presence of crescent microliths (taken to be elements of some light projectile).

After viewing the design elements of the Susa A pottery from approximately 3000 B.C., Adams (1962:113) concluded that "members of the *Capra* and *Gazella* genera are very numerous, while bovids and equids are decidedly rare." Such a statement would characterize the faunal remains from prehistoric Deh Luran during all periods of our sequence. It is a reflection of the extreme importance this one wild genus had in the diet of ancient Khuzistan.

Butchering Technique

Gazelle were brought back to the village intact, and butchered there. In 1963 we recovered virtually every bone in the body. Although we doubted our ability to distinguish most vertebrae of gazelle from those of goat, presumably a good many of the 1800 vertebrae of small bovids we uncovered were from *Gazella.* In addition, there were 300-odd ribs and 1300 fragmentary teeth which were either goat, sheep, or gazelle.

Gazelle were not butchered with flint pebble choppers, so far as we could determine. Instead, they were disjointed with flint blades, whose traces are evident at some of the points where ligaments or tendons had to be cut: for example, on the upper surface of the distal end of the radius (probably to free the extensor carpi radialis), and on the side of the proximal end of the first phalanx (to sever a suspensory ligament?). Disjointing of the limbs does not always seem to have been complete, however, and many components remained in articulation. The head was removed by cutting between the occipital condyles and the atlas, but the atlas and axis sometimes remained in articulation. Other articulated bones recovered were groups of carpals and tarsals, especially the calcaneum and astragalus. Bones were broken open and tapped to shake out the marrow; the proximal end of a femur from the Ali Kosh phase clearly shows unintentional chipping along its broken edge where this was done.

Our 1961 report stated that bones "of large as well as small animals" showed signs of roasting (Hole and Flannery, 1962:132). With the larger sample we recovered in 1963 it is now possible to say that roasting was much more common with small ungulates (goat and gazelle) than with larger ones. A few ox and onager bones did get carbonized, but in most cases the meat must have been cut off the bone before cooking. In the case of gazelle, however, some 50 to 60 bones were definitely carbonized, as if a haunch of gazelle meat had been roasted over hot coals. The "roasting pit" we recovered in 1961 (see Fig. 11*c*) may have served that purpose during the Ali Kosh phase.[4]

ONAGER

Sample: 495 fragments (see Table 64 and Fig. 124)

Temporal distribution: All phases

Introduction

The onager or wild ass of southwestern Asia (*Equus hemionus*) was hunted throughout the sequence at Deh Luran. Onager bones were most common in the Ali Kosh and Mohammad Jaffar phases, but there were even a dozen or so from the Bayat phase. Nothing remains today of the large herds which once roamed the steppe and desert of the lower Euphrates (Hatt, 1959:54), but groups of four or five can still be found around the base of small mountain ranges in the Kavir desert of central Iran. The animal was temporarily

[4]Of course, it is possible that the bones we found had been secondarily burned in hearths or smouldering ash piles after eating.

Table 64

REMAINS OF ONAGER (*EQUUS HEMIONUS*) FROM ALI KOSH AND TEPE SABZ
(By Stratigraphic Zone)

Phase	Site	Zone	Number of Identified Fragments	Minimum Number of Individuals	Individual Fragments Recovered																			
					Maxilla	Mandible	Stray Teeth	Scapula	Humerus	Radius	Ulna	Femur	Patella	Tibia	Carpal	Tarsal	Calcaneum	Astragalus	Metapodial	First Phalanx	Second Phalanx	Third Phalanx	Vertebra	Other
Bayat	TS	A_1	4	(1)	...	...	2	...	...	1	...	...	...	...	1	...	...	...	...	...	...	...	...	...
	TS	A_2	1	(1)	...	...	...	...	...	...	...	...	...	...	...	...	...	...	...	...	...	...	...	1
	TS	A_3	8	(2)	...	...	4	...	...	...	...	...	...	1	...	...	...	...	3	...	...	...	...	...
Mehmeh	TS	B_1	1	(1)	...	...	...	...	...	...	...	...	...	...	...	...	...	...	...	...	...	...	...	1
	TS	B_2	1	(1)	...	...	...	...	...	...	...	...	...	1	...	...	...	...	...	...	...	...	...	...
	TS	B_3	...	...	...	...	...	...	...	...	...	...	...	...	...	...	...	...	...	...	...	...	...	...
Khazineh	TS	C_1	2	(1)	...	...	1	...	...	...	...	...	...	...	...	...	...	...	1	...	...	...	...	...
	TS	C_2	...	...	...	...	...	...	...	...	...	...	...	...	...	...	...	...	...	...	...	...	...	...
	TS	C_3	...	...	...	...	...	...	...	...	...	...	...	...	...	...	...	...	...	...	...	...	...	...
Sabz	TS	D	2	(1)	...	...	1	...	...	1	...	...	...	...	...	...	...	...	...	...	...	...	...	...
Mohammad Jaffar	AK	A_1	44	(2)	...	...	7	1	1	4	1	1	...	...	3	...	2	2	6	3	2	1	5	5
	AK	A_2	99	(2)	...	...	15	3	3	2	...	1	1	2	2	4	2	2	7	8	5	2	22	18
Ali Kosh	AK	B_1	84	(2)	2	1	17	4	6	1	3	2	...	3	5	3	2	2	6	5	2	3	12	5
	AK	B_2	199	(10)	1	2	15	5	12	9	...	10	4	10	20	9	7	5	16	7	5	3	42	17
Bus Mordeh	AK	C_1	30	(2)	...	...	1	...	...	...	...	2	1	1	4	2	1	...	1	4	4	4	2	3
	AK	C_2	20	(1)	...	...	2	...	...	1	1	1	1	1	4	...	...	1	1	...	...	...	4	3
Totals			495	(27)	3	3	65	14	22	19	5	17	7	19	39	18	14	12	41	68	18	13	87	53

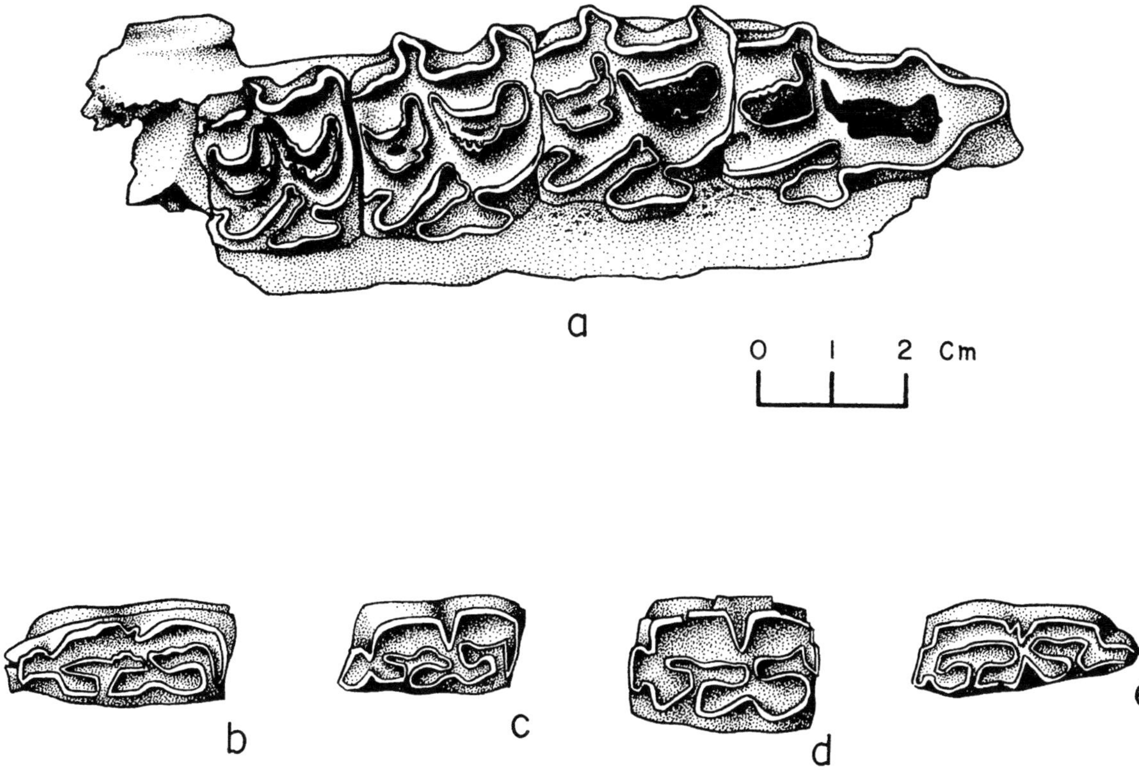

Fig. 124. Dentition of onager (*Equus hemionus*) from Ali Kosh phase levels, Tepe Ali Kosh: *a*, right maxilla fragment showing P^2-M^1 (zone B_2); *b-e*, lower left cheek teeth (*b,d,e*, zone B_1; *c*, zone B_2).

domesticated by the ancient Sumerians, but later abandoned in favor of the horse. There is no evidence of its domestication during any part of our sequence.

We do not know how the onager was hunted at Ali Kosh and Tepe Sabz. *E. hemionus* is a swift runner whose protective coloration (tan above, white below) blends into the alluvium at any great distance. In Baluchistan they are known to migrate to the hills during the driest part of the summer (Lydekker, 1912:185), and they may have done much the same thing in Khuzistan. Herds would have been bigger and fatter when the winter grass sprouted on the Deh Luran plain, and many were probably killed during that season.

At times we thought we could detect two sizes of onagers in our faunal collections, but this may be no more than a size difference between males and females, such as we observed in *Bos primigenius*.

Butchering Technique

In many respects the technique used to cut up onagers resembles that used on the wild ox. However, the numbers of vertebrae and skull fragments recovered suggest that entire onagers were often brought back to the village intact, in contrast to *Bos primigenius*. Almost every part of the skeleton is represented in our collections.

First, the villagers freed the muscle from the bone with flint blades. They may have used slicing slabs under the tendons and ligaments to facilitate cutting. Up to fifteen blade marks have been found on areas such as the back of the distal end of the humerus, where the "elbow" joint was disarticulated, and the back of the distal femur, where the knee joint was disarticulated. Other, more inedible portions of the skeleton were discarded without being cut apart; bone elements found in articulation included (1) strings of up to thirteen cervical vertebrae; (2) the proximal end of the metatarsal, with all tarsals still in place; (3) the distal tibia, astragalus, and calcaneum; (4) the proximal radius and ulna; and (5) the first, second, and third phalanges. From this we conclude that the feet were chopped off and discarded as a unit, as well as joints which were mostly gristle. Areas like the pelvis, scapula, upper humerus, and femur, where large areas of "steaks" or "tenderloin" could be removed, were virtually never recovered intact.

The villagers then split open the stripped limb bones with flint pebble choppers for marrow extraction. Several metapodials were also divided by a cleaver blow in such a way as to suggest that the distal metapodial was the point below which the limb was considered inedible, and discarded. Elements like the distal humerus show scalelike chipping marks where they were tapped until they released their plug of marrow.

Almost none of the onager bones are carbonized. We suspect the villagers roasted or boiled the onager meat only after they had cut it away from the bone. There is no evidence that onagers or *Bos primigenius* were ever "barbecued" the way small goat or gazelles seem to have been.

CATTLE, WILD AND DOMESTIC

Sample: 275 fragments from all periods (see Tables 65 and 66 and Fig. 125)

Introduction

On the basis of present evidence, it is generally accepted that all domestic cattle are derived from one or another subspecies of the aurochs or wild ox of Eurasia, *Bos primigenius,* an animal whose range included the Near East (Zeuner, 1963). Teeth of the aurochs antedating 75,000 B.C. have been identified from the site of Barda Balka, Iraq; wild cattle were still hunted by the Assyrian kings in the ninth century B.C., and the European aurochs only became extinct about 1627 A.D. (Hatt, 1959:66; Zeuner, 1963:12). The wild ox was an enormous bovid, standing more than a meter and a half at the shoulder, and with a horn span of up to a meter in males. The dangers of hunting such an animal were probably weighed against the amount of meat a single individual would yield.

The Problem of *Bos* and *Bison*

The archeological faunal analyst in many parts of the world is faced with the almost impossible task of separating postcranial bones of cattle and bison. How can we be sure that our "cattle" from Ali Kosh are really *Bos primigenius* and not *Bison bonasus,* the Old World bison? It has been suggested by Hatt (1959:67) that the latter was an inhabitant of the "fringing forested hills" of Mesopotamia, and if so, any identification of "cattle" remains must be done with caution (Reed, 1960:142). Our feeling on this subject is as follows:

1) There really seems to be no skeletal evidence that the European bison ever

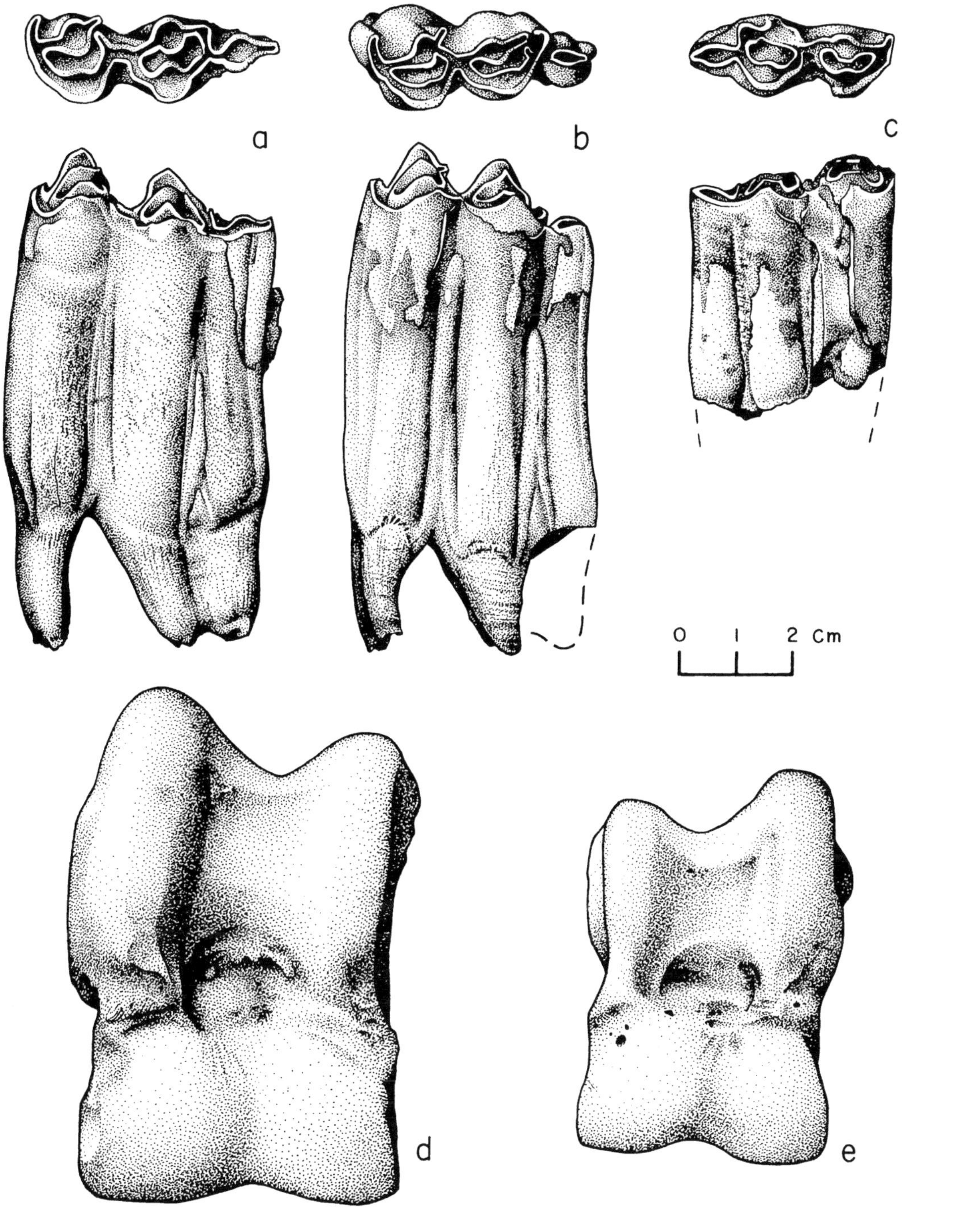

Fig. 125. Cattle remains from the Deh Luran sites, both wild and domestic: *a,b,* lower third molars of wild aurochs from Tepe Ali Kosh (Ali Kosh phase); *c,* lower third molar of domestic ox from Tepe Musiyan "E," 480 to 530 cm. (Mehmeh phase); *d,* astragalus of wild aurochs from Tepe Ali Kosh, zone A_2 (Mohammad Jaffar phase); *e,* astragalus of domestic ox from Tepe Sabz, zone D (Sabz phase).

Table 65

REMAINS OF WILD AUROCHS (*BOS PRIMIGENIUS*) FROM ALI KOSH
(By Stratigraphic Zone)

Phase	Site	Zone	Number of Identified Fragments	Minimum Number of Individuals	Individual Fragments Recovered																	
					Mandible	Stray Teeth	Humerus	Radius	Ulna	Carpal	Sesamoid	Femur	Tibia	Calcaneum	Astragalus	Metapodial	1st Phalanx	2nd Phalanx	3rd Phalanx	Vertebra	Rib	Other
Mohammad Jaffar	AK	A_1	17	(1)	...	3	...	1	...	1	2	...	...	...	1	1	3	1	...	2	2	...
	AK	A_2	15	(1)	1	3	...	...	...	...	1	...	...	...	1	...	2	...	1	2	2	2
Ali Kosh	AK	B_1	37	(2)	1	7	1	1	1	2	4	1	1	1	...	3	2	3	1	4	2	2
	AK	B_2	139	(4)	1	8	8	4	2	15	6	7	2	6	3	12	13	13	8	12	5	14
Bus Mordeh	AK	C_1	16	(2)	...	...	...	...	2	1	3	...	...	...	...	1	1	4	2	2	...	...
	AK	C_2	8	(1)	...	...	...	...	1	3	1	...	...	...	...	...	...	3	...	...	...	...
Totals			232	(11)	3	21	9	6	6	22	17	8	3	7	5	17	21	24	12	22	11	18

Table 66

REMAINS OF DOMESTIC CATTLE (*BOS TAURUS*) FROM TEPE SABZ
(By Stratigraphic Zone)

Phase	Site	Zone	Number of Identified Fragments	Minimum Number of Individuals	Individual Fragments Recovered															
					Horn Core	Mandible	Stray Teeth	Scapula	Radius	Ulna	Femur	Metapodial	Astragalus	Calcaneum	1st Phalanx	2nd Phalanx	3rd Phalanx	Rib	Vertebra	Other
Bayat	TS	A_1	5	(1)	1	...	...	...	...	...	1	...	...	...	1	1	...	1	...	...
	TS	A_2	9	(1)	...	...	2	1	...	...	...	1	1	1	1	...	...	1	1	...
	TS	A_3	5	(1)	...	...	1	...	...	...	...	1	...	...	1	...	1	1	...	...
Mehmeh	TS	B_1	3	(1)	...	...	1	...	...	...	...	1	1	...	...	...	...	...	...	...
	TS	B_2	2	(1)	...	...	1	...	...	...	...	...	...	...	...	...	1	...	...	...
	TS	B_3	2	(1)	...	...	...	...	...	...	...	...	...	...	...	...	...	...	...	2
Khazineh	TS	C_1	1	(1)	...	...	1	...	...	...	...	...	...	...	...	...	...	...	...	...
	TS	C_2	...	...	...	...	...	...	...	...	...	...	...	...	...	...	...	...	...	...
	TS	C_3	...	...	...	...	...	...	...	...	...	...	...	...	...	...	...	...	...	...
Sabz	TS	D	16	(2)	...	2	7	...	1	1	...	2	1	...	1	...	...	...	...	1
Totals			43	(9)	1	2	13	1	1	1	1	5	3	1	4	1	2	3	1	3

reached Mesopotamia or the southern Zagros, let alone Khuzistan. The animal is not known with any certainty south of the Caucasus (Ellerman and Morrison-Scott, 1966:383). No bone or horn core from any archeological site in Kurdistan, Luristan, Khuzistan, or Assyria has ever been identified as *Bison*.

2) The "evidence" on which Hatt bases his admittedly cautious suggestion consists of painted representations on potsherds, plus cylinder seals and statuettes, from Uruk through Akkadian times (Hatt, 1959:67-8). Whether these representations are really bison is open to question.

3) On the other hand, *Bos* remains are definitely known from the whole area under consideration. Specimens include a horn core from Jarmo (Reed, 1960:142), and a lower third molar (and other teeth) from Barda Balka (Hatt, 1959:67), which are believed to be *Bos primigenius*.

4) All measurable postcranial bones of bovine from Ali Kosh compare with measured *Bos primigenius* from England and Denmark (see Osteometric analysis, below). However, we also compared them for qualitative characters with skeletons of *Bison bonasus* and large *Bos taurus* in the collections of the U. S. National Museum. Our guide to this comparison was Olson's paper (1960) on postcranial skeletal characters of *Bos* and *Bison*. Olson's characters were worked out on specimens of *Bison bison*, but most of them seem to work on *Bison bonasus* as well.

According to Olson (1960:5), "although *single* individual 'key characters' may vary and intergrade when a large series of skeletons is examined, making the separation of *Bison* and *Bos* difficult, in no instance was it observed that *all* key characters followed this course and prevented positive separation of the 2 genera." If Olson is right, then it would seem that all our large Bovines from Ali Kosh are *Bos primigenius*, for they repeatedly matched the characters he gives for *Bos*, and differed from those observed in *Bison bonasus* and *Bison bison*.

By way of example, we might cite the following *Bos* characters, all of which are described in Olson's manual, and which appeared in the Ali Kosh bovine material:

On the distal humerus, the fossa for muscle attachment on the lateral condyle is a nearly round pit, rather than an elongate irregular trench. The distal end of the metacarpal is not swollen at the area of contact between the shaft and the articular condyles, and its nutrient foramina are relatively small. The proximal end of the first phalanx has a deeper pit on its dorsal face than is typical of either *Bison bison* or *Bison bonasus* specimens examined, and its lateral margin is relatively straight, rather than curved. The second phalanx has a dorsal prominence on its proximal end, giving its dorsal margin the "dished" surface of *Bos* rather than the straighter margin of *Bison*. The third phalanx has a slightly curved plantar margin, and its anterior margin is concave. The sustentaculum of the calcaneum, viewed posteriorly, forms a lateral right angle rather than showing the downward deflection seen in Olson's *Bison* specimens; and the facet on the calcaneum for the tibia is oval, as in most *Bos* specimens, rather than being round (as in *Bison bison*) or absent (as in *Bison bonasus* specimens in the U.S.N.M.).

5) On the basis of the qualitative characters, plus the osteometric analysis to be described below, plus the lack of skeletal evidence for *Bison* anywhere in the southern Zagros to date, we are therefore regarding the large bovines from Ali Kosh as *Bos primigenius*.

6) We have eliminated water buffalo (*Bubalus bubalis*), to our own satisfaction at least, through essentially the same process. The evidence that its range, in the wild, ever reached Khuzistan is meager indeed, and its bones did not match our specimens.

The Deh Luran Sequence

On the basis of osteometric data to be presented below, we believe that our Deh Luran sequence brackets the appearance of domestic cattle in the area. Cattle bones from the Bus Mordeh, Ali Kosh, and Mohammad Jaffar phases all seem to be from large wild aurochs hunted by the prehistoric villagers. They compare in size with *Bos primigenius* specimens from Star Carr, England (Frazer and King, 1954; Jewell, 1963) and from Danish peat bogs (Degerbøl, 1963). Wild cattle bones constitute less than 1 per cent of the animal remains from the Bus Mordeh phase; they increase during the Ali Kosh phase to 2.6 per cent of the fauna, and this slight increase in cattle hunting seems to be accompanied by a proliferation of flint pebble choppers and slicing slabs for use in butchering. The Mohammad Jaffar phase has much the same aspect, with large wild cattle remains constituting 1.4 per cent of the identifiable faunal debris.

With the Sabz phase, cattle increase suddenly to 5 per cent of the animal remains, and there is a noticeable decrease in size. From the Sabz phase through to the Bayat phase, osteometric analysis shows that our cattle fall within the size range of domestic *Bos taurus* from Neolithic Europe and Denmark (see Figs 126-127). In this respect they resemble the cattle from Banahilk in Iraqi Kurdistan (a site contemporary with the Khazineh phase), where measurements are sufficiently small so that Reed (1961:33-34) considers them domestic. Equally small are the cattle from Ras al Amiya, a central Mesopotamian site contemporary with the Mehmeh phase, whose measurements we include with ours (below).

We conclude, therefore, that domestic cattle (derived from *Bos primigenius*) made their initial appearance in Khuzistan between 5500 and 5000 B.C. with no previous evidence of "incipient cattle domestication." We do not know yet from which adjacent area they may have been introduced. At 5000 to 4500 B.C. we have evidence for them in both central Mesopotamia and Kurdistan, and there is no reason why they should not ultimately prove to have been there by 5500 B.C. as well; in fact, cattle bones form a higher proportion of the fauna at Ras al Amiya than in contemporary levels at Tepe Sabz.

We note, however, that nowhere in the Zagros area do our studied collections from 5800 to 6000 B.C. contain bones of domestic cattle. Neither the Mohammad Jaffar phase, nor upper Tepe Guran (Flannery, unpublished data), nor upper Jarmo (Reed, 1960:142-143) have anything but wild cattle, and at all three sites cattle bones are a very small proportion of the faunal remains. We can therefore point with some confidence to 5500 B.C. as a crucial date for the appearance of domestic cattle in the Zagros-Mesopotamian region. We note with interest that cattle were domestic perhaps 1000 years earlier than this at Argissa in Thessaly (Miločić, Boessneck, and Hopf, 1962).

We do not know what specific uses the ancient Deh Luranis made of their cattle, although certainly their wild ancestors had been eaten for centuries. By the end of the fourth millenium B.C. (800 years or so after the abandonment of Tepe Sabz), the existence of the plow can be demonstrated in Khuzistan, according to various interpretations of the proto-Elamite tablets (Adams, 1962:113); thus cattle probably served as draft animals as well as food by that period.

Osteometric Analysis

The problems of measuring cattle to distinguish wild from domestic forms are set forth by Degerbøl (1963) and Jewell (1963) in the symposium volume on *Man and Cattle* (Mourant and Zeuner, eds., 1963). Briefly, their principal points are as follows:

1) There is considerable sexual dimorphism in *Bos primigenius,* the males being

so much larger than females that many bone measurements show a bimodal distribution (cf. Jewell, 1963:Fig. 18).

2) Male *Bos primigenius* is conspicuous by the prodigious size it may reach, but the smaller females may overlap in size with the larger male domestic cattle.

3) Domestic cattle may not show such a bimodal distribution of measurements, since castrated domestic bullocks may be intermediate in size between bulls and cows.

4) Tooth measurements may be useful in distinguishing size changes after domestication, for sexual dimorphism seems to be less pronounced in the teeth than in horn cores or limb bones.

5) Both Degerbøl and Jewell find measurements of the metacarpal useful for distinguishing wild and domestic cattle, when a sufficiently large series is present. In addition, Jewell has made use of the humerus and astragalus for comparative measurements.

Both Degerbøl and Jewell have presented useful charts and diagrams showing size changes after domestication, and our osteometric study is deliberately patterned after theirs:

Lower third molar (Fig. 126).—As the figure shows, three specimens from Ali Kosh (Ali Kosh and Mohammad Jaffar phases) range from 45 to 49 mm. in basal length, comparing well with the wild *Bos primigenius* from Denmark; Degerbøl's 34 wild specimens had a range of 45 to 55 mm. A single lower third molar from our test at Tepe Musiyan "E" (Mehmeh phase levels) measured only 36 mm. in length, comparing well with a modern domestic specimen we collected in Luristan, and some of the smaller Danish neolithic cattle (Degerbøl, 1963).

Distal humerus and distal metacarpal (Fig. 126).—Once again, all specimens from Ali Kosh (Bus Mordeh through Mohammad Jaffar phases) lie well within the size range of wild *Bos primigenius* (Star Carr specimens, as diagrammed by Jewel, 1963). There is considerable overlap in size between wild and early domestic cattle with regard to the distal humerus width, but none of Jewell's British neolithic specimens exceeded 88 mm.; a single specimen from Ras al Amiya also measures 88 mm. in width. The width of the distal metacarpal shows much the same overlap between small wild and large domestic cattle. A single distal metacarpal from Ras al Amiya, however, only 59 mm. wide, falls outside the range of *Bos primigenius* and is presumed to be domestic.

Astragalus (Fig. 126).—It is when we turn to measurements of the length of the astragalus that we begin to get the clearest break between our wild and domestic cattle. Thirteen *Bos primigenius* specimens from Star Carr ranged from 81 to 92 mm. in length; four specimens from Ali Kosh range from 77 to 89 mm., and are presumably wild. All later specimens are noticeably smaller: two from Ras al Amiya are 70 and 76 mm. in length, and two from Tepe Sabz (including a specimen from the Sabz phase) are 69 and 71 mm., which compares well with astragali of British Neolithic domestic cattle (Jewell, 1963). Our modern Luristan domestic cow had the smallest astragalus of all those we measured (57 mm.). Tentatively, it appears that 76 to 77 mm. may be a useful "rule of thumb" for the break in length of astragalus between wild and domestic Iranian cattle, although it would certainly be necessary to have a larger series of specimens before relying on it. We still have so few measurements that we are generalizing only from isolated specimens, rather than populations.

Phalanges (Fig. 127).—First, second, and third phalanges were the most common

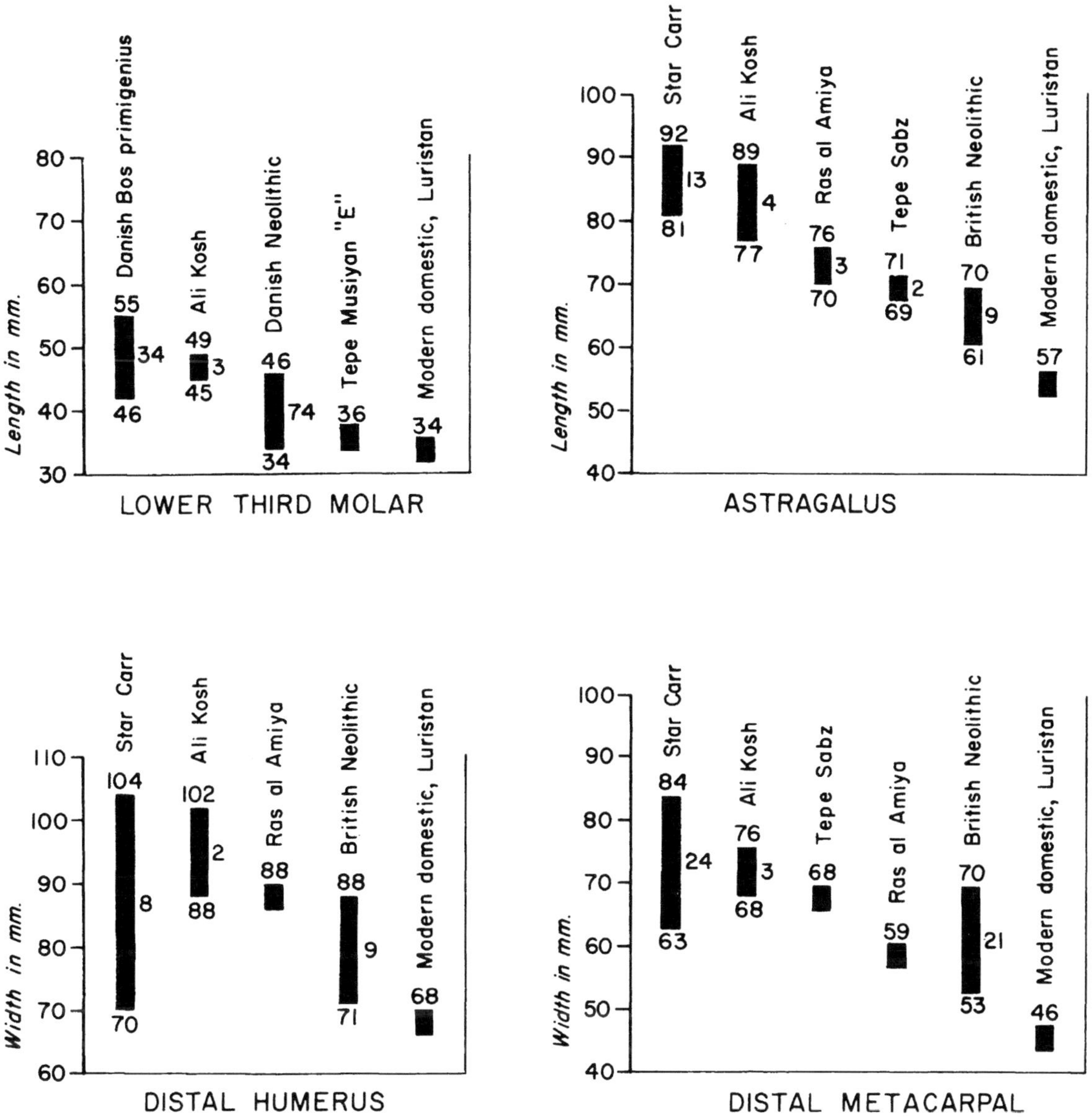

Fig. 126. Measurements of wild and domestic cattle bones from the Deh Luran sites, compared with modern and prehistoric Near Eastern cattle, and specimens from the European Mesolithic and Neolithic. Figures to the right of each heavy bar give the number of specimens measured; figures at the ends of each bar give the extreme measurements of the sample. Where only one measurement is given, only one specimen was present. European measurements after Degerbøl (1963) and Jewell (1963). Danish *Bos primigenius,* Star Carr specimens, and those from Ali Kosh are wild; all others are domestic.

Measurements applied to the Deh Luran bones, here and elsewhere in the text, were the maximum length (antero-posteriorly), maximum width (medio-laterally), and maximum height (dorso-ventrally.)

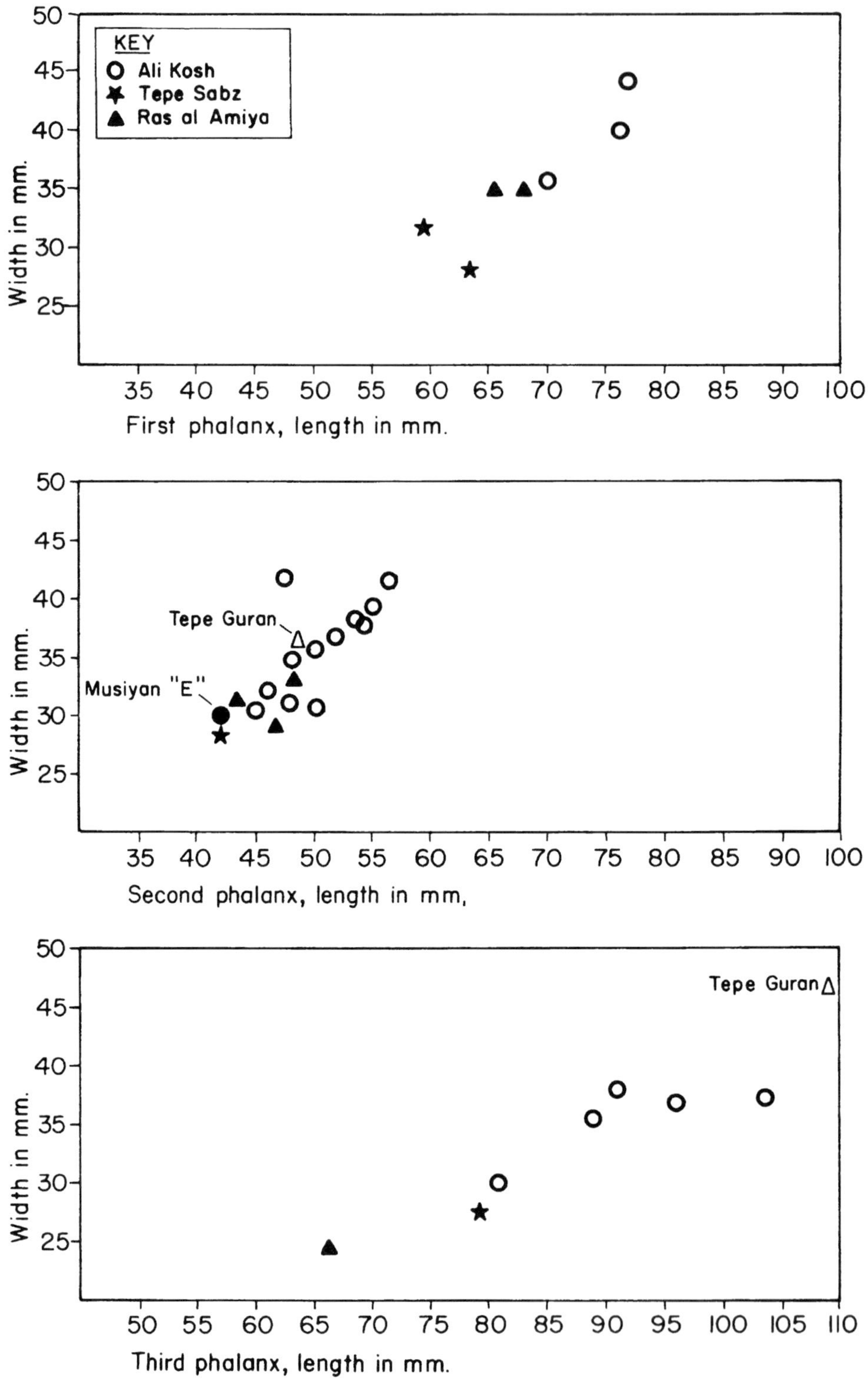

Fig. 127. Scatter diagrams giving length and width of cattle phalanges from Ali Kosh, Tepe Sabz, Tepe Musiyan "E," Ras al Amiya, and Tepe Guran. Specimens from Ali Kosh and Tepe Guran are wild; all others are domestic.

elements of the cattle skeleton we recovered, and they proved as useful as astragali for differentiating wild and domestic forms. As the accompanying figures suggest, the first and third phalanges showed a more striking reduction in size after domestication than did the second phalanx. Thirteen second phalanges from Ali Kosh varied between 45 and 57 mm. in length, overlapping slightly with five specimens from Tepe Sabz, Musiyan "E," and Ras al Amiya, which varied between 42 and 49 mm. The Mehmeh and Bayat phase specimens were the smallest measured.

No overlap was noted in measurements of first phalanges, however; three Ali Kosh specimens ranged from 70 to 77 mm. in length, while the range of presumably domestic specimens from Tepe Sabz and Ras al Amiya was only 59 to 68 mm. Similarly, six third phalanges from Ali Kosh and Tepe Guran ranged from 81 to 109 mm. in length, while Tepe Sabz and Ras al Amiya specimens were only 66 and 79 mm. long. Lengths and widths of all phalanges measured are plotted in Fig. 127.

Horn Core.—A single horn core fragment from the Bayat phase at Tepe Sabz is too small to be very informative. It would have been only about 45 mm. in diameter, however, and from somewhere relatively near the base. What is left of it corresponds fairly well to domestic (*Bos taurus*) specimens in the United States National Museum.

Butchering Technique

Our report on the 1961 test pit at Ali Kosh suggested a possible correlation between bones of wild cattle and onager and the numerous flint pebble choppers found on house floors of the Ali Kosh and Mohammad Jaffar Phases (Hole and Flannery, 1962:131-32). Excavations in 1963 only reinforced our impression that these tools were associated with the butchering of large ungulates. The floor plan of zone A_1 at Ali Kosh (see Fig. 12 and Pl. 10*b*) shows only a few of the many instances in which clusters of 5 to 10 choppers were found in a pile along with butchered *Equus* and *Bos*. The temporal distribution of these choppers (Table 33, Chap XI) even suggests that they were a tool whose use increased during the Ali Kosh and Mohammad Jaffar phases in response to increased hunting of large herbivores.

We do not know how wild *Bos primigenius* was hunted by the villagers at Deh Luran. A scarcity of ribs and vertebrae, as compared with lower limb bones, suggests that the kill sites sometimes were a good distance away, and that the initial butchering was done there, with only selected limbs being carried back to the village (see Table 65). No complete skulls or horn cores of *Bos primigenius* were recovered, although teeth are present (mostly from the lower jaw). Either the crania were left at the site of the kill, or else—as at Çatal Hüyük—all our cattle skulls were kept as trophies in a room we have not yet uncovered (cf. Mellaart, 1964*a*:103).

Limb bones were brought back to the village, often apparently in an articulated condition. Frequently, the articulated foot (with all three phalanges intact) was discarded as a unit. The muscle was freed with flint knives, which frequently left blade marks (e.g., on the back of the distal humerus and femur), and then the long bones were broken open with flint pebble choppers for marrow extraction, much in the way a piece of kindling might be split with a wedge. Scale-like "retouch" marks along the broken edges of some long bones show where they were repeatedly tapped against a hard surface until the plug of marrow fell out of its cavity. The flat limestone discs scattered through the house floor debris at Ali Kosh would have served as convenient anvils for such activity. So few of the cattle bone from the pre-pottery horizons show charring that we suspect most beef was cooked only after it has been cut away from the bone.

The domestic cattle remains from Tepe Sabz were not treated so roughly. Bones were more frequently found in articulation (even long bones like the radius and ulna), although evidence of the use of the cleaver or chopper persists even into the early part of the Bayat phase. Teeth and other cranial elements are more common, and our impression is that had our excavations been more extensive we would have recovered examples of every bone in the skeleton, since domestic cattle were butchered (or died) in or near the village.

PIGS, WILD AND DOMESTIC

Sample: 40 fragments (see Table 67 and Fig. 128)

Temporal distribution: 35 out of 40 fragments came from Bus Mordeh through Sabz phases

Introduction

Wild pigs (*Sus scrofa*) were sporadically hunted from the Bus Mordeh phase through to the Sabz phase, and after that their remains are extremely rare. Nor do the ancient Deh Luranis seem to have been very interested in domesticating them. This was not because pigs were particularly scarce in the region, for they can be hunted today anywhere along the lower reaches of the Dawairij and Mehmeh Rivers, and they even invade the grain fields in the spring. In the fall of 1963, the son of the mayor of Musiyan presented us with a 100-kilo specimen, shot only a few minutes' drive east of Ali Kosh. Obviously, the prehistoric villagers did not consider pig-hunting as economically rewarding as the hunting of onager and gazelle.

It was a surprise to find that, as late as 4000 B.C., domestic pigs were still rare at Deh Luran. Two thousand years earlier, at Jarmo, in upper (pottery-bearing) levels contemporary with the Mohammad Jaffar phase, domestic pigs were already abundant; measurements of pigs from the early Neolithic of Greece show they may have been domestic just as early there (Flannery, 1961; Reed, 1961:31-32; Higgs, 1962:273). By 5000 B.C. the domestic form was widespread from Iraqi Kurdistan

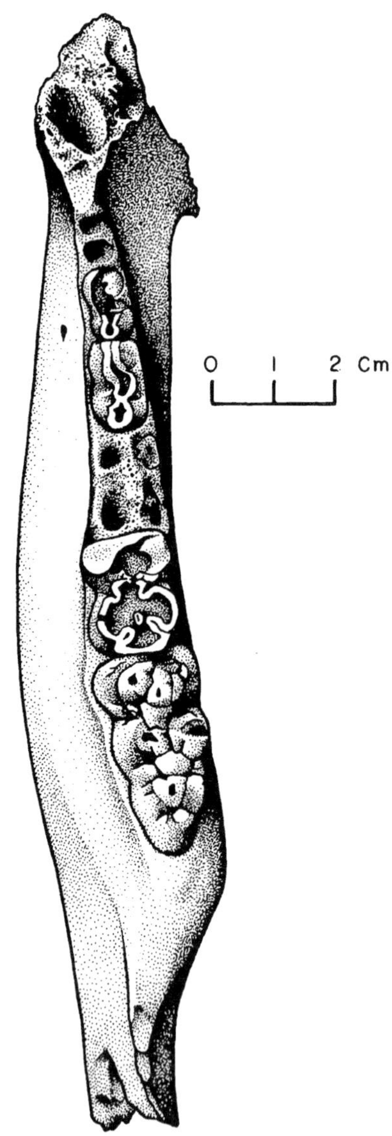

Fig. 128. Left side of mandible of possible domestic pig (*Sus scrofa*) from Tepe Sabz, zone A_1 (Bayat phase).

Table 67

REMAINS OF PIG (*SUS SCROFA*) FROM ALI KOSH AND TEPE SABZ
(By Stratigraphic Zone)

Phase	Site	Zone	Number of Identified Fragments	Minimum Number of Individuals	Individual Fragments Recovered											
					Tusk	Maxilla	Mandible	Stray Tooth	Scapula	Humerus	Radius	Ulna	Tibia	Metapodial	Phalanx	Other
Bayat	TS	A_1	3	(1)*	...	...	1	2	...	...	...	...	...	...	...	...
	TS	A_2	...	...	...	...	...	...	...	...	...	...	...	...	...	...
	TS	A_3	1	(1)	...	...	...	...	...	...	...	...	...	...	1	...
Mehmeh	TS	B_1	1	(1)	...	...	...	...	...	...	...	...	...	...	...	1
	TS	B_2	...	...	...	...	...	...	...	...	...	...	...	...	...	...
	TS	B_3	...	...	...	...	...	...	...	...	...	...	...	...	...	...
Khazineh	TS	C_1	...	...	...	...	...	...	...	...	...	...	...	...	...	...
	TS	C_2	...	...	...	...	...	...	...	...	...	...	...	...	...	...
	TS	C_3	...	...	...	...	...	...	...	...	...	...	...	...	...	...
Sabz	TS	D	8	(2)	...	...	...	1	...	2	1	...	...	...	...	4
Mohammad Jaffar	AK	A_1	3	(2)	1	1	...	1	...	...	...	...	...	...	...	...
	AK	A_2	2	(1)	...	...	...	...	...	...	...	...	...	...	2	...
Ali Kosh	AK	B_1	...	...	...	...	...	...	...	...	...	...	...	...	...	...
	AK	B_2	18	(3)	2	3	...	...	1	2	...	1	1	...	4	4
Bus Mordeh	AK	C_1	2	(1)	...	1	1	...	...	...	...	...	...	...	...	...
	AK	C_2	2	(1)	...	1	...	...	...	...	...	...	...	1	...	...
Totals			40	(13)	3	6	2	4	1	4	1	1	1	1	7	9

*The asterisk indicates a possible domestic specimen.

to the Mediterranean—but *not* in Khuzistan. And neither Tepe Sarab nor Tepe Guran show evidence of pig domestication in levels contemporary with Jarmo. It has been suggested that this lack of pig domestication was due, at least in part, to southwest Iran's dependence on transhument herding, with its seasonal movements of flocks from plains to mountains (Flannery, 1965:1254). Such seasonal movements are incompatible with swineherding (Krader, 1955:315).

Domestic pigs at Jarmo were originally distinguished on the basis of the greatly reduced length of their cheek-tooth row, especially the third molar. Twenty-one specimens of wild *Sus scrofa* from Southwest Asia were measured as a control group (Flannery, 1961). Their lower third molars ranged from 38.8 to 49.3 mm. in length, with a mean of 41.3 mm., and their lower molar row (M_1 - M_3) ranged from 75.2 to 88.6 mm., with a mean of 81.6 mm.

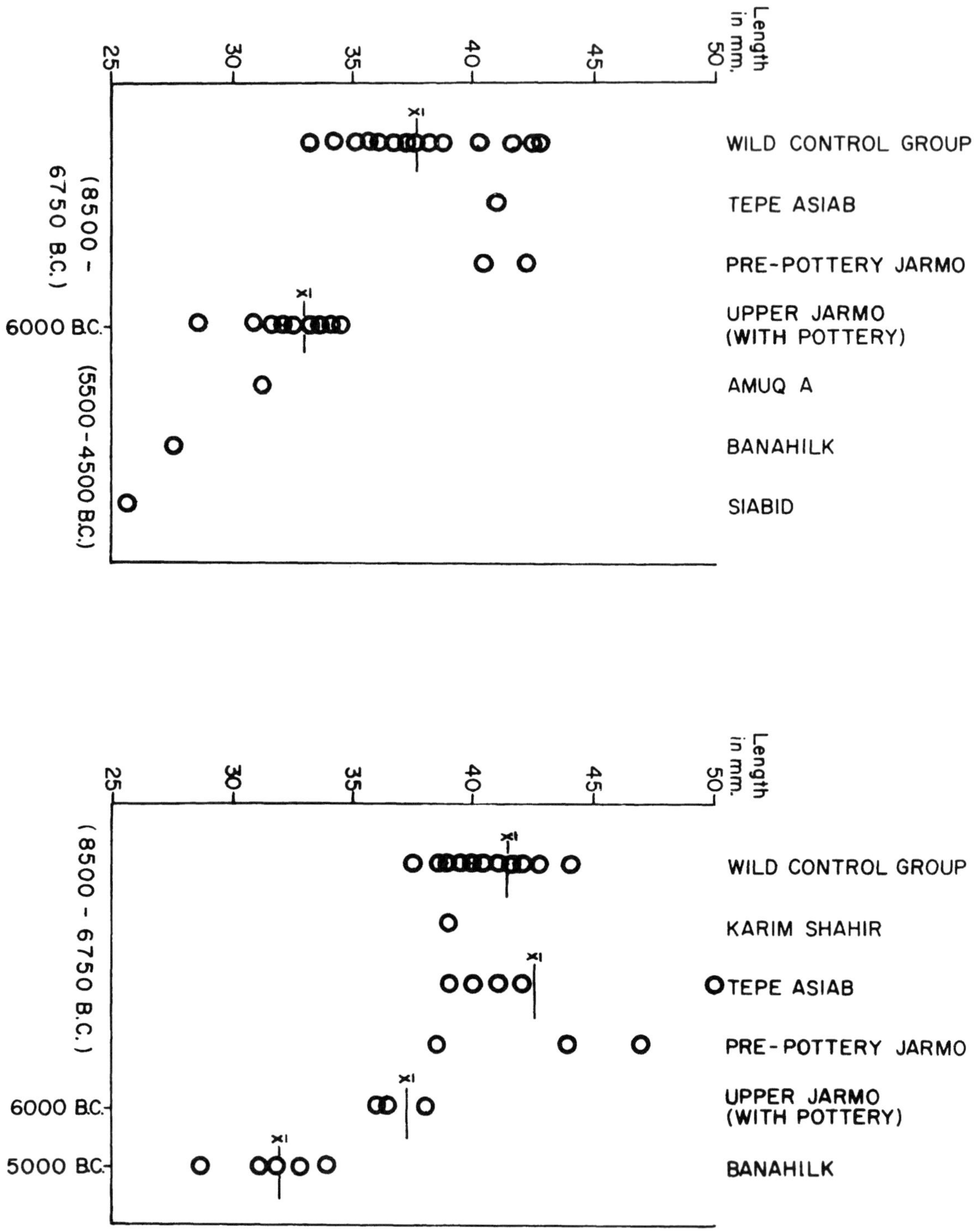

Fig. 129. Measurements of third molars of wild and domestic pigs (*Sus scrofa*). A sample of 21 modern wild specimens from the Near East ("control group") is compared with pigs from archeological sites in the same area. Left, measurements of upper third molars. Right, measurements of lower third molars; $\bar{x}$ = mean. Pigs from Tepe Asiab, Karim Shahir, and pre-pottery Jarmo are wild; all others are domestic. (Data taken from Flannery, 1961.)

Zone A_1 at Tepe Sabz (Bayat phase, *ca.* 3800 B.C.) produced a pig mandible whose tooth measurements fall outside this range; its lower third molar is only 45 mm. long, and the molar row (M_1 - M_3) measures only 66.3 mm. This compares well with the domestic pigs from upper Jarmo (see Fig. 129). Was this domestic pig locally raised, or was it traded into Tepe Sabz from some nearby area? It would be difficult to resolve this question without further evidence. We cannot believe that domestic pigs were common in the Deh Luran plain even in the Bayat phase, because there are so few specimens of pig (only 5 fragments in the upper 9 levels of Tepe Sabz); at the same time, we do know that some adjacent areas of Iranian Kurdistan had domestic pigs in levels contemporary with the Bayat phase (Flannery, 1961). It may be that domestic pigs were occasionally obtained from mountain villagers.

WOLVES AND DOMESTIC DOGS

Sample: 88 fragments (13 wolf or dog, 75 probably dog)

Temporal distribution: Wolf, Ali Kosh-Mohammad Jaffar phases; dogs, Sabz through Bayat phases (see Table 68 and Fig. 130)

Introduction

The problem of distinguishing early domestic dog from wolf by means of skeletal remains from archeological sites has been one of the most frustrating tasks facing the Near Eastern specialist. The difficulty lies in the fact that the Southwest Asian wolf, *Canis lupus pallipes,* is a race showing wide variability and including relatively small individuals. The difficulty of clearly segregating the Jarmo "dogs" from wild *C. lupus pallipes* has already been discussed by Reed (1961:36-37), and the same difficulty obtained with the specimens from Ali Kosh. At that time, Reed concluded (*Ibid.*): "one wonders if there exists any good osteological evidence for dogs in southwestern Asia until their skeletons are actually found buried with humans in the Ubaid period in Mesopotamia."

Here Reed has put his finger on one possible approach to the problem—cultural, rather than osteological. When there is overlap in nearly all skeletal characters between the wild and domestic forms of a given species, we must turn to its archeological context for evidence. We feel that archeological context allows us to suggest that dogs were domestic at Deh Luran by the Sabz phase. Our reasoning is as follows:

There were only 13 fragments of *Canis* from the entire site of Ali Kosh. This is a very small amount, especially when one considers that foxes were three times as common (42 fragments). There were never more than 5 bones of *Canis* in a given zone, and none were articulated; most were stray foot bones. One specimen from the Mohammad Jaffar phase had been roasted. Thus there is little evidence at Ali Kosh for anything beyond the occasional hunting and eating of wolves.

Abruptly in the Sabz phase, we recovered 50 bones of *Canis,* the remains of at least 4 semiarticulated individuals. The canids of the Sabz phase (and subsequent periods) are about the size of the modern Kurdish guard dog (they also compared in size with skeletons of Irish setter in the U.S. National Museum). In precisely the same levels, we recovered Susiana Black-on-buff pots with painted designs showing a canid with a fluffy, "feathered" tail which curves up over its back (Fig. 131*d*). No wolf carries its tail in such a position, but the modern Kurdish guard dog *does* (see Hatt, 1969:Plate I). We conclude that the 4 partial skeletons recovered from

Table 68

DOMESTIC DOGS (*CANIS FAMILIARIS*) AND UNIDENTIFIED LARGE CANIDS FROM ALI KOSH AND TEPE SABZ
(By Stratigraphic Zone)

Phase	Site	Zone	Canis Species Indeterminate		Domestic Dog		Total Bones	Total Individuals	List of Skeletal Components, Domestic Dog												
			Number of Bones	Number of Individuals	Number of Bones	Number of Individuals			Maxilla	Mandible	Stray Teeth	Scapula	Humerus	Radius	Ulna	Femur	Tibia	Metapodial	Phalanx	Vertebra	Other
Bayat	TS	A_1	...	...	...	...	...	...	...	...	...	...	...	...	...	...	...	...	...	...	...
	TS	A_2	...	...	12	(2)	12	(2)	...	2	...	...	2	1	1	...	...	1	...	5	...
	TS	A_3	...	...	6	(1)	6	(1)	...	1	...	...	...	...	...	...	...	...	...	5	...
Mehmeh	TS	B_1	...	...	...	...	...	...	...	...	...	...	...	...	...	...	...	...	...	...	...
	TS	B_2	...	...	...	...	...	...	...	...	...	...	...	...	...	...	...	...	...	...	...
	TS	B_3	...	...	...	...	...	...	...	...	...	...	...	...	...	...	...	...	...	...	...
Khazineh	TS	C_1	...	...	3	(2)	3	(2)	...	2	1	...	...	...	...	...	...	...	...	...	...
	TS	C_2	...	...	4	(1)	4	(1)	...	1	1	...	...	...	...	...	...	1	...	...	1
	TS	C_3	...	...	...	...	...	...	...	...	...	...	...	...	...	...	...	...	...	...	...
Sabz	TS	D	...	...	50	(4)	50	(4)	1	5	14	1	4	...	...	1	2	7	6	3	6
Mohammad Jaffar	AK	A_1	4	(1)	...	...	4	(1)	...	...	...	...	...	...	...	...	...	...	...	...	...
	AK	A_2	5	(1)	...	...	5	(1)	...	...	...	...	...	...	...	...	...	...	...	...	...
Ali Kosh	AK	B_1	2	(1)	...	...	2	(1)	...	...	...	...	...	...	...	...	...	...	...	...	...
	AK	B_2	2	(1)	...	...	2	(1)	...	...	...	...	...	...	...	...	...	...	...	...	...
Bus Mordeh	AK	C_1	...	...	...	...	...	...	...	...	...	...	...	...	...	...	...	...	...	...	...
	AK	C_2	...	...	...	...	...	...	...	...	...	...	...	...	...	...	...	...	...	...	...
Totals			13	(4)	75	(10)	88	(14)	1	11	16	1	6	1	1	1	2	9	6	11	7

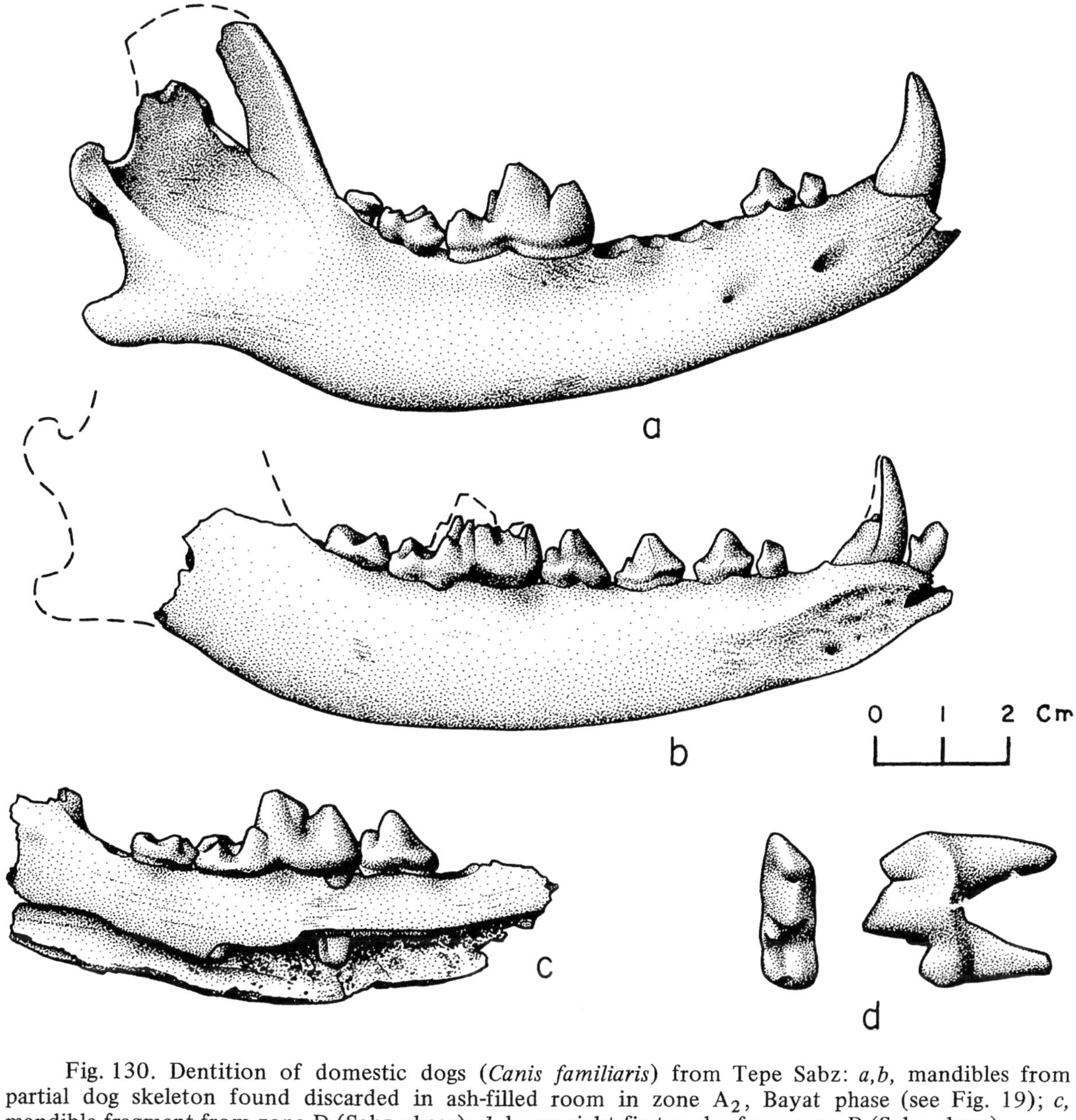

Fig. 130. Dentition of domestic dogs (*Canis familiaris*) from Tepe Sabz: *a,b,* mandibles from partial dog skeleton found discarded in ash-filled room in zone A_2, Bayat phase (see Fig. 19); *c,* mandible fragment from zone D (Sabz phase); *d,* lower right first molar from zone D (Sabz phase).

zone D at Tepe Sabz were probably domestic dogs who lived in the village. None appears to have been butchered or cooked. Some do show "crowding" of the teeth, a possible result of muzzle-shortening in domestication (cf. Lawrence, 1967).

Dog remains appeared in 4 other zones at Tepe Sabz, and they represent a *minimum* of 6 more individuals. In zone A_2 (Bayat phase) we found a dog which had been thrown into the corner of an abandoned room (see Fig. 19). The right and left mandibles; the atlas and 4 other vertebrae; and the left humerus, radius, and ulna had remained in articulation. Bones of still another dog appeared in the same refuse-filled room. In all, we recovered 75 fragments of such canids from Tepe Sabz (nearly 6 times the number found at Ali Kosh).

One interesting archeological by-product of dog domestication is a great decrease in other animal bone fragments. Tens of thousands of splinters from the long bones of goat and gazelle lay on the floors of houses at Ali Kosh, and none of them showed the kind of gnawing one would expect if domestic dogs were present. Tepe Sabz, however, did not show such proportions of splintered long bone; usually, all that remained after the dogs had finished were the least edible parts of the skeleton, like teeth, horns, hooves, and particularly hard and compact articular ends. The number of "chewable" bone midsections was much smaller, relative to Ali Kosh.

Dog Domestication in Khuzistan

On the basis of the evidence presented above, we presume that by 5500 B.C. in Khuzistan, canids resembling the Kurdish guard dog were already inhabiting the dump-heaps of our early villages. In all probability they were descendents of the local wild *Canis lupus pallipes,* who had been allowed by the villagers to become semi-domestic scavengers.

The curly-tailed "dogs" painted on pottery of the Sabz Phase are reminiscent of the curly-tailed "dog" figurines from Jarmo illustrated by Braidwood, Howe, *et al.* (1960:Plate 16:2). Representations in prehistoric art are always dangerous evidence on which to base zoological conclusions, but coupled with the bones from Tepe Sabz they suggest what the early dogs of Khuzistan might have looked like.

During the next 3000 years, as pointed out by Hatt (1959:35-36), some of these early domestic dogs seem to have been selectively bred to produce two specialized races: (1) a large mastiff used in war (and somewhat resembling the Kurdish guard dog), and (2) a lean, greyhoundlike hunting dog which was probably the ancestor of the modern *seluki. Seluki*-like dogs are painted on Susa I sherds from Khuzistan, dating to about 3000 B.C. (Fig. 131*e*); some sherds show them hunting or attacking wild goats (Fig. 131*f*). Such was the history of dogbreeding in Khuzistan during the millenium after the abandonment of Tepe Sabz. In addition to the specialized mastiff and *seluki,* however, the large, nondescript village dog of southwestern Iran apparently continued its role as guard and scavenger on the local dump heaps, where it can still be found today.

RED FOX

Sample: 54 fragments from nearly all phases (see Table 69 and Fig. 132*a*)

The red fox (*Vulpes vulpes*) was by far the commonest small mammal eaten by the prehistoric villagers at Deh Luran. Their bones show that they were often roasted, but not necessarily broken open for marrow. The bulk of our fox remains came from the Ali Kosh and Mohammad Jaffar phases, as many as 5 individual animals occurring in zone A_2 at Ali Kosh. Foxes were also eaten regularly at Jarmo (Reed, 1961:36) and Tepe Guran (Flannery, unpublished data), and are still eaten today in the winter in Kurdistan (Reed, quoted in Hatt, 1959:38).

Reed (1961:36) suggests that at Jarmo "foxes and wolves were captured and eaten, but that jackals never were." Interestingly enough, this is precisely the situation at Ali Kosh and Tepe Guran. We sighted (and heard) jackals much more frequently than foxes during our stay at Deh Luran, yet not a single jackal bone appeared in the prehistoric refuse; and jackals are absent also at Tepe Guran, although foxes

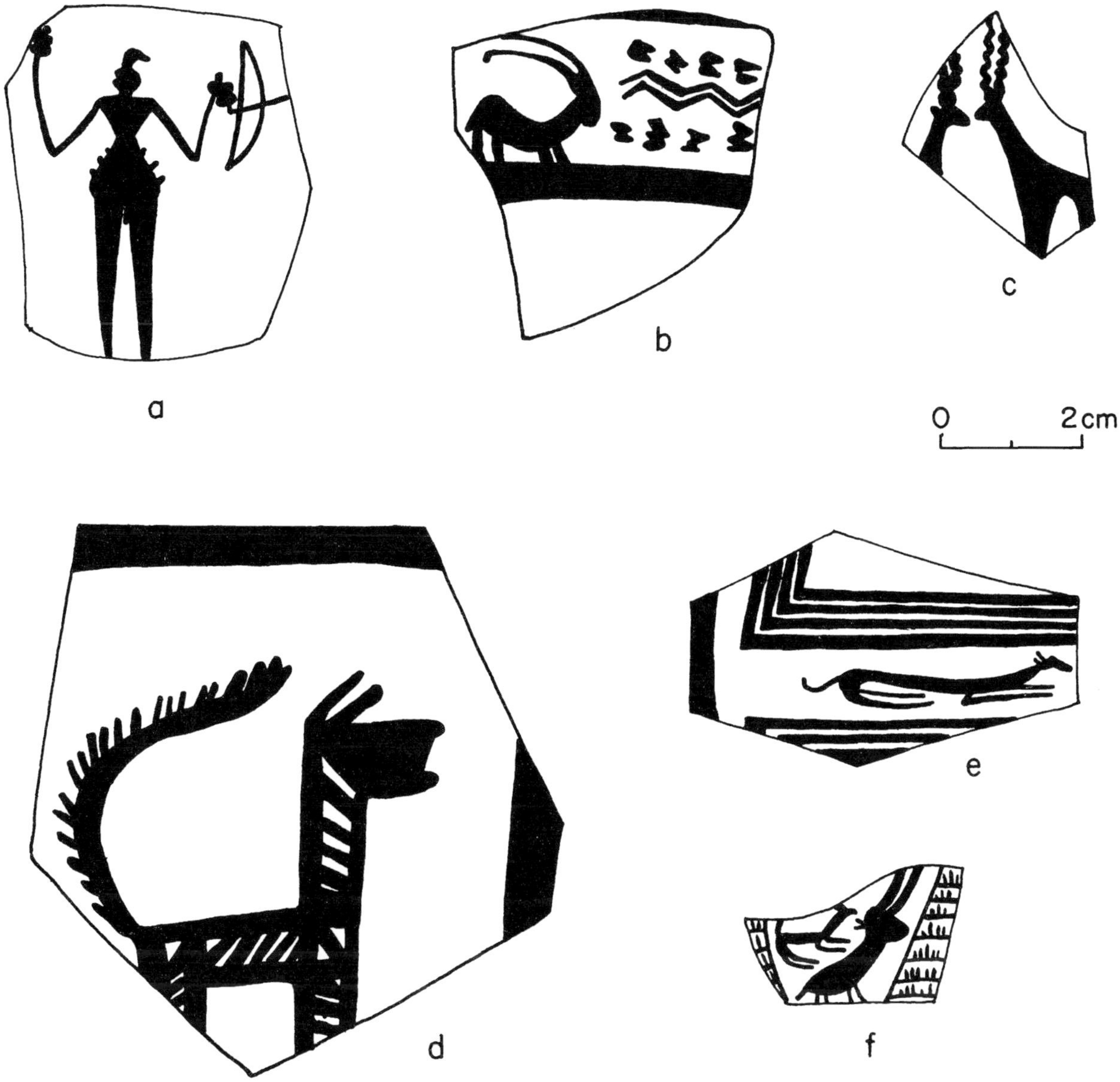

Fig. 131. Susiana Black-on-buff pot sherds from sites in Khuzistan, providing data relevant to the faunal analysis: *a,* man with bow and arrow, Tepe Jowi (Le Breton, 1947: Fig. 30: 16). Probably Mehmeh phase (= Susiana *b*); *b,* wild goat accompanied by what appear to be hoof prints, Tepe Musiyan "E," Mehmeh phase; *c,* male gazelles, Tepe Bandibal (Le Breton, 1947: Fig. 40: 12). Probably Mehmeh phase; *d,* domestic dog with tail curled over back, Tepe Sabz, zone D (Sabz phase); *e,* seluki-like dog, Susa I (Le Breton, 1947: Fig. 49: 12); *f,* seluki-like dog apparently attacking wild goat or gazelle, Susa I (Le Breton 1947: Fig. 50: 15).

and wolves were often eaten. The law of averages would seem to suggest that some human selection factor was operating here. It may be that more strictly nocturnal habits of the jackal made it difficult to hunt. We sighted foxes at almost any hour of the day, but jackals approached our camp only under cover of darkness.

Table 69

OTHER WILD CARNIVORES FROM ALI KOSH AND TEPE SABZ
(By Stratigraphic Zone)

Phase	Site	Zone	Hyaena		Red Fox		List of Skeletal Components, Red Fox											
			Number of Bones	Number of Individuals	Number of Bones	Number of Individuals	Maxilla	Mandible	Stray Teeth	Humerus	Radius	Ulna	Femur	Tibia	Metapodial	Vertebra	Sacrum	Other
Bayat	TS	A_1	...	...	...	...	...	...	...	...	...	...	...	...	...	...	...	...
	TS	A_2	...	...	1	(1)	...	...	...	...	...	...	...	1	...	...	...	...
	TS	A_3	...	...	8	(3)	...	4	...	...	1	2	...	1	...	...	...	...
Mehmeh	TS	B_1	...	...	...	...	...	...	...	...	...	...	...	...	...	...	...	...
	TS	B_2	...	...	...	...	...	...	...	...	...	...	...	...	...	...	...	...
	TS	B_3	...	...	1	(1)	...	...	...	...	...	...	...	...	...	1	...	...
Khazineh	TS	C_1	...	...	...	...	...	...	...	...	...	...	...	...	...	...	...	...
	TS	C_2	...	...	...	...	...	...	...	...	...	...	...	...	...	...	...	...
	TS	C_3	...	...	...	...	...	...	...	...	...	...	...	...	...	...	...	...
Sabz	TS	D	...	...	2	(1)	...	...	...	...	1	...	...	1	...	...	...	...
Mohammad Jaffar	AK	A_1	...	...	4	(2)	...	1	3	...	...	...	...	...	...	...	...	...
	AK	A_2	1	(1)	15	(5)	2	6	2	...	1	...	1	1	1	...	...	1
Ali Kosh	AK	B_1	...	...	1	(1)	...	...	...	...	...	...	...	...	1	...	...	...
	AK	B_2	...	...	15	(2)	...	...	...	...	...	...	...	...	4	4	2	5
Bus Mordeh	AK	C_1	...	...	6	(1)	...	1	...	1	...	...	1	...	...	3	...	...
	AK	C_2	...	...	1	(1)	...	1	...	...	...	...	...	...	...	...	...	...
Totals			1	(1)	54	(18)	2	13	5	1	3	2	2	4	6	8	2	6

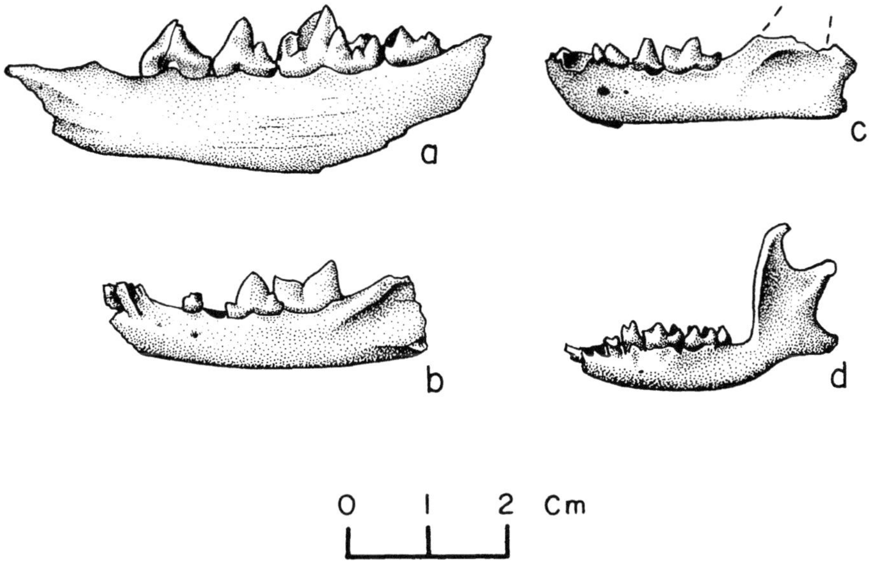

Fig. 132. Mandibles of small mammals from Tepe Ali Kosh: *a*, red fox (*Vulpes vulpes*), zone C_2 (Bus Mordeh phase); *b*, wild cat (*Felis* cf. *libyca*), zone B_1 (Ali Kosh phase); *c*, weasel (*Mustela* cf. *nivalis*), zone A_2 (Mohammad Jaffar phase); *d*, hedgehog (*Hemiechinus auritus*), zone B_1 (Ali Kosh phase).

HYAENA

Sample: 1 fragment from the Ali Kosh phase.

Hyaena hyaena is not uncommon at Deh Luran today, but it seems to have played no role in the prehistoric diet. We sighted hyaenas on several occasions while driving between Ali Kosh and Tepe Sabz, and collected one elderly, arthritic male who had become trapped in the asphalt spring. The police at the Bayat border inspection post reported that a hyaena ransacked their garbage pit every night and regularly carried away dead donkeys. Thus its virtual absence in the ancient faunal remains is not due to its scarcity in the region.

OTHER SMALL CARNIVORES

Wild Cat (Possibly *Felis lybica*, the Indian desert cat)

Sample: 11 fragments (Ali Kosh through Sabz phases); see Fig. 132*b*

Our fragmentary remains of wild cat were difficult to identify, and our assignment of them to *Felis lybica* is mainly on the basis of size. They seem too small to be *F. chaus,* the other likely candidate. *F. libyca* is known from the lower Tigris near Kut al Imara (Hatt, 1959:46).

Weasel (Probably *Mustela nivalis*)

Sample: 1 mandible from the Ali Kosh phase (Fig. 132*c*)

This is the only species of weasel listed by Hatt (1959) whose range might extend into Khuzistan.

Table 70

SMALL MAMMAL REMAINS FROM ALI KOSH AND TEPE SABZ
(By Stratigraphic Zone)

Phase	Site	Zone	Long Eared Hedgehog		Wild Cat		Weasel		Beech Marten		Unidentified Small Mammals
			Number of Bones	Number of Individuals	Number of Bones	Number of Individuals	Number of Bones	Number of Individuals	Number of Bones	Number of Individuals	
Bayat	TS	A_1	...	...	...	...	...	...	...	...	...
	TS	A_2	...	...	...	...	...	...	...	...	...
	TS	A_3	...	...	...	...	...	...	...	...	1
Mehmeh	TS	B_1	...	...	...	...	...	...	...	...	...
	TS	B_2	...	...	...	...	...	...	...	...	...
	TS	B_3	...	...	...	...	...	...	...	...	...
Khazineh	TS	C_1	...	...	...	...	...	...	...	...	...
	TS	C_2	...	...	...	...	...	...	...	...	1
	TS	C_3	...	...	...	...	...	...	...	...	2
Sabz	TS	D	1	(1)	1	(1)	...	...	5	(1)	...
Mohammad Jaffar	AK	A_1	...	...	...	...	...	...	...	...	1
	AK	A_2	1	(1)	8	(2)	1	(1)	...	...	2
Ali Kosh	AK	B_1	1	(1)	1	(1)	...	...	...	...	1
	AK	B_2	1	(1)	1	(1)	...	...	...	...	...
Bus Mordeh	AK	C_1	...	...	...	...	...	...	...	...	...
	AK	C_2	...	...	...	...	...	...	...	...	...
	Totals		4	(4)	11	(5)	1	(1)	5	(1)	8

Beech Marten (*Martes foina*)

Sample: 5 fragments (all from one individual) in the Sabz phase.

The beech marten was also eaten at Jarmo (Braidwood, Howe, *et al.* 1960:48), although presumably it was as rare an element there as it was at Tepe Sabz.

Hedgehog

Sample: 4 fragments (Ali Kosh through Sabz phases); see Fig. 132*d*

Mandibles of the long-eared hedgehog (*Hemiechinus auritus*) were an uncommon element in our faunal remains. Presumably these shy, nocturnal animals were rarely encountered.

SMALL RODENTS

Sample: 352 mandibles or maxillae (all levels)

Introduction

Small rodents do not appear to have been eaten at Ali Kosh and Tepe Sabz, but they used both sites as burrowing areas. Literally thousands of rodent bones were recovered by our excavations, but owing to a lack of comparative postcranial material, only the skulls, jaws, and teeth could be identified to species.

Recent intrusive rodents could be distinguished by their pale white color, their articulated condition, and often by their accompanying seed caches. By far the majority of the rodent remains from the lowest levels, however, were as dark-colored as the rest of the prehistoric animal bone. A few carbonized mandibles may have been from rodents who burrowed into the site in ancient times, died in their burrows, then were accidentally dug up by prehistoric villagers, and eventually burned accidentally in debris around hearths or smouldering middens.

We suspect that the bulk of our rodents date to the prehistoric period, but since rodents are notorious burrowers, we make no claims that those found, for example, in zone B_2 actually are contemporary with B_2. They may have burrowed down from A_1 or A_2, or been accidentally brought up from C_1 or C_2. What is interesting to us, as stated in the chapter on local ecology, is that no species are found (even in the lowest levels) which would not still be present in the area today. That includes specimens which were carbonized by fires that smouldered on middens of the Bus Mordeh phase, and *Tatera* specimens found in the sterile soil below the site.

Commensal House Mouse

Sample: 1 fragment

A single mandible of the commensal house mouse, *Mus musculus,* was found in zone A_2 of Ali Kosh. Since it occurred just a little over a meter below the surface—and since no house mouse remains appeared in later levels—we assume it is a relatively recent intrusive. There were no house mouse remains at Tepe Sabz, even in the Bayat phase levels. As late as 3800 B.C., therefore, there is still no evidence that the house mouse (originally native to eastern Asia) had begun to occupy human settlements in Khuzistan.

Wild Rodents (Table 71)

The Indian Gerbil (*Tatera indica*)

Sample: 331 mandibles or maxillae (Fig. 133*a*)

This was the most common rodent encountered in the excavations; it was clear

Table 71

REMAINS OF SMALL WILD RODENTS FROM ALI KOSH AND TEPE SABZ
(By Stratigraphic Zone)

Site	Zone	Indian Gerbil				Karun Desert Gerbil				Bandicoot-Rat				Grand Total
		Maxillae		Mandibles		Maxillae		Mandibles		Maxillae		Mandibles		
		R	L	R	L	R	L	R	L	R	L	R	L	
TS	A_1	...	...	...	1	...	...	...	...	...	...	...	...	...
TS	A_2	...	1	2	...	...	...	...	...	...	...	...	...	...
TS	A_3	1	...	2	4	...	...	...	...	...	...	...	...	...
TS	B_1	1	...	1	1	...	...	...	...	...	...	...	...	...
TS	B_2	...	...	2	1	...	...	...	...	...	...	...	...	...
TS	B_3	1	...	3	4	...	...	...	...	...	...	...	...	...
TS	C_1	...	...	1	...	...	...	...	...	...	...	...	...	...
TS	C_2	...	...	...	...	...	...	...	...	...	...	...	...	...
TS	C_3	...	1	...	...	...	...	...	...	...	...	...	...	...
TS	D	...	1	...	1	...	...	1	...	...	...	...	...	...
AK	A_1	6	2	8	8	2	2	2	2	...	...	1	...	...
AK	A_2	3	3	12	13	2	2	2	2	...	...	...	...	...
AK	B_1	1	2	4	5	...	...	...	...	...	...	...	...	...
AK	B_2	9	12	53	55	...	...	...	...	...	...	1	...	...
AK	C_1	2	3	33	37	...	...	1	...	...	...	...	...	...
AK	C_2	...	...	18	13	...	...	...	...	...	...	...	...	...
Totals		24	25	139	143	4	4	6	4	...	...	2	...	351

that *Tatera* had been present at Deh Luran long before Ali Kosh was founded, making burrows in the sterile soil where the Bus Mordeh villagers later settled. The Indian gerbil is a semi-desertic species inhabiting wadis, riverine thickets, and rocky hillsides from northern Arabia to Ceylon. Type locality for one of its subspecies is the Jebel Hamrin (Hatt, 1959:89). *Tatera* does not avoid human habitations. We collected a specimen at Tepe Sabz in the fall of 1963.

The Karun Desert Gerbil (*Meriones crassus*)

Sample: 18 mandibles or maxillae (Fig. 133*b*)

This rodent appeared in some of the lowest levels at both sites, and there were nearly complete skeletons in the uppermost strata at Ali Kosh. *Meriones crassus* occupies hot, dry areas from the Sahara to northern India, and the type locality of one of its subspecies is the archeological mound of Susa, some 100 km. east of Deh Luran. Two *Meriones* lived under the ice chest in our field camp, so it is entirely possible that they inhabited the village of Ali Kosh while it was still occupied.

The Bandicoot-rat (*Nesokia indica*)

Sample: 2 mandibles (Fig. 133*c*)

Both fragments of this species appeared at Ali Kosh, and both were within the depth range (6 meters) to which this animal is known to burrow. Both are, however, stained the same mahogany brown as the other faunal material from the levels in

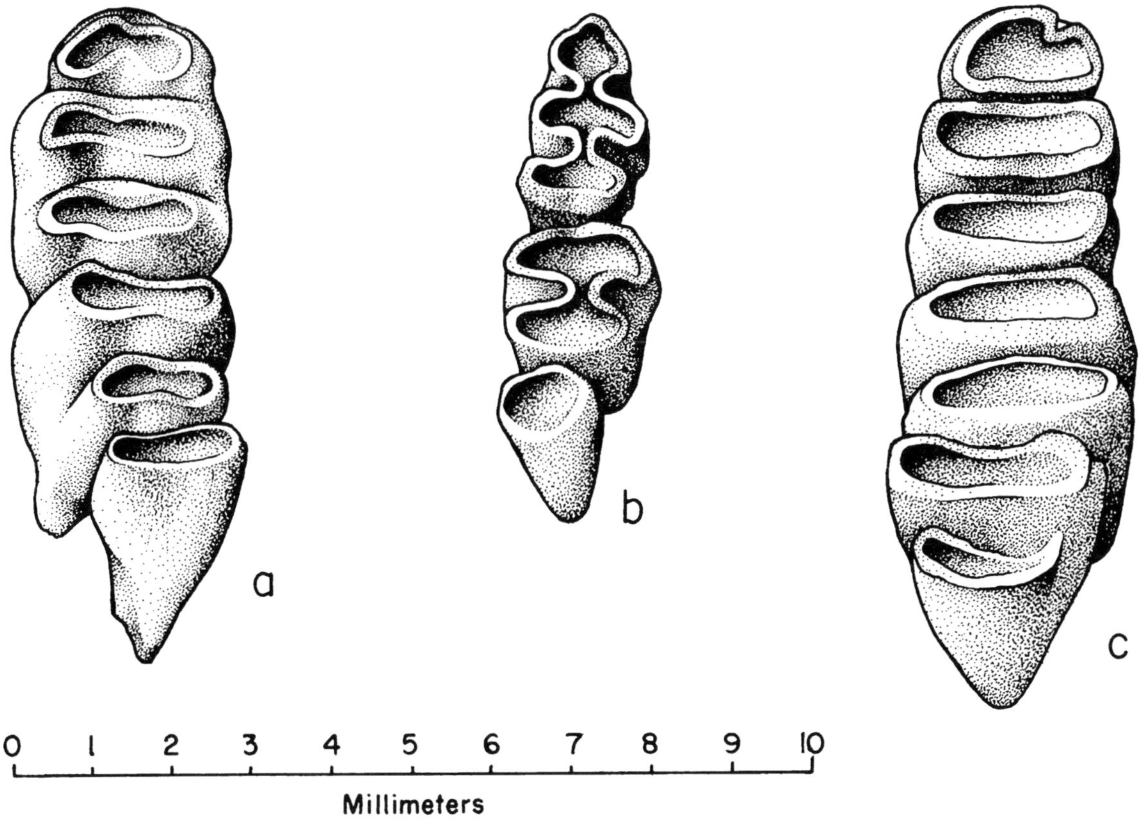

Fig. 133. Lower molars of small wild rodents from Tepe Ali Kosh, shown many times natural size: *a,* Indian gerbil (*Tatera indica*), zone C_2; *b,* Karun desert gerbil (*Meriones crassus*), zone A_2; *c,* bandicoot-rat (*Nesokia indica*), zone A_1.

which they occurred, and from the context in which they were found it appears that both were redeposited specimens, disturbed in ancient times, rather than modern intrusives. The bandicoot-rat is a crop pest which ranges from Egypt and northern Arabia to India and Pakistan, occupying moist microhabitats within desertic areas.

BIRD REMAINS

Sample: 30 fragments, all phases

Introduction

Birds formed part of the diet of the prehistoric inhabitants of the Deh Luran plain. A variety of species were eaten, with no evidence of specialization on any one particular bird. Ducks, geese, cranes, herons, storks, partridges, eagles and hawks were among the types whose bones could be identified by comparison with specimens in the U. S. National Museum. Drs. George Watson and Richard Zusi of the Division of Birds, Smithsonian Institution, greatly facilitated our work.

Some of the species eaten at Ali Kosh and Tepe Sabz (in particular, the partridges) are year-round inhabitants of Khuzistan. Nine of the species, however, are winter visitors (see below). Their presence in the refuse from all zones at Ali Kosh indicates that residence in the Bus Mordeh, Ali Kosh, and Mohammad Jaffar phases definitely included the period from November to March. This is no surprise, since the winter rainy season would have been a period of considerable agricultural activity; nevertheless, it is valuable to have tangible proof in the form of winter water-fowl.

Ducks are still seen in the Deh Luran area during the winter, but the numbers of seasonal water birds cannot compare with those in the Amara marshes, just across the Jebel Hamrin in Iraq. Notes on the avifauna of southern Iraq by Allouse (1953) form the basis for our comments on the individual species recovered by our excavations (below).

Seasonal Water Birds

Gray Goose (*Anser anser*)

Sample: 1 humerus from the Bus Mordeh phase

Allouse (1953:14) describes the gray goose as a very common winter visitor to the marshes of southern Iraq. It arrives in late October, and most geese have left for the north again by the end of March, although a few have been known to stay on through the summer and breed in marshes like the Haur al-Hammar.

White-Fronted Goose (*Anser albifrons*)

Sample: 1 carpometacarpus from the Bus Mordeh phase

This is also a common winter visitor to the area, its dates of arrival and departure being similar to those of the gray goose. It seems to be more frequently found north of Baghdad than south.

Mallard Duck (*Anas platyrhynchos*)

Sample: 1 ulna from the Mohammad Jaffar phase

The mallard is a common winter visitor in the region of Amara on the Tigris River (just across the Jebel Hamrin from Deh Luran). So far there is no definite proof that these ducks stay through the whole summer to breed in southern Mesopotamia, but some years they may arrive as early as July-August, or leave as late as May (Allouse, 1953:16). We collected a specimen from the Dawairij River in November, 1963.

Diving Duck (*Aythya* sp.)

Sample: 1 coracoid from the Mohammad Jaffar phase

Several species of diving ducks are reported to be common winter visitors (October through April) in the rivers and deep marshes of southern Mesopotamia.

Crane (*Grus grus*)

Sample: 1 tarsometatarsus from the Ali Kosh phase

Cranes begin to fly south into the Persian Gulf area in November, and they are fairly common winter visitors on the marshy plains of Mesopotamia. Some merely pass through on their way farther south.

White Stork (*Ciconia ciconia*)

Sample: 1 carpometacarpus from the Ali Kosh phase

North of Baghdad, storks can be seen at any time of the year, often nesting on the rooftops of mud-walled houses. South of Baghdad, however, it appears that they are only winter visitors and passage migrants from mid-September to early April (Allouse, 1953:11). Presumably, this pattern would apply in Khuzistan as well.

Heron (*Ardea cinerea*)

Sample: 2 fragments, from the Mohammad Jaffar and Mehmeh phases

Herons fly south into Iraq in September, and are very common in winter. They may occasionally be seen in summer in certain suitable localities, like the marshes at the head of the Persian Gulf; so their pattern is not rigidly one of winter occupation, as in the case of some of the other birds.

OTHER WINTER VISITORS

Eagle (*Aquila* sp., *sensu latu*)

Sample: 1 individual (several fragments) from the Sabz phase

Most locally-occurring members of this genus are winter visitors to the steppes and marshes of the Karun and lower Tigris, between September and March. Our specimen could not be identified to species.

Hawk or Kite (Family Accipitridae, genus uncertain)

Sample: 1 carpometacarpus from the Khazineh phase

Most locally-occurring members of this family visit the southern Mesopotamian and southwest Persian area between October and April. Our specimen could not be identified further.

PERMANENT RESIDENTS

Black Partridge (*Francolinus francolinus*)

Sample: 2 fragments, from the Ali Kosh and Mohammad Jaffar phases

The black partridge or francoline is a common year-round resident from Kurdistan to Basra, most frequently found in thick scrub (especially tamarisk and licorice) or dense grass near water (Allouse, 1953:36). Loftus (1857:346) mentions this bird as being abundant in the vicinity of Susa. The most suitable habitats for francolines in the Deh Luran plain are the tamarisk thickets of the Mehmeh and Dawairij Rivers.

Seesee partridge (*Ammoperdix griseogularis*)

Sample: 1 tarsometatarsus from the Khazineh phase

This partridge is a common resident of stony, hilly country (including the Jebel Hamrin), but rarely inhabits open plains (Allouse, 1953:35). It hides during the day, but comes out to feed and drink in the morning and evening throughout the year.

Hooded crow (*Corvus corone*)

Sample: 1 ulna from the Mohammad Jaffar phase

At least one race of hooded crow is a year-round resident of the plains and date palm groves from the Persian Gulf to the upper Tigris; other races come down seasonally from the Iranian central plateau.

Table 72

BIRD BONES FROM ALI KOSH AND TEPE SABZ
(By Stratigraphic Zone)

			Seasonal Water Birds									Permanent Residents					
Phase	Site	Zone	Gray Goose	White-fronted Goose	Mallard Duck	Diving Duck	Crane	Stork	Heron	Eagle	Hawk	Black Partridge	Seesee Partridge	Hooded Crow	Songbird	Unidentified Birds	Totals
Bayat	TS	A_1	...	...	...	...	...	...	...	...	...	...	...	...	...	...	...
	TS	A_2	...	...	...	...	...	...	...	...	...	...	...	...	...	1	1
	TS	A_3	...	...	...	...	...	...	...	...	...	...	...	...	...	...	...
Mehmeh	TS	B_1	...	...	...	...	...	...	...	...	...	...	...	...	...	...	...
	TS	B_2	...	...	...	...	...	...	...	...	...	...	...	...	...	...	...
	TS	B_3	...	...	...	...	...	...	1	...	...	...	...	...	...	2	3
Khazineh	TS	C_1	...	...	...	...	...	...	...	...	...	...	1	...	1	1	3
	TS	C_2	...	...	...	...	...	...	...	...	...	...	...	...	...	...	...
	TS	C_3	...	...	...	...	...	...	...	...	1	...	...	...	...	...	1
Sabz	TS	D	...	...	...	...	...	...	...	1	...	...	...	...	...	...	1
Mohammad Jaffar	AK	A_1	...	...	...	...	...	...	1	...	...	...	...	...	1	2	4
	AK	A_2	...	...	1	1	...	...	...	...	...	1	...	1	...	2	6
Ali Kosh	AK	B_1	...	...	...	...	...	...	...	...	...	1	...	...	...	2	3
	AK	B_2	...	...	...	...	1	1	...	...	...	...	...	...	...	3	5
Bus Mordeh	AK	C_1	...	1	...	...	...	...	...	...	...	...	...	...	...	1	2
	AK	C_2	1	...	...	...	...	...	...	...	...	...	...	...	...	...	1
Totals			1	1	1	1	1	1	2	1	1	2	1	1	2	14	30

UNIDENTIFIED PASSERINES

Bone fragments of songbirds are notoriously difficult to identify. One humerus from the Mohammad Jaffar phase may be a member of the thrush family, and a larger humerus from the Khazineh phase resembles the starling group.

OTHER UNIDENTIFIED BIRDS

Fourteen fragments of bird bone from all phases remain to be identified. Some are so fragmentary that it may never be possible to key them out, others are almost certainly songbirds, but which family would be very difficult to say.

REPTILES

Remains of turtles and lizards were common in the refuse at Ali Kosh, but less so at Tepe Sabz. In all, 433 fragments of reptile bone were identified by Dr. James Peters, Division of Reptiles and Amphibians, Smithsonian Institution.

Turtles

Sample: 71 fragments of carapace or plastron, 3 limb bones

Temporal distribution: Most abundant in the Bus Mordeh phase, continuing in diminishing numbers through the Ali Kosh and Mohammad Jaffar phases; sporadically present in later periods.

Discussion

The common fresh-water turtle of western Iran, *Clemmys caspica,* was one of the aquatic resources exploited by the early villagers on the Deh Luran plain. This turtle occurs in rivers of the Tigris, Karkheh, and Karun drainages, throughout the mountain valleys of Kurdistan and Luristan and down to the Khuzistan plain; we have collected live specimens in the Kermanshah Valley, the Khorramabad Valley, and the Ain Girzan spring, near Musiyan. However, the number of fragments present in early levels at Ali Kosh suggests there was more fresh water available in the vicinity of the site than today. This is supported by the evidence of freshwater mussels, crabs, and fish in the Bus Mordeh, Ali Kosh, and Mohammad Jaffar phases (see below).

While these water turtles are present in small numbers at fresh-water springs, we did not observe any of the saline rivers of the Deh Luran plain. Did the Bus Mordeh villagers travel six km. to Ain Girzan to obtain turtles and mussels, or was the seasonally-flooded central depression of the Deh Luran plain a permanent freshwater slough?

Lizards

Sample: 359 vertebrae, limb bones, and jaws

Distribution: Abundant at Ali Kosh in all levels; rare at Tepe Sabz

Discussion

Two species of large lizard frequent the Deh Luran plain. One is the Desert Monitor Lizard (*Varanus griseus*), one specimen of which we managed to capture alive in 1963 as it made for its burrow in a road cut near the Dawairij River ford. The other is the Spiny Tailed Agamid Lizard (*Uromastix* cf. *hardwickii*). *Uromastix* is known archeologically from Shanidar Cave in Iraq (Reed and Marx, 1959:99) and from descriptions in Sumerian texts (Landsberger, 1934). One of these fearsome creatures, which may reach a meter in length, was undoubtedly the lizard which fascinated William Kenneth Loftus during his trip through Susiana in the 1840's. According to Loftus (1857:306):

> They live chiefly on snakes, which they pounce on suddenly, shake as a terrier does a rat, and cranch from tail to head; then they suck the mangled body down their throats, somewhat after the manner of a Neapolitan swallowing his national maccaroni! I once saw a lizard of this species attack, kill, and attempt to swallow a serpent six feet long. After gulping for a length of time to get down the tip end of its victim's tail, which hung out of its mouth, it disgorged its meal, repeated the process of mastication, and, ultimately, after some hard gasping, succeeded in overcoming its difficulty.

Today, both *Uromastix* and *Varanus* excavate burrows in well-drained areas such as archeological mounds. Ali Kosh was obviously a prime locality, and lizard burrows (with partial skeletons of their occupants) were frequent in upper levels of the site. We suspect that most lizard remains were introduced into the site in this way. Tepe Sabz does not seem to have been as favorable a den locality.

Not all the specimens are recent, however. Lizard bones from Bus Mordeh phase levels are often the same mahogany color as the other fauna, implying a certain degree of antiquity when contrasted with the pale white bones of more recent specimens. Further, some lizard bones were burned in prehistoric time, and some are even burned and broken as if the lizard had been eaten.

We find it impossible to decide what proportion of the *Varanus* and *Uromastix* specimens burrowed into the site, and what proportion were eaten; but we suspect that their role in the diet of prehistoric man was a small one. First of all, the number of *individual specimens* is relatively small. A single lizard may leave behind many vertebrae, but when one examines the number of jaws (a more diagnostic element), it appears there were only five to twenty per stratigraphic zone. Considering that many of these probably burrowed into the site, the number eaten is further reduced. As in the case of the small rodents already discussed, the lizard remains are less important to an understanding of the ancient diet than to a study of the similarities between today's environment and that of the prehistoric period.

Table 73

REPTILE REMAINS AT ALI KOSH AND TEPE SABZ
(By Stratigraphic Zone)

Phase	Site	Zone	Freshwater Turtle		Lizard				Grand Total
			Carapace or Plastron Fragments	Limb Bones	Vertebrae	Limb Bones	Jaws, Uromastix	Jaws, Varanus	
Bayat	TS	A_1	...	...	...	...	...	...	...
	TS	A_2	5	...	...	...	...	...	...
	TS	A_3	3	...	7	...	...	...	...
Mehmeh	TS	B_1	...	...	3	...	...	...	...
	TS	B_2	...	...	...	...	...	...	...
	TS	B_3	3	...	...	...	...	...	...
Khazineh	TS	C_1	...	...	...	...	...	...	...
	TS	C_2	...	...	...	...	...	...	...
	TS	C_3	...	...	...	...	...	...	...
Sabz	TS	D	1	...	...	...	...	...	...
Mohammad Jaffar	AK	A_1	4	...	35	3	15	...	...
	AK	A_2	6	...	54	8	22	...	...
Ali Kosh	AK	B_1	9	...	11	2	9	...	...
	AK	B_2	8	...	65	4	9	1	...
Bus Mordeh	AK	C_1	10	2	69	3	8	...	...
	AK	C_2	22	1	24	2	5	...	...
Totals			71	3	268	22	68	1	433

FISH REMAINS

Sample: 275 fragments

Temporal distribution: Bus Mordeh through Sabz phases (with 1 exception)

Introduction

Fish played a role in the food supply of the early villagers at Deh Luran, but they ceased to be economically important by 5000 B.C. Literally hundreds of fish bones were found in the middens of the Bus Mordeh, Ali Kosh, and Mohammad Jaffar phases. Along with the fresh-water turtles and mussles, they constitute one more line of evidence for the relatively greater use of aquatic resources in our earliest periods.

All our prehistoric remains are from fish whose length probably did not exceed 15 to 30 cm. Today, fish of this size can only be found in the Mehmeh and Dawairij rivers during the high water period of the winter rains. In the summer, the water level is too low and the salt concentration too high for all but the hardiest species. One of these hardy types is the catfish *Heteropneustes* (= *Saccobranchus*), one small specimen of which we collected from the Mehmeh River in the autumn. This catfish can live in very shallow warm water with little oxygen (Khalaf, 1961), a prerequisite for the Deh Luran rivers all summer. It also protects itself with a poison gland at the base of its pectoral spine.

The Musiyanis fish only with dynamite today, applying it occasionally to parts of the Dawairij River between Musiyan village and the Jebel Hamrin. One wonders if the yield even balances the cost of a stick of dynamite.

Types of Fish Represented (Table 74)

The fish of Khuzistan have never been extensively studied. One of the nearest rivers for which we have any information is the Tigris, 75 km. away, and we have drawn on the reports of Khalaf (1961) and Mahdi (1961) in this regard. Dr. William R. Taylor of the Division of Fishes, Smithsonian Institution, patiently identified our fish remains to family, and explained the impossibility of carrying the identification farther because of an almost total lack of comparative material from the region involved.

Our fish bones fall into three main categories. The most abundant are vertebrae and miscellaneous fin rays which cannot even be identified to family. The second most numerous group includes pectoral spines and skull fragments of catfish, which form the bulk of the identifiable remains from the Ali Kosh and Mohammad Jaffar phases. Lastly, we have pharyngeal arches (with teeth) and serrated dorsal spines from members of the Cyprinidae (or carp family), which are more abundant in the Bus Mordeh and early Ali Kosh phases than elsewhere.

Our "carp" pose a complex identification problem. At least two species, and possibly three, are represented. None are the "true" carp, *Cyprinus*. The pharyngeal arches show one species with a single tooth row, and others with three tooth rows. Possible genera listed by Khalaf, all of which have serrated dorsal spines, are *Varichorhinus, Cyprinion,* and *Barbus.* These are, however, no more than possibilities.

The catfish situation is equally unclear. Since *Heteropneustes* is known for the Mehmeh River, remains of that genus are probably included in our collection. But *Heteropneustes* is a member of the Bagridae, and there are other Bagrids (e.g., *Mystus*) listed for the lower Tigris. On the basis of the comparative material presently available, one cannot specify further what types of catfish we have at Ali Kosh.

Table 74

FISH REMAINS FROM ALI KOSH AND TEPE SABZ
(By Stratigraphic Zone)

Phase	Site	Zone	Carp Family		Catfish		Unidentified Vertebrae	Miscellaneous Fin Rays and Other Fragments	Grand Total
			Pharyngeal Arches	Dorsal Spines	Pectoral Spines	Other Fragments			
Bayat	TS	A_1	...	...	...	...	...	...	...
	TS	A_2	...	...	...	...	...	...	...
	TS	A_3	...	...	...	...	...	1	...
Mehmeh	TS	B_1	...	...	...	...	...	...	...
	TS	B_2	...	...	...	...	...	...	...
	TS	B_3	...	...	...	...	...	...	...
Khazineh	TS	C_1	...	...	...	...	...	...	...
	TS	C_2	...	...	...	...	...	...	...
	TS	C_3	...	...	...	...	...	...	...
Sabz	TS	D	...	...	...	...	4	3	...
Mohammad Jaffar	AK	A_1	...	...	14	2	16	3	...
	AK	A_2	1	2	15	2	48	5	...
Ali Kosh	AK	B_1	1	3	6	1	9	4	...
	AK	B_2	4	4	13	1	49	10	...
Bus Mordeh	AK	C_1	3	2	3	...	20	1	...
	AK	C_2	3	...	5	...	5	12	...
Totals			12	11	56	6	151	39	275

INVERTEBRATES

Freshwater Mussels

Sample: 408 (Bus Mordeh through Bayat phases)

Introduction

Our prehistoric villagers collected three species of Unionidae, or pearly fresh-water mussels. Counts of mussel shells ran into the hundreds in the Bus Mordeh, Ali Kosh, and Mohammad Jaffar phase levels. These shells were also occasionally cut and polished into mother-of-pearl ornaments. All were species which are known from the Tigris River or its tributaries.

All fragments of mussel shell were counted, but only those which preserved some portion of the shell margin were submitted for identification. They have been identified by Dr. Joseph P. E. Morrison, Division of Mollusks, Smithsonian Institution (see Table 75).

a) *Pseudodontopsis euphraticus* (55 specimens, Bus Mordeh through Mohammad Jaffar phases). Known from the Tigris River near Baghdad.

b) *Unio tigridis,* large river form (26 specimens, Bus Mordeh through Bayat phases). Common in the Tigris River drainage. This is the fresh water mussel eaten at Ras al Amiya, Tepe

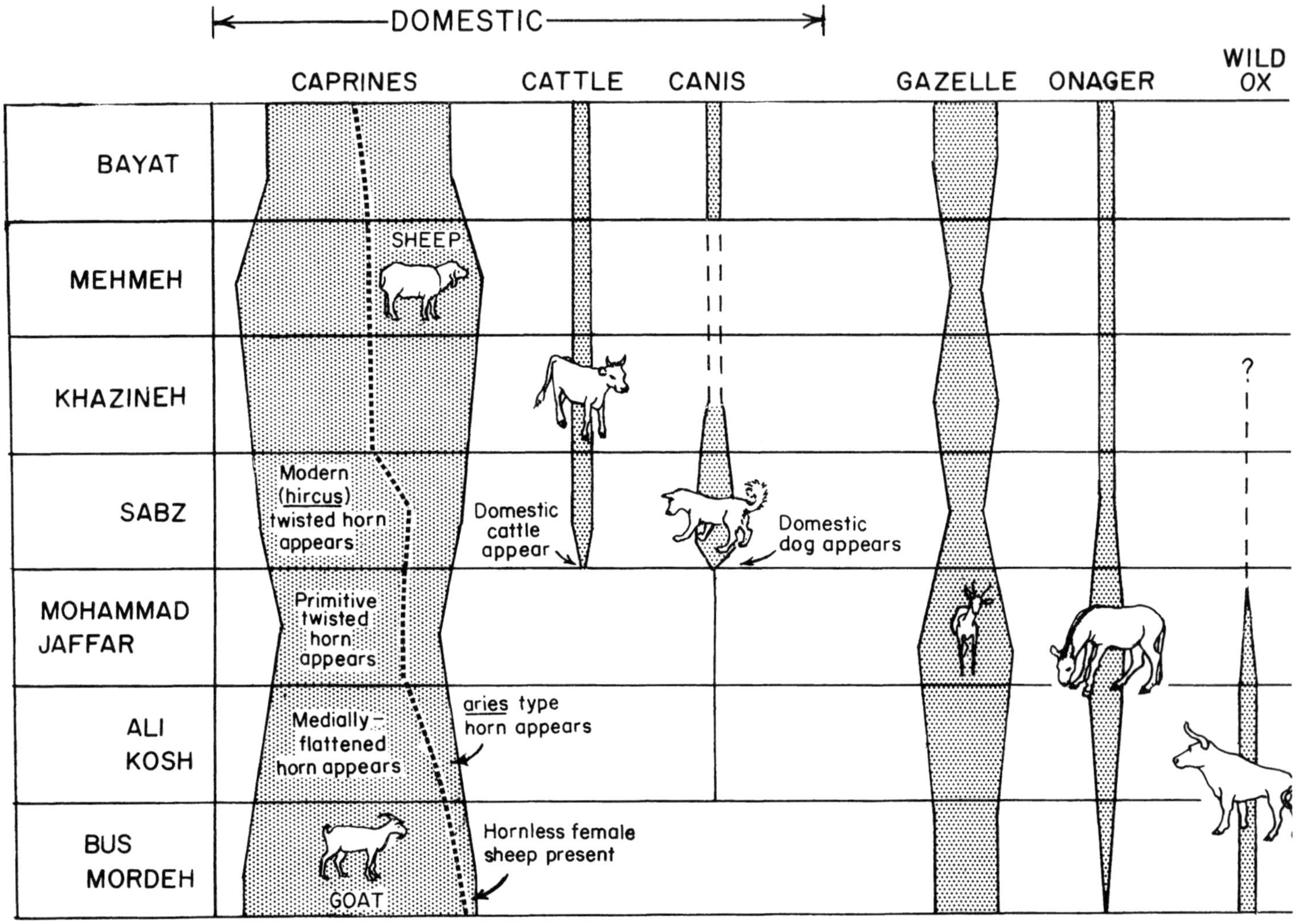

Fig. 134. Animal bones from the Deh Luran sequence: ch
showing changes in percentages of various types of animals thr
and Tepe Sabz. Frequency of each animal reflects the number o
total sample of identified bones from a given cultural phase. (Gr
of individuals, or weight of meat represented by each species.)

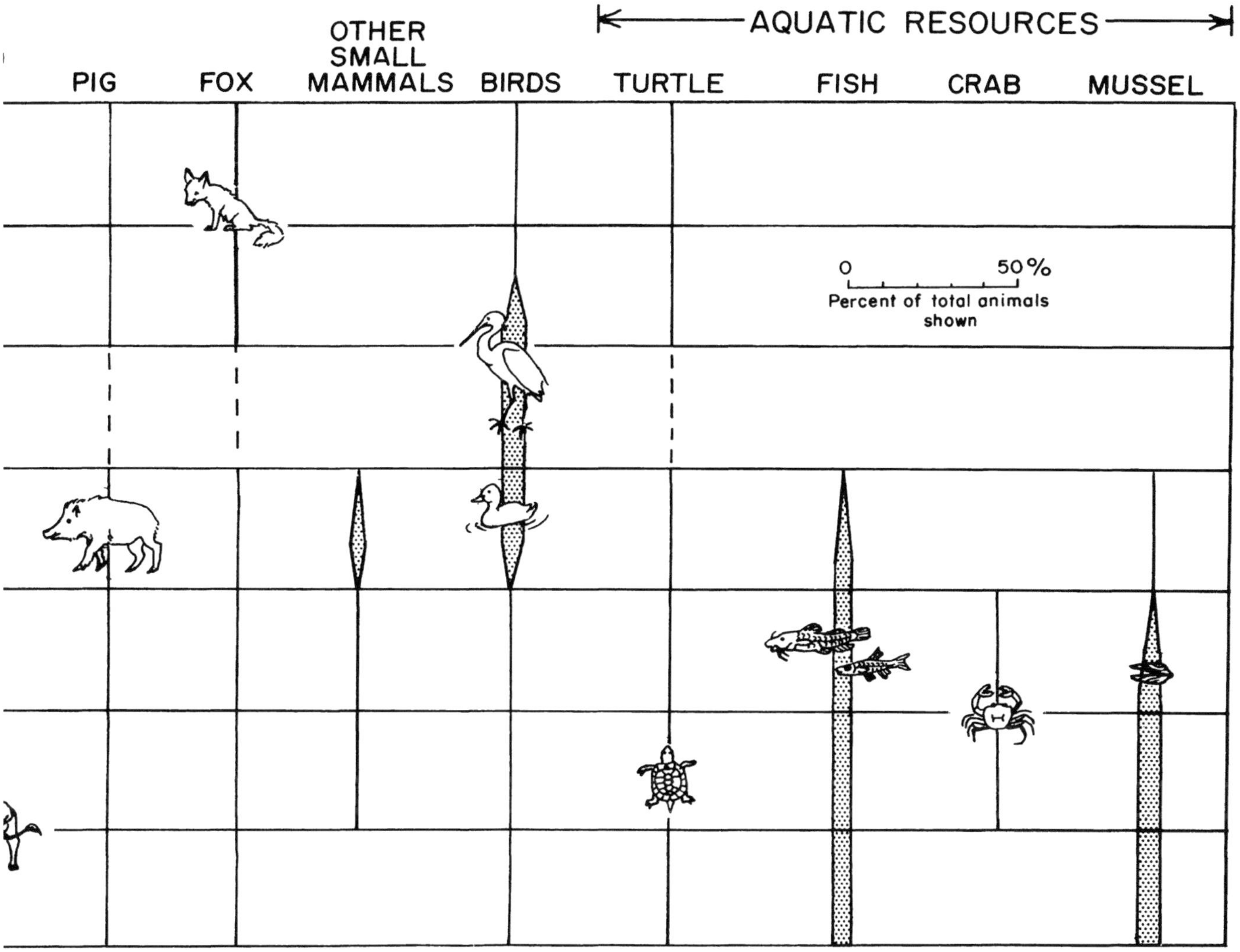

ıanges through time. Frequency polygons
rough all cultural phases at Tepe Ali Kosh
ıf identified bones of that type within the
raph does *not* indicate minimum numbers

Guran, and Palegawra Cave (Braidwood, Howe, *et al.* 1960:59; Flannery, unpublished data).

c) *Leguminaia wheatleyi* (3 specimens, Ali Kosh phase). Known also from the Tigris.

In addition, we collected modern mussels from the pool in front of the Ain Girzan spring near Musiyan. These were identified as *Unio mussolianus,* a form known from the Tigris River near Mosul, Iraq. R. Morrison cautions us that when the internal anatomy of this group is better known, *U. mussolianus* may turn out to be only a smaller stream form of *U. tigridis.* What is interesting, however, is the fact that all the prehistoric *Unio* from Ali Kosh belong to the large river forms; none are *mussolianus.* Thus the ancient villagers must have collected their mussels from the Dawairij River rather than the Ain Girzan spring. Moreover, the Dawairij in those days was evidently a suitable environment for the large river form, which means that its salt content and substratum could not have been drastically different from parts of the Tigris.

Our failure to find *Unio, Pseudodontopsis,* or *Leguminaia* in the bed of the Dawairij in 1963 may mean nothing, for all three species lie hidden under rocks, or buried in the sand between gravel particles or cobbles, with less than a fifth of their length exposed. It would take an experienced eye to detect their presence unless they were there in great density. It is not known precisely what level of salt content would prohibit their growth.

All three species would have been available throughout the year, but could most easily have been found and collected at the time of low water (June-October).

Freshwater Snails

Sample: 15 (Bus Mordeh through Mohammad Jaffar phases)

Introduction

Dr. Morrison also identified three species of fresh-water snail from deposits at Ali Kosh. These snails were probably introduced into the site by being brought back accidentally in drinking water containers. One species, *Melanoides tuberculatus,* has probably been carried around widely by man from northwest Africa to southern China. Since all individuals of the species are parthenogenic females, a single snail could start a new colony by hitching a ride in a goatskin water bag. Our find spots within the prehistoric village may only indicate places where a water bag was shaken out after emptying, and the snail dropped out.

Two other forms, *Melanopsis nodosa* and *Melanopsis* cf. *doriae,* appear to be common Mesopotamian water snails. They were less numerous in the refuse (see Table 75.).

Freshwater Crabs

Sample: 6 claw fragments (Ali Kosh and Mohammad Jaffar phases)

Introduction

The prehistoric villagers used crab claw to make ornaments, and presumably ate the crabs as well. The crab (unidentifiable to species) appears to belong to the genus *Potamon,* which is the common freshwater genus from the eastern Mediterranean coast to the Persian Gulf (Pretzmann, 1962). We are grateful to Dr. Fenner A. Chace, Jr. and Mr. Henry B. Roberts, Division of Marine Invertebrates, Smithsonian Institution, for examining our badly preserved specimens.

Potamon was also eaten at Paleolithic sites in Luristan; at Tepe Guran; and at Jarmo (Braidwood, Howe, *et al*, 1960:48; Flannery, unpublished data). It inhabits the rivers of Mesopotamia and Khuzistan, including tributaries of the Kharkheh in Luristan, and there is no reason why we should doubt its presence in the Dawairij and Mehmeh.

Table 75

INVERTEBRATE REMAINS FROM ALI KOSH AND TEPE SABZ
(By Stratigraphic Zone)

Phase	Site	Zone	Freshwater Mussels					Freshwater Snails				Freshwater Crab	Grand Total
			Pseudodontopsis euphraticus	*Unio tigridis*	*Leguminaia wheatleyi*	Unidentified Fragments	Total Mussels	*Melanoides tuberculatus*	*Melanopsis nodosa*	*Melanopsis* cf. *doriae*	Total Snails	(*Potamon* sp.)	
Bayat	TS	A_1	...	1	...	1	2	...	...	...	...	...	...
	TS	A_2	...	...	...	1	1	...	...	...	...	...	...
	TS	A_2	...	1	...	1	2	...	...	...	...	...	...
Mehmeh	TS	B_1	...	...	...	...	...	...	...	...	...	...	...
	TS	B_2	...	...	...	...	...	...	...	...	...	...	...
	TS	B_3	...	...	...	...	...	...	...	...	...	...	...
Khazineh	TS	C_1	...	...	...	...	...	...	...	...	...	...	...
	TS	C_2	...	...	...	...	...	...	...	...	...	...	...
	TS	C_3	...	...	...	...	...	...	...	...	...	...	...
Sabz	TS	D	...	...	...	3	3	2	...	...	2	...	...
Mohammad Jaffar	AK	A_1	5	2	...	36	43	1	...	...	1	3	...
	AK	A_2	7	2	...	59	68	1	...	...	1	...	...
Ali Kosh	AK	B_1	16	5	1	48	70	2	...	...	2	3	...
	AK	B_2	18	13	2	63	96	6	1	1	8	...	...
Bus Mordeh	AK	C_1	4	1	...	53	58	1	...	...	1	...	...
	AK	C_2	5	1	...	59	65	...	...	...	...	...	...
	Totals		55	26	3	324	408	13	1	1	15	6	429

XX

RADIOCARBON DATING OF THE DEH LURAN SEQUENCE

Deposits from all seven phases in our Deh Luran sequence yielded carbon samples, from which we have obtained thirty-one radiocarbon age determinations. Some of these age determinations fit very well with previously-published dates for artifactually similar (and therefore presumably contemporaneous) materials in the Zagros Mountain area; many others, however, fall outside the expected age range.

The method of radiocarbon dating, at least as a laboratory process, is well established and relatively routine. The theoretical basis for radiocarbon dating, however, is being held in question (e.g., Stuiver and Suess, 1966), and we cannot yet control with any real certainty the various sources of "geobiochemical" contamination that may occur in archeological situations (Braidwood, 1964). It is clear, to judge from the erratic behavior of many of our dates, that some samples were affected by one or more of the possible sorts of contamination.

In this chapter we will list all thirty-one of our radiocarbon dates, with relevant data on their laboratory treatment, and compare them with previously-published dates from contemporary levels at other prehistoric sites. Detailed data on our samples are given in Table 77.

Before proceeding with the comparisons, we should emphasize that any conclusions we reach concerning the dependability of the dates in a calendric sense must remain tentative, in view of the uncertainties now surrounding radiocarbon dating. It is presently impossible to determine, on theoretical grounds, what the relationship is between a radiocarbon date and the true age of a sample (Stuiver and Suess, 1966:536). This means that the true chronological limits of our phases cannot be determined in calendric years, although they can be specified in "radiocarbon years." Unfortunately, a radiocarbon age may correspond to more than one calendric age; consequently, a series of samples from the same phase which are not absolutely consistent internally may not necessarily be incorrect in "radiocarbon years."

Moreover, chronological gaps in a long sequence may be more apparent than real. For example, the apparent hiatus between our date of some 7900 B.C. for the Bus Mordeh phase and the 6500 B.C. date of the subsequent Ali Kosh phase may ultimately be explained as a consequence of the erratic behavior of radiocarbon. It is clear that, under these circumstances, we cannot say much about rates of change, and we should not unconsciously relate radiocarbon dates to the calendar. The problems of dating are manifold, and can be settled only with further theoretical studies (and renewed efforts to obtain the best possible samples for dating).

In our comparisons, we use only dates from sites in eastern Iraq and western Iran, geographically contiguous areas in which there is enough similarity in artifacts to permit reasonably accurate attributions of relative age. After inspecting Table 76, one is struck by the lack of correspondence in dates between sites which on archeological grounds should be contemporaneous. For some ranges of time (e.g., Mehmeh phase) it is even difficult to infer a useable order of magnitude, if we consider the dates for this phase in isolation.

Since the Bayat phase seems to be the most reliably dated, we will consider our seven phases in ascending order of age, regarding the Bayat period as the most securely fixed point in our dating sequence.

BAYAT PHASE

Expected date: *ca.* 3500 to 4000 B.C.

Radiocarbon dates: Eight, all falling between 3750 and 4220 B.C.

These age determinations have a gratifying internal consistency. The samples were all of solid charcoal, often tamarisk wood from clean building debris, an optimum situation. We have no way of determining the duration of the phase, since it may have gone on after Tepe Sabz was abandoned. We note that the dates of deeper samples were not necessarily older than the uppermost samples. Hence, we are probably dealing here with a series of building levels covering only about four hundred years.

Dates for sites with similar material (Table 76) are not entirely consistent, and some (e.g., those from Tell-i-Ghazir) seem very improbable. We have a problem here, however, in that we may be encountering instances where there was a time lag between the lowlands and the highlands. This could be a factor in the dates from north Iran (RY-2, Rezaiyeh Road, and Pisdeli Tepe), but probably would not explain the date of Ghazir, which lies in nearby eastern Khuzistan.

MEHMEH PHASE

Expected date: *ca.* 4500 to 4000 B.C.

Radiocarbon dates: Two (4520 B.C. and 3460 B.C.)

On the grounds of our dates alone, the Mehmeh phase could not be dated readily; we know, however, that it immediately preceded, and led into, the Bayat phase. On this basis, our date of 4520 B.C. seems reasonable, and compares well with the Bakun B determination. Other dates for similar material are of little help. The Dalma Tepe date, if correct, places Dalma IV as contemporary with Mehmeh, although (typologically) we would have expected Dalma Tepe to be earlier. Once again, if correct these dates suggest a time lag between lowland southern Iran and the northern highlands.

KHAZINEH PHASE

Expected date: *ca.* 5000 to 4500 B.C.

Radiocarbon dates: Three (4975, 5250, and 5510 B.C.)

All Khazineh phase samples were small, and came from deposits of ash midden and decomposed walling. The date of 4975 B.C. seems to us most reasonable; in view of the Tepe Sarab and Upper Tepe Guran dates, which are internally consistent, the Khazineh phase could hardly have been as early as 5510 B.C. The same is true of the date from Tell Halaf. One Arpachiyeh date (5077 B.C.) may be relevant to Khazineh.

SABZ PHASE

Estimated date: *ca.* 5500 to 5000 B.C.

Radiocarbon dates: Three, ranging from 7100 B.C. to A.D. 490

The Sabz phase is a crucial one, and unfortunately is poorly dated. None of our dates seem good, and we suspect this is partly due to the fact that they came from a level three meters below the surface of the plain, where they had been frequently subjected to ground water. The sherds from this level, for example, were heavily crusted with calcareous material.

On the basis of the Tell es-Sawwan dates (Table 76), we have selected the estimated date given above; the Matarrah date seems a bit early in view of the Sarab determinations, but may not be far wrong.

MOHAMMAD JAFFAR PHASE

Estimated date: *ca.* 6000 to 5600 B.C.

Radiocarbon dates: Three (5270, 5870, and 6940/6970 B.C.)

On the basis of our dates alone, it would be hard to determine the age of the Mohammad Jaffar phase; but our date of 5870 B.C. agrees with Tepe Sarab, Upper Tepe Guran, and Sayid Hammadani. This is probably a reasonable date for Upper (pottery-bearing) Jarmo, as well. The latter site, whose samples were processed early in the development of the radiocarbon technique, has too wide a spread to shed any light on the dating of this period.

ALI KOSH PHASE

Expected date: *ca.* 6750 to 6000 B.C.

Radiocarbon dates: Nine, of which five fall between 6150 and 6475 B.C.

This is one of our more reliably-dated phases, and correlates well with the date from Lower (preceramic) Tepe Guran. Our Ali Kosh phase samples consisted of ash, seeds, minute bits of reed charcoal, and other types of organic debris, suggesting that materials other than solid wood charcoal can give consistent dates. We cannot explain the incredible spread of the determinations from prepottery Lower Jarmo, and suggest that those levels probably date in the 6500 B.C. time range on comparative grounds.

BUS MORDEH PHASE

Expected date: *ca.* 7500 to 6750 B.C.

Radiocarbon dates: Three (5430, 5720, and 7950 B.C.)

The Bus Mordeh phase is of considerable interest to us, representing the oldest known traces of sedentary life in Khuzistan. Unfortunately, our samples from Bus Mordeh levels (like those from the Sabz phase) came from depths subject to the action of ground water. The date of 7950 B.C. would seem to be the most reasonable, based on determinations from Zawi Chemi Shanidar and Tepe Ganj-i Darreh (Table 76). However, typological similarities between sites of this time period are very general, and cannot be expected to yield precise relative chronologies. For the time being, we offer a tentative (and perhaps conservative?) maximum date of 7500 B.C. for the Bus Mordeh phase.

SUMMARY

The thirty-one radiocarbon determinations from Deh Luran can not be relied upon to serve as a chronological yardstick for Khuzistan unless they are placed in the context of dates from contemporary sites in adjacent areas. Some phases, like Bayat and Ali Kosh, seem relatively securely dated; others are still an open question. All of which merely strengthens our impression that single radiocarbon dates are to be regarded with suspicion.

Our data suggest that large chunks of carbonized tamarisk wood are more reliable for dating than carbonized reeds, and that samples from clean mud wall debris high up in an archeological mound are more reliable than those from levels at (or below) ground water. It seems likely that most of the apparent trouble with our dates stems from the samples themselves having been poor, even though this was not recognized in the field. Finally, until the dating process itself is better understood, we should not be too quick to translate radiocarbon dates into calendric dates for purposes of interpreting rates of change, gaps in sequences, or the fine-scale relative ages of separate sites.

Table 76

CORRESPONDENCE OF AVAILABLE RADIOCARBON DATES FOR TYPOLOGICALLY RELATED ARCHEOLOGICAL HORIZONS

Deh Luran Phases	Deh Luran Radiocarbon Dates*	Radiocarbon Dates from Sites with Typologically Similar Material*
Bayat	4100 (15), 4220 (17), 4110 (17), 3750 (17), 3910 (15), 3820 (6), 4110 (15), 4120 (1)	Ghazir, 5812 (10); Tall-i-Gap, 3920 (4), 3490 (4); Pisdeli, 3510 (7), 3568 (9), 3688 (9); RY-2, 3780 (16); Rezaiyeh Road, 3495 (10)
Mehmeh	3460 (15), 4520 (15)	Siabid, 3865 (9); Bakun B, 4040 (9), 4314 (10); Dalma IV, 4036 (9)
Khazineh	4975 (1), 5250 (17), 5510 (15)	Gawra, 3450 (5); Halaf, 5620 (12); Arpachiyeh, 5077 (11), 6114 (11)
Sabz	A.D. 490 (17), 4790 (15), 7100 (1)	KR-20, 4250 (15); Sawwan, 4858 (11), 5349 (11), 5506 (11); Matarrah, 5620 (8)
Mohammad Jaffar	5270 (15), 5870 (15), 6940-6970 (6)	Guran H, 5810 (18); Sarab, 5655 (9), 5694 (9), 6006 (9); Hajji Firuz, 4945 (9), 5319 (9); Sayid Hammadani, 5850 (16); Jarmo: II 2, 3316 (5), II 4, 6880 (8)
Ali Kosh	5790 (17), 5820 (14), 6150 (15), 6300 (14), 6460 (16), 6475 (14), 6475 (14), 6900 (16), 8000 (15)	Guran U, 6400 (18); Jarmo: II 5, 4700 (2), 4745 (5); JPQ-14, 7090 (8), 9290 (8); JN-18, 9250 (8); JI-7, 4656 (5), 4757 (5), 6000 (8); JI-8, 4620 (2); JPQ-14, 5800 (8); JI-7, 8525 (3)
Bus Mordeh	5430 (15), 5720 (15), 7950 (1)	Ganj-i Darreh, 8450 (13); Zawi Chemi, 8850 (8)

*All dates are B.C. and calculated with the 5570 year half-life. Numbers in parentheses refer to the source of the date (see Table 79).

Table 77

INVENTORY OF RADIOCARBON SAMPLES FROM DEH LURAN

Phase, Site, and Zone	Sample Number	Field Description	Laboratory Comments and Reference	Laboratory Number and Date in Radiocarbon Years	Date B.C.
Bayat .... (Tepe Sabz, zone A_1)	TS4-95	Bits of charcoal from midden. Collected by J.A. Neely, October, 1963.	None	I-1499 6050±140	4100
Bayat .... (Tepe Sabz, zone A_1)	TS4-85	Chunks of charcoal from midden area. Collected by J.A. Neely, October, 1963.	For treatment of sample, see Long and Mielke 1966. (Unpublished to date)	SI-203 6170±200	4220
Bayat .... (Tepe Sabz, zone A_2)	TS1-125	Charcoal fragments from midden area. Collected by J.A. Neely, October, 1963.	For treatment of sample, see Long and Mielke 1966. (Unpublished to date)	SI-204 6060±200	4110
Bayat .... (Tepe Sabz, zone A_2)	TS9-156	Carbonized wood (*Tamarix*) from midden area. Collected by J.A. Neely, October, 1963.	For treatment of sample, see Long and Mielke 1966. (Unpublished to date)	SI-205 5700±250	3750
Bayat .... (Tepe Sabz, zone A_2)	TS9-167	Carbonized wood. Collected by J.A. Neely, October, 1963.	None	I-1503 5860±230	3910
Bayat .... (Tepe Sabz, zone A_3)	TS14-301	Charcoal, seeds and sheep or goat dung from midden area. Collected by J.A. Neely, October, 1963.	For treatment of sample, see Long and Mielke 1966. (Published in Long and Mielke 1966)	SI-156 5770±120	3820
Bayat .... (Tepe Sabz, zone A_3)	TS15-312	Carbonized seeds, sheep or goat dung and ash. Collected by J.A. Neely, October, 1963.	None	I-1502 6060±140	4110
Bayat .... (Tepe Sabz, zone A_3)	TS14-278	Carbonized wood and sheep or goat dung from ash lens. Collected by J.A. Neely, October, 1963.	Berger, Fergusson and Libby 1965	UCLA-750A 6070±100	4120
Mehmeh ..... (Tepe Sabz, zone B_1)	TS7-380	Chunks of carbonized wood. Collected by J.A. Neely, October, 1963.	Samples combined	I-1500 5410±160	3460
Mehmeh ..... (Tepe Sabz, zone B_3)	TS25-501	Chunks of charcoal. Collected by J.A. Neely, November, 1963.	None	I-1493 6470±160	4520
Khazineh .... (Tepe Sabz, zone C_1)	TS21-680	Charcoal. Collected by J.A. Neely, November, 1963.	None	I-1501 7460±160	5510
Khazineh .... (Tepe Sabz, zone C_3)	TS25-860	Carbonized grains of barley, unidentifiable as to race. Washed in H_2O by Helbaek. Collected by J.A. Neely, November, 1963.	Berger, Fergusson and Libby 1965	UCLA-750B 6925±200	4975

(Continued on next page)

Table 77 (Cont'd)

Phase, Site, and Zone	Sample Number	Field Description	Laboratory Comments and Reference	Laboratory Number and Date in Radiocarbon Years	Date B.C.
Khazineh .... (Tepe Sabz, zone C_3)	TS34-623	Carbonized wood from midden area. Collected by J.A. Neely, November, 1963.	Sample very small. For treatment of sample, see Long and Mielke 1966. (Unpublished to date)	SI-206 7200±1000	5250
Sabz ...... (Tepe Sabz, zone D)	TS20-968	Carbonized wood. Collected by J.A. Neely, December, 1963.	None	I-1497 6740±190	4790
Sabz ...... (Tepe Sabz, zone D)	TS29-1020	Chunks of carbonized wood. Collected by J.A. Neely, December, 1963.	Berger, Fergusson and Libby 1965	UCLA-750C 9050±160	7100
Sabz ...... (Tepe Sabz, zone D)	TS20-946	Charcoal fragments from midden. Associated with cultivated flax, wheat, barley, almond seeds and Sabz pottery. Collected by J.A. Neely, December, 1963.	Sample was very small, and apparently contaminated. For treatment of sample, see Long and Mielke 1966.	SI-255 1460±400	A.D. 490
Mohammad Jaffar .... (Ali Kosh, zone A_2)	AK85-90	Bits of charcoal and ash. Collected by F. Hole and K. Flannery, September, 1963	None	I-1495 7220±160	5270
Mohammad Jaffar .... (Ali Kosh, zone A_2)	AK67-117	Ash and *Prosopis* seeds in midden area. Associated with Mohammad Jaffar pottery. Collected by F. Hole and K. Flannery, September, 1963.	See Long and Mielke 1966	SI-160 8920±100	6970
		Ash and *Prosopis* seeds in midden area. Associated with Mohammad Jaffar pottery. Collected by F. Hole and K. Flannery, September, 1963.	Replicate analysis of SI-160. (Published in Long and Mielke 1966)	SI-160R 8890±200	6940
Mohammad Jaffar .... (Ali Kosh, zone A_2)	AK59-150	Bits of charcoal and ash. Collected by F. Hole and K. Flannery, October, 1963.	None	I-1494 7820±190	5870
Ali Kosh..... (Ali Kosh, zone B_1)	AK89-280	Charcoal from midden just above ancient mound surface of courtyard. Associated with prepottery occupation. Collected by F. Hole and K. Flannery, October, 1963.	Sample was very small. For treatment of sample, see Long and Mielke 1966. (Unpublished to date)	SI-207 7740±600	5790
Ali Kosh..... (Ali Kosh zone B_1)	AK69-260	Bits of charcoal from midden overlying ancient surface or courtyard. Collected by F. Hole and K. Flannery, October, 1963.	None	I-1491 8100±170	6150

Ali Kosh. . . . . (Ali Kosh, zone B_1)	AK73-270	Bits of charcoal from midden overlying ancient mound surface or courtyard. Collected by F. Hole and K. Flannery, October, 1963	None	I-1490 9950±190	8000
Ali Kosh. . . . . (Ali Kosh, zone B_2)	A-32	Organic material from ash layer under clean building debris. A thin scatter of organic material over one-half meter square. Collected by F. Hole and K. Flannery, December, 1961.	This sample was examined by Prof. Elso Barghoorn. He writes: "The material is a brownish earthy-looking matrix with fragments of carbonate indiscriminantly mixed in with the matrix proper. I treated fragments of the material with ten per cent Potassium Hydroxide and respectively another sample with strong Hydroflouric Acid. The first sample was boiled in the caustic potash solution for a few minutes, decanted and then washed by centrifugation. The acid treated sample was treated similarly after removal of the acid. Both samples yielded a copious brown residue, which upon examination in the microscope revealed the presence of triturated fragments of plant and animal tissue, all of which exhibited a light brown to dark brown humic appearance. There is absolutely no evidence of charcoal or burned tissue in the sample. The material looks in fact more or less what one might expect to find in a well decomposed compost pile. The alkali extracts after acidification precipitated a copious amount of flocculent material which might be considered humic acids. The supernatent liquid was almost clear and very light colored. The mineral matter with exception of the carbonates is almost entirely silica or siliceous material soluble in Hydroflouric Acid. This was quite evident when the residue was examined in polarized light, although some fragments of the organic matter showed optical activity, i.e., anisotropy. It would appear to me that the material is the remains of a mixture of organic materials of both plant and animal origin including insects and fragments of calcareous invertebrates. The paucity of fungal remains is a bit puzzling, although some pollen grains occur. It is certainly completely unrelated to charcoal or any evidence of burning."	Humble Oil and Refining Co. Run No. 0-1845 8250±175	6300

(Continued on next page)

Table 77 (Cont'd)

Phase, Site, and Zone	Sample Number	Field Description	Laboratory Comments and Reference	Laboratory Number and Date in Radiocarbon Years	Date B.C.
Ali Kosh. . . . . (Ali Kosh, zone B_2)	A-26	Organic material from hearth underlying a collapsed brick wall. Collected by F. Hole and K. Flannery, December, 1961.	None	Humble Oil and Refining Co. Run No. 0-1848 7770±330	5820
Ali Kosh. . . . . (Ali Kosh, zone B_2)	A-33, #8	Charcoal from hearth underlying clean mud building debris. Collected by F. Hole and K. Flannery, December, 1961 (same hearth as samples A-33 #9, #10, below).	None	Humble Oil and Refining Co. Run No. 0-1833 8425±180	6475
Ali Kosh. . . . . (Ali Kosh, zone B_2)	A-33, #10	Charcoal from hearth underlying clean mud building debris. Collected by F. Hole and K. Flannery, December, 1961 (same hearth as samples A-33 #8, #9).	None	Humble Oil and Refining Co. Run No. 0-1816 8425±180	6475
Ali Kosh. . . . . (Ali Kosh, zone B_2)	A-33, #9	Charcoal from hearth underlying clean mud building debris. Collected by F. Hole and K. Flannery, December, 1961 (same hearth as samples A-33 #8, #10).	None	Shell Development Co. Book Number 1246 8410±200	6460
Ali Kosh. . . . . (Ali Kosh, zone B_2)	A-22	Charcoal from lens in a layer of relatively sterile mud building debris. Collected by F. Hole and K. Flannery, December, 1961.	None	Shell Development Co. Book Number 1174 8850±210	6900
Bus Mordeh . . (Ali Kosh, zone C_1)	AK91-525	Black organic material from extensive midden at top of zone. Collected by F. Hole and K. Flannery, December, 1963.	None	I-1496 7380±180	5430
Bus Mordeh . . (Ali Kosh, zone C_2)	AK94-691	Black ash and seeds from midden, on top of sterile white sand, at base of zone. Collected by F. Hole and K. Flannery, December, 1963	None	I-1489 7670±170	5720
Bus Mordeh . . (Ali Kosh, zone C_2)	A76-680	Bits of charcoal from midden filling collapsed house. Collected by F. Hole and K. Flannery, December, 1963.	Berger, Fergusson, and Libby 1965	UCLA-750D 9900±200	7950

Table 78

PREVIOUSLY-UNPUBLISHED RADIOCARBON SAMPLES TAKEN FROM OTHER SITES IN IRAN

Site	Sample Number	Field Description	Laboratory Comments and Reference	Laboratory Number and Date in Radiocarbon Years	Date B.C.
Sayid Hammadani . . (Solduz Valley, Azerbaijan)	NQ-6	Charcoal and ash taken from vertical face cut into mound by villagers. Associated with pottery similar to that found at nearby Hajji Firuz. Collected by F. Hole and K. Flannery, November, 1961.	None (Unpublished)	Shell Development Co. 7800±210	5850
Bog-i-No . . . . . (site near Khorramabad, Iran; see Young, 1966)	KR-20	Charcoal and ash taken from vertical face cut in mound by brickmakers. Associated with new type of pottery, possibly contemporary with early part of Tepe Sabz sequence. Collected by F. Hole and K. Flannery, August, 1963.	None (Unpublished)	I-1492 6200±140	4250
RY-2 . . . . (site near Rezaiyeh, North Iran)	RY-2	Charcoal and ash taken from vertical face cut in mound by brick makers. Associated with pottery similar to that found at Pisdeli Tepe. Collected by F. Hole and K. Flannery, November, 1961	None (Unpublished)	Shell Development Co. 5730±190	3780

Table 79

SOURCES OF RADIOCARBON DATA
(Based on half-life of 5570 years)

Source of Date	Site and Stratum	Laboratory Number	Date in C-14 Years
(1) Berger, Fergusson and Libby, 1965	Tepe Sabz A_3	UCLA-750A	6070±100
(2) Braidwood, 1958*b*	Jarmo II5	F-44	6650±170
	Jarmo I8	F-45	6570±165
(3) Braidwood, 1958*b*	Jarmo I7	H-551/491	8525±175
(4) Kigoshi and Endo, 1963	Tall-i-Gap (GAT-II)	Gak-198	5440±120
	Tall-i-Gap (GAT-I)	Gak-197	5870±160
(5) Libby, 1955	Tepe Gawra 17-18	C-817	5400±325
	Jarmo II-2	C-744	5266±450
	Jarmo II-5	C743	6695±360
	Jarmo I-7	C742	6606±330
	Jarmo I-7	C-113	6707±320
(6) Long and Mielke, 1966	Tepe Sabz A_3	SI-156	5770±120
	Ali Kosh A_2	SI-160+	8920±100
	Ali Kosh A_2	SI-160R	8890±200
(7) Ralph, 1959	Pisdeli Tepe	P-157	5460±160
(8) Rubin and Alexander, 1960	Matarrah (VI-4)	W-623	7570±250
	Jarmo II-4	W-651	8830±200
	Jarmo PQ-14	W-657	11,240±300
	Jarmo PQ-14	W-608	7750±250
	Jarmo PQ-14	W-607	9040±250
	Jarmo N-18	W-665	11,200±200
	Jarmo I-7a	W-652	7950±200
	Zawi Chemi Shanidar	W-681	10,800±300
(9) Stuckenrath, 1963	Pisdeli Tepe (II,10)	P-505	5638±85
	Pisdeli Tepe (II, 5)	P-504	5518±81
	Tall-i-Bakun B	P-438	5990±81
	Siabid	P-442	5815±83
	Dalma Tepe IV	P-503	5986±87
	Hajji Firuz (D-15)	P-455	7269±86
	Hajji Firuz (V)	P-502	6895±83
	Tepe Sarab (5)	P-466	7956±98
	Tepe Sarab (4)	P-465	7605±96
	Tepe Sarab (1)	P-467	7644±89
(10) Stuckenrath, Coe, and Ralph, 1966	Tell-i-Ghazir 5, 6	P-930	7762±98
	Bakun B	P-931	6264±70
	"Rezaiyeh Road" Tepe	P-866	5445±72
(11) Stuckenrath and Ralph, 1965	Arpachiyeh (well)	P-585	8064±78
	Arpachiyeh (tholos)	P-584	7027±83
	Tell es-Sawwan (pre-I)	P-855	7456±73
	Tell es-Sawwan (I)	P-857	6808±82
	Tell es-Sawwan (III)	P-856	7299±86
(12) Vogel and Waterbolk, 1964	Tell Halaf	GrN-2660	7570±35
(13) Young and Smith, 1966	Ganj-i Darreh (lower)	Gak-807	10,400±150
(14) Unpublished (Humble Oil and Refining)	Ali Kosh B_2	O-1848	7770±330
	Ali Kosh B_2	O-1845	8250±175
	Ali Kosh B_2	O-1816	8425±180
	Ali Kosh B_2	O-1833	8425±180

Table 79 (Cont'd)

Source of Date	Site and Stratum	Laboratory Number	Date in C-14 Years
(15) Unpublished (Isotopes, Inc.)	Tepe Sabz A_1	I-1499	6050±140
	Tepe Sabz A_2	I-1503	5860±230
	Tepe Sabz A_3	I-1502	6060±140
	Tepe Sabz B_1	I-1500	5410±160
	Tepe Sabz B_3	I-1493	6470±160
	Tepe Sabz C_1	I-1501	7460±160
	Tepe Sabz D	I-1497	6740±190
	Ali Kosh A_1	I-1495	7220±160
	Ali Kosh A_2	I-1494	7820±190
	Ali Kosh B_1	I-1491	8100±170
	Ali Kosh B_1	I-1490	9950±190
	Ali Kosh C_1	I-1496	7380±180
	Ali Kosh C_2	I-1489	7670±170
	Bog-i-No(Kr-20)	I-1492	6200±140
(16) Unpublished (Shell Development) . .	Ali Kosh B_2	1246	8410±200
	Ali Kosh B_2	1174	8850±210
	RY-2	No number	5730±190
	Sayid Hammadani	No number	7800±210
(17) Unpublished (Smithsonian)	Tepe Sabz A_1	SI-203	6170±200
	Tepe Sabz A_2	SI-204	6060±200
	Tepe Sabz A_2	SI-205	5700±250
	Tepe Sabz C_3	SI-206	7200±1000
	Tepe Sabz D	SI-255	1460±400
	Ali Kosh B_1	SI-207	7740±600
(18) Unpublished (personal communication from Peder Mortensen)	Tepe Guran (H)	Copenhagen (?)	7760±150
	Tepe Guran (U)	Copenhagen(?)	8350±200

XXI

SUMMARY AND CONCLUSIONS

In this chapter we will sum up the evidence for architecture, artifacts, way of life, and population density during each of the seven phases we have defined for the Deh Luran plain. These "capsule summaries" for each phase are based on the detailed descriptive material already presented in earlier chapters. We have, however, made an effort to present them in relatively nontechnical terms, and free of bibliographic references, feeling that in this way they may be of greater interest to the general reader. The Near Eastern specialist can find the technical data and references he wants in the appropriate previous chapter. The summaries which follow are intended as a culture history of the Deh Luran plain in particular, and Khuzistan in general.

But culture history is not the sole purpose of archeology. Archeology, we feel, should also be the study of long-term cultural and ecological processes. Therefore in this chapter we will also advance some hypotheses about the relationship of man to the steppe environment of Khuzistan: how he adapted his agriculture to it, how agriculture and grazing altered the vegetational cover, and how man re-adapted to a landscape that was now partly of his own making. At this stage we do not have easy answers to all that happened in Khuzistan, but we feel that one of our main purposes should be to present an explanatory model to be tested by future archeologists.

THE BUS MORDEH PHASE

7500 to 6750 B.C.

Nine thousand years ago, much of the surface of the Deh Luran plain was an undulating expanse of sandy loam and reddish clays, derived in part from the sandstone hills of the Jebel Hamrin and the gypseous marls of the Kuh-i-Siah range. The center of the plain, a seasonally-inundated natural depression today, may at that time have been a semi-permanent slough bordered with sea club-rush, sedge, and feather grass. The villagers of the Bus Mordeh phase settled in the southeastern part of the plain, in a sandier and better-drained area only two kilometers from the Jebel Hamrin.

Out of a natural red clay deposit in the floor of the plain, the Bus Mordeh group cut slabs averaging 15 by 25 by 10 cm., which they used as unfired "bricks" in the construction of small houses or huts. The rooms they constructed were often no more than 2 by 2.5 meters, with walls 25 to 40 cm. thick and doorways a meter-and-a-half wide. As yet there are no certain indications—such as floor features and other architectural details—that prove these structures were dwellings rather than storage rooms. Size is not the critical factor here, for many prehistoric dwellings in the Southwestern United States are no more than 1.5 meters on a side.

The floors were of stamped mud or clay. No plaster of any kind is yet known from this period, but there is a suggestion of simple, over-one, under-one matting which may have been used as a floor covering or in roof construction (based on the way roofs are made in the area today). The clay-slab brick architecture is unlike anything known from the Zagros Mountains at this time (compare, for example, the "hut circles" of Zawi Chemi, the "pit houses" at Asiab, or the "wooden huts" of prepottery Tepe Guran). This suggests that it is a type of architecture native to the lowland steppe, where building materials other than mud or clay have always been scarce.

The subsistence pattern of the Bus Mordeh phase also shows a relative independence from the Zagros Mountains. The tens of thousands of carbonized seeds and broken animal bones left behind by these people show a high degree of orientation to the steppe environment. Nine-tenths of the seeds found in Bus Mordeh levels were from annual legumes and wild grasses native to northern Khuzistan. They systematically and intensively collected the seeds of medic or wild alfalfa, spiny milk vetch, *Trigonella* (a small plant of the pea family), canary grass, oat grass, and goosefoot, and ate the fruit of the wild caper. Since some of these plants have seeds no larger than clover seed, the amount of work involved in these harvests—which had to take place some time after the peak growing season in March—must have been considerable.

In addition, the Bus Mordeh folk planted emmer wheat and two-row hulled barley, two annual grasses which are not native to Khuzistan. Although constituting less than a tenth of the carbonized seeds left by these people, wheat and barley have significantly larger grains than most of the wild plants mentioned above, and were probably two of the preferred foods. They underscore the fact that the Bus Mordeh development, for all its peculiar architecture and its steppe collecting pattern, was not unrelated to developments in the highlands of the Near East, where the wild ancestors of wheat and barley are at home.

Wheat and barley were not the only "foreign" plants eaten by the people of the Bus Mordeh phase; three other grasses, which were probably weeds in the wheat fields, come from outside Khuzistan. These were goat-face grass, ryegrass, and wild einkorn wheat, all of which were probably introduced into the Deh Luran area in imperfectly-cleaned batches of wheat seed. Once established, at least ryegrass and einkorn were probably eaten along with wheat and barley. We do not know from which area of the mountains all these seeds were first introduced into the Khuzistan diet, nor do we yet know at what time they first arrived. Harlan and Zohary (1966) have recently presented evidence suggesting that the large-seeded Palestinian race of wild emmer—and not the Zagros Mountain race—may be the ancestor of cultivated emmer wheat. If this proves to be the case, then the events antecedent to the Bus Mordeh phase may be even more complex than we suspected at first.

Carbonized seeds of club-rush (*Scirpus*) included with the grains indicate that the fields must have been very near the margins of our postulated marsh or slough. The cultivated cereals were harvested with flint sickles, roasted to render the glumes brittle, and then "threshed" by grinding with flat-topped or saddle-shaped grinding slabs of pitted limestone, a few of which were found in the rooms of this phase. "Groats," or coarsely-ground grits of wheat and barley, were recovered in some quantity.

Apart from their seed-gathering and wheat-harvesting in the late winter and spring, the people of the Bus Mordeh phase were herdsmen. A major aspect of their subsistence was the herding of goat, an animal not occurring normally on the plain (although wild goats inhabit the cliffs of the Kuh-i-Siah and Jebel Hamrin, not far away). North Khuzistan is excellent winter grazing land, a fact which may have had a great deal to do with the beginnings of food production there.

Most of the goats eaten during the Bus Mordeh phase were young; only a third of the flock reached the age of three years, and there were virtually no elderly goats represented in the bone remains. Judging by the discarded horn cores, mostly young males were eaten, presumably to conserve the females for breeding. Numbers of small, lightly-baked figurines resembling goats suggest that "magical" means may also have been resorted to in an effort to increase the herds. The goats of the Bus Mordeh phase differed barely, if at all, from the wild phenotype, having horns whose cross-sections were either quadrangular or lozenge-shaped; but the age-ratio of the herd differed strikingly from that of a wild goat population, not merely in terms of yearlings, but also in terms of the survivorship of two-year-olds, three-year-olds, and so on.

The Bus Mordeh villagers also herded sheep, but in much smaller numbers. One sheep skull from a basal Bus Mordeh phase house floor is hornless, indicating that sheep had been domestic for some time prior to the Bus Mordeh period. Our evidence tentatively suggests that horn loss by female sheep was one of the first osteological changes to follow domestication, and that male sheep underwent a change in horn core cross-section at a later date. There is no evidence that male sheep ever lost their horns at any time in our sequence. It is difficult to estimate the relative proportions of sheep to goat in the Bus Mordeh phase herds, but goats were certainly more than ten times as numerous. This would seem to be typical of the Southern Zagros. Similarly high proportions of goats (relative to sheep) characterized Tepe Guran (Flannery, unpublished data), Sarab (Bökönyi, personal communication), and Jarmo (Reed, personal communication).

Hunting and fishing constituted the fourth major component of Bus Mordeh subsistence. The common ungulate of the Khuzistan steppe is the Persian gazelle, which was brought down by the villagers in tremendous numbers. Onager, wild ox, and wild boar were also taken; small mammals, like the red fox, were a very small part of the diet. In particular, the Bus Mordeh phase stands out in the Deh Luran sequence for its use of aquatic resources like carp, catfish, mussel, and water turtle. Seasonal waterfowl, which visit the Deh Luran region between November and March, were also eaten, and, along with the harvested wild legumes, indicate the real importance of the winter resources of northern Khuzistan. On the basis of plants and animals recovered, we could not prove beyond a shadow of doubt that the Bus Mordeh folk were in the Deh Luran plain during the hot, dry summer months.

The flint tools manufactured by the Bus Mordeh villagers were varied and abundant, but for the most part it is impossible to separate those designed to deal with hunting and those designed to deal with domestic animals. Possibly the diagonal-ended-and-backed microliths served as parts of composite hunting tools, but the scores of endscrapers could have served as well for working the hides of domestic goats and sheep as for those of gazelles and onagers. Drills were also abundant, and the assemblage included reamers, burins, and retouched blades of various kinds.

From narrow, bullet-shaped cores, the Bus Mordeh people struck tens of thousands of flint blades, some of them only a few millimeters wide. A relatively small percentage of these were turned into other tools by means of bone pressure-flakers. Flint nodules from the bed of the Dawairij River served as raw material for the flint-knappers, and waste flakes were strewn through the rooms we found. About one per cent of the chipped stone was obsidian, identified through trace element analysis as native to the Lake Van region of eastern Turkey.

Other tools used by the Bus Mordeh villagers for dealing directly with problems of subsistence included pounders made from flint nodules or chunky, only partially-used flint cores; small abraders made from gritty slabs of sandstone; small "picks" of chipped flint; and bone awls made from the metapodials of goat or gazelle. The only evidence of containers so far recovered from this phase are three fragments of bowls ground from soft stone. Baskets may have been present, but our limited exposure did not reveal any evidence beyond the weaving of simple reed or club-rush mats. Compared with the phases which were to follow, the Bus Mordeh tool assemblage is lacking in variety, especially in the category of ground stone and heavy chipped-stone tools.

We have not yet recovered a burial that can with any assurance be assigned to the Bus Mordeh phase. We do know, however, that the villagers ornamented themselves with pendants of boar tusk, mussel shell, and polished flat pebbles; wore small "buttons" of tusk and mother-of-pearl which may have been sewn onto garments of some kind; and had necklaces of tubular stone beads, or flat disc beads which were red, white, and black. They also used cowrie shells which presumably came from the Persian Gulf.

On the basis of artifactual cross-ties and resemblances, the Bus Mordeh phase is probably broadly contemporary with sites like Zawi Chemi Shanidar, Karim Shahir, Asiab, and Tepe Ganj-i Dareh. Our chronological placement is supported by at least one of the Bus Mordeh radiocarbon dates, which was 7900 B.C. So far as we can tell from our excavations and surface survey, there is only one village of this phase in the Deh Luran plain; in fact, sites of this age are rare anywhere in western Iran, and no two of the sites known are exactly alike. That the Bus Mordeh folk had relations with people outside Deh Luran is evident from the occurrence of Turkish obsidian, and from the cultivated emmer wheat whose natural habitat lies elsewhere. Neither of these implies much in the way of systematic trade, but the Bus Mordeh villagers had at least a few local raw materials, like natural asphalt, which they could have exchanged for obsidian.

The relative scarcity of summer-season products in the refuse, plus the abundance of goats, suggests that the Bus Mordeh people may have been at least partially transhument. Within a few days' travel from Deh Luran are mountain valleys like that of the Saimarreh River, which even today serve as summer pasture for Khuzistan herders. Transhumence would have been one mechanism for preventing total isolation of the Deh Luran villagers from happenings in the uplands, and it would have given them the opportunity to exchange new products or ideas with their neighbors. And yet, beyond the few items mentioned above, there is little tangible evidence to show an awareness, on the part of the Bus Mordeh folk, of the world beyond the plains of Khuzistan.

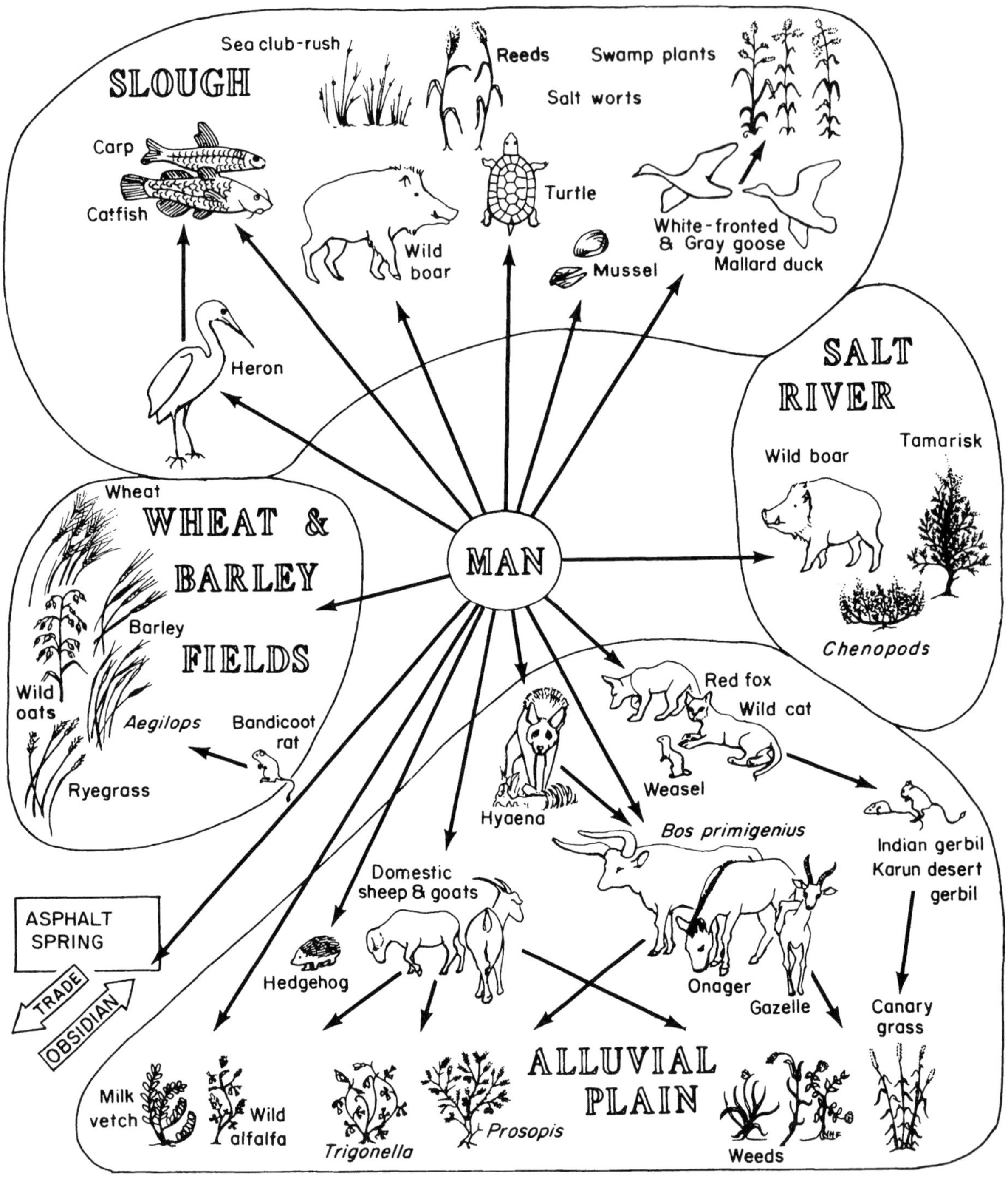

Fig. 135. Simplified diagram of man's exploitation of wild and domestic resources in northern Khuzistan during the seventh and eighth millenia B.C. Also shown are major imports, exports, and a part of the food chain of some of the animal species involved, by "micro-environment."

THE ALI KOSH PHASE

6750 to 6000 B.C.

The Bus Mordeh adaptation was a successful one, and by comparing it with the Ali Kosh phase we can isolate those components which were most successful, for they were on the increase between 6500 and 6000 B.C. Cultivation of winter-grown cereals and hunting of large ungulates increased during the Ali Kosh phase, and there was a slight increase in numbers of domestic sheep. During the phase there seems to have been a real tapering-off in the collection of small-seeded wild legumes.

About 40 per cent of the carbonized seeds left behind in the hearths and middens of the Ali Kosh phase were grains of emmer wheat and two-row hulled barley. These were the same plants grown in the Bus Mordeh phase; only their amount had increased. Quite probably, in increasing the acreage under cultivation around Ali Kosh, the villagers had reduced the number of small wild legumes and useful wild grasses, since these have roughly the same growing season and compete for the same kind of soil as the cereals: sandy, well-drained loam with low salinity. We are uncertain to what extent grazing by goats and sheep also contributed to a reduction in the native wild flora. The effects of this land-use were to become apparent in later phases, but the Ali Kosh period was one of apparent prosperity.

Small legumes like those collected in the Bus Mordeh phase had dropped to just under twenty per cent of the seeds. Goat-face grass, ryegrass, and einkorn wheat, the crop weeds, were well established now; and the villagers collected wild oats, canary grass, goosefoot, caper, and others. A single lentil has so far been identified from this phase, suggesting that the Ali Kosh farmers were in contact with villagers in the mountains which, like Jarmo, had begun to cultivate some of the large-seeded annual legumes (Helbaek, 1960*a*:115). Studies of the carbonized plants suggest that reeds or club-rushes may have been the most popular fuel for hearths.

The prosperity of the Ali Kosh phase is perhaps best reflected in its architecture. We do not know, because of our limited exposure, whether or not the village had grown larger, but the multiroomed houses evidently had. The rooms we found were larger than 3 by 3 meters, and the walls were up to a meter thick. The walls, built up of large, untempered, clay-slab bricks averaging 40 by 25 by 10 cm., were held together by mud mortar and often finished on both sides by a coat of smooth mud plaster. Where two walls came together, they simply "butted," with no interlocking of bricks. House floors were of stamped mud, often surfaced with a layer of clean clay, and apparently topped with over-two, under-two woven mats of reed or club-rush. There were apparent courtyards, which contained domed brick ovens and brick-lined roasting pits. No ovens were found inside rooms, and considering the heat of the Khuzistan summer, it would have been no advantage to have them inside. There were also doorways and small niches in walls, and narrow alleyways separating houses.

Domestic goats were the animals most commonly eaten by the villagers of the Ali Kosh phase. Showing clear osteological evidence of domestication, these goats had horn cores which might be quadrangular, lozenge-shaped, or plano-convex (medially flattened) in cross-section. Most were still eaten while quite young, though 40 per cent reached the age of three years—an increase over the Bus Mordeh phase. The few domestic sheep appearing in the Ali Kosh phase were still outnumbered heavily by goats; and male sheep horn cores still indicate no osteological deviation from the wild phenotype.

The Ali Kosh phase saw increased hunting of gazelle, onager, and wild cattle. To deal with the heavier ungulates, the villagers used a set of specialized butchering tools: flint pebble choppers for fracturing limb bones, small "slicing slabs" which could be inserted under tendons or ligaments to facilitate cutting with flint blades, and of course, blades and scrapers by the hundreds. Included in butchering areas are more enigmatic tools, like chipped limestone discs which (among other possible uses), may have been the "anvils" on which ungulate limbs were tapped to release their marrow. Chipping scars on the bones themselves suggest that this technique, common among some hunting peoples of the New World, was also used at Deh Luran. Scarred, chipped, fractured ox and onager bones were left in piles in the corners of the Ali Kosh phase rooms in association with such tools; gazelles and domestic goats were differently dealt with.

Use of aquatic resources went on in the Ali Kosh phase. Catfish, carp, water turtle, mussels, ducks, geese, cranes, herons, and river crabs were among the animals they collected. Their interest in small land mammals was relatively slight, although foxes were eaten.

The Ali Kosh villagers harvested their cereals with flint sickles, which were set into hafts by means of asphalt. They ground up wheat, barley, and crop weeds on saddle-shaped or shallow-basin grinding slabs, using simple discoidal handstones of pitted limestone. An innovation was the use of the stone mortar and pestle. Some grinding stones show traces of red ochre, an iron oxide pigment which was used in a variety of ways.

Besides chipping flint nodules into butchering choppers, the Ali Kosh folk produced tens of thousands of flint blades struck from narrow, conical, bullet-shaped polyhedral cores, and wider "tongue-shaped" cores. Some of the blades were secondarily retouched into diagonal-ended and backed bladelets for use in composite hunting tools, or into end-of-blade scrapers for hide-working. Chunkier cores were also used in the production of flakes, some of which eventually became scrapers. Drills, reamers, burins, and other tools were manufactured. Some of the finer retouching seems to have been done with small mussel-shell pressure flakers. Particularly characteristic of the phase were domed or keeled scrapers made from chunky cores, and resembling the "scraper planes" used in the prehistoric southwestern United States or Mexico for extracting the edible pulp from tough fiber plants. Obsidian from Lake Van constituted about two per cent of the chipped stone during Ali Kosh times.

The villagers used pounders made from flint nodules or crude flint blade cores (some of which were also used as pestles). We have already mentioned the flint pebble choppers and slicing slabs which were abundant in houses of this phase. Bone awls or bodkins and bone needles were manufactured, and at least some of them were sharpened on grooved rubbing stones made from gray, gritty sandstone. Chipped limestone discs, pecked balls of limestone which may have been light-duty pounders, and other heavy-duty ground-stone tools were common.

The use of containers is much clearer in the Ali Kosh phase than in the preceding levels of the Bus Mordeh period. In addition to over-two, under-two and over-one, under-one floor mats, the villagers made simple twined ("wicker") baskets with an over-one, under-one weave. Some of these seem to have been waterproofed with asphalt. A curious tool used (it would seem) in the stirring and spreading of asphalt resembles a limestone "sashweight." These roughly cigar-shaped stones, smeared at one end with asphalt and occasionally with red ochre as well, occurred by the hundreds.

Stone bowls greatly increased in number and variety during the Ali Kosh phase. Some were carved out of stone as soft as gypsum, while others were made with painstaking care from stone as hard as marble. Flat-based bowls with a simple rounded rim, or a "beaded" rim were commonest, but there were also shallow "trays" of limestone. None of these stone vessels were large enough to have served for storage; each would have held only a single meal for a single individual. Possibly they may once have held the gruel cooked up from the ground and roasted wheat and barley; it is worth noting that emmer wheat and hulled barley are largely unsuitable for bread-making, and that the ovens in the Ali Kosh phase courtyards were more likely for roasting or parching grain than for baking.

Lightly-baked, perhaps in the same ovens, were a variety of figurines. These included the small, goatlike figures already made in Bus Mordeh times, which may have functioned as charms connected with the increase of domestic herds. But the Ali Kosh villagers also made a few human figurines, preserved only in very fragmentary condition. Clay cylinders of various kinds (some of which may have been parts of figurines) occurred in great quantity—some have pinched ends, some appliqué blobs, some show punctations that may depict tatooing such as that seen occasionally (when the opportunity presents itself) on the native women of Khuzistan even today.

These figurines are not complete or realistic enough to show us how the Ali Kosh villagers dressed; but the burials provided clues. The women of the phase practiced annular skull deformation and wore strings of beads composed of flat black or white stone discs, sea shells, or tubular stones. Men wore some sort of pubic covering, the imperishable part of which was a bell-shaped cover of polished stone, asphalt, or lightly-baked clay. Other ornaments, worn perhaps by either sex, included boar tusk or mussel-shell pendants, plummet-shaped or flat pebble pendants, and strings of disc beads with tubular bead spacers. Turquoise, imported from at least as far away as the Iranian Plateau, was made into small irregular beads. Native copper, perhaps from the Iranian Plateau as well, appeared in the form of a tubular bead which had been cold-hammered, cut with a chisel, and rolled into shape.

When an individual died during the Ali Kosh phase, his body (sometimes coated with red ochre) was tightly flexed and wrapped in a twilled, over-two, under-two reed or club-rush mat. An excavation was made under the floor of his house, and the bundled body placed (often in a sitting position) under the floor at no great depth, accompanied by articles of personal adornment. A few individuals, however, seem to have been reburied at a later date, after their flesh had decomposed. Perhaps in the case of a few persons of relative prestige, the bundled bodies were saved for a delayed, more elaborate burial (as in the case of a number of American Indian groups). Alternatively, certain individuals may have been disinterred and reburied at a later date, either purposefully or through accidental disturbance of a long-forgotten burial. Not all components of the skeleton were present in these secondary burials.

Ali Kosh is the only site in the Deh Luran plain which is definitely known to have been occupied during this period; the village was approximately a hectare in extent. Given the size and spacing of the Ali Kosh houses, it was probably not occupied by more than one hundred individuals. This would give us an estimated population density for the Deh Luran plain of perhaps 0.3 persons per square kilometer.

The network of exchange participated in by the people of the Ali Kosh phase, however, was greater than that of the preceding Bus Mordeh phase. Sea shells (from the Persian Gulf?), copper (from central Iran?), turquoise (from the Mashed region, near the Afghanistan border?), and obsidian from eastern Turkey, all reached Ali Kosh at this period. In addition, the domestic goats raised by these villagers were in contact with other herds, from whom they had presumably picked up some of the genes responsible for the medially-flattened horn core. It may be that this gene flow took place late in the summer, when the Deh Luran herds may have been taken up to the summer grazing lands of Luristan and came into proximity with other domestic herds.

Typologically, the Ali Kosh phase would seem to be contemporary with prepottery levels at Jarmo in Iraqi Kurdistan, and Tepe Guran in Iranian Luristan. Several radiocarbon dates in the 6500 B.C. time range would tend to support this placement.

THE MOHAMMAD JAFFAR PHASE

6000 to 5600 B.C.

The Mohammad Jaffar phase saw innovations in subsistence, architecture, and artifacts. The villagers of this phase lived in houses whose foundations were built of river pebbles, with some use of larger cobbles and even river boulders. Above these foundations, the walls were of clay-slab bricks, plastered with mud; a few crumbled wall fragments indicate that in some cases this plaster was painted with red ochre. The walls were up to a meter thick, and floors were of stamped mud or clean clay, covered with over-two, under-two reed or club-rush mats.

More than a thousand years of agriculture had preceded this phase, and the carbonized plant remains reflect the changed land surface of this part of the Deh Luran plain. Emmer wheat and two-row hulled barley were still virtually the only crops known, although an occasional lentil indicates contact with mountain farming groups. But practices of fallowing and grazing had removed a great deal of the natural vegetational cover in the vicinity of the site, and its place was taken by pasture plants like plantain, mallow, vetch, oat grass, and canary grass. In particular, the area had seen an increase in the woody perennial legume *Prosopis,* a plant related to American mesquite and known to the Arabs as *shauk.* The fleshy pods of this plant are edible, and the discarded seeds (which are not eaten) appeared in carbonized form by the hundreds in Mohammad Jaffar phase middens. Adams (1965:5) points out that *shauk* tends to increase with cultivation because it matures so late in the year that it competes hardly at all with winter-sown crops, and hence does not suffer the fate of winter-maturing weeds.

This increase in *Prosopis,* which somewhat reduced the percentage of wheat and barley grains in the total assemblage of carbonized plants, was not the chance occurrence of a single bonfire: it characterized ash samples from outside houses, inside houses, in middens, in asphalt-coated baskets, everywhere. Other plants which seem to have been on the increase were fumitory (*Fumaria*) and goose-grass (*Galium*), both field weeds. Wild ryegrass, goat-face grass, vetchling, and caper still appeared in the refuse.

In other words, farming in the Mohammad Jaffar phase, while obviously successful, required careful weeding and a reasonable fallowing system, which had altered the landscape to a noticeable degree. Similar problems must have beset the herdsman as he sought to find adequate pasture for his flocks in a region where the amount of land given over to cultivation was on the increase. For herding was also expanding, to judge by the animal bones, and sheep along with it. Sheep were outnumbered by goats at the start of the Mohammad Jaffar phase, but gaining on them rapidly by 5500 B.C. In later periods, they were to overtake and pass them by a wide margin, becoming the most common domestic animal of prehistoric and early historic Khuzistan (Adams, 1962:115). Sheep, after all, have a panting mechanism which enables them to survive better than some domesticated animals under the hot climatic regime of the steppe (Schmidt-Nielsen, 1964:99).

Osteologically, both the sheep and the goats of the Mohammad Jaffar phase can be considered as highly domesticated. Some goats had already begun to exhibit the helically-twisted or "corkscrew" horn core of modern Iranian domestic goats, although most individuals preserved the straight, medially-flattened, or quadrangular horn core cross-section. Male sheep of this period had the "goatlike" horn core cross-section typical of domesticates, and not the anteriorly-broad cross-section of wild Luristan sheep. The Mohammad Jaffar villagers still liked to eat their goats and sheep at the young stage, and only about forty per cent of the herd reached the age of three years.

Mohammad Jaffar phase hunters brought down gazelle, onager, aurochs, and wild pig, possibly using projectiles whose heads were barbed with backed and diagonal-ended microliths set in asphalt. As in earlier periods, piles of onager and aurochs bones are accompanied by the flint pebble choppers, flint blades, and scarred "slicing slabs" which were probably used in butchering. Broken limb-bone ends show chipping scars which may have been produced when the marrow was tapped out, perhaps on the chipped limestone discs abundant in the butchering refuse. Cut marks near tendon attachments show that limbs were disarticulated with flint blades; most bones show no evidence of burning, while a few are charred, as if some haunches had been roasted over hot coals. The villagers continued their use of winter water birds, and fished for catfish and some carp, as well as collecting crabs, water turtles, and freshwater mussels. As the grazing of domesticated animals increased, it would have reduced the amount of forage available for the wild ungulates; no real decrease in the number of such animals is noted until after the Mohammad Jaffar phase, but it may be significant that more small mammals seem to have been eaten in this period. Fox, hedgehog, and wild cat were included in the diet. Large canids were only rarely eaten, and there is no concrete evidence as yet for the domestic dog.

The hulled barley and emmer wheat were harvested with flint blades set in a haft, with asphalt as the principal mastic; grains were roasted before grinding up for use in gruel. The difficulty of removing the glumes of these early cereals had been countered by the Mohammad Jaffar people through an array of grinding implements which, in terms of variety and number, was never matched in later periods. Besides the saddle-shaped and shallow-basin grinding slabs inherited from the Ali Kosh phase, the Mohammad Jaffar folk made implements which were combination shallow-basin grinding slabs and mortars; these were used in conjunction with implements appearing to be combination handstones and pestles. They also used pebble mortars; boulder mortars; flat-topped boulder slabs; discoidal, loaf-shaped, or irregular elongate handstones; and stubby, bell-shaped mullers. The difficulty of processing in bulk cereals which were not yet genetically "free-threshing" is reflected in the lengths to which the Mohammad Jaffar people had gone in evolving an adequate ground-stone industry for coping with the problem. In later periods, with free-threshing cereals, such variety of grinding implements rapidly dwindled.

The Mohammad Jaffar villagers continued to produce flint blades in the remarkable quantity as in preceding phases; more than a hundred sickle blades were recovered from levels of this period. An innovation was the practice of trimming sickle blades so that they would fit into a particular slot in the handle, a custom that was to become common in later phases. Drills, reamers, and endscrapers made either on blades or on flakes were also tools typical of the period. It may be that many of the drills and reamers were for use in making wooden tools which have not been preserved; others, like some of the bone awls and needles, may have been for perforating hides. Nearly two per cent of the chipped stone from this phase was obsidian.

Bone awls, needles, and chisels may have been sharpened on grooved rubbing stones. Flat spatulas were ground out of ribs or flat slabs of animal bone. The villagers' kitchen areas were filled with discarded choppers, flint nodule pounders, "sashweight" asphalt stirrers, slicing slabs, chipped limestone discs, and pecked stone balls. They also ground up red ochre on pitted limestone slabs.

Twined baskets (either over-two, under-two or over-one, under-one) were coated with asphalt for waterproofing; some baskets had "floors" of plaited matting rather than twined centers, and most appeared to be shallow trays which may have served in seed-collecting. Many of the same stone-bowl types seen in the Ali Kosh phase continued, including flat-based bowls with a simple or beaded rim. The villagers also manufactured oval bowls and a few highly polished miniature vessels.

The most striking innovation in the field of containers was pottery, which made its first appearance in the Mohammad Jaffar phase. The pottery of this period was soft, friable, and straw-tempered, made of clay which differed but little from that used in previous periods to make figurines. The techniques used to finish and decorate the surface were not so far removed from those used in wall-surfacing: a smoothing or burnishing of the clay, followed by a coating of red ochre. The tempering material, straw, was a by-product of agriculture. Several of the vessel shapes are shared by stone bowls of the same period. The pots themselves could easily have been baked in an oven like that used for centuries previously to roast grain or bake figurines. In other words, although pottery appears rather abruptly in the Mohammad Jaffar phase, virtually all the concepts needed to manufacture it had already existed previously in southwestern Asia: clay working, smoothing and ochre-painting of clay, firing, and container forms. We do not know where this type of pottery, introduced into the Deh Luran plain early in the Mohammad Jaffar phase, was first manufactured. We simply point out that, like all innovations, it was simply a recombination of previously existing techniques.

The pottery of the Mohammad Jaffar phase was basically of three types, all of which were made with poorly cleaned clay tempered with chaff. First, there were plain buff bowls with pinkish or blackish firing clouds; these might be round and deep, with slightly everted lips, or else large and oval. Second, there was a variety of deep bowl whose surface was decorated with geometric motifs in fugitive red ochre paint; zig-zags, chevrons, or pendant triangles and lozenges. A few of these pots had small troughtlike spouts at the lip. Third, there were small bowls, either hemispherical or carinated, some with beaded rims, covered with a soft, red ochre wash or slip which had been burnished. A few red globular jars with dimpled bases and constricted "hole-mouths" appeared later in the phase, but never in great frequency.

Lightly baked clay figurines were made in great numbers. Most appeared as fragmentary cylinders, broken limbs and torsos, but there was at least one recognizable human figure depicted in a squatting position with hands on knees—the kind frequently referred to as a "mother goddess." A number of stalk- or T-shaped figurines may have been highly stylized human figures also. Clay polishers (possibly for burnishing pottery) were manufactured, and in fact, far greater and more varied use of clay was made during the Mohammad Jaffar phase than in previous periods. The villagers even chipped broken sherds of pottery into small perforated discs, which may be crude spindle whorls, or fly wheels for pump-type drills. If they were truly spindle whorls, we do not know what their use implies, for it is not yet known when wool and flax first came to be spun in Khuzistan.

The Mohammad Jaffar folk wore pendants of flat polished pebbles, mussel shell, or crab claw, and bracelets of white, black, and red stone disc beads, interrupted by tubular stone spacers. They imported cowrie shells and turquoise nodules which were also used as ornaments, and they made smooth-surfaced stone bracelets of marblelike stone. Particularly characteristic were lip plugs of asphalt, clay, or polished stone, one of which was found *in situ* on the lower jaw of a burial. Men wore girdles or G-strings decorated with a fringe of flat black stone disc beads, and a pubic covering with a bell-shaped artifact of stone, asphalt, or lightly baked clay. No purposeful skull deformation is known from this phase so far, but our number of skeletons recovered is very small and consists mostly of males. In the realm of exotica, there were stone "phalli" made from limestone or alabaster, often carefully polished. Numerous similar highly polished alabaster "phalli" were found in graves of the earliest occupation as Tell as-Sawwan near Samarra in Iraq, apparently equivalent in time to the Sabz Phase (El-Wailly, 1963, 1964). Their appearance during the Mohammad Jaffar phase in the Deh Luran plain gives us our first real evidence of interaction between the Khuzistan steppe and the Tigris River region—an interaction which is more strongly manifested during the Sabz phase, with the arrival of many new products and techniques of possible northeast Mesopotamian origin.

When an adult male died during the Mohammad Jaffar phase, his body was taken outside the house and buried in semiflexed position on its left side, facing west. No evidence of mat-wrapping was detected on the burials we found, but red ochre appeared in some graves and at least one individual seems to have had a basket (with perishable foodstuffs?) at the shoulder. The individual was accompanied by his articles of personal adornment, including as many as three or four turquoise beads. At the hips were traces of a beaded G-string and the usual bell-shaped artifact.

Ali Kosh was a village of approximately one hectare in extent during this period. On the basis of our surface collections, it is possible that there were two other small villages in the Deh Luran plain at that time, north of Tepe Sabz; this will, of course, have to be confirmed by future excavations. We might therefore tentatively estimate the population density of the plain as approximately 1.0 person per square kilometer.

The Mohammad Jaffar people participated in an ever-widening trade network at this time, although the amount of material exchanged was fairly small, and there is no evidence of a medium more sophisticated than balanced reciprocity. They had obsidian from eastern Turkey, turquoise possibly from northeastern Iran, specular hematite which may have come from Fars, and sea shells from the Persian Gulf. The designs on their pottery, made in red ochre, show some relationship to designs on the contemporary pottery at Tepe

Guran in Luristan and Tepe Sarab in southern Kurdistan; some ties can also be seen with later pottery from the alluvial lowlands, namely Samarra and Matarrah in the Tigris drainage of Iraq. The dimple-based, hole-mouth vessels of red burnished pottery suggest later jars from Tepe Sialk, near the Anarak copper lode on the high Iranian Plateau, and the convex-walled bowls in plain buff and fugitive ochre-painted buff are reminiscent of Qalat Jarmo in northern Kurdistan and Hajji Firuz Tepe in Azarbaijan. Speaking generally about the Zagros Mountains and Khuzistan, this was a time of population increase and settlement into a variety of habitats. Surface surveys hint at transhument herding patterns with summer and winter settlements, and active exchange which linked the peoples east of the Tigris and its tributaries into a loose network along which new ideas traveled rapidly.

THE SABZ PHASE

5500 to 5000 B.C.

Midway through the sixth millenium, the Deh Luran plain (and perhaps Khuzistan in general) went through a rapid and crucial transition which was to set it clearly in the path toward population expansion and urban life. The two major innovations of that period were (1) the beginnings of competent irrigation, and (2) the first local evidence for the use of domestic cattle. Our evidence suggests that irrigation was still a small-scale affair, and that cattle were probably used mainly for food; but within the next two thousand years, more advanced irrigation and the cattle-drawn plow led the lowlands into civilization.

We do not know yet whether or not the Sabz phase was an indigenous development out of the Mohammad Jaffar phase. Numbers of artifact types bridge the gap between the two phases, but there are also striking differences. Certain pottery types, ornaments, and tools continued into the Sabz phase, but the whole aspect of the chipped-stone industry changed drastically, and new tools appeared in significant quantity. Were the tools which show continuity merely those which were of wide distribution throughout the steppe in the early sixth millenium, or do they really indicate a local origin for tne Sabz phase?

In Susiana proper—the rolling plain drained by the Karkheh and Diz Rivers, only a hundred km. to the east of Deh Luran—Robert Adams (1962:112) found at least thirty-four villages belonging to this general period of time. We find it hard to believe that this many farmers and herders suddenly descended on Khuzistan at about 5500 B.C. And since the environment in Susiana proper was at least as favorable for early village settlement as that of the Deh Luran plain, we suspect that Susiana must have been occupied during the Mohammad Jaffar phase, although sites of that age have yet to be found there.

Only future excavations will be able to solve the problem of whether the Sabz phase is indigenous to Khuzistan. If indeed it consists, in part, of an influx of new peoples, our guess would be that the area most likely to contain its origins is the adjacent Tigris River steppe of northeast Mesopotamia. In the latter region, sites like Tell as-Sawwan had already assumed unprecedented proportions and evidently included the residences of important persons whose status was expressed in the form of rich burial equipment. Our limited exposure of the Sabz phase revealed no high status graves, but the agricultural complex we recovered is identical to that of Tell as-Sawwan (Helbaek, 1964), which suggests that both areas lie within the same farming province.

One aspect of the Sabz phase is clear. It cannot be derived from the highlands. Its tools, its pottery, its complex of domestic plants are already within the tradition which was to lead on to the Ubaid. Its ceramic ties are with Eridu I, Samarra, Matarrah, Jaffarabad, and the southern lowlands, and not with sites in the Zagros Mountains like Siabid, Dalma Tepe, Mushki, or Jari, nor with sites in far northern Mesopotamia like Hassuna or Halaf. In one sense, the Sabz phase is a redefinition of the period Le Breton (1957) called "Susiana *a.*" Its new definition is based on more than pottery.

Because our 1963 trench hit only midden deposits of this phase, we know nothing about its architecture. A few traces of plaited reed or club-rush matting, and some possible "door pivot stones" like those of later phases, were our only clues. The middens were rich enough in carbonized sheep and goat dung, tamarisk firewood, carbonized seeds, and broken animal bones to tell us something about the village, however.

The people of the Sabz phase planted "free-threshing" hexaploid bread wheat as well as emmer. They had hulled six-row barley, which was to become with time the most successful cultivated cereal of the Mesopotamian lowlands. In addition, they raised two-row hulled barley, lentils, vetch, and vetchling. They left behind almonds which may have been cultivated, or else gathered wild on the upper slopes of the Kuh-i-Siah. And they grew linseed or flax (*Linum*) whose seeds are too large to have come from plants raised on rainfall alone; they are in the size range of irrigated flax seeds from lowland Mesopotamian sites (see Helbaek, 1960*b*:192-93 and this volume).

Accompanying this agricultural development came a shift in settlement pattern. Instead of occupying well-drained, low rises near the margins of the seasonally-flooded central depression of the Deh Luran plain, many sites of the Sabz phase (including Tepe Sabz itself) are located where they could have taken advantage of the many small stream channels coming down off the mountains to the north of the plain. These natural drainages could have been used as sources for irrigation water during the winter rainy season, and enlarged or diverted with a minimum of effort. Many of them, even today, drain into small, low-lying areas of the plain, which are presently farmed by the nomads who visit the Deh Luran plain in the winter (see Plate 2*a*).

But not all Sabz phase villages used irrigation; as pointed out by Adams (*loc. cit.*), some villages of this period in Susiana proper were located in situations where irrigation could not have been practiced, from which he concludes that agriculture at this time must have been mainly dependent on rainfall. Artificial water control during the Sabz phase may have been principally an insurance policy against a bad year, a supplement to rainfall farming. Its implications for the future of lowland steppe agriculture, however, are obvious. Adams, for one, should not be surprised to learn of its inception by 5500 B.C., for he had already ventured that "the high early density of settlement in this region can perhaps be traced to the exceptionally favorable circumstances the region would have offered for the transition from dry farming to irrigation agriculture. . ." (Adams, *loc. cit.*).

Appearing in this phase for the first time is an implement known, for want of a better term, as a "polished celt". It is a flat, elongate limestone pebble which had been chipped into shape and ground until smooth. The upper end shows traces of the asphalt which held it in its handle; the lower end shows the kind of polish which accumulates on flint hoes used in regions of alluvial soil. From the Sabz phase on through the whole of the Tepe Sabz sequence, not only in Deh Luran but throughout the Khuzistan steppe, this was one of the most common tools recovered. It is a tool, to the best of our knowledge, unknown from the mountains at this time, although roughly chipped hoes are found in the contemporary Hassuna context in northern Mesopotamia. Its appearance, simultaneously with the first evidence of irrigation, is probably no coincidence, or else why would it be absent in the rain-fed uplands? Several possibilities for its use exist, and at present we have no way to decide between the alternatives. It could be, purely and simply, a hoe for breaking the surface of the alluvium. It could, on the other hand, be an instrument which functioned in the opening of breaches in stream levees and in the digging of small channels for water. Still another, more intriguing hypothesis has been advanced by a paleobotanist colleague, James Schoenwetter. Schoenwetter feels that perhaps, under conditions of digging-stick agriculture, weeds may not have constituted much of a problem; nor would they have been as much of a problem when cattle-drawn plows made large-scale cultivation a possibility. The time when weeds were most annoying might have been the period between the start of irrigation and the adoption of the plow. It is probably in that period of time that the so-called "polished celt" fits stratigraphically. Perhaps future investigations will make the role of this instrument more clear.

The villagers of the Sabz phase also raised goats, whose small, helically-twisted horn cores are indistinguishable from those of the modern Iranian domestic goat. In somewhat smaller numbers, they also raised domestic sheep with small, curled, and anteriorly-keeled horns. To these animals they had now added the domestic ox. The cattle of the Sabz phase were much smaller than the wild aurochs, and constituted only five per cent of the animal bones recovered from levels of that period, but they represent another landmark in the prehistory of Khuzistan.

Hunting continued during the Sabz phase, with gazelle still the most popular quarry; some onagers and wild boar were occasionally taken. The Sabz phase villagers continued the fishing and collecting of mussel and water turtle which had characterized the earlier periods at Deh Luran, perhaps an aspect of subsistence which indicates continuity from the Mohammad Jaffar phase. Birds, and small mammals like the fox and hedgehog, were also a part of their diet.

The domestic dog had now become a scavenger around the villages of the Deh Luran plain. Paintings on pottery vessels show that the Sabz phase dogs had erect ears and a long, fluffy tail which curled up over the back like that of the modern Kurdish shepherd's dog. Their bones show that they were nearly as large as the wolves of the Zagros Mountains, and the intact, semiarticulated condition of their remains indicates that they were not eaten.

Although they grew free-threshing wheat, the Sabz villagers dealt with their hulled barley and emmer wheat with many of the same grinding stone types as the folk of the Mohammad Jaffar phase: saddle-shaped slabs, combination mortar-and-shallow-basin slabs, simple discoidal handstones, and irregular sausage-shaped pestles. They used flint nodule pounders, or hammerstones made from crude flint cores, much as the Mohammad Jaffar villagers. They used similar slicing slabs in butchering sheep, goat, and gazelle, and other animals, but (perhaps due to reduced hunting of onager and wild ox) they seem not to have needed so many flint pebble choppers. They stirred asphalt with "sash-weight"-shaped stones, and made bone awls, spatulas, and gouges not unlike those of the earlier phases in our sequence.

One of the most dramatic changes from the pattern of the Mohammad Jaffar phase is in the quantity and quality of flint tools. The Sabz phase villagers chose to use a new source of flint of uniformly low quality for most of their tools (although a few blades of good quality flint appear). Gone for the most part are the finely-chipped bladelet cores which are so characteristic of the preceding phases, and so clear an indication of the mastery of flint chipping. Where flint blades had been counted in the thousands during the Mahammad Jaffar phase, their numbers were reduced to less than one hundred in excavations of comparable magnitude in the Sabz phase. In neither this period nor the subsequent Khazineh phase did we recover obsidian.

The principal tools of the Sabz phase were plain blades, and sickle blades which had been trimmed to fit into particular slots in a handle. Equipment for composite hunting tools included crescent-shaped microliths, while use of items like drills, reamers, and scrapers had begun to taper off. We do not yet know whether or not this decrease in hide-working tools is related to the increase in spindle whorls and the growing of irrigated flax, a situation which suggests that woven wool or plant fiber may have been replacing leather for certain items. Generally speaking, the change in flint also suggests a shift away from a preoccupation with hunting, a trend which is further supported by the other evidence we have cited.

Although they made a few stone bowls with simple or "beaded" rims, like their Mohammad Jaffar predecessors, the villagers of the Sabz phase had entered into a tradition of pottery-making which, though changing gradually through time, was to characterize Khuzistan for the next two thousand years. In quality and complexity their ceramics far surpassed those of the Mohammad Jaffar phase. They still made oval bowls and holemouth jars of soft, chaff-tempered pinkish-tan pottery, but they had ceased to decorate it with fugitive red ochre paint. They still made red-slipped, burnished bowls with simple or beaded rims, but grit particles now constituted a greater part of the temper than previously. In addition, the Sabz potters had begun to make a hard, sand-tempered, yellowish-buff pottery which was far sturdier and less friable than anything seen in the Mohammad Jaffar phase. It appears to have been fired at a higher temperature than the soft, chaff-tempered wares of the Mohammad Jaffar phase—possibly even in a true kiln—and although still handmade, it was a clear technological advancement. Literally thousands of sherds appeared in excavations of this phase: it was the first point in our sequence during which fragments of pottery outnumbered fragments of flint.

In undecorated form, this sand-tempered buff ware was made into oval basins (not unlike the oval bowls in chaff-tempered pottery), convex-walled bowls (not unlike their chaff-tempered counterparts), small hemispherical bowls with simple or beaded rims (not unlike their stone counterparts), hole-mouth jars with dimple bases, and several new shapes—perhaps the most distinctive being a bowl supported by a short pedestal.

Appearing for the first time in this phase, however, were numbers of vessels of this same grit-tempered yellowish-buff ware to which designs had been added with paint. Most designs were geometric, and the paint used was an iron oxide or peroxide, like red ochre, but fired at such a temperature that it almost always turned tawny brown or grayish-black, rather than red. Moreover, it was far from fugitive, except in the case of a few reddish variants (possibly accidental). The paint was applied in a broad-line, free-hand manner, with a great deal of individualism, yet the vessels have a more professional quality about them than those of the Mohammad Jaffar phase. At the same time, they lack the standardization and extremely precise painting of later phases in the sequence.

Vessels in this type of pottery included large oval basins with black bands at rim and base, or convex-walled bowls whose exteriors were covered with painted designs: herringbones, chevrons, vertical panels of wiggly-line motifs, checkerboards, screens, or crosshatching. There were bowls on pedestal bases, some of which had little triangular or diamond-shaped "windows" cut in them A few small bowls with incurved rims were covered with designs which resembled knotted cords or basketry; some of these were so densely painted that the design, instead of appearing in black on a buff background, appeared as buff designs in a black field—a technique known as "reserve" or "negative" decoration, and which was to increase with time.

The Sabz phase villagers made numerous items of clay and fired pottery. They continued the tradition of stylized, T-shaped or "stalk" figurines seen in the Mohammad Jaffar phase, and they made spindle whorls of a very distinctive kind, in the shape of a star or asterisk. They chipped or ground pot sherds into scrapers of various sizes; some may have been used to scrape the sides of pots that were being shaped from plastic clay, while others may possibly have replaced the flint scrapers of previous periods.

The people of this phase ornamented themselves with lip-plugs of lightly-baked clay, asphalt, or stone, as in the Mohammad Jaffar phase. They made stone bracelets or anklets, but not of the smooth polished kind seen in Mohammad Jaffar times. Their bracelets were flattened bands whose outer surface bore deeply-incised parallel lines which followed the circular course of the bracelet.

Materials of the Sabz phase are widespread in Khuzistan, but lie principally north of the isohyet indicating 300 mm. of rainfall. They were competent at irrigation, but they preferred to stay within the area where rainfall farming was possible, an area still sparsely-enough inhabited so that there was room for many villages. In the Deh Luran plain, there were at least six villages of this phase, each containing perhaps one hundred persons. This would give us an estimated population density of approximately two persons per square kilometer. As mentioned earlier, Adams' survey in Susiana proper found thirty-four villages which pertain to this period, of which only two (Jaffarabad and Chogha Mish) have been excavated. Most are in the neighborhood of one hectare in size, but a few may have been considerably larger—we have verbal reports that Chogha Mish, for example, may have been a sizeable settlement already in the Sabz phase. A conservative estimate for the population of Susiana proper at this time period would, therefore, be on the order of 3400 inhabitants.

The Sabz phase thus extended geographically from at least as far as Deh Luran in the northwest to perhaps as far as Ram Hormuz in the southeast. Nowhere in this entire region were sites as abundant as in the "Little Mesopotamia" between the Karkhah and Diz Rivers, where sufficient rain and surface water plus good drainage provided the ideal situation for the transition to irrigation farming. To the southwest, the Eridu I culture—related but not identical—found its own environmental setting and had its own geographical distribution in the arid Tigris-Euphrates plain. To the northeast, Iranian mountain cultures—also related but different—seem to have been farming in the valley plains and perhaps sharing the mountain grazing lands with herders of the Sabz phase.

This was a crucial period of Iranian prehistory, about which we would like to know more. It has shown us the earliest clear evidence of irrigation, of cattle-herding, and possibly of kiln-fired pottery in southwestern Iran. With it we enter the Susiana sequence, heretofor defined on the basis of ceramics alone, which led on the emergence of town life and civilization in the land between the Karkheh and the Diz. What eludes us still is a clear-cut picture of its origins.

THE KHAZINEH PHASE

5000 to 4500 B.C.

Villagers of the Khazineh phase lived in houses of mud brick whose walls were sometimes founded on a single layer of pebbles of cobbles. On the floors were twilled mats of reed or club-rush, and the doors swung on pivots which fitted into stone sockets. Villages reaching two hectares in size are known from the Deh Luran plain, and much larger villages may well be buried under later deposits on some of the really big sites in the area—like Tepe Musiyan.

Khazineh phase farmers cultivated free-threshing wheat, two-row and six-row barley (both hulled and naked), lentils, vetch, vetchling and flax. Their herds consisted of sheep and goats in about equal numbers, with a few cattle as well. The horn cores and bones of these animals are indistinguishable from modern Iranian domestic breeds: goats had tightly twisted horns, and female sheep were probably mostly hornless. Domestic dogs scavenged on the village dumps, and there was a little hunting of gazelle and onager.

Ground stone was lacking in variety, possibly because the "naked" grains made mechanical husking unnecessary. There were saddle-shaped grinding slabs, boulder mortars, simple discoidal handstones, and irregular sausage-shaped pestles in use. Plain flint blades were chipped from cores (often from one side only, not using the whole periphery of the core), and some flakes and blades were retouched into other tools. Some sickle blades were both backed and truncated for fitting into hafts. No microlithic tools or obsidian appeared in the various building levels of the Khazineh phase we exposed. Polished celts, hafted with bitumen, continued as tools of considerable importance, and pounders made from flint nodules or from roughed out flint cores were also typical of the Khazineh phase.

In the Khazineh phase appeared the first evidence of coiled basketry we have seen in southwestern Iran. A larger exposure of Sabz phase levels might show that the manufacture of coiled basketry actually began in that period, but our earliest clear-cut impressions in asphalt date to about 5000 B.C. Coiled basketry occurs much earlier in the Anatolian region (Mellaart, 1962:56), along with coiled pottery; apparently it took a millenium or more for the technique to reach the southern Zagros. We conclude that in early periods—about 6000 B.C.—there were two distinct vessel making traditions in the Near East, one involving coiled basketry and coiled pottery (in Antolia) and the other concentrating on twilled and twined basketry and pottery built up by lamination (in the Zagros). By 5000 B.C. the distribution of the two traditions overlapped.

The pottery of the Khazineh phase was related to that from Qala't Hajji Muhammad, near Warka (Ziegler, 1953), and phase *b* of the Susiana sequence as defined by Le Breton. Decorative motifs were shared with a number of sites ranging over all of southern alluvial Mesopotamia and the Khuzistan steppe; ties with the mountains are much more tenuous, but some correspondences can be seen with Halaf, Banahilk, Siabid and other early fifth millenium sites.

Chaff-tempered red pottery continued in domestic usage. The predominant form was a hole-mouthed jar with dimple base, but there were also open bowls and carinated bowls in burnished red. Much of this type of pottery may have been made locally in the village households.

In the same levels occurred thousands of sherds of decorated buff pottery which may have been made by craft specialists. Included were large carinated bowls with complicated geometric patterns painted (primarily in black) on the inside of the base—"sundials," "flowers," and "wheels" were common motifs. There were also many small hemispherical bowls with exterior patterns resembling knotted cords or basketry designs. "Bow-ties," rows of lozenges, or diamonds were also favorite designs. The Khazineh phase potters made "sauce boats" with handles, and convex-walled bowls like those already seen in the Sabz phase. Many of the latter were covered with "close" patterns, "screens" or "checkerboards" so densely painted that the design appears "in reserve." In fact, the Khazineh phase represented a climax in "reserve" or "negative" geometric patterns; never again was such a large proportion of the vessel surface so densely covered with black, greenish-black, or reddish-black paint.

For the most part, plain buff pottery appeared in the same shapes as black-on-buff painted ware, but it was less common.

The Khazineh phase villagers still used star-shaped spindle whorls and wore nail-shaped and cuff-link-shaped labrets, as had their Sabz phase predecessors. They manufactured scrapers (and pot lids?) from chipped sherds, and made awls and pressure-flakers from bone. A few fragments of bone appear to have come from broken hafts for flint tools.

Most of the activities indicated in the "kitchen debris" are those still carried on by the small villages of Khuzistan: hoeing, harvesting, grinding grain, roasting and cooking cereals and legumes, spinning fiber, tending and butchering sheep and goats, and working their hides.

In the Deh Luran plain at this time there were six to eight villages; Adams' survey in Susiana proper located 102 contemporary sites, some of which appear to have covered many hectares. Some villages were in areas where irrigation is possible; others were not. Dry farming, small-scale irrigation, and herding, with probable transhumant movements to the valleys of mountainous Luristan and Fars, were the main subsistence activities.

The geographic range of the Khazineh phase includes all of Khuzistan; to the southwest lay the Hajji Mohammad culture area, which had related pottery, but not necessarily related economic and social activities, as we shall see when we discuss the subsequent Mehmeh phase.

At this point it is clear that Tepe Sabz was near the small end of a size continuum which must have included much larger and more important villages elsewhere in Khuzistan. The debris of the Khazineh phase yielded few of the exotic imported items and raw materials one might expect from this period. This suggests to us that differential access to these exotic raw materials was a real factor, and that these items are most likely to be found at the more important sites, where persons of somewhat higher status resided.

There are at least twelve sites of the Khazineh phase in the Deh Luran plain, giving us an estimated population density of four persons per squre km. Adams' surveys in Susiana proper disclosed 102 sites, suggesting a total population for Khuzistan of more than 10,000.

THE MEHMEH PHASE

4500 to 4100 B.C.

Through a series of accidents, we know more about the architecture of the Mehmeh phase than that of any other period. The house plans visible on the surface of Tepe Ashrafabad, and the architectural features recovered in the step trench at Tepe Sabz, tell essentially the same story. Houses were rectangular, reaching at least 5 by 10 in size, and with a door which pivoted on a perforated stone on one of the long sides. The outer walls were nearly a meter thick, founded on two parallel rows of cobbles separated by a band of closely-set river pebbles. Above this, the outer walls were of untempered sun-dried clay bricks perhaps 20 by 50 by 10 cm. in size; they were finished with a layer of mud plaster. Inside the houses were platforms with cobble foundations, possible storage areas, and a number of walls of tamped clay which probably were room dividers. The floors were covered with twilled (over-two, under-two) reed or club-rush mats. Three to five persons could have lived comfortably in such a house, to judge by present dwellings in the Deh Luran plain.

Villagers in the Mehmeh phase cultivated roughly the same crops as in Khazineh times: two-row and six-row barley, free-threshing wheat, lentils, vetch, vetchling, grass peas, and flax, with some evidence of irrigation reflected in the size of the flax seeds. Sheep and goats, in approximately equal numbers, were by far the most common domestic animals; some cattle were herded, and domestic dogs were present. Onager, wild pig, small mammals, birds, and turtles made up a small percentage of the diet.

Representations of bowmen, gazelles, and gazelle and wild goat tracks on pottery of the Mehmeh phase suggest that these villagers hunted gazelle with bow and arrow, probably by ambush hunting along known gazelle trails. Such trails are abundant near Tepe Sabz, and follow tamarisk-filled *wadis* where a bowman could crouch in wait for the gazelle.

Most grinding stones from Mehmeh phase levels were saddle-shaped slabs; a few of these also had "sockets" in them for use as mortars. They were used in conjunction with simple discoidal handstones or irregular, sausage-shaped handstones or pestles. Pounders made from flint nodules or roughed-out cores, and combination pounder-rubbing stones were also typical of the phase.

The Mehmeh phase flint knappers struck hundreds of plain blades from cores, using only one side of the striking platform rather than the whole periphery. Some of these blades were retouched, truncated, or backed, often for use in sickles; still others were made into drills. Obsidian, used for blades, was very rare, representing less than one per cent of the chipped stone. Polished and hafted limestone celts and heavy grooved mauls made up the remainder of the stone tools.

Coiled basketry had now become a normal part of the artifact assemblage, as indicated by impressions in asphalt. These baskets were typically made on a grass bundle foundation, laced together with split grass stems.

The pottery of the Mehmeh phase overlaps with phase *c* of the Susiana sequence as defined by Le Breton, and has strong ties with Oates' "early Ubaid" at Eridu, and the Ras al Amiya pottery as described by Stronach. Specifically, this period featured a new pottery type, Mehmeh Red-on-red, which appeared also at Ras al Amiya (though in smaller quantities). This straw-tempered ware, which looked "Iranian" to Stronach (1961:122) had a soft pale red slip and was painted with geometric designs in dark red or purplish paint. Surprisingly, affinities of this pottery type seem to be with sites like Tepe Hissar and others on the Iranian Plateau rather than with nearer sites in the Zagros. Typical shapes were hole-mouth jars with dimple bases, covered with net or screen patterns, rows of tally marks, or other designs. Some of these jars had small spouts at the lip. Wide, shallow bowls or dishes with stripes (both inside and out), and small painted cups were also present. The temper included both chaff and grit. This type of pottery is a real "index fossil" for the Mehmeh phase.

Utility wares, presumed to be locally made, continued in much the same form as in Khazineh times. Soft, red pottery with chaff and grit tempering appeared in the form of hole-mouth jars with dimple bases, open bowls, and carinated bowls. However, the use of this soft red pottery was on the decline and it was destined to be abandoned altogether in subsequent periods. Khazineh Red wares represented a link with the earliest pottery-making periods in Khuzistan, a tradition which took many millenia to run its course.

To judge by the painted, black-on-buff pottery of the Mehmeh phase, ties between the Iranian Plateau and the Khuzistan steppe had never been stronger. Many large open bowls had naturalistic motifs like "rows of wild goats" or "dancing men" which can be traced as far as Sialk III, Hissar I*a*, and Tepe Giyan; these were also common at Tepe Jowi in Susiana proper, but did not appear at Eridu or Ras al Amiya. However, ties with the latter site can be clearly seen in globular jars with interior ledges at the rim, and fine bell-shaped bowls with meander or "wavy ladder" designs. Some carinated bowls with closely-painted "Hajji Muhammad" motifs or "sundial" interior bases persisted into the Mehmeh phase (just as they did at Ras al Amiya) but they were on the wane. Such designs were clearly in the process of being replaced by more "open" patterns such as typified in the later Ubaid pottery. And lastly, the extremely fine quality of some of the deep bowls of the Mehmeh phase suggests not only professional craftsmanship but use of at least a "slow" wheel.

Other distinctive artifacts of the Mehmeh phase were the "bent ceramic nails" so common at sites like Tepe Gawra, Eridu and al Ubaid. Almost all of these implements (whose function is still unknown) appeared in Mehmen phase levels.

Villagers manufactured bone awls and needles, and flat knives cut from cattle ribs. Sherds were chipped into scrapers or pot lids (some of which probably were used to cover the mouths of ledge-rim jars). They used spindle whorls which were either star-shaped, oval-discoidal, or (more commonly) shaped like a small "chariot wheel." The "chariot wheel" type was made from buff pottery and painted in a variety of individualistic designs, most of which were not common on the black-on-buff pottery.

Mehmeh phase farmers ornamented themselves with T-shaped labrets and rings made from buff ware sherds of of lightly fired clay. They also had copper pins with slightly diamond-shaped heads, like those used at Tepe Sialk in period III.

At least nine villages of the Mehmeh phase are known from the Deh Luran plain. The smallest are one to two hectares in extent, but there are hints that a very large village of this phase may lie buried under the south half of Tepe Musiyan. Adams found more than one hundred sites of this age in Susiana proper, most in the 1 to 2 hectare size range but some (like Chogha Mish) considerably larger. We estimate the population density of the Deh Luran plain at five persons per square kilometer, and the total population of Susiana proper at over 12,000 inhabitants during the Mehmeh phase.

It is clear from excavations in Iraq that there were towns of this period already in existence, some of them with temples. It is just as clear that by the Mehmeh phase, Deh Luran was a provincial backwater and Tepe Sabz a relatively small site with little evidence of ceremonial activities or political importance. The dramatic developments of this age were taking place in the Diz-Karheh plain, near Susa, and on the lower Euphrates near Eridu and Ur where much larger concentrations of population could be maintained. The marginal location of the Deh Luran plain kept it out of the mainstream of these developments, although extensive excavations at Musiyan might show that there was at least one important town in the area during the Mehmeh phase.

THE BAYAT PHASE

4100 to 3700 B.C.

Architectural details were well-preserved in Bayat phase levels at Tepe Sabz, but our step trench was too narrow to recover a complete house plan. The houses were large, with exterior walls up to a meter in thickness, composed of clay slab bricks and coated with a layer of mud plaster. Corners, where two walls came together, were "bonded" by interlocking the bricks from both walls. Smaller interior walls, possibly room dividers, were of compacted clay. In some cases, rooms were 3 m. wide and over 3 m. long, and the floors had a covering of twilled (over-two, under-two) reed or club-rush mats. Doors pivoted on perforated stones.

As houses aged and collapsed, they were used as dumps for refuse from adjacent houses: ash, hearth sweepings, broken pottery, the bones of butchered animals, even carcasses of dead dogs. Open areas between houses were used for burials. The Bayat phase villagers buried their dead in the extended position, lying on the right side and oriented roughly east-west. The graves were covered by stone slabs, some of which were discarded worn-out grinding stones. No ornaments were observed in our limited sample, but women were accompanied by saddle-shaped grinding slabs and simple discoidal handstones.

At this same time period, at Eridu in southern alluvial Mesopotamia, there is considerable evidence for high-status burials in brick tombs, accompanied by offerings of well-made pottery. This suggests that the Bayat phase burials we found may be typical only of the persons of lowest status (and possibly only of females?).

Bayat phase middens were rich in carbonized grains, spikelet forks, and internodes of barley, both hulled and naked. Both the six-row and two-row strains were grown. Since barley was the dominant cereal of later times in southern Mesopotamia (Helbaek, 1960*a,b*) it is interesting to note that its rise to prominence may have begun in Ubaid times. Factors favoring barley over wheat are low rainfall and high soil salinity, as well as the salinity of the water used for irrigation. All these factors may have applied in the Deh Luran plain, where today the soil salinity in some areas is so high that only sesame can be grown.

Other crops grown in the Bayat phase were wheat, lentils, vetch, grass peas, and flax, the same complex which had characterized Khuzistan since the beginnings of the Sabz phase.

Tamarisk was used as firewood in preference to reeds and club-rushes.

Helbaek notes a curious aspect of later Bayat phase samples of carbonized seeds: just as in the uppermost strata at Ali Kosh, agricultural products show signs of a recession, and weedy or salt-resistant plants come to the fore. By the time of Tepe Sabz' abandonment at around 3700 B.C., almost the only plants left are those which would have survived in salty fallow land or abandoned irrigation canals. We conclude that during the course of their two thousand year occupation, the farmers of Tepe Sabz so modified the immediate vicinity of the village that equilibrium was destroyed and the balance tipped toward salinity. Decreased agricultural productivity made it necessary eventually to abandon Tepe Sabz and move to a new location – in this case, perhaps only 5 km. away, to some site like Tepe Farukhabad.

It is interesting that the total duration of occupation at Tepe Sabz was similar to that of Ali Kosh; this suggests to us that two thousand years may be roughly the length of time required to reduce soil productivity in the Deh Luran plain to such a level that shifting of settlement becomes necessary—at least in areas where the soil is tenuously balanced on the verge of prohibitive salinity. More favorable localities (like that of Tepe Musiyan?) may have had a longer cycle of productivity, although our modern soil samples taken in 1961 indicate that even that area is now dangerously saline (see p. 20).

Sheep (some hornless) and goats (of the modern twisted-horn type) were herded in large numbers. There is evidence that sheep were becoming the dominant herd animals of the area, as we know they were during later periods of Khuzistan's history (Adams, 1962:113). Cattle herding continued as a relatively minor activity. A single maxilla of what is probably a domestic pig indicates that Bayat phase villagers were in contact with pig-raising peoples—possibly the village farmers of Zagros Mountains, who are known to have had domestic pigs at this time (Flannery, 1965:1254). There is little evidence for pig raising on the Deh Luran plain during the Bayat phase, however, possibly because seasonal transhumance was still an important part of the subsistence pattern. Hunting of gazelle, onager, and small game continued.

Saddle-shaped grinding slabs and simple discoidal handstone were the common grinding implements. The Bayat phase villagers produced hundreds of flint blades, only a few of which were ever retouched by design, although many show chipping from use. They made sickles by hafting blades which were either unmodified, or backed, or backed and truncated, probably depending on where they were to fit in the haft. Cores were chipped only around part of the periphery of the striking platform. Drills, and—very rarely—geometric microliths appeared. Less than one per cent of the chipped stone was obsidian.

Polished and hafted limestone celts were no longer as common as they had been. The manufacture of bone awls and spatulas continued, for metal was still an extremely rare item, at least at villages as small as Tepe Sabz. As in previous periods, the Bayat folk chipped out sherd scrapers and pot lids and wove baskets and mats from grasses of various kinds.

The pottery of the Bayat phase was squarely within the Ubaid tradition, and corresponds roughly to phase *d* of the Susiana sequence as defined by Le Breton. Ties were overwhelmingly with southern alluvial Mesopotamia and the Susiana sites of the Diz-Karheh River area; the naturalistic motifs of the Mehmeh phase had vanished, along with most of the other "Iranian Plateau" ceramic characteristics. Chaff-tempered pottery reached its lowest frequency in our entire sequence, and the painting of buff ware swung away from the earlier densely-covered style and took on the more open, "cursive" look of later Ubaid ceramics.

As chaff-tempered, soft red pottery disappeared, it was replaced by the hard, grit-tempered salmon red ware common in period A at Susa. Carinated bowls, hole-mouth jars, and a few necked jars were the only shapes in which this utility ware appeared. At this point we began to doubt that *any* of the pottery used at Tepe Sabz during Bayat times was produced in village households; even the "cooking wares" had the mass-produced, standardized look of craft pottery. Sherds of this salmon-colored pottery from Tepe Sabz were literally indistinguishable from those at Chogha Mish, more than 100 km. away—they could easily have come from the same kiln in the same pottery-making town.

The black-on-buff painted pottery was no longer as common as unpainted buff. On the larger bowls, decoration was limited to a series of hanging loops painted around the rim, or a simple wavy line between two pairs of straight lines. Large ring-based bowls with a simple painted band at rim and base were common; so were deep plain bowls with only a very cursive horizontal band of tally marks at the rim, or a plain black band. "Reserve" decoration or dense screen patterns were no longer in vogue. Perhaps the most abundant reminder of earlier ceramic styles was the fine, egg-shell-thin, bell-shaped bowl, which actually reached maximum frequency in the Bayat phase. This is the type of bowl which Stronach (1961:112) called "the finest product of the Ras al'Amiya potter."

Plain buff ware—in the form of carinated bowls, ring base bowls, and deep plain bowls—was the type of ceramic most abundantly represented in the trash piles of the Bayat phase. Standardized, technically competent, and aesthetically uninteresting, it nevertheless provided us with many of the most useful "index fossils" of the period.

A few rare sherds from vessels obtained by trade appeared in Bayat phase levels. All were types known from Mesopotamia: painted bichromes, fine black-on-tan, and highly burnished black.

Villagers of the Bayat phase used spindle whorls which were oval-discoidal or "chariot wheel"-shaped. Some whorls had appliqué blobs or rows of punctation. T-shaped labrets and ceramic "rings" appeared in small numbers. An innovation of the Bayat Phase were the small biconical objects of unfired clay which have generally been referred to as "sling missiles." These "missiles," which occurred by the hundreds at sites like Tepe Gawra (Tobler, 1950:16) never really became common at Tepe Sabz, and we wonder about their true functions.

The Bayat folk had definite ideas about property, which were reflected in their sealing of jars. Throughout the upper levels of Tepe Sabz occurred clay plugs which had evidently once been used to stopper pottery vessels. All had been stamped with cylindrical seals, and no two designs were alike. A few cylindrical bead seals appeared in the trash, bearing incised patterns like stylized, branching trees, or rows of herringbones. Apparently, the wet clay was pushed into the mouth of the jar and then the bead pressed into it two or three times and rolled from side to side. Whether the designs were specific to individuals, lineages, or merchants is not clear, but the Bayat phase was the earliest point in our sequence when such property-marking became evident.

At least nine villages or towns (some reasonably large) are known from the Deh Luran plain at this time period. One of these has an apparent series of temples within it, but it is not known yet whether this series reaches back into the Bayat phase. Adams found 116 sites of all sizes in Susiana proper dating to the Bayat phase. Since this part of the "Ubaid" sequence includes everything from hamlets to towns with temples and high-status cemeteries, it is clear that Tepe Sabz throws very little light on the social and political complexity of the period.

The Ubaid "oikumene," of which the Bayat phase is just one regional variant, stretched from Syria and eastern Palestine to the Turkoman Steppe. It represented some sort of plateau on the road toward urban civilization. This final phase of our Deh Luran excavations, while telling us little politically, makes it clear that by 4000 B.C. the basic "barley and sheep" economy of the early Mesopotamian–Khuzistan civilizations was in the process of formation. We estimate the population density of the Deh Luran plain at this time at possibly six persons per square kilometer. The total population of Susiana proper probably exceeded 15,000.

MAN'S PLACE IN THE KHUZISTAN ECOSYSTEM

A Model for Consideration of the Evidence

Our data from the Deh Luran plain, combined with those of Adams (1962), suggest a model for the internal dynamics of prehistoric Khuzistan, which can be investigated and modified by future workers in the area. The model is as follows.

At 8000 B.C. the original post-Pleistocene environment of Khuzistan lay unmodified: a rolling steppeland with 300 mm. of rainfall concentrated in the winter months, and a growing season which climaxed in March. Physiographically, the region as a whole is an unstable geosyncline, but because it tends to fill with alluvium at approximately the same rate at which it settles, the general ecology remained stable for thousands of years. Khuzistan provides a number of biotopes which were exploited by early man: (1) open sandy plains, (2) reed-bordered marshes, (3) gypseous or saline depressions, (4) slow-moving streams and rivers, and (5) sandstone foothills. Each of these "microenvironments" had a complex of edible plants and animals which characterized it and which were available either year-round or at certain well-defined seasons.

Our hypothetical picture of life in Khuzistan during the food-collecting era is one of plains hunters who stalked gazelle, onager, and aurochs, and made use of the aquatic resources of the marshes and rivers, which were available year-round. If the onager herds moved up to the lower mountains during the heart of the summer (as they are known to do in Baluchistan), some hunter bands may have followed them. When winter rains reached the steppe, it turned into meadows of Bermuda and Canary grass, attracting the ungulate herds back down to lower elevations. The rich leguminous vegetation of late winter months—wild alfalfa, spiny milk vetch, *Trigonella,* and others—was intensively collected by early man. In those days human population was so scanty[1] and the effects of human predation so slight that the steppe was in equilibrium. Man was simply one species in a large and stable ecosystem.

We note, however, that the original Khuzistan environment included two different types of alluvial plain. One, because of its excellent natural drainage and underlying gravels, had only a mild tendency toward salinity; this was the type found in much of Susiana proper, between the Diz

[1]Braidwood and Reed (1957:21), for example, estimate the population density of Late Paleolithic hunter-gatherers in Iraq as 0.125 persons per square mile.

and Karkheh. The other, found at Deh Luran and elsewhere in Khuzistan, was balanced just at the threshhold of salinity. This distinction was of little importance during the food-collecting era, but was to become critical at a later date.

The first change in the Khuzistan ecosystem came sometime before 7000 B.C., with the introduction of cereal cultivation and the herding of Caprines. What this process involved is rather interesting, in terms of man's capture of solar energy through environmental exploitation. The intense summer heat of southern Iran inhibits the growth of perennial vegetation; most plants there are annuals which come ripe after the cool winter rains. The annuals include most of the grasses and legumes edible by man; the perennials are often tough and thorny species of little direct human food value. What man did, before 7000 B.C., was to domesticate the annuals he could eat, and then domesticate the animals who lived on the perennials. This intensified his access to both energy sources, either directly or through an animal converter.

It is clear from the species involved—emmer wheat, two-row hulled barley, goats, and sheep—that the first food-production in Khuzistan involved plants and animals introduced from the mountains, not native to the steppe. Their success on the steppe, however, was such that a kind of "positive feedback" was established: the more wheat planted, the more mutants with a tough rachis were selected for; the greater the yield, the more farmers survived; the greater the population, the more wheat had to be planted. And so the system of cultivation was amplified, and between 7000 and 6000 B.C. cultivated grains grew from less than 5 per cent of the seeds consumed to roughly 40 per cent.

It may be that early farmers were first attracted to the steppe because of its great potential as winter grazing land, and that they stayed in the area only long enough to harvest a winter cereal crop before taking their herds up to summer pasture in the mountains. (There is little evidence that, at the outset, they exploited Khuzistan's summer-maturing plants.) But the productivity of the steppe, with its friable alluvium and its marshy areas of high water table, where grain could be planted in moist soils, led eventually to sedentary communities with permanent storage facilities. Helbaek's evidence suggests that they planted in areas so wet that carbonized club-rush (*Scirpus*) even showed up among the wheat and barley grains.

Once stabilized, however, this early domestic plant and animal complex allowed for only slow and limited population growth; as late as approximately 5800 B.C., population density in the Deh Luran plain was still probably no more than one person per square kilometer. We suggest that this early complex, which involved mainly emmer wheat and goats (augmented by barley and sheep, but in smaller numbers) was basically an upland-mountain adaptation, imposed, with limited success, on the lowland steppe.

Our preliminary surveys in the intermontane basins of western Iran—Luristan and southern Kurdistan—suggest that while some valleys were nearly unoccupied during the Mohammad Jaffar phase, others may have had a population double that of the Deh Luran plain (*cf.* Hole,1962). Such populations might well be expected in the well-watered uplands, where wheat and barley grow wild, and the returns of dry farming greater than in northern Khuzistan. Yet even if we postulate a density of two to three persons per square kilometer for certain of Kurdistan's intermontane plains during the Mohammad Jaffar phase, a rather sparse population is implied.[2] Moreover, neither Khuzistan nor Kurdistan at this time period exhibit much in the way of surpluses, social stratification, or craft specialization. We conclude that neither Kurdistan, nor Luristan, nor the upper plains of Khuzistan managed to support stratified societies on the basis of the early wheat-goat-dry farming complex. The difference was this: Kurdistan and Luristan had reached an equilibrium which was to change but little in the subsequent two millenia, while Khuzistan was to change drastically.

One thing the early complex did was to modify the vegetational pattern of Khuzistan. First, imperfectly cleaned batches of grain from the mountains introduced several new plants into the lowlands as field weeds; among these were goat-face grass, ryegrass, and wild oats. Second, land clearance and grazing removed the native grass cover in the vicinity of villages and replaced it with fallow-land and pasture plants like mallow, plantain, fumitory, goosegrass, and wild vetch. At least some of the field weeds and fallow-land plants were harvested and eaten. Their increase was at the expense of wild plants which would normally grow during the winter, and which competed for the very soils needed by the cultivated cereals: fine-grained alluvium. Ironically, it was the small legumes which had once figured in early man's diet (like milk vetch, *Trigonella,* and wild alfalfa) which suffered the most from land clearance; summer-maturing plants, like *Prosopis,* actually increased once their competition had been removed, because they did not conflict with the winter-maturing cereals. And with year-round occupation of villages, summer-available plants like *Prosopis* were eaten in much larger numbers. Thus man's food habits changed as the vegetation of the steppe was altered by the early agricultural regime.

In areas like Deh Luran, there were some deleterious aspects to early agriculture. After 1500 to 2000 years of farming, the site of Ali Kosh was abandoned— and there are hints in the plant remains from the terminal occupation that one reason was soil exhaustion. Two millenia of steady cultivation in an area delicately balanced at the limits of prohibitive salinity had eventually tipped the balance, and left the immediate vicinity a mildly saline waste of low productivity. However, there were still vast areas of the plain lying unoccupied, uncultivated, and in equilibrium; any overcultivation problem could be solved by shifting settlement a few miles away.

During the early "wheat-goat" phase of Khuzistan agriculture, productivity was sufficiently low so that there were always virgin lands available, allowing disturbed and salinized areas time to recover. The social unit produced was the small (one by two hectare) multifamily community, which stayed at approximately the same size but shifted to new localities at intervals of perhaps two millenia. This pattern might have persisted for many centuries, except for another systemic change which took place between 5500 and 5000 B.C.

This second major change was a crucial one for Khuzistan. It may have been an outgrowth of the wheat-goat complex, but this could not be proved on the basis of our data from Deh Luran; too many intervening steps are missing.

The change involves the addition of some simple irrigation techniques to cereal cultivation. This innovation took advantage of Khuzistan's pattern of braid-

[2] We find Braidwood and Reed's (1957:22) estimate of 25 persons per square mile for the Chemchemal Valley during the Jarmo phase much too high: note that it is based, not on the number of Jarmo-age sites in the valley, but on the present density of farming villages.

ed, aggrading stream channels (Adams, 1963:113), many of which flow so close to the plain that water can easily be diverted from them without lifting devices. One of the immediate ecological results was the stabilizing of a hulled six-row strain of barley, which was destined to become the most important cereal of the lowlands. Irrigated six-row barley initiated another "positive feedback" situation which, once begun, continued to reinforce itself and increase the area under cultivation dramatically when compared with previous periods.

A second systemic change of this period was an increase in the relative proportions of sheep, slowly at first but growing with geometric rapidity toward the end of our sequence. The ability of sheep to withstand the high summer temperatures of the steppe probably had something to do with this—and if only we had concrete data on the start of wool-bearing in sheep, we might find that this was also a factor, for wool is known to act as a cooling device for sheep in desertic environments (Schmidt-Nielsen, 1964:96-98).

These innovations of the Sabz phase (5500-5000 B.C.) ultimately led to a basic change in the whole food-producing pattern of Khuzistan. Instead of a wheat-goat complex, more suitable to the uplands, one can see the beginnings of the "barley-sheep" complex which was to typify the later Elamite civilization.

Still another innovation of the Sabz phase—and one without apparent local antecedents—was the introduction of domestic cattle. Faunal remains from Ras al Amiya and Eridu (Flannery and Wright, n.d) suggest that cattle were more important in southern alluvial Mesopotamia than in Khuzistan. At our sites they seem never to have exceeded 5 per cent of the animal bone debris. Why cattle were not more numerous is not clear; for literally millenia they remained at the same frequency. But the potential for yet another "positive feedback" situation was there, and when finally cattle were harnessed to the plow, sometime prior to 2000 B.C., agriculture went through another geometric expansion which supported the growth of walled towns and cities (Adams, 1962:114). The period of this climax is, however, outside the time limits of our Deh Luran sequence.

The expansion of the irrigation-barley-sheep complex was at the apparent expense of wild ungulate hunting and wild legume collecting. Each village must now have been surrounded by an intensively cultivated "infield" and a grazed and sporadically cultivated "outfield" (Wolf, 1966:21). This extensive destruction of the habitat on which the wild steppe legumes and large herbivores had previously subsisted seems to have been associated with a decline, first of wild oxen, then of the other wild ungulates. Gazelle and onager survived, probably, because they could exploit the saline fallow lands which were of low farming and grazing potential; but the plants and animals of the sandy well-drained alluvium could not compete with the new agricultural complex, well-suited as it was to the lowlands.

At this point, a population explosion is clearly reflected in our graph (Fig. 136) showing increase in occupancy of the Deh Luran plain through time. Although irrigation was introduced during the Sabz phase, its cumulative effects were really felt in the Khazineh and Mehmeh phases, when the number of occupied sites shot up to a dozen, and the estimated population went from 600 to 1500 persons. Similar trends can be seen in Adams' data from central Khuzistan, where the number of sites increased from thirty-four to one hundred and two between Sabz phase (= Susiana *a*) and Mehmeh phase (= Susiana *c*) times.

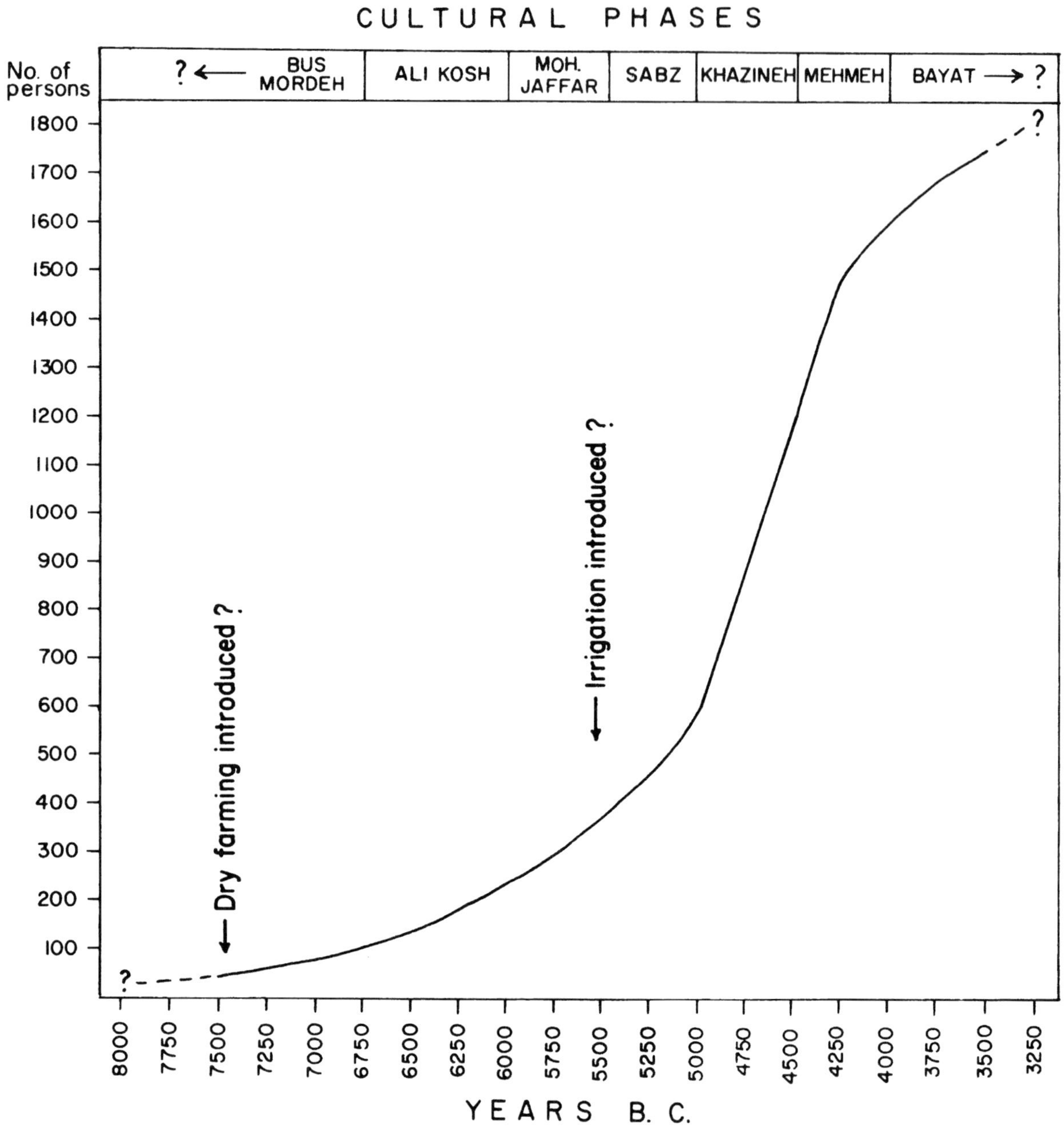

Fig. 136. Theoretical population curve for the Deh Luran plain during the period 7500 to 3500 B.C. Based on number of village sites recovered per cultural phase, plus a rough estimate of 100 persons per one-hectare village (see text).

The population trend of the Khazineh and Mehmeh phases took the form, not so much of increase in village size, but of increase in numbers: by Bayat phase times (= Susiana *d*), Adams (1962:110) notes "a grid of villages fully comparable to that of the present day in spacing." In other words, colonization of virgin lands and wide geographic distribution of 1-5 hectare multifamily villages over the landscape was the rule; and many of Adams' villages are strung out along the fossil courses of stream channels where simple irrigation was possible.

The difference in potential of this irrigation-barley-sheep complex is evidenced by our population density estimates of up to six persons per square km. at Deh Luran, and a total population estimate of 15,000 for Susiana in the Bayat phase (*ca.* 3750 B.C.). This represents a density at least six times that of the Mohammad Jaffar phase, and greater than that of any part of prehistoric Kurdistan we have seen. It may be that Kurdistan, committed to the rainfall-wheat-goat complex because of its early success, had reached a plateau which could not be exceeded without some basic change in agricultural pattern.

Here the differing potential of the plains soil types of Khuzistan began to make a difference, however. The plain of the Shaur and Karkheh rivers in central Khuzistan, with its good drainage and underlying gravels, stayed productive. The site of Susa, apparently founded late in the Bayat phase, grew to a metropolis within whose walls the density of population reached an estimated four hundred persons per hectare (Adams,1962:115). Here the agricultural complex supported social stratification, craft specialization, and urban life. At sites like Tepe Sabz, there is every reason to believe (on the basis of plant remains) that the "infield" surrounding the village had lost so much fertility that agriculture was no longer profitable. Many areas with too tenuous a balance and poor drainage remained fallow wasteland. The story of areas like Deh Luran is one of slowly shifting settlement which barely kept ahead of the destruction of the local environment.

Following the Bayat phase, Adams notes a decrease in number and an increase in size of sites. It appears that the population of Khuzistan had begun to concentrate itself behind the walls of a few very large towns or small cities. Adams (1962:114) suggests that this was a process of "the drawing together of the population into larger, more defensible political units." We wonder if there might not have been contributory processes at work here also: that is, the concentration of agricultural populations in those areas where salinization was less of a problem, and the intensified cultivation of those key areas by means of irrigation and the plow, leaving the worst salinized areas open for grazing land.

Ultimately, these pasture lands were to become "buffer zones" between the early city-states. Following the lead of Hickerson (1965), we might even postulate that competition between city-states was a regulatory mechanism which maintained these buffer zones, and counteracted deviations from the ecologically effective "walled-city" settlement system of the Early Dynastic period. Such competition effectively prevented a return to the dispersed settlement pattern of the Bayat phase, which may have reached the limits of its ecological potential by 3500 B.C.

CONCLUSION

The developmental model just presented cannot do justice to the complexity of ancient Khuzistan, but it is offered in the hope that future investigators, by testing it, will bring to light some of the processes which set the stage for urban civilization in southwestern Iran. We have collected a multitude of facts on prehistoric Deh Luran, but collection of facts in itself cannot lead on to understanding. As Coe (1963) has recently reminded us, facts never speak for themselves; they must be cross-examined. Without a developmental model, all the artifacts and carbonized seeds in southwestern Iran could not explain how the Elamite empire evolved in the Khuzistan ecosystem, where only five or six thousand years previously man had lived by hunting onager and gazelle, and gathering wild legumes.

REFERENCES

Adams, Robert McC.

1962 Agriculture and Urban Life in Early Southwestern Iran. Science, Vol. 136, No. 3511, pp. 109-22. Washington.

1965 Land Behind Baghdad: A History of Settlement on the Diyala Plains. The University of Chicago Press. Chicago.

Allouse, Bashir E.

1953 The Avifauna of Iraq. Iraq Natural History Museum, Publication No. 3. Al-Tafayyudh Press. Baghdad.

Berger, Rainer; Fergusson, G.J.; and Libby, Willard F.

1965 UCLA Radiocarbon Dates IV. Radiocarbon, Vol. 7, pp. 336-71. New Haven.

Bialor, Perry A.

1962 The Chipped Stone Industry of Çatal Hüyük. Anatolian Studies, Vol. 12, pp. 67-110. London.

Boessneck, Joachim; Müller, Hanns-Hermann; and Teichert, Manfred

1964 Osteologische Unterscheidungsmerkmale zwischen Schaf (*Ovis aries* Linne) und Ziege (*Capra hircus* Linne). Kühn-Archiv, Band 78, Heft 1-2, pp. 1-129. Akademie-Verlag. Berlin.

Bökönyi, Sándor

1964 A Moroslele-Panai Neolitikus Telep Gerinces Faunája. Különlenyomat az Archaeologiai Értesíto, Vol. 91, No. 1, pp. 87-94.

Braidwood, Robert J.

1951 From Cave to Village in Prehistoric Iraq. American School of Oriental Research, Bulletin No. 124, pp. 12-18. South Hadley & Baltimore.

1952 The Near East and the Foundations for Civilization. Condon Lecture Series. University of Oregon. Eugene.

1958a Near Eastern Prehistory. Science, Vol. 127, No. 3312, pp. 1419-30. Washington.

1958b Über die Anwendung der Radiokarbon-Chronologie für das Verständnis der ersten Dorfkulture-Gemeinschaften in Südwestasien. Osterreichischen Akademie der Wissenschaften, Phil.-hist. Klasse, Anzeiger (Jahrgang 1958), No. 19, pp. 249-59.

1960 Seeking the World's First Farmers in Persian Kurdistan: A Full-scale Investigation of Prehistoric Sites Near Kermanshah. Illustrated London News, Vol. 237, No. 6325, pp. 695-97. London.

1964 Further Remarks on Radioactive Carbon Age Determination and the Chronology of the Late Prehistoric and Protohistoric Near East. Vorderasiatische Archäologie: Studien und Aufsätze (Anton Moortgat Festschrift), Verlag Gebr. pp. 57-67. Mann, Berlin.

Braidwood, Robert J., *et al.*

1952 Matarrah: A Southern Variant of the Hassunan Assemblage, Excavated in 1948. Journal of Near Eastern Studies, Vol. 11, pp. 1-75. Chicago.

Braidwood, Robert J. and Braidwood, Linda S.

1953 The Earliest Village Communities of Southwestern Asia. Journal of World History, Vol. 1, pp. 278-310.

1960 Excavations in the Plain of Antioch, I. The Earlier Assemblages, Phases A-J. Oriental Institute Publications, Vol. 61. The University of Chicago Press. Chicago.

Braidwood, Robert J. and Howe, Bruce

1962 Southwestern Asia beyond the Lands of the Mediterranean Littoral. *In* Courses Toward Urban Life, edited by R.J. Braidwood and G.R. Willey. Viking Fund Publications in Anthropology, Vol. 32, pp. 132-46. Wenner-Gren. New York.

Braidwood, Robert J.; Howe, Bruce; *et al.*
1960 Prehistoric Investigations in Iraqi Kurdistan. Oriental Institute of the University of Chicago, Studies in Ancient Oriental Civilization, No. 31. The University of Chicago Press. Chicago.

Braidwood, Robert J. and Reed, Charles A.
1957 The Achievement and Early Consequences of Food-Production: A Consideration of the Archeological and Natural-Historical Evidence. Cold Spring Harbor Symposia on Quantitative Biology, Vol. 22, pp. 19-31.

Brainerd, George W.
1951 The place of Chronological Ordering in Archaeological Analysis. American Antiquity, Vol. 16, pp. 301-13.

Buechner, Helmut K.
1960 The Bighorn Sheep in the United States: Its Past, Present, and Future. Wildlife Monographs, No. 4. The Wildlife Society, Chestertown, Maryland.

Butzer, Karl W.
1964 Environment and Archeology: An Introduction to Pleistocene Geography. Aldine Publishing Co. Chicago.

Childe, V. Gordon
1957 The Bronze Age. Past and Present, No. 12, pp. 2-15. Kendal.

Clark, John Grahame Douglas
1963 Neolithic Bows from Somerset, England, and the Prehistory of Archery in North-west Europe. Proceedings of the Prehistoric Society n.s. Vol. 29, pp. 50-98. London.

Clark, John Grahame Douglas; and Piggott, Stuart
1965 Prehistoric Societies. Alfred A. Knopf. New York.

Coe, Michael D.
1963 Olmec and Chavín: Rejoinder to Lanning. American Antiquity, Vol. 29, pp. 101-04.

Coe, Michael D.; and Flannery, Kent V.
1964 Microenvironments and Mesoamerican Prehistory. Science, Vol. 143, No. 3607, pp. 650-54. Washington.

Colton, Harold S.
1953 Potsherds: An Introduction to the Study of Prehistoric Southwestern Ceramics and Their Use in Historical Reconstruction. Museum of Northern Arizona Bulletin, No. 25. Flagstaff.

Contenau, Georges
1927-47 Manuel d'Archéologie Oriental depuis les Origines jusqu'a l'Époque d'Alexandre. A. Picard, Paris.

Contenau, Georges; and Ghirshman, Roman
1935 Fouilles du Tépé Giyan, présde Néhavend, 1931 et 1932. Musée du Louvre, Départment des Antiquites Orientales, Série Archéologique, Tome III. Paris.

Coon, Carleton S.
1951 Cave Explorations in Iran, 1949. University of Pennsylvania, The University Museum. Philadelphia.

Cressey, George B.
1960 Crossroads: Land and Life in Southwest Asia. J.B. Lippincott Co. Chicago.

Curwen, Cecil E.
1930 Prehistoric Flint Sickles. Antiquity, Vol. 4, No. 14, pp. 179-86. Gloucester.

Degerbøl, Magnus
1963 Prehistoric Cattle in Denmark and Adjacent Areas. *In* Man and Cattle: Proceedings of a Symposium on Domestication, edited by A.E. Mourant and F.E. Zeuner. Occasional Paper No. 18, Royal Anthropological Institute of Great Britain and Ireland, pp. 69-79.

Delougaz, Pinhas
1952 Pottery from the Diyala Region. Oriental Institute Publications, Vol. 53. The University of Chicago Press. Chicago.

Dyson, Robert H., Jr.
1960 Hasanlu and Early Iran. Archaeology, Vol. 13, No. 2, pp. 118-29. New York.
1964 Sciences Meet in Ancient Hasanlu. Natural History, Vol. 73, No. 8, pp. 16-25. New York.
1965 Problems in the Relative Chronology of Iran 6000-2000 B.C. *In* Chronologies in Old World Archaeology, edited by Robert W. Ehrich, pp. 215-56. The University of Chicago Press. Chicago.

Dyson, Robert H., Jr.; and Young, T. Cuyler, Jr.
1960 The Sôlduz Valley, Iran: Pisdeli Tepe. Antiquity, Vol. 34, No. 133, pp. 19-28. Newbury.

Eggan, Fred
1954 Social Anthropology and the Method of Controlled Comparison. American Anthropologist, Vol. 56, pp. 743-63.

Ehrich, Robert W., editor
1954 Relative Chronologies in Old World Archaeology. The University of Chicago Press. Chicago.
1965 Chronologies in Old World Archaeology. The University of Chicago Press. Chicago.

Ellerman, J.R.; and Morrison-Scott, T.C.S.
1966 Checklist of Palaearctic and Indian Mammals. 2nd edition. British Museum (Natural History). London.

El-Wailly, Faisal
1963 Tell as-Sawwan (Foreword). Sumer, Vol. 19, Nos. 1 and 2, pp. 1-2. Baghdad.
1964 Tell as-Sawwan (Foreword). Sumer, Vol. 20, Nos. 1 and 2, pp. 1-2. Baghdad.

El-Wailly, Faisal; and Abu es-Soof, Behnam
1965 The Excavations at Tell es-Sawwan: First Preliminary Report (1964). Sumer, Vol. XXI, Nos. 1-2, pp. 17-32.

Ewbank, J.M.; Phillipson, D.W.; Whitehouse, R.D.; with Higgs, E.S.
1964 Sheep in the Iron Age: A Method of Study. Proceedings of the Prehistoric Society, n.s. Vol. 30, pp. 423-26.

Fairservis, Walter A., Jr.
1961 Archeological Studies in the Seistan Basin of Southwestern Afghanistan and Eastern Iran. Anthropological Papers, American Museum of Natural History, Vol. 48, Pt. 1. New York.

Flannery, Kent V.
1961 Skeletal and Radiocarbon Evidence for the Start and Spread of Pig Domestication. Unpublished Master's Thesis, Files, University of Chicago Department of Anthropology.
1965 The Ecology of Early Food Production in Mesopotamia. Science, Vol. 147, No. 3663, pp. 1247-56. Washington.

Flannery, Kent V.; and Wright, Henry T.
n.d. Faunal Remains from the "Hut Sounding" at Eridu, Iraq. Unpublished ms. submitted to Dr. Fuad Safar, Department of Antiquities, Baghdad.

Ford, James A.
1962 A Quantitative Method for Deriving Cultural Chronology. Pan American Union, Technical Manual, No. 1. Washington.

Frankfort, Henri
1924-27 Studies in Early Pottery of the Near East. Occasional Papers, Nos. 6-8, Royal Anthropological Institute. London.

Fraser, F.C.; and King, J.E.
1954 Faunal Remains. *In* Excavations at Star Carr, by J.G.D. Clark, pp. 70-95. Cambridge University Press. Cambridge.

French, D.H.
1964 Recent Archaeological Research in Turkey. Anatolian Studies, Vol. 14, pp. 35-37. London.

Garrod, Dorothy A.E.
1930 The Palaeolithic of Southern Kurdistan: Excavations in the caves of Zarzi and Hazar Merd. American School of Prehistoric Research, Bulletin No. 6, pp. 8-43. New Haven.

Garstang, John
1953 Prehistoric Mersin, Yümük Tepe in Southern Turkey. The Clarendon Press, Oxford. London.

Gautier, J.E.; and Lampre, G.
1905 Fouilles de Moussian. Mémoires de la Mission Archéologique de Perse, Vol. 8, pp. 59-148. Paris.

Ghirshman, Roman
1938 Fouilles de Sialk, prés de Kashan, 1933, 1934, 1937. Vol. I. Musée du Louvre, Département des Antiquites Orientales, Série Archéologique, Tome IV. Paris.

Griffin, James B.
1964 The Northeast Woodlands Area. *In* Prehistoric Man in the New World, edited by Jesse D. Jennings and Edward Norbeck pp. 223-58. The University of Chicago Press (for William Marsh Rice University). Chicago.

Gromova, Vera I.
1953 Osteologiceskie Otlicija Rodov Capra (kozly) i Ovis (barany). Trudy: Komissii po Izuc. Cetverticn. Perioda, Vol. X, No. 1. Moscow.

Haltenorth, Theodor
1961 Lebensraum, Lebensweise und Vorkommen des Mesopotamischen Damhirsches, Cervus mesopotamicus Brooke, 1875. Säugetierkundliche Mitteilungen, BLV-Verlagsgesellschaft München 3, 9. Jhg., No. 1, pp. 15-39.

Harlan, Jack R.; and Zohary, Daniel
1966 Distribution of Wild Wheats and Barley. Science, Vol. 153, No. 3740, pp. 1074-80. Washington.

Hatt, Robert T.
1959 The Mammals of Iraq. Miscellaneous Publications, Museum of Zoology, University of Michigan, No. 106. Ann Arbor.

Helbaek, Hans
1960*a* The Paleoethnobotany of the Near East and Europe. *In* Prehistoric Investigations in Iraqi Kurdistan, by Robert J. Braidwood and Bruce Howe. Studies in Ancient Oriental Civilization No. 31, pp. 99-118. University of Chicago (Oriental Institute).
1960*b* Ecological Effects of Irrigation in Ancient Mesopotamia. Iraq, Vol. 22, pp. 186-96.
1963 Textiles from Çatal Hüyük. Archaeology, Vol, 16, No. 1, pp. 39-46. New York.
1964 Early Hassunan Vegetable Food at Es-Sawwan Near Sammara. Sumer, Vol. 20, Nos. 1 and 2, pp. 45-48. Baghdad.

Herzfeld, Ernst
1930 Die Vorgeschichtlichen Töpfereien von Samarra. Die Ausgrabungen von Samarra V. Berlin.

Hickerson, Harold
1965 The Virginia Deer and Intertribal Buffer Zones in the Upper Mississippi Valley. *In* Man, Culture, and Animals, edited by Anthony Leeds and Andrew P. Vayda. Publication No. 78, American Association for the Advancement of Science, pp. 43-65. Washington, D.C.

Higgs, Eric S.
1962 Fauna. *In* Excavations at the Early Neolithic Site at Nea Nikomedeia, Greek Macedonia (1961 season) by Robert J. Rodden. Proceedings of the Prehistoric Society, n.s. Vol. 28, pp. 271-74.

Hodges, Henry W.M.
1964 Artifacts: An Introduction to Primitive Technology. F.A. Praeger. New York.

Hole, Frank
1961 Chipped Stone Analysis and the Early Village Farming Community. MS, doctoral dissertation, University of Chicago. Chicago.
1962 Archeological Survey and Excavation in Iran, 1961. Science, Vol. 137, No. 3529, pp. 524-26. Washington.
1966 Investigating the Origins of Mesopotamian Civilization. Science, Vol. 153, No. 3736, pp. 605-11. Washington.

Hole, Frank; and Flannery, Kent V.
1962 Excavations at Ali Kosh, Iran, 1961. Iranica Antiqua, Vol. 2, pp. 97-148. Leiden.

Hole, Frank; Flannery, Kent V.; and Neely, James A.
1965 Early Agriculture and Animal Husbandry in Deh Luran, Iran. Current Anthropology, Vol. 6, No. 1, pp. 105-06. Chicago.

Hole, Frank; and Shaw, Mary
1967 Computer Analysis of Chronological Seriation. Rice University Studies, Vol. 53, No. 3. Houston.

Huckriede, Reinhold
1962 Jung-Quartär und End-Mesolithikum in der Provinz Kerman (Iran). Eiszeitalter und Gegenwart, Vol. 12, pp. 25-42. Hannover.

Jewell, Peter
1963 Cattle from British Archaeological Sites. *In* Man and Cattle: Proceedings of a Symposium on Domestication, edited by A.E. Mourant and F.E. Zeuner. Occasional Paper No. 18, Royal Anthropological Institute of Great Britain and Ireland, pp. 80-100.

Khalaf, Kamel T.
1961 The Marine and Fresh-water Fishes of Iraq. ar-Rabitta Press. Baghdad.

Kigoshi, Kunihiko; and Endo, Kunihiko
1963 Gakushuin Natural Radiocarbon Measurements II. Radiocarbon, Vol. 5, pp. 109-17. New Haven.

Krader, Lawrence
1955 Ecology of Central Asian Pastoralism. Southwestern Journal of Anthropology, Vol. 11, pp. 301-26.

Kroeber, Alfred L.
1953 Cultural and Natural Areas of Native North America. University of California Press. Berkeley and Los Angeles.

Landsberger, Benno
1934 Die Fauna des Alten Mesopotamien. Leipzig.

Lawrence, Barbara
1967 Early Domestic Dogs. Zeitschrift für Säugetierbunde, Vol. 32, pp. 44-59.

Le Breton, Louis
1947 Note sur la Céramique Peinte aux Environs de Suse et à Suse. Mémoires de la Mission Archéologique de Perse, Vol. 30, pp. 193-217. Paris.

1957 The Early Periods at Susa, Mesopotamian Relations. Iraq, Vol. 19, Pt. 2, pp. 79-124. London.

Lees, G.M.; and Falcon, N.L.
1952 The Geographical History of the Mesopotamian Plains. Geographical Journal, Vol. 118, pp. 24-39. London.

Libby, Willard F.
1955 Radiocarbon Dating. Second Edition. The University of Chicago Press. Chicago.

Lines, Joan L.
1953 The Al 'Ubaid Period in Mesopotamia and its Persian Affinities. MS, doctoral dissertation, Girton College. Cambridge.

Loftus, William Kenneth
1857 Travels and Researches in Chaldaea and Susiana. James Nisbet & Co. London.

Long, Austin; and Mielke, James E.
1966 Smithsonian Institution Radiocarbon Measurements III. Radiocarbon, Vol. 8, pp. 413-22. New Haven.

Lydekker, Richard
1912 The Horse and its Relatives. George Allen and Co. Ltd. London.

Mahdi, Nuri
1961 Fishes of Iraq. Baghdad, Ministry of Education.

Mac Neish, Richard S.
1964*a* Ancient Mesoamerican Civilization. Science, Vol. 143, No. 3606, pp. 531-37. Washington.
1964*b* The Origins of New World Civilization. Scientific American, Vol. 211, No. 5, pp. 29-37. New York.

Mallowan, Max E.L.
1936 The Excavations at Tall Chagar Bazar, and an Archaeological Survey of the Habur Region, 1934-1935. Iraq, Vol. 3, pp. 1-86. London.

Mallowan, Max E.L.; and Rose, J. Cruikshank
1935 Prehistoric Assyria: Excavations at Tall Arpachiyah, 1933. Iraq, Vol. 2, pp. 1-178. London.

Mc Cown, Donald E.
1942 The Comparative Stratigraphy of Early Iran. Oriental Institute of the University of Chicago, Studies in Ancient Oriental Civilization, No. 23. The University of Chicago Press. Chicago.

Mecquenem, Roland de
1928 Notes sur la Céramique Peinte Archaique en Perse. Mémoires de la Mission Archéologique de Perse, Vol. 20, pp. 99-132. Paris.

Mellaart, James
1962 Excavations at Çatal Hüyük. Anatolian Studies, Vol. 21, pp. 41-65. London.
1963 Çatal Hüyük in Anatolia: Excavations which Revolutionize the History of the Earliest Civilizations. Part III - Pottery and Textiles. Illustrated London News, Vol. 242, No. 6445, pp. 196-98. London.
1964*a* Excavations at Çatal Hüyük, 1963, Third Preliminary Report. Anatolian Studies, Vol. 14, pp. 39-120. London.
1964*b* A Neolithic City in Turkey. Scientific American, Vol. 210, No. 4, pp. 94-104. New York.
1965 Earliest Civilizations of the Near East. Thames and Hudson. London.

Miločić, V.; Boessneck, J.; and Hopf, M.
1962 Die Deutschen Ausgrabungen auf der Argissa-Magula in Thessalien. I. Das Präkeramische Neolithikum sowie die Tier- und Pflantzenreste. Beiträge zur Ur- und Frühgeschichtlichen Archäologie des Mittelmeer–Kulturraumes, Vol. 2. Bonn, Habelt Verlag.

Morgan, Jacques de
1900 Étude Géographique sur la Susiane. Mémoires de la Mission Archéologique de Perse, Vol. 1. Paris.

Morris, Earl H.; and Burgh, Robert F.
1941 Anasazi Basketry, Basketmaker II through Pueblo III: A Study Based on Specimens from the San Juan River Country. Carnegie Institution of Washington, Publication 533. Washington.

Mortensen, Peder

1964 Early Village-farming Occupation. *In* Excavations at Tepe Guran, Luristan, by Jørgen Meldgaard, Peder Mortensen and Henrik Thrane. Acta Archaeologica, Vol. 34, pp. 110-21. Copenhagen.

Mourant, A. E.; and Zeuner, F. E. (Eds.)

1963 Man and Cattle: Proceedings of a Symposium on Domestication. Occasional Paper No. 18, Royal Anthropological Institute of Great Britain and Ireland.

Munsell, Albert H.

1961 A Color Notation. An Illustrated System Defining all Colors and Their Relations by Measured Scales of Hue, Value, and Chroma. 11th. Edition. Munsell Color Co. Baltimore.

Murie, Adolph

1944 The Wolves of Mount McKinley. U.S. National Park Service, Fauna Series, No. 5. U.S. Government Printing Office. Washington.

Oakley, Kenneth P.

1956 Man the Tool-Maker. British Museum (Natural History). London.

Oates, Joan

1960 Ur and Eridu, the Prehistory. Iraq, Vol. 22, pp. 32-50. London.

Olson, Stanley J.

1960 Post-cranial Skeletal Characters of *Bison* and *Bos*. Peabody Museum Papers, Harvard University, Vol. XXXV, No. 4. Cambridge, Massachusetts.

Oppenheim, Baron Max F. von

1931 Tell Halaf. New York, Putnam.

1933 Tell Halaf, Vol. 1. Die Prähistorische Funde. Bearbeitet von Hubert Schmidt, 1943. Berlin.

Pabot, H.

1960 The Native Vegetation and its Ecology in the Khuzistan River Basins. Khuzistan Development Service, Ahwaz, Iran. (Mimeographed.)

Perkins, Ann L.

1949 The Comparative Archeology of Early Mesopotamia. Oriental Institute of the University of Chicago, Studies in Ancient Oriental Civilization, No. 25. The University of Chicago Press. Chicago.

Perkins, Dexter, Jr.

1964 Prehistoric Fauna from Shanidar, Iraq. Science, Vol. 144, pp. 1565-66.

Petter, F.

1961 Repartition Geographique et Ecologie des Rongeurs Desertiques: du Sahara Occidental à l'Iran Oriental. Mammalia, Tome 25, No. spécial. Museum National d'Histoire Naturelle. Paris.

Pretzmann, Gerhard

1962 Die Mediterranen und Vorderasiatischen Süsswasserkrabben (Potamoniden). Annals, Natur-historisches Museum, Vienna, No. 65, pp. 205-40.

Ralph, Elizabeth K.

1959 University of Pennsylvania Radiocarbon Dates III. Radiocarbon, Vol. 1, pp. 45-58. New Haven.

Rawlinson, Henry C.

1839 Notes on a March from Zohab through Luristan to Kirmanshah, in the year 1836. Journal of the Royal Geographic Society, Vol. 9, pp. 26-116. London.

Reed, Charles A.

1959 Animal Domestication in the Prehistoric Near East. Science, Vol. 130, pp. 1629-39.

1960 A Review of the Archeological Evidence on Animal Domestication in the Prehistoric Near East. *In* Prehistoric Investigations in Iraqi Kurdistan, by Robert J. Braidwood and Bruce

Howe. Studies in Ancient Oriental Civilization, No. 31, pp. 119-45. University of Chicago (Oriental Institute).

1961 Osteological Evidences for Prehistoric Domestication in Southwestern Asia. Zeitschrift für Tierzüchtung und Züchtungsbiologie, Vol. 76, No. 1, pp. 31-38.

1963 Osteo-Archaeology. *In* Science in Archaeology, edited by Don Brothwell and Eric Higgs, pp. 204-16. Basic Books. New York.

Reed, Charles A.; and Marx, Hyman

1959 A Herpetological Collection from Northeastern Iraq. Transactions of the Kansas Academy of Science No. 62, pp. 91-122.

Renfrew, Colin; Dixon, J. E.; and Cann, J. R.

1966 Obsidian and Early Cultural Contact in the Near East. Proceedings of the Prehistoric Society, n.s. Vol. 32, pp. 30-72. Cambridge.

Robinson, W.S.

1951 A Method for Chronologically Ordering Archaeological Deposits. American Antiquity, Vol. 16, pp. 293-301.

Rubin, Meyer; and Alexander, Corrine

1960 U.S. Geological Survey Radiocarbon Dates V. Radiocarbon, Vol. 2, pp. 129-85. New Haven.

Schmidt, Erich F.

1937 Excavations at Tepe Hissar, Damghan. University Museum, The University of Pennsylvania Press. Philadelphia.

Schmidt-Nielsen, Knut

1964 Desert Animals: Physiological Problems of Heat and Water. The Clarendon Press. Oxford.

Scott, Sir Lindsay

1954 Pottery. *In* A History of Technology, Vol. 1, edited by Charles Singer, E.J. Holmyard and A.R. Hall, pp. 376-412. Oxford University Press. London

Shepard, Anna O.

1956 Ceramics for the Archaeologist. Carnegie Institution of Washington, Publication 609. Washington.

Silver, I.A.

1963 The Ageing of Domestic Animals. *In* Science in Archaeology, edited by Don Brothwell and Eric Higgs, pp. 250-68. Basic Books, New York.

Sisson, Septimus; and Grossman, James D.

1953 The Anatomy of the Domestic Animals. (4th edition, revised). W.B. Saunders. Philadelphia.

Smith, R. N.

1956 Fusion of the Epiphyses of the Limb Bones of Sheep. Veterinary Record, Vol. 68, No. 18, pp. 257-58.

Solecki, Ralph S.

1963 Prehistory in Shanidar Valley, Northern Iraq. Science, Vol. 139, No. 3551, pp. 179-93. Washington.

1964 Shanidar Cave, a Late Pleistocene Site in Northern Iraq. Report of the VI th. International Congress on Quaternary, Vol. 4, pp. 413-23.

Solecki, Rose L.

1964 Zawi Chemi Shanidar, a Post-Pleistocene Village Site in Northern Iraq. Report of the VI th. International Congress on Quaternary, Vol. 4, pp. 405-12.

Steensberg, Axel

1943 Ancient Harvesting Implements: A Study in Archaeology and Human Geography. Nationalmuseets Skrifter, Arkoeologisk-Historisk Roekke, I. Copenhagen.

Stronach, David
1961 The Excavations at Ras al 'Amiya. Iraq, Vol. 23, Pt. 2, pp. 95-137. London.

Struever, Stuart
1965 Flotation: a Method for Recovery of Small-Scale Archaeological Remains. Northwestern University (mimeographed).

Stuiver, Minze; and Seuss, H.E.
1966 On the Relationship between Radiocarbon Dates and True Sample Ages. Radiocarbon, Vol. 8, pp. 534-40.

Stuckenrath, Robert, Jr.
1963 University of Pennsylvania Radiocarbon Dates VI. Radiocarbon, Vol. 5, pp. 82-103. New Haven.

Stuckenrath, Robert, Jr.; and Ralph, Elizabeth K.
1965 University of Pennsylvania Radiocarbon Dates VIII. Radiocarbon, Vol. 7, pp. 187-99. New Haven.

Stuckenrath, Robert, Jr.; Coe, William R.; and Ralph, Elizabeth K.
1966 University of Pennsylvania Radiocarbon Dates IX. Radiocarbon, Vol. 8, pp. 348-85. New Haven.

Tobler, Arthur J.
1950 Excavations at Tepe Gawra, Vol. II. Museum Monographs, University of Pennsylvania. The University of Pennsylvania Press. Philadephia.

Todd, T.W.; and Todd, A.W.
1938 The Epiphyseal Union Pattern of the Ungulates with a Note on Sirenia. American Journal of Anatomy, Vol. 63, No. 1, pp. 1-36.

Van Zeist, Willem; and Wright, Herbert E., Jr.
1963 Preliminary Pollen Studies at Lake Zeribar, Zagros Mountains, Southwestern Iran. Science, Vol. 140. No. 3562, pp. 65-67. Washington.

Vayson, Andre
1919 Faucille Préhistorique de Solferino. L 'Anthropologie, Tome 29, pp. 393-422. Paris.

Vogel, J.C.; and Waterbolk, H.T.
1964 Groningen Radiocarbon Dates V. Radiocarbon, Vol. 6, pp. 349-69. New Haven.

Watson, Patty Jo
n.d. Test Excavations at M'lefaat, Ali Agha, El-Khan, and Banahilk. Manuscript, files, Oriental Institute, University of Chicago.

Wertime, Theodore A.
1964 Man's First Encounters with Metallurgy. Science, Vol. 146, No. 3649, pp. 1257-67. Washington.

Wolf, Eric
1966 Peasants. Prentice-Hall, Inc., Englewood Cliffs, N.J.

Woolley, Sir Charles Leonard
1955 Ur Excavations, Vol. 4: The Early Periods. University Museum. Philadelphia.

Wright, Herbert E., Jr.
1961 Pleistocene Glaciation in Kurdistan. Eiszeitalter und Gegenwart, Vol. 12, pp. 131-64. Hannover.

Young, T. Cuyler, Jr.
1962 Taking the History of the Hasanlu Area Back Another Five Thousand Years: Sixth and Fifth Millenium Settlements in Solduz Valley, Persia. Illustrated London News, Vol. 241, No. 6431, pp. 707-09. London.
1966 Survey in Western Iran, 1961. Journal of Near Eastern Studies, Vol. 25, No. 4, pp. 228-39.

Young, T. Cuyler, Jr.; and Smith, P.E.L.
1966 Research in the Prehistory of Central Western Iran. Science, Vol. 153, No. 3734, pp. 386-91. Washington.

Zeuner, Frederick E.
1963 A History of Domesticated Animals. Hutchinson & Co. London.

Ziegler, Charlotte
1953 Die Keramik von der Qal'a des Haggi Mohammad, Uruk-Warka, Vol. 5.

Appendix I

PLANT COLLECTING, DRY-FARMING, AND IRRIGATION AGRICULTURE IN PREHISTORIC DEH LURAN

Hans Helbaek
Danish National Museum, Copenhagen[1]

INTRODUCTION

Deh Luran, the northwestern extremity of Iranian Khuzistan, is a small alluvial plain wedged in between the low Jebel Hamrin, the watershed of which is the frontier with Iraq, and the higher range of Kuh-i-Siah, north of which is Luristan. Its latitude is approximately the same as that of Baghdad. The river Mehmeh cuts along the northwest end of the plain, through a canyon in the Jebel Hamrin and ends, under the name of the Tib, in the salt marshes north of Amara in Iraq. This river, like others crossing the plain, is charged with salts, principally gypsum and lime; but east of the hamlet Musiyan there is a moderately clean spring from which the inhabitants of the plain are supplied, by truck, with drinking water.

Jebel Hamrin is a worn sandstone, conglomerate and gravel ridge, sparsely grown with Zizyphus, but otherwise rather barren. The calcareous Kuh-i-Siah that rises to an altitude of 1100 m. above the plain, which itself is elevated some 145 m. above sea level, would be well-wooded naturally, but now rather exhibits the symptoms of heavy grazing and fuel hunting. However, much more is still left of the natural vegetation than in so many other parts of the lower Zagros range. Low on the mountain small Zizyphus shrub (*Zizyphus spina-christi*) occur sporadically, Pistachio (*Pistacia atlantica*) appear some 450 m. above the plain, joined by Oak at 600 m. While all Pistachio observed are old, but badly mauled by fuel hunters and goats, many of the Oak trees (*Quercus pubescens*) are fine although small specimens, quite untouched and over 4 m. high, with trunks of a diameter up to 35 to 40 cm. In the upper reaches the two species are, if not densely distributed, at least quite frequent on shelves and among rocks.

The middle of the Deh Luran plain is occupied by a large depression characterized by a fairly rich growth of Tamarisk (*Tamarix* sp.). Its central part is marshy even in the dry season, and densely populated with a variety of species of mainly the Goosefoot family (Seablite, Orache, etc.), many of which are succulent, salt-loving and flood-resistant. In less marshy areas Camel thorn is very common, gradually mingling with Prosopis as the groundwater table recedes. The typical plant association on the fringe of the swamp consists of Camelthorn (*Alhagi maurorum*), Prosopis (*P. stephaniana)* and Caper (*Capparis spinosa*); the two latter species increasing in frequency on drier land and the former eventually restricted to the slight, salty depressions that occur sporadically all over the plain. Shrubby Zizyphus up to a couple of metres high are the largest members of the steppe vegetation. The local population call it Titika.

This Tamarisk depression represents the last remains of an old lake, eventually

[1]Manuscript received April, 1967.

filled in by erosion material from the surrounding mountains. Some parts of the plain, notably the eastern fringe along the Kuh-i-Siah, are still very alive erosionally, the faintly sloping land strewn with boulders to such a degree that walking is difficult, and driving a vehicle out of the question. The Tamarisk swamp drains principally across this slope. On the other hand, some silting up with the winter rain takes place in certain other areas.

Near the foot of Kuh-i-Siah, south-east of the village of Deh Luran, there is an area of bitumen springs, the most active of which is a stinking, bubbling pool, 12 to 15 metres across. From under the bitumen, sulphurous water carrying an oily film, is drained away by a small creek along which Sea club-rush (*Scirpus maritimus*) and large Orache (*Atriplex* sp.) grow in dense formations. In the tract around this spring a succession of gypsum outcrops penetrate the surface as white humps.

Apart from these special features, Deh Luran is a sparsely vegetated steppe, hot as a furnace in the summer, utterly desolate on rainy days and during winter dust storms.

No precipitation and temperature figures are available for the Deh Luran valley itself, but the average data given below, covering the Dizful area (the same altitude, but some 115 km. to the east) during the years 1952 to 1960, may give a rough idea of the climatic conditions (Gremliza, 1962). Higher maximum summer temperatures than those stated in the original table (50.5 C°) have been heard of for Deh Luran, and our experience of having to break ice, which covered our water barrels on December mornings, tends to show that, at least near the Tamarisk swamp, the winter temperature may drop below the absolute minimum of + 0.5 degrees centigrade as stated in the original table.

The plain, except for the boulder-strewn drainage area, is littered with mounds dating from the Early Neolithic up to recent times. After surveying the plain and testing certain sites in 1961 (Hole, 1962), the Rice University team decided to investigate one small mound, Ali Kosh, east of the Tamarisk depression, evidently the earliest visible site, and another somewhat larger, Tepe Sabz, west of the depression, that seemed to promise a link-up with the top levels of Tepe Ali Kosh. This plan was put into operation in the autumn 1963 (Hole, Flannery, and Neely, 1965) and I was invited to join the team when things had got moving. Arriving in the middle of November I found a small, close-knit, hard-working party of a most inspiring spirit and of obvious competence.

Table 1

DIZFUL CLIMATOLOGICAL DATA FOR 1952-1960
(Monthly Averages)

Month	Rain (mm.)	Temperatures (C°)	Month	Rain (mm.)	Temperatures (C°)
May	6.8	30.7	November	86.9	20.6
June	...	35.7	December	73.0	14.8
July	...	38.2	January	66.6	13.6
August	...	37.9	February	46.8	14.7
September	...	34.4	March	50.9	17.9
October	8.5	28.8	April	37.2	24.3

Plants Represented in the Deh Luran Material

The volume of the carbonized plant debris from the Deh Luran excavations has not been measured, but it hardly exceeded half a litre. Tepe Sabz contributed the major portion, but since that material has not been finished and a proper count made of the determinable plant parts, no figures can be given for the investigation as a whole.

However, the sorting of the lesser volume from Tepe Ali Kosh, involving examination of millions of particles, resulted in some 45,000 grains, seeds and spike fragments being picked out.

For lack of local comparison material a satisfactory identification of many species was impossible. Another decisive drawback for a precise determination is the circumstance that all the material comes from what may best be conceived as midden deposits. If it had been food stores from burned houses, seed coats and other indispensable diagnostic criteria might have been preserved, ensuring a higher degree of definition.

As it is, the following list (Table 2) gives the family, most often also the genus, and in some cases the actual species of the plants. Their ratio of occurrence is laid down in the ecologically arranged chart, Table 3.

TEPE ALI KOSH

After the test sounding of Tepe Ali Kosh made by Hole and Flannery in 1961, it appeared probable that no concentrated deposits of plant material could be expected. Therefore, when called in on the excavation I made up my mind to transfer to the field, for the first time, the laboratory technique for segregating plant remains from mineral samples by means of bouyancy. This process in its most primitive form,[1] is carried out by drying the soil or ash sample and then pouring it into a basin with water. Under cautious stirring, the water is slowly poured through a fine mesh sieve, the plant matter floating on the surface and being retained in the sieve. When the mineral matter approaches the lip of the basin, the process is stopped and the sediment, as circumstances indicate, either thrown away, or dried again and subjected to other kinds of examination. After drying in shade, the plant material is ready for the microscope.[2]

As it turned out, no concentrated deposit was in fact found during the 1963 campaign. The material picked out by the excavators came from dark patches, ashy layers and other promising or doubtful occurrences (Fig. 137). These samples were then probed by floating, with a negative as often as positive result.

Eventually it became clear that the plant material was spillings from meals dropped into the fire or ash fringe, sometimes heated more than once and consequently badly misshapen and puffed. Swept up with ash and dirt, the plant re-

1 The floating technique employed in the field was, of course, a makeshift arrangement. The principle in segregation is to exploit the difference in specific weight between the plant matter and the fluid. This difference is not very great when water is used. Carbon tetrachloride (C C*14*) is 1.8 times as heavy as water and is therefore the agent used at the laboratory. It is neutral as opposed to concentrated sulphuric acid which also is very heavy. During excavations in outlying districts and hot climates it would, however, not be easy to keep up supply since loss by evaporation of the highly volatile tetrachloride would almost prohibit filtering and reuse.

2 The microscope used for the seed analysis, a stereoscopic, low-power Wild M4 instrument, was supplied by the Danish Carlsberg Foundation. I wish to extend my sincere thanks to the Foundation for its unfailing support of my research work.

Table 2

PLANTS REPRESENTED IN THE DEH LURAN SITES

Family	Common Name	Latin Name
GRAMINEAE	Goat-face grass	*Aegilops crassa*
	Wild einkorn wheat	*Triticum boeoticum*
	Einkorn wheat	*T. monococcum*
	Emmer wheat	*T. dicoccum*
	Bread wheat	*T. aestivum*
	Wild barley	*Hordeum spontaneum*
	Two-row barley	*H. distichon*
	Six-row hulled barley	*H. vulgare*
	Six-row naked barley	*H. vulgare* var. *nudum*
	Canary grass	*Phalaris* cf. *paradoxa*
	Wild oat species	*Avena ludoviciana* *Avena* sp.
	Rigid ryegrass	*Lolium rigidum*
	Unspecified ryegrass	*Lolium* sp.
CYPERACEAE	Sea club-rush	*Scirpus maritimus*
LILIACEAE	Grape hyacinth ?	*Muscari* sp ?
CHENOPODIACEAE	Seablite	*Suaeda* sp.
CARYOPHYLLACEAE	Unspecified (catchfly?)	
CRUCIFERAE	Unspecified	
FUMARIACEAE	Fumitory	*Fumaria* cf. *parviflora*
CAPPARIDACEAE	Caper	*Capparis spinosa*
ROSACEAE	Wild almond	*Amygdalus spartioides*
MIMOSACEAE	Prosopis	*Prosopis stephaniana*
PAPILIONACEAE (LEGUMINOSAE)	Trigonella	*Trigonella* spp.
	Ray-podded medick	*Medicago radiata*
	Unspecified medick	*Medicago* spp.
	Melilotus	*Melilotus* sp.
	Clover	*Trifolium* spp.
	Milk vetch	*Astragalus* spp.
	Horseshoe vetch	*Hippocrepis* sp.
	Unspecified vetch	*Vicia* spp.
	Grass pea	*Lathyrus cicera*
	Unspecified vetchling	*Lathyrus* sp.
	Lentil	*Lens esculenta*
LINACEAE	Pale flax	*Linum* cf. *bienne*
	Flax, linseed	*L. usitatissimum*
ANACARDIACEAE	Pistachio	*Pistacia atlantica*
MALVACEAE	Mallow	*Malva parviflora* *M. nicaeensis*
VIOLACEAE	Unspecified	
PRIMULACEAE	(Blue?) pimpernel	*Anagallis arvensis*
BORAGINACEAE	Gromwell	*Lithospermum* cf. *arvense*
	Bugloss	*Echium* sp.
	Heliotrope	*Heliotropium persicum*
PLANTAGINACEAE	Plantain	*Plantago ovata* *P.* cf. *lanceolata*
RUBIACEAE	Bedstraw	*Galium* sp.

mains were thrown into some place where they were often trodden upon and therefore excessively fragmented. Incidentally, no carbonized wood occurred at Tepe Ali Kosh, and bits and pieces of reed seem to indicate that the fuel was reed and stems of other herbaceous plants of the marshy environ. Probably the "cooking" was done then just as I saw the nomads doing it when I stayed with them: a thin sheaf of long stems was pushed little-by-little into the fire, lit in a tiny pit in the floor, keeping the kettle boiling. In that case the stems were of sesame grown by the nomads.[3]

The investigation has been a matter of examining literally millions of particles from each of the two mounds, and this time-consuming process, combined with other obstructive circumstances, has made it impossible to finish the whole work on Tepe Ali Kosh and Tepe Sabz within the available time. However, so as to present at least the fundamental ideas about the stage of plant collection and agriculture, and the dietary habits of the ancient peoples, it was decided to add to the present archaeological report this brief, preliminary survey of the results so far gained.

In this connection it deserves mentioning that Frank Hole, the director of the excavation, exhibited great generosity in supplying all the water wc sloshed away on the floating, every pint of which was brought in by truck and dearly paid for. Also, that the back-breaking job of the

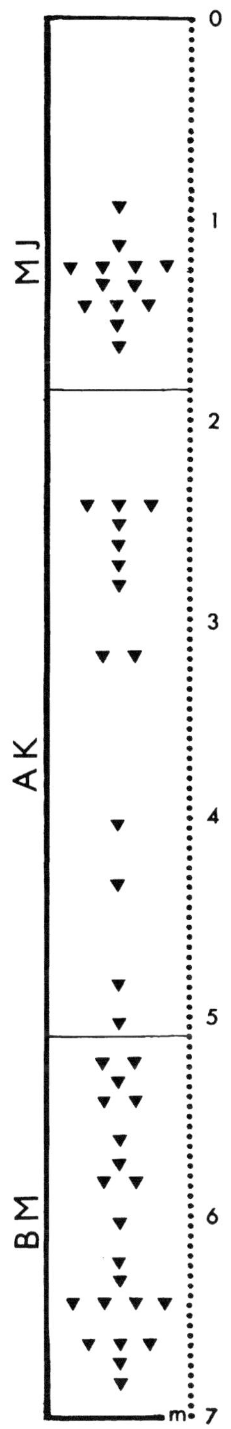

Fig. 137. Distribution of seed-bearing ash samples throughout Tepe Ali Kosh. The solid black triangles indicate depth from surface of the upper edge of the sample, but not its vertical extension, which may vary from 5 to 20 cm. (scale in metres). Letters indicate cultural phase (Bus Mordeh, Ali Kosh, Mohammad Jaffar).

[3] The nomad family referred to was in the process of settling. They lived in a tent, but they cultivated an isolated little plot by exploiting a trickling stream from the mountains nearby. They never moved the tent outside the vicinity of their fields.

actual floating was taken over cheerfully by the already hard-pressed Kent and Nancy Flannery in their so-called "spare time." This arrangement left me time to make a superficial survey of the ecology of Deh Luran and the mountains, as well as to reduce the prehistoric plant material to essentials by means of the microscope.

The tabularization of a mixed material like this is something of a problem. A table is a mechanism for comparison of items, but in the present case the items are in many respects incommensurable. Ideally, one would seek to express the proportional nutritive value of the various seeds, the leading principle for growing or gathering them. This is, however, impossible because of the widely diverging volume and chemical properties of the individual seeds or categories of seeds, as also because the influence on these factors by carbonization is incalculable. The specific values found in the Ali Kosh material for one thousand cereal grains is 9.0 g., while one thousand seeds of the small, endemic legumes weigh no more than 0.28 g., on the average. Besides, it also makes a difference in the evaluation that the former are principally a source of starch, the latter of plant protein.

Since the items cannot be boiled down to a common standard of expression, the vertical columns (the phases) can best be employed for qualitative consideration. The horizontal, ecologically-inspired arrangement of species (the Ecological Groups) intimate the quantitative importance of the several categories, whether collected or cultivated, as it changes from one phase to another, expressed per cent in brackets.

The original plant list, such as it stands now, comprises 1950 squares, so Table 3 is just a generalized condensed extract. It is arranged in such a way as to show (Ecological Groups 1-2) plants occurring in cultivated soil, cultivars and weeds presumably foreign to the environment; the other groups (Ecological Groups 3-7) comprise plants belonging to the several ecological niches of which the plain is made up, indicating collection of additional plant food—incidentally, of course, also comprising certain species which can have been of no economic interest whatever and thus fortuitous in the material.

Even though the number of recovered items differs very much from phase to phase, the statistical value of the figures is unquestionable. The smallest number, 917 seeds for the Ali Kosh phase, is much more than in so many other sites and would in any case constitute a fair basis for evaluation; the Bus Mordeh phase, with its 31,210 seeds of more than 30 species, is prodigious indeed. The Mohammad Jaffar phase material is shown in Table 3 in its direct form; additionally, in Table 4 (p. 413), it is then paranthetically subdivided into two columns, because the distribution and composition of the various samples are so obviously different that they must reflect a change in some domestic practice from the two earlier phases. However, this investigator cannot account for its reason.

Some of the horizontal figures, mainly those of the cereals, rest on calculation, not direct count, because very few intact grains were found. In the first place, threshing was clearly done by means of mortars and querns, a process in which most grains and larger seeds must inevitably be cracked. In the second place, as mentioned above, the material has probably also been subjected to rough treatment on the garbage heaps. The effects of the different ways of fragmentation, one before, the other after carbonization, are easily distinguished in the microscopic image of the fracture surfaces. Therefore, the fragments obviously belonging to cereal grains were picked out; determinable bits were sorted as to species and the amount of particles of each species was weighed and the number of whole grains to which the weight corresponded, calculated on the basis of the average grain weight: one cereal grain = 9 mg. The unspecifiable particles of grain were, again by weight, converted into the corresponding number of whole grains. These are the figures entered into the plant list (the latter category designated "groats") and the values integrated into the total items.

Although by their element of specific uncertainty the groats may be said to work against the evaluation of the relative importance of the several cereals, they are necessary as a factor in estimating the proportional relation between collected and cultivated plant food. Weight calculation was also employed for Prosopis that has clearly not been ground, but which cracks easily on carbonization. The resulting fragments of seed and shell are readily recognizable on account of a mode of tar formation typical of the species, as well as very good diagnostic criteria. Altogether some 45,000 grains, seeds and spikelet fragments have been, if not identified in the strict sense of the term, at least classified, from Tepe Ali Kosh alone.

This is the first time such a long record of food plants and evidence for their changing utilization has been recovered by archaeological excavation. The duration of the habitation of Tepe Ali Kosh is at present considered to cover the time from at least 7000 B.C. to about 5600 B.C., and the lifetime of the three cultural phases, designated the Bus Mordeh, the Ali Kosh, and the Mohammad Jaffar, does not seem to differ substantially. It is also the first time we see—as in a flash—the whole complexity of an early stage of the long-drawn-out transition in plant economy, from roaming cave dwellers to settled, collecting-farming hunting-herding human society.

The general trend during the occupation and its individual phases appears plainly from Table 3. The colonizers[4] came to the valley from uplands where emmer wheat (*Triticum dicoccum*) was already domesticated and two-row wild barley (*Hordeum spontaneum*) had been in cultivation long enough to have produced and stabilized a mutant in which the grains are loose within the husks (naked barley) and which, as opposed to its wild progenitor, is six-row (*H. vulgare* var. *nudum*) (see Plate 40 and Figs. 138-139). Einkorn (*Triticum monococcum*) occurs sparsely, that also being the domesticated form (Fig. 141). Three weed grasses, Goat-face grass (*Aegilops crassa*), Wild einkorn (*Triticum boeoticum*) and Rye-grass (*Lolium rigidum*) were brought in with the seed, maybe not wholly unintentionally. Two local wild grasses, Canary grass (*Phalaris* cf. *paradoxa*) and a small-grained species of oat (*Avena* sp.) were collected beyond the cultivated plots and on the fallow land. It is interesting to note, by their great number in the Ali Kosh phase, how well the weed grasses adapted to their new ecology.

Treatises theorizing upon the plant food of Palaeolithic man consistently emphasize the large-grained wild barley and wheat as his primary or exclusive goal. The Bus Mordeh phase material makes a serious dent in this one-sided concept, unprovable since not a single Palaeolithic plant find exists. Of course man would go for easily collected plant food, and wheat and barley would be obvious targets where they occurred, but here, quite unexpectedly, we find an enormous la-

[4] When in this and following chapters I use expressions such as "colonizers," "foreigners," "migrating," or "invading" tribes, they should be understood purely as figures of speech, intended to enliven the narrative. I do not mean to take a stand in the discussion of physical movement of populations *versus* dissemination of ideas and techniques by means of direct contact or wandering traders, although the latter are proven beyond doubt both by the botanical and the archaeological material.

bour reflected in the collection of small plants with tiny seeds (1.05 by 0.75 to 1.85 by 0.60 mm.), exceedingly difficult to unhusk. Evidently the early collector-farmers recognized the importance of a balance between starch (grasses) and plant protein (leguminous seeds) in a healthy diet, and this lesson was hardly learned on the salty, arid plain immediately upon their arrival in that novel ecological world. It certainly reflects very ancient experiences in regard to plant food. Even in the following Ali Kosh phase, when tilling supplied a comparative abundance of cultivated cereals and weed grasses, the small legumes, collected in the open steppe, were of a not inconspicuous importance.

The plant remains of the Bus Mordeh phase contain quite a few seeds of plants belonging to water-logged ground or edges of streams. These species, Sea blite (*Suaeda* sp.) and Sea club-rush (*Scirpus maritimus*), suggest that the settlement was originally founded near the edge of the lake and that the fields ran down to the marshy zone to which these swamp species belong. The one seed of Sea blite

Fig. 138. Analytic diagram of cereal spike. The black, composite column is the axis or rachis. Its component parts, the internodes, are separated by white interstices denoting the points at which, in the wild cereal, the axis comes apart in sections or units consisting of the internode with attached spikelet(s) (brittle spike). These disintegration points may become solid by mutation; then the axis does not fall apart, but remains one tough column. The toughness of the spike is the most significant property in domestication.

The spikelet consists of two glumes (the hatched area) enclosing one or more florets (white area). A vestigial spikelet is shown at the base of the axis.

The floret consists of two inner bracts (paleas) within which the ovary, styles and anthers are placed, eventually developing one fruit (caryopsis or grain). Anatomically the grain is a seed vessel containing one seed, but the two organs, the seed case and the seed coat, are fused into one (grain shell).

Table 3

RATIO OF OCCURRENCE OF PLANTS IN THE DEH LURAN SITES
(+ = number of fragments; number of x's indicates relative abundance)

Ecological Group	Plants Represented	Tepe Ali Kosh			Tepe Sabz	Tepe Musiyan
		Bus Mordeh Phase	Ali Kosh Phase	Mohammad Jaffar Phase	General	Mehmeh Phase
Ecological Group 1 (Cultivated plants)	Einkorn grains	1	2	...	x	1
	Emmer grains	300	135	36	x	x
	Einkorn emmer spikelets+	2812+	905+	957+	xxx+	87
	Hulled barley, straight grains	154	34	138	xxx	
	Hulled barley, twisted grains	...	...	2	xx	x
	Naked barley, straight grains	13	7		x	2
	Naked barley, twisted grains			...	x	...
	Groats, unspecified	601	189	102	x	...
	Linseed	(3)	(1)	(1)	xx	5
	Hexaploid wheat, grains	...	...	...	xx	1
	Lentil	...	1	1	xx	16
	Grass pea	...	...	...	x	...
	Total cultivated plants	1072 (3.4 per cent)	369 (40.1 per cent)	280 (3.5 per cent)	xxx	xxx
Ecological Group 2 (Introduced weeds)	Goat-face grass	38	81	21	xx	...
	Ryegrass	25	47	18	xx	6
	Wild einkorn	8	2	...	x	...
	Weed legumes	...	...	...	xx	7
	Total introduced weeds	71 (o.3 per cent)	130 (14.1 per cent)	39 (0.5 per cent)	xx	xx
Ecological Group 3 (Endemic grasses)	Feather grass	...	...	73	...	..
	Wild oat	19	14	881	x	3
	Canary grass	258	26	299	x	7
	Miscellaneous grasses	...	...	...	x	...
	Total endemic grasses	277 (0.9 per cent)	40 (4.4 per cent)	1253 (15.4 per cent)	x	x
Ecological Group 4	Total endemic legumes	29421 (94.2 per cent)	171 (18.8 per cent)	4771 (59.0 per cent)	x	...
Ecological Group 5	Total swamp plants	53 (0.2 per cent)	1 (0.1 per cent)	...	x	...
Ecological Group 6 (Other wild plants)	Heliotrope	81	...	4	x	...
	Bugloss	38	...	...	...	...
	Gromwell	171	2	18	x	...
	Vetch etc.	16	4	59	x	...
	Mallow	4	2	462	x	2
	Plantain	9	4	800	x	...
	Incidentals	91	6	16	x	...
	Total other wild plants	310 (1.0 per cent)	18 (2.0 per cent)	1359 (16.6 per cent)	x	x
Ecological Group 7 (Arboreal fruits)	Prosopis	3	184	396	xx	...
	Caper	3	4	7	x	...
	Pistachio	x	x	x	x	...
	Wild almond	...	...	...	x	...
	Total arboreal fruits	6 (0.- per cent)	188 (20.5 per cent)	401 (5.0 per cent)	x	...
	Grand totals	31210 items	917 items	8103 items	...	137 +x

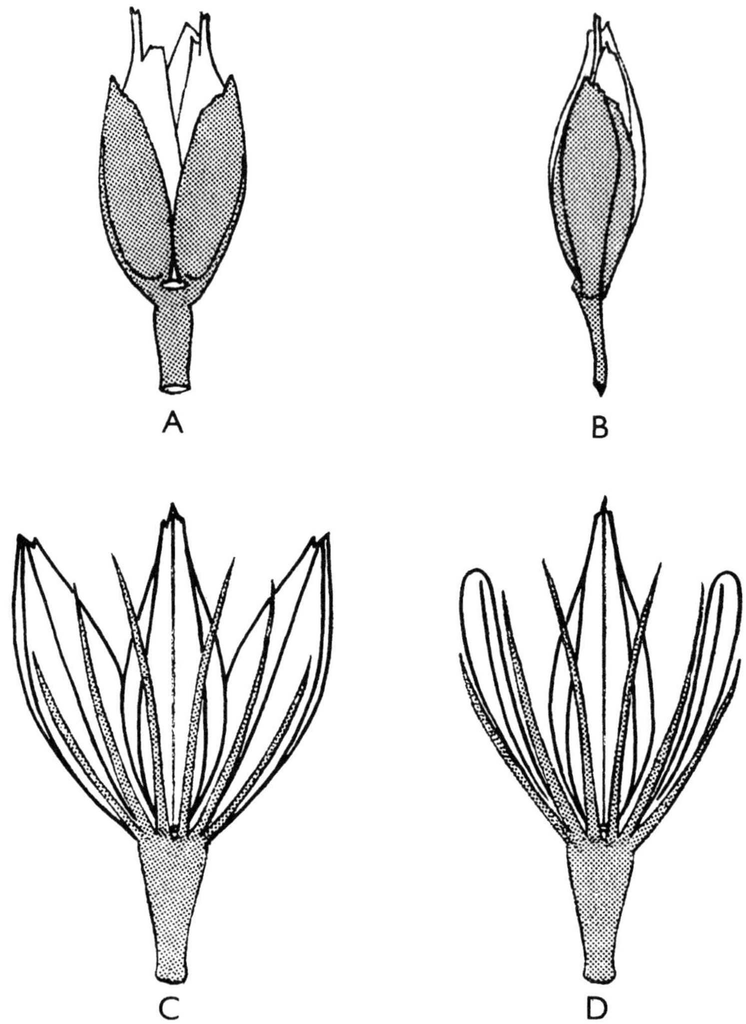

Fig. 139. Diagrams of wheat and barley spike sections. (Internodes and glumes are shown hatched, florets are white); *A*, emmer wheat spikelet with internode, ventral view; *B*, emmer wheat spikelet with internode, lateral view.

The white ovals at the upper and lower end of the internode are the disintegration scars. In wheats the internode bears only one spikelet which, however, may contain from one to many florets (grains). In einkorn, one grain is developed; in emmer, two; and in bread wheat, three to five. Besides, one or more rudimentary florets will usually be present; *C*, six-row barley, dorsal view of spike section or triplet; *D*, two-row barley, dorsal view of spike section or triplet.

As opposed to wheat, the barley internode bears three spikelets, each with its own pair of reduced glumes and each containing only one floret. Structurally, the two forms are identical; the difference is a matter of morphological and physiological development in the lateral florets.

In two-row barley—the ancestral form—only the median spikelet bears a fertile floret developing a grain; the two lateral organs are sexually imperfect (male) and thus sterile. By mutation, physiological actuation of the female sex organs in the lateral florets may happen. Hence all three florets of the spike section will bear a grain, and thus the spike has become six-row. All fertile florets are awned; the sterile ones in the two-row form are not.

The casing of a hulled barley grain is very complex: the seed is covered by the seed coat (testa, consisting of an inner and an outer integument). To this the seed case (pericarp) is fused anatomically; finally, the paleas are fused chemically to the seed case. In naked barley the last-mentioned condition is cancelled by mutation.

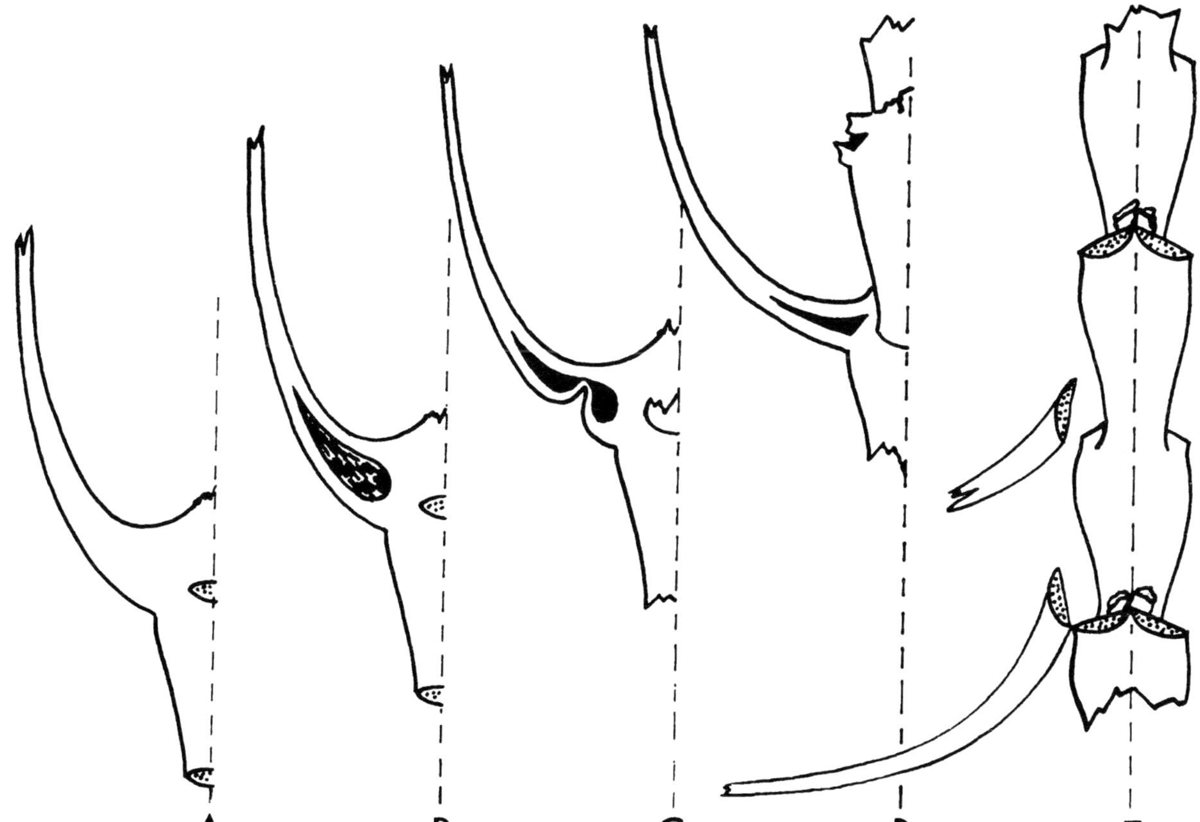

Fig. 140. Tentative representation of the mechanical transformation in the emmer spikelet in consequence of hybridization leading to the free-threshing wheat spike: *A*, shows the solid and sturdy junction between the glume base and the internode (the "shoulder"), the resistance of which is the reason why emmer, wild and domesticated, does not release the grains by normal threshing. The drawing shows brittleness of the axis (cf. Fig. 138); *B* and *C*, represent transitional conditions, the solid shoulder has become hollow or spongy; in *C* the outer tissue has collapsed into the medial tissue, forming a sharp crease that weakens the shoulder decisively. At the same time, the disintegration of the axis becomes irregular and the break often happens somewhere above the natural fracture point, or not at all; *D*, shows the initial free-threshing condition: the glume is more delicate and by its weakness is adaptable to an increasing number of grains in the spikelet; the shoulder is now brittle and breaks up on threshing. Eventually the spike axis develops complete toughness and remains one piece, adhering to the straw.

By now the glume-internode junction is reduced to a thin, brittle, crescent-shaped area, as shown in *E*; glumes and grains are easily detached by pounding.

As opposed to the schematized drawings *A* to *D*, *E* is a fairly naturalistic illustration of the most advanced axis type found in the late sixth millennium. Photographic documentation is available in Helbaek, 1966*d*, Figs. 6 and 7.

The crucial diagnostic features in identification of the early bread wheat are the crease in the shoulder and the occurrence of conjoint, glumeless internodes.

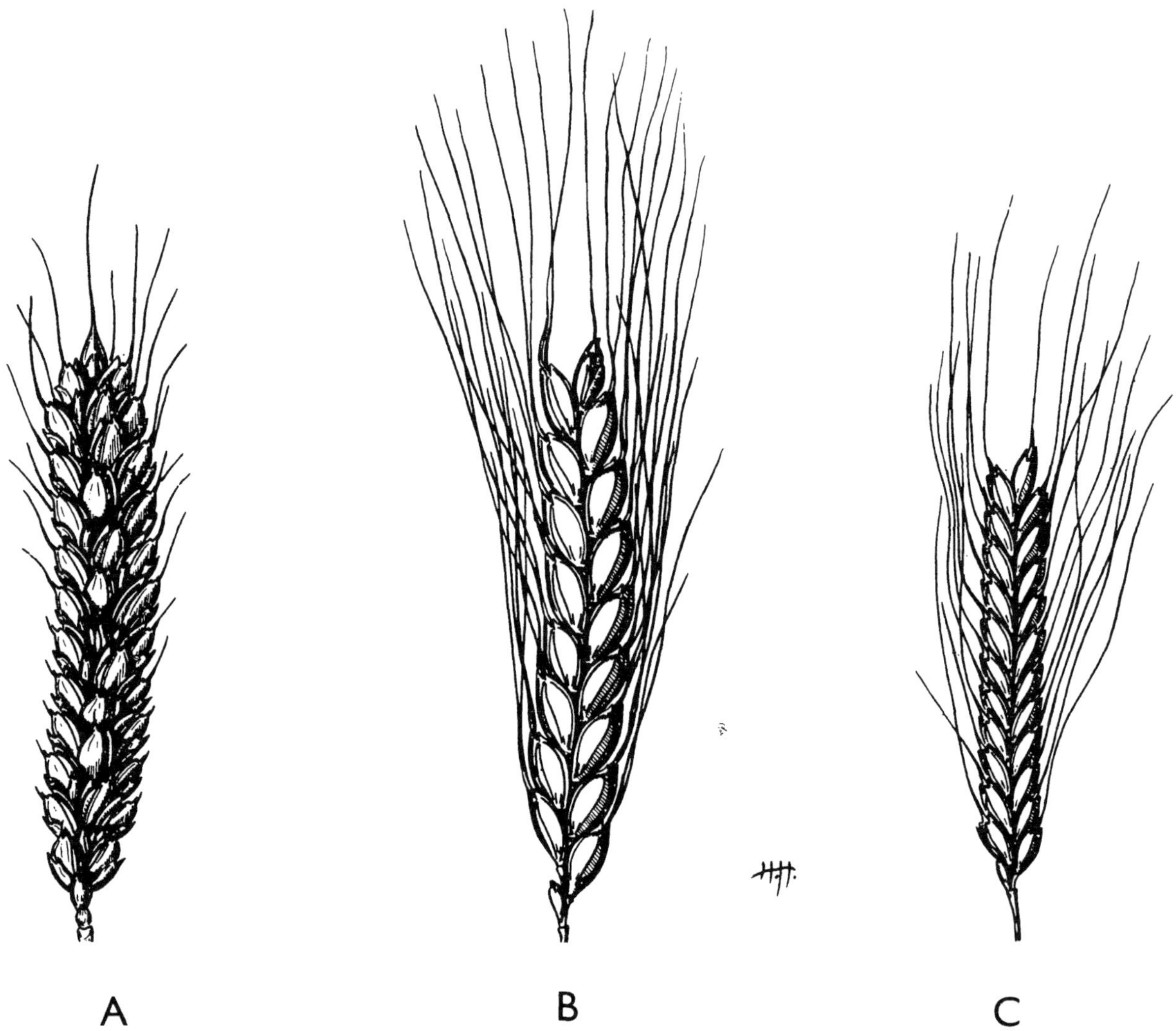

Fig. 141. Modern spike types of wheat: *A*, bread wheat (hexaploid, free-threshing); *B*, emmer (tetraploid); *C*, einkorn (diploid).

in the Ali Kosh phase cannot be accepted as evidence, while the complete absence of swamp flora in the Mohammad Jaffar phase may well mean that the lake at that time had retreated substantially from the site.

Taking the Mohammad Jaffar seeds for what they are worth, a principal change of economy seems to have taken place. Cultivated plants and their attendant weeds fall off, indicating that the plant-producing activity during the period became secondary to other occupations, pastoralism and hunting, in tendency if not in detail reminiscent of the colonization phase. We leave this aspect to the zoologist, but from the plant list it appears that collection of the wild plants of the steppe increased on a huge scale. Field output declines from some 55 per cent in the Ali Kosh phase to 4 per cent in the Mohammad Jaffar phase, while the wild plants supply 96 per cent of the number of items as opposed to the 45 per cent in the preceding phase.

A glance at Ecological Group 6 in the plant table reveals this intensification of the hunt for wild plant food in that two species, Plantain (*Plantago ovata*) and Mallow (*Malva parviflora*), demonstrably available in the steppe almost from the beginning of settling, but appearing in very modest numbers in the two previous phases, suddenly are collected in such volume during the Mohammad Jaffar phase as to swell this group from 2 per cent to about 17. Both are plants that thrive in disturbed if not actually tilled soil, occurring in and about the village, along paths and goat tracks. Simultaneously the weed grasses fall off almost to insignificance.

This probably means that the lake with its extended groundwater table had by now receded too far from the village for agriculture to be practical and profitable enough, and after this period of material deflation, the site was given up as a permanent base.

It is further interesting to note that, according to the calculated figures, barley had supplanted Emmer as the principal cereal. Of considerable genetic interest is the occurrence, in the middle of the Mohammad Jaffar phase, of the first traces of a new mutant in barley, the hulled, six-row form, *Hordeum vulgare*. The evidence consists of two small and poorly developed grains, but definitely twisted and curved like the lateral grains in a six-row spike should be. The sample comes from about 1.40 m. below the surface and would thus be dated to some 5800 B.C. In other areas in the Near East (Iraq and Anatolia) this mutation has been noted for the same general period, but the Mohammad Jaffar phase comes to an end without any further evidence for the mutant. Only in Tepe Sabz do we come across evidence of more substantial occurrence of this form of barley, and this has probably something to do with irrigation. Another feature of note in the Mohammad Jaffar phase is the absence of naked barley which occurred consistently, if in minority, in the two preceding phases.

In the plant table, Ecological Group 7 is concerned, among others, with Prosopis. This plant, seemingly lacking an English name in spite of its enormous distribution, is a small, straggling shrub belonging to the Mimosa family. It is a valuable grazing plant because, being extremely deep-rooted, it persists during the hot summer when most other plants in its principal environment, semidesert and dry steppe, have withered and lost most of their nutritive value. Its fruit is a swollen pod varying up to the size of a grown man's thumb, containing rather large, bone-hard seeds which pass through the digestive canal of man and animal without losing their viability. Prosopis pods are eaten eagerly by sheep and goats.

Our material contains these seeds throughout the duration of the village. They turn up so late and are so few in the Bus Mordeh phase as to show that the plant was hardly exploited. Late in the Ali Kosh phase their frequency increases steeply, but in the top phase the seeds become so alarmingly common in most of the samples that, for lucidity, it was considered expedient also to list the Mohammad Jaffar phase material in two separate groups, characterized by a low ('*a*') and a high ('*b*') percentage of Prosopis (Table 4, p. 413). We have already referred to Group "*a*" in the discussion of cultivated versus collected plant food; Group "*b*" is so inconsistent with everything else that a plausible explanation seems almost unattainable (see also Fig. 142).

Distribution of plant samples in the Mohammad Jaffar phase is rather insufficient for a confident account to be given of the plant foods of the time. Looking at the detailed (not published) plant list, we find the depth from the top to 0.90

m. (zone A_1) completely devoid of plant remains. At that point an isolated sample appears, mostly consisting of Prosopis seeds. After another empty space, the strata from 1.20 to 1.50 m. yield ten samples of the same character, by number altogether consisting of 93 per cent of Prosopis seeds, practically no cereal grains and very few small legumes. Then, within the 0.35 m. between 1.40 and 1.75 m., we encounter three samples of a perfectly reasonable composition, the material that was discussed above. Thereafter, from 1.75 to the bottom of the Mohammad Jaffar levels, not a single seed of any kind was produced in spite of strenuous efforts on the part of the excavators, and much floating.

It seems, at any rate, as if new domestic practices as regards garbage disposal were introduced by the Mohammad Jaffar people. They only slipped up in the comparatively brief period that yielded the material of Group "*a*." But why the concentrated samples of Prosopis? One must object to the idea of the seeds having been left by goats housed in the village, because in the first place, there would be no reason for the goats to leave the seeds carbonized, and further, there appear to be no Prosopis seeds in the abundant carbonized goat droppings in the site. Besides, even if the seeds had passed through the goats unscathed, how come that the few other seeds which are soluble in the intestines of both man and animal, were also not digested? On the other hand, if goat herders collected the pods and roasted them in the evening and had a meal on them, spitting the seeds into the fire, why did they leave the refuse on the spot since it was not customary at the time? Were it not for the substantial traces of architecture in zone A_1 at Tepe Ali Kosh, one would be tempted to suggest that there were no Mohammad Jaffar phase houses near the 1963 excavation area.

Without solving this particular problem, other finds may be introduced here which tend to show that indeed Prosopis was exploited for human food, even in times and places of the highest sophistication.

In one of the store rooms in the palace of Late Assyrian Nimrud, of the seventh century B.C., a collection of slightly immature pods were found (Helbaek, 1966*a*). They cannot have been brought into the food store accidentally or as animal fodder, and no other reason can be proposed except that they were destined for human consumption. Also, at Early Hassunan Tell es-Sawwan near Samarra, a deposit of carbonized plant food was found in a ditch dated to approximately the same time as the plant-carrying levels in the Mohammad Jaffar phase (Helbaek, 1964*a*; el-Wailly, 1964; el-Wailly and es-Soof, 1965). The plant remains consisted of three separate samples: one of wheat and barley, one of Prosopis seeds and one of the seeds of Caper, the fruits of which are eaten by people even in our day (Guest, 1933:18). Apart from this, stray Prosopis seeds are found in other prehistoric sites, associated with cereals. So, on the accumulated evidence, there seems to be good reason for including the species among the collected human foods.

Thus far we have considered the generalized plant table mostly from the viewpoint of quantity; the quality of the various groups should, however, be briefly touched upon, if for no other reason than to be of assistance to other investigators of similar matters. Also there are certain details of slight numerical weight which by implication indicate conditions of considerable ecological and cultural significance.

Having referred to the cereals of the first group, Ecological Group 1, in such detail as necessary in this summary, some rare items which have their own little story to tell, should be pointed out so as not to get lost among the more prominent figures.

However modest in number, the occurrence - stated in brackets - of linseed (flax, *Linum* sp.) is highly interesting. It being only fragments of seeds and pods, a definite identification cannot be undertaken, but judging by such dimensions as can be ascertained, it seems to be the wild Pale flax (*L. bienne*), common in the higher and moister terrain of the foothills and intermontane valleys of the Zagros mountains. It cannot grow in an ecology like that of Deh Luran, and no other species of the genus is at home in such environment. In the Bus Mordeh phase traces appear in three samples, in the other two phases (Ali Kosh and Mohammad Jaffar) only one each. This may be taken as evidence for trading contacts and repeated import of foreign seed from the mountains to the north, especially as the flax appears in initial levels of all three phases. The species did not survive; on the average, there is several hundred years between the occurrences. Later on, when irrigation was introduced, a high-quality, domesticated flax was grown consistently by the Tepe Sabz people a few miles east of Ali Kosh.

More or less the same interpretation must be applied to the two lentil seeds found in the Ali Kosh and Mohammad Jaffar phases. The first specimen came out of the 1961 test trench and belongs to a fairly early stage of the Ali Kosh phase (zone B_2) whereas the other occurred among the Group "*a*" samples of the Mohammad Jaffar phase, again most of half a millennium between the two. The lentil is another plant that would not put up with the dry, saline conditions of the early times. Later, races were selected that could be grown in such environment, upheld by irrigation, again a fact demonstrated by the plant finds at Tepe Sabz and Tepe Musiyan.

The Goat-face grass occurring continuously in Deh Luran (Ecological Group 2) is the coarse species, *Aegilops crassa.* Some whole and full spikelets have been found in both sites. It is one of the ever-occurring grasses in prehistoric finds from the Zagros mountains, the foothill region and the Mesopotamian plain, still a common weed in wheat fields from western Iran to Syria and beyond. The heavy, but variable spike tapers from a thick and sturdy, cylindrical base to a slender, sterile top spikelet, and the size of grain corresponds more or less to the decreasing diameter of the spikelet bases. Thus the topmost grain is often as small as Ryegrass while that of the primary floret in the base spikelets may be as large - albeit of a different shape - as an Emmer grain. Because of this fluctuation it is not always possible to be sure that only one species of Goat-face grass is involved, and besides, there is little doubt that the distinction between the puffed grains of Ryegrass and the upper grains of Goat-face grass may occasionally have been rather subjective, not least because the former also vary considerably in size.

In the dehusked state, Ryegrass is extremely difficult to specify when it is puffed as well. There is, however, a strong probability that the species introduced in Deh Luran was Rigid ryegrass (*Lolium rigidum*). It is a widespread pest both in irrigation and dry-farming, and a few grains with the sharkskin-like paleas preserved, found at Tepe Sabz, seem to confirm this determination.

The massive increase of oat (*Avena* sp.) after the Ali Kosh phase presents a striking feature in Ecological Group 3. Most of the seeds are very small and their specification is doubtful. Such species as *A. clauda, A. sterilis* and others bear the small type of grain which we find in the earlier phases, but whether or not they are native to Deh Luran can be ascertained only by studying the present day flora in detail and at the right season, April and May. However, among the oat of the Mohammad Jaffar phase some fragments of a larger grain occur which correspond to the common weed oat, *A. ludoviciana.* That species may in the meantime have been introduced as a contamination in foreign seed. Doubtful as is the specification of these grains, the generic classification is safe enough; no other grass fruit is deformed on carbonization in just the way of oat.

Ecological Group 3 includes two other native grasses, one of which, Feather grass (*Stipa capensis*), found only in one sample, certainly is fortuitous. It is a widely distributed, wind-dispersed steppe and desert grass and may have got into the house as material for thatch or some such. The other, Canary grass (*Phalaris* cf. *paradoxa*), is extremely common in the whole of the Near East and thrives in a wide range of ecological conditions. It was collected throughout the lifetime of Tepe Ali Kosh, but, together with oats, made up the most conspicuous proportion in the Mohammad Jaffar phase.

Most important to the wider understanding of what went on in Deh Luran at 7000 B.C. is the content of Ecological Group 4, endemic legumes. The group probably comprises a large number of species, but without proper field collection scanty specification can be done. The average size of these items is about 1.25 mm., and morphologically they may be segregated into three main groups: *a*) a slender cylindrical type corresponding to a large number of species of Trigonella (*T. auranthiacum, T. brevidentata, T. monspeliaca, T. monantha* and others); *b*) a flat, squarish to rhombic type corresponding to certain Milk-vetch species, such as *Astragalus cruciata, A. tribuloides* and others; *c*) an oval, flat type with softly corrugated surface, varying greatly in dimensions; only this one can be determined with certainty, it is the Ray-podded medick, *Medicago radiata.* All such species belong to the dry steppe and many could probably be found in the Deh Luran valley if a proper excursion were made from early spring to harvest time. For our present purpose, however, the crucial common feature is that this whole family has a much higher protein content than most other seeds available in the steppe (Earle and Jones, 1962; Smith, *et al.* 1959; Van Etten, Miller, and Wolf, 1963), and that the nutritive consequences of this fact must have been recognized empirically by ancient peoples. Later on the same property has been eagerly sought for in the domestication of larger-seeded species of the family, as for instance pea, lentil, chickpea, bean and many others which today are of immense importance in the diet of the peoples of the arid, south-temperate zone.

Ecological Group 6 contains a group, incidentals. These comparatively few seeds come from such species as Field pansy (*Viola* sp.), Bedstraw (*Galium* sp.) and Fumitory (*Fumaria* sp.). It seems as if two species of Mallow are present, at least in the Tepe Sabz material. They are the closely related *Malva parviflora* and *M. nicaeensis.* The distinguishing mark is a slightly different formation of the seed case, very rarely preserved, but the seeds cannot be told apart on size. The former grows around the Ali Kosh mound today.

Although only *Plantago bellardi* was in evidence in the steppe during the winter of 1963, the species of Plantain that occurs in both sites is *Plantago ovata* and possibly, on closer investigation, *P. lanceolata.*

Fragments of small round seeds turn up irregularly in both Tepe Ali Kosh and Tepe Sabz; they are the cotyledons of a small vetch or related species, maybe one type could be Yellow vetchling (*Lathyrus aphaca*). But here again, without the hilum and at least part of the seed coat, the question of identity is somewhat unapproachable.

Bits of shells or occasionally whole fruits of Pistachio (*Pistacia atlantica*) appear with a certain frequency during the Bus Mordeh phase, more rarely later on. This tree cannot grow in the valley; as mentioned above it belongs hundreds of metres up the slopes of Kuh-i-Siah. This reminds us of the peculiarity that oleaginous seeds are practically absent from the plant list, as also that the Pistachio represents the only contact with the mountains we can see. If such fatty fruits were easily accessible, acorns, almonds and Pistachio would certainly have shown up with reasonable frequency in the table. Since the mountains are less than half a day's walk away from the site there must have been hard reasons for the collector-farmers not to go and get them. Probably the mountains were, at the time, inhabited by fierce hunters who envied and therefore detested the soft, settled farmers on the plain, and only approached them with evil intent. However, some trade must have occurred, or maybe the Pistachio were brought in by the same barter contacts from the north who traded the seed corn contaminated with flax and lentil. So, while the Ali Kosh people depended upon their own ecological niche for vegetable protein and starch, the third principal vegetable element, fat, seems to have been unobtainable and to have been replaced with fat from animal sources, mainly domestic goats, sheep, and wild ungulates.

The Caper (*Capparis spinosa*) is a straggling, thorny shrub, distributed all over the steppe. Its fruits look like small, slender figs containing a number of comparatively large seeds (2 to 3 mm.) embedded in a red jelly. Herdsmen and other passers-by eat the fruits in the autumn when they are mature. That they were sometimes brought home is indicated by the seeds found in all three phases at Tepe Ali Kosh. Incidentally, it is peculiar that no remains of Zizyphus fruits have been established for ancient Deh Luran; in the Khorramabad Valley (Luristan) in 1963, the Rice University team found Zizyphus fruit pits together with carbonized Pistachios and cereal grains at the site of Bog-i-No, whose pottery resembles that of the Sabz phase but which yielded a radiocarbon date of 4250 B.C.[5] On high gravel land between Deh Luran and Dizful, Zizyphus occur in park-like groves, large and finely developed trees, while in Deh Luran of today the species occurs as small, rather puny individuals. The question cannot be avoided: did it grow at all in the low steppe under the conditions obtaining nine to seven millennia ago? At present the small, berry-like fruits, of a bitter-sweet taste, are picked by people on the plain and they can be bought in the bazar.

Now we arrive at a hurdle which seems difficult to jump. The Borage family (*Boraginaceae*) is represented in our finds by three members, two of which, Gromwell (*Lithospermum* sp.) and Bugloss (*Echium* sp.) have not been named specifically. The third, the Heliotrope (*Heliotropium persicum*), is such a common plant in the steppe and fields of Deh Luran that its occurrence in two of the phases may be fortuitous; but then again, it may not, we cannot say. However, both Gromwell and Bugloss appear with such a conspicuous concentration in the lowest building level (zone C_2) of the Bus Mordeh phase that it can hardly be without special reason. Gromwell does turn up occasionally during that and the following phase, but it is extraordinary that the first half metre yielded 106 seeds in six samples, whereas the following eleven samples, covering the rest of the period

5 The Zizyphus pits were examined by Helbaek in the Ali Kosh field camp, but are not published.

(1.30 m.), contained altogether only nine seeds. Even more striking is the distribution of Bugloss; the same, deep building level gave thirty-seven seeds, and some centuries later a single seed occurs. That is all we see of it.

Since the actual species are not determined it is difficult to discuss the matter on ecological grounds. There is, however, a property common to many species of the Borage family, namely that their roots contain chemicals which may be extracted in primitive ways and used for red and yellow dyes. Did the first Bus Mordeh people stain their bodies - or maybe their corpses before funeral such as was the practice at Çatal Hüyük and in other places - or their vegetable utensils? There can be no reason for collecting the seeds for food, and their stems would be of much lower fuel value than most other available vegetation, beside being very prickly in handling. It may, in this connection, be mentioned that seeds of this family occur frequently in other very early sites in the Near East, Aceramic Haçilar, Çatal Hüyük and Beidha, but not, for instance, in such a rich, but late find as Assyrian Nimrud.

Finally, a matter that probably bears on threshing practices is the occurrence of crushed spikelet forks of Emmer and Einkorn. When threshed, especially in a mortar, the solid structure of the spikelet base with attached glumes and internode will be somewhat fragmented, but usually a fork-like particle will survive, consisting of the base of the spikelet and the glumes, sometimes even the internode. This does not really apply to the Tepe Ali Kosh material. Very few forks have been found, but numerous small bits are present in practically every sample of the two earlier periods, and in the Mohammad Jaffar phase Group "a" as well.

It was calculated by weight that on the average the bits correspond to one-eighth of the fork structure such as it commonly occurs, for instance, in nearby Tepe Sabz, among carbonized Emmer and Einkorn grain. If the grain and the spikelet parts had been ground up together, there would be a certain relation between the number of fragments and the number of grains in each sample. Eight particles making a spikelet fork, two grains should go with them; or rather, each grain should be accompanied by at least four spikelet fragments - in the case of Einkorn, by eight.

But there is no such correlation. Most often there are too many spikelets per grain, and sometimes spikelet fragments and no grain at all. The dilemma is illustrated by a constellation of the number of Emmer mentioned in the table, with the fact that almost 4700 fragments of spikelets have been counted, corresponding to some 1175 grains, or two and a half times as many as found. Even though admittedly these speculations rest on a somewhat shaky basis, mathematically speaking, the discrepancy is too prominent to be relegated to the world of fortuitous coincidence.

Apart from some samples with spikelet fragments but no grain at all, there are such extremes as 25 grains to 794 fragments in the Mohammad Jaffar phase, and even two grains to 647 fragments in the Ali Kosh phase. In a rich Bus Mordeh sample, 1430 fragments go with 124 grains and not the 360 with which the spikelets correspond; in another slightly smaller, but also very rich sample there is a discrepancy from 52 to the 184 grains that should occur with the 733 fragments in that case. Now, these same two Bus Mordeh phase samples contain respectively 12,750 and 1,800 seeds of small legumes, and by and large there seems to be a correlation between the number of excess spikelet fragments and the seeds of small legumes. Even in the Mohammad Jaffar Group "a" (Table 4) this coincidence is striking: seven grains (and no groats), 137 spikelet fragments and 2083 small legumes in one sample; 25 grains, 794 fragments and 2322 seeds of small legumes in another. Altogether, even if we take it that the unidentified cereal grains listed as "groats," are in fact fragments exclusively of Emmer grains, we arrive at a total just over two-thirds of the number necessary to cover the requirements for correlation.

Any field botanist with interest in collecting type samples of seeds in the Near East is familiar with the extreme toughness of the pods of many genera. It is often impossible to dehusk the seeds in the field without special equipment. This applies to many species of the family *Leguminosae.* One can roll the pods between one's hands - and get the hands torn, but no seed dehusked. Most specifically this is the case with many genera such as Trigonella, Milk-vetch, Medick and other small-seeded species.

The ancient collectors have been up against this particular difficulty, and they found the ideal solution: the mortar. When a reasonable amount of pods are pounded in a mortar, the pod valves will slowly be shredded and broken up; the seeds will accumulate more or less intact on the bottom. Separation is easy then.

Seeing how substantial the solid, woody spikelet base looks in the "glume wheats" (Einkorn, Emmer, and Spelt), it is not difficult to imagine that primitive people did not always realize that this portion of the spike is completely devoid of food value. In order to relieve the spikelets, already broken in the quern of mortar, of their flimsy edges and other obvious "trash," they may have put the half-treated spikelets in with the legume pods and given them the same pounding. The solid portions, just those bits we find in the carbonized material, would, together with the seeds, concentrate by gravity on the bottom of the mortar. Winnowing would remove the pulverized portions both of spikelets and pods. Such a procedure would explain this peculiarity about the Tepe Ali Kosh plant deposits.

In support of this suggestion it may be pointed out that, although many pods of the leguminous genera represented in the material are extremely substantial and tough, not one particle in the whole lot could be referred to any pod. If it were possible to remove these, there is no reason why the Emmer and Einkorn spikelets and their fragments should be difficult to get rid of if it were desired. Further, at this stage of development, each grain of hulled barley has it own internode and, in case it were impracticable to dispose of this kind of object, we might expect a large number of them, while, in fact, barley internodes are generally utterly rare in the Tepe Ali Kosh material. They are thin, sharp, and certainly not suggestive of any nutritive value whatsoever. Even so, one of the Mohammad Jaffar phase samples, containing 218 of them, proves that they did not automatically disappear in winnowing. It might be noted, although slightly out of place, that about 10 to 15 per cent of these internodes show fractures characteristic of a tough axis (*c.* 6000 B.C.)

An analogous case might be quoted even if it may seem farfetched. A man was murdered, probably sacrificially, in the second century A.D. and thrown into a disused peat cutting in Denmark where, by the humic acid the body was kept more or less fresh until a few years ago. When, in 1952, his intestinal duct was removed and subjected to an analysis, seeds and grains from about 65 species were established (Helbaek, 1958). Also many fragments of the spikelets of Emmer and Spelt wheat, but it was conspicuous that the easily recognizable remains of grain shells of wheat were very rare, much too few to account for all the spikelet fragments. Here there seems no doubt that the woody parts were considered nourishing, or, at any rate, deliberately added to the meal.

In what state the Ali Kosh people consumed their vegetable diet remains subject to conjecture. Not until the Mohammad Jaffar phase does pottery appear at the site, implying the possibility of actual boiling. It is difficult to imagine any other kind of receptacle in which proper, necessarily prolonged cooking of farinaceous food could be accomplished. Nor is there evidence for raw materials from which vessels could be made that would stand boiling of water. In all probability, plant food was consumed in the roasted state, presumably suspended in water. It is also not improbable that some degree of roasting or parching preceded the mortar threshing.

Here we shall, like the impoverished Mohammad Jaffar people, leave Tepe Ali Kosh and turn our attention towards the other side of the Tamarisk swamp where foreigners arrived and settled, furnished with new knowledge of plant husbandry and land management. However, in describing the plant economy of the ancient settlers of Tepe Ali Kosh and the evolution of the plants they cultivated, certain phrases and terms have been employed which perhaps may seem inconsistent and carelessly chosen. In order to facilitate the reading of the second part of this economic-botanical report, an explanatory chapter is now inserted which, it is hoped, will clear up any doubt so far arisen, and make the writer's concepts of the consequences of irrigation lucid above doubt.

TERMINOLOGICAL INTERLUDE

In trying to describe novel phenomena in scientific experience a difficulty is encountered with which all present-day archaeologists are familiar: proper logical, unambiguous terminology.

With the insight gained from Ali Kosh we move into a similar situation of inadequate, misleading, or plain senseless terms as regards the botanical aspect of human life, employing common, every-day phrases in expressing highly specific ideas and phenomena, words which in daily speech are used in a vague and indeterminate sense. Thus in the more-or-less theoretical discussion of later years, acquisition of plant food by Upper Palaeolithic and later man has been described, implying a typological sequence, in such words as "plant collecting," "incipient plant gathering," or "intensified plant collecting," ending with "incipient agriculture" by the Mesolithic period. This technical phraseology is based upon not one single find of material evidence, and the nomenclature conveys little rational meaning to the general reader, none at all to the professional student of prehistoric plant food.

Indeed, when dealing with specific, demonstrable facts it is necessary to employ special words and phrases, but too often the wear of time and the progress of science will undo their validity. Thus Gordon Childe's "Neolithic Revolution" (Childe, 1939:59-86) with emphasis on the food production aspect of the New Stone Age has become obsolete and illusory. In 1936 nobody knew from where the principal crop plants came, what their progenitors were; nobody had any idea how long ago their "production" first took place, let alone how long a period was involved in the trasitional process. But, at the time the phrase had its mission in that, for the first time, it turned the prehistorian's mind towards recognition of the fundamental fact that man had to eat while he produced the architecture and artifacts which hitherto had been the archaeologist's sole preoccupation. However, the word "revolution" has about it a tone of suddenness that, in this context, cannot any more be accepted. We now recognize the fact that we are observing a typical slow evolution of a duration of at least 2000 years.

The plant finds at Tepe Ali Kosh furnish a broad practical hint as to what went on in this sphere before man became conscious of his own power to influence the growth conditions and propagation for some of the plants he had hitherto been seeking in their natural stands. At Ali Kosh we see two contemporaneous elements of early agriculture: on the one hand, a heavy dependence upon collection of seeds of wild, endemic plants; on the other, cultivation of both wild and domesticated forms of wheat and barley, introduced from uplands where embryonic agriculture had reached a certain stage of development (Helbaek, 1966*c*)

The bulk of the Bus Mordeh phase barley is the wild, two-row, hulled *Hordeum spontaneum* in which the spike axis is brittle. But besides that we find the earliest known domesticated form, the six-row, naked-grained barley (*H. vulgare* var. *nudum*), numerically amounting to less than 10 per cent of the determinable grains. This mutant had emerged somewhere else and was probably not yet segregated for separate cultivation.

Wild einkorn, *Triticum boeoticum*, was among the introduced seed, and at an early stage of the Bus Mordeh phase a few grains of the domesticated mutant, *T. monococcum,* appear. This mutation may have taken place in Deh Luran - as well as other places in the Near East.

Insofar as one can judge from the specified grains, Emmer wheat, *T. dicoccum*, was the principal crop plant during the Bus Mordeh and Ali Kosh phases. It is the thoroughly domesticated species, and no trace of its wild progenitor, *T. dicoccoides,* is in evidence.

During the Mohammad Jaffar phase, presumably about 5800 B.C., another mutant of the wild barley makes a sporadic appearance. Two small, twisted grains with the inner husk attached to the surface were picked out from a collection of 138 otherwise straight, hulled grains. This is one of the three earliest known, but all roughly contemporaneous, occurrences of the later so important six-row, hulled *Hordeum vulgare.* This mutant evidently did not agree with the prevailing ecological conditions and did not show up again at Tepe Ali Kosh. Simultaneously the naked barley disappears.

In this brief summary we again come up against the conflict between general and specific meanings of the words applied when speaking of the newly tamed plants. I shall try to define the sense in which I use the words "cultivation" and "domestication" in this report.

In daily speech the word cultivation means particular and persistent interest in something, mostly aiming at improving the relationship to the cherished subject. In the instance of plant husbandry, cultivation means promotion of favourable growth conditions for one or more species: changing the microbiology of the topsoil through hoeing or ploughing and, in many regions, by controlling water supply; further, by artificial dispersal of seeds and by keeping out competition from animals and plants that may infringe upon the maximum prosperity of the chosen species - in the hope that these endeavours will prove profitable also to the benefactor. But the word cultivation does not intrisically imply that the cherished species will die if the care of the cultivator comes to an end.

Thus wild barley may have been cultivated for hundreds of years without losing its ability to revert to its original status, able to propagate independently and fight its natural battle for existence against competing vegetation and predatory animals. That is, as long as it is not moved into a materially different environment (Helbaek, 1966*b*).

Experience shows that physiological changes take place in wild plants (and domesticated, too, for that matter) by random combination of genes that traditionally do not interact, but which in their new alliance express novel, inheritable qualities in the plant. Although rarely, these mutations do happen again and again in nature. Many results of mutation are not viable under the ecological conditions obtaining where the change takes place and thus the mutant, even if not sterile, will die out from environmental pressure. However, if man improves growth conditions for a species, more individuals may be accommodated in the same area unit, and this enables some mutants that in the untended state would have perished from competition, to survive in consequence of "relaxed selection pressure" (Hutchinson, 1958:3). If attractive, such mutants may be picked out for special attention, and at that moment their status has changed: they cannot return to an independent existence in nature; they are domesticated, that is, tied to man (*lit.* to his house).

A common genetic change in plants is the loss of ability to disperse the seeds or fruits, the mechanism upon which their propagation is dependent. This is, of course, fatal to a wild plant. On the other hand, it can be an immense gain to man in that, if the plant is profitable to him, he can now reap the whole pod, spike or inflorescence instead of collecting the individual seeds, or having to reap the plant before it has attained its maximum development and economic value. This is conspicuous for instance in grasses (cereals), some leguminous plants and flax.

If a pea looses the contortion mechanism in its pod valve, a prerequisite for dispersal of its mature seeds at random, it is doomed as a wild plant; its propagation can continue only by man's intervention. Thus it is now domesticated. The grasses are in the same case. In the independent state the spike of wild barley disintegrates at maturity and the units are dispersed by wind or animal transport. The units, or spike sections, are admirably built for wind transport, of an aerodynamic design reminiscent of modern aircraft and with appendages for anchoring and self-planting. Only the median of three florets bears a grain, the two empty lateral organs act as stabilizers. The moment a mutation happens making the two lateral florets loaded with developed grains, the unit becomes a clumsy structure that will fly no more than a bulldozer; it drops limply to the ground and, *nota bene*, all the units will drop in the same place, creating a quite impossible situation of growth competition.

If man takes a hand, this otherwise hopeless impasse can be overcome, and then only in a useful way if another mutation happens, keeping the spike axis articulate at maturity, and not disintegrating. Consequently, barley having suffered these two physiological changes would be absolutely helpless in nature; but would, in the hands of man, yield a large surplus over and above the grain necessary to reproduce the field with the same or even increased density of individuals. Most conspicuous is, of course, the case of the naked-grained six-row barley.

This is the fundamental meaning of domestication. So it may be concluded that a cultivated plant need not necessarily be domesticated—cannot by any means so be from the outset—while on the other hand, a domesticated plant can exist only as a cultivated plant. Cultivation is a matter of directing ecology, whereas domestication depends upon some physiological inefficacy in a plant, advantageous to man.

By cross pollination it may happen that two related species or varieties produce a new species differing from either parent. Such hybrids may be sterile or fertile as the genetic circumstances dictate, but even if the latter, the final decision of survival and propagation lies with the environment. In natural conditions many otherwise successful hybrids do not come off, and here is another situation where man by creating suitable ecology may keep the species alive. This applies to some of the world's most important cereals, as for instance free-threshing wheat and corn (maize). Solely due to man's intervention these two hybrids, hopelessly deprived of dispersal capabilities, have adapted to widely differing climates, day lengths and soils, and are being grown in various parts of the world in innumerable varieties. Both would disappear from the surface of the earth a few years after man's removal from this planet.

Generally speaking, domestication is a conscious effort on man's part. By selecting, nursing and propagating the subject of his endeavours he institutes a reciprocal dependency, almost a symbiosis: the domesticated plant cannot exist without his help, and, considering humanity comprehensively, man cannot exist without his domesticated plants.

In a manner of speaking, however, unitentional and unprofitable domestication that by detrimental competition is obstructive to the prime motive, must also be taken into account. This applies to the weeds, and has taken place ever since the first sod was turned in order to accommodate useful food plants.

Weeds are plants belonging to the ecological habitat that is turned into cultivated soil. They invade the arable, thrive on the improved conditions and adapt to the vegetational rhythm organized by man. Sowing time, harvesting time and threshing technique will in the long run select special genetic strains or races of certain species which, under constant mutative adaptation and spontaneous selection, can follow agriculture into remote areas, climatically vastly different from their homelands. Many such weed varieties are domesticated in the sense that they will be extinct if agriculture is given up. Thus Scandinavia, and even America, owe many of their common field weeds to unintended import of members of the wild flora of the Near East and the Mediterranean region, over the millennia transported as impurities in batches of seed.

In primitive agriculture man accepted the *status quo* he was unable to influence, and took what advantage he could of the weeds. We see this reflected in the occurrence of Goat-face grass and Ryegrass in Tepe Ali Kosh, and in the exploitation of these and the introduced leguminous weed species at Tepe Sabz. The practice has been common throughout the ages wherever agriculture was introduced. Weed exploitation actually went on up to the quite recent industrialization of agriculture, and it is still being performed in primitive society (Helbaek, 1950, 1951, 1954, 1958).

Rye and oat became physiologically domesticated in this roundabout way, only at a late stage selected and deliberately cultivated after having lost their natural dispersal capability (Helbaek, 1955). It is also quite possible that, from the start, barley was not an invited inhabitant of the arable land man had prepared in his attempt to harness the wild wheat. However, as yet no early prehistoric find affords the means for settling this question; they all contain both species. In Tepe Ali Kosh we perceive a typologically quite early stage of agriculture, indeed the earliest hitherto, but we are still too far from the first pioneering effort.

TEPE SABZ

Tepe Ali Kosh was abandoned before the middle of the sixth millennium, and the present archaeological investigation takes up the thread in Tepe Sabz, which seems to have been founded just about the same time.

James A. Neely, who ran the excavation of the mound, took great care not to neglect even the remotest possiblity of recovering material bearing on the ancient plant economy. The result is an almost continuous series of samples through the two earliest periods, the Sabz and the Khazineh phases. Represented by a deposit of almost three metres, the following time span, designated the Mehmeh phase, is poorly illuminated by only three samples. When we come to the latest cultural period, the Bayat phase, we find the lower half well sprinkled with information while, like at Tepe Ali Kosh, the final habitation, accumulating almost a metre and a half of debris, yielded but a few samples, indicative of economic breakdown and collapse of social cohesion.

Tepe Sabz was founded by a foreign people, already equipped upon their arrival in Deh Luran with a radically different agricultural technique, a much wider choice of crop plants and, incidentally, weeds. By that time pottery was in abundant use.

They settled on the opposite side of the lake, some 12 km. west of Ali Kosh, in a tract that even today displays certain botanical traits indicating a high, obviously man-made soil salinity. Tamarisk form a quite copious growth over a large not particularly moist, flat area, and dense populations of Common peganum (*Peganum harmala*) cover open patches, interspersed with Camelthorn and, more moderately, Prosopis and a bushy Mullein (*Verbascum* sp.). In the direction towards the Mehmeh River, near the mound, a certain line, probably representing an ancient canal or river bed, separates the Tamarisk area from an open desertic plain, in which the most conspicuous features are widely dispersed Zizyphus and Caper. No Tamarisk at all, but here and there the trailing vines of the wild poisonous melon, the Colocynth (*Citrullus*) are encountered.

The newcomers did not decide the placement of their village with special reference to the lake, but reckoned with water on its way from the mountains. They brought the independence in settlement and field planning spelled out by artificial canals.

The use of controlled irrigation through a canal system, and the consequent extension of water surface and high evaporation rate, entail a progressive concentration of salts from the water into the soil. This fact is painfully conspicuous in the state of the plant material from Tepe Sabz. Although evidently the grain was no longer threshed by mortar and quern, and therefore should be much better preserved than the Ali Kosh material, its identification presents difficulties sometimes amounting to complete frustration.

The irrigation water came directly from calcareous mountains with considerable salt deposits and passed through country with solid veins of gypsum in the surface. Owing to the mineral-loaded groundwater, most carbonized plant objects are coated with a heavy gypseous and calcareous deposit, seriously restricting observation of morphological and anatomical details. The crystalline coating cannot be removed; in some cases even the surface tension of plain water is enough to split the carbonized body into atoms, a fact that undoubtedly has cost us great loss through the floating process, particularly in cereal grains that are the most susceptible of all. The use of hydrochloric or acetic acid develops internal pressure from the liberated carbon dioxide that also explodes the fragile object.

Even before the crystallization took effect, the plant material was in a delicate state, in that it appears from the carbonized debris that now more efficient fuel was used than the reed at Ali Kosh. Fragments of twigs of shrubs, especially of Tamarisk, abound among the grain, and even more substantial pieces of wood up to 2 cm. in diameter are met with. The higher temperature thus engendered in the hearth has left seeds, and especially cereal grains dropped into the fire, in a badly puffed and internally fissured state.

All these circumstances have made the plant material so different from that from Tepe Ali Kosh that a quantitative comparison is quite impossible. At Ali Kosh we knew that the particles salvaged by floating were all that the soil sample contained; at Tepe Sabz it is evident that much of the material was comminuted in floating after excavation, and disappeared through the sieve. Also, it appears that small leguminous seeds, Prosopis and certain other elements have survived rather well, while cereals and other grasses have suffered very badly and do not at all make up their original percentage of the sample such as deposited. They are also to a large extent indeterminable.

All attempts similar to those employed at Ali Kosh at reconstructing the original state of affairs by counting, microweighing and use of the slide rule, would bog down in complete loss of realism. Therefore it has not been done, and thus no analogous and commensurable plant table can be produced. All we can conscientiously do is to compare the various Ecological Groups of the Ali Kosh table, with the findings at Tepe Sabz, and in this way get a notion of the qualitative influence of irrigation in the same environment.

Opportunities have not permitted the Tepe Sabz material to be fully worked up in time for this publication. Therefore it was decided to include in the present account principally the information gained from the complete examination of the earliest phase of the occupation, the Sabz phase, and the plant remains recovered through the final 2.30 m., the last few centuries of the Bayat phase. We are, on this basis, able to follow the rise and fall of plant husbandry through the centuries by referring to sporadic observations of samples of intermediate stages.

As it happens, the earliest deposits in the Tepe Sabz sequence constitute an excellent signpost, both to the plant inventory of the whole Tepe Sabz occupation, as also to the place, or rather type of environment from which the emigrants set out.

As noted, the impurity of the water has proved a serious drawback as regards the identification of the carbonized material, but in another way it has furnished the most excellent and extraordinary documents we could wish for.

The very last days' work at Tepe Sabz revealed a pit dug into virgin soil, either in a house or the courtyard of a house. This is the oldest evidence for the fundamentally different exploitation of the ecological possibilities introduced by the newcomers. By floating the fill of the pit, a small amount of carbonized matter was recovered, even for Tepe Sabz in a pretty poor state of preservation. But the sediment left after floating proved to contain about two hundred fossilized plant bodies, isolated by straight washing through the sieve.

The pit was used for storage of plant food and probably became flooded rather soon. It contained almonds, linseed, seeds of Caper, some grasses and seeds of a cruciferous plant, besides rather large fragments of reed and several other plant remains too fragmentary for identification. These objects would have had no chance of survival over several millennia in the damp ground. However, because of the special quality of the water they have turned into calcareous-gypseous casts, revealing their original shape and size to a degree practically unseen in any other type of material. The actual mechanism of the pertrification cannot be accounted for in detail; some seeds are cast in their entirety, others only fragmentarily although it is clear that the whole object was there. In some cases even the outer tissues are reflected in the microstructure of the mineral, in others elements as heavy as almond shells have disappeared without trace. In general, it seems as if the operative constituent was the integument (seed coat) that is often semipermeable, and in this instance has acted as a oneway filter, retaining the minerals under a fluctuating condition of absorption and evaporation of groundwater.

This phenomenon of substitution of organic matter by mineral deposit is, of course, nothing unheard of, but it is the first time I have come across it on a scale like this in palaeoethnobotanical material. After all, geologically speaking, these fossils have been created on the instant.

Culturally, the most important of the contents are thirty-one whole or fragmentary linseeds. They are minutely cast, even the epidermal cells may be caught in the microscope. In two of them the reproduction is perfect, displaying all the traits typical of the species: the oblique, beak-like protrusion above the micropyle, the sharp edges and the dimensions in the fresh state. They prove to belong to the largest linseed found in irrigation agriculture prior to about 3000 B.C. Comparison is based on imprints in baked clay that may be supposed to correspond reasonably well with the dimensions of the seed in the fresh state (Table 5). The largest linseed imprints found in ancient, non-irrigated agriculture, in Halafian Brak and Arpachiyah in Iraq, are 3.84 to 4.03 mm. long, while ours vary from 4.67 to 4.83 mm. in length and from 2.25 to 2.67 mm. in width. This by itself proves that the Tepe Sabz people came from lands where irrigation was practiced; linseed must have been grown by this technique for a long time to have developed such an impressive size (Helbaek, 1959).

Practically all subsequent samples of this and the following phases contain carbonized remains of linseeds and pods, and some seeds from the middle of the Mehmeh phase are well enough preserved for the length to be ascertained. They vary from 3.33 to 3.58 mm., and the shrinkage on carbonization being something like 15 to 17 per cent it means that in the fresh state they were 4.00 to 4.25 mm. long. This is sensibly smaller than the originally introduced seeds, a fact that undoubtedly is related to increased salinity of the arable land.

The shell-less, drop-shaped almonds vary in length from 7.33 to 11.67 mm., in width from 5.17 to 6.67 mm. This corresponds to the dimensions of the fresh seeds of a wild almond, *Amygdalus spartioides,* a common shrub in mountains all over the Near East, and the small fruits are collected even today in the Zagros range and elsewhere and on sale in the bazar of many places. Thus I bought them myself in Dizful, a local market center, and collected them, in 1955, in northern Kurdistan. Small fragments of shells occur in some of the later samples, but only in a few instances is enough preserved for identification. The almonds found in the pit probably belonged to the immigrants' travel provisions.

As we saw in Ali Kosh, Caper fruits were exploited at all times, and the seeds from the pit may well be of local origin, so much the more as the shrub is common about Tepe Sabz. But they occur very rarely in the carbonized material; this could, however, be due to destruction in floating.

Four large, finely reproduced seeds belong to a cruciferous plant presumably introduced by the new people; it was not found among the Ali Kosh plants. For lack of comparative material it cannot be named, but it would seem to be a plant related to cress or Hoary cress (*Lepidium* or *Cardaria*).

Also the carbonized plant matter from the pit contained other items indicative of irrigation. One well-preserved grain and an internode of the hexaploid Bread wheat (*Triticum aestivum*), proving a tough spike axis, usher in a new era in wheat cultivation. This hybrid species appears in Iraq (Helbaek, 1964*a*) and Anatolia (Helbaek, 1964*b*, and n.d.) during the first half of the sixth millennium, and at Tepe Sabz it persists and prospers all the way up until salinity reached a critical level. In contrast to Einkorn and Emmer, its grain is loosely fitted within the husk and is much more easily threshed than the former two. Judging by axis fragments preserved in later phases, consisting of as many as four articulate internodes, the type of Bread wheat was unstable and quite diversiform, except that the ultra-short internode of the variety Club wheat (*T. compactum*) has not been observed.

It has been pointed out that the lentil introduced into the plain during the initial stages of the Ali Kosh and Mohammad Jaffar phases did not survive. Now we find a lentil on the bottom of the Sabz phase pit, the first among many occurring throughout the occupation of the site up to the time of deterioration. Some of the later seeds reach the quite opulent size of 4.17 mm., a diameter that is better than most examples of the subsequent two or three millennia. Most later prehistoric lentils in Antolia and Europe belonged to another, distinctly small-seeded race of a maximum diameter between 2.5 and 4 mm.

Another very useful, large-seeded legume, the Grass pea or Dwarf vetchling (*Lathyrus cicera* or *L. sativus*) appears in the earliest architectural level, but it never attained quite the same importance as the lentil. In the Sabz phase it is found in five consecutive 10-cm. levels within the zone D midden, but after that it only reappears in mid-Bayat phase levels. It belongs to the wild flora of the moister country of the upper plain and foothills, but it migrated widely with lentil and other domesticated legumes. It even appears in Switzerland with Neolithic pea (Helbaek, unpublished investigation), and in Pre-urban Rome among horsebean (Helbaek, 1956).

Although documented by innumerable spikelet fragments, Einkorn and Emmer do not take up any conspicuous position among the identified cereal grains. Maybe these wheats were finely ground for consumption, or perhaps their grains are more sensitive to the surface tension of water and thus have perished in floating. However this may be, the established number of spikelet fragments just from the Sabz phase exceeds that of all the phases of Tepe Ali Kosh together. At this junction it should be pointed out that here the spikelets are much less fragmented than in Tepe Ali Kosh, and that the number of particles represent an appreciably greater number of spikes. In almost all samples whole spikelet forks are present, consisting of the spikelet base with attached internode and the lower portions of the glumes. In the largest Tepe Sabz sample, one from the Bayat phase, not yet fully processed, several thousand forks and fragments may be anticipated. The proportional frequency within two dimensional ranges indicate that Einkorn was at least as important as Emmer, possibly more so. All this goes to prove that new threshing methods were introduced together with irrigation. It seems obvious, however, that the spikelets still went into the food; now at least they could be softened by proper cooking.

Twisted hulled barley grains appear with increasing frequency from the pit to the top of the mound. Although these lateral grains are still inferior in size, this means that the hulled, six-row form thrived under irrigation. Some internodes of the two-row, hulled barley with a tough axis demonstrate that this form was not yet extinct. A few grains and internodes of the wild barley suggest that the species persisted as a weed, but by and large brittle-spike barleys were from the beginning replaced by tough-axis, properly domesticated forms. (Plate 41).

Pondering the earliest appearance of certain definitely artifactual (domesticated) plants, it is conspicuous that the first half of the sixth millennium saw the emergence of such important and lasting additions to man's agricultural inventory as six-row, hulled barley, free-threshing, hexaploid wheat, and large-seeded lentil and flax. There seems to be no reasonable doubt that this coincidence stems from the inception and development of irrigation, the greatest ecological improvement man has ever achieved in the arid tracts, adjacent to the homelands of the wild cereals and other important food plants (Fig. 143). Inevitably the thought comes up that this also was the crucial period in the transition from simple hoeing to furrow-cutting by means of a hoe, gradually modified into the plough, drawn by man or animal. Only by furrowing can irrigation water be evenly and simultaneously distributed throughout a larger area.

Having now considered the first section of Table 3 (p. 391), the cultivated plants, we shall turn to the weed section, Ecological Group 2. Goat-face grass and Ryegrass are still of a certain importance, probably more or less of the same frequency as in the Bus Mordeh phase. But a new category has been added to the section: weed legumes. In Tepe Ali Kosh we saw that all the leguminous species belong to the ecological habitat of the site, while now the majority of the seeds are larger and belong to genera we did not previously encounter. They are natural inhabitants of the foothill country to the north, and they were spread as weeds in agriculture to the lower steppe and river plains.

The small types described above as being of the genera Trigonella, Milk-vetch and Medick (*Medicago radiata*) do still occur, but now only occasionally, except that a few seeds of the latter persist in most samples.

What we now find is somewhat larger seeds (1.30 to 2.50 mm. long) of two general types: one, the smaller, is blunt, oval-rounded, has a long radicle and the hilum near one end. This seed shape is characteristic of the genera *Trifolium* and *Melilotus* (Clover and Melilot). Many of these species are common field and fallow weeds, the latter in some areas a typical irrigation weed.

The other type is larger, oblong-reniform, with a shorter radicle and the hilum placed on the concave edge. That is the specific shape of seed in a great number of Medick species, represented by *Medicago hispida, M. rigidula, M. minima* and other common weeds.

There is no evidence that these seeds were collected with the all-pervading intensity evinced by the great number of steppe legumes in the Ali Kosh deposits; they only make up a modest proportion of the classified seeds, even though they obviously withstood the stresses of floating comparatively unmolested. Probably they were not collected at all, but were reaped together with the cereals, now that harvesting technique necessarily must have become more wholesale and effective. The following numbers may be quoted from the Sabz phase, as an expression of the proportional frequency: steppe legumes, 60; weed legumes, 396 seeds. And even the endemic steppe species may by now have adapted to irrigation conditions and have turned into weeds.

For the section Ecological Group 3, wild grasses is by now a somewhat doubtful designation. The number of items is not large, and a species like oat is probably no longer wild, but a weed, and thus unavoidable. Also the indeterminate grasses have become more important proportionally, but less obvious of classification. They seem to belong to a greater number of species, among which there is some reason to suspect Brome grass (*Bromus* sp.) and Medusa-head grass (*Taniaetherum crinitum*). They are, however, so fragmented that a proper analysis and identification is out of the question. Canary grass still persists, but in insignificant volume; it may easily have joined up with the weeds of the irrigated area.

Swamp plants are represented by only one species, the Seablite, (*Suaeda* sp.), presumably growing along the canals. That also is quite inconspicuous numerically, except in one of the Bayat samples where ten seeds were concentrated.

Ecological Group 6 has dwindled to the status of the fortuitous. We still note the Heliotrope, a small Vetch, Mallow and Plantain, but none of them appears in force. Thus Mallow, which in the Mohammad Jaffar phase occurred in a number of 462, and Plantain 800, are represented in the Sabz phase by ten and one specimens respectively. Incidentals include a few seeds of an unspecified Bedstraw, in shape and size corresponding to the European Marsh bedstraw, *Galium palustre*.

Prosopis is met with in almost all the samples from the Sabz phase storage pit upwards; not in such a heavy way as in the Mohammad Jaffar phase, but still frequent enough to be considered as having been collected intentionally.

Gromwell, suggested as a dye plant in the Bus Mordeh phase, occurs dispersedly with a low number throughout Tepe Sabz. Now its presence may be explained by the fact that it is a plant apt to appear along canal banks.

All the way up through the mound, bits and pieces of shells of fruits have been noticed. Mostly the fragments are too small for identification, but as mentioned above, almond was established for a few late samples. In one case it was possible to determine a fragment of a Pistachio that in the carbonized state had been approximately 6 mm. long. It may be observed that the easily recognizable fragments of the pits of Zizyphus still are conspicuous by their absence. It is feasible that more species could be identified eventually, but this will be a special commitment requiring a better collection of type samples than at present available.

TEPE MUSIYAN "E"

In Table 3, along with Tepe Sabz, is listed a small deposit of carbonized plant remains from Tepe Musiyan, operation "E," 480 to 530 cm. below surface. In 1963, Flannery reopened the old cut "E" made by the French in 1903, and reached undisturbed prehistoric debris beneath their pit at a depth of 480 cm. below the surface of the tell (and still many metres above the surface of the surrounding plain). These undisturbed levels dated to the Mehmeh phase (4500 to 4000 B.C.), and yielded two samples of seeds. The plant inventory discloses a situation just like that of the Mehmeh phase at Tepe Sabz: linseed, lentil and hexaploid wheat prove that irrigation was employed, and it is characteristic that all small leguminous seeds are of the introduced, not native species. Apart from this slight glimpse of corroborative evidence, Tepe Musiyan "E" does not add to the general picture.

This is not quite as far as development proceeded in ancient Deh Luran. Other communities succeeded Tepe Sabz, some founded already before its abandonment. But it was beyond the scope of the present investigation to elucidate the activities during the Uruk Period, the later, poorly-represented Sassanian Period and the brief renaissance of agriculture in Early Islamic times.

What is left now is to recapitulate the salient features of plant collecting and subsequent rational plant production as put forth in this fragmentary report. Also, to try to draw some general conclusions and to suggest possible solutions to the many problems raised by the excavated material itself.

In the following chapter an attempt will be made at concentrating the ideas about plant introduction, land use, and genetic evolution, in order to establish a basis, however tentative, for interpretation and discussion of future findings. Our complex of experiences in Deh Luran was the first of its kind, but it will not for long remain the only one.

COMPARATIVE CONCLUSIONS

It is, of course, not possible to describe with any degree of exactitude the topographical, hydrological and floristic details of a locality after the lapse of 9000 years. Left to itself, the terrain would have changed even if, as here presumed, the climatic conditions remained more or less stable. Exposed to man's exploitation, nothing would be untouched. Even primitive agriculture is apt to influence microbiology, soil structure, fauna and flora, and Deh Luran is an extreme example rather than an exception (Flannery, 1965).

It may be taken for granted that none of the grasses enumerated in Table 3 as cultivated or weed species, are indigenous in the steppe. Also considering their complete absence from the plant deposits of the whole of Tepe Ali Kosh, a span of at least 1500 years, the larger-seeded leguminous species described for Tepe Sabz and Tepe Musiyan, may safely be regarded as human introductions. If we do not find some particular plant in the cultural debris, it may not inevitably mean that it did not exist in the locality. But, if the species was customarily exploited by ancient peoples, then its absence in a period of intense plant collecting would seem suspicious.

The Tepe Ali Kosh people came from uplands where *Hordeum spontaneum* was indigenous and where it had been cultivated together with Emmer long enough for the latter to have changed into the typical domesticated species; in the barley, complex mutations had happened and a form, or species, was established which, by its incapacity of self-dispersal, must be classified as domesticated. The sterile lateral florets had become fertile and grain-bearing, the natural adhesion of the grain surface to the inner husk (palea) was lost, and, at some still indeterminate stage, the spike axis became tough. How long a time should be allotted for these changes to be accomplished cannot be suggested. A mutation happens overnight, but it may take centuries for a new species to stabilize.

A further qualification for the locale of emigration is the presence of Ryegrass and Goat-face grass, again pointing at the foothills or the higher intermontane valleys of, say, Kurdistan. Up there both the wild cereals and the two typical weed grasses are at home. On the other hand, there are so many more weed species which might be expected in the same composition, and which certainly would have been found in Tepe Ali Kosh had the migrating people been dependent on agriculture to a high degree. As it is, one rather visualizes herders-collectors coming in with a small bag of hand-picked agricultural products for seed, but plotting their existence on plant collecting more than cultivation of the land.

At their arrival they found what they needed: good pasturage and ample opportunities for seed collecting, water, generous availability of desirable game,[6] and an even shore area regularly flooded in the winter.

[6] See Chapter XIX, "The Animal Bones."

Table 4

EXTRAORDINARY FREQUENCY OF PROSOPIS IN CERTAIN SAMPLES OF PLANT REMAINS FROM MOHAMMAD JAFFAR PHASE LEVELS AT TEPE ALI KOSH

	Mohammad Jaffar "*a*" Samples No. 38, 40, 43		Mohammad Jaffar "*b*" Samples No. 39, 41, 42, 44-50	
	Items	Per Cent	Items	Per Cent
Ecological Group 1. Cultivated plants	275	(3.6)	3	(1.3)
Ecological Group 2. Introduced weeds	38	(0.5)	1	(0.4)
Ecological Group 3. Endemic grasses	1252	(15.9)	1	(0.4)
Ecological Group 4. Endemic legumes	4766	(60.4)	5	(2.1)
Ecological Group 5. Swamp plants	...	...	...	...
Ecological Group 6. Other wild plants	1352	(17.2)	7	(2.9)
Ecological Group 7. Caper	7	(0.1)	...	...
Ecological Group 7. Prosopis	174	(2.2)	222	(92.9)
Totals	7864		239	

While it is possible to account for the absence in Tepe Ali Kosh of certain species as followers of irrigation, the non-occurrence of Zizyphus and the peculiar pattern in which Prosopis appears, call for special attention. In deliberating the ancient ecology of the steppe these features are not insignificant.

Zizyphus is one of the most conspicuous absentees from the plant table. On higher land around the valley the species occurs as quite large trees, occasionally in wide-spread, forest-like formation. On the plain it is represented by widely dispersed, shrublike individuals, branching from the ground up, and hardly ever exceeding a height of 2m.[7] The small fruits are eaten by the people in the winter. They were also eaten by Neolithic peoples elsewhere in the general area (Khorramabad). But we do not find the slightest trace of them in Tepe Ali Kosh or Tepe Sabz. Inevitably the suggestion presents itself that Zizyphus did not grow in Deh Luran during these early times, and that it only intruded from the surrounding heights at a time when soil texture, groundwater level and other ecological factors had changed in some particular direction. The Deh Luran steppe must still be described as its ecological border zone.

From a food point of view another shrub, Prosopis, has been discussed in detail in a previous chapter. In order to emphasize its suspiciously uneven distribution in the plant deposits, Table 4 is inserted here to show its frequency at the various times.

The first two hundred years, a period of intense plant collecting, Prosopis does not appear at all. Almost a metre of cultural debris had accumulated before we come across a sample containing three seeds. After a long interval, presumably about five hundred years, another sample, well into the predominantly agricultural Ali Kosh phase, yields another three seeds. Some hundred years after that, but still long before the Ali Kosh phase culture changes, we run into a continuous series of

[7] At present Zizyphus does not seem to be sought for fuel in Deh Luran. I found only one mishandled individual on my excursions in the valley. The shrub is so fiercely prickly that the Tamarisk, abundantly available, is preferred for practical reasons; the local nomads were seen collecting it for fuel.

occurrences, the number of seeds increasing steadily as time passes, and with no break at the transition to the Mohammad Jaffar phase. In fact, the seeds increase in frequency as long as we have evidence of vegetable food from the mound (0.90 m. from the top), the latest samples, as previously noted, consisting of practically nothing else.

How can this be interpreted? A number of answers might be suggested, none of them entirely satisfactory, but at least one seems worth putting up for discussion.

The obvious explanation is, of course, that the plant was not at all available when the eagerly plant-collecting Bus Mordeh tribe came to their new home. It may be admitted at once that I subscribe to this view, but also that I am prepared to see it vigorously contested. However, no valid material evidence can be obtained to prove the detailed distribution of plants so long ago, particularly not of species which profited greatly by agricultural activities.

In any case, if originally not available, Prosopis must have been introduced by strangers coming from areas where it was naturally distributed or already introduced as a weed. Would this also go for Kurdistan? We have no means of knowing. It is one of the most tenacious weeds even in modern, non-mechanized agriculture in the climatic zone with which we are concerned, also in the much moister uplands. Thus it is difficult to determine how far its occurrence at any specific time and place is natural or caused by man's mixing-up activities.

However, the sample in which the first Prosopis seeds occur, coming from about 0.80 above virgin soil, is unique in other ways, too. It contains the first and only seeds of mallow in the Bus Mordeh phase and, more significant, it comprises one of the three widely spaced occurrences of linseed during that phase. That flax was introduced by visiting traders from mountainous environment may be considered beyond question.

Half a millennium later, the second occurrence of three Prosopis seeds is noted, this coming from a medium-rich Ali Kosh phase sample, although without corroborative evidence for outside influence. Still, it may have been brought into the valley as a traveller's pocket provision.

Centuries passed before it appeared again. Only after the accumulation of four metres of cultural debris in the mound, do the seeds come into the picture with such frequency and consistency as to cut off the discussion of their origin. Now the plant is plainly common in the steppe, in cultivated and fallow areas. From there it would have spread with goat droppings all over the pasturage and thus been abundantly available for collecting. Straddling the line of demarcation between the Ali Kosh and Mohammad Jaffar phases, it does not afford a basis for the concept

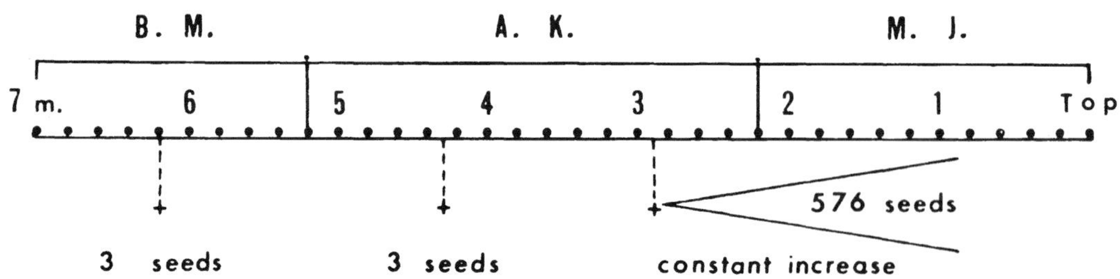

Fig. 142. Distribution of occurrences of *Prosopis* seeds in ash deposits at Tepe Ali Kosh. Letters indicate cultural phases (Bus Mordeh, Ali Kosh, and Mohammad Jaffar).

that its exploitation was initiated by collecting-minded newcomers; it was in full use while agriculture was still, as far as we can see, in a healthy state.

So, in concluding, it is propounded that Prosopis is another plant not indigenous in the steppe, repeatedly introduced in vain from abroad, but not taking root because the ecological circumstances were not yet propitious. As time passed and hydrological, edaphic and other conditions were corrupted by man's influence, the species moved in and became one of the most frequent and important plants of the valley.

The leguminous weed, Caterpillar *(Scorpiurus sulcata)* furnishes a parallel example. Its fairly large and very characteristic seeds do not at any time appear in our series, covering more than three millennia. In our day it is one of the most obnoxious weeds in the Deh Luran field and fallow, as indeed over huge stretches of the Near East. It must have been dragged into our valley at a later occasion, possibly as late as Parthian or Sassanian times when irrigation agriculture was brought to a high pitch of efficiency in the province (Adams, 1962).

In a terrain like Deh Luran, some salinity is naturally inevitable; undrained catchment depressions would contract excess minerals and, in spite of their more than average humidity would be useless for agriculture, while offering favourable spring grazing. The shore belt, on the other hand, would be washed out by run-off and by annual floods which kept the soil salinity at a level low enough for agriculture to be profitable. This situation seems to be illustrated by the plant table (Table 3).

During the millennium and a half of the duration of Tepe Ali Kosh, the growing-in and silting-up of the lake progressed so far that, in the end, the village was too far from the cultivatable belt. And probably even without systematic irrigation, the agricultural activities had caused a topographical transformation serious enough to favour increasing salt concentration and leaching in the original arable zone. The somewhat imponderable factor of tectonic movements in the whole of the Mesopotamian basin must also be taken into account when considering the drying-up of the lake and possible changes in the drainage regime of the valley. Even a local movement far away might affect the drainage datum of the rivers on which, ultimately, the Deh Luran agriculture depended.

While controlled canal irrigation was a decisive step forward in arid zone agriculture, it was by no means a basic invention. It was a sophisticated stage of evolution of the fundamental qualification for moving plant husbandry out of the natural habitat region, the higher rainfall zone. Natural, uncontrolled flooding of rivers and lakes would have been an absolute requirement for the earliest farmers who moved to the low steppe country. Eventually they would have taken to experimenting with blocking the retreating flood water in order to gain another week or two of humid soil conditions after the natural shrinkage of the lake or river in the spring. Every step in this direction improved the crop outlook, but it also contained the evil germ of land destruction which presently became the hallmark of the whole Mesopotamian basin and Deh Luran of today (Jacobsen and Adams, 1958).

As conditions deteriorated within the agricultural enclave of Tepe Ali Kosh, crops fell off. The wheats weakened and naked barley suffered enough not to show in our plant table for the Mohammad Jaffar phase. Hulled barley was the only cereal that stood up to the hardships, and during this period the new mutant, the six-row, hulled form, makes its first appearance. However, it does not seem to have stabilized and endured the general neglect which must have characterized the time. Its prolific potentialities are not very noticeable in the early mutant, the lateral grains of which are most inconspicuous of size. Thus its selection was probably missed by the Mohammad Jaffar people.

Straying about the plain looking for potsherds, flints, or plants, one is impressed by the unending and confusing pattern of traces of watercourses. Shallow, narrow ditches evidently of more recent origin overlie faint, but persistent depressions obviously denoting long disused watercourses, canals, or rivers. At the foot of Tepe Sabz a small river or canal still carries enough water in the rainy season to indicate that here, a long time ago, the volume and current of water was enough to account for considerable erosion of the south flank of the mound. However, it would be an illusion to connect any present-day surface trace of watercourses with the motives for the first settlers in choosing the site of Tepe Sabz for their future home. The land surface of those days is now 3 m. below the present valley floor and, during the intervening ages, horizontal erosion would have changed the pattern of rivers and canals as the land silted up. Further, new irrigation systems have repeatedly been laid out by succeeding peoples, probably intermittently up to Early Islamic times.

However the landscape looked 7500 years ago, it is a fair assumption that Tepe Sabz was passed by a natural perennial watercourse at a not too great distance. The settlers would not have started with digging a canal from the Mehmeh River at its present course, several kilometres away. There could have been a stream coming from the mountains near the present village of Deh Luran, running into the Mehmeh, possibly by way of the lake. On such a feeder the canal system must have been based.

It was suggested above that eventually the peoples of Tepe Ali Kosh exercised some primitive influence upon the natural water resources. They were not, however, able to suit their needs at will; they were bound by the immediate meteorological circumstances. They had to obstruct the retreat of the flood when it was at a suitable height, whenever that might be during the late winter.

Now, with a calculated irrigation system behind them, the Tepe Sabz farmers were free to block their watercourse at the exact place that suited their purpose. They could divert and distribute the water through the canals over the area they had levelled off and prepared; and they could do it at the time most useful to the crops. Also, it was now feasible to repeat the process and control its volume by leading off excess water, thus delaying the dangerous build-up of salinity in the arable. So, even though the irrigation water, as shown by our experience with the plant remains, was far from pure, the water control itself meant an immense advantage above the simple exploitation of restricted inundation.

If the present-day traces of irrigation systems around Tepe Sabz must be regarded as unrelated to the foundation of the village, what, then, is the evidence upon which the postulate is based, that the founders employed this novel technique?

We need not, in fact, look beyond the plant table to find proof of significant changes in crop choice, indisputably pointing at an intensification of human mastery of growth conditions, an advance that can only be ascribed to control of water supply.

It is considered probable that the Mohammad Jaffar phase of Tepe Ali Kosh petered out about the same time as the Sabz tribe moved into the valley. If so, the then existing environmental factors were the same for both tribes. To the ancient inhabitants these factors spelled ruin, whereas to the newcomers they meant a promising outlook. In other words, the difference was a matter of exploitation of opportunities, a matter of combining the natural prerequisites in different ways. And the two ecological factors which were recombined were water and temperature.

In the uplands rainfall is more generous and protracted in the late spring and temperatures are lower. Thus the ripening of the crops takes place in a not too long period of severe drought. In the low steppe, on the other hand, rain is practically non-existent in May and temperatures rise steeply. This combination causes forced ripening with attendant decrease in grain weight, withering of less well established plants and other adverse effects - and certain species cannot at all be grown. If water supply can be kept up while the temperature rises, an important improvement is gained in growth condition, a higher utilization of the fertility of the alluvium, reflected in crop density, quality of grain and seeds, and in various biological opportunities not furnished by the natural balance between humidity and temperature.

Without controlled irrigation it is not possible to make up for failing precipitation during the winter - a misfortune that may hit these low, arid tracts as often as every four to six years. Nor is it feasible to extend the period of humid soil conditions into the hot late spring. Both these unfortunate situations can be counteracted artificially if water is at hand, and if their technical skill enables the farmers to distribute it according to the best interests of the various crop species.

That is what the Sabz people knew before they left their previous home. This knowledge is reflected in their cultivated plants, species which were either not grown in Deh Luran previous to their arrival, or which had appeared sporadically and disappeared again for lack of propitious growth conditions.

Let us consider a few examples and try to define their biological requirements, unattainable under the old agricultural practices, but complied with by the new methods of land use - or rather, water use.

The seeds of the wild progenitor (*Linum bienne*) of the domesticated flax or linseed (*L. usitatissimum*), are very small; in Iraqi Kurdistan they vary from 2.4 to 2.7 mm. in length. Judging by the fragments of seeds and pods of flax found at Tepe Ali Kosh, this is probably the species that, unsuccessfully, was introduced from its natural habitat in the higher rainfall zone.

Wild flax undoubtedly belongs to the group of plants that were collected for their oleaginous seeds. It became domesticated in the uplands, and a conspicuous improvement in seed size is noticeable already in the earliest known finds, coming from the early fifth millennium sites in the Habur area in the northwestern Iraq. After the transplantation of flax to the hot lowlands, however, its seeds move into a much superior dimensional bracket. According to modern manuals on flax cultivation, the plant cannot be grown in the hot alluvia of the Near East without careful irrigation (Guest, 1930:5-6; Nazif, 1958:8-10). This must, of course, also have applied in ancient times.

Table 5, below, is a modified extract from the most recent monograph on the phylogeny and cultural history of flax (Helbaek, 1959). It comprises only such items as may be regarded as reasonably commensurable, i.e. imprints in baked clay, fossil replicas and actual seeds from permanently waterlogged localities. All these may be regarded as reflecting the size of the fresh seeds. Carbonized and dried items are not employed because their original size cannot be calculated with confidence.

As it appears from the table, the maximum seed length remained the same as long as the domesticated plant was grown without irrigation, whether in the Iraqi foothills at Brak, 5000 B.C., or at Windmill Hill in southern England, about 3000 B.C. (Helbaek, 1952). It never exceeds 4 mm.

Table 5

DEVELOPMENT OF LINSEED IN DIFFERENT HYDROLOGICAL CONDITIONS

RAINFALL			IRRIGATION	
length of seed (mm.)		AGE B.C.	*length of seed* (mm.)	
		5500 - 5000	4.67; 4.83:	Tepe Sabz
Arpachiya Brak	3.84 4.03	5000 - 4500		
		4500 - 4000	4.39 4.76	Ur Hama
		4000 - 3500		
Brak	4.03	3500 - 3000		
		3000 - 2500	4.94	Hama
		2500 - 2000		
Switzerland England Holland Scotland Denmark Eire	3.11-4.03	2000 - 1500	4.76	Khafajah
		1500 - 1000		
		1000 - 500		

In contrast to this, all linseed coming from localities where effective agriculture was possible only by means of irrigation, are consistently much larger.

The range of dimensions is headed by an imprint from Hama on the Orontes, of the Jemdet Nasr Period. But our much older seeds from Tepe Sabz, indeed one of the earliest examples of domesticated linseeds as yet reported, compete very favourably with it. Thus, in entering them into the table, there is no possible doubt as to the group in which they belong. Wherever they were grown, they came from irrigated land. Being present in the very base stratum of the settlement, the Tepe Sabz seeds were either grown locally in the first year or two, or they were brought in from another irrigation area as the basic seed stock of the newcomers.

A few linseeds were found in the grain deposits at Tell es-Sawwan, of approximately the same age (Helbaek, 1964*a*). Since they are carbonized their exact original size cannot be stated, but one of them is 4 mm. long. This means that in the fresh state it must have been at least 4.5 to 4.6 mm.

Also the small plant deposit excavated at Tepe Musiyan "E," belonging to the Mehmeh Phase, contained several linseeds, although they were too badly damaged for estimates of their lengths to be made. The fragments are, however, much too large to be referred to the wild species, Pale flax.

By improved technique, irrigation farming eventually succeeded in producing considerably larger seeds. In the first millennium B.C. Iraq and Egypt we find linseeds exceeding 6 mm. (Helbaek, 1959). It may thus be concluded that it was the higher temperatures in the low alluvia combined with artificial, carefully timed watering, that made possible the development and selection of flax races bearing seeds of increasing size.

Lentil affords another, quite analogous instance. In two samples, one of the Ali Kosh phase, the other of the Mohammad Jaffar phase, 1.70 m. and hundreds of years apart, we encounter an isolated seed of this plant. To the primitive farmers it must have been most attractive, and they certainly would have jumped to its cultivation had it been possible. These large seeds contain very much protein and would have made up for a lot of time-consuming collecting of the tiny wild legumes of the steppe. But they were unable to keep them alive. The lentil belongs to the higher rainfall zone and cannot endure the fiercely hot, rainless spring in Deh Luran. So the Ali Kosh site was abandoned before the cultivation of this leguminous species succeeded.

One seed of lentil was found together with the linseeds in the storage pit in zone D of Tepe Sabz, and a sprinkling of the species characterizes the whole series of samples throughout that mound, as also the samples from Tepe Musiyan. It belonged to the staple crops of these peoples. Again, only one explanation for its persistence is possible: it was carried through the desiccation period in the spring by irrigation.

That the plant thrived during the occupation of Tepe Sabz is proved by the size of the seeds, up to 4.2 mm., which is much more than the earliest known seeds of the species. Lentils from Aceramic Haçilar, of about 7000 B.C., vary from 2.5 to 2.9 mm. in diameter (Helbaek, 1963).

The diagram, Fig. 143, is an attempt at concentrating the conclusions based on identifications and datings of the early finds of different forms of barley at present available. In its actual form, the diagram must, of course, be taken with a certain reserve. The finds are few, and there are still too many unknown factors of evolutionary stages and their chronological cross roads for the development to be expressed confidently in black and white. But in principle it represents what for the time being may be considered the most reasonable genetical and chronological schema. While I am convinced that *Hordeum spontaneum* is the sole progenitor of all forms of domesticated barley, the digression from the main hereditary line of the naked six-row barley is probably more complicated than here shown. Several mutations and subsequent spontaneous selection may well be involved in the formation of naked barley. Thus the diagram expresses what we see, but possibly not all that actually happened.

The dotted lines represent the condition of brittle axis; how long this continued cannot be determined and the duration would not have been the same everywhere. The evidence suggests that this condition in naked barley was on its way out already about 7000 B.C., while we have no proof of a tough axis in hulled barley until some time, probably late, in the seventh millenium. Thus the suggested transitional period from 7000 to 6000 B.C. is somewhat arbitrary.

The three early finds, put jointly at 7000 B.C. do, in fact, cover a period of several hundred years, both before and after that date. In the same way, the three later finds are considered to stretch from about 5800 B.C. to slightly after the middle of the millennium. Mohammad Jaffar and Bus Mordeh are the latest and earliest phases respectively of Tepe Ali Kosh (A.K.).

In spite of a certain divergence of view among modern geneticists, it is widely accepted that the physiological qualifications for the concepts expressed in the diagram are, in reality, proved through practical hybridization experiments and cytological studies.

As we have seen, the one and only occurrence of six-row, hulled barley in the Mohammad Jaffar phase was agriculturally abortive; it did not lead to selection and cultivation of the species—or form. Now,

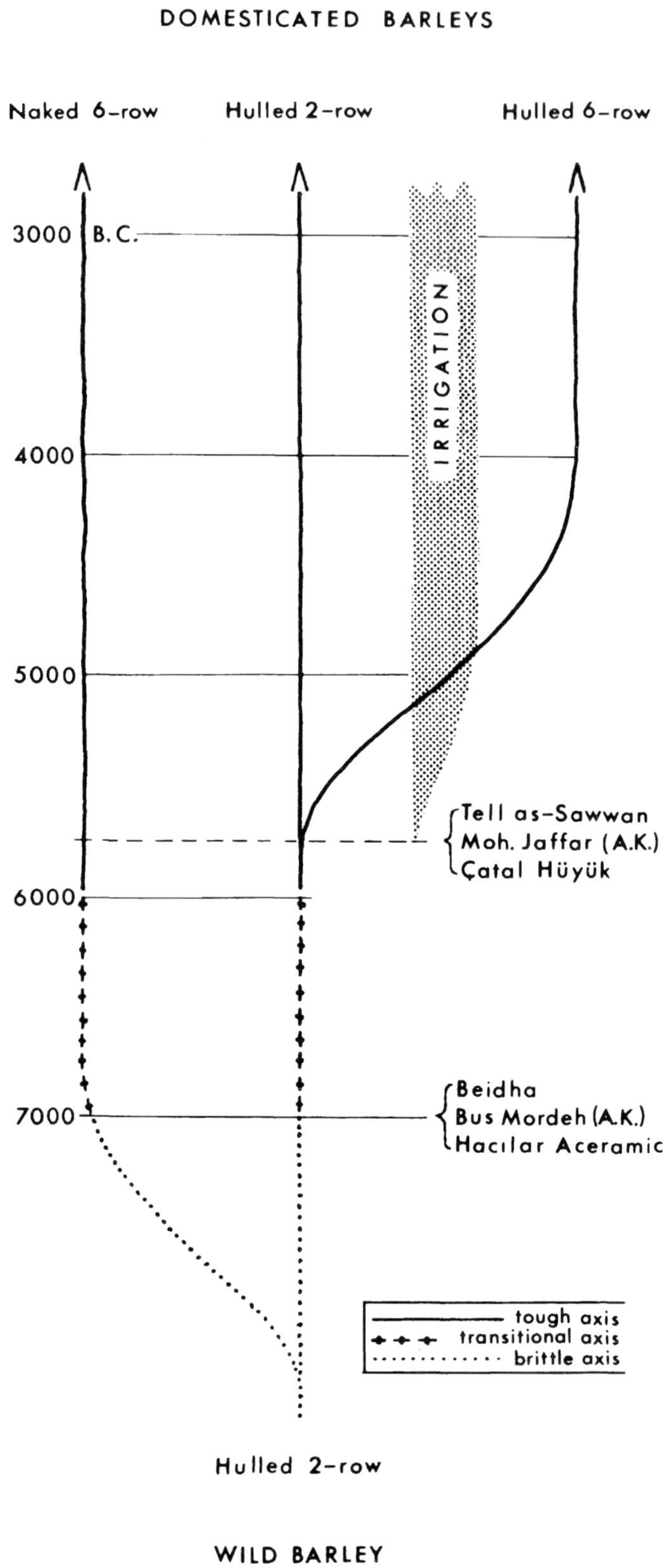

Fig. 143. The evolution of domesticated barley.

Inserted in proof: Further study of the rather few hulled barley grains from Çatal Hüyük makes it doubtful whether any grain is genuinely twisted, i.e. if the six-row, hulled variety did in fact exist there at the stated time.

scanning the barley grains from Tepe Sabz, the six-row, hulled form appears from the very beginning. Not in great numbers, but persistently in sample after sample, witnessed both by twisted grains and the typical internodes. During the successive phases its importance increased steadily, by the middle of the Bayat phase, some 4500 B.C., probably outweighing the two other forms. The lateral grains are still sensibly smaller than the median ones, and the internodes prove the spike to have been narrow and lax with a tough axis.

It is not unreasonable to suppose that a six-row mutant always has appeared spontaneously in wild barley populations, but because of its clumsy triplet it has been unable to stand up to competition from the two-row *Hordeum spontaneum*. Although it would also have occurred in the mountains in fields of cultivated barley of early ages, it was, as far as we know, never selected for special attention, and thus suppressed environmentally.

But as soon as we encounter plant finds in lowland regions where irrigation may be presumed to have been practised, the six-row, hulled barley begins to appear. At Tell es-Sawwan there is one twisted specimen among 180 grains of hulled barley, and at late sixth millennium Haçilar a deposit of some 3400 hulled grains contained 22 twisted examples. The latter proportion shows that by then about 1 per cent of the hulled barley spikes were six-row.

Judging by these instances it seems that the six-row, hulled form required a higher water supply, a need that could only be complied with when irrigation was introduced. This impression is supported by the fact that later on, in the fourth and subsequent millennia, all barley so far established for the irrigated Mesopotamian and Egyptian river basins, was the six-row, hulled form (Helbaek, 1960). One reason for this phenomenon may be suggested—for all it is worth.

Until otherwise demonstrated, it may be taken for granted that the lateral, grain-bearing florets in the fresh mutant were awned. Two-row barley having only awns on the median florets, this means that a six-row spike had three times as many awns as a two-row one with the same number of internodes.

The physiological function of the awn is that of a transpiration organ. Its loose interior tissue in connection with the strongly developed veins and the densely distributed stomata (respiration cells), makes it well adapted to dealing with a heavy transpiration flow, as also to step up the transportation of nourishing matter to the grain. It has been shown that barley spikes with the awns cut off, pass only 20 to 25 per cent of the water compared with spikes with the awns intact (Smith, 1951; Nilan, 1964:120-21). If thus a six-row barley spike evaporates more than a two-row one, it is logical to conclude that the plant needs a more generous water supply. This could be the significance of late, artificial watering under severe evapotranspiration conditions.

Why the same should not apply to the naked form is difficult to say, but it obviously did not. As far as our present experience goes, it thrived from the earliest times in the moist uplands, on the low steppe without irrigation, and in irrigation agriculture. This is all that can be inferred from the material at present available. Naked barley - presumably always six-row - occurs at Aceramic Beidha (Helbaek, 1966*b*) and Haçilar (Helbaek, n.d.) about 1000 m. above sea level, also without irrigation; at Çatal Hüyük (Helbaek, 1964*b*) at 1000 m. and at Tell es-Sawwan (Helbaek, 1964*a*) at, say, 50 m. above the sea, under some form of controlled irrigation conditions. And now at Tepe Sabz on the low steppe, irrigated. The quality rather than the quantity of water seems to be the crucial factor to the prosperity of naked barley. It disappeared from the plant list for the Mohammad Jaffar phase, and at the end of the Bayat phase it also became conspicuously scarce at Tepe Sabz. The large city states of later Mesopotamia did not know the naked form, nor has it ever been demonstrated - although often enough claimed - for Egypt. Probably everywhere because salinity had reached a level with which the plant was unable to cope. In this respect the hulled form proved quite otherwise hardy.

One is disposed to consider unconventional biological behaviour in cultivated plants as results of human interference. This may sometimes be the case, but as often as not the consequence of man's activities is secondary. Mutation and hybridization happen in nature, but usually the products are unnoticed and, if the immediate ecological circumstances do not favour the mutant or hybrid, it will quietly disappear. If, on the other hand, the biological process takes place in a cultivated crop kept under constant observation, human selection and special care may give rise to useful agricultural novelties.

The hexaploid, free-threshing wheat that, here in Deh Luran, we meet for the first time at Tepe Sabz, is a hybrid between Emmer and one or more species of Goat-face grass (*Aegilops squarrosa* and *A. speltoides* are suggested) (Peterson, 1965). The cross pollination between these species, and subsequent other processes such as gene mutation, recombination and chromosome doubling, caused a product to emerge that is of remarkable genetical complexity. The hybridization may have happened anywhere within the common area of distribution of the parent species and at any time, also long before agriculture was thought of.

But no free-threshing wheat has ever been found in natural stations or in very early cultural contexts. We find its first traces in cultures contemporaneous with those that yield the first hulled, six-row barley and the first large-seeded flax. As argued above, the common denominator for the success of these and other species seems to be the introduction of controlled irrigation.

In the wild state a free-threshing wheat would be predestined to extinction because of lacking dispersal power. In early dry-farming it would presumably have fallen victim to the same adversity as suggested for the hulled, six-row barley: desiccation in the late stages of ripening.

With the advent of irrigation, the last mentioned inadequacy was neutralized. In the event of the suggested Goat-face grasses having been introduced in the arid lowlands as weeds in the Emmer crop, irrigation would have transformed the whole situation. Augmented crop density in the fertile and properly watered fields occasioned an increased mutation and hybridization incidence and enabled some hybrids to survive and make themselves conspicuous, even if the weed partners proved unable to endure irrigation for very long. With this larger scope for selection, the farmer might pick out any strange-looking spikes, propagate them under special supervision and eventually discover their advantages: they were much more easily threshed, and their grain was in certain ways of different cooking qualities.

This, in rough and hypothetical outline, may be how the free-threshing wheat was enlisted in the ranks of domesticated plants.

At Tepe Sabz, as at the approximately contemporaneous sites of Catal Hüyük and late Haçilar, we find evidence of a primitive, ancestral type of hexaploid, free-threshing wheat. As the internodes and other details vary rather much in all three finds, both in respect of length and sturdiness, it is not possible to refer this wheat to any of the three main varieties recognized today, namely, *Triticum vulgare, T. compactum,* and *T. sphaerococcum.* For convenience the hybrid species will therefore be referred to under the general name Bread wheat, *Triticum aestivum.* It should, however, be noted that no present-day form of *T. aestivum* corresponds in structural detail to the ancient forms established for the first time in the three abovementioned sixth-millennium finds. Here we are dealing with a transitional and intermediate series (Helbaek, 1966*c*).

The ancient wheat is determined in a general way by its grain shape that corresponds to *T. aestivum* alone. It is shorter, wider and flatter than the grains of any other group of wheat. Details of spikelets, however, permit the definition of certain transitional features, suggesting the structural and anatomical evolution from the Emmer spike to that of the free-threshing species.

In the diagram, Fig. 140, an attempt is made to show what happened by the hybridization, how the new gene combination affected the structure of the Emmer spike.

Even in domesticated Emmer, the glume junction is extremely tough and the spike axis is still semibrittle; on threshing the spike falls to pieces consisting of the grain pair still in the grip of the glumes. Further measures are necessary to free the grains from their husks.

In the hybrid, the axis became tough and articulate, while the glume junction turned fragile and brittle. Moderate threshing broke off the glumes and the grains were released, at the same time shedding their inner husks. This labour-saving development is one of the reasons why Emmer today is in the process of extinction.

However, it took a long time and many cultural changes for Bread wheat to gain supremacy in the family. At this writing, the existence of the ancestral form of the species can be proved only for four ancient communities: Tell es-Sawwan is maybe the earliest, dated to 5800 to 5600 B.C. Contemporaneous or close at its heels are Çatal Hüyük and Tepe Sabz, roughly of the middle of the sixth millennium; finally Late Neolithic Haçilar, slightly later. Thus the finds are restricted within some two or three centuries. And one conspicuous qualification is common to all of them: the four settlements were placed on the banks of perennial watercourses easily exploitable in canal construction, all situated in areas of very severe spring temperatures. That the Sabz river has disappeared in the meantime does not influence this definition; its one-time existence is a logical prerequisite to the plant finds.

The further fate of Bread wheat is only imperfectly known. It appeared but briefly and sporadically in the cultures of the river basins of Egypt and Mesopotamia and, as far as known, not at all in their culmination period in the third and second millennia. During those times there is indication of its cultivation in the Near East in mountainous environment - and especially in Europe.

The known circumstances lead to the conclusion that the fixation of Bread wheat as a definite species is attributable to irrigation, but that eventually increasing salinity put an end to the well-being of the early forms in their original area of emergence. In the meantime, through its complex genetical constitution, Bread wheat - in our general sense - has developed a multitude of varieties and races which succeed in highly differing environment.

Many more details could be picked out that would underline the difference between the early and the later human economy in Deh Luran, but, for the time being, these few examples will have to suffice.

The initial pattern of existence of the Bus Mordeh tribe demonstrates that these people came from uplands with only faintly developed agricultural attitudes; but with a long tradition of plant collecting behind them, principally linking them up with their forefathers of remote Palaeolithic times.

With equal distinctness, the assemblage of domesticated plants and their attendant weeds show that the Sabz tribe came from arid lowlands, made agriculturally manageable by controlled utilization of perennial water resources. The evolutionary stage of some of the introduced domesticates prove that the land from where they came, had been under irrigation for a long time, maybe for centuries.

Accepting the estimated dates for the Anatolian, Mesopotamian, and Deh Luran settlements here discussed, it seems justifiable to suggest that controlled irrigation was initiated in many places about or not long after 6000 B.C. From this it may be inferred, that such modern-type cereals as six-row hulled barley and free-threshing hexaploid wheat need not have spread by cultural diffusion, but may have emerged independently in many widely-spaced areas in consequence of the artificial hydrological regime. The natural qualifications for their metamorphosis were present almost everywhere in the Near East.

The place whence the Sabz tribe brought their plants need not be sought far away. They may have come from the western side of the Jebel Hamrin, or any other place in lower Mesopotamia. At present too few finds and plant analyses are at hand on which to base surmises of this kind, but current and future investigation of the alluvial aprons along the Zagros range, and in the river basin itself, will eventually bring us closer to a definite answer.

Beside a general extension in knowledge of early human economy and social organization, the Deh Luran investigation has served to emphasize some fundamental principles in the scholarly approach to the problems concerned with the history of man. The enterprise is a classical example of the value of following up the cultural development within a confined, ecologically uniform area over as long a time span as possible. All aspects were included in the enquiry and, for one thing, the gains in palaeoethnobotanical knowledge from this comparatively limited undertaking, are unique and out of all proportion to the negligible volume of plant material recovered.

Parallel cultural development may take place in widely-spaced areas, but at different times; simultaneous evolution may take distinctly different courses in neighbouring districts because of diverging ecological conditions. Only within one uniform ecological habitat is it possible to distinguish between the undercurrents of environmental and cultural qualifications for what happened and understand why events took the course they did.

The Deh Luran material has told the story of advances in plant economy within this small locality in south-western Iran; but it has also served to tie together into an intelligible pattern numerous isolated, fortuitous findings from all over the Near East, hitherto without a definable place in the chain of comprehension.

REFERENCES

Adams, Robert Mc.
1962 Agriculture and Urban Life in Early Southwestern Iran. Science, Vol. 136, No. 3511, pp. 109-22.

Childe, V. Gordon
1939 Man Makes Himself. (1936). Mentor Books, pp. 59-86.

Earle, F.R.; and Jones, Quentin
1962 Analysis of Seed Samples from 113 Plant Families. Economic Botany, Vol. 16, (4), New York. pp. 221-50.

Flannery, Kent V.
1965 The Ecology of Early Food Production in Mesopotamia. Science, Vol. 147, No. 3607, pp. 1247-56.

Gremliza, F. G. L.
1962 Ecology of Endemic Diseases in the Dez Irrigation Pilot Area; a Report to Khuzistan Water and Power and Plan Organization, Government of Iran. New York, Development and Resources Corporation.

Guest, E.
1930 The Cultivation and Marketing of Linseed. Bull. No. 21, Dept. of Agriculture, Government Press, Baghdad.
1933 Notes on Plants and Plant Products with their Colloquial Names in Iraq. Bull. No. 37, Dept. of Agriculture, Government Press, Baghdad.

Helbaek, Hans
1950 Botanical Study of the Stomach Contents of the Tollund Man. Aarboger, 1950, pp. 311-41.
1951 Seeds of Weeds as Food in the Pre-Roman Iron Age. Kuml, 1951, pp. 65-74.
1952 Early Crops in Southern England, Proc. Prehist. Soc., Vol. 18. London. pp. 194-233.
1954 Prehistoric Food Plants and Weeds in Denmark. Danmarks Geologiske Undersøgelse, Vol. II R, 80, Copenhagen. pp. 250-61.
1955 The Botany of the Vallhagar Iron Age Field. In Stenberger, M. *et al.*: Vallhagar, a Migration Period Site on Gotland, Sweden. Munksgaard, Copenhagen, pp. 653-99.
1956 Vegetables in the Funeral Meals of Pre-Urban Rome. *In* Gjerstad, E., Early Rome, Vol. 2. Acta Inst. Rom. Regni Sueciae, Ser 4°, 17 (2). pp. 287-94.
1958 The Last Meal of the Grauballe Man: an Analysis of the Food Remains in the Stomach. Kuml, 1958, Aarhus, pp. 83-116.
1959 Notes on the Evolution and History of *Linum*. Kuml, 1959, Aarhus. pp. 103-29.
1960 Ecological Effects of Irrigation in Ancient Mesopotamia. Iraq, Vol. 22, London. pp. 186-96.
1963 Late Cypriote Vegetable Diet at Apliki. Acta Inst. Athen. Regni Sueciae, Ser. 4°, Vol. 8, Lund, pp. 171-86.
1964*a* Early Hassunan Vegetable Food at Tell as-Sawwan near Samarra. Sumer 20, Baghdad. pp. 45-48.
1964*b* First Impressions of the Catal Hüyük Plant Husbandry. Anatolian Studies 14. London. pp. 121-23.
1966*a* The Plant Remains from Nimrud. *In* M. E. L. Mallowan, Nimrud and its Remains, Vol. 2. Collins, London. pp. 613-20.
1966*b* Pre-Pottery Neolithic Farming at Beidha. *In* Kirkbride, D., Five Seasons at the Pre-Pottery Neolithic Village of Beidha in Jordan. Palestine Exploration Quarterly 1966, 1. London. pp. 61-66.
1966*c* 1966-Commentary on the Phylogensis of *Triticum* and *Hordeum*. Economic Botany, Vol. 20 (4). New York. pp. 350-60.
n.d. The Haçilar Plant Remains. In press.

Hole, Frank
1962 Archaeological Survey and Excavation in Iran 1961. Science, Vol. 137, pp. 524-26.

Hole, Frank; and Flannery, Kent V.
1962 Excavations at Ali Kosh, Iran 1961. Iranica Antiqua, Vol. 2 (2), pp. 97-148.

Hole, Frank; Flannery, Kent; and Neely, James
1965 Early Agriculture and Animal Husbandry in Deh Luran, Iran. Current Anthropology, Vol. 6 (1), pp. 105-6.

Hutchinson, Sir Joseph
1958 Genetics and the Improvement of Tropical Crops. Cambridge University Press.

Jacobsen, Thorkild; and Adams, Robert Mc.
1958 Salt and Silt in Ancient Mesopotamian Agriculture. Science, Vol. 128, No. 3334, pp. 1251-58.

Nazif, Selim
1958 Fibre Crops in Egypt. Ministry of Agriculture. Government Printing Office, Cairo.

Nilan, A. Robert
1964 The Cytology and Genetics of Barley. Monogr. Suppl. No. 3, Reserach Studies, Washington State University.

Peterson, R.T.
1965 Wheat: Botany, Cultivation and Utilization. Interscience Publications Inc., New York

Smith, L.
1951 Cytology and Genetics of Barley. Botanical Review, Vol. 17. pp. 133-202.

Smith, C.R.; Shekleton, M.C.; Wolf, I.A.; and Jones, Quentin
1959 Seed Protein sources - Amino Acid Composition and Total Protein Content

of Various Plant Seeds, Economic Botany, Vol. 13 (2), New York. pp. 132-50.

Van Etten, C.H.; Miller, R.W.; and Wolf, I.A.
1963 Amino Acid Composition of Seeds from 200 Angiospermous Plant Species. Agricultural and Food Chemistry, Vol. 11 (5). pp. 399-410.

el-Wailly, Faisal
1964 Tell as-Sawwan. *Sumer,* Vol. 20. Baghdad.

el-Wailly, Faisal; and Behnam, Abu es-Soof
1965 The Excavations at Tell as-Sawwan: First Preliminary Report. Sumer, Vol. 21, pp. 17-32.

Appendix II

ANALYSIS OF THE COPPER BEAD FROM ALI KOSH

Cyril Stanley Smith
Massachusetts Institute of Technology

The bead was heavily corroded. A general view is shown in plate 42*a* at a slight magnification. It was clearly made by taking a small piece of metal strip and rolling it into a hollow cylinder. A radiograph of this bead (Plate 42*b*) was not very informative, although it does suggest the presence of a denser part in one section. The bead was mounted in a transparent cold-setting plastic (E-Z Mount brand) and sectioned for metallographic examination. Two sections, separated only by the width of a saw cut, are shown in plate 42*c* and *d*, slightly magnified. These sections are not etched.

Examination under the microscope showed that the bead was composed entirely of mineralized corrosion products. There was no trace of metal. The lightest-colored phase seen in the following photomicrographs is a dense mineral, supposedly cuprite. Both inside and outside of this are other areas which are of a slightly transparent greenish mineral (gray in the photographs), supposedly malachite, though the compactness of this is much greater outside than inside. In this "malachite" there are few patches of other minerals, including small areas probably of azurite, but I have not been able to identify these as our experience here is mostly metallic.

My impression is that the corrosion product that is quite dark in plate 43*b* is actually the same as the outer gray phase which I believe to be malachite. It is of much smaller grain size, however, (almost powder), and very soft. Under polarized light it appears red, probably simply because the "cuprite" is seen through it, for a similar color appears at the interface between the "cuprite" and larger "malachite" crystals.

The general appearance of the cross section at both low and high magnifications confirms the impression that the bead was made by rolling up a metallic strip. There are no features that would hint at the structure of the metal before corrosion. In some corroded samples of metal there are residual slag inclusions or a corrosion pattern inheriting some of the grain size and shape of the original metal. It is quite impossible, therefore, to say what heat treatment, if any, the original metal had received.

The generally laminar nature of the corrosion products does suggest that the original metal itself had been somewhat laminated, and there is a clear suggestion from the shape of the ends of the section shown in plate 42*c* or at larger magnifications in plate 43, that the strip had been cut in some way, for the structure is turned down as if by the deformation that would accompany a chisel cut. One end indeed, plate 43*b*, even has what seems to be the remains of an actual uncut sliver of metal which has been folded back.

It is possible that the generally laminated structure of the corrosion product originated as a result of the corrosion process but it is, I think, more likely to have arisen from laminations in the original copper. Had a piece of native copper containing some bits of rocky matter been extensively hammered, it is quite likely that the copper would have been laminated. The laminations would not seriously interfere with the cutting and rolling up into the bead, but they would provide paths for corrosion to start, producing the laminated structure as observed.

I can only reach the disappointing conclusion that corrosion has proceeded too far for any positive metallurgical statements to be made. There is no doubt that the bead, currently completely mineral, was once metal. It was probably cut from a piece of heavily hammered sheet copper about half a millimeter thick, the cutting being done with a chisel which distorted the edges of the cut piece. Unless a subsequent (but not recent) accident is responsible for the discontinuities, the rolling of the strip into the coiled bead did not give a uniform cylindrical section, but the metal may have split longitudinally. The conversion of the metal to corrosion product has resulted in considerable swelling and this too may have been responsible for the obvious mechanical damage.

The preparation of this specimen and the photography were done by Katharine Clapp, though she should not be held responsible for the poverty of the interpretation.

Appendix III

THE SOURCES AND SUPPLY OF THE DEH LURAN OBSIDIAN

Colin Renfrew
University of Sheffield

The Deh Luran obsidian provides positive evidence of movement, and presumably of cultural contact over a considerable distance. Thanks to the very careful record of chipped stone, including obsidian, kept by the excavators, it is possible to make a detailed comparison of the utilization of obsidian and chipped stone in the different phases of occupation. The comparison involves a number of approximations, but this need not detract from the validity of the results as orders of magnitude.

THE SOURCES

Seven pieces of obsidian from Deh Luran have been analysed in collaboration with Dr. J.R. Cann and Mr. J.E. Dixon. The figures, with a discussion of the sources have already been published (Renfrew, Dixon, and Cann 1966: 39*f*). They were selected on the basis of appearance from a larger sample made available by Dr. Frank Hole. It had already been realised (Cann and Renfrew, 1964: 121) that a green colour in transmitted light is a good indicator of peralkaline obsidians, and four such green pieces (two from the Ali Kosh Phase, two from the Mohammad Jaffar Phase) were chosen for analysis. All three had the high zirconium and low barium characteristic of peralkaline obsidians of Group 4*c*. The three grey pieces analysed (one from the Ali Kosh Phase, two from the Mohammad Jaffar) fell within Group 1*g*. These results must be taken in conjunction with those from other sites in the Zagros area - Zarzi, Shanidar, Jarmo, Sarab, Tepe Guran and Tell Shemsharah - with which they are in close agreement.

The principal source of Group 4*c* obsidian has been identified as Nemrut Dagh, at the western end of Lake Van, some 900 km. northwest of Deh Luran. A second source of similar obsidian has been identified recently near Bingöl, 150 km. west of Nemrut Dagh, and the existence of further sources in this general area cannot yet be excluded. The source of the Group 1*g* obsidian has not yet been precisely located. The distribution of finds, however, which is much like that of 4*c*, being centered in the Zagros area, suggests that this source also will prove to lie in Armenia, perhaps also in the Van area. It remains to be seen whether the obsidian from these two sources reached Deh Luran via the Tigris Valley (travelling perhaps first to somewhere near Siirt) or along the Zagros foothills, probably via the Hakari region. The very early use of obsidian during the Zarzi period at Shanidar, Zarzi, and Palegawra probably favours the second alternative.

In either case it is significant that no obsidian whatever reached the Zagros from the important source region of south Anatolia, which was already supplying the Levant. This is particularly notable since small quantities of Group 4*c* obsidian have been identified from aceramic Neolithic levels at Tell Ramad and Beidha.

Nor has any Group 3 obsidian, from sources in the Lake Urmia (Rezaiyeh) region, been identified in the Zagros, although it reached Arpachiyah and Chagar Bazar in the Halaf period. This would seem to argue against contact on any large scale across the Zagros range in Neolithic times.

The results from Deh Luran thus compare well with those from other Zagros sites, all of which stand in marked contrast, in this respect, to the early sites in the Levant.

CHRONOLOGICAL VARIATION

The find of obsidian in significant quantities in the Bus Mordeh phase in Deh Luran is interesting, and a little puzzling. For this site has been equated chronologically with the Karim Shahir phase in Kurdistan, where obsidian, although known, was extremely rare. Professor Braidwood has stated that obsidian was not present in significant quantity at Karim Shahir itself, about six pieces being recovered.[1] Two bladelets which certainly belong to this period (one grey, one green) were recovered at M'lefaat.[1] In Kurdistan at this time the obsidian supply seems hardly greater than in the earlier Zarzi period, when it is similarly rare. For example, of the thirteen pieces of obsidian from Palegawra (none of them grey), only two can be assigned with certainty to the Zarzi period.[1] It is difficult to see why Bus Mordeh should have a better obsidian supply than the contemporary sites further north, nearer the sources. Perhaps Bus Mordeh is a little later than some of the Karim Shahir period sites, or possibly the chipped-stone industry recovered from the latter was not sufficiently large to give a representative sample.

No grey obsidian has been recovered from Bus Mordeh[2]. This is certainly of considerable significance, for, in general, Group 4*c* obsidian is green (although a small proportion of it is, in fact, grey) while Group 1*g* obsidian is grey (although 4 pieces of the 16 analysed had a greenish tinge). With a uniform criterion for deciding which pieces are green (sometimes no easy decision), meaningful generalisations can certainly be drawn (Table 1).

It appears that little or no Group 1*g* obsidian was reaching Deh Luran in the Bus Mordeh phase. The proportion increased in the Ali Kosh phase, when it was comparable with that at Sarab, and again in the Mohammad Jaffar Phase. But Group 4*c* obsidian was always the more common.

Until we know the exact location of the Group 1*g* source, this variation cannot satisfactorily be interpreted. Presumably the Group 4*c* source was always the easier of access. But there appear to have been steadily improving relations with the Group 1*g* region - with which Jarmo, apparently, was always in good contact.

The variation also in abundance of obsidian in the Deh Luran area is marked. The chipped-stone industry declined sharply at the end of the Mohammad Jaffar period, and only nine pieces of obsidian from the Sabz to the Bayat period (Hassuna-Susiana *a* to Late Ubaid) were recovered. Probably stone tools were at this time largely replaced by metal ones, and the obsidian trade came to an end.

Table 2 indicates the variation of obsidian in relation to the volume of material excavated from the early phases in Deh Luran, with figures from Sarab and

[1] Personal communication, April, 1967.

[2] All colour identifications quoted are based on my own observation. I am very grateful to Dr. and Mrs. Braidwood and to Dr. and Mrs. Hole for the opportunity to study the available material, and for their very kind hospitality.

Jarmo for comparison. The volumes excavated are approximate estimates by the excavators[3]. None of the figures is exact. In Deh Luran the total chipped-stone industry declined at the end of the Bus Mordeh phase, while the obsidian component of it increased both relatively and absolutely. The increased number of obsidian fragments per excavated cubic metre correlates with an increase in the mean weight of the pieces. Although this might at first sight be explained best by the increased abundance of the obsidian supply, the mean weight does not decrease greatly when obsidian becomes rarer again in the succeeding Mohammad Jaffar phase. The increase in mean weight probably reflects instead a functional or culturally determined change in the lithic industry rather than the fluctuation in supply.

Table 1

THE PROPORTION OF GREY OBSIDIAN (GROUP 1*g*) IN THE OBSIDIAN ASSEMBLAGE

	Deh Luran				
Assemblage	Bus Mordeh	Ali Kosh	Mohammad Jaffar	Sarab	Jarmo
Total in sample.	196	578	367	498	683
Number of grey pieces	0	72	107	82	251
Percentage of grey	0.0	12.4	29.4	16.8	35.7

Note.—The figures for Sarab are from Sarab 1C - 2*a*. Those for Jarmo are amalgamated from seven samples from both Jarmo I and Jarmo II. One sample from J1 - E28, possibly a chipping floor, had 2 grey pieces and 50 green. A sample from J1, 7 had 71 grey and 28 green. In view of this variation the figures of 39.6 per cent grey and 30.4 per cent grey in Jarmo I and Jarmo II respectively probably do not differ significantly.

Table 2

VARIATION IN QUANTITIES OF OBSIDIAN PRESENT

	Deh Luran				
	Bus Mordeh	Ali Kosh	Mohammad Jaffar	Sarab	Jarmo
Total chipped stone	19,574 (40,114)	23,231	23,934	40,864	93,239
Volume excavated (cu.m.) . .	70	144	165	50	2,700
Chipped stone/cu.m.	279 (573)	162	144	817	34
Obsidian/cu.m.	2.8	4.0	2.2	14.5	14.3
Percentage of obsidian in total chipped stone . . .	1.0 (0.5)	2.5	1.6	1.8	42.0
Mean weight of obsidian fragments (gm.).	0.30	0.41	0.39	0.53	0.20

Note:—The Deh Luran data are from figures kindly provided by Dr. Frank Hole. Deh Luran material was sifted through a 0.3 cm. mesh. Sarab and Jarmo material was unsifted. Figures for Bus Mordeh exclude a cache of flint from the base of the site, while those in parentheses include it. The weighings of Sarab and Jarmo material are from samples of 729 and 3150 pieces respectively.

[3] Personal communication. For Jarmo see Braidwood and Howe, 1960: 38.

COMPARISON WITH OTHER SITES

At Sarab, chipped stone was found more abundantly than in Deh Luran, although the proportion of obsidian to flint was much the same as at Ali Kosh or Mohammad Jaffar. At Jarmo, on the other hand, there was very much less chipped stone per unit volume, while obsidian represented fully 42.0 per cent of the lithic assemblage recovered.

These differences, especially those between Sarab and Jarmo, require explanation, and several factors must be considered which reflect on the validity of the figures in general. In the first place the practice of sieving in the Deh Luran excavations makes these differences difficult to compare with Jarmo and Sarab. Contrary to expectation, however, the mean weight of the pieces recovered at Jarmo is actually less than in Deh Luran. This will have to be explained in terms of differences in the lithic industry, but it does not suggest that the absence of sieving at Sarab and Jarmo resulted in any serious loss of the smaller artifacts. It is possible, on the other hand, that manual collection of the chipped stone, in the absence of sieving, favours the retention of obsidian rather than of flint which would help to explain the low figure of thirty-four pieces of chipped stone per cubic metre of soil at Jarmo, although not the high figure at Sarab.

Probably a more serious problem is the validity of comparing the industries in terms of the concentration by volume of excavated material. At Jarmo the houses were of tauf, so that in a given period of occupation, much more excavation debris is to be expected than for the same period on a site with flimsier dwellings. The concentration of chipped stone per unit volume would consequently be smaller. The high value for chipped stone per cubic metre of soil at Sarab, and to a lesser extent at Bus Mordeh, may reflect chiefly a lack of bulky occupation debris contributed by collapsed mudbrick structures. Braidwood has referred to the disparity in the nature of the settlements at Jarmo and Sarab (Braidwood, 1962:122) and in their probable difference in function. These parameters of chipped stone per cubic metre, obsidian per cubic metre, and mean weight of obsidian fragments may thus be sensitive indicators, determined by the nature of the site in question, and not solely by differences in sampling procedure.

THE OBSIDIAN SUPPLY

The comparison of the total quantities of obsidian buried at each site has not previously been made. The figures are extrapolations from the excavated material, and depend on the excavators' estaimates for the proportion of the site left unexcavated. They are themselves approximations, therefore. In computing them the mean weight of obsidian fragments at each site has been used (Table 3).

One's first reaction to these weights is perhaps surprise that they are not greater. Originally, when the total weight of obsidian at Jarmo was calculated (Renfrew, Dixon, and Cann, 1966: 52) a figure of 4 kilograms per 1,000 pieces was taken as a mean weight. It was based on weighings of obsidian at the Neolithic site of Saliagos in the Cyclades, where obsidian was the principal material for an important flake industry. Weighings of Jarmo material now show that a figure of 200 grams per 1,000 pieces is more realistic for the Jarmo industry, and it was a mistake to regard the blade industry of Jarmo as comparable with the flake industry of Saliagos, where obsidian was evidently in much more abundant supply. (The greater abundance

Table 3

THE TOTAL WEIGHTS OF OBSIDIAN REPRESENTED

Obsidian Fragments	Deh Luran			Sarab	Jarmo
	Bus Mordeh	Ali Kosh	Mohammad Jaffar		
Number of pieces in sample . .	196	578	367	723	39,211
Sample as fraction of total site	1/338	1/338	1/135	1/50	1/25
Size of site (cu.m.)	24,000	49,000	22,000	2,500	68,000
Total calculated weight of obsidian (kilograms) . .	20	80	19	18	196

at Saliagos is eloquently indicated by the mean weight of 8.0 grams for worked-out cores, compared with 0.75 gms at Sarab.) The new mean weight yields an over-all total for the site of about 200 kilograms instead of the former estimate of 4,000 kilograms (4 tons). Sarab, a much smaller site, has correspondingly less, while Bus Mordeh, Ali Kosh and Mohammad Jaffar, although of the same order of size as Jarmo, have distinctly smaller quantities of obsidian. This is satisfactorily explained by their greater distance from the sources.

The mechanism of transport has already been discussed (Renfrew, Dixon, and Cann 1966:50). In the absence of beasts of burden - unless the sheep was used as a pack animal at that time, as sometimes in Tibet today - traders presumably carried their own merchandise. What is as yet unexplained, however, is why the prehistoric knappers troubled to obtain obsidian at all when it could only be used to provide a small proportion of the total lithic industry. The mechanical properties of obsidian, as contrasted with the various types of flint utilised, have not yet been sufficiently investigated. In addition, an exhaustive breakdown of the lithic industry into forms and tool types, by obsidian and flint variety, may well reveal the preferential use of specific materials for particular functions. It may be that obsidian was superior to flint for the manufacture of small parallel-sided blades in particular, which form a large part of the lithic assemblages. In this case the need for a continuing supply would be comprehensible, while the more abundant flint would be used for other types for which it was as well suited as obsidian. Perhaps it is along these lines that the small but steady supply of obsidian which passed along the foothills and valleys of the Zagros Mountains to Deh Luran is to be explained.

REFERENCES

Braidwood, R.J.
1962 The Earliest Village Communities of Southwestern Asia Reconsidered. Atti del VI. Congresso Internazionale delle Scienze Preistoriche e Protoistoriche, Vol. 1, pp. 115. Rome.

Braidwood, R.J., Howe, B., *et al.*
1960 Prehistoric Investigations in Iraqi Kurdistan. Studies in Ancient Oriental Civilization, No. 31. University of Chicago Press.

Cann, J.R. and Renfrew, C.
1964 The Characterization of Obsidian and its Application to the Mediterranean Region. Proceedings of the Prehistoric Society, Vol. 30, pp. 111-33. Cambridge.

Renfrew, C., Dixon, J.E. and Cann, J.R.
1966 Obsidian and Early Cultural Contact in the Near East. Proceedings of the Prehistoric Society, Vol. 32, pp. 30-72. Cambridge.

Appendix IV

THE FAUNA FROM RAS AL AMIYA, IRAQ: A COMPARISON WITH THE DEH LURAN SEQUENCE

Kent V. Flannery
University of Michigan
I. W. Cornwall
Institute of Archaeology, University of London

SETTING OF THE SITE

The prehistoric village of Ras al Amiya lies in the plain of southern Mesopotamia, midway between the Tigris and Euphrates, and 240 kilometers west of Deh Luran. The site, which has 3 meters of stratified mud-walled architecture, had been completely covered by alluvium and only appeared by chance when a drainage canal was cut through the area. It was excavated by David Stronach (1961).

Ras al Amiya, like its neighboring sites of Kish, Jemdat Nasr, and Babylon, belongs in the northern part of Hatt's "alluvial plains" biotic province (Hatt, 1959:14). Its elevation is less than 40 meters above sea level, and annual precipitation in the area is under 150 mm. annually, generally considered inadequate for dry farming (Adams, 1962:110).

The area is mostly treeless plain, with few perennials except the hardiest, like *Prosopis* and camel-thorn (*Alhagi* sp.); exceptions are areas subject to seasonal inundation, which have some growth of trees and brush (Hatt 1959:94). River bottoms have dense thickets of tamarisk, popular, bramble, and wild licorice like those of Khuzistan, but the flats in between are barren and desertic. There were herds of onager here until the arrival of the Model A Ford, with its mobilized hunting techniques, and gazelle can still be sighted. Wild sheep and goats are *not* native, and could not have been encountered by the inhabitants of Ras al Amiya without a journey of over 150 kilometers.

THE FAUNA

Stronach's excavations produced 194 fragments of animal bone or shell, which were shipped to he University of London Institute of Archaeology. There, Cornwall was able to sort out the various species involved, and mention of his results appeared in the report on Ras al Amiya (Stronach, 1961:124).

The Ras al Amiya collection is particularly important because so few animal bone samples have ever been saved for analysis from sites of this age in southern Mesopotamia. The Deh Luran plain is literally the nearest region from which abundant specimens of comparable age are available. In view of this, the Ras al Amiya collection was shipped on to the Smithsonian Institution, where Flannery compared it with animal remains from Tepe Sabz.

It is the Mehmeh Phase (4700-4100 B.C.) which shows the strongest ties with Ras al Amiya, both in ceramics and artifacts. Ceramic "bent nails," polished celts, and oval-discoidal spindle whorls characterize both areas at this time, as well as Stronach's painted bowl types nos. 1, 11, 12, 13, 14, 15, 18 and 20 (see chapter on ceramics). Ras al Amiya also had some unfired mud-slab "brick" architecture reminiscent of that found at Tepe Sabz (Stronach, 1961:100).

All the fauna identified from Ras al Amiya occurred also at Tepe Sabz. Cattle (*Bos taurus*), sheep (*Ovis aries*), and possibly goat (*Capra hircus*) were present as domesticates. Five fragments of *Canis* sp. are perhaps from dogs, although it would be difficult to prove they were not small *Canis lupus pallipes* (see chapter on fauna from Ali Kosh and Tepe Sabz). There is no evidence that the rare remains of pig (*Sus scrofa*) were anything but local wild boar. The villagers at Ras al Amiya, like those at Tepe Sabz, hunted gazelle (*Gazella subgutturosa*) and onager (*Equus hemionus*), and collected fresh-water mussels (*Unio tigridis*). Counts of all these remains appear in Table 1.

Domestic herbivores account for approximately 80 per cent of the faunal remains in the Mehmeh phase at Tepe Sabz, and at Ras al Amiya. When the two areas are compared, however (see Fig. 144), the most striking difference noticed is the greater percentage of cattle bones, relative to sheep and goat, at Ras al Amiya. Cattle were, in fact, the most common animals recovered by Stronach's excavation: they comprised 45 per cent of the fragments. In contrast, there is no period in the Deh Luran sequence during which cattle constitute more than 5 per cent of the animal bone.

We doubt that so great a difference can be attributed to mere sampling error. In the first place, the collection consists of all bone fragments recovered by Stronach, not a "selected" sample. Second, the Ras al Amiya fauna, like that from Tepe Sabz, has internal consistency when examined level by level. In virtually all five building levels which produced bone fragments, cattle predominate, with fragments of sheep or goat not far behind (Table 1, below).

That the Ras al Amiya cattle were domestic is clearly indicated by the size of their bones. The astragalus (3 specimens), distal metacarpal, and phalanges (6 specimens) all fall within the size range of domestic cattle from Tepe Sabz and the British Neolithic, rather than *Bos primigenius;* the distal humerus falls at the borderline between small *Bos primigenius*

Table 1

COUNTS OF ANIMAL BONE FROM RAS AL AMIYA, BY BUILDING LEVEL

Level	Sheep/Goat	Cattle	Pig	Gazelle	Onager	Dog (or wolf)	Mussel	Unidentified Fragments	Total
I	5	5	...	...	1	...	...	14	25
I-II	...	2	...	...	...	...	...	1	3
II	4	3	...	1	1	...	4	17	30
III	28	29	3	1	1	5	...	51	118
IV	1	6	1	...	...	...	...	3	11
IV	...	1	...	...	...	...	...	6	7
Total ..	38	46	4	2	3	5	4	92	194
Per Cent	37.3	45.1	3.9	1.96	1.4	4.9	3.9	...	...

and early domestic cattle (see Figs. 126-7 and pp. 304-7). In addition, a number of complete, unbroken long bones could be measured. A complete radius from III b CW 45-50 had an overall length of 316 mm.; a complete metacarpal from III CE 70-75 measured 203 mm. in length; and a complete metatarsal from III b CW 45-50 was 247 mm. long. The length of the metacarpal compares with Neolithic domestic cattle from northern Europe, and is much smaller than *Bos primigenius* metacarpals listed by Degerbøl (1963:Fig. 17) and Jewell (1963:Fig. 19).

Few of the 38 fragments of caprines from Ras al Amiya were helpful for distinguishing sheep from goat. A single distal metapodial from III b CW 65-70 fell in the range given by Gromova (1953:77-78) for *Ovis*. The diameter of the lateral articular surface of the condyle was 64.3 percent of the diameter of the medial articular surface (see pp. 267-70). No horn cores or metapodials of goat appeared, and although it is quite possible that goats were present at the site, concrete evidence is lacking. Most remains therefore had to be listed simply as "sheep or goat."

Since *wild* sheep and goats are not available within 150 kilometers of the site, we see little possiblity that any of the Ras al Amiya caprines could have been anything but domestic animals. No diagnostic horn core sections were present in the collections, so our evidence is presumptive rather than osteological.

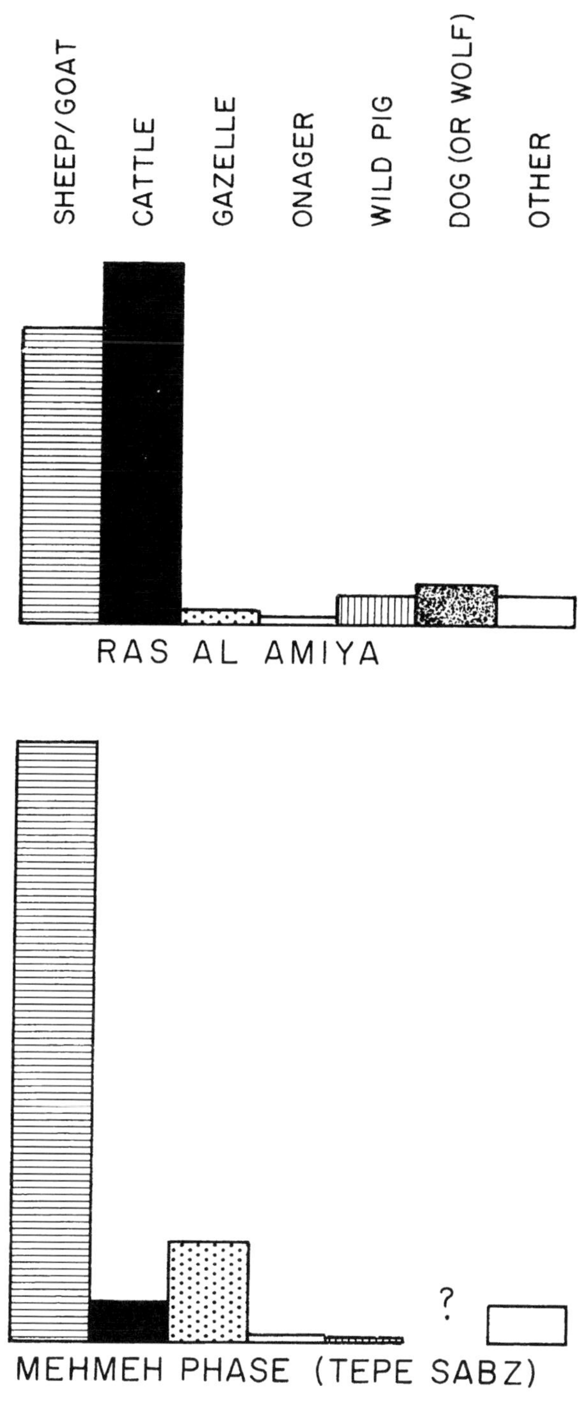

Fig. 144. Bar graphs showing differences in faunal remains between Ras al Amiya (Iraq) and Mehmeh phase levels at Tepe Sabz (Iran), which are roughly contemporary. Height of bar indicates percentage which each animal constitutes in the total faunal assemblage (calculated on the basis of total identifiable bones).

CONCLUSIONS

Any conclusions drawn from the small sample at Ras al Amiya must be considered tentative, pending recovery of more animal bones from contemporary sites in the Jemdat Nasr-Nippur area of Mesopotamia. If such sites yield bones in the same frequencies as Ras al Amiya, we shall be forced to conclude that at 4500 B.C., cattle herding was of relatively greater economic importance in central Mesopotamia than in the steppeland at the base of the Zagros Mountains.[1] The latter area, perhaps because of the accessibility of summer pastures in the adjacent mountains, seems to have relied more heavily on goat (and sheep) grazing. Tepe Sabz and Ras al Amiya are definitely related by ceramic designs and forms, as well as shared artifact types, but their economies may have been as different as their environmental settings.

Evidence of prehistoric cattle domestication in southern alluvial Mesopotamia has, until recently, been limited to representations on cylinder seals from relatively late sites like Warka (Reed 1960:144). Two or three more faunal collections like that from Ras al Amiya would do a lot to clarify the relationships between the alluvium and the Zagros Mountains.

[1]Since this writing, it has been possible to examine bones from Ubaid levels at Eridu. They show similar high frequencies of cattle.

PLATES 2-30

PLATE 2

a

b

Patterns of land use in the Deh Luran plain: *a*, plowing seasonally-flooded depression near Tepe Sabz; *b*, grazing sheep and goats on the plain near Tepe Farukhabad. View north toward the Kuh-i-Siah range.

PLATE 3

a

b

Modern fauna and vegetation of the Deh Luran plain: *a*, female gazelle running through area of low herbaceous vegetation (chenopods, legumes, and wild caper) near Tepe Ali Kosh; *b*, dromedary grazing in patch of camel thorn (*Alhagi*) near Tepe Sabz.

PLATE 4

a

b

Excavations at Tepe Ali Kosh (1963 season): *a*, exposing Mohammad Jaffar phase levels. In foreground is eroded 1961 test pit; *b*, split-level excavation. To the right, area at 460 cm. depth has been left while sub-floor burials of zone B_2 (Ali Kosh phase) are cleaned. To the left, workmen dig initial exploratory squares into Bus Mordeh phase levels (zone C_1).

a b

Excavations at Tepe Ali Kosh (1963 season): *a*, in the background, workmen are exposing wall of Ali Kosh phase house (zone B_2). In the foreground, men are removing ash samples for flotation. Edge of 1961 pit shows in foreground; *b*, the southeast corner of 1963 excavations, taken to sterile soil. Bus Mordeh phase strata appear at the bottom.

PLATE 6

Tepe Ali Kosh. West end of 1963 pit, showing Bus Mordeh phase walls and ash beds.

PLATE 7

Tepe Ali Kosh. Southwest corner of 1963 pit, showing stratigraphy of Bus Mordeh phase levels. The cards indicate depths of 5, 6, and 7 meters.

PLATE 8

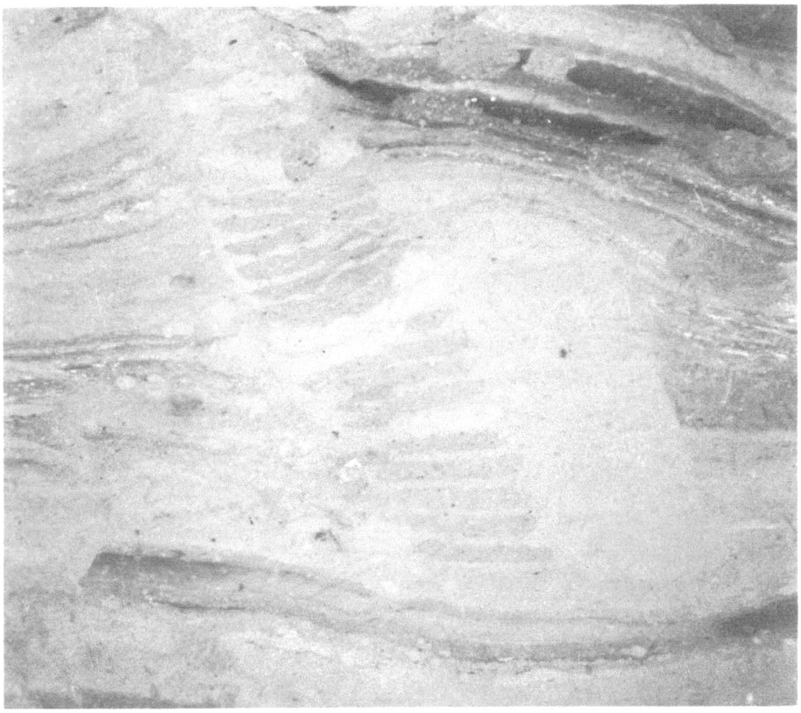

a

b

Tepe Ali Kosh. Cross-sections of two kinds of Bus Mordeh phase walls: *a*, green clay slab-brick wall, with packed-mud wall resting against it to the right; *b*, small room made of thin, red clay slab-bricks.

PLATE 9

a

b

Tepe Ali Kosh. Exposing Ali Kosh phase walls in zone B_2 : *a*, workmen picking up the edge of wall; *b*, scraping wall to clarify color differences between bricks and mud mortar.

PLATE 10

Features of houses at Tepe Ali Kosh: *a*, Pebble wall foundation from Mohammad Jaffar phase, zone A_1. (Notches in wall are from intrusive "Iron Age" burials.) To the right of the wall (foreground) are scatters of heavy stone tools on house floor; *b*, removing pile of pebble choppers, in association with bones of onager and aurochs, from the corner of a Mohammad Jaffar phase house; *c*, view of Ali Kosh phase wall foundation in zone B_1, 1961 test pit. Inside the house are scatters of heavy stone tools; *d*, section through brick-lined roasting pit in zone B_2, 1961 test pit.

PLATE 11

a

b

Excavations at Tepe Ali Kosh (1963 season): *a*, workman collecting samples of ash from midden of the Mohammad Jaffar phase (zone A_2) for flotation to recover carbonized seeds; *b*, workman cleaning subfloor burial (Burial 34) associated with Ali Kosh phase house in zone B_2.

PLATE 12

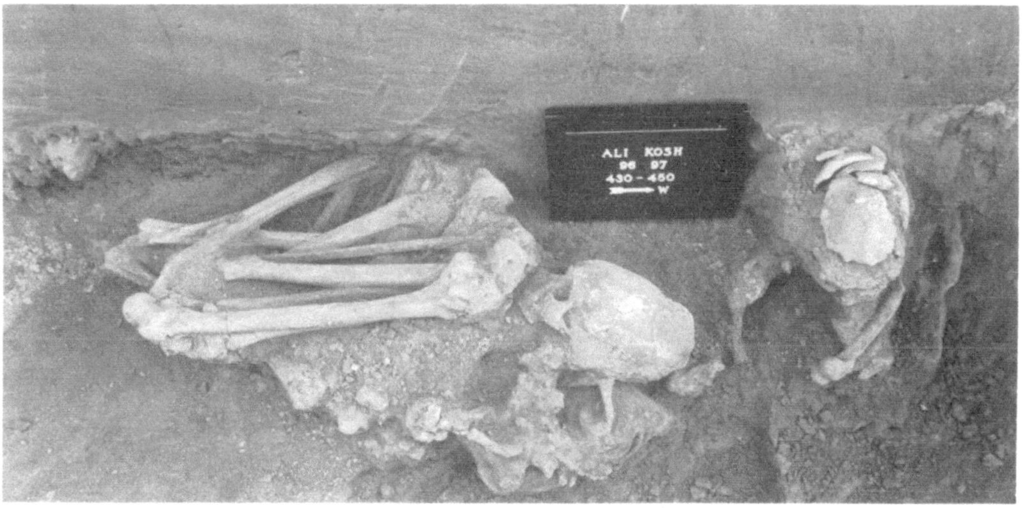

a

b

c

Tepe Ali Kosh. Examples of burials: *a*, group of subfloor burials in zone B_2 (Burials 34, 34*a*, and limb bones of secondary burial). Ali Kosh phase; *b*, close-up of skull of Burial 34, showing annular skull deformation; *c* burial 8, Mohammad Jaffar phase (zone A_1), accompanied by stone "bell" between the thighs, strings of beads near the pelvis, and turquoise beads in neck and shoulder region.

PLATE 13

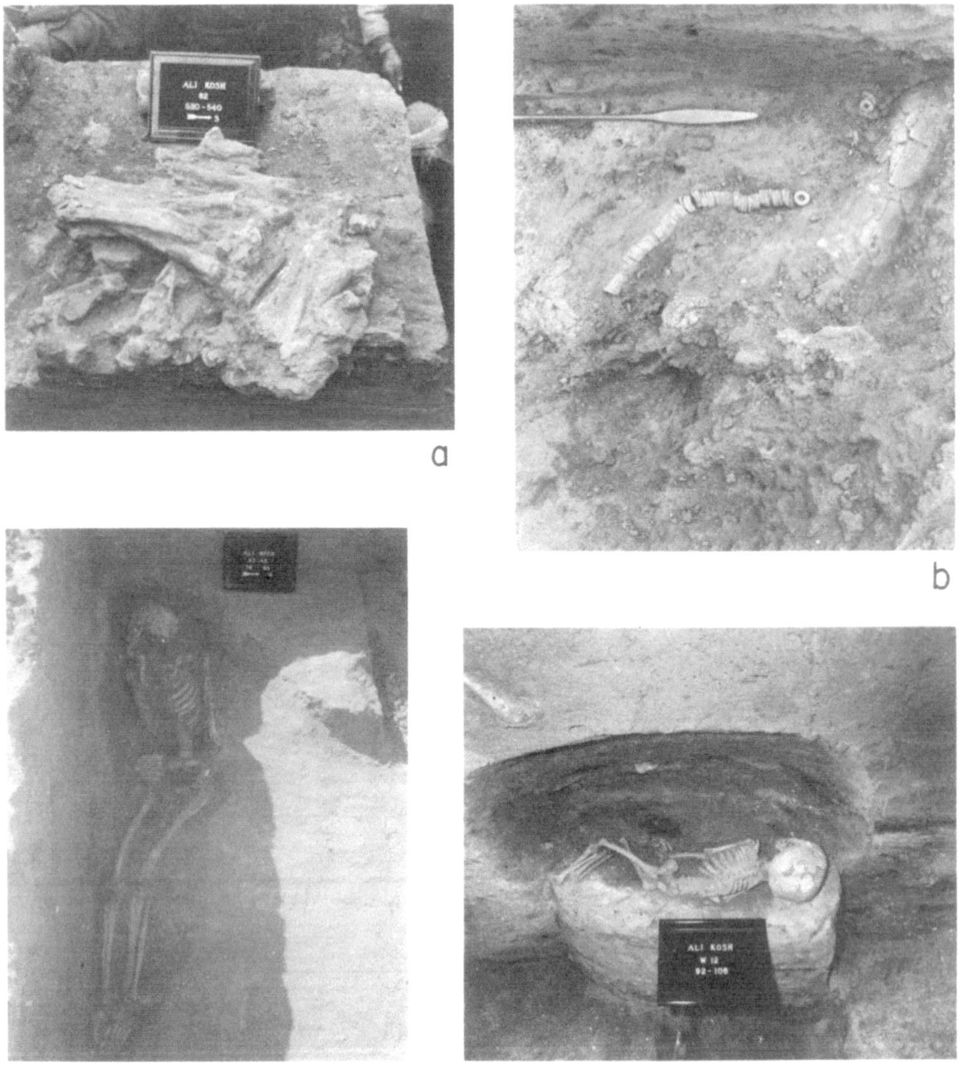

Miscellaneous burials at Tepe Ali Kosh: *a*, mass of secondarily-buried limb bones in zone C_1, probably intrusive from zone B_2 (Ali Kosh phase); *b*, close-up of string of white disk beads on pelvis and femur of Burial 9, zone A_1, Mohammad Jaffar phase; *c*, adult intrusive "Iron Age" burial, Burial 14; *d*, infant intrusive "Iron Age" burial, Burial 4.

PLATE 14

a

b

Tepe Sabz, general views: *a*, view of the east side of Tepe Sabz; *b*, tamarisk trees mark the course of an abandoned irrigation canal just west of Tepe Sabz.

View of step trench at Tepe Sabz. Workmen are standing on center row of one-meter squares, left as a "balk" for stratigraphic purposes.

PLATE 16

a

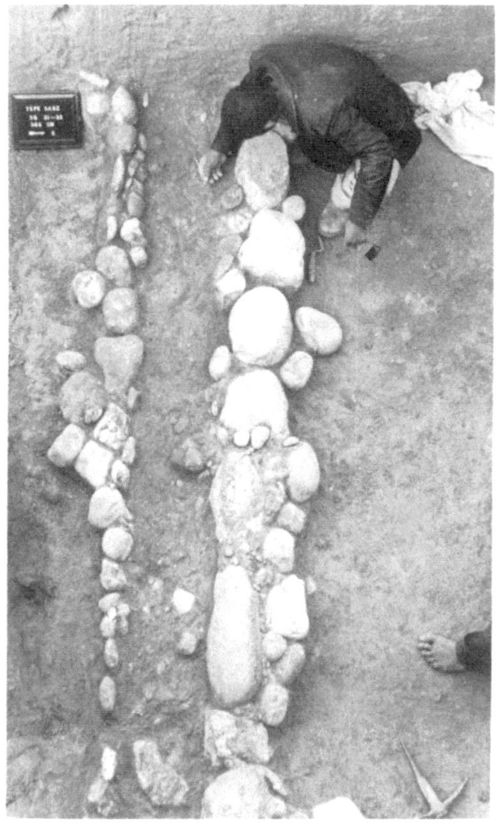

b

c

Details of Mehmeh phase house at Tepe Sabz, zone B_3: *a*, workman cleaning platform of cobbles; *b*, workman cleaning wall foundation composed of two rows of cobbles and boulders, with an intervening band of pebbles; *c*, detail of wall foundation, showing tightly-set pebbles.

PLATE 17

a

b

c

Bayat phase burials at Tepe Sabz: *a*, Burial 5, adult; *b*, Burial 4, infant; *c*, Burial 3, adult female, accompanied by saddle-shaped grinding slab and large discoidal handstone.

a

b

Other sites in the Deh Luran plain: *a*, Tepe Ashrafabad. Mehmeh phase house foundation stones exposed by sheet erosion at surface of mound; *b*, Tepe Musiyan as seen from Tepe Ali Kosh, about one-and-a-half km. to the west.

PLATE 19

a

b

Tepe Musiyan, 1963 excavations: *a*, removing washed-in materials from eroded pit in area "E" made by Gautier and Lampre in 1903; *b*, stratigraphy in north face of 1963 test pit, showing outline of Gautier and Lampre's 1903 pit, A Mehmeh phase brick wall stub may be seen in undisturbed levels below the 1903 pit.

PLATE 20

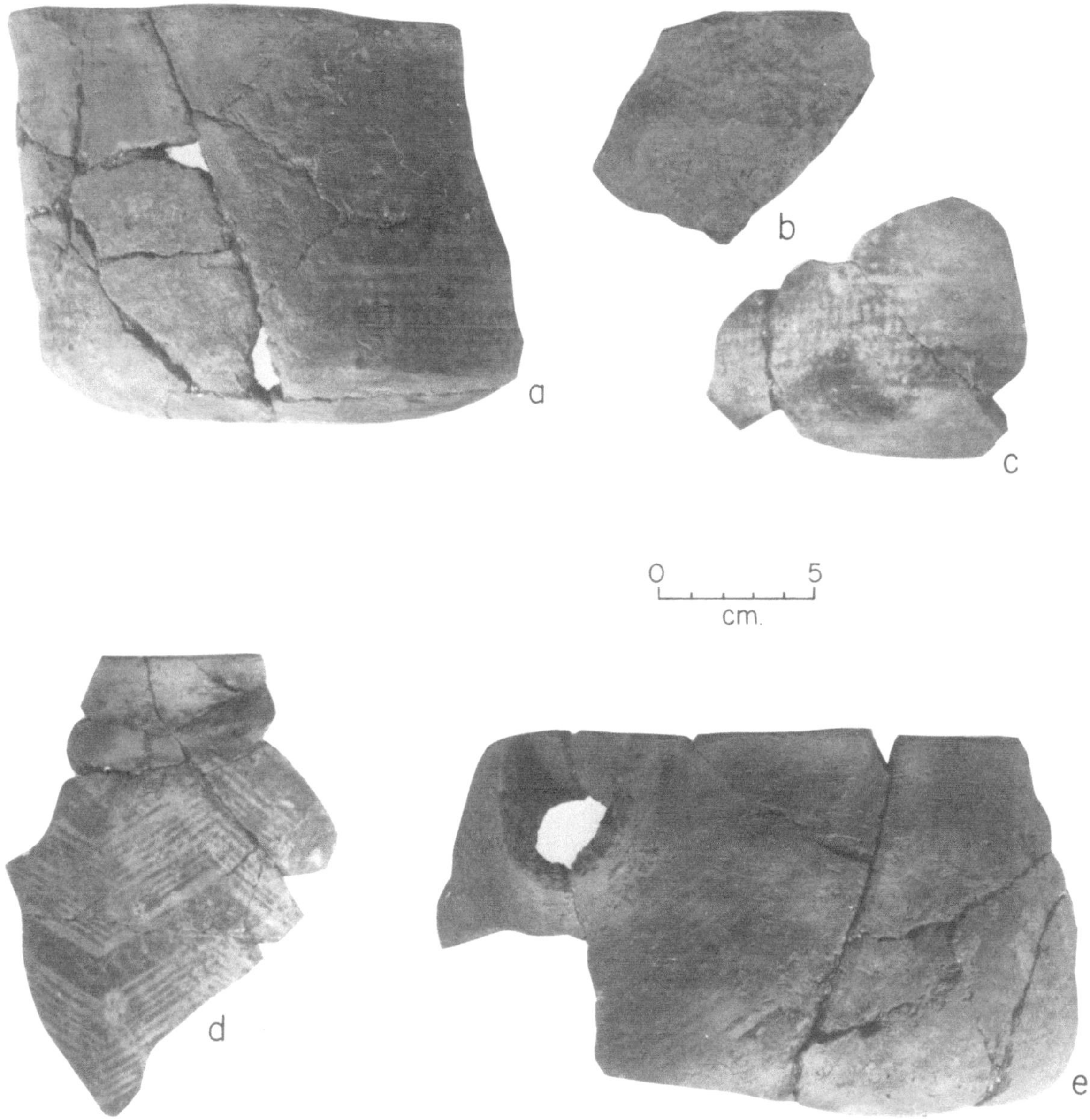

Jaffar Painted pottery, Mohammad Jaffar phase (Tepe Ali Kosh). All are fragments of deep, convex-walled bowls; *e* shows the remains of a small trough spout.

PLATE 21

Susiana Black-on-buff pottery: forms and motifs typical of the Sabz phase (Tepe Sabz): *a-f*, "Sabz pots." *e*, painting of dog with tail curled over its back; *g*, bowl with trough spout; *h*, early form of ring base.

PLATE 22

Pottery from the Deh Luran sequence: *a-c*, sherds from Khazineh Red vessels of the Mohammad Jaffar phase (Tepe Ali Kosh): *a*, Hole-mouth jar; *b*, trough spout; *c*, deep bowl; *d-h*, sherds from Mehmeh Red-on-red vessels typical of the Mehmeh phase (Tepe Sabz); *d*, hole-mouth jar; *e*, hole-mouth jar with trough spout; *f*, interior design on a shallow dish; *g*, exterior design on a bowl; *h*, cup.

PLATE 23

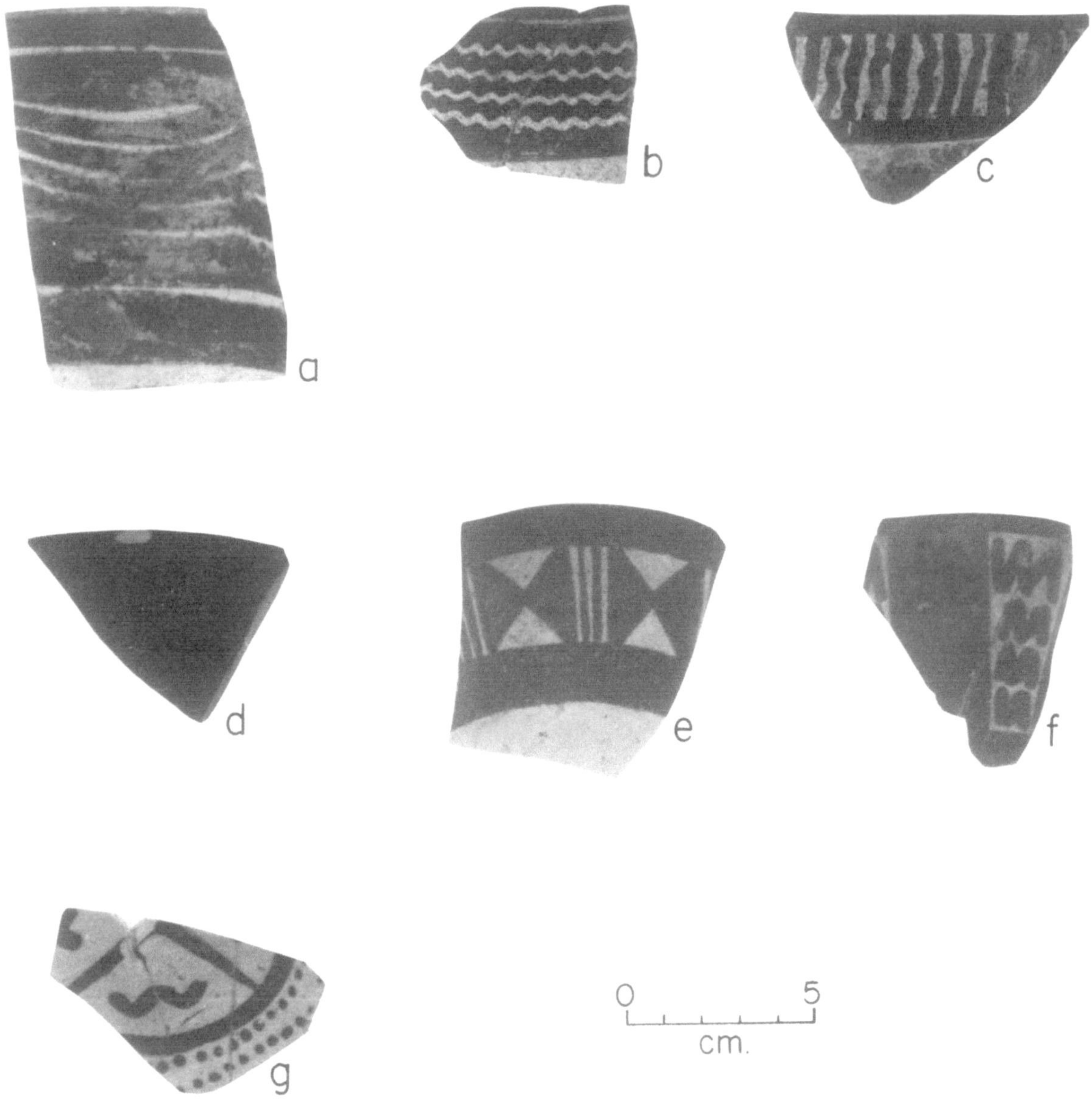

Susiana Black-on-buff pottery. Sherds show motifs typical of the Khazineh phase (Tepe Sabz).

PLATE 24

Susiana Black-on-buff pottery. Decorations on "Type 13" bowls typical of the Khazineh phase (Tepe Sabz).

PLATE 25

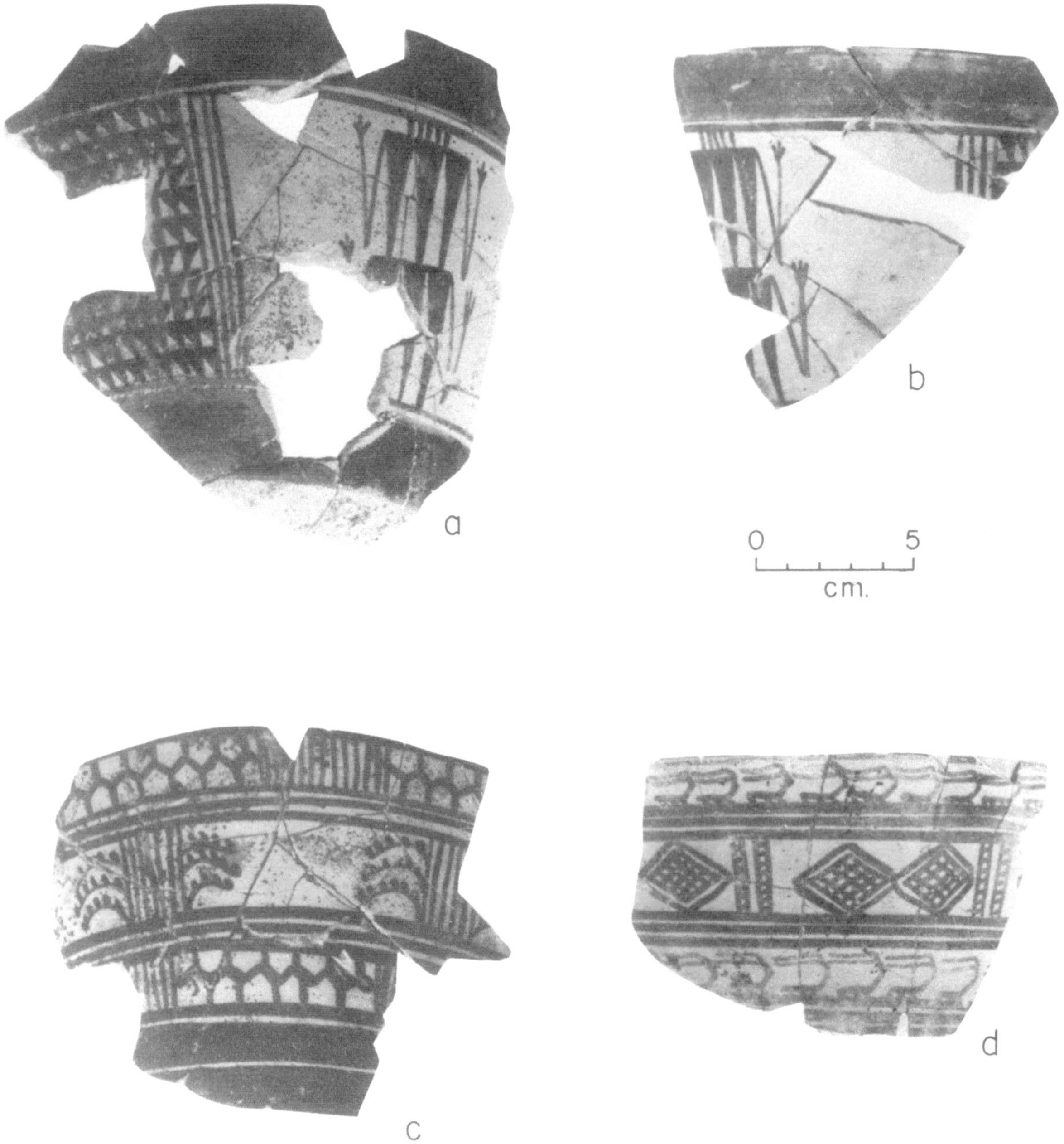

Susiana Black-on-buff pottery. "Type 11" bowls with decoration typical of the Mehmeh phase (Tepe Sabz).

PLATE 26

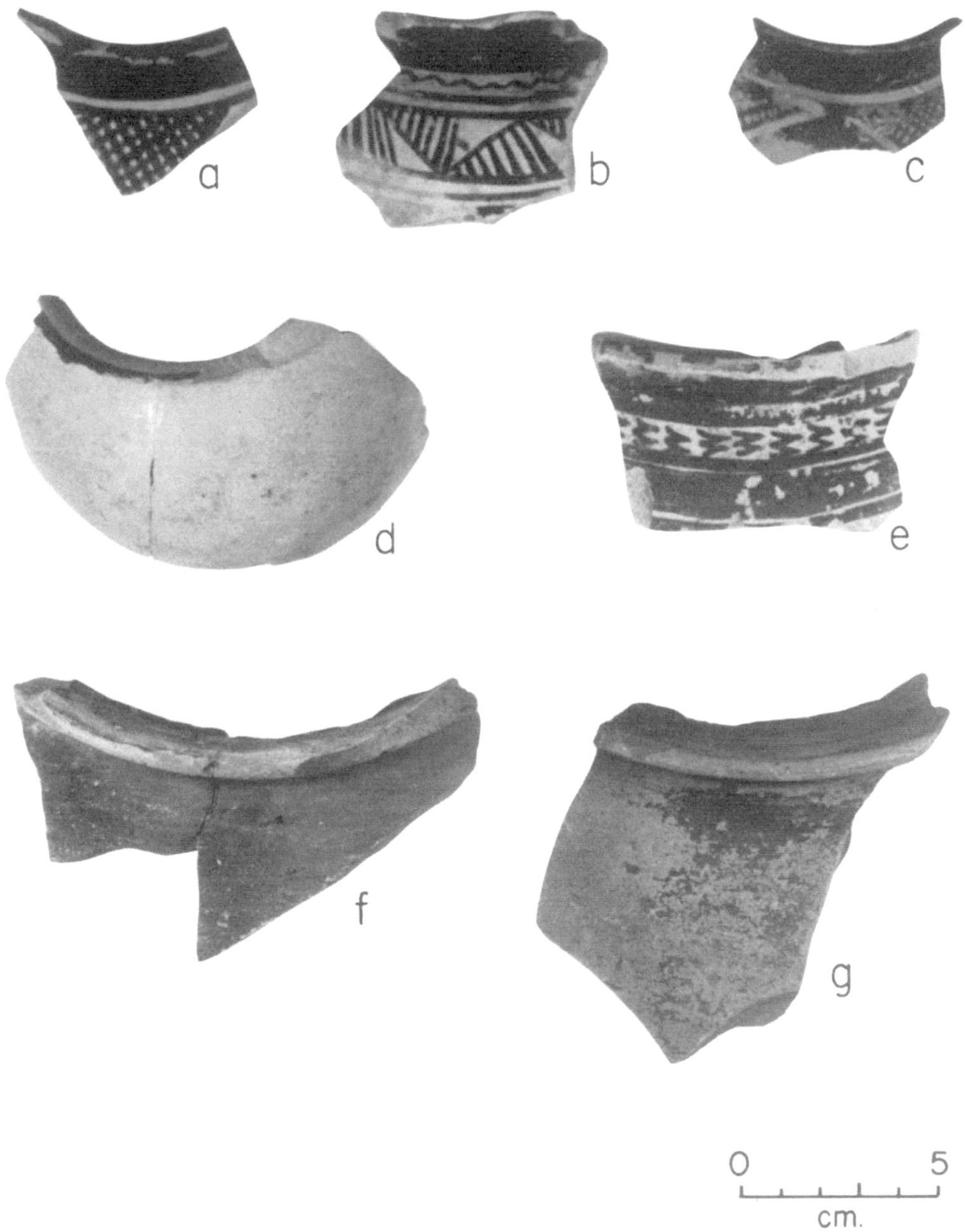

Susiana Black-on-buff pottery. Sherds from ledge-rim jars typical of the Mehmeh phase (Tepe Sabz).

PLATE 27

Susiana Black-on-buff pottery. Exterior designs on bowls typical of the Mehmeh phase (Tepe Sabz).

PLATE 28

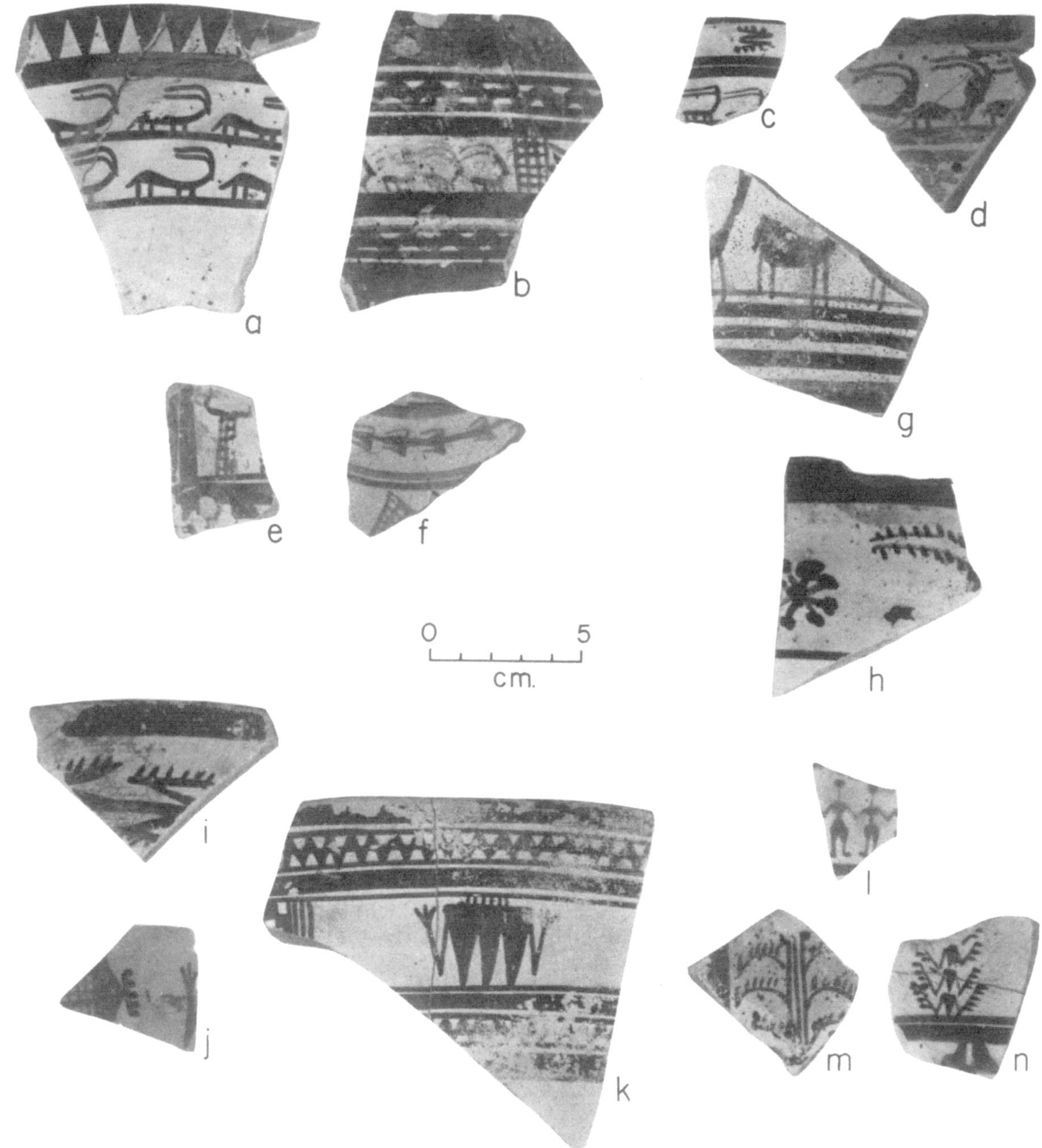

Susiana Black-on-buff pottery. Naturalistic motifs typical of the Mehmeh phase (Tepe Sabz): *a-g*, rows of wild goats; *e-f*, "bukrania;" *j-l*, "dancing men."

PLATE 29

Susiana Black-on-buff pottery. Painted motifs typical of the Bayat phase (Tepe Sabz).

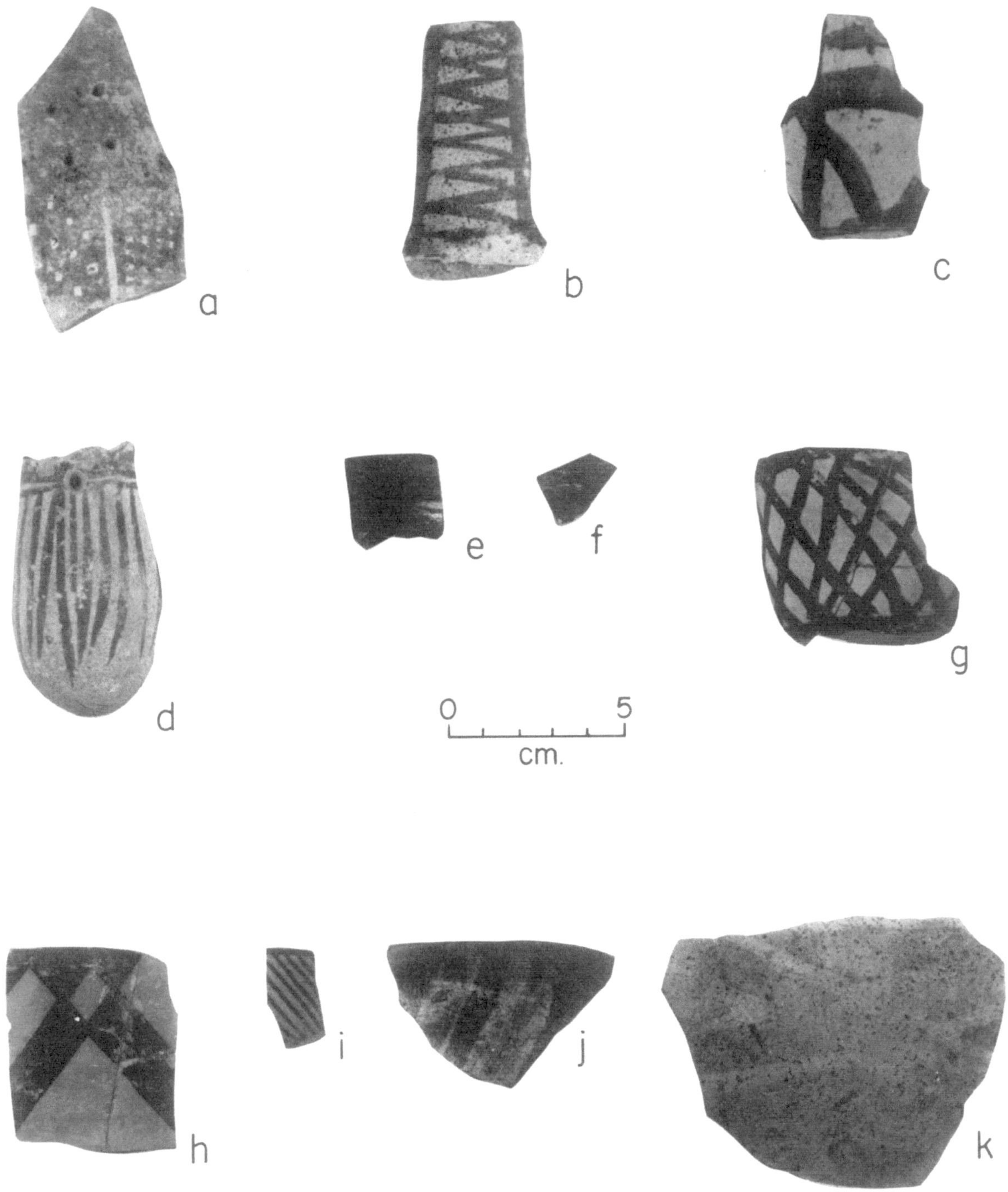

Miscellaneous pottery from various phases at Tepe Sabz and Tepe Musiyan: *a,b*, "handles" of Susiana Black-on-buff "sauce boats" (*a*, Tepe Sabz, zone D, Sabz phase; *b*, Tepe Musiyan "E", Mehmeh phase); *c*, fragment of a small Susiana Black-on-buff "sauce boat," Tepe Sabz, zone B_3 (Mehmeh phase); *d*, small Susiana Black-on-buff vessel (complete), found in Khazineh phase levels of clearing trench; *e, f*, Burnished Black sherds from zones A_1 and A_2 at Tepe Sabz (Bayat phase); *g*, Susiana Black-on-buff cup, Tepe Sabz, zone A_2 (Bayat phase); *h,i*, Fine Black-on-tan sherds from zone A_1, at Tepe Sabz (Bayat phase); *j,k*, Bichrome Painted sherds from zone A_3 at Tepe Sabz (Bayat phase).

PLATE 31

Stone artifacts typical of the Ali Kosh and Mohammad Jaffar phases at Tepe Ali Kosh: *a-d*, sickle blades with asphalt (used for hafting) still adhering to them (various levels); *e-h*, flint pebble choppers (*e*, *h*, Ali Kosh phase; *f,g*, Mohammad Jaffar phase); *i-l*, core pestles (all from zone B_2, Ali Kosh phase).

PLATE 32

Stone artifacts typical of the Ali Kosh and Mohammad Jaffar phases at Tepe Ali Kosh: *a-e*, "sashweight" asphalt-stirrers (*a*, zone A_1, Mohammad Jaffar phase; *b-e*, zone B_2, Ali Kosh phase); *f-h*, chipped limestone discs, zones B_1 and B_2 (Ali Kosh phase).

PLATE 33

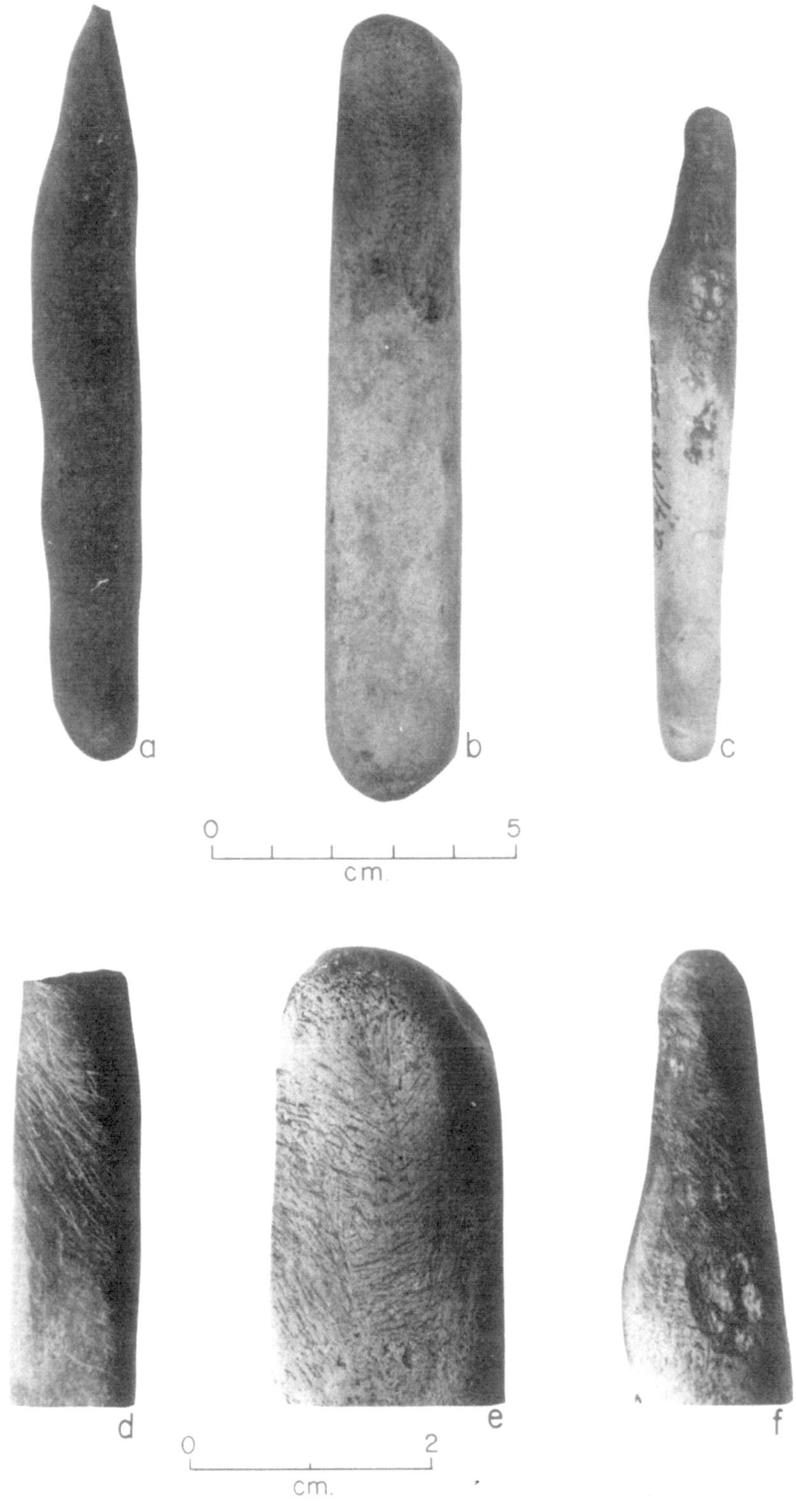

Slicing slabs from the Ali Kosh and Mohammad Jaffar phases at Tepe Ali Kosh: *a-e*, 5/6 natural size (*a*, zone A_2, Mohammad Jaffar phase; *b-c*, zones B_1 and B_2, Ali Kosh phase); *d-f*, distal ends magnified to show scratches left by cutting tools.

PLATE 34

Stone artifacts typical of Tepe Sabz: *a,b*, chipped stone hoes (*a*, zone A_3, Bayat phase; *b*, zone D, Sabz phase); *c*, blank for polished limestone celt, zone B_3 (Mehmeh phase); *d-g*, polished limestone celts (*d*, Mehmeh phase; *e*, Khazineh phase; *f*, Bayat phase; *g*, Sabz phase); *h*, polished limestone celt, showing asphalt mastic on proximal end impression of haft, zone B_2 (Mehmeh phase).

PLATE 35

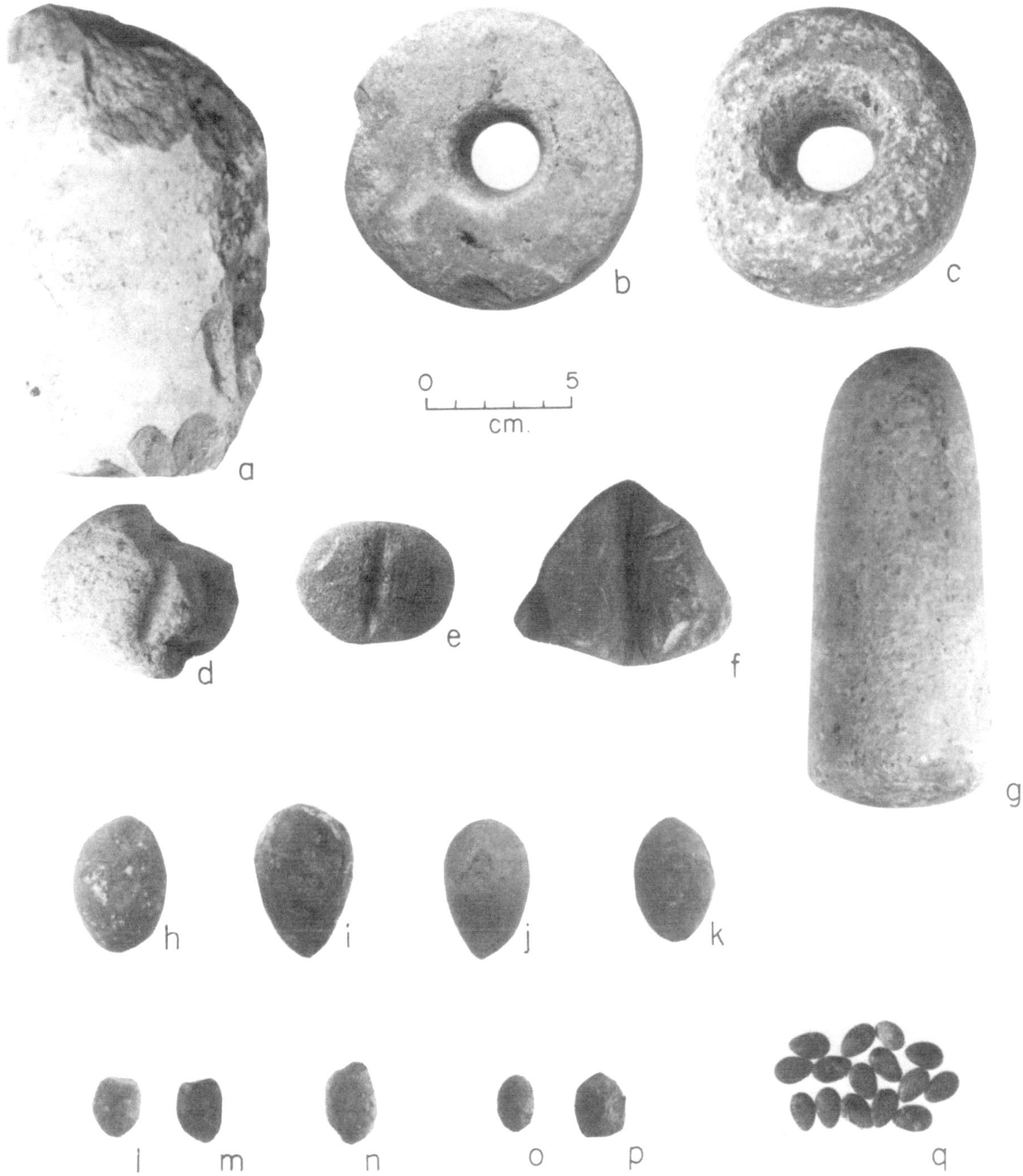

Miscellaneous objects from the Deh Luran excavations: *a*, limestone cleaver/rubbing stone, found in house in zone B_2 at Tepe Ali Kosh (Ali Kosh phase). See also Fig. 83*i* and Fig. 10 (center); *b,c*, perforated stones which may have served as sockets for door pivots (*b*, Tepe Sabz, zone B_1, Mehmeh phase; *c*, Tepe Musiyan "E", Mehmeh phase); *d,f*, grooved rubbing stones from Tepe Ali Kosh (*d,e*, zone B_2, Ali Kosh phase; *f*, zone A_2, Mohammad Jaffar phase); *g*, combination conical pestle and rolling handstone (Ali Kosh phase), Tepe Ali Kosh; *h-k*, "sling missiles" (Bayat phase), Tepe Sabz; *l-p*, carbonized pellets of goat or sheep dung, all phases (Tepe Sabz); *q*, carbonized *Prosopis* seeds (Mohammad Jaffar phase), Tepe Ali Kosh.

PLATE 36

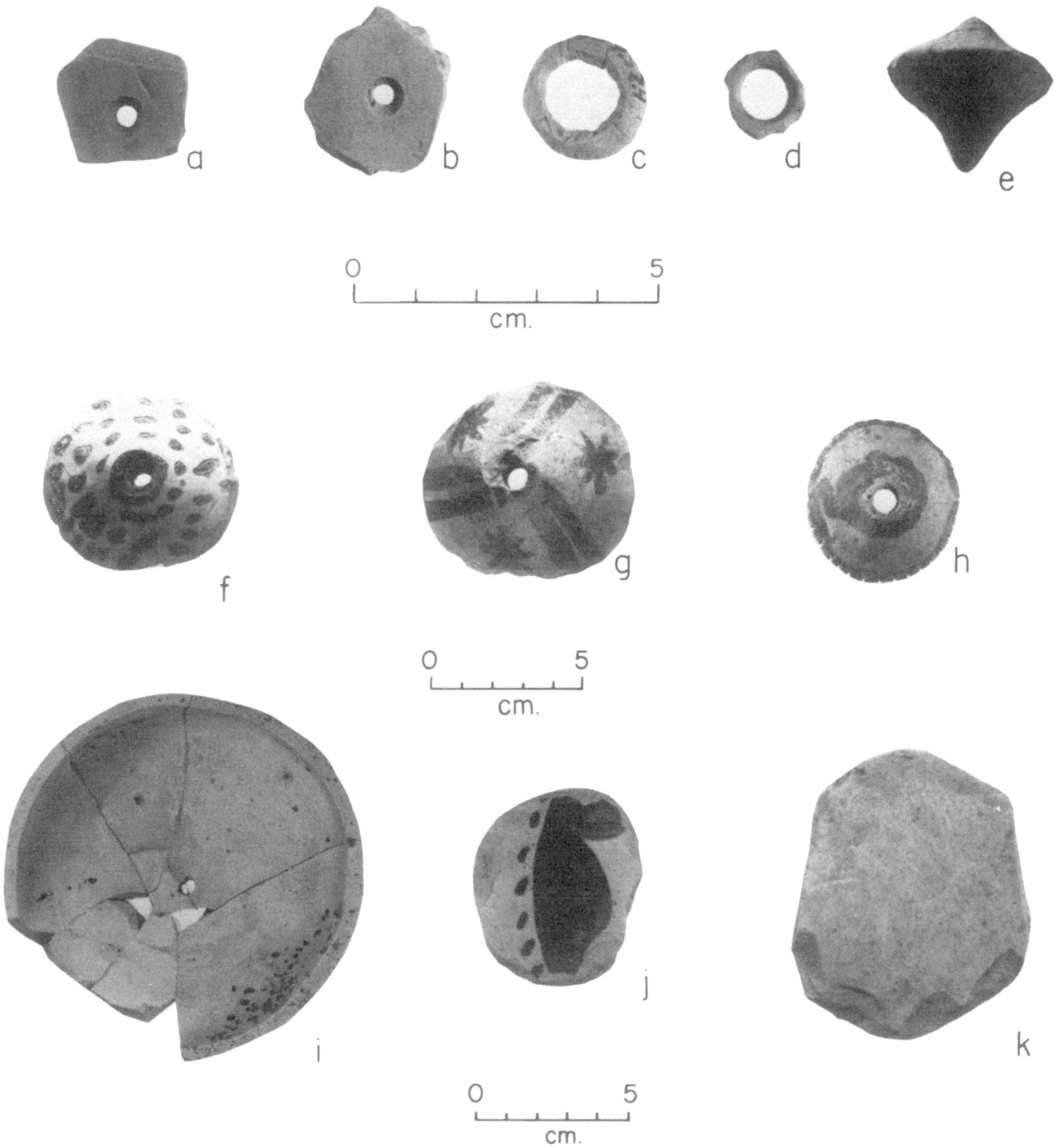

Miscellaneous ceramic artifacts from Tepe Sabz: *a,b*, drilled sherds, possibly "blanks" for rings, zone A_3 (Bayat Phase); *c,d*, ceramic "rings" (*c*, zone C_1, Khazineh phase; *d*, zone B_1, Mehmeh phase); *e*, toy "top," zone A_3 (Bayat phase); *f,g*, spindle whorls of the "chariot wheel " type (*f*, zone B_1, Mehmeh phase; *g*, zone A_2, Bayat phase); *h*, spindle whorl of the "oval-discoidal" type, zone C_3 (Khazineh phase); *i*, pot lid made from chipped and ground sherd, zone B_1 (Mehmeh phase); *j,k*, chipped sherds (*j*, zone B_2, Mehmeh phase; *k*, zone D, Sabz phase).

PLATE 37

Matting and basketry from Tepe Ali Kosh and Tepe Sabz: *a*, Silica "ghost" of coiled basket found just to west of Mehmeh phase house, zone B_3, Tepe Sabz; *b*, asphalt impression of twined basket associated with Burial 9, zone A_1 at Tepe Ali Kosh (Mohammad Jaffar phase); *c*, magnification of wall of twined basket shown in *b*; *d*, asphalt impression of over-two, under-two reed or club-rush floor mat from Tepe Ali Kosh, zone B_1 (Ali Kosh phase); *e*, magnification of asphalt impression of similar over-two, under-two matting from Tepe Ali Kosh (Ali Kosh phase);

PLATE 38

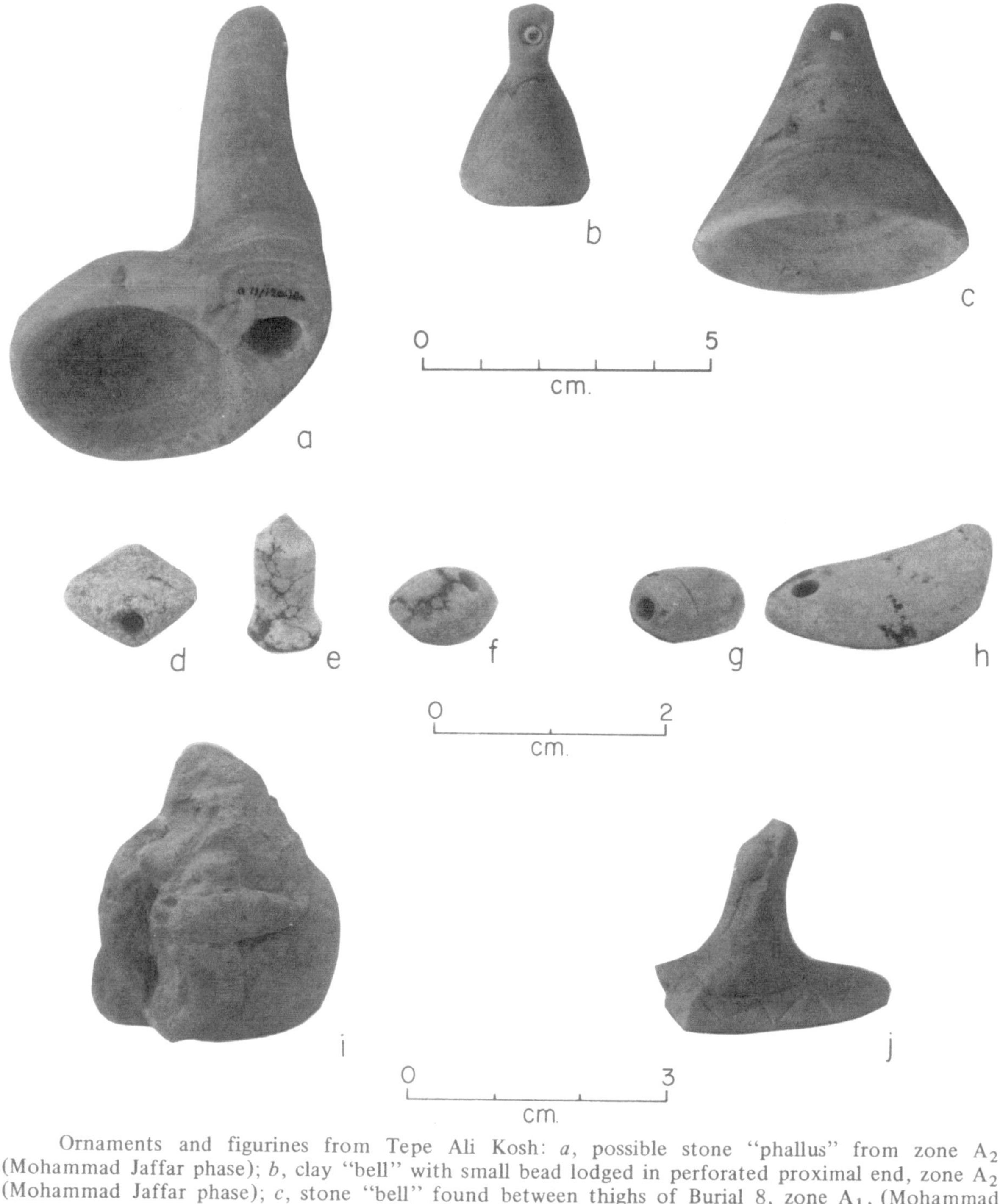

Ornaments and figurines from Tepe Ali Kosh: *a*, possible stone "phallus" from zone A_2 (Mohammad Jaffar phase); *b*, clay "bell" with small bead lodged in perforated proximal end, zone A_2 (Mohammad Jaffar phase); *c*, stone "bell" found between thighs of Burial 8, zone A_1, (Mohammad Jaffar phase); *d-f*, turquoise ornaments associated with Burial 8, zone A_1, (Mohammad Jaffar phase); *g-h*, turquoise bead (*g*) and pendant (*h*) associated with Burial 25, zone A_1, (Mohammad Jaffar phase); *i*, lightly-baked clay "mother goddess" figurine, seated, hands on knees, zone A_2 (Mohammad Jaffar phase); *j*, lightly-baked clay "stalk" figurine, zone A_1 (Mohammad Jaffar phase), found in ash-filled borrow pit in Square 98.

PLATE 39

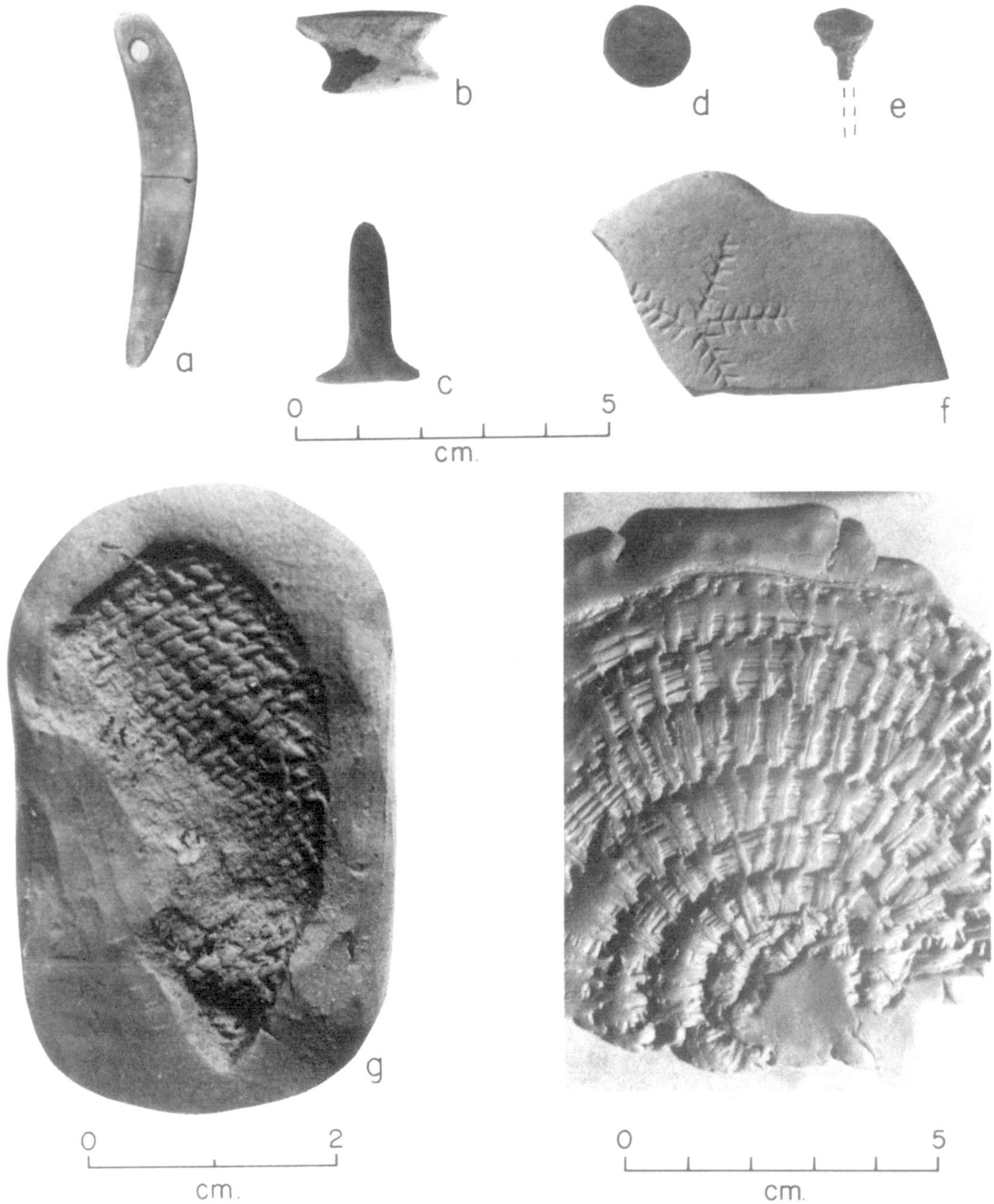

Miscellaneous items from Tepe Ali Kosh and Tepe Sabz: *a*, mussel-shell pendant found with mass of secondarily-buried limb bones near Burial 34, zone B_2 at Tepe Ali Kosh (Ali Kosh phase); *b*, cuff-link-shaped stone labret, Tepe Sabz, zone C_3 (Khazineh phase); *c*, T-shaped stone labret, Tepe Sabz, zone B_1 (Mehmeh phase); *d*, small stone spool, Tepe Ali Kosh, zone B_2 (Ali Kosh phase); *e*, head of copper pin, Tepe Sabz, zone B_2 (Mehmeh phase); *f*, incised pebble, Tepe Sabz, zone B_2 (Mehmeh phase); *g*, "positive" modeling-clay impression of lightly-baked clay fragment, which showed "negative" impression of plain weave textile, Tepe Sabz, zone A_3 (Bayat phase); *h*, "positive" modeling-clay impression made from "negative" asphalt impression of a coiled, grass-bundle foundation basket, Tepe Sabz, zone B_2 (Mehmeh phase).

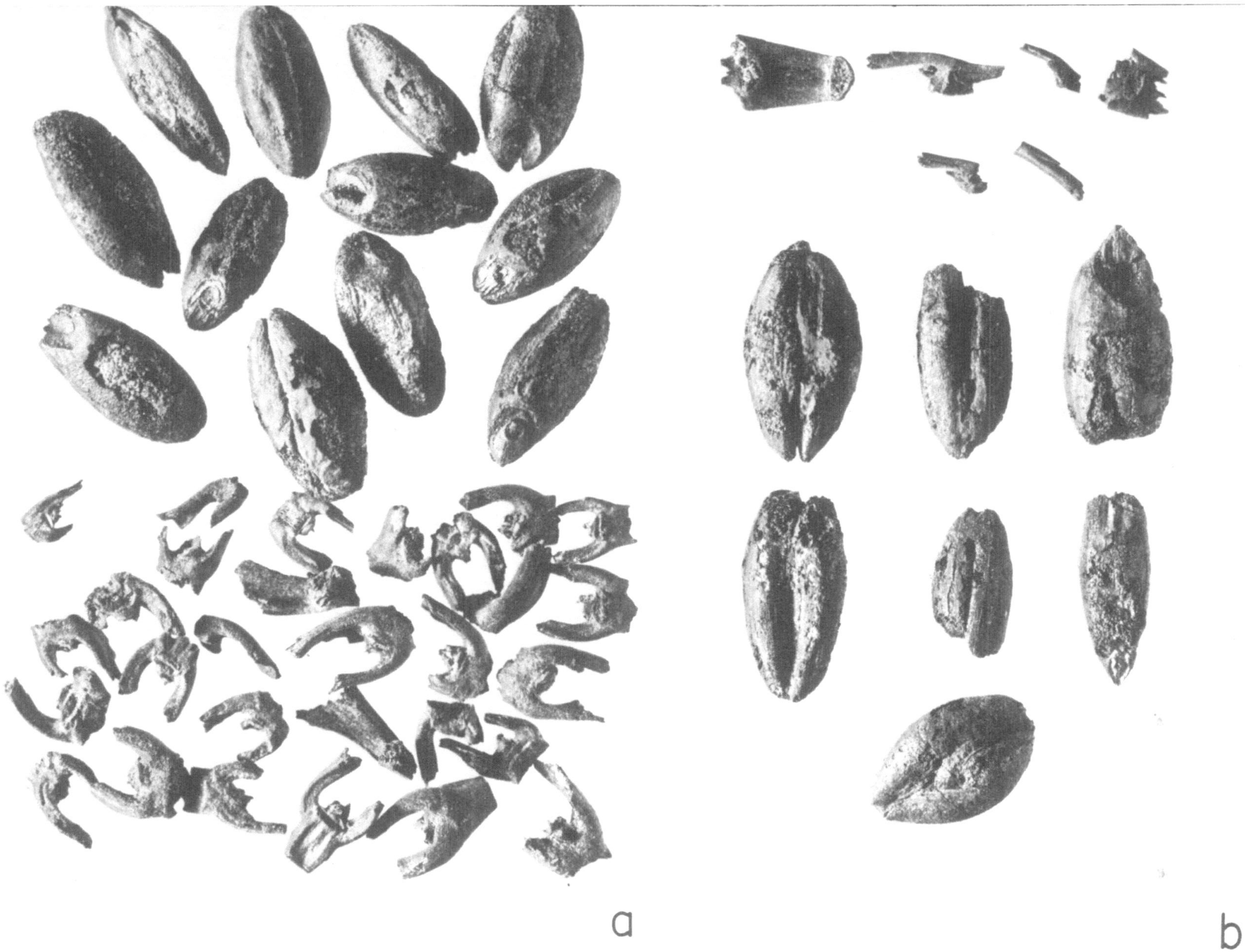

Carbonized grain from the Bus Mordeh phase, Tepe Ali Kosh (Hans Helbaek, Appendix I): *a*, collection of the best preserved Emmer wheat grains and spikelet parts from the Bus Mordeh phase, (six times natural size); *b*, barley from the Bus Mordeh phase: Top; four lateral floret pedicels, and two internodes of barley (two-row) showing clean, brittle fracture surfaces; Middle; six straight grains of hulled barley; Bottom; straight grain of naked barley; all six times natural size.

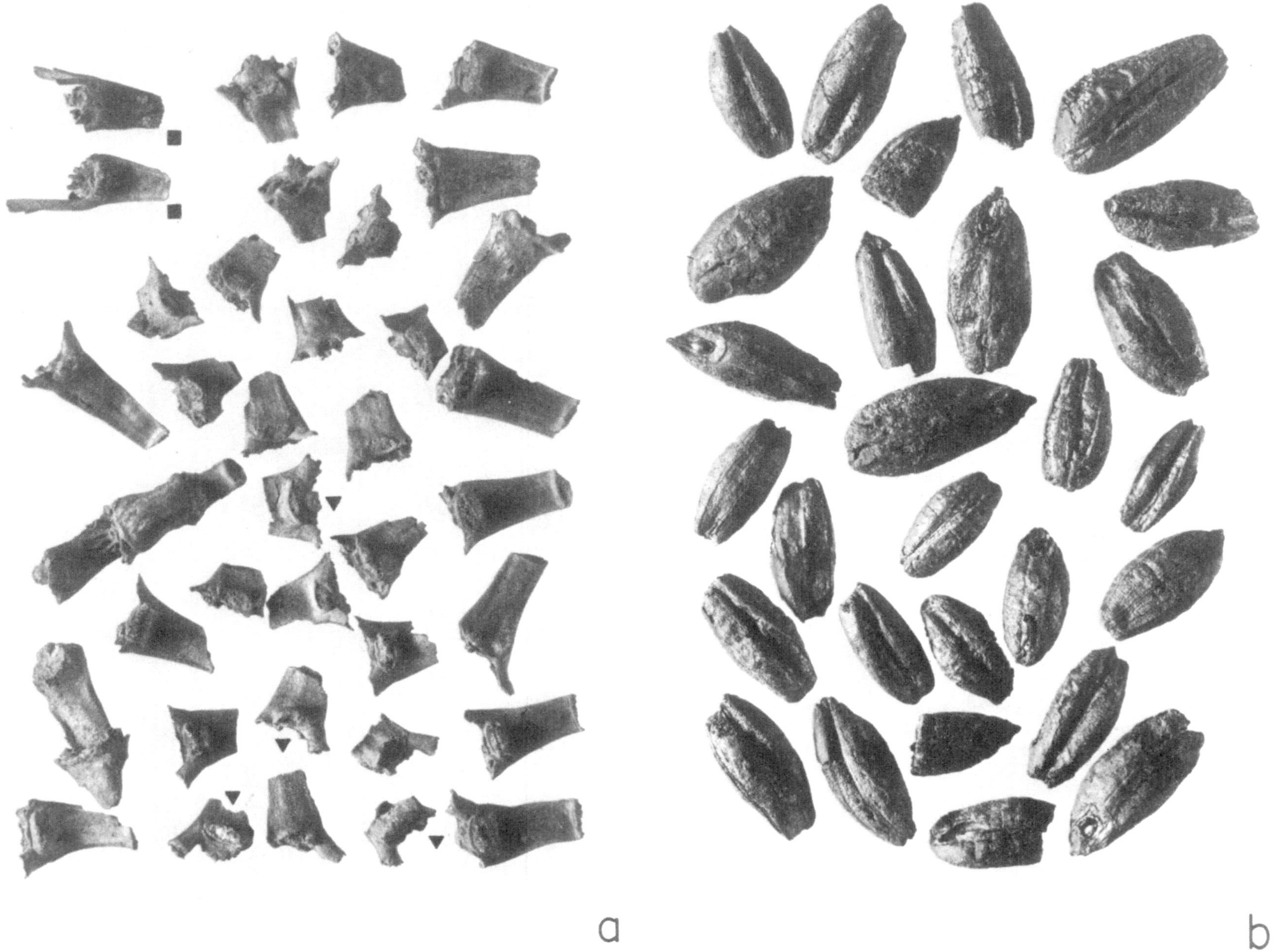

Carbonized grain from the Bayat phase, Tepe Sabz. (Hans Helbaek, Appendix I): *a*, barley internodes, mainly of the hulled, six-row form: two from the hulled, tough-axis, two-row form are marked (■) and some typical examples of the naked six-row form are marked (▲). Six times natural size; *b*, twisted (lateral) grains of hulled, six-row barley, same provenience as internodes shown in Pl. 41*a*. Six times natural size.

PLATE 42

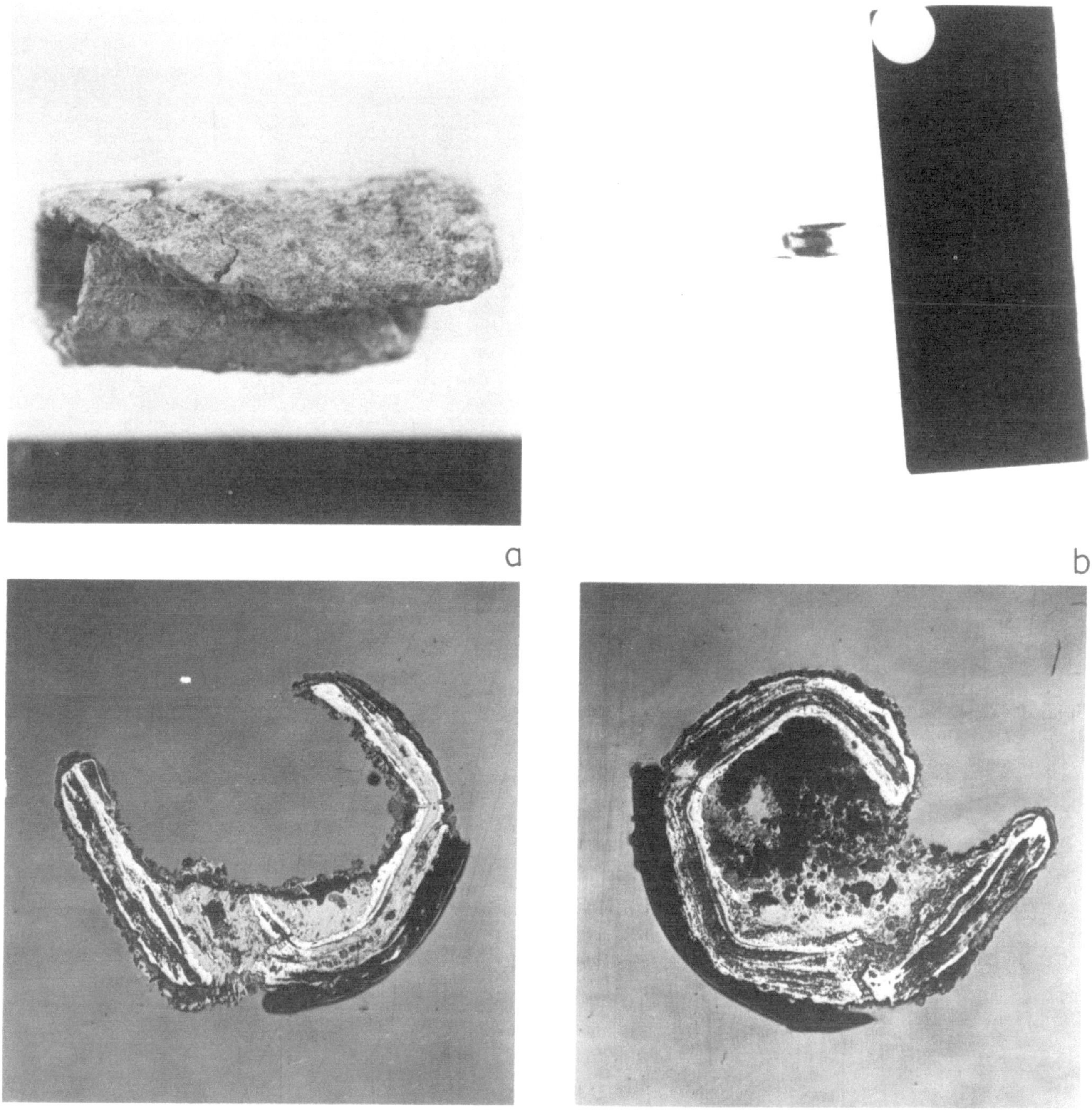

Copper bead from zone B_2 at Tepe Ali Kosh (Ali Kosh phase). (Cyril S. Smith, Appendix II): *a*, general view, five times natural size; *b*, radiograph; *c*, section A, ten times natural size, no etching; *d*, section B, ten times natural size, no etching.

PLATE 43

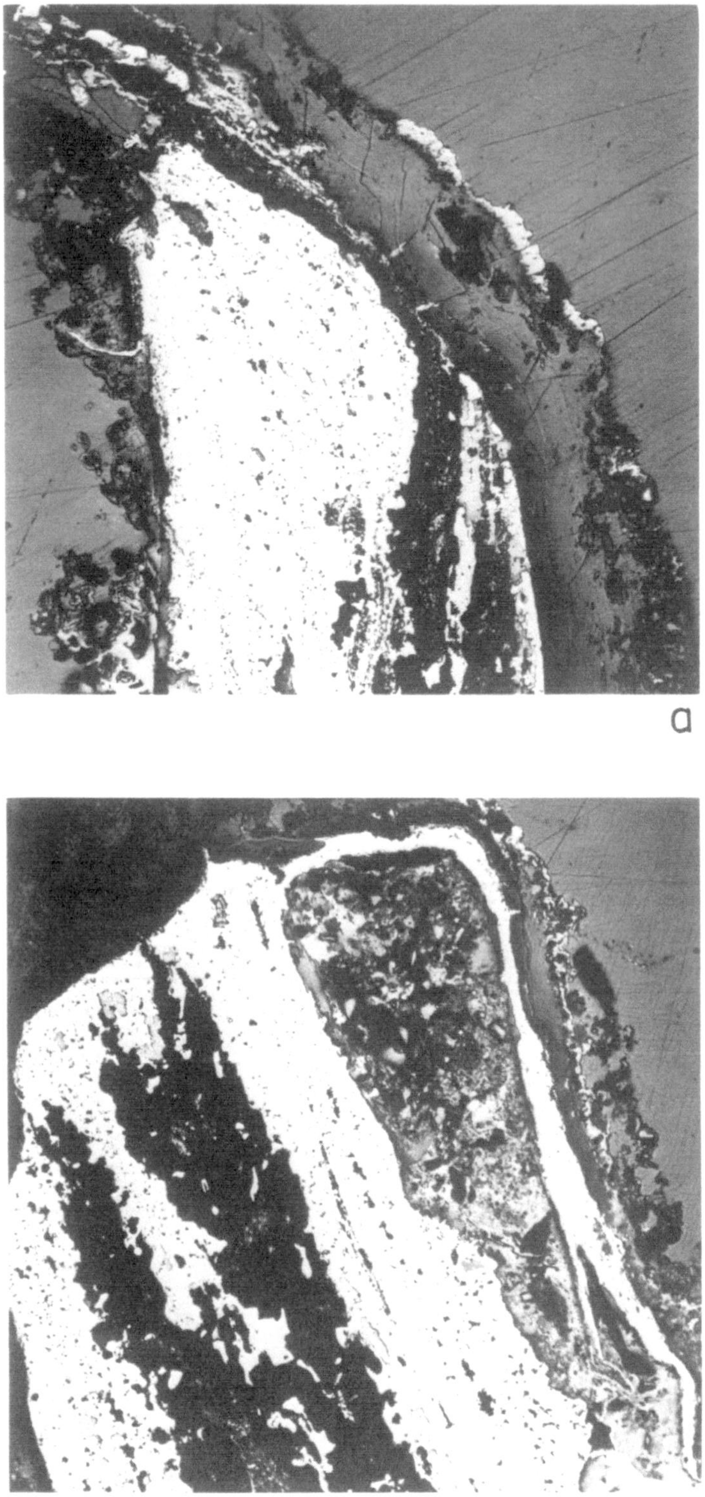

a

b

Copper bead from zone B_2 at Tepe Ali Kosh (Ali Kosh phase). (Cyril S. Smith, Appendix II): *a*, section A, 100 times natural size, no etching; *b*, section A, 100 times natural size, no etching.